STONE AGE ARCHAEOLOGY

Essays in honour of John Wymer

Stone Age Archaeology

Essays in honour of John Wymer

Edited by
Nick Ashton, Frances Healy and Paul Pettitt

Oxbow Monograph 102
Lithic Studies Society Occasional Paper 6
1998

Published by
Oxbow Books, Park End Place, Oxford OX1 1HN

© Oxbow Books and the individual authors 1998

ISBN 1 900188 66 X

This book is available direct from
Oxbow Books, Park End Place, Oxford OX1 1HN
(Phone: 01865–241249; Fax: 01865–794449)

and

The David Brown Book Company
PO Box 511, Oakville, CT 06779, USA
(Phone: 860–945–9329; Fax: 860–945–9468)

The cover illustration is by Hazel Martingell

The photo on the back cover shows John Wymer at West Tofts in 1982
(Photo: R. J. MacRae)

Printed in Great Britain at
The Alden Press
Oxford

Table of Contents

List of Contributors

Stephen Aldhouse-Green
Department of Humanities & Science, University of Wales College Newport, Caerleon Campus, PO Box 179, Newport NP6 1YG

Nick Ashton
Quaternary Section, Department of Prehistoric and Romano-British Antiquities, British Museum, Franks House II, 38-46 Orsman Road, London N1 5QJ

Nick Barton
Department of Anthropology, Oxford Brookes University, Oxford OX3 0BP

David Bridgland
Department of Geography, Durham University, South Road, Durham DH1 3LE

Jill Cook
Quaternary Section, Department of Prehistoric and Romano-British Antiquities, British Museum, Franks House II, 38-46 Orsman Road, London N1 5QJ

A. David
Ancient Monuments Laboratory, English Heritage, 23 Savile Row, London W1X 1AB

H. J. Deacon
Department of Archaeology, University of Stellenbosch, PB XI Matieland, 7602 South Africa

Phil Dean
Department of Prehistoric and Romano-British Antiquities, British Museum, Franks House II, 38-46 Orsman Road, London N1 5QJ

John Evans
Department of Environmental Sciences, University of East London, London E15 4LZ

John Gowlett
Department of Archaeology, University of Liverpool, Brownlow Street, Liverpool L69 3BX

Clive Gamble
Department of Archaeology, University of Southampton, Avenue Campus, Southampton SO17 1BJ

Bruce G. Gladfelter
Program in Geography, M/C 027, University of Illinois at Chicago, 1007 W. Harrison St., Chicago, Illinois, 60607-7139 USA

P. A. Harding
Wessex Archaeology, Portway House, Old Sarum Park, Salisbury, Wilts SP4 6EB

Frances Healy
20 The Green, Charlbury, Oxon OX7 3QA

Roger Jacobi
c/o Quaternary Section, Department of Prehistoric and Romano-British Antiquities, British Museum, Franks House II, 38-46 Orsman Road, London N1 5QJ

Andrew J. Lawson
Wessex Archaeology, Portway House, Old Sarum Park, Salisbury, Wilts SP4 6EB

Simon G. Lewis
School of the Environment, Cheltenham and Gloucester College of Higher Education, Francis Close Hall, Swindon Road, Cheltenham GL50 4AZ

John Lord
The Old Mill House, Chalk Row Road, Gooderstone, King's Lynn, Norfolk PE33 9BW

R. J. MacRae
Kirby Cottage, Low Street, Hardingham, Norfolk NR9 4EL

John MacNabb
Institute of Prehistoric Sciences, University of Liverpool, Brownlow Sreet, Liverpool L69 3BX

Paul Pettitt
Radiocarbon Accelerator Unit, Research Laboratory for Archaeology and the History of Art, 6 Keble Road, Oxford OX1 3QJ, and Keble College, Oxford, OX1 3PG

Michael J. Reynier
Department of Classics and Archaeology, University of Nottingham, University Park, Nottingham NG7 2RD

Alison Roberts
Department of Antiquities, Ashmolean Museum, University of Oxford, OX1 2PH

Peter Robins
53 Aylsham Road, North Walsham, Norfolk NR28 0BL

Derek Roe
Donald Baden-Powell Quaternary Research Centre, 60 Banbury Road, Oxford OX2 6PN

Andrew Rogerson
Field Archaeology Division, Norfolk Museums Service, Union House, Gressenhall, East Dereham, Norfolk NR20 4DR

Alan Saville
Department of Archaeology, National Museums of Scotland, Chambers Street, Edinburgh EH1 1JF

Katherine Scott
Donald Baden-Powell Quaternary Research Centre, 60 Banbury Road, Oxford OX2 6PN

Martin Street
Forschungsbereich Altsteinzeit, Römisch-Germanisches Zentralmuseum Mainz, Schloss Monrepos, 56567 Neuwied, Germany

Elaine Turner
Forschungsbereich Altsteinzeit, Römisch-Germanisches Zentralmuseum Mainz, Schloss Monrepos, 56567 Neuwied, Germany

Francis F. Wenban-Smith
Institute of Archaeology, University College London, 31-34 Gordon Square, London WC1H 0PY

Mark J. White
Department of Archaeology, Downing Street, Cambridge CB2 3DZ

Peter C. Woodman
Department of Archaeology, National University of Ireland, Cork, Cork, Ireland.

1. Bifaces, Booze and the Blues. Anecdotes from the Life and Times of a Palaeolithic Archaeologist

Andrew J. Lawson and Andrew Rogerson

SWANSCOMBE

Saturday 30 July 1955 was a very significant day. The discovery of a small bone 'with the consistency of wet soap' in a long-disused gravel pit could hardly be expected to excite anyone at all. Yet it changed the career of its finder and the course of British archaeology.

The place was Swanscombe, an otherwise undistinguished settlement on the fringe of London's south-eastern industrial suburbs, built on the edge of the '100 ft' gravel terrace which rises from the southern margin of the Thames estuary with occasional views of Thurrock and Tilbury to the north. The bone was a right parietal, the third bone from the skull which at that time was the oldest example of ancient 'fossil man' (more accurately 'fossil woman') in Britain. The finder was 27-year-old John James Wymer, a man who was to become a leading prehistoric archaeologist and student of ancient hunter-gatherers in Britain and beyond.

John's father had first visited the gravel pits of northwest Kent in search of palaeoliths in 1910, long before John or his brother were even thought about. With this legacy, John was captivated from the start by the great antiquity of Man, and the even longer story told by geology. While John was at school the war raged but the holidays provided an opportunity to escape the suburban streets of Richmond. The uncluttered roads were safe for cyclists and the young John toured the length and breadth of the country, rations carefully stowed, with a target of 50 miles a day, and a ten shilling note sewn by his mother into the lining of his jacket for emergencies. One trip totalled a thousand miles, but what better way to experience first hand the effects of geology on geography and topography?

Prior to the discovery of the parietal, John had visited the gravel pits around Swanscombe on various occasions, accompanying his parents in pursuit of their joint interest in the discovery of Palaeolithic implements. They had a particular interest in the Barnfield Pit, which stemmed from the large collections of flint implements made there

since the 1870s and above all the discoveries in 1935–6 by a Clapham dentist, who rejoiced in the name of Alvan Theophilus Marston, of the first two bones of the fossil skull (Wymer 1985a). The Wymer family located an undisturbed area of the gravel layer in which Marston had found his bones (the Upper Middle Gravel) and set to work.

In 1956 John was awarded a teaching certificate and took a job at Wokingham. He continued his regular research at Swanscombe, but now only at weekends, until November 1960. The now familiar correlation of train timetables enabled John still to travel from Wokingham via Waterloo and the stopping service to Swanscombe, although this added to the difficulty of his arduous working weekends. The parietal had been found on the second day of the campaign; as luck would have it no further human remains came to light, although 487 bifaces and other implements were recorded (Wymer 1964).

READING

John Wymer had no formal qualifications in archaeology. Nonetheless, armed with his already extensive knowledge of Pleistocene geology, enthusiasm for fieldwork, eagerness to pursue archaeology and, of course, the famous parietal, he was interviewed for the post of archaeologist at Reading Museum and Art Gallery. Much to his surprise, the then Director, W.A. Smallcombe, offered him the position in which he could follow in the footsteps of George Boon and his predecessor, Stuart Piggott. Thus commenced an archaeological career with many highlights. Although it was not without its share of difficulties and frustrations, the priority in John's work has remained the study of the Palaeolithic and Mesolithic. His unswerving dedication to these early periods has unquestionably enhanced their place in British prehistory. Our knowledge of them is much greater as a result of his outstanding contribution, not least because of the links he forged with other sciences with a common interest in the period.

The industrial growth of Reading was due to three main products: biscuits (Huntley and Palmers), bulbs (Suttons) and beer (Simonds). A town whose prosperity was based on booze must have appealed to John, as his metabolism seems to thrive on a regular supply of good beer. Many of the collaborative, multi-disciplinary strategies which have been a hallmark of John's excavations were fermented in the company of like-minded souls in the relaxed surroundings of a public bar. Happily for John, The Elephant just round the corner from the Museum (and now demolished) ran a blues club.

From his base at Reading Museum John was able to catalogue and study the collections of hand-axes in a range of institutions while continuing to observe the exposures of gravel in active pits such as Little Thurrock, Grays, Essex (Wymer 1957) or Highlands Farm, Henley. This latter site was the stimulus for a reconsideration of the date of the former channel of the Thames between Caversham and Henley (Wymer 1961a). From the start John wrote with clarity of expression and, combined with his fine skills as an illustrator of flint implements in the style of the great W.O.Waterhouse, created a succession of prompt publications.

As early as 1951, John had been visiting gravel pits in the Kennet Valley, but once installed at Reading Museum his attention was drawn to the abundant microlithic flints found beneath peat at Thatcham. Trial excavation in December 1957 revealed bone and flint in mint condition: work continued intermittently until 1961. The final year saw the innovation of a steel coffer dam built to enable excavations to take place in the reed swamp which flanked the site. The construction required overlapping steel sheets to be driven through the waterlogged swamp in an area where exploration with a mechanical excavator (itself something of an innovation at the time) had located pristine flint, bone and plant macrofossils (Wymer 1959; 1962).

The setting would have discouraged many with a less strong constitution. The nearby Newbury Sewage Works were overpoweringly apparent when the wind was from the north. No sooner had the din from the pounding of steel sheets relented than the clatter of diesel pumps would sound all day long. If the smell of sewage were not enough, the black sludge now taken from the coffer dam and lovingly searched for the traces of Mesolithic fishermen stank almost as much. The campsite was squeezed between the reed swamp, the excavation and a seemingly abyssal water-filled gravel pit. Each morning the drowsy campers and the myriad *Daphnia* which filled the merest spoonful of pit water, already awoken by the clamour of thoughtless schoolboy campers, were alarmed at the sight of Wymer teetering on the precipitous, crumbling edge of the pit as he performed his daily shaving ritual. It was a miracle that nobody, especially if they had been trying to keep pace with John in the pub, ever ended up in the local Coroner's statistics for 'persons missing and dredged from lakes'. Despite all this, Thatcham remains one of the most impor-

tant Mesolithic sites excavated in Britain, and with the more famous Star Carr in Yorkshire, one of the few sites to produce a reasonable assemblage of contempor–aneous animal bone.

The Mesolithic site which John investigated in 1964 at Wawcott was also situated adjacent to a reed swamp. However, the setting beside the Kennet and Avon Canal was a pleasant contrast to Thatcham's sewage works. Delving in the reed swamp disturbed swarms of mosquitos. Although every bottle of citronella in southern Berkshire was requisitioned to repel the voracious insects, few of the diggers escaped huge rashes of irritating bites. However, compensation took a very different, edible form. Whilst the diggers toiled, men were observed dragging nets along the adjacent canal. From time to time the nets were pulled out full of writhing, silvery fish and the men set to work dividing up the catch. The object of the exercise was solely to improve the lot of the trout by exterminating their competitors, mainly grayling, The trout were repatriated to the waters while the grayling were left floundering on the bank. John was uncomprehending, not at the carnage, but at the waste of food. How could only three or four campers possibly eat all this bounty before it rotted? The solution was as much experimental archaeology as it was in Mesolithic tradition. We would smoke them. Fires were lit and barbed wire procured on which to hang the gutted fish. The kippered grayling, or 'grippers' as they were called, were excellent, not only tasty but lastingly edible. Quantities were transported with the tents, equipment and diggers, like refugees, on a Reading Corporation lorry to the next site at Lambourn.

Despite all these activities, John's role in Reading Museum was not primarily as an excavator. His duties included the display of the outstanding collections such as the newly discovered Moulsford torc (Wymer 1961b) and most importantly, with his colleague Bill Manning, the Roman finds from Silchester. For these he painstakingly created small dioramas, such as a carpenter's workshop in which even the miniature iron tools were forged as the originals may have been.

Research-orientated rescue excavations were undertaken with volunteers from the Berkshire Field Research Group and the Archaeological Society amongst others, requiring John to embrace the archaeology of later periods. For example, the threat of motorway construction prompted the excavation in 1963 of a Bronze Age ring ditch at Englefield (Healy 1994). The work was conducted at Easter. After the removal of topsoil the rain was so relentless day after day that the trenches totally filled with water: all the miserable volunteers could do was peer out of their damp tents and John out of his sectional site hut – until the roof blew off. Eventually a break in the weather demanded action, which in turn exposed John's immense capacity for motivating his helpers. With the weather still spitting at the workers, and scenes more reminiscent of the Somme than Sir Mortimer Wheeler's neatly ordered

Figure 1.1. 1964: J.J.W. points to the primary chalk rubble in the base of the south ditch of the Lambourn long barrow

boxes, the now liquid alluvial subsoil was bucketed from the trenches and some sense of normality returned.

John has always worked in a most orderly fashion. One suspects this is a natural talent rather than the outcome of conscription into the RAF, working as an audit clerk, or his training as a teacher. Nonetheless, for the investigation and reconstruction of the megalithic tomb of Wayland's Smithy by Richard Atkinson and Stuart Piggott in 1962–3, John was enlisted to use these organisational skills in the establishment and control of the site camp. Knowledge gained at Wayland's Smithy was put to good use the following year as the Inspectorate of Ancient Monuments continued its programme of investigation of long barrows by inviting Reading Museum to investigate the monument at Lambourn.

The Lambourn long barrow, on the north-western fringe of the extensive 'Seven Barrows' group, had fallen to the ravages of the plough but early reports of protruding sarsen

boulders implied a complex structure, possibly similar to the tomb at Wayland's Smithy. During a long hot summer the volunteers stripped the thin chalky ploughsoil to reveal the last remnants of the mound, and the somewhat better preserved, albeit disturbed, sarsen cairn at the eastern end of the monument. Sorties were led on foot (because John had not yet mastered driving) to The George in Lambourn, The White Horse in Woolston (ostensibly to ponder whether the large sarsen outside might have been removed from a chambered tomb) or even to Ashbury (to check that the quality of the 'sustenance' had not deteriorated since the Wayland's Smithy days). Responsibility of the site director always goes beyond the excavation itself and at Lambourn John was faced with a series of distractions which might test the mettle of many: stubble fires which threatened to engulf the excavation, motorcycle crashes that fortunately did more damage to machine than riders, the arrival of lady helpers dressed more for Ascot than the field, and the unwitting ensnaring of very, very expensive race horses in measuring tapes on the brink of deep ditch sections (Wymer 1966).

All these activities, though enthusiastically undertaken, seem to have been a sideline for the main thrust of John's interest, namely the gathering of details of the Palaeolithic objects from the Thames gravels. The outcome of this study was the weighty publication *Lower Palaeolithic Archaeology in Britain as Represented by the Thames Valley* (1968). As well as discussion and interpretation, it presented an immense gazetteer of sites with catalogues of the implements found classified according to John's own typological scheme and illustrated with huge numbers of his distinctive drawings.

MUSICAL ACCOMPANIMENT

The virtuosity of John 'Summer Lightning' Wymer, blues-boogie pianist, is not legendary but real. For many of his friends John's skill as a tickler of the ivories comes to the mind as quickly as his deep knowledge of prehistory. Much influenced by his mother, a professional pianist in the silent picture palaces of the 1920s, and by one Snelling, a champion drummer and school colleague, John started to play piano in 1942 at the age of 15. At about this time he acquired his first record, a 78 rpm single of *Boogie-Woogie Prayer* by the (literally) immense trio of Albert Ammons, Pete Johnson and Meade Lux Lewis.

The boogie boom had begun after Ammons, Johnson and Lewis had appeared in John Hammond's 'Spirituals to Swing' concert at the Carnegie Hall, New York, in December 1938. This event soon unleashed upon white America, and subsequently Europe, a form of fast and predominantly 12-bar piano blues, characterised by rolling repetitive left-hand bass figures, which had long been a favourite amongst American black or 'race' audiences. Although the style was soon to be watered down into a limp cliché by many a white swing band, a few enthusiasts around the world, notably young Wymer, were able to pick up the true spirit of this exciting music and to avoid rendering it down to banal neutrality.

John thus came to the blues some two decades or more before this form of music began to be appreciated in Britain for its own sake and not merely as a less sophisticated adjunct to, or light relief from, jazz. Unlike most younger blues enthusiasts, John has scarcely been influenced by the many so-called primitive, and often understandably ill-known, country bluesmen of the pre-war period. In the main they were guitarists whose scratchy renditions began to fill up countless LPs in the later 1960s and onwards. By becoming involved with the music when he did, John has avoided any tendency towards obsessions with disco-graphical detail and biographical obscurity, both great pitfalls for many followers of the blues. John simply loves to play and to listen, and it is remarkable that although his music sounds so much like the 'real thing' (he would

Figure 1.2. 1997: Play it again, John!

modestly deny this), he has never played with any American bluesmen. He is proud, though, of having met two of them, Champion Jack Dupree and Memphis Slim, both of whom found homes in Europe.

John is at his best playing the music of Jimmy Yancey, the most idiosyncratic and original of blues-boogie pianists, who, although he had been playing for many years, did not become well-known to a wide audience until the boogie boom had got under way. Yancey's intricate and sensitive playing of his own compositions is frequently interpreted with beautiful clarity by John whose versions of numbers such as *Yancey's Special* always create a storm. Other standards with which John can produce similar responses amongst his listeners are *Pinetop's Boogie Woogie* (first recorded by Clarence 'Pine Top' Smith in 1928) and Meade Lux Lewis' 1927 classic *Honky Tonk Train Blues*. Interest-ingly the latter, a fast and extremely difficult piece which most pianists do not even attempt to play, has been known to give John problems in the maintaining of an even tempo, his train tending to run away at an increasing and seemingly uncontrollable speed before coming to a dramatic and unscheduled halt. Another pianist specially favoured by John is Cripple Clarence Lofton. Wymerian versions of Lofton numbers such as *Strut That Thing* can liven up proceedings and may often have powerfully destructive effects on British reserve.

When he feels temporarily sated with the keyboard John sometimes turns to the acoustic guitar (he owns two), and, accompanied by a stand-in pianist or another guitarist, will lay out sweet blues in his own style, most reminiscent of that bottleneck wizard of the 1930s and 40s, Tampa Red. After a suitable interval of plucking he returns to his piano. Sessions can be extended, although they never seem long. On one wonderful Norfolk summer's day in 1978 John played, with only a few natural stops, for almost twelve hours, ending in the 'wee midnight hours long before the break of day' surrounded by exhausted revellers and sporting a full set of bleeding fingertips.

Whether it is the hesitant atmosphere of a private party, or the smoky stillness of an unsuspecting public house on a quiet midweek evening, any environment lucky enough to be disturbed by John's music will soon be transformed into something memorable. Some good beer or red wine is all that is required to prepare the maestro for work, and a steady supply of the same ensures a quality performance. A characteristic chuckle at the end of each number will provoke a roar of approval from the crowd and on occasions listeners find themselves inspired by the Wymer sound to sing the blues. This is not always very kind to the ear, but can result in minor modern classics like *Retouch Me Mama*, first heard at the Yaxley Cherry Tree (Suffolk) in 1973.

It is remarkable to consider that Jimmy Yancey at one time had to make the choice between the two careers of base-ball player and blues pianist. We are all glad that John chose archaeology, and relegated the piano to his leisure hours. However, any prehistorians who have not yet experienced the Wymer phenomenon should make efforts to plug this major gap in their experience. This may be the only way to ensure that they no longer wake up in the morning with those mean ol' hand-axe blues.

AFRICA

Ronald Singer, a stocky, cigar smoking anatomist with a rrrolling South African accent, had long been interested in the evolution of Pleistocene mammals, in particular the human race, the latter being something of a sensitive issue in the home of apartheid. Throughout the 1950s he had drawn attention to the prolific mineralised Pleistocene animal bone and stone artefacts exposed during erosion in the Hopefield district inland from Saldanha Bay, some 60 miles north north west of Cape Town. The site was all the more important for the discovery of a human skull which at the time was 'the only other skull in sub-Saharan Africa, apart from the Broken Hill skull . . . which shows distinct Neanderthaloid characteristics' (Singer & Wymer 1968). In 1962 Singer was appointed to a chair at the University of Chicago and from there was able to secure grants to continue fieldwork in pursuit of his continuing interests in South Africa. John Wymer was recruited to direct the fieldwork and in August 1965 work commenced, building

upon the initial work of Singer, Ray Inskeep and Mr (now Professor) and Mrs Hilary Deacon.

Elandsfontein Farm, the site of the Saldanha Bay skull, was a far cry from the rolling downland and verdant valleys of Berkshire. It is situated on the extensive *Sandveld* which, with low annual rainfall, encourages little more than sparse grazing for sheep and goats. One pictures the scene from the report of the work: 'Elandsfontein is particularly impoverished as some two square miles of the farm have been transformed by erosion into a sandy desert; once the thin bush is removed the sand is subject to the full force of the strong winds which frequently blow over this part of the Cape. Series of *barchan* dunes have formed, some to a height of 50 feet or more . . .'. With the help of local workers frequently drunk on *boerwyn* or high on *dagga* (pot), and based in a small hut (Chippindale 1997), seventeen new cuttings were made, exposing the sequence of coastal sediments and establishing the contexts of the eroded Palaeolithic tools. The workers withstood the sandblasting until May 1966.

The next challenge was to investigate the fossil sand bar sediments at Langebaanweg, another remote location dominated by dust-spewing industrial works which converted dazzlingly white fossil guano reclaimed from the sediments into phosphate fertiliser. Here, as at Hopefield, vast quantities of well-preserved animal bone had led to reconsiderations of the Pleistocene development of many extinct mammal genera (Boné & Singer 1965). Great sections were cut through the sediments to record the geological sequence but with the absence of artefacts, deposits which might shed light on human evolution could be more profitably explored elsewhere.

Four hundred miles east of Cape Town, the brown-grey cliffs of the Tzitzikama coast tower nobly above the blue waters of the southern Indian Ocean. Clear skies, fringed with a distinctive purply-pink hue in the crisp, early morning light, present a distinctive canvas upon which the bright greens of the abundant vegetation and the gold of beach sands are luxuriantly daubed. Here and there, at different levels in the cliff face, dark shadows mark the gaping mouths of cavernous recesses cut millennia ago when the seas, altered by the cycles of universal glacial events, pounded the metamorphic rock at varying altitudes. Wave-cut platforms fed with natural spring waters and interspersed with sandy or pebbly coves appear like lawns spread-out at the foot of the cliffs. The air is filled both with the sound of shrieking monkeys and glimpses of exotically coloured birds of a hundred or more different species. This spectacle, blessed with a balmy Mediterranean climate and enhanced by the sound of foaming, white-topped waves breaking against the craggy sandstone cliffs, must have seemed like paradise after the desert of the western Cape, but such was the scene just east of Klasies River Mouth.

From the 1920s onwards, rich stone age remains had been recorded from the caves of the South African coast, human burials providing the basis for limited anthropo-

Figure 1.3. 1968: J.J.W. (second from left) with Ronald Singer (second from right), staff, visitor and workmen at Klasies River Mouth

logical study but the overall chronological framework was extremely vague. The potential of the caves at Klasies River Mouth to answer questions about human physical and cultural evolution in the Late Pleistocene had been noted since 1955 and they were therefore chosen by Ronald Singer to further his research aims. Through two seasons (1967 and 1968), John directed a party of three archaeologists, two from England, one from the South African Museum, and an average of four local workmen.

The choice of site was excellent and the results exceeded expectations. The site has since become a yardstick against which to measure the results of both earlier and later excavations, having provided a largely unbroken sequence throughout the local Middle and Late Stone Age. Prior to

the excavations, it was assumed that the archaeological deposits which had accumulated on the floors of the caves at different heights in the cliff were totally independent of each other, their sequences possibly overlapping or being contemporaneous. However, as the excavations progressed it became apparent that they were really remnants of a single sequence.

The mother of all middens had once formed in front of the cliff, choking the lower caves and affording access to the upper. The midden had been largely eroded away as the seas came and went, but its talus remained inviolate against the cliff face. Traces of former brecciated layers could be traced between the deposits in different areas and so it was possible to visualise the huge size of the original midden. The deposits represented a 20m thick stratigraphic sequence! The base had formed on an early beach and sterile storm deposits were interspersed with the shell middens of the ancient beachcombers. Artefact and faunal remains abounded: excluding debitage 255,244 artefacts were recorded during the excavations.

The basic aim of the excavation was to establish a broad framework for the development of the cultural material. Had a more complex strategy, for example one requiring the three-dimensional recording of every find, been attempted, the small team would still be there today. It was impossible, therefore, to attempt to dig separately every lens of the deposit. Instead, trenches which would offer representative sections through the deposits were divided into transects and excavated strictly stratigraphically or, in the upper part, in convenient thin spits through the laminated deposits. This technique had served Palaeolithic archaeology well since the pioneering work of Pengelly and Piette and there seemed little point in attempting time-consuming alternatives.

Progress was slowed by the need to sieve all the soil and to collect carefully every element of debitage. Accordingly, John improvised a novel method of sieving. A stone's throw from the edge of the trench, the ocean crashed upon the shore; the sea regularly came and went, so, thought John, why waste energy pushing a sieve to and fro when the sea would do it for you. Stout, wooden framed boxes with wire mesh sides were preconstructed in Cape Town. On site a system of ropes, running through pulleys hung from vertical posts allowed the boxes to be lowered rapidly from the excavation to the wave-cut platform and, using a second array, into the swirling sea beneath. After initial teething problems, the system worked admirably. The sea-washed contents of each basket were tipped onto sorting tables and the finds easily picked out from the worthless residue.

The four man team stayed for each six-month season at the site, John and one other in a pitch-covered fisherman's hut, the other two in tents. The expedition had two four-wheel-drive vehicles, but these could not be brought the final mile and a half along the cliff path and down the steep final descent. Every morsel of food and every ounce of fuel had to be carried that final mile and a half to the site. Consequently, almost all cooking was done *al fresco* on driftwood fires and the diet was supplemented by shellfish gathered from the nearby rocks and fish expertly caught by the workmen. By the end of the season, a new, modern midden of mussel shells and charcoal had been created outside the hut.

Of more serious concern to John was the fact that drink also had to be man-handled down the cliff. Booze is extremely heavy stuff to carry anywhere other than in the stomach, and it often comes in very breakable bottles. Alas, beer was rationed to one small can of Lion lager per day – but Friday was *wyndaag*. In the evening around a blazing fire, entertained by the workmen enthusiastically strumming improvised guitars and chanting the genre of

songs introduced to the wider world by Miriam Makeba, all could indulge in generous quantities of South African wine. Liebestein, a sweet white wine, was imported in gallon jars – supposedly because they would break less easily than bottles – and because it was very cheap. Residents and occasional visitors alike came to appreciate the mellowing qualities of this 'nerve tonic'. At some stage, a visitor had embroidered a tea-towel with the quintessentially sixties mantra 'Lovers of Liebestein shake it'. In truth, it was the Liebestein that left its sippers shaking. Nonetheless, the towel hung like a limp flag inside the hut as a welcome reminder that the next *wyndaag* was at most only a week away.

One of the greatest rewards to the research programme was the discovery of human bones scattered throughout the stratigraphic sequence. The antiquity of the oldest was well beyond the range of radiocarbon dating, but by analogy with other Middle Stone Age industries and the correlation of the basal beach deposits with the high sea level of the last interglacial (OIS 5e), it was probably older than 100,000 years. This was by far the earliest *Homo sapiens sapiens* in southern Africa, or for that matter in the world. This was all the more surprising because the more substantial, Neanderthal-like mandibles were higher in the sequence (Singer & Wymer 1982).

Much remained to be done in South Africa, but Singer had already experienced difficulties with the authorities and the politics placed restrictions on John's liberty. It was time to beat a retreat to the northern hemisphere.

EAST ANGLIA

The golf club officials decided to tolerate the presence of diggers provided its members didn't have to be confronted with the sight of them. The only option, therefore, was to conceal the excavation in the middle of a thicket. In the early morning the motley party who were normally camped on a village green in deepest Essex would scurry across the fairways and into the hawthorn bushes, not to be seen until evening. From time to time this cover was penetrated by wayward golf balls and the regular warbling of a distant holiday camp tannoy 'Come and get your ice cream, come and get your ice cream nowowow'. In this isolating *enceinte*, tons of Pleistocene gravel and clay were being removed in search of flint flakes and cores which had once been manufactured on the banks of a meandering stream channel. Associated animal bones suggested that this had occurred in a relatively warm stage of the Pleistocene, but frost-heaving of the gravel showed that much colder conditions had followed (Wymer & Singer 1970; Singer *et al.* 1973; Wymer 1974). There were no sophisticated bifaces, of course, because this was Clacton-on-Sea, Edwardian holiday resort, type site, and source of the only Palaeolithic wooden spear in Britain.

Two seasons of excavation at Clacton (in 1969 and 1970) marked John's return to England, still as an employee of the University of Chicago under Ronald Singer. Many further seasons of work were in prospect in eastern England, so he relocated home, first wife and five children to the area. It may have been no coincidence that at a time when the English brewing industry was at its nadir, the new family home was in Bury St Edmunds, the source of Greene King's Abbot Ale. Appropriately enough the large garden of the house had produced a hand-axe, but the family must have wondered what sort of place the new home would be when they learned that early in its history, it had been a 'house of correction' for wayward young women, next to the prison.

John's ability to collect, order and publish data promptly made him the obvious choice to co-ordinate reviews of the evidence for hunter-gatherer sites in Britain. Between 1968 and 1973 he acted as the editorial hub of a circle of regional fact-finders engaged in the production of a gazetteer of all recorded Mesolithic collections in England and Wales (Wymer 1977). In those pre-database days, file cards must have filled every crevice of his study, not least because in 1969 he also initiated a gazetteer of the numerous Palaeolithic sites of East Anglia.

After Clacton, John's attention swung to other sites where *in situ* material might be found to research the economy, culture and environment of early hunter-gatherers through multi-disciplinary approaches. What better site than the one at which the great antiquity of Man, beyond the biblical account, had first been suggested. For decades, most academics had ignored the 'curious and most interesting communication' from John Frere of Roydon Hall, near Diss, placed before the Society of Antiquaries in 1797, concerning his observations on the discovery of 'some flints' at a brickpit at Hoxne, Suffolk. The potential of the lacustrine deposits at Hoxne was later realised and by the end of the 1950s it had become the 'stratotype locale' for the interglacial which bears its name.

John began his five-season excavation in the Oakley Park pit in May 1971. Two principal periods of occupation were apparent from artefacts *in situ*, the later (or Upper Industry) with coarser technology and the earlier (Lower Industry) with much more elegant technology. The Lower Industry was in pristine condition, the artefacts spread along a shore line next to clusters of cobbles undoubtedly representing some deliberate human action. Such a find immediately swept the rug from the feet of those who argued for a smooth typological development of the Acheulian, from coarse to fine. Microwear studies suggested the range of activities that the artefacts had actually been used for. The work culminated in a monograph with contributions from a dozen different specialists who debated the ancient landscape, the processes of burial, absolute dating, and so on, never previously possible from the limited sampling of the sedimentary sequence (Wymer 1983; Singer *et al.* 1993).

With the success of Hoxne, Ronald Singer was intent on continuing his collaboration with John and plans were considered for further excavation both at Hoxne and at Swanscombe. Unfortunately, these schemes were blocked and the long-running machine which had so successfully conducted worthwhile Pleistocene research was turned off.

Between 1979 and 1980, an S.E.R.C. grant funded John in the post of Senior Research Associate in the Department of Environmental Sciences at the University of East Anglia. The grant enabled him to complete the gazetteer of East Anglian Palaeolithic sites started in 1969, work which involved much travelling, consultation with colleagues and 'incarceration within dusty museum cellars' to document the 'large and hitherto somewhat archaeologically uncharted' region. The ensuing publication was a mine of information illustrated with location plans and drawings of artefacts in John's distinctive style, all used to underpin an interpretation of the Pleistocene evolution of the landscape (Wymer 1985b). With an eye on the broader perspective, John also devoted time to the preparation of a global overview of the Palaeolithic Age (Wymer 1982).

Grants are hard to win and don't last for long. Finding outstanding staff is equally problematic. No sooner had the grant that supported John run out than someone else was keen to employ an adaptable and capable prehistorian. In this case, the someone was John Hedges, County Archaeological Officer for Essex. Twenty-four hectares of the archaeologically rich, brickearth-covered, billiard-table-flat terrace north of the Thames at North Shoebury were earmarked for development. Wymer was probably as interested in the contents of the terrace as he was in that which lay on its surface. Nonetheless, between January and November 1981 he directed the excavation of a 7ha palimpsest now covered with a supermarket and housing. The original intention was to continue the North Shoebury excavations for at least four years, but funding could not be secured for more than a single season. Post-excavation analysis followed and, in due course, the report of the excavations appeared (Wymer & Brown 1995).

At times when others might despair, John would be heard to exclaim 'Allah will provide': not because his 1970 trip to Iran (Singer & Wymer 1978) had led to a religious conversion, but more from a belief in fate. And so it was in 1983. He had moved first to Stowupland and then Bildeston in Suffolk and, now with his second wife, Mollie, to Breckland wilds at Great Cressingham in Norfolk. A vacancy for a prehistorian had arisen in the Norfolk Archaeological Unit and, bearing in mind John's formative role in the regional advisory committee established in the early 1970s (the Scole Committee), he was the obvious choice. MSC teams were supervised and round barrows soon excavated at Bawsey, Longham, Lyng and Southacre (Wymer 1996).

The normal unit routines and rounds of committee meetings were broken by things closer to John's heart. Much earlier, he had drawn attention to the potential for Late Glacial sites in East Anglia with his publication of tanged flint points from Cranwich (1971). Similarly, he had reported on the long blade industry and barbed points which had been recovered from a gravel pit at Sproughton in Suffolk, only for the more detailed investigation of the relict stream channel to be frustrated in December 1974 when the River Gipping burst its banks, flooding the pit (Wymer *et al.* 1975; Wymer & Rose 1976). Throughout the 1970s a number of beachwalkers had collected jet-black flints from the beach at Titchwell in north Norfolk. The flint from which the enormous blades and cores had been worked was actually grey, so their colour was clearly a stain. Some flints were found in the fan of sand behind sand dunes, caused when extra strong tides had surmounted the sandy barrier. From this evidence, it became clear that the flints were not eroding from the dunes themselves but from a layer of peat below the normal low tide level. The might of the sea was wrenching blocks of peat from the sea bed together with the clay surface to which they had been attached and hurling them onto the beach where they slowly degraded leaving their Late Glacial lithics to be collected. Eventually material was found *in situ* but the location could only be reached at times of exceptionally low tide, every three or four months, and then only for about an hour. Nonetheless, a dedicated group of enthusiasts encouraged by John managed to plot a spatial distribution of finds and the associated stratigraphy was sampled (Wymer & Robins 1994).

John paid similar attention to Norfolk's Mesolithic sites. A newly discovered early Mesolithic site at Great Melton was excavated in 1986–7 'in the absence of any site of this nature in the county ever having been dug in an unselected and controlled manner . . .' (Wymer & Robins 1995). Earlier the later Mesolithic site at Banham had been investigated, but neither site had produced an undisturbed assemblage associated with animal bone and environmental indicators as Thatcham had done more than 35 years earlier.

CLIMAX

Arguably the finest achievement of John's career has been his most recent. Since 1990 John has worked with Wessex Archaeology, spearheading a team in a strategic project. The Southern Rivers Palaeolithic Project and the English Rivers Palaeolithic Survey sponsored by English Heritage, together with the Welsh Lower Palaeolithic Project sponsored by Cadw, have necessitated a consideration of every known Earlier Palaeolithic site in the country (*Past* 13; Lawson 1995). The distinctive figure, now bearded, habitually crowned with a well-worn brown trilby and striding with a somewhat loping gait, has been seen throughout the length and breadth of the country. The end product of his work, soon to be distilled into a unique topographically-based assessment of Pleistocene archaeology, has been an incomparable national survey, providing curators and researchers alike with a complete national overview. The seven weighty reports from these projects have created a baseline study which will help any interested person when they wish to assess the relative importance of any particular discovery or the potential for new discoveries in sensitive Pleistocene deposits.

John was uniquely qualified to undertake such a complex project. Its prompt completion marks yet another success in a very singular and brilliant career won by dedication, professionalism and down right hard graft. Most people look forward to a quiet retirement but the more John learns the more he seems to want to do, so who knows to what he will next turn his attentions.

REFERENCES

Boné, E. L. & Singer, R. 1965. *Hipparion* from Langebaanweg, Cape Province and a revision of the genus in Africa. *Annals of the South African Museum* 48, 314 –97

Chippindale, C. 1997. Editorial. *Antiquity* 71(272), 255–6.

Healy, F. 1994. The excavation of a ring-ditch at Englefield by John Wymer and Paul Ashbee, 1963. *Berkshire Archaeological Journal* 74, 9–25.

Lawson, A. 1995. Palaeolithic Archaeology – a geological overlap. *Earth Heritage* 4, 3–5.

Singer, R., Gladfelter, B.G. & Wymer, J. J. 1993. *The Lower Palaeolithic Site at Hoxne, England.* Chicago & London: University of Chicago Press.

Singer, R. & Wymer, J. J. 1968. Archaeological investigations at the Saldanha Skull site in South Africa. *South African Archaeological Bulletin* 23, 63–74.

Singer, R. & Wymer, J.J. 1978. A hand-ax from northwest Iran: the question of human movement between Africa and Asia in the Lower Paleolithic period. In L. Freeman (ed.), *Views of the Past*, 13–27. Chicago: Mouton.

Singer, R. & Wymer, J.J. 1982. *The Middle Stone Age at Klasies River Mouth in South Africa.* Chicago: University of Chicago Press.

Singer, R., Wymer, J.J., Gladfelter, B.G. & Wolff, R. Excavation of the Clactonian industry at the golf course, Clacton-on-Sea, Essex, *Proceedings of the Prehistoric Society* 39, 6–74.

Wymer, J.J. 1957. A Clactonian flint industry at Little Thurrock, Grays, Essex. *Proceedings of the Geologists' Association* 68, 159–77.

Wymer, J.J., 1959. Excavations on the Mesolithic site at Thatcham: interim report *Berkshire Archaeological Journal* 57, 1–24.

Wymer, J.J., 1961a. The Lower Palaeolithic succession in the Thames valley and the date of the ancient channel between Caversham and Henley. *Proceedings of the Prehistoric Society* 27, 1–27.

Wymer, J.J. 1961b. The discovery of a gold torc at Moulsford. *Berkshire Archaeological Journal* 59, 36–7.

Wymer, J.J. 1962. Excavations at the Maglemosian sites at Thatcham, Berkshire, England. *Proceedings of the Prehistoric Society* 28, 329–61.

Wymer, J.J. 1964. Excavations at Barnfield Pit, 1955–60. In C.D. Ovey (ed.), *The Swanscombe Skull: a Survey of Research at a Pleistocene Site*, 19–61. London: Royal Anthropological Institute Occasional Paper 20.

Wymer, J.J. 1966. Excavations of the Lambourn long barrow, 1964. *Berkshire Archaeological Journal* 62 [for 1965–6], 1–16.

Wymer, J.J. 1968. *Lower Palaeolithic Archaeology in Britain as Represented by the Thames Valley.* London: John Baker.

Wymer, J.J. 1971. A possible late Upper Palaeolithic site at Cranwich, Norfolk. *Norfolk Archaeology* 35(2), 259–63.

Wymer, J.J. 1974. Clactonian and Acheulian industries in Britain: their chronology and significance. *Proceedings of the Geologists' Association* 85, 391–421.

Wymer, J.J. 1977. *Gazetteer of Mesolithic Sites in England and Wales.* London: Council for British Archaeology Research Report 20.

Wymer, J.J. 1982. *The Palaeolithic Age.* London: Croom Helm.

Wymer, J.J. 1983. The Lower Palaeolithic site at Hoxne. *Proceedings of the Suffolk Institute of Archaeology and History* 35(3), 169–89.

Wymer, J.J. 1985a. The archaeology of Barnfield Pit. In K.L. Duff (ed.), *The Story of Swanscombe Man*, 20–27. Kent County Council and Nature Conservancy Council.

Wymer, J.J. 1985b. *Palaeolithic Sites of East Anglia.* Norwich: Geo Books.

Wymer, J.J. 1996. *Barrow Excavations in Norfolk 1984–88.* Gressenhall: East Anglian Archaeology Report 77.

Wymer, J.J. & Brown, N.R. 1995. *Excavations at North Shoebury: Settlement and Economy in South-east Essex 1500 BC–AD 1500.* Chelmsford: East Anglian Archaeology Report 75.

Wymer, J.J. & Robins, P.A. 1994. A long blade flint industry beneath Boreal peat at Titchwell, Norfolk. *Norfolk Archaeology* 42(1), 13–37.

Wymer, J.J. & Robins, P.A. 1995. A Mesolithic site at Great Melton. *Norfolk Archaeology* 42(2), 125–47.

Wymer, J.J., Jacobi. R.M. & Rose, J. 1975. Late Devensian and early Flandrian barbed points from Sproughton, Suffolk. *Proceedings of the Prehistoric Society* 41, 25–41.

Wymer, J.J. & Rose, J. 1976. A long blade industry from Sproughton, Suffolk. Ipswich: *East Archaeology Report* 3, 1–10.

Wymer, J. & Singer, R. 1970. The first season of excavation at Clacton-on-Sea, Essex, England: a brief report. *World Archaeology* 2(1), 12–16.

2. J. J. W. A Tribute from the Upper Thames

R. J. MacRae

ABSTRACT

The following offering to John Wymer's festschrift is in essay form rather than a formal archaeological paper. The first part recalls some of the ways in which he has been invaluably helpful to the author in Palaeolithic activities. The second part records, very briefly, how collections of palaeoliths were made in gravel pits in the Upper Thames Valley, with some observations on provenance, technology and possible chronology. The whole is presented in a way which is more personal than is customary, and the author hopes to be forgiven for this necessary style.

MEMORIES FROM THE OXFORD REGION

In this book others will honour John in a more orderly, sequential way than ever I can, tracing his rise to eminence in British and international archaeology. They will praise his profound scholarship, his excavating skills, and his rare ability to clarify Palaeolithic problems in language all can understand. They will pay tribute to one whose contribution to Quaternary science is uniquely valuable. In this we all concur.

For my part I would like to say something about John's impact on my own life during the 30 years or more I have counted him as a friend; and to acknowledge how he has generously shared his knowledge and experience with one less gifted, less erudite, than himself. I am told I am to write about some aspects of the remote prehistory of the Upper Thames Valley. This I will do presently. Meanwhile (now my 83rd birthday is past) I am permitted to sketch a personal background to John's influence, and I think he will smile at shared recollections.

My packed folder of letters from John begins in 1966 when he showed interest in an untutored tyro who was able to travel around on business over much of southern England and find time to pick up handaxes and flakes from gravel pits. John's letters and laconic five-line postcards, and occasionally his company, spurred me on. Romsey, Henley, Maidenhead, Cookham, Taplow, Remenham, Warren Hill and Kentford were all fruitful. Palaeoliths were piling up! John introduced me to Highlands Farm in the 'Ancient Channel' of the Thames above Henley which he knew so well, and I enjoyed many days of muscular gravel-shifting there. Two classic guide books to the Palaeolithic appeared in 1968 – Derek Roe's 'Gazetteer' and John's survey of the Thames Valley and they were riches indeed.

I moved to Oxford in 1969 and in scant leisure helped Donald Baden-Powell sort the Pitt Rivers Museum Palaeolithic collections. Derek Roe had come to Oxford and persuaded me to transfer all my finds to the museum. Despite his heavy committments, John kept in touch. The seventies were exciting. A new Oxfordshire site at Berinsfield added 250 handaxes and flakes to 'Mac's room' at No. 60, Banbury Road where the Donald Baden-Powell Quaternary Research Centre had been established, and where for more than 20 years I enjoyed as a privileged amateur the facilities of a university department.

John had moved from Berkshire to East Anglia and I often went over from Oxford, once to show him seven handaxes and 200 flakes I had rescued from a pit at Kentford in basal silt below glacial outwash. These, with

Figure 2.1. J. J. Wymer and R. J. MacRae at Lynford Pit, Norfolk, Summer 1994. (Photograph by Terry Hardaker)

two twisted ovates and two fine Acheulian scrapers from that pit, were later figured by John in his East Anglia Palaeolithic sites record (Wymer 1985). Sometimes he and I would have a day together in the Breckland for the sheer pleasure of flint-hunting without really serious intent except to ensure that the lunchtime beer was a good brew. When he and Mollie settled at Great Cressingham I sometimes stayed with them, and not only was there satisfying 'handaxe talk' but what Chaucer would call 'genial revelrie'.

Talking of handaxes what a pleasure it is to watch John's fingers sensitively tracing the flaking pattern on one's latest find – assessing the skill of its maker and paying silent tribute to a fellow-craftsman, for he is a master of replication, deft with stone and soft-hammer, and self-taught as with his other skills. His illustrations (and there must be hundreds of them) are done with artistry and accuracy. He and I share the quite unscientific belief that symmetry of form often meant as much to the handaxe-makers as did utility. The aesthetic principle (perhaps Man's most enduring discovery) is evidenced in an Acheulian's elegant handaxe as much as in Donatello's David. One wonders, did visual imagery come before articulate speech? Shall we ever know?

Here are just one or two 'flashback' memories of enjoyable days with John...

– Cutting a section at Furze Platt, one of Britain's finest sites before its owner, breaking his promise to preserve the old pit, sold it for building, leaving only a remnant of the SSSI.
– A Quaternary Research Association trip to Highlands Farm, with John and I on separate mounds of gravel declaiming to our audiences and shouting against the wind like market men. A pub lunch that same

day with Russell Coope in hilarious story-telling mood.
– At Pinkney's Green, near Maidenhead, together cutting a section in Winter Hill gravels. After two hours – not a flake! We needed invocation to a fertility goddess, so I made one from clay and set her up. Three minutes later a nice sharp ovate emerged. We looked at each other, wondering.
– From Switchback, Cookham, towards sunset, a rare sight. Four of the Thames terraces folded down the hill to the west of us. 'Must have been a mighty river once' said John.
– An enigmatic and technologically unclassifiable collection of over 500 small crude flakes and haphazard cores from solution hollows in Lynch Hill terrace gravel at Remenham was discussed with John (I had seen the only parallel in Peyrony's 'Tayacian' in Les Eyzies Museum). 'Must have been a sort of remedial school for mentally-retarded Acheulians', concluded John.

John is good fun to be with. I had found three heavy-butted sharp handaxes quite close to Cannon Court Farm, and decided to look again at the overgrown Furze Platt pit. I unearthed the very rusty head of a pickaxe. I gave it to John, who declared it might well have belonged to Deffy Cooper, who found Britain's biggest handaxe back in 1912. John put the relic by, but a month or so ago he joined me at Southacre in Norfolk, brandishing Deffy's pick, newly-hafted. It brought us luck.

We all, veterans and young lions alike, have such memories; and we should cherish them. Sooner or later at meetings, excursions and digs one meets nearly everybody in the Palaeolithic business, and a wonderfully friendly lot they are. No wonder, with John setting such an example.

In the eventful time of the late eighties there was the production of a volume all about quartzite and non-flint; my Gravelly Guy pit was still yielding handaxes; a big new Floodplain pit just west of Oxford was packed with Devensian reindeer and bison, and Kate Scott was the right person in the right place at Stanton Harcourt, opening up the richest mammoth site in Britain. A little later, John began collecting information for his Southern Rivers Project and I was able to supply details of pits I knew and the finds therefrom. It was some small repayment for his unstinting help over the years. For me, retirement meant more time for prehistory, but sadly, just short of our golden wedding, my wife Joan died in 1991. Lukewarm towards archaeology, but a fine photographer and a dedicated nature conservationist.

I left Cassington two years ago and bought a rural cottage in mid-Norfolk with a big garden, a little river at the bottom, and next door to my daughter. John Wymer lives half-an-hour's drive away and the pit at Southacre is also handy. I get there often, and the bag so far is 15 handaxes, 4 Levallois cores and 230 flakes. Other pits, too, are promising. John sometimes comes along, taking a break from his desk where the monograph to follow his English Rivers Palaeolithic Survey steadily grows. Not long ago modest John was given a belated Honorary Doctorate.

RICHES FROM THE OXFORD REGION

At editorial command, I must now contribute a much abbreviated account of what I was able to do towards the early Palaeolithic record in the Upper Thames Valley, and in extending awareness of the significance of quartzite artefacts found in the valley and indeed in the rest of Britain. The continuous work of geologists in the Oxford region has lately been summarised by David Bridgland (1994) and the terrace chronology (with almost everything else) remains controversial. As for the archaeology I wonder I have the temerity to write about it at all when from time to time Derek Roe, in his inimitable style, does the job infinitely better. He has a sort of stewardship over the region and its place 'on the extreme north-western edge of human settlement'.

The Upper Thames total of palaeoliths listed by Roe in his Gazetteer in 1968 was just over 400, including 300 handaxes. There were only 30 quartzite implements. Up to 1988 the record was increased by more than 300 palaeoliths Among these more recent finds were 65 artefacts of non-flint materials. Nearly all these additions came from Berinsfield and Stanton Harcourt. I am still puzzled by the indifference of archaeologists to the potential wealth in the valley between the early years of the century and the seventies. Roe records only three handaxes from Berinsfield and only two from Stanton Harcourt. Yet there had been big gravel pits at both places for 40 years or more. Only eight handaxes are known from the formerly extensive pits west of Stanton Harcourt, where the hunter-gathering environment must have been much the same as down-river (Briggs 1988), and the periglacial and fluvial processes similar. My own search had to be limited to two small areas, as time and chance dictated. The only other active handaxe-hunter has been Jeffrey Wallis in the Abingdon area, with nearly 25 palaeoliths.

The oldest and most important assemblage in the region is that from the Wolvercote brick-pit. Most of us have seen and handled the truly magnificent plano-convex specimens and the rest of the 133 handaxes, described so well by Joyce Tyldesley (1986). The battle of the geologists over the age of the buried Wolvercote channel continues, though the site is now quite inaccessible. Bridgland sums up this key site, opting for OIS 9. Valuable collections came early in the century from Iffley, and from the Wallingford fan gravels before the destructive onset of mechanical aggregate extraction. During the seventies geologists were quite busy in the Upper Thames, notably David Briggs and his colleagues. I was lucky to be with David one morning in Dix pit, Stanton Harcourt, when he discovered the OIS 7 interglacial channel, the remarkable story of which is told elsewhere in this volume.

Before he left for other spheres of action, David Briggs produced a British Archaeological Report entitled rather grandly *The Chronology and Environmental Framework of Early Man in the Upper Thames Valley* (Briggs et al. 1985). With guidance from Derek Roe and John Wymer I wrote the chapters on the Palaeolithic. The theme was much expanded three years later in a wide-ranging BAR (MacRae & Moloney 1988).

Luck plays a great part in artefact collection and the co-operation of gravel companies and their workmen is essential. One is haunted by the horrifying thought of the hundreds of Palaeolithic treasures that at Berinsfield, for instance, were carried away to roads and building sites. At that site more than half of the 250 handaxes and debitage recovered were spotted on a moving conveyor belt by Colin Winterbourne, engineer at the grading plant, and he gave me all he rescued. I had the rest from pit floors and reject heaps. Unstratified they remain, but so are 95% of all known British palaeoliths (Wymer 1968). We ended up with a very mixed bag of handaxes, pointed and ovate: 21 butts and tips; 7 Levallois flakes; and 2 cores. Even more exciting were the 36 artefacts of quartzite – one seventh of the total assemblage. The pits closed in 1981.

The Berinsfield flint finds were often rolled and frost-cracked, but some were fresh. Roe has described (1994) them as 'good Middle Acheulian', cautiously placing them in 'the record of intermittent human occupation of Britain from OIS 11 to 6'. The origin of flint raw material is always worth looking for. Although the great soliflucted mass of the Wallingford flint fan gravels, accumulated during the Anglian, lies only a few kilometres away, those gravels are now badly frost-shattered. Were they so when the Berinsfield Acheulians were around? Was there an accessible source of good flint in the Chiltern foothills and now swept away or buried? Or could the implements pre-date the fan gravels? A source of sound, workable flint must also be postulated for the Stanton Harcourt handaxes up-river. They are thermally undamaged. At both sites it is obvious that visiting groups turned to the plentiful Northern Drift quartzite pebbles to supplement flint supplies. So did the Wolvercote and Iffley people. The Acheulians, by the very nature of their existence, had to be masters of expediency.

It is not now possible to find, on the surface or in any exposures along the 50km stretch of the Thames between Wallingford and Stanton Harcourt, a nodule of sound flint fit to make anything bigger than a very small ovate. There are plenty of small flint pebbles reworked from the Northern Drift, but these are all decayed and frost-cracked, useless for implements, and must have been so long before the Acheulians came. It is evident that flint blanks and roughouts, but mainly finished tools, were carried from some Chilterns source up the valley to all the hunter gatherer locations of which we know (MacRae 1989).

After Berinsfield, I was able to concentrate on a newly-opened pit in OIS 6 gravels at Stanton Harcourt. Who 'Gravelly Guy' was I never found out, but he and his pit kept me entertained for the next nine years. The pit (now closed) was in charge of my good friend Vic Griffin, without whose help I could not have rescued many of the 49 flint handaxes, plus a few broken pieces and some resharpening flakes. In additon there were 19 handaxes, choppers and flakes of quartzite. The flint tools made up an orthodox mix of Middle Acheulian styles, pointed handaxes predominating with some sub-cordates and one extraordinary ficron – the third largest handaxe known in Britain, at 27cm long. There was no trace of Clactonian or Levallois.

As for trying to date these Stanton Harcourt finds the most likely probability is that they pre-date the cold climate gravels, and were the losses or discards of groups visiting the valley in one or more of the warm or cool-temperate phases now recognised in the Anglian. Or they may be later – there are so few certainties in current ideas of the Thames chronology. The artefacts are likely to have lain a long time on river-banks or adjacent hill-slopes and were swept into stream-channels, and, as Briggs has concluded (1988) were 'armoured by mud and sand and protected by a veneer of other lag materials'. Certainly most came from the lowest levels and some were embedded in the bedrock Oxford Clay. Nearly all the flint handaxes were only very slightly abraded, but, strangely, many of the quartzites were rolled, some heavily.

The recovery of such a large proportion of quartzite artefacts from Berinsfield and Stanton Harcourt led to the idea of a wider survey of their significance. In 1987 Norah Moloney and I jointly compiled and edited the first comprehensive work on non-flint artefacts and materials in the British palaeolithic. I had little difficulty in persuading a dozen well known archaeologists and geologists to contribute. Derek Roe wrote the preface and John Wymer laid the ground for the study in a re-assessment of the geographical range of Lower Palaeolithic activitiy in Britian, showing that the absence of familiar raw materials was no bar to early man's penetration into the Midlands and beyond.

It is pleasing to think that one has provided material for further study, and that Terry Hardaker, a Palaeolithic enthusiast, now keeps watch over the Upper Thames. Also gratifying is the progress Hyung Woo Lee from Korea is making towards his doctorate at No. 60 Banbury Road – his subject is 'The MacRae Collection from the Upper Thames'. He is, in addition, making a detailed examination of the several thousand artefacts I brought from Highlands Farm.

Some facts and figures have crept into this chronicle, but a lot more are recorded elsewhere. They are merely markers in a crowded and often exciting life. Quite unashamedly I still value the thrill of discovery. To unearth something that was last held by a human or hominid countless thousands of years ago is rather like shaking hands with him. I have heard John Wymer saying much the same thing. The sheer pleasure of finding an object so awesomely ancient remains with me, even after it may ignominiously end up in other hands as computer-fodder.

REFERENCES

Bridgland, D.R. 1994. *Quaternary of the Thames*. London: Chapman & Hall. Geological Conservation Review Series 7.

Briggs, D.J. 1988. The environmental background to human occupation in the Upper Thames Valley during the Quaternary period. In R.J.MacRae & N.Moloney, (eds), 1988. *Non-Flint Stone Tools and the Palaeolithic Occupation of Britain*, 167–85. Oxford: British Archaeological Reports British Series 189.

Briggs, D.J., Coope, G.R. & Gilbertson, D.D. (eds), 1985. *The Chronology and Environmental Framework of Early Man in the Upper Thames Valley*. Oxford: British Archaeological Reports British Series 137.

MacRae, R.J. 1989. Belt, shoulder-bag or basket? An enquiry into handaxe transport and flint sources. *Lithics* 10, 2–8.

MacRae, R.J. & Moloney, N. (eds) 1988. *Non-Flint Stone Tools and the Palaeolithic Occupation of Britain*. Oxford: British Archaeological Reports British Series 189.

Roe, D.A. 1968. *A Gazetteer of British Lower and Middle Palaeolithic Sites*. London: Council for British Archaeology Research Report 8.

Roe, D.A. 1994. The Palaeolithic Archaeology of the Oxford Region. The Tom Hassall Lecture 1994. OXONIENSIA Vol LIX 1994.

Tyldesley, J.A. 1986. *The Wolvercote Channel Handaxe Assemblage*. Oxford: British Archaeological Reports British Series 153.

Wymer, J.J. 1985. *The Palaeolithic Sites of East Anglia*. Norwich: Geo Books.

Wymer, J.J. 1968. *Lower Palaeolithic Archaeology in Britain as Represented by the Thames Valley*. London: John Baker.

3. On the Move. Theory, Time Averaging and Resource Transport at Olduvai Gorge

John McNabb

ABSTRACT

This paper explores some ideas about how the implications of time averaging may be overcome by a more realistic understanding of the nature of the archaeological record. The inter-relationship between resource transport and raw material behaviour for Plio-Pleistocene hominids at Olduvai Gorge, Tanzania, is taken as an example of what can be done with time averaged assemblages.

We shall not cease from exploration
And the end of all our exploring
will be to arrive where we started
and know the place for the first time.

The words of T.S. Elliot from *Little Gidding* remind us that all knowledge is a journey whose ultimate purpose is to help us understand. Nowhere is this more apparent than in archaeology where knowledge is used to structure stories about the past which we hope will help to explain human behaviour. So the journey is an ontogenetic development. The archaeology of the late twentieth century bears little resemblance to what it was even forty years ago. But how far have we come? What can we really say about past behaviour?

Until we can invent the proverbial time machine and learn to wind the clock backwards we will never be absolutely certain of anything. Until we can ask people what was going through their minds when they did this or that, we can never be certain if the attributes we select as important for study really are. Modern ethnography has shown that even when we can observe and question living people, the motivations for their actions are not always apparent, even to them. (An excellent example of this is Nigel Barley's *Innocent Anthropologist*.). So there can be no truth in anything we do, individual lives and their motivations are for the most part lost to us. Our pasts are only as good as our methodologies and our imaginations. Archaeological explanations are not so much neutral and obvious windows on the past, rather they are the choice of which window to look through.

WHAT DOES THIS MEAN FOR THE PALAEOLITHIC?

In the study of earliest humans the most pressing issue that new awareness has highlighted in recent years is that of time averaging, based on the work of people like Stern (1993; 1994). Here is as serious a challenge to our myths of history as ever there was, and its implications have not as yet been fully realised. The nightmare scenario implied by Stern's work is that in 9 cases out of 10 archaeological sites tell us almost nothing. In brief, Stern's arguments are as follows. At a landscape level it is difficult to develop ideas of hominid behaviour because individual sites may not be genuinely contemporary. One site may lie exposed for a long period of time, and be the product of repeated visits by hominids, another may be the product of one visit and be buried relatively quickly. Yet both lie on the same land surface, and commonly archaeologists would make comparisons between the two in reconstructing subsistence behaviour. In these circumstances Stern argues that we can only look at behaviour from the point of view of a gross sedimentological timescale; by identifying unambiguous 'ceiling' and 'floor' deposits, such as tuffs, which bracket archaeological sediments. We can then say that within a block of sedimentological time such and such happened, but any finer temporal resolution on those constituent archaeological components is not possible.

The traditional goal of recognising and interpreting a landscape of behaviour is only as good as the interpretation of individual units of behaviour within that landscape, in other words reconstructing what is going on at individual sites. At this level the implications of Stern's work raise some profound difficulties for behavioural reconstructions.

Methodological difficulties

One of the most common mechanisms for validating site based reconstructions of behaviour is that promoted by Binford (1981) who argued that Middle Range Theory provides a bridging argument between the present and the past, as uniformitarianist principles can empower the use of modern actualistic studies and their results to explain past signatures in the archaeological record, thus explaining them by reference to modern counterparts. The crux of Middle Range Theory is the empowering of the bridging argument itself. But there are all sorts of problems with this. How do we know that past mechanisms do operate like those of today? Is uniformitarianism justified in explaining extinct species behaviour where no modern analogue exists? Can two or more mechanisms produce the same signature?

Difficulties with site development

Two levels of difficulty operate here. If sites are open over a long time they are subject to a number of potential agencies of disturbance; partial destruction/removal of material by natural processes, disturbance by animals, disturbance by hominids etc.. Alternatively, natural agencies can combine to create sites at points in a landscape where no hominid activity actually took place (Schick 1987). Secondly, and here we come to the real issue, if a site does have something of a *long durée* it could be the focus of repeated visits by tool making and using hominids. They could practice the same activity at the site, but not necessarily in the same precise spot thus blurring any evidence of individual activities. Or they may practice a number of activities at the site, perhaps over repeated visits with no regard for habit. The result would be a homogenised assemblage of artefacts. The recognition of behaviour now takes on the qualities of a contextual minestrone; chuck it all in then give it a stir.

NEW DIRECTIONS?

Four areas of analysis transcend time averaging, since they are independent of how many episodes of activity make up a site.

1) Technology. The study of how an artefact was made. Synchronic and especially diachronic changes in this aspect of archaeology can be especially revealing about changes in tool behaviour. These kinds of studies are particularly useful in inter-site comparative analysis.
2) Typology. In this instance taken to mean what was being made.
3) Raw material studies. Data generated from the effects of raw material studies on how artefacts are made, and on the catchment potential of the raw materials used on sites can be particularly informative.
4) Transport studies. Generating data on gross resource movement and manipulation is possible even on time averaged surfaces. The method outlined and developed below is one possible way of doing this.

Clearly the above are all inter-related, and possibly significant patterning in the data will be apparent when the relationships between the three are analysed. Another area of analysis in which elements of the above may be studied, independent of time averaging, is the context in which tool behaviour and resource manipulation are embedded. This is shown in the table below.

	Why	*How*	*Where*	*When*
Resources used		X	X	X
Tools made		X	X	X
Tools used		?	X	X

Through the contextual analysis of the how, where and when of tool behaviour, the all important questions in the why column may be speculated upon.

CASE STUDY

Above I asserted that our pasts are only as good as our methodologies and our imaginations. As an example of how behavioural studies can be practised on time averaged assemblages, at least at site level, I wish to look at the inter-related nature of the raw material and transport behaviour of hominids at Olduvai Gorge during Oldowan and Early Acheulian times.

Methodology

The analysis is based on a number of assumptions, and a simple premise. A *flaked piece* (any block of raw material from which pieces have been detached) will be knapped a minimum of three times and a maximum of fifteen. Each flake of lava will be accompanied by two pieces of shatter, and each flake of non-lava raw materials, primarily quartz or quartzite, will be accompanied by four pieces of shatter. Bifaces will be made with a minimum of three removals and a maximum of fifty. These figures are assumptions based on my own (unrecorded) experimental knapping with these kinds of raw materials and these types of artefact. Given the number of flaked pieces at a site it is possible to calculate the number of *detached pieces* (all flakes including retouched flakes, shatter, chips and fragments etc.) that would be expected from *in-situ* flaking. The number of actual pieces recovered during the excavation of these localities is then looked at to see whether it falls above, below, or within the estimated parameters.

A brief synopsis of each of the localities used is given in Tables 3.1 and 3.2. (data drawn from Leakey 1971; Hay 1976; Peters & Blumenschine 1995; Monahan 1996; Walter *et al.* 1991). The sites have been chosen because they represent the least disturbed contexts. EF–HR and FC West show more potential for being disturbed than the remainder and these should be treated with more caution. FLKNN 1 and 3 were interpreted by Leakey (1971) as the edges of bigger occupation loci destroyed by erosion. While this is possible, it is equally possible that they represent less intense activity on a surface (Leakey 1971, 43; the scatter between the patches?). As with any sites, all interpretations are relevant only to the excavated area.

Tables 3.3 and 3.4 present the results of the analysis. The data was extracted from Leakey's excellent Olduvai Gorge volume 3 (1971). In some cases raw totals of artefact categories as given have been used, and in some cases totals have been generated from the percentages in Leakey's Table 7 (1971, 264).

Results (summarised in Table 3.5)

The Olduvai Bed I and II sites group into three. Those with too many flaked pieces, those with too many detached pieces, and those that fall within the model's predicted limits. But within these groups there are some interesting sub-patterns.

Four sites (DK and FLKNN 1 – non biface; TK Upper Floor and EF–HR – biface [because the totals for FLKNN 1 lava and non-lava are so small I have assumed the null hypothesis that there is a small enough number of cores to explain the small number of flakes]) form a distinct group, where approaches to both raw material types are identical. Here lava and non-lavas were brought to these sites, flaked, and left *in-situ*. Any subsequent transport from these localities was not enough to upset this pattern. At EF–HR it is certain that some of the bifaces were knapped at this spot because thinning flakes form a significant part of the debitage (Leakey 1971, 124; a fact not observed at any of the other biface sites). All the other sites in the study show a difference in the treatment of lava vs non-lava raw materials.

There are four sites where there are too many lava cores and bifaces to explain the number of detached pieces

present (see Table 3.5). Either pre-flaked cores were brought to the site, of which only some were then knapped, or flakes have been removed from the immediate vicinity. Stiles (1991) argues a convincing case for the transport of flakes from site to site at Olduvai. Toth has argued the same for Koobi Fora (1987). The question of the import of pre-knapped artefacts is particularly noticeable in the TK Lower Floor data, where only 8 flaked lava pieces are present. There were no lava flakes found at this locality, and only 1.9 pieces of lava debitage were recovered! There are two lava bifaces from this floor (Leakey 1971, 175). A glance at the illustrated lava biface from this horizon (Leakey 1971, fig. 82) indicates that not only is it on a flake blank itself, but, at a conservative estimate, its shape has been achieved by at least 20 blows. The remaining biface and 6 flaked lava pieces (2 side choppers, 1 end chopper, 1 polyhedron, 1 sub-spheroid, 1 heavy duty scraper) are still too numerous to explain the small flake count at this site. In terms of the model, the lack of flakes and virtual absence of detached pieces suggests that at least the bifaces, as well as the majority of the cores were probably brought to this site already flaked.

For all four of these sites where flaked lava pieces were either imported, or lava flakes have been exported, all the non-lava raw material appears to have been flaked and left *in situ*.

The patterning in the data for sites with too many detached pieces is more distinctive, and reverses that just described. There are only two assemblages here, and both lack bifaces. Both of them show that the amount of lava knapped can be explained by the number of cores present (because the numbers of flaked and detached pieces are so small I have assumed the null hypothesis for FLKNN 3 that there are enough cores to explain the small number of detached pieces), but now it is the non-lava raw materials that are being treated differently. Each of these two is quite dramatic in its way. *All* of the non-lava cores from FLKNN 3 have either been removed from the vicinity of the excavated area, or all the flakes were brought to the site.

With FLK Zinj the situation is less ambiguous. The number of detached pieces present exceeds the maximum expected total by 790.4 pieces. Given that the number of non-lava flaked pieces is 20 (and exceeds the lava total by only two), and that the non-lava detached pieces comprise over 95% of the entire knapped component of the site, it is difficult to draw any other conclusion than that the non-lavas have been brought to the site, knapped on the spot, and then the cores removed.

Support from this comes from the small size of the debitage, as well as the spatial distribution of the archaeological material excavated (Leakey 1971, fig 24 – pull out). The majority of the detached pieces as plotted cluster within the north east corner of the site and form a distinct concentration. In addition to the small size of these pieces and the high concentrations of bone fragments, there were numerous smaller non-lava chips and fragments that were

Site	Bed	Depth of archaeology	Stratigraphic context	Degree of disturbance	Age	Location	Environment
DK Non-biface	I	1.5–2.0 m from 3 levels. Majority from base of lowest	1.5–2.2 m below Tuff IB. On a land surface	Minimal. Small frags bone present, small coprolites. Overlain by clay	>1.8 mya	In eastern edge of eastern lake margin zone, < 1km from alluvial fans, > 3km from permanent lake shore.	Time of occupation shore close by, crocs, water loving fauna, flora etc. Lake margin zone indicates occasional flooding. Trees near.
FLKNN 1 and FLKNN 3 Non-biface	I	c. 10 cm or less	FLKNN 1 stratig. equivalent of FLK Zinj. FLKNN 3 on Tuff IB. Both on land surfaces as indicated by palaeosols.	Minimal. 1 – bone in fresh condit., artefacts unrolled 3 – no mention of weathering, frags and rodent bones present. Some carnivore gnawing and coprolites. Both overlain by tuffs	<1.8 mya	In eastern lake margin zone, c. 1 km from permanent lake shore, and c. 2km from alluvial fans.	Flora, fish and fauna indicator proximity of water, either lake shore or marsh environment
FLK Zinj Non-biface	I	< 7 cm or less	Below Tuff IC On a land surface as indicated by palaeosol	Minimal – articulated bones, minute frags of bone and stone chips. Small channel present	> 1.76 mya	In eastern lake margin deposits, same location as FLKNN 1 and 3	Marsh vegetation present below Tuff IC. Freshwater snails, bovids both water and dry land species. Trees near by.
FLKN 1–2 and FLKN 3 Non-biface	I	1–2 from < 80cm, artefacts concentrated near top. 3 <25 cm	Below Tuff IF, level 1–2 (top) overlain by IF. Artefacts sunk into clay from occupied surface.	Minimal. Micro fauna and rodent bones present in large quantities. A few bones articulated. Artefacts and bone fresh. Overlain by tuff – lacustrine origin	< 1.75 mya	Brief phase of lake expansion after shrinking period. Site c. 1.5–2 km away from alluvial fans. Lake shore possibly close, c. 1 km.	General climate drier than previous e.g. open country bovids and increasing incidence of dry land rodents. Lake possibly very saline indicated by fish. Some bovids suggest proximity of closed tree cover nearby

Table 3.1. Archaeological, stratigraphic and environmental context of Bed I sites, Olduvai Gorge (after Leakey 1971; Hay 1976).

Site	Bed	Depth of archaeology	Stratigraphic context	Degree of disturbance	Age	Location	Environment
FC West Biface	II	< 7 cm	Stratigraphically above Tuff IIB + below U. Augitic Sandstone. Locally below Bird Print Tuff. On clay surface	Bones unweathered, some artefacts abraded or weathered. Poss. some material removed (or emplaced) by water. Possibly some disturbance	1.4 mya	In eastern lake margin zone. Possibly less than 1 km from permanent lake shore. Streams draining from south in close proximity	Earth movements cause lake and adjacent marshland to shrink. To west of lake major westward flowing drainage way feed into lake, this is in lake margin zone so occasionally flooded. General drier more arid climate of Bed II (post Lemuta Member) prevail.
EF–HR Biface	II	10 cm	Between the Brown Tuffaceous Silt layer and Tuff IIC. Implication is that site is on a landsurface.	Artefacts on either side of a small channel cut into clay. Artefacts on this surface mostly unabraded. Gravel infills channel and buries site. Rolled artefacts in gravels. Unabraded material *in-situ?* Small flakes	1.4 mya	Within lake margin/flood zone, during period of lake expansion. Hay terms this site inland. > 1.5 km from permanent lake margin and c. 2 km from the area of mudflows to west of site. Site in drainageway area.	Dry climate of Bed II. Proximity to numerous local streams, northern draining streams bringing big clasts into drainageway. At times of flooding the lake is brackish
TK Upper Floor and TK Lower Floor Biface	II	Upper on contact with clay unit, Lower on contact with clayey tuff < 7 cms both	Above Tuff IID. Implication is both sites on landsurfaces.	Minimal. No mention of weathering or rolling on artefacts Both overlain by waterlain tuff	1.2 mya	Shortly after deposition of Tuff IID Lake Olduvai disappears. Uncertain whether TK floors associated with last gasp of lake or extensive ponding in former bed. Site in marshy area in eastern drainageway which is still flowing westwards	Semi-arid climate. In marshy zone. Close proximity to streams draining from north.

Table 3.2. Archaeological, stratigraphic and environmental contexts of Bed II sites, Olduvai Gorge (after Leakey 1971; Hay 1976).

Site	Bed	Flaked pieces (actual)	Flake range (extrap.)	Debitage range (extrap.)	Detached pieces, max range (extrap.)	Detached pieces (actual)
DK	1	Core 122	366–1830	732–3660	366–5490	600.5
		Biface				
FLK Zinj	1	Core 18	54–270	108–540	54–810	77.4
		Biface				
FLKN 1–2	1	Core 105	315–1575	630–3150	315–4725	152.5
		Biface				
FLKN 3	1	Core 24	72–360	144–720	72–1080	14
		Biface				
FLKNN 1	1	Core 3	9–45	18–90	9–135	1
		Biface				
FLKNN 3	1	Core 4	12–60	24–120	12–180	8
		Biface				
FC West	2	Core 43	129–645	258–1290	129–1935	52.2
		Biface				
TK Upper Floor	2	Core 26	78–390	156–780	98.1–2175	120.9
		Biface 6.7	20.1–335	40.2–670		
TK Lower Floor	2	Core 6	18–90	36–180	24–570	1.9
		Biface 2	6–100	12–200		
EF–HR	2	Core 28	84–420	168–840	198–6960	266.2
		Biface 38	114–1900	228–3800		

Extrapolated flake range for cores based on minimum of 3 flakes per core and a potential maximum of 15.
Extrapolated flake range for bifaces based on minimum of 3 flakes per biface and a potential maximum of 50
Extrapolated debitage range based on assumed 2 pieces of shatter/chips etc. for every lava flake
Example – at DK 122 cores produce a minimum of 366 flakes (122x3) and a possible maximum of 1830 (122x15) flakes.
Accompanying this is a minimum of 732 shatter fragments (366x2) and a potential maximum of 3660 (1830x2) pieces of debitage. For
DK the potential range of detached pieces is therefore 366 (flakes unaccompanied by debitage) – 5490 (max. flakes+max. debitage).

Table 3.3. Predicted quantities and actual archaeological quantities of flakes and debitage from core and biface working on lava *at selected sites from Olduvai Gorge (after Leakey 1971).*

not plotted (*ibid.*, 50). These are the debris of on the spot flaking. Yet within the confines of this scatter there are only four flaked pieces!

IMPLICATIONS AND DISCUSSION

My main theme in this paper is to explore an aspect of time averaged surfaces, palimpsest activities, through a single behavioural mechanism, transport. The aim of the paper is to show that first impressions of the problems that time averaged surfaces present need not be so gloomy.

As a palimpsest, the final pattern of artefacts on an activity surface can not be assumed to be the result of a one to one relationship between one activity episode and its residue. But transport allows us to overcome this difficulty at certain locations. Even on time averaged surfaces it is clear that over the whole life span of some sites, gross import has exceeded gross export, or *vice versa*. The overall pattern may be the result of a number of transport episodes, or just one, either way at sites with

minimal disturbance, transport remains the best explanation for these asymmetries. The robust patterning in the data allows for the recognition of a behavioural trend to be extracted from a time averaged surface.

Part of the fun of archaeology is exploring patterns in data. In this section I wish to briefly explore some of the implications of the data in the tables by setting up possibilities and questions, that others can answer or dismiss as they see fit. Again, the purpose of this is to show how palimpsest data can be employed in behavioural reconstructions despite the inherent problems with these sites.

1. These data support suggestions by Stiles (1991) and Leakey (1971) that artefacts which have already been knapped, are being moved around the landscape. The data imply this is the case for finished tool forms like bifaces, as well as for core forms, and flakes. This is especially clear when we take into account 'exotic' raw materials. These data are presented for the sites discussed in Table 3.6. These are raw material types which were incorporated in the non-lava data, but which are not quartz or quartzite.

Site	Bed	Flaked pieces (actual)	Flake range (extrap)	Debit'ge range (extrap)	Det'ched pieces, max range (extrap)	Detached pieces (actual)
DK	1	Cores 7	21–105	84–420	21–525	317.7
		Bifaces				
FLK Zinj	1	Cores 20	60–300	240–1200	60–1500	2290.4
		Bifaces				
FLKN 1–2	1	Cores 24	72–360	288–1440	72–1800	772.5
		Bifaces				
FLKN 3	1	Cores 4	12–60	48–240	12–300	90.9
		Bifaces				
FLKNN 1	1	Cores 2	6–30	24–120	6–150	2
		Bifaces				
FLKNN3	1	Cores 0	0	0	0	30
		Bifaces				
FC West	2	Cores 73	219–1095	876–4380	234–6725	869.8
		Bifaces 5	15–250	60–1000		
TK Upper Floor	2	Cores 89	267–1335	1068–5340	318.9–1100	4811.1
		Bifaces 17.3	51.9–865	207.6–3460		
TK Lower Floor	2	Cores 35	105–525	420–2100	144–5875	2066.1
		Bifaces 13	39–650	156–2600		
EF–HR	2	Core 9	27–135	108–540	60–3425	153.8
		Biface 11	33–550	132–2200		

Extrapolated flake range for cores based on minimum of 3 flakes per core and a potential maximum of 15.
Extrapolated flake range for bifaces based on minimum of 3 flakes per biface and a potential maximum of 50
Extrapolated debitage range based on assumed 4 pieces of shatter/chips etc. for every non-lava flake
Example – at DK 7 cores produce a minimum of 21 flakes (7x3) and a possible maximum of 105 (7x15) flakes. Accompanying this is a minimum of 84 shatter fragments (21x4) and a potential maximum of 420 (105x4) pieces of debitage. For DK the maximum range of detached pieces is therefore 21 (flakes unaccompanied by debitage) – 525 (max. flakes+max. debitage)

Table 3.4. Predicted quantities and actual archaeological quantities of flakes and debitage from core and biface working on non-lavas at selected sites from Olduvai Gorge (after Leakey 1971).

Behavioural pattern	Lava	Non-lava
TOO MANY FLAKED PIECES Bringing pre-flaked cores to the site for flaking and/or taking flakes away	FLKN 1–2 (non-biface) FC West (biface) TK Lower Floor (biface) FLKN 3 (non-biface)	
ENOUGH FLAKED PIECES TO EXPLAIN THE NUMBER OF DETACHED PIECES Cores brought to a site, knapped, flakes and cores left where they are	DK (non-biface) TK Upper Floor (biface) EF–HR (biface) FLKNN 1 (non-biface) FLK Zinj (non-biface) FLKNN3 (non-biface)	DK (non-biface) TK Upper Floor (biface) EF–HR (biface) FLKNN 1 (non-biface) FLKN 1–2 (non-biface) FC West (biface) FLKN 3 (non-biface) TK Lower Floor (biface)
TOO MANY DETACHED PIECES Bringing flakes to a site and/or taking flaked cores away after in-situ knapping		FLK Zinj (non-biface) FLKNN3 (non-biface)

Table 3.5. Summary of results in Tables 3 and 4 for sites in Beds 1 and 2 Olduvai Gorge.

Site	Pegmatite			Chert			Gneiss			Welded Tuff		
	FP	DP	UFP	FP	DP	UFP	FP	DP	UFP	FP	DP	UFP
FLKN 1–2							x1					
FC West			x1	x1			x2		x4			
EF–HR	x1				x5							
TK Upper Floor							x2		x2			x1
TK Lower Floor							x1		x1			

- FP = flaked pieces; DP = detached pieces; UFP = unflaked pieces (i.e. manuports and utilised pieces (*sensu* Leakey 1971).
- Empty cell indicates no examples present.
- x1 or x2 indicates number of examples.

Table 3.6. Table to show import and export of exotic raw materials from the non-lava data set, for sites in Bed I and Bed II, Olduvai Gorge.

The table clearly shows the asymmetry in flaked pieces and detached pieces, and reinforces the notion of the movement of already flaked artefacts from place to place. The movement of flaked artefacts lies at one end of a continuum of such behaviours since the presence of manuports and unflaked raw materials also implies the movement of resources from place to place. In many instances the distances involved may only be a few hundred meters or so, but what is significant is the scale at which this is happening. At *every site* we see the presence of raw materials brought to a place for flaking. Hammerstones must also be brought since at none of these sites are cobbles of lava, or quartz and quartzite, part of the immediate substrate. But then at some sites certain products of flaking are moved out of the vicinity of the excavated area. This behaviour pattern cross-cuts so called cultural boundaries (i.e. Acheulian vs Oldowan), and could be labelled as a long term hominid behavioural pattern since it appears in both Beds I and II, a potential time span of over 600ky. This fully supports suggestions by Potts (1991) that habitual transport may represent one of the only real differences between early hominid behaviour and that of modern chimps.

2. At some localities different raw materials are being treated differently. In some cases lava is the subject of transport activity while the non-lavas at the site appear to have been flaked and discarded in place. At other localities the reverse is true. Why should this be? Did hominids use some raw materials for some tasks and not others? Are we seeing choices in raw material preference, or simply diachronic changes in availability or access to different raw materials? We will probably never know. But it should be noted once again that this occurs at sites in both Beds I and II, and is not solely tied to Oldowan or Acheulian sites.

3. Many Olduvai localities show repeated re-use of one spot, for example six levels at FLKN, or two floors at TK. The repeated transport of raw materials to a particular place also shows this. What might this imply? The precise circumstances of each locality are now lost to us, but what ever their significance was, the fact of persistent return implies some advantage to their position. Possibly they were close to the stream beds from which raw materials could be procured; or perhaps they were close to clumps of trees or good vantage points. Alternatively they were ingrained into the consciousness of certain hominids who went back to the same spot time and time again as part of a pattern of foraging from which they could not deviate. Whatever the reason for these localities being significant, they indicate that hominids possessed a definite *sense of place*. The fact of transporting raw materials across a landscape to a specific location shows this, and the *long durée* of many of these localities could imply a sense of *persistent places* within the wider landscape consciousness.

4. As a speculative exercise we could take this one step further. Grounding any ideas in the fact of transport and the significance of persistent places, as presented here, we could argue that hominids possess a conscious sense of *place and space*. It should be recalled that the distance between most of these sites is only a few kilometres. In many cases the localities would have been within sight of each other, for example FLKNN1 and FLK Zinj are on the same land surface. (Naturally not all the sites are contemporary of course.) Can we then speculate that the awareness of significant places is embedded within a web of awareness concerning the broader landscape, and other places within it – a cobweb of persistent places. Why might the web of place and space be conscious? Because the same things are not being done at these persistent places every time they are visited by hominids. Table 3.7 repeats the data in Table 3.5, but for three stratified multi-occupation sites. At FLKN the same pattern persisted over two visits; the import and/or export of lava pieces, and the

Site	Assemblage character	Lava	Non-lava
FLKN 1–2	Too many cores	*	
	Enough cores		*
	Too many flakes		
FLKN 3	Too many cores	*	
	Enough cores		*
	Too many flakes		
FLKNN 1	Too many cores		
	Enough cores	*	*
	Too many flakes		
FLKNN3	Too many cores		
	Enough cores	*	
	Too many flakes		*
TK Upper Floor	Too many cores		
	Enough cores	*	*
	Too many flakes		
TK Lower Floor	Too many cores	*	
	Enough cores		*
	Too many flakes		

Table 3.7. *Raw material behaviours at stratified site in Bed I and Bed II, Olduvai Gorge.*

on the spot flaking and discard of non-lavas. However at the nearby FLKNN locality different behaviours occurred. At FLKNN 1 all the raw material flaked was left where it was (contrast this with the possibly contemporary movement of non-lava flaked pieces away from the FLK Zinj. floor), but in the underlying FLKNN 3 the transport of non-lavas occurred. At TK a variation on this is seen. On the Upper Floor everything is left, but on the Lower Floor the import or export of lava occurs. Whether or not hominids are going back to the same places for purely mechanical or hard-wired reasons, what they are doing at these places is not pre-programmed.

The above falls into two categories; discussion on patterns seen in the data, and speculations generated on what those patterns may mean. Both have incorporated a site-based awareness as well as a broader landscape awareness. But both have been done so from the understanding that the sites being used are palimpsests of activity, and that archaeologists have not been able to assume a one to one relationship between action and its residue. Whether you agree with it is up to you.

CONCLUSIONS.

This is not a paper about transport, nor is it one that is about reconstructing hominid lifestyles. It is more about

methodology than anything else. With some notable exceptions, all archaeological sites are time averaged one way or another. This simple fact presents us with a considerable problem if we wish to use these sites as important building blocks in behavioural reconstructions. I have tried to argue that time averaging need not be a stumbling block to progress – just another challenge. As I said earlier, our archaeology is only as good as our imaginative potential.

ACKNOWLEDGEMENTS

I am grateful to Lisa Marlow for her constructive criticism on earlier drafts of this paper. I should also thank the editors. *Pax Cambrensis.*

REFERENCES

Binford, L. 1981. *Bones: Ancient Men and Modern Myths.* New York: Academic Press.
Barley, N. 1983. *The Innocent Anthropologist.* London: British Museum Publications. (Re-issued in Penguin Books, 1986)
Hay, R.L. 1976. *Geology of the Olduvai Gorge.* Berkeley: University of California Press.
Leakey, M.D. 1971. *Olduvai Gorge.* Volume 3. Cambridge: Cambridge University Press.
Monahan, C.M. 1996. New zooarchaeological data from Bed II, Oluvai Gorge, Tanzania: implications for hominid behaviour in the Early Pleistocene. *Journal of Human Evolution* 31, 93–128.
Peters, C.R. & Blumenschine, R.J. 1995. Landscape perspectives on possible land use patterns for Early Pleistocene hominids in the Olduvai Basin, Tanzania. *Journal of Human Evolution* 29, 321–62.
Potts, R. 1991. Why the Oldowan? Plio-Pleistocene tool making and the transport of resources. *Journal of Anthropological Research* 47, 153–76.
Schick, K.D. 1987. Modelling the formation of Early Stone Age artefact concentrations. *Journal of Human Evolution* 16, 789–807.
Stern, N. 1993. The structure of the Lower Pleistocene archaeological record. *Current Anthropology* 34, 201–24.
Stern, N. 1994. The implications of time averaging for reconstructing the land-use patterns of early tool making hominids. *Journal of Human Evolution* 27, 89–105.
Stiles, D. 1991. Early hominid behaviour and culture tradition: raw material studies in Bed II, Olduvai Gorge. *The African Archaeological Review* 9, 1–19.
Toth, N. 1987. Behavioural inferences from Early Stone Age artefact assemblages: an experimental model. *Journal of Human Evolution* 16, 763–87.
Walter, R.C., Manega, P.C., Hay, R.L., Drake, R.E., & Curtis, G.H. 1991. Laser fusion 40/ Argon/ 39/Argon dating of Bed I, Olduvai Gorge, Tanzania. *Nature* 354, 145–9.

4. Elandsfontein and Klasies River Revisited

H. J. Deacon

ABSTRACT

The evidence from the Acheulean site of Elandsfontein and the Middle Stone Age Klasies River main site are contrasted. At Elandsfontein deflation of the sandy substrates to the level of the water table can account for the local wetland around which the Middle Pleistocene fossil fauna and artefacts accumulated. A wetland focus is the norm for Acheulean sites most frequently found in river valley, spring and pan situations. It is concluded that archaic Middle Pleistocene humans were stenotopic, living in a narrow range of ecological conditions. By contrast, early anatomically and cognitively modern humans, recorded from the earliest Late Pleistocene at Klasies River main site, were eurytopic. They occupied the same hunter-gatherer niche as Later Stone Age people but one different from archaic humans.

INTRODUCTION

There is an abominable sandy track that leads from the village of Hopefield, north of Cape Town, to the farm Elandsfontein. It was here in 1953 that Ronald Singer, assisted by Keith Jolly, had found the sixty odd fragments of the Saldanha skull among the many thousands of bones and rather fewer Acheulean and younger artefacts that littered the bays between the dunes. In 1964 Singer asked me to carry out excavations to learn about the stratigraphic context of the artefacts in the sands. The following year the programme of excavation was extended on a larger scale by John Wymer. This was the beginning of the long and productive collaboration between Ronald Singer and John Wymer and it was with considerable interest that I followed the progress of their work at Elandsfontein.

In 1967 John had transferred his base to a creosoted wooden shack on a cove, 100m from the Klasies River main site. This was a further Singer-Wymer collaborative effort; in this case searching for makers of the Middle Stone Age artefacts. Singer (1958) had effectively de-frocked 'Boskop Man', as the progenitor of the San leaving no one to 'man' the Middle Stone Age. Artefacts and bones of appropriate age, glued to the wall of the cliff at main site, promised some hope of finding evidence to fill the lacuna.

The excavations of the 1967 season at main site were well underway when I took off a few days from my own excavation at Wilton to visit Klasies River with Janette Deacon. Work was going on in cave 1 and the initial cutting in 1A had been completed. One of the points of interest was the 'Magosian' artefacts that John had recovered from the carbonized layer in the upper part of the sequence in 1A. We had recently re-excavated the Howiesons Poort name site (J. Deacon 1995), and Charles Keller (1973) and Erich Wendt (1972) had found similar assemblages at Montagu and Apollo 11 respectively. Here was the Howiesons Poort interstratified in the Middle Stone Age sequence, looking for all like a macro-Wilton with its backed tools. That visit included a sortie to Laidler's (1947) Geelhoutboom open site in the dunes inland of the coastal cliffs where Acheulean and Middle Stone Age artefacts lay scattered over several kilometres on deflated surfaces. I still think it is significant that Acheulean groups living in the area did not go down to the sea, a point taken up later in this paper. The down side of that visit was that after the long walk to Geelhoutboom we gulped down copious quantities of water from the polluted spring at cave 5. It made the next few days working below the reflecting shelter wall at Wilton difficult and sent the team at Klasies scurrying off to Humansdorp for medical help.

As I was overseas the following year I could not follow the progress of the excavation. It was several years later that I guided Richard and Gail Klein there and visits in 1979 and 1983 showed progressive collapse of standing sections. Conservation measures were needed but could only be funded through research. A 10 year programme of the excavation of a Holocene-Late Pleistocene sequence at Boomplaas cave had just been completed. This site sequence covered the last 80ky with the Howiesons Poort as the culture stratigraphic marker at the base. This marker is in the top of the Klasies River main site sequence which has a basal dating of 120kya. Main site and Boomplaas are complementary and together span the whole of the Late Pleistocene and Holocene, the last interglacial, last glacial and present interglacial cycle (H.J. Deacon 1995). In 1984 it seemed appropriate to extend the same high resolution sampling developed at Boomplaas to main site by excavation of a column through the sequence. This has occupied the subsequent years. In the process, sections have been stabilized by sand bags sewn in geotextile, work that is still in progress. I well remember John's suggestion that I might encourage future students to take on more detailed study of the artefact samples he was sorting and cataloguing in that creosoted hut at Klasies River. They are still productively engaged in that task.

In this paper I wish to offer a perspective that links the evidence from Elandsfontein and Klasies River, sites which were central to John Wymer's years of archaeological research in South Africa. The sites illustrate the contrasting archaeological traces left by archaic and modern humans at the respective locations.

ELANDSFONTEIN AND PALAEOENVIRONMENTS

A rectangular area of mobile sands, 3km long by 1.5km wide, forms the Elandsfontein site. Since the 1960s when John Wymer excavated there, the invasion of exotic acacias and conscious planting of vegetation has reduced dune mobility. The bulk of the finds including the human remains have been collected from deflated surfaces between the dunes. It is a palaeontological rather than an archaeological site with faunal remains more abundant than artefacts.

Excavations have been carried out for stratigraphic purposes and to establish the association of the materials. From an archaeological perspective the most productive excavation has been cutting 10 (Singer & Wymer 1968) which established the occurrence of a series of small but well finished bifaces, cores and flakes buried below a brown sand layer. The bifaces are so similar and their occurrence

so localised that there is no doubt about the integrity of the artefact sample. The fauna from the cutting (Klein 1978) is not well preserved and includes a number of taxa represented by different body parts. The artefacts and the fauna may not be directly associated, leaving open the interpretation of the site as a butchery or kill site. A study of damage marks (Milo 1994) on the admittedly poorly preserved bone surfaces suggests accumulation of the bone through carnivore rather than human agencies. Establishing associations between artefacts and faunal elements has proved difficult at Acheulean sites everywhere. This notwithstanding, the high percentage of bifaces in the sample (25%), tools made kilometres away where stone was available and imported to the sandveld for a specific task, makes interpretation of the artefacts as a butchery toolkit reasonable. Any other function in this context is improbable. This leaves open the question of what animals may have been butchered with such a toolkit, a point taken up later in this paper.

The site is dated through associations of fauna and artefacts. The fauna includes some archaic elements, a sabre-toothed cat and a sivathere (an antlered, short necked giraffid) that represent a Plio-Pleistocene component (Hendey & Deacon 1977). The bulk of the fauna is Middle Pleistocene in age (Klein & Cruz-Uribe 1991), dominated by bovids, with a high proportion of grazers relative to browers among the antelopes, and large herbivores including hippopotamus, rhinoceros, and elephant. The dating of the Middle Pleistocene component is unlikely to be less than 250kya, the presently indicated dating for the beginning of the Middle Stone Age, and estimates range as old as 400–700kya (Klein & Cruz-Uribe 1991). In addition there is a Late Pleistocene component indicated by Middle Stone Age artefacts including Stillbay points and younger fauna and artefacts, noted by Singer & Wymer (1968) who concluded that the common attraction was the presence of water holes in an otherwise dry sandy environment.

My own interest has been in the formation and some palaeoecological implications of the Elandsfontein site. Set in the Saldanha embayment, the site is underlain by a thickness in excess of 100m, of Mio-Pliocene sands and a cover of Pleistocene sands of the Bredasdorp Formation (Rogers 1980). A calcrete ridge, exposed in the south eastern part of the site and possibly related to the northerly to north westerly trending dune plume complex (Hendey 1983, 50, fig. 3) would be included in the Langebaan Limestone Member of the latter formation. The surficial geology of the site was originally mapped in detail by Jack Mabbutt (1956), best known for his later contribution to arid land geomorphology in Australia. He recognised a sequence, from the base, of silver grey sands, calcareous sands, dark or brown sands and calcrete. The interpretation was biased towards recognising a succession of wet and dry climatic pulses, associated with ferricrete and calcrete formation respectively, in line with the then prevailing pluvial hypothesis. More importantly Mabbutt interpreted

Stage 1: Accumulation of Middle Pleistocene fossils

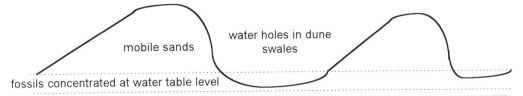

Stage 2: Late Pleistocene stabilisation of the sands and pedogenesis

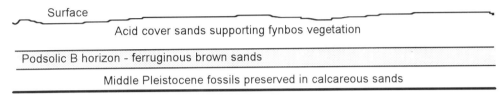

Stage 3: Present-day remobilisation of the sands

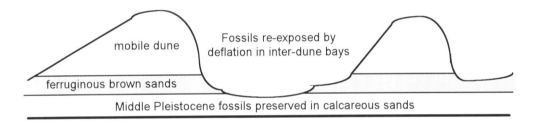

Figure 4.1. Model of site formation at Elandsfontein.

the site as formed by the deposition of different generations of sands with their contents on landsurfaces in a stratigraphic sequence. He has been followed in this interpretation by others (Butzer 1973; Klein & Cruz-Uribe 1991). Singer & Wymer (1968) stressed the integrity of the main fossil horizon associated with the Acheulean artefacts but concede the importance of fluctuations of the water table and deflation in site formation.

From sections excavated through the brown sand plains and ferricrete ridges in 1964, I concluded that the brown sands are a pedogenic feature, the B horizon of a podsol, and not a stratigraphic unit (see also Partridge 1982). This suggested that the process of site formation involved alternate episodes of mobilisation of the sands and stabilisation by vegetation. Under this model the Middle Pleistocene fauna and Acheulean artefacts accumulated around water holes formed where deflation intersected the water table. As the water table is the limit of deflation the fossil materials occur in a horizon reflecting the position of the then seasonally fluctuating water table. The modern water table is only slightly below that in the Middle Pleistocene. Although a deflation model opens the prospect of repeated episodes of deflation, the tight clustering of carnivore molar lengths (Klein 1986) suggests the bulk of the Middle

Pleistocene fossils accumulated under temperature conditions like the present, possible during a single prior interglacial. The model suggests that subsequent stabilization of sands under vegetation, a higher water table and pedogenesis formed not only the brown sand horizon but led to the decalcification of the cover sands. The ecological consequences can be seen in that the acid sands in the modern surrounds of the site support a fynbos vegetation with a low carrying capacity whereas a non-fynbos vegetation (Cowling & Holmes 1992, 50), probably allied to strandveld, would have been found on the Middle Pleistocene calcareous substrates. To explain the predominance of grazers in the bovid fauna, Klein & Cruz-Uribe (1991) have suggested an increase in summer rainfall in the Middle Pleistocene. The underlying assumption is that higher temperatures in the growing season would favour the spread of C-4 grasses (Vogel *et al.* 1978) creating a grassland habitat. Although stable isotope analysis can potentially test this postulate, a more economical assumption is that the Middle Pleistocene vegetation alliances offered sufficient graze and possibly minerals and trace elements to attract grazers. The major ecological change at the site was the Late Pleistocene establishment of restiod fynbos.

The different reconstructions of the Middle Pleistocene palaeoenvironment at Elandsfonein are in agreement that this was an area of wetland and water holes. It is a pattern throughout southern Africa that Acheulean sites are associated with wetland habitats along river valleys, at pans and springs and the occurrence at Elandsfontein conforms to this pattern. Although the bovids represented in the fossil fauna are diverse and explain the presence of carnivores and the incidence of carnivore damage on the bone recorded by Milo (1994), they do not necessarily explain the presence of humans. Given that African bovids are notoriously lean they may not have been the main prey of humans. The question posed by Elandsfontein and other Acheulean sites is what were archaic humans doing at such wetland locations? In the final discussion an attempt is made to answer this question but part of the answer follows from considering the niche occupied by early modern humans and this is best exemplified at Klasies River main site.

KLASIES RIVER MAIN SITE

The excavations carried out by Singer & Wymer (1982) at the Klasies River sites established the culture stratigraphy of the Middle Stone Age and provided diverse faunal materials and significant finds of human remains. Together these represent a substantial contribution. Subsequent research reviewed here briefly has provided added information on the dating, the taphonomy of the human remains and, more relevant to the argument developed here, the archaeological interpretation at what is termed main site, the depository that includes caves 1, 1A, 1B, 1C and 2.

Properly speaking, main site is not a series of cave sites but an open site. It is now very exposed but would have been protected by a barrier dune associated with the last interglacial high sea-level. A radiocarbon date of some 6000 years on flowstone, high up in 1A, is considered to date the Holocene high sea-level that destroyed all traces of this dune and caused the erosion of the bulk of the original deposits. The formation of this barrier dune with the regression from that sea level some 125kya puts a limit on the age of the oldest deposits. Association of the initial occupation with the last interglacial, OIS 5e, was shown by Nick Shackleton's (1982) original oxygen isotope analysis of opercula of the marine turban shell. Through collaboration with Siep Talma and John Vogel (Deacon *et al.* 1988) it has been possible to establish a minimum age of 110kya for the lowest LBS member (levels 38–40), a maximum age of 100kya for the SAS member (levels 17 upwards) in cave 1. Further, from an oxygen isotope profile through the sequence reported in this research it has been shown that the Howiesons Poort (levels 10–21) in the Upper member correlates with OIS 5a–4. This is the basis for suggesting an age centred on 70kya for the Howiesons Poort artefacts (Deacon 1992). There are ongoing attempts

to refine the precision of the dating of the sequence using appropriate alternative methods to radiocarbon and make this one of the best dated early Late Pleistocene sites.

The present investigation has added to the 1967–8 finds of human remains, notably in two maxillary fragments from the base of the sequence in the LBS member, an ulna and teeth from the SAS member and isolated teeth from the Upper member. The dating of these finds would be 120, 90 and 70kya respectively. The Singer & Wymer (1982) assessment of the remains as representing a single dimorphic, anatomically modern population is supported (Rightmire & Deacon 1991). My interest has been in the taphonomy of the finds. The two fragments recovered from the LBS member were found within a square metre of each other and in the same shell midden layer. They are a burnt piece of a maxilla of a young, probably male, individual and a fragment of maxilla retaining a worn molar of an older, gracile and probably female individual. The latter was protected under a patellid shell and shows angular breaks. The discard in a refuse heap, the fragmentary nature of these and indeed all remains from the site and the burning are pointers to interpersonal violence, as suggested by Tim White (1987).

The finds in the SAS member which would include all the 1967–8 finds from cave 1 and 1B and the more recent finds are now thought to represent a second discrete episode of accumulation of human remains. Although the 1967–8 finds in cave 1 were referred to stratigraphic layers 37 and 17–14, there is reason to argue that they are all from the same horizon. One indicator is that layers 15 and 14 are steeply dipping talus slope deposits formed when the cave was no longer habitable while layers 17 and 16 include primary occupation horizons. The clustering of the finds in cave 1 (Singer & Wymer 1982, figs 3.20–3.24) is inconsistent with such different modes of deposition and the clustering itself indicates they were associated with habitation rather than transported down a slope. The implication is that the human fossils in the LBS and SAS members are not low frequency, chance finds, randomly distributed through the deposits but occur in specific horizons as a consequence of episodic interpersonal violence. It is debatable whether this behaviour was motivated by dietary or ritual needs but a ritual component can be assumed.

The natural section through the main site deposits, masked by slope wash but exposed by the initial and other 1967–8 cuttings, is a remarkable sequence of multiple short human occupation events separated by the accumulation of natural sediments. Dissecting the micro-stratigraphy has only been possible in smaller sections than John Wymer and his team excavated because it is so time consuming. The justification for giving attention to finer details like plotting features such as hearths and individual finds is to get an insight not only into what people living at the site were doing but why they were doing it. What I have found impressive is the parallels that can be drawn between the archaeological traces of Middle Stone Age occupation at main site and that at Later Stone Age sites in the region. The deposits have built up in the same way. Occupation horizons at main site are marked by the carbonized surrounds to small circular hearths representing burnt plant food residues, separate midden heaps of shell and bone and, numerous artefacts. Elsewhere (Deacon 1995) it has been argued that the evidence in the Middle Stone Age for the use of individual domestic hearths, the collecting and managing of plant food resources, hunting bovids of all body sizes (Milo 1994), the harvesting of marine resources, the use of ochre and making artefacts to a standardised design (Deacon & Wurz 1996) are consistent with modern cognitive abilities.

Apart from providing secure dating for the presence of anatomically modern humans, the evidence from main site raises questions on the emergence of modern cognition. If modern kinds of people were living at Klasies River 120kya what were they doing that was different from what archaic people at Elandsfontein and Geelhoutboom were doing?

PERSPECTIVE

The questions posed in this paper serve to contrast the habitats occupied by the Acheuleans and Middle Stone Age groups. The demonstrable difference is in the distribution of sites in the landscape. Acheulean peoples can be termed stenotopic, meaning that they were terrain specialists, occupying valley bottom-wetland habitats. Elandsfontein and Geelhoutboom are two examples with perhaps the best known occurrences in the valleys like the Vaal River. Main site is a single Middle Stone Age occurrence but it can be typologically correlated with other coastal and inland sites in all terrain positions. Early anatomically modern people in contrast to the Acheulean groups were eurytopic; they had the ability to disperse across the landscape and occupied a hunter-gatherer niche that was the same as that in the Later Stone Age but different from and far broader than that occupied by people in Acheulean times. Whereas modern hunter-gatherer analogues and norms of behaviour have relevance for the interpretation of the evidence from the Klasies River and other Middle and Later Stone Age sites, none may be appropriate to the interpretation of Acheulean sites like Elandsfontein.

The niche occupied by Acheulean foragers is as intriguing a problem as the function of bifaces (Deacon 1993). Preservational biases and taphonomic problems mean that this problem cannot be resolved at present but it can be conjectured as a working hypothesis that archaic humans lacked the social mechanisms for groups to disaggregate and disperse and that their habitat preference and their toolkits reflect the importance of the fatty tissues of the largest class of herbivores, animals like hippopotamus and elephant, in their ecology.

Although it may seem that John Wymer's involvement in excavations at Elandsfontein and the Klasies River sites were distinct commitments, both were back breaking

efforts for which he deserves considerable credit, they are linked in an important way. To understand what it means to claim that the people living at Klasies River were anatomically and cognitively modern, it has to be shown that there were earlier people, the Acheulean outgroup, who were not modern. Elandsfontein is part of interpreting Klasies River and *vice versa*. I hope it gives John satisfaction to see the sites linked in this way.

ACKNOWLEDGEMENTS

Research reported here has been supported by the Centre for Science Development, Pretoria, the University of Stellenbosch and the L.S.B. Leakey Foundation. I am grateful to Ronald Singer for originally involving me in the research at Elandsfontein and to John Wymer for interesting discussions on these sites. Some of the ideas presented here have been stimulated by discussions with Janette Deacon, Rob Foley, Richard Klein, Philip Rightmire, Ian Tattersall, John Vogel and Sarah Wurz.

BIBLIOGRAPHY

Butzer, K.W. 1973. Re-evaluation of the geology of the Elandsfontein (Hopefield) site, south-western Cape, South Africa. *South African Journal of Science* 69, 234–8.
Cowling, R. M. & Holmes, P. M. 1992. Flora and vegetation. In R.M. Cowling (ed.), *The Ecology of Fynbos: Nutrients, Fire and Diversity,* 23–61. Cape Town: Oxford University Press.
Deacon, H. J. 1992. Southern Africa and modern human origins. *Philosophical Transactions of the Royal Society, London* B 337, 177–83.
Deacon, H. J. 1993. Planting an idea: an archaeology of Stone Age gatherers in South Africa. *South African Archaeological Bulletin* 48, 86–93.
Deacon, H. J. 1995. Two late Pleistocene-Holocene archaeological depositories from the Southern Cape, South Africa. *South African Archaeological Bulletin* 50, 121–31.
Deacon, H. J., Talma, A.S. & Vogel, J.C. 1988. Biological and cultural development of Pleistocene people in an Old World southern continent. In J. R. Prescott (ed.), *Early Man in the Southern Hemisphere,* S23–S31. Adelaide: Department of Physics and Mathematical Physics, University of Adelaide.
Deacon, H. J. & Wurz, S.J.D. 1996. Klasies River main site, cave 2: a Howiesons Poort occurrence. In G. Pwiti & R. Soper (eds), *Aspects of African Archaeology: Papers from the 10th Congress of the PanAfrican Association for Prehistory and Related Studies,* 213–8. Harare: University of Zimbabwe Publications.
Deacon, J. 1995. An unsolved mystery at the Howieson's Poort name site. *South African Archaeological Bulletin* 50, 110–20.
Hendey, Q. B. 1983. Cenozoic geology and palaeogeography of the Fynbos region. In H. J. Deacon, Q. B. Hendey & J. J. N. Lambrechts (eds), *Fynbos Palaeoecology: a Preliminary Synthesis,* 35–60. South African National Scientific Programmes Report No. 75. Cape Town: Council for Scientific and Industrial Research.
Hendey, Q. B. & Deacon, H. J. 1977. Studies in palaeontology and archaeology in the Saldanha region. *Transactions of the Royal Society of South Africa* 42, 371–81.
Keller, C. M. 1973. *Montagu Cave in Prehistory: a Descriptive Analysis.* University of California Anthropological Records 28.

Klein, R. G. 1978. The fauna and overall interpretation of the "Cutting 10" Acheulean site at Elandsfontein (Hopefield), Southwestern Cape Province, South Africa. *Quaternary Research* 10, 69–83.

Klein, R. G. 1986. Carnivore size and Quaternary climate change in southern Africa. *Quaternary Research* 26, 153–70.

Klein, R. G. & Cruz–Uribe, K. 1991. The bovids from Elandsfontein, South Africa, and their implications for the age, palaeoenvironment, and origins of the site. *The African Archaeological Review* 9, 21–79.

Laidler, P. W. 1947. The evolution of the Middle Palaeolithic technique at Geelhoutboom, near Kareedouw in the southern Cape. *Transactions of the Royal Society of South Africa* 31, 283–313.

Mabbutt, J. A. 1956. The physiography and surface geology of the Hopefield fossil site. *Transactions of the Royal Society of South Africa* 35, 21–58.

Milo, R. G. 1994. Human-Animal Interactions in Southern African Prehistory: a Microscopic Study of Bone Damage Signatures. Unpublished PhD. thesis, University of Chicago.

Partridge, T. C. 1982. The chronological positions of the fossil hominids of southern Africa. In H. de Lumley & M. de Lumley (eds), *L'Homo erectus et la Place de Tautavel parmi les Hominidés Fossiles*, 617–75. Nice: 1er Congrès International de Paléontologie Humaine.

Rightmire, G. P. & Deacon, H. J. 1991. Comparative studies of Late Pleistocene human ramains from Klasies River Mouth, South Africa. *Journal of Human Evolution* 20, 131–56.

Rogers, J. 1980. *First Report on the Cenozoic Sediments between Cape Town and Elands Bay.* Pretoria: Geological Survey, Open File Report 165.

Shackleton, N. J. 1982. Stratigraphy and chronology of the KRM deposits: oxygen isotope evidence. In R. Singer & J. J. Wymer (eds), *The Middle Stone Age at Klasies River Mouth in South Africa*, 194–9. Chicago: University of Chicago Press.

Singer, R. 1958. The Boskop 'race' problem. *Man* 58, 231–50.

Singer, R. & Wymer, J. J. 1968. Archaeological investigations at the Saldanha skull site in South Africa. *South African Archaeological Bulletin* 25, 63–74.

Singer, R. & Wymer, J. J. 1982. *The Middle Stone Age at Klasies River Mouth in South Africa.* Chicago: University of Chicago Press.

Vogel, J. C., Fuls, A. & Ellis, R. P. 1978. The geographical distribution of Krantz grasses in South Africa. *South African Journal of Science* 74, 9–15.

Wendt, W. E. 1972. Preliminary report on an archaeological research programme in South West Africa. *Cimbebasia (B)* 2, 1–61.

White, T. D. 1987. Cannibalism at Klasies? *Sagittarius* 2, 6–9.

5. The Pleistocene History and Early Human Occupation of the River Thames Valley

David R. Bridgland

ABSTRACT

The terrace deposits of the Thames are an important repository for stone artefacts, which provide evidence for human occupation of south east England during the Pleistocene. Revised dating of the terrace sequence, based on biostratigraphy, geochronology and modelling of climatically generated terrace formation, allows correlation with the globally applicable oceanic sequence of oxygen isotope stages. The terraces thus provide, indirectly, a valuable chronological framework for the archaeological record they contain. With reference to this framework, significant changes within the archaeological sequence can be dated, such as the first appearance of the Levallois technique (OIS 8). The record from the Thames suggests depopulation during OIS 6, with recolonization occurring during the last glacial.

INTRODUCTION

The River Thames is the main agent of drainage within the synclinal London Basin, in which it forms the axial valley. At the western end of the syncline, the axial river is the Kennet, which joins the Thames at Reading. The upper catchment of the Thames lies outside the London Basin, between the Cotswolds and Chilterns escarpments. The river enters the London Basin through a gap in the Chilterns at Goring. The range of rocks making up the Lower Pleistocene gravels of the Thames suggests that the Thames once drained an even larger area, perhaps including much of the West Midlands and even parts of Wales (e.g. Hey 1986; 1996; Whiteman & Rose 1992; Bridgland 1994a).

An excellent record of the history of the Thames river system during the Pleistocene is to be found in the deposits laid down by it and its tributaries. All such deposits were formed on the valley floors, but the rivers have repeatedly cut down through their valley bottoms to ever lower levels, so that their earlier deposits now form staircases of terrace remnants on the valley sides. The process of alternating sedimentation and downcutting that has given rise to the Thames terrace system is thought to have been driven by the repeated climatic oscillation that characterized the Pleistocene, well documented from sediment records from the deep oceans (Fig. 5.1).

In the catchment of the Thames, the most complete sequence of Quaternary terraces is preserved on the north side of the valley in the Slough-Beaconsfield area (Hare 1947; Gibbard 1985; Fig. 5.2). Whatever the cause of the southward migration implied by this pattern of preservation (Bridgland 1985), it has been accelerated by the glacial diversion of the river during the most extensive of the Quaternary glaciations, during the Anglian Stage. This event, illustrated in Figure 5.3, took the river directly from a course through what is now Hertfordshire and central Essex into its modern valley through London. Much of the new route was, in all probability, already in existence before the Anglian glaciation, as part of the tributary Darent-Medway system. The lower part of this diverted course, downstream from London, provides important evidence

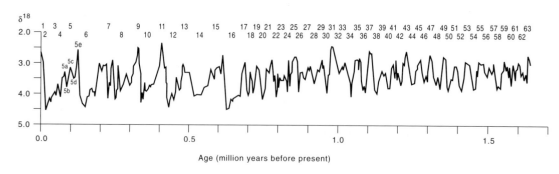

Figure 5.1. The climatic record as determined from deep ocean sediments laid down during the last 1.6 million years. From drilling at a site in the mid-Atlantic at latitude c. 41°N. Significant climatic episodes are numbered as 'Oxygen Isotope Stages', counting backwards from the present temperate episode, the Holocene, which is Stage 1. Warm stages therefore have odd numbers and cold ones have even numbers. Compiled from data published by Ruddiman et al. (1989).

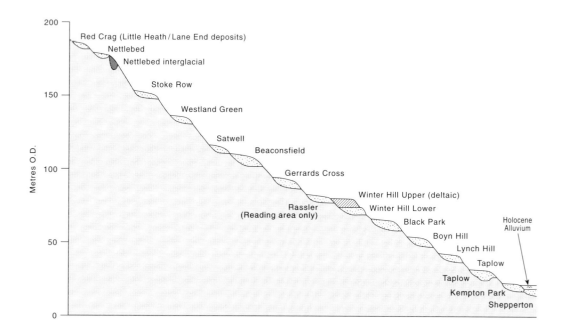

Figure 5.2. Idealized transverse section through the north side of the Thames valley in the Slough area. Those terraces from which Palaeolithic artefacts have been obtained are shown with a coarser stipple. The lower density of stipple in the lowest terraces is to convey the information that artefacts from these are less common and are primarily derived.

for repeated climatic change since the Anglian, as well as for early human occupation of the valley, and will therefore receive particular attention below. Before the Thames was diverted southwards, the Medway flowed beyond its present catchment in Kent across eastern Essex to join the early Thames near Clacton (Fig. 5.3). This glaciation introduced characteristic rocks from the north into the London Basin for the first time. The appearance of these exotic rocks within the staircase of Thames deposits, as well as the change in the river's course in the eastern half of its catchment, means that the Anglian glaciation provides an important stratigraphical marker.

THE EARLIEST HUMAN OCCUPATION OF THE THAMES VALLEY

Until a few years ago, it was thought that the earliest human occupation of the Thames valley, and of Britain as a whole, followed the Anglian. It is now known that humans were present in southern England, the Midlands and East Anglia prior to the Anglian, based on evidence from sites such as Boxgrove, West Sussex (Roberts 1986; Roberts *et al.* 1994), Waverley Wood Farm, Warwickshire (Shotton *et al.* 1993) and High Lodge, Suffolk (Ashton *et al.* 1992). This occupation is believed to have

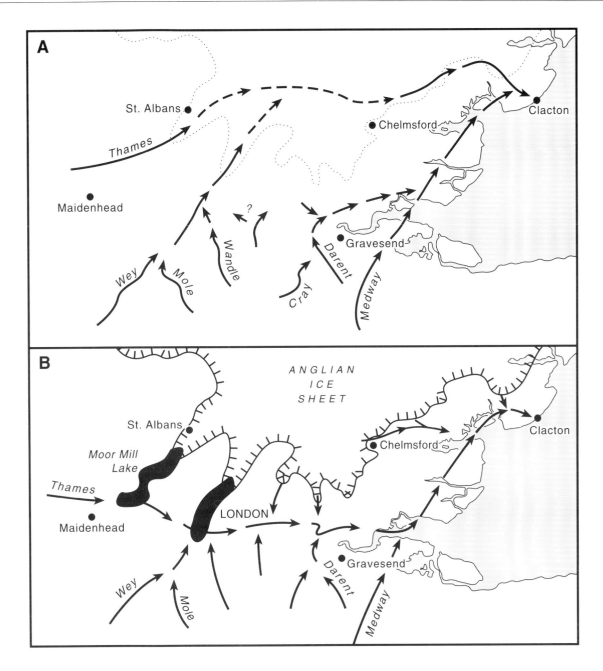

Figure 5.3. The course of the River Thames immediately before (A) and immediately after (B) its diversion as a result of the Anglian glaciation (maximum glacial limit indicated in B).

coincided with an interglacial that preceded the Anglian, late within the 'Cromerian Complex' (as recognized in the Netherlands). Pre-Anglian interglacial sediments are poorly represented within the Thames sequence; most of those that have been recorded are probably older than the late Cromerian Complex and have failed to produce artefacts. A site at Wivenhoe, in Essex, is thought to represent the last pre-Anglian interglacial (Bridgland *et al.* 1988; Bridgland 1994a), but the sediments there have yielded only two small flakes (Bridgland 1994a) that might easily be the product of natural breakage within the fluvial environment.

Occurrences of artefacts within Anglian gravels of the Thames system are quite common, however, and these might have been reworked from earlier sediments or land surfaces. Sites in such gravels include Highlands Farm Pit and other localities in the 'Ancient Channel gravel' (= Black Park Gravel) of the Caversham-Henley area (Wymer 1961; 1968; Bridgland 1994a) and sites in the Silchester Gravel of the Kennet, such as Sulhamstead (Wymer 1977) and Hamstead Marshall, west of Newbury (Bridgland 1994a). The pre-Anglian occupation may have continued into the early part of the glacial, although no primary context Anglian sites have been discovered to date. It can probably be assumed, however, that the advance of ice sheets into the London area during the glacial maximum was sufficient to cause the early humans to migrate southwards from the 'British peninsula'.

THE LOWER THAMES SEQUENCE OF POST-ANGLIAN TERRACES

The term Lower Thames is generally applied to that part of the river downstream from central London. This stretch of the valley is within the tidal influence of the southern North Sea at the present day, although an offshore continuation of it has been recognised beneath the sea-floor, extending towards the north east (D'Olier 1975; Bridgland *et al.* 1993; Bridgland & D'Olier 1995). In the Lower Thames valley and the coastal margins of eastern Essex are preserved terrace deposits laid down by the Thames (in the latter area the Thames-Medway) subsequent to the glacial diversion of the river. These are dominated by cold-climate gravels, but interbedded with these are interglacial sediments (Fig. 5.4), which occur here more commonly than in other parts of the valley. In some cases, particularly in eastern Essex, they occur in restricted channels beneath the widespread sheets of terrace gravel (Bridgland 1988). Some of these interglacial sediments appear to represent earlier periods of estuarine deposition, recording high sea-level episodes between the Anglian and the Holocene and showing that the latter is not the first interglacial to bring a tidal influence to this part of the valley.

Three terraces have been identified east of London, based on the New Series mapping of the Geological Survey (especially their sheets 257, Romford, and 271, Dartford; see appropriate memoirs: Dewey *et al.* 1924; Dines & Edmunds 1925). Because of a confusion of nomenclature, described below, it is perhaps best to use the descriptive terms 'high', 'middle' and 'low' terraces to describe these in this opening discussion. It used to be believed, partly on the basis of artefact types found in the various deposits, that the Thames cut down from the 'high terrace' to the 'middle terrace' level soon after the initiation of Lower Thames drainage, only to aggrade back up to the 'high terrace' level once more, before cutting down to the 'middle terrace' level for a second time (King & Oakley 1936). These ideas persisted until quite recently, largely because of the belief that only two interglacials were represented in the terrace sequence in the London area (see above). The old artefact-based scheme was helpful in explaining this apparent anomaly, since it allowed deposits dating from the same interglacial to occur in both the 'high' and 'middle' terraces, and it also allowed two different interglacials to be represented in the 'middle terrace'.

Dating the terraces

The idea that the Thames terraces have formed in synchrony with climatic fluctuation during the Quaternary, recently promoted by the author and others (Bridgland 1994a; 1995; Bridgland & Maddy 1995; Bridgland & Allen 1996), is by no means new. It was one of the mechanisms envisaged by Zeuner (1945; 1946; 1959; 1961), who was one of the first to attempt to explain terrace formation, recognizing tectonic movements, sea-level change and climatic variation as the main causes. He regarded the climatic mechanism as the most widespread and the most important from a stratigraphic point of view. He claimed that 'the sequence of climatic river terraces ... gives the number of cold phases that occurred in the course of time represented by it, which in many cases means the duration of the Pleistocene'. Thus climatic terraces could provide a record of the sequence of climatic events during the Quaternary. This view fell from favour in the face of the scheme for Quaternary chronology, based principally on palynology, that was erected during the 1950s and 60s and eventually summarized by Mitchell *et al.* (1973). This pollen-based scheme placed the diversion of the Thames in the antepenultimate glacial and, therefore, identified just two interglacials since that event occurred, the Hoxnian and Ipswichian of what can be called the 'traditional' British chronology. There are too many terraces in the Lower Thames (which entirely post-dates the diversion) for the idea of climatically generated terraces and the 'traditional' chronology to be reconciled. There were, however, later advocates of climatic generation as the main mechanism behind terrace formation, notably John Wymer (1968), in his seminal work on the Palaeolithic record from the deposits of the Thames.

In recent years it has become apparent that the 'traditional' chronology is inadequate and that there have been more oscillations of climate between the Anglian and the Holocene than were recognized in the pollen-based scheme. This realisation has come about mainly through the analyses of sediment cores from the deep oceans, which provide a proxy record of Quaternary climate from fluctuations in the oxygen isotope content of foraminifera contained in the sediments (for explanation, see Patience & Kroon 1991). The resultant 'oxygen isotope curve' (Fig. 5.1) is thought to be the best available record of global climatic fluctuation. The current aim of much Quaternary research is to correlate this oceanic record with the various fragmentary terrestrial sequences, amongst which the Thames terraces perhaps represent the most important in Britain.

Even before the oceanic record came to be used as the template for Quaternary 'climatostratigraphy', questions had been raised about the ability of the traditional chronology to explain the Lower Thames sequence. First, Sutcliffe (1960; 1964; 1975) recognized two post-Hoxnian mammalian faunas of interglacial character, whereas the traditional chronology allowed for only a single post-Hoxnian interglacial, the Ipswichian. Sutcliffe regarded

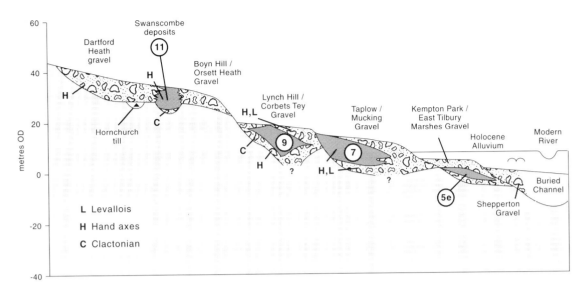

Figure 5.4. Idealized transverse section through the Lower Thames terrace sequence, showing the interbedding of cold-climate sands and gravels with interglacial sediments (darker tone). Certain individual beds of specific importance are identified separately. The stratigraphic positions of Palaeolithic occurrences are indicated.

the deposits at Ilford and Aveley, both attributed to the Ipswichian on the basis of pollen (West *et al.* 1964; West 1969), as older than other supposed Ipswichian deposits at Trafalgar Square in central London. Subsequently Allen (1977) suggested that the molluscan assemblage from Purfleet implied deposition in an interglacial that was neither the Hoxnian nor the Ipswichian. Wymer (1985) suggested that the Ilford-Aveley deposits were emplaced during a previously unrecognized interglacial, which he termed 'Ilfordian', intermediate in age between the Hoxnian and the Ipswichian. Keen (1990) and Preece (1995) have presented more detailed cases against the traditional chronology on the basis of Mollusca, whereas recent work by Schreve (1997a) suggests that mammalian assemblages provide sufficient biostratigraphical resolution to confirm that four post-Anglian interglacials can be recognized in the Lower Thames.

Eventually it has become apparent that the Purfleet deposits, as well as those at Ilford and Aveley, represent climatic cycles additional to the Hoxnian, as recognized at Swanscombe, and the Ipswichian, as recognized at Trafalgar Square (Bridgland 1994a; 1995; Schreve 1997a). In fact the four interglacials now identified within the Lower Thames sequence occur in four different terraces, allowing Zeuner's idea of climatic terrace generation in the Thames to be reintroduced. Thus recent reviews of terrace formation have emphasized the role of climate, which controls fluvial activity indirectly through its influence on discharge and sediment supply, the latter also influenced by vegetation cover, which is another indirect climatic factor (Green & McGregor 1980; 1987; Bridgland 1994a; 1995; Bridgland & Allen 1996). The recognition of four different interglacials in the Lower Thames, within

discrete terrace formations, is supported by amino acid geochronology (Bowen *et al.* 1995).

The revised Lower Thames sequence

In the revised interpretation of the Lower Thames terrace sequence, based on the notion that terrace formation has been driven by climatic fluctuation (see above), terraces are considered to have formed as a result of punctuated but progressive downcutting by the river, without the complex sequence of rejuvenation and aggradation envisaged in the earlier artefact-based scheme. The terraces originally identified by the Geological Survey have been reclassified as lithostratigraphic formations, the Boyn Hill/Orsett Heath Gravel, the Lynch Hill/Corbets Tey Gravel and the Taplow/Mucking Gravel (Bridgland 1988; 1994a; 1995; Gibbard *et al.* 1988). In addition, a fourth formation has been recognized, buried beneath the Holocene alluvium of the modern floodplain, the Kempton Park/East Tilbury Marshes Gravel (Fig. 5.4).

It should be noted that terraces identified by the names Taplow Gravel and Floodplain Gravel on the above-mentioned Geological Survey maps are not the equivalents of the Taplow and Floodplain terraces west of London, where the names originate. Thus only the Boyn Hill Gravel is correctly identified east of London, although the mapping in the latter area is basically sound. The fault lies in the original failure to recognize an additional terrace, formed by the Lynch Hill Gravel, between the Boyn Hill and Taplow formations west of London. The additional terrace was recognized on the Romford and Dartford sheets, but was miscorrelated with the Taplow Gravel of the type area near Slough. The true Taplow Gravel in the Lower Thames is the deposit mapped as Floodplain Gravel. To alleviate the confusion caused by this error, an alternative system of local nomenclature has been applied to the Lower Thames, although here both names are used, in downstream sequence separated by a slash, as in Boyn Hill/Orsett Heath Gravel. This correction to the terrace mapping west and east of London has important implications, not least because the Lynch Hill Gravel is widely regarded as the richest source, amongst the Thames formations, of Palaeolithic artefacts (Wymer 1988).

Correlation with the oceanic sequence

Each of the four terrace formations recognized east of London (Fig. 5.4) incorporates locally preserved interglacial sediments sandwiched between cold-climate gravel deposits (in the lowest terrace, interglacial sediments have yet to be found downstream from central London). Four separate, post-Anglian interglacials are thus represented, as described above (Fig. 5.4). As stated already, a principal aim in any current stratigraphic reconstruction of a lengthy terrestrial sequence must be correlation with the global oceanic record for the Quaternary. Most recent authors have regarded OIS 12 of the deep-sea record as the most likely correlative of the Anglian Glacial (Bowen *et al.* 1986; Campbell & Bowen 1989), during which Lower Thames drainage was initiated. This has led to the suggestion that the above-mentioned four interglacials correspond with the four odd-numbered stages recognized in the oxygen isotope sequence after OIS 12, namely OIS 11, 9, 7 and 5 (Fig. 5.1). In fact the last interglacial, the Ipswichian, is now well established as the correlative of substage 5e, on the basis of absolute dating (Gascoyne *et al.* 1981; Stringer *et al.* 1986; Bowen & Sykes 1988), leaving the later warm episodes within OIS 5, substages 5c and 5a, together with the poorly developed OIS 3, to be related to ameliorations of climate within what has been regarded on land as the last glacial. There is good evidence from amino acid ratios to support the correlation of interglacial deposits within the Boyn Hill/Orsett Heath Formation, the Taplow/Mucking Formation and the Kempton Park/East Tilbury Marshes Formation with OIS 11, 7 and substage 5e respectively (Bowen *et al.* 1989; Bridgland & Harding 1993; Bridgland 1994a; Fig. 5.4). Similarly convincing evidence to link Corbets Tey Formation interglacial sediments with OIS 9 has been more elusive, but ratios indicative of such a correlation have been obtained from the deposits of this terrace at Belhus Park (Bowen 1991; Bowen *et al.* 1995), while Schreve (1997a; 1997b) has assigned the Purfleet deposits to OIS 9 on the basis of mammalian biostratigraphy.

THE PALAEOLITHIC SEQUENCE FROM THE THAMES

On the basis of the revised chronology of the Thames sequence, certain changes in artefact types within the terrace staircase can now be related to the oceanic sequence with some degree of confidence. Undiluted Clactonian assemblages occur only within the oldest two terrace formations of the Lower Thames, their last appearance being in the lower gravel of the Lynch Hill/Corbets Tey Formation, which is ascribed to late OIS 10 (Fig. 5.4). The prolific site at Globe Pit, Little Thurrock (Wymer 1957; Bridgland & Harding 1993; 1994a), is the best-known such occurrence, but Clactonian material has also been recovered from the same stratigraphic level at Purfleet (Palmer 1975; Wymer 1985; Bridgland 1994a; 1994b). The first use of the Levallois technique is seen in later deposits within the same terrace formation, although these are believed to date from OIS 8. Thus a 'protolevallois' element was identified within the Palaeolithic assemblage from Botany Pit, Purfleet, by Wymer (1968), in gravel believed to represent the later, upper part of the Corbets Tey Formation (Bridgland 1994a; 1994b). Levallois technique is seen in Palaeolithic assemblages from a number of sites in the basal gravel of the next terrace (formed by the Taplow/Mucking Formation), which is also believed to date from OIS 8. Thus the assemblages from Crayford (e.g. Kennard 1944; Wymer 1968) and West Thurrock (Bridgland & Harding 1994b) are from this position within the terrace staircase, while the famous Levallois site at Northfleet probably represents the same stratigraphic level in the tributary Ebbsfleet (Bridgland 1994a). It seems, therefore, that a significant change in Palaeolithic technology occurred in the Lower Thames between OIS 10 and 8, with the first appearance in the latter episode of the Levallois technique.

Handaxes (bifaces), belonging to the Acheulian Industry, range from the earliest human occupation, which pre-dated the diversion of the Thames, throughout the sequence described above, potentially occurring in the same stratigraphic levels as Clactonian and Levallois assemblages. Fresh, as opposed to rolled and reworked artefacts, seem to disappear from the terrace sequence at the level of the upper (post-interglacial) gravel of the Taplow/Mucking Formation, which has yielded no evidence of primary context archaeology – in marked contrast to the lower gravel of the same formation, described already (Fig. 5.4). This upper Mucking Gravel is thought to date from OIS 6, which appears to have been the most severely cold glacial since the Anglian. Although there is evidence for human occupation of the valley during the OIS 7 interglacial, from the Crayford brickearth (Kennard 1944), there is no convincing evidence for a Palaeolithic presence during substage 5e. Many sites in the Thames and elsewhere attributed originally to the last interglacial are now believed to be older, so only sites for which there is corroboration, from absolute dating or biostratigraphy, of a substage 5e age can be included in this argument. None has produced evidence for human presence (Currant & Jacobi 1997). It is thus possible to suggest that humans migrated south from the 'British peninsula' in the face of the severe cold of OIS 6 and were prevented from returning in the Ipswichian, substage 5e, by the rapid rise in sea level that flooded the Dover Strait.

Regardless of whether humans were absent from Britain during the Ipswichian, it is clear that there was human occupation during the last glacial. This cold episode saw both Neaderthals and modern humans occupying continental Europe, the former being associated with artefacts of Mousterian type. The evidence for Neanderthals in Britain is scanty (Stringer & Gamble 1993), with none yet known in the Thames. Modern humans are certainly known to have appeared in Britain during a low sea-level phase of the last glacial, establishing an Upper Palaeolithic culture, although again evidence from the Thames is generally lacking. By this time the River Thames had established the course of its modern floodplain, which is everywhere underlain, at a greater or lesser depth, by Devensian (last glacial) gravels. East of London these gravels decline beneath the floodplain, eventually to extend out into the southern North Sea as the basal infill of the buried and submerged valley system originally described by D'Olier (1975; Bridgland *et al.* 1993; Bridgland & D'Olier 1995). It is here that the evidence for last glacial human occupation would have to be sought, so perhaps its failure to come to light is unsurprising. Following the Pleistocene, the Holocene marine transgression inundated the downstream end of this Devensian valley, leading eventually to the modern limits of the tidal estuary being established.

CONCLUSIONS

Studies of the depositional record of the River Thames have revealed it to be a river of considerable antiquity, very much older than the earliest human occupation of Britain. The valley of the Thames through London, on the other hand, is a relatively recent feature, adopted by the river in response to glacial diversion during the most severe of the Quaternary glaciations. Humans had been present slightly earlier that this event; subsequently the evolution of the river and the development of human endeavour, or what we can tell of it from the stone artefacts that survive, go hand in hand. The deposits of the river provide an important repository for the artefacts, while the latter represent a significant potential means of dating and classifying the former.

The major part of this record, from terraces on the side of the valley, relates to landscapes very different to that of the present day. This is not just because the climate was often different, but also because the river was flowing at a very different level to the modern Thames: higher, in the case of the terraces, or lower, in the case of the gravels laid down during the last glacial, which lie deeply buried beneath the modern floodplain. Although the confines of the modern valley floor were established during the last glacial, it is only with the rise in sea level during the Holocene that the present level of the floodplain and the configuration of the modern tidal estuary were developed.

REFERENCES

Allen, T. 1977. Interglacial sea-level change: evidence for brackish water sedimentation at Purfleet, Essex. *Quaternary Newsletter* 22, 1–3.

Ashton, N.M., Cook, J., Lewis, S.G. & Rose, J. (eds) 1992. *High Lodge. Excavations by G.de G. Sieveking, 1962–8, and J. Cook, 1988.* London: British Museum Press.

Bowen, D.Q. 1991. Amino acid geochronology. In S.G. Lewis, C.A. Whiteman & D.R. Bridgland (eds), *Central East Anglia and the Fen Basin*, 21–24. London: Quaternary Research Association Field Guide.

Bowen, D.Q., Hughes, S.A., Sykes, G.A. & Miller, G.M. 1989. Land-sea correlations in the Pleistocene based on isoleucine epimerization in non-marine molluscs. *Nature* 340, 49–51.

Bowen, D.Q., Rose, J., McCabe, A.M. & Sutherland, D.G. 1986. Correlation of Quaternary glaciations in England, Ireland, Scotland and Wales. *Quaternary Science Reviews* 5, 299–340.

Bowen, D.Q. & Sykes, G.A. 1988. Correlation of the marine events and glaciations on the north-east Atlantic margin. *Philosophical Transactions of the Royal Society of London* B318, 619–35.

Bowen, D.Q., Sykes, G.A., Maddy, D., Bridgland, D.R. & Lewis, S.G. 1995. Aminostratigraphy and amino acid geochronology of English lowland valleys: the Lower Thames in context. In D.R. Bridgland, P. Allen & B.A. Haggart (eds), *The Quaternary of the Lower Reaches of the Thames Field Guide*, 61-63. Durham: Quaternary Research Association.

Bridgland, D.R. 1985. Uniclinal shifting; a speculative reappraisal based on terrace distribution in the London Basin. *Quaternary Newsletter* 47, 26–33.

Bridgland, D.R. 1988. The Pleistocene fluvial stratigraphy and palaeogeography of Essex. *Proceedings of the Geologists' Association* 99, 291–314.

Bridgland, D.R. 1994a. *Quaternary of the Thames*. London: Chapman & Hall. Geological Conservation Review Series 7.

Bridgland, D.R. 1994b. Dating of Lower Palaeolithic industries within the framework of the Lower Thames terrace sequence. In N. Ashton & A. David (eds), *Stories in Stone*, 28-40. London: Lithic Studies Society Occasional Paper 4.

Bridgland, D.R. 1995. The Quaternary sequence of the eastern Thames basin: problems of correlation. In D.R. Bridgland, P. Allen & B.A. Haggart (eds), *The Quaternary of the Lower Reaches of the Thames Field Guide*, 35-52. Durham: Quaternary Research Association.

Bridgland, D.R. & Allen, P. 1996. A revised model for terrace formation and its significance for the lower Middle Pleistocene Thames terrace aggradations of north-east Essex, U.K. In C. Turner (ed.), *The Early Middle Pleistocene in Europe*, 121-34. Rotterdam: Balkema.

Bridgland, D.R., Allen, P., Currant, A.P., Gibbard, P.L., Lister, A.M., Preece, R.C., Robinson, J.E., Stuart, A.J. & Sutcliffe, A.J. 1988. Report of Geologists' Association field meeting in north-east Essex, May 2nd-24th, 1987. *Proceedings of the Geologists' Association* 99, 315–33.

Bridgland, D.R. & D'Olier, B. 1995. The Pleistocene evolution of the Thames and Rhine drainage systems in the southern North Sea Basin. In R.C. Preece (ed.), *Island Britain: a Quaternary Perspective*, 27-45. London: Geological Society of London Special Publication 96.

Bridgland, D.R., D'Olier, B., Gibbard, P.L. & Roe, H.M. 1993. Correlation of Thames terrace deposits between the Lower

Thames, eastern Essex and the submerged offshore continuation of the Thames-Medway valley. *Proceedings of the Geologists' Association* 104, 51-8.

Bridgland, D.R. & Harding, P. 1993. Middle Pleistocene Thames terrace deposits at Globe Pit, Little Thurrock, and their contained Clactonian industry. *Proceedings of the Geologists' Association* 104, 263-83.

Bridgland, D.R. & Harding, P. 1994a. Globe Pit, Little Thurrock (TQ 625783). In D.R. Bridgland, *Quaternary of the Thames*, 228-37. London: Chapman & Hall. Geological Conservation Review Series 7.

Bridgland, D.R. & Harding, P. 1994b. Lion Pit tramway cutting (West Thurrock; TQ 598783). In D.R.Bridgland, *Quaternary of the Thames*, 237-51. London: Chapman & Hall. Geological Conservation Review Series 7.

Bridgland, D.R. & Maddy, D. 1995. River terrace deposits: long Quaternary terrestrial sequences. *Abstracts, XIV INQUA Congress*, 37. Berlin.

Campbell, S. & Bowen, D.Q. 1989. *Quaternary of Wales*. Geological Conservation Review Series, Nature Conservancy Council.

Currant, A. & Jacobi, R. 1997. Vertebrate faunas of the British Late Pleistocene and the chronology of human settlement. *Quaternary Newsletter* 82, 1-8.

Dewey, H., Bromehead, C.E.N., Chatwin, C.P. & Dines, H.G. 1924. *The Geology of the Country around Dartford*. Memoir of the Geological Survey of Great Britain.

Dines, H.G. & Edmunds, F.H. 1925. *The Geology of the Country around Romford*. Memoir of the Geological Survey of Great Britain.

D'Olier, B. 1975. Some aspects of late Pleistocene-Holocene drainage of the River Thames in the eastern part of the London Basin. *Philosophical Transactions of the Royal Society of London* A279, 269-77.

Gascoyne, M., Currant, A.P. & Lord, T.C. 1981. Ipswichian fauna of Victoria Cave and the marine palaeoclimatic record. *Nature* 294, 652-4.

Gibbard, P.L. 1985. *The Pleistocene History of the Middle Thames Valley*. Cambridge: Cambridge University Press.

Gibbard, P.L., Whiteman, C.A. & Bridgland, D.R. 1988. A preliminary report on the stratigraphy of the Lower Thames Valley. *Quaternary Newsletter* 56, 1-8.

Green, C.P. & McGregor, D.F.M. 1980. Quaternary evolution of the River Thames. In D.K.C. Jones (ed.), *The Shaping of Southern England*, 172-202. London: Academic Press. Institute of British Geographers, Special Publication No. 11.

Green, C.P. & McGregor, D.F.M. 1987. River terraces: a stratigraphic record of environmental change. In V. Gardiner (ed.), *International Geomorphology 1986 Part 1*, 977-87. Chichester: Wiley.

Hare, F.K. 1947. The geomorphology of a part of the Middle Thames. *Proceedings of the Geologists' Association* 58, 294-339.

Hey, R.W. 1986. A re-examination of the Northern Drift of Oxfordshire. *Proceedings of the Geologists' Association* 97, 291-302.

Hey, R.W. 1996. The origin and early history of the Upper Thames. *Quaternary Science Reviews* 15, 407-11.

Keen, D.H. 1990. Significance of the record provided by Pleistocene fluvial deposits and their included molluscan faunas for palaeoenvironmental reconstruction and stratigraphy: case study from the English Midlands. *Palaeogeography, Palaeoclimatology, Palaeoecology* 80, 25-34.

Kennard, A.S. 1944. The Crayford Brickearths. *Proceedings of the Geologists' Association* 55, 121-69.

King, W.B.R. & Oakley, K.P. 1936. The Pleistocene succession in the lower part of the Thames Valley. *Proceedings of the Prehistoric Society* 1, 52-76.

Mitchell, G.F., Penny, L.F., Shotton, F.W. & West, R.G. 1973. *A Correlation of Quaternary Deposits in the British Isles*. London: Geological Society of London Special Report 4.

Palmer, S. 1975. A Palaeolithic site at North Road, Purfleet, Essex. *Transactions of the Essex Archaeological Society* 7, 1-13.

Patience, A.J. & Kroon, D. 1991. Oxygen isotope chronostratigraphy. In P.L. Smart & P.D. Francis (eds), *Quaternary dating methods, a user's guide*, 199-222. London: Quaternary Research Association Technical Guide 4.

Preece, R.C. 1995. Mollusca from interglacial sediments at three critical sites in the Lower Thames. In D.R. Bridgland, P. Allen & B.A. Haggart (eds), *The Quaternary of the Lower Reaches of the Thames Field Guide*, 53-60. Durham: Quaternary Research Association.

Roberts, M.B. 1986. Excavation of the Lower Palaeolithic site at Amey's Eartham Pit, Boxgrove, West Sussex: a preliminary report. *Proceedings of the Prehistoric Society* 52, 215-45.

Roberts, M.B., Stringer, C.B. & Parfitt, S.A. 1994. A hominid tibia from Middle Pleistocene sediments at Boxgrove, UK. *Nature* 369, 311-3.

Ruddiman, W.F., Raymo, M.E., Martinson, D.G., Clement, B.M. & Backman, J. 1989. Pleistocene evolution: northern hemisphere ice-sheets and north Atlantic ocean. *Paleoceanography* 4, 353-412.

Schreve, D.C. 1997a. Mammalian bistratigraphy of the later Middle Pleistocene in Britain. Unpublished PhD thesis, University of London.

Schreve, D.C. 1997b. Excavations at the later Middle Pleistocene site of Greenlands Pit, Purfleet, Essex. *Quaternary Newsletter* 82, 30-1.

Shotton, F.W., Keen, D.H., Coope, G.R., Currant, A.P., Gibbard, P.L., Aalto, M., Peglar, S.M. & Robinson, J.E. 1993. The Middle Pleistocene deposits of Waverley Wood Pit, Warwickshire, England. *Journal of Quaternary Science* 8, 293-325.

Stringer, C.B., Currant, A.P., Schwarcz, H.P. & Colcutt, S.N. 1986. Age of Pleistocene faunas from Bacon Hole, Wales. *Nature* 320, 59-62.

Stringer, C. & Gamble, C. 1993. *In Search of the Neanderthals*. London: Thames and Hudson.

Sutcliffe, A.J. 1960. Joint Mitnor Cave, Buckfastleigh. *Transactions of the Torquay Natural History Society* 13, 1-26.

Sutcliffe, A.J. 1964. The mammal fauna. In C.D. Ovey (ed.), *The Swanscombe skull. A Survey of Research on a Pleistocene Site*, 85-111. London: Royal Anthropological Institute of Great Britain and Ireland, Occasional Paper 20.

Sutcliffe, A.J. 1975. A hazard in the interpretation of glacial-interglacial sequences. *Quaternary Newsletter* 17, 1-3.

West, R.G. 1969. Pollen analyses from interglacial deposits at Aveley and Grays, Essex. *Proceedings of the Geologists' Association* 80, 271-82.

West, R.G., Lambert, J.M. & Sparks, B.W. 1964. Interglacial deposits at Ilford, Essex. *Philosophical Transactions of the Royal Society of London* B247, 185-212.

Whiteman, C.A. & Rose, J.1992. Thames river sediments of the British Early and Middle Pleistocene. *Quaternary Science Reviews* 11, 363-75.

Wymer, J.J. 1957. A Clactonian flint industry at Little Thurrock, Grays, Essex. *Proceedings of the Geologists' Association* 68, 59-177.

Wymer, J.J. 1961. The Lower Palaeolithic succession in the Thames Valley and the date of the ancient channel between Caversham and Henley, Oxfordshire. *Proceedings of the Prehistoric Society* 27, 1-27.

Wymer, J.J. 1968. *Lower Palaeolithic Archaeology in Britain, as Represented by the Thames Valley*. London: John Baker.

Wymer, J.J. 1977. Sulhamstead. In E.R. Shephard-Thorn & J.J.

Wymer (eds), *South-east England and the Thames Valley*. Guide book for Excursion A5, 10th INQUA Congress, Birmingham, 24–8. Norwich: Geoabstracts.

Wymer, J.J. 1985. *The Palaeolithic Sites of East Anglia*. Norwich: Geo Books.

Wymer, J.J. 1988. Palaeolithic archaeology and the British Quaternary sequence. *Quaternary Science Reviews* 7, 79–98.

Zeuner, F.E. 1945. *The Pleistocene Period: its Climate, Chronology and Faunal Successions*. London: Ray Society.

Zeuner, F.E. 1946. *Dating the Past: an Introduction to Geochronology*. London: Methuen.

Zeuner, F.E. 1959. *The Pleistocene Period: its Climate, Chronology and Faunal Successions* (2nd edition). London: Hutchinson.

Zeuner, F.E. 1961. The sequence of terraces in the Lower Thames and the radiation chronology. *Annals of the New York Academy of Sciences* 95, 377–80.

6. As Represented by the Thames Valley

Derek A. Roe

ABSTRACT

This article is a brief and necessarily very selective tribute to John Wymer's fine work on the Lower Palaeolithic of the Thames Valley over the best part of fifty years. Its theme is the way his work there reflects so many things of importance that have happened to British Lower Palaeolithic Archaeology and Quaternary Research, during the second half of the 20th century. The Wolvercote Channel site is used to represent his interest in the Upper Thames, while Highlands Farm Pit is selected for the Middle Thames, and mention is also made of Barnfield Pit, Swanscombe, for the Lower Thames.

INTRODUCTION

John Wymer's long devotion to the Lower Palaeolithic of the Thames Valley is one aspect of his work that will always retain special importance. His first substantial publication on it, about the Caversham Ancient Channel (1956), reports fieldwork carried out in 1955, but he had been familiar with working Thames gravel pits for some while before that. Publications of Thames Valley interest related to the English Rivers project will certainly carry him on to the start of the new millenium, and the longer into it he continues to keep a firm eye on the Thames Palaeolithic, the better for us all.

While the sheer quality of Wymer's publications on the Palaeolithic and Pleistocene successions of the Thames Valley would ensure their relevance for future generations of British Palaeolithic archaeologists, the inherent importance of the Thames Quaternary sequence is an additional factor, to which I have referred elsewhere (e.g. 1995). There is, alas, no single Thames Valley site with quite the capacity of, say, Boxgrove, to provide a detailed picture of early humans in action, and indeed the large majority of Thames Valley Palaeolithic sites have yielded artefacts in secondary contexts or worse. But it is the long

geological and archaeological succession that is so important, and the chance, whether locally in the Upper, Middle or Lower sections of the valley, or more generally after combining their evidence, to examine the broad picture of human settlement in Britain from before the Anglian glaciation until some time within the Devensian (Bridgland 1994; Gibbard 1985; 1994). This is still a vital central framework of reference to which other British sites need to be related, whatever their individual quality. Besides, the Thames Valley itself, with the main river and its tributaries, seems likely always to have been an important route for human groups moving around the British peninsula. The British Isles of today, and the sea-filled southern North Sea basin, offer only a misleading guide to the former possibilities for human settlement in Pleistocene north west Europe. The Thames is not the river it was at various times in the past: all the more reason for doing the best we can, following John Wymer's lead, to extract good information from our present Thames Valley.

The title of this article is a sometimes overlooked part of the full title of John Wymer's first book (1968), *Lower Palaeolithic Archaeology in Britain as Represented by the Thames Valley*. When he wrote it, much of his work elsewhere in Britain (including East Anglia) still lay in the future. Partly for that very reason, it was possible in the 1960s to offer an account of the British Lower Palaeolithic based just on the Thames Valley sites and not miss too much. That is hardly achievable today, so many things having changed, but one could still go some way towards it, and it is certainly often possible to cite Thames Valley parallels, some of them found long ago, for situations that have only recently been identified or made understandable elsewhere in Britain.

SOME THAMES VALLEY LOWER PALAEOLITHIC SITES

Over the years, Wymer has carried out practical fieldwork at numerous Thames Valley Palaeolithic sites, ranging from major excavations to the simple clearing of typical sections for congress excursions. Few others can still exist, in whatever form, that he has not personally visited at some stage; in the earlier years, former gravel pits were often clearly identifiable and could be recorded quite fully, while today many have been completely obliterated by modern residential or commercial development. Comparison of the 1968 volume with the relevant reports of the Southern Rivers and English Rivers Projects shows the extent of such destruction, but these publications, decades apart, recognizably belong to the same careful programme of record and interpretation, with some but not all of the aims having changed.

The Upper Thames

While less fully involved in excavation upstream of the Goring Gap than downstream, Wymer has at various times faithfully recorded the growing number of Lower Palaeolithic find-spots in the Upper Thames Valley, most recently for the Southern Rivers and English Rivers Projects. The increase over recent years has been dramatic – thanks largely to the efforts of his good friend R.J. MacRae, another contributor to this volume. In 1968, Wymer described the Wolvercote Brick Pit as the most important Palaeolithic site in the Upper Thames Valley, commenting on its peculiar plano-convex handaxes, found in an interglacial stream channel context, and discussing whether they belonged to the Hoxnian or to the interglacial which followed what was then called 'the Gipping Glaciation'; he expressed the hope that pollen analysis might make possible a comparison with Hoxne, and that an answer would soon be obtained (*op. cit.* 87–90).

Plus ça change... For many, thirty years later, Wolvercote is still the most important site in the Upper Thames region, but its problems, though perhaps now better understood, are far from solved. British awareness of the Oxygen Isotope Stages and their significance for the British Pleistocene succession really starts only in the late 1970s; for Wolvercote, the effect was to provide far more than two warm periods to choose from, in considering the age

of the interglacial channel feature (cf. Bridgland 1994, 58–65). Strenuous efforts to find a decent new exposure of the Wolvercote Channel have surprisingly drawn blank, and no good pollen samples exist. As it happened, Wymer himself was to be instrumental in changing our views of Hoxne, too (Singer *et al.* 1993). The Wolvercote plano-convex handaxes remain as unusual in Britain as ever they were (Tyldesley 1986), but there are now new attitudes to biface morphology and the factors that cause handaxes to look the way they do (see for example White 1996). We are still only guessing at the source of the large units of fine flint used by the makers of the Wolvercote handaxes and, if we still wish to make direct comparison with certain plano-convex handaxe industries from continental Europe (Tyldesley *op. cit.*; Roe 1981, 123–28), the dating of those has been thrown into equivalent confusion by the lengthening of the Pleistocene succession. An Ipswichian date for Wolvercote (in the sense of OIS 5e) has become rather unlikely, in the absence of any definite sign of human presence at that time in Britain, which was probably temporarily an island (cf. Preece 1995). Indeed, controversy has grown over whether any evidence for Lower Palaeolithic occupation in Britain exists in a situation that unequivocally indicates contemporaneity with the warmest part of any interglacial. Was the Wolvercote site an exception? Only a new exposure of the Channel, with artefacts in place, could help us establish the true relationship between the artefacts and the beaches and swirl-holes of the stream, or whether the stream does indeed belong to the maximum of the interglacial. It is not easy, meanwhile, to see where a direct solution to the problems of Wolvercote will be found.

For the Upper Thames Valley more generally, perhaps a consistent picture is beginning to emerge of occasional penetration by humans, following the river upstream, bringing ready-made flint artefacts with them, but prepared to turn subsequently to local rock types for implement manufacture during their stay (cf. Buckingham *et al.* 1996, 412–14). This touches on another great interest of John Wymer's: the extent to which more northerly areas of Britain were occupied during the Lower Palaeolithic, and how toolmakers fared in non-flint areas (see for example Wymer 1988a). The area where that topic can be addressed certainly starts in the Upper Thames Valley, but unfortunately we cannot follow it further north on this occasion.

The Middle and Lower Thames

During John Wymer's time at Reading Museum, particularly, the Middle Thames Valley was his home territory, and much useful fieldwork resulted from this. There is space here to refer only to a minimal number of sites, and I will choose Highlands Farm Pit at Rotherfield Peppard as the main one.

This pit was cut into the gravels of the Caversham Ancient Channel, now identified as part of the Black Park

Terrace of the Middle Thames. It was the last active pit in these gravels, and Wymer not only visited it over many years, but carried out various excavations and close observation during the period 1955–60, which enabled him to form views on the nature and age of the deposits and the artefacts they contained. The previous account of the Ancient Channel, by Treacher *et al.* (1948) was based mainly on finds in earlier gravel pits; the Highlands Farm Pit had existed at this time, but it was reopened in 1955, and the important discoveries there begin then. Treacher *et al.* had concluded (*op. cit.*, 153) that the Ancient Channel deposits contained 'the largest and most valuable geologically-dated assemblage of artefacts of Abbevillian and Early Acheulian culture yet brought to light in Britain'. In two important early accounts of his own work at Highlands (1956; 1961), Wymer concluded that there was actually a mixture of artefact assemblages in the Ancient Channel Gravels there, the major components being Clactonian (the most prolific) and Late Middle Acheulian; he also identified a separate small group of crude handaxes, which he tentatively attributed to an Early Acheulian. Since these disparate elements could hardly be contemporary, and occurred mixed together at all levels of the gravel at Highlands Farm, Wymer concluded that the deposit, whatever the age of its original formation, had in this part of the Ancient Channel at least been drastically resorted at or after the time when the youngest of these industries, the Late Middle Acheulian, was current in Britain – probably late in 'the Hoxnian Interglacial', as that term was then understood.

To a reader in the late 1990s, this probably seems a nightmare case of typology running riot and being used to date geological deposits. Not at all, even though Wymer himself later referred to it (1988b, 82) as 'an unjustifiable typological mistake'. In his 1961 paper, he drew the conclusions just summarised specifically on the basis of work by himself and many others at the most important of all the Thames Valley sites, Barnfield Pit, Swanscombe. Here, there was a stratified sequence of deposits, many containing artefacts, providing an actual sequence of Lower Palaeolithic industries, which could at that time be summarised (*op. cit.*, 6) as beginning with the Clactonian industry of the Lower Gravel, characterized by 'crude pebble tools, chopper-cores and the flakes removed in their manufacture', continuing with the Middle Acheulian industry of the Middle Gravels, with pointed handaxes 'usually crudely made but sometimes of fine workmanship', and followed by the Late Middle Acheulian of the Upper Loam, with 'a greater proportion of well-wrought implements and new types: cordates and ovates, with straight or twisted edges, often finished by a tranchet blow.'

In considering the artefacts from Highlands Farm in the light of this stratified Swanscombe sequence, Wymer diagnosed the presence of Clactonian at Highlands on the basis of the characteristic cores, and not just the heavy flakes, which could have belonged to almost any Lower

Palaeolithic industry; with the ovates, it was specific aspects of their technology which most impressed him. Certainly, typological considerations were at the heart of the argument – this was 1961 – but so was the stratigraphy of the only site, Barnfield Pit, capable at the time of offering a clear relevant sequence. In my own view, Barnfield Pit is still the best starting point for anyone seeking to understand the contents of the British Lower Palaeolithic, and all the work there since 1961 has simply enhanced its importance. Today, one approaches the Swanscombe sequence with rather different questions to ask, and there is abundant evidence of many kinds from other British sites to help provide answers, but the way in which Wymer structured the arguments in his 1961 paper still strikes me as of fundamental importance.

His new interpretation of the archaeological contents of the Caversham Ancient Channel had quite an effect at the time. Among those particularly interested by it were two Cambridge students, Glynn Isaac and the present author, who in 1960 had quite independently been trying out various metrical analyses on the handaxes in the Treacher Collection, at the suggestion of their supervisor, Charles McBurney, somewhat before such an approach became widespread. Their results had been quite contrary to what one would have expected of an 'Abbevillian and Early Acheulian' assemblage. But that is another story.

Following the particular theme of this paper, I must turn to what might now be thought of the Highlands Farm artefacts. I believe that Wymer was quite correct in picking out three separate series of implements, even if we cannot satisfactorily prove it, because they are mixed together in the Ancient Channel gravels. An assemblage of hard-hammer cores and flakes is numerically dominant, perfectly acceptable as Clactonian. Many finely made ovate handaxes are also present, their overall condition probably a little fresher than the bulk of the Clactonian material, though that assertion would need checking by re-examination of much now quite widely dispersed material. Such examples as I have seen of the third, much smaller, group of crude, thick handaxes, which Wymer tentatively attributed to an Early Acheulian, seem the most heavily worn pieces of all.

What is new, or at least only about ten years old, is that it is now acceptable for artefacts of all these kinds to occur together in a gravel of Anglian age, which is what the Black Park Terrace is. It is no longer necessary to suggest that the ovates were added later, with resorting of the deposits, because we know from many sites that finely made ovates were amongst the earliest handaxes to be made in Britain. Wymer himself is amongst those who have expounded this, in his later writing (e.g. 1988b): for key sites that document the altered thinking, one need look no further than Boxgrove (Bergman *et al.* 1990; Roberts *et al.* 1995, 171–2) or High Lodge (Ashton *et al.* 1992), though there are plenty more. If the gravels at Highlands Farm contain artefacts swept up together by various processes around the time of melting of the great

Anglian ice sheets, which had reached as far south as the Thames Valley, those artefacts must represent various human occupations in this general area, either before the Anglian glaciation or perhaps during its milder periods, or both. Evidently, various different sets of artefacts were made by these earliest visitors to Britain, however one may wish to interpret that situation: some specialized in fine ovates, some in 'hard hammer' cores and flakes, and perhaps also some in crude thick handaxes, achieved without 'soft-hammer' flaking. At Highlands Farm, such industries are inextricably mixed, but elsewhere we can see good separate occurrences, of comparable age, certainly in the case of the fine ovates, and the 'Clactonian'. Can we also find any intact occurrences of crudely made handaxe industries, their morphology and technology not necessarily attributable entirely to the effects of the available raw material, for example at Kent's Cavern, Fordwich, Warren Hill (the worn series), or, rather nearer to Highlands Farm, at Hamstead Marshall in a Kennet Valley gravel equivalent to the Black Park Terrace? Or is it only the sole survivor of those two 1960 Cambridge undergraduates who would persist in believing something so unfashionable (cf. Roe 1996)?

To conclude these comments on Highlands Farm, did Wymer really make what he called 'an unjustifiable typological mistake' over the ovates? I don't think so: where at the time was there clear evidence of an early date for any of the sites that we can now perceive to contain a pre-Anglian ovate industry? Boxgrove was undiscovered; the re-excavation of High Lodge had not begun. For the others, dating evidence was scarce, and the British Quaternary Sequence was not the one we now know, let alone the one we may eventually end up with. Expectations based on available accounts of French sites were for ovates to be younger rather than older. It was perfectly true that there were fine ovate industries occurring, as Wymer knew, in the Upper Loam at Swanscombe and other sites of equivalent age. Only if we now compare in detail the early and the rather later British ovate industries can we, with the hindsight that is our privilege, see certain consistent (though hardly dramatic) differences. For example, the early group tends to have rather square-ended handaxe plan-forms, a high frequency of tranchet finishing blows, and a minimal occurrence, if any at all, of deliberately twisted profiles. The later group has more pointed plan-forms, and in many of its industries twisted profiles are remarkably frequent. Seventeen years after his 1961 paper, John Wymer observed (1988b, 82) that it might be significant that no handaxes with twisted edges had ever been found at any of the Ancient Channel sites. I do not believe that such a comment could have been forthcoming in 1961.

CONCLUSION

My allotted space has of course been inadequate to do justice to John Wymer's work on the Palaeolithic of the Thames Valley. Dozens more sites where he has worked could have been discussed at some length; even Barnfield Pit has been mentioned only in passing, and the Swanscombe skull, of which John found a part, not at all. I can only hope that the chosen examples give just a hint of the quality and significance of his work, whether in the field or as author. As extraordinary as anything is the fact that the Thames Valley work is only a small part of John Wymer's personal contribution to Palaeolithic Archaeology, as the rest of this volume will make abundantly clear.

REFERENCES

Ashton, N.M. Cook, J., Lewis, S.G. & Rose, J. 1992. *High Lodge. Excavations by G. de G. Sieveking, 1962–8 and J. Cook, 1988.* London: British Museum Press.

Bergman, C.A., Roberts, M.B., Collcutt, S.N. & Barlow, P. 1990. Refitting and spatial analysis of artefacts from Quarry 2 at the Middle Pleistocene Acheulian site of Boxgrove, West Sussex, England. In E. Cziesla, S. Eickhoff, N. Arts & D. Winter (eds), *The Big Puzzle*, 265–82. Bonn: Holos.

Bridgland, D.R. 1994. *Quaternary of the Thames.* London: Chapman & Hall. Geological Conservation Review Series 7.

Buckingham, C.M, Roe, D.A. & Scott, K. 1996. A preliminary report on the Stanton Harcourt Channel Deposits (Oxfordshire, England): geological context, vertebrate remains and Palaeolithic stone artefacts. *Journal of Quaternary Science* 11(5), 397–415.

Gibbard, P.L. 1985. *Pleistocene History of the Middle Thames Valley.* Cambridge: Cambridge University Press.

Gibbard, P.L. 1994. *Pleistocene History of the Lower Thames Valley.* Cambridge: Cambridge University Press.

Preece, R.C. (ed.) 1995. *Island Britain: a Quaternary Perspective.* London: The Geological Society Special Publication 96.

Roberts, M.B., Gamble, C.S. & Bridgland, D.R. 1995. The earliest occupation of Europe: the British Isles. In W. Roebroeks & T. van Kolfschoten (eds), *The Earliest Occupation of Europe: Proceedings of the European Science Foundation Workshop at Tautavel (France) 1993,* 165–91. Leiden: University of Leiden.

Roe, D.A. 1981. *The Lower and Middle Palaeolithic Periods in Britain.* London: Routledge & Kegan Paul.

Roe, D.A. 1995. Father Thames and the British Pleistocene. *The Review of Archaeology* 16(1), 9–15.

Roe, D.A. 1996. The start of the British Lower Palaeolithic: some new and old thoughts and speculations. *Lithics* 16, 17–26.

Singer, R., Gladfelter, B. & Wymer, J.J. 1993. *The Lower Palaeolithic Site at Hoxne, England.* Chicago: University of Chicago Press.

Treacher, M.S., Arkell, W.J. & Oakley, K.P. 1948. On the Ancient Channel between Caversham and Henley, Oxfordshire, and its contained flint implements. *Proceedings of the Prehistoric Society* 14, 126–54.

Tyldesley, J.A. 1986. *The Wolvercote Channel Handaxe Assemblage: a Comparative Study.* Oxford: British Archaeological Reports British Series 153.

White, M.J. 1996. Raw materials and biface variability in Southern Britain: a preliminary examination. *Lithics* 16, 1–20.

Wymer, J.J. 1956. Palaeoliths from the gravel of the Ancient Channel between Caversham and Henley at Highlands, near Henley. *Proceedings of the Prehistoric Society* 22, 29–36.

Wymer, J.J. 1961. The Lower Palaeolithic Succession in the Thames Valley and the date of the Ancient Channel between Caversham and Henley, Oxon. *Proceedings of the Prehistoric Society* 27, 1–27.

Wymer, J.J. 1968. *Lower Palaeolithic Archaeology in Britain as Represented by the Thames Valley*. London: John Baker.

Wymer, J.J. 1988a. A reassessment of the geographical range of Lower Palaeolithic activity in Britain. In R.J. MacRae & N. Moloney (eds), *Non-Flint Stone Tools and the Palaeolithic Occupation of Britain*, 11–23. Oxford: British Archaeological Reports British Series 189.

Wymer, J.J. 1988b. Palaeolithic Archaeology and the British Quaternary Sequence. *Quaternary Science Reviews*, 7(1), 79–97.

7. Quaternary Stratigraphy and Lower Palaeolithic Archaeology of the Lark Valley, Suffolk

Simon G. Lewis

ABSTRACT

This paper describes briefly aspects of the Quaternary geological sequence in the valley of the River Lark between Bury St Edmunds and Mildenhall. The sequence is divisible broadly into three: pre-Anglian fluvial sediments, Anglian glaciogenic deposits and post-Anglian river terrace deposits. The distribution of these deposits, their altitudinal relationships and their lithological characteristics are summarised. The latter property is a particularly useful means of distinguishing the various deposits. The development of drainage in this area is discussed and the evidence for drainage into central East Anglia, approximately along the line of the current River Lark, is reviewed. This geological sequence provides a framework for discussion of the large quantity of Palaeolithic archaeological data for the area. The utility of the archaeological evidence is constrained in many cases due to derived context and/or poorly known provenance of old collections. However, a number of sites have yielded important archaeological information from in situ artefact assemblages, which can be placed securely within the stratigraphic framework. Palaeolithic material is known from pre-Anglian deposits of the Bytham River, which flowed into this area from the English Midlands, most notably at High Lodge. A limited quantity of derived artefacts are known from Anglian glaciofluvial sediments. Artefacts from post-Anglian sequences are known from the in situ assemblage at Beeches Pit and from derived contexts associated with the terrace deposits of the River Lark.

INTRODUCTION

In 1990 John Wymer introduced the author and Dr David Bridgland to a number of sites of geological and archaeological interest in the Icklingham and West Stow district. These sites proved to be worthy of further investigation and since then sections have been dug at several of these localities with the objective of establishing the geological sequence in the area and also establishing the position of the archaeology within that lithostratigraphic sequence. Results of some of this research may be found in Preece *et al.* (1991), Wymer *et al.* (1991) and Bridgland *et al.* (1995). This paper summarises some aspects of that work, together with a review of selected published records of archaeological sites and attempts to place the archaeological data within a geological framework for the area.

At the present time drainage of this area consists of small rivers draining into the Fen basin or to the North Sea (Fig. 7.1). The River Lark rises in the central plateau area of Suffolk, south east of Bury St Edmunds (Fig. 7.1) and flows north westwards into the Fen basin. The drainage pattern in this area has undergone significant alteration during the Pleistocene, particularly as a consequence of glaciation during the Anglian. Prior to the Anglian the region was drained by large rivers flowing from Midlands England to the southern North Sea basin. The main rivers were the ancestral River Thames and the Bytham River (Rose 1994). The area now occupied by the River Lark is approximately coincident with the route of the Bytham River which drained in the opposite direction to the modern river, into central East Anglia. During the earlier part of the existence of the Bytham River (Early Pleistocene), it was a north bank tributary of the River Thames. During the latter part of its history (early Middle Pleistocene) it occupied a separate course across East Anglia, coincident further downstream with the line of the modern River Waveney, probably joining the Thames somewhere off-shore (Fig. 7.1a).

The area of the Lark valley between Bury St Edmunds and the Fen edge also contains a number of Lower Palaeolithic archaeological sites (Wymer 1985). Many of these are surface find-spots with little or no stratigraphic information. However, there are a number of important archaeological localities, including High Lodge, Warren Hill and Beeches Pit, together with a number of further sites from which artefacts have been recorded and for which a reasonable degree of stratigraphic control has been established (for example Rampart Field, Weatherhill Farm Pit and Devereux's Pit). This paper examines some of the main sites in the Lark valley and attempts to provide a stratigraphic framework, based upon the pre-Anglian deposits, the glacial sequence and the post-Anglian terrace deposits and associated fine-grained sediments, for these archaeological data.

THE PRE-ANGLIAN SEQUENCE

Prior to the Anglian glaciation a major river system entered north west Norfolk from the English Midlands and flowed south and then eastwards across Norfolk and Suffolk (Fig. 7.1). This river deposited a characteristic suite of quartz and quartzite rich sands and gravels, which were named the Ingham sand and gravel (Clarke & Auton 1982; 1984) but have recently been referred to as the Bytham sands and gravels by Rose (1994). Deposits associated with this river system can be identified at a number of sites in the Lark valley (Fig. 7.2). These sediments contain abundant (in some cases in excess of 50%) quartzose material derived form the Triassic pebble beds of the Midlands in addition to locally derived flint. In addition, sediment body geometry and available palaeoflow data from a number of sites (Fig. 7.2) shows that the flow direction is west to east, which is opposite to that of the modern river. The ability to distinguish between pre-Anglian, Anglian and post-Anglian gravels in this area on the basis of detailed clast lithological analysis is discussed by Bridgland *et al.* (1995). A number of lithologies that characterise Anglian glaciofluvial gravels are absent from the gravels at all these sites. For example, the interpretation of the deposits at Hall Heath, Lackford (TL 799693) (Fig. 7.2) as Anglian outwash (Hamblin & Moorlock 1995; Mottram 1994) is not substantiated by the detailed clast lithological data (Bridgland & Lewis 1991) which shows that the gravels contain none of these indicator lithologies. The absence of some of these (chalk, limestone and derived shell fragments) may be accounted for by decalcification, however some lithologies are more durable, in particular *Rhaxella* chert, which is an ubiquitous component of

glacial outwash gravels in the region, but is not present in the gravels at Hall Heath.

The height distribution of these deposits (Fig. 7.3) shows that, in this area, at least three distinct altitudinal levels can be identified which represent separate phases of aggradation by the river punctuated by periods of incision. These were identified over a wider area by Lewis (1993). A fourth, higher remnant can also be identified (Lewis 1993), though at a very few sites and the reconstruction of the sediment body geometry is therefore more tentative. These various aggradations were suggested to represent terraces of the pre-Anglian Bytham River. In the area under discussion, the two highest terraces are present at Ingham. These are represented by the deposits at The Folley (TL 845716) (Fig. 7.2) and at the large gravel pit to the north of the village (TL 855715) (Fig. 7.2). The altitudinal position of these sequences is shown in Fig. 7.3. The next level is represented here by the sites at Hengrave (TL 816679) (Rose & Wymer 1994) and Hall Heath, Lackford (Lewis 1993). These sites form a west-east sloping body of sediment (Fig. 7.3). The lowest level is represented by Rampart Field (TL 789715) (Bridgland *et al.* 1995) and Timworth (TL 853692) (Lewis & Bridgland 1991) and also lie on a west-east sloping gradient (Fig. 7.3).

The sequence at Warren Hill (TL 744743) (Fig. 7.2) is of interest. Contrary to the earlier interpretation of these deposits as outwash gravels (Solomon 1933), it has been suggested by Bridgland *et al.* (1995) that these gravels form part of the suite of Ingham-type gravels and are probably early Anglian in age. However the altitudinal position of this sequence does not fit well with the lowest of the gradients that can be plotted through the other sites as it is too low (Fig. 7.3). The sequence at Warren Hill rests on Chalk bedrock at an altitude of *c.*10m OD. This is overlain by sands and silts, and coarse gravels. The contact between the latter two units is at *c.* 14m OD (Bridgland *et al.* 1995).

The altitudinal position of the pre-Anglian deposits at High Lodge (TL 739754) is a result of glaciotectonic movement and deformation during the Anglian (Lewis 1992). The High Lodge clayey-silts represent fine-grained floodplain deposits of the Bytham River formed during a pre-Anglian temperate phase, which were transported by an ice sheet to their current position (Ashton *et al.* 1992). They cannot therefore be fitted on to the reconstructed gradients for the Bytham River (Fig. 7.3).

Artefacts have been recovered from a number of sites associated with this river system, which provide important information concerning the earliest occupation of the region (Roberts *et al.* 1995). Of particular note is the material from High Lodge (Ashton 1992) which occurs within the High Lodge clayey-silts. This assemblage offers compelling evidence not only for the antiquity of human occupation but also vouches for the ability of flint-knappers during this period as it includes scrapers and other flake tools which show a considerable degree of technological refinement. The High Lodge assemblage is significant because

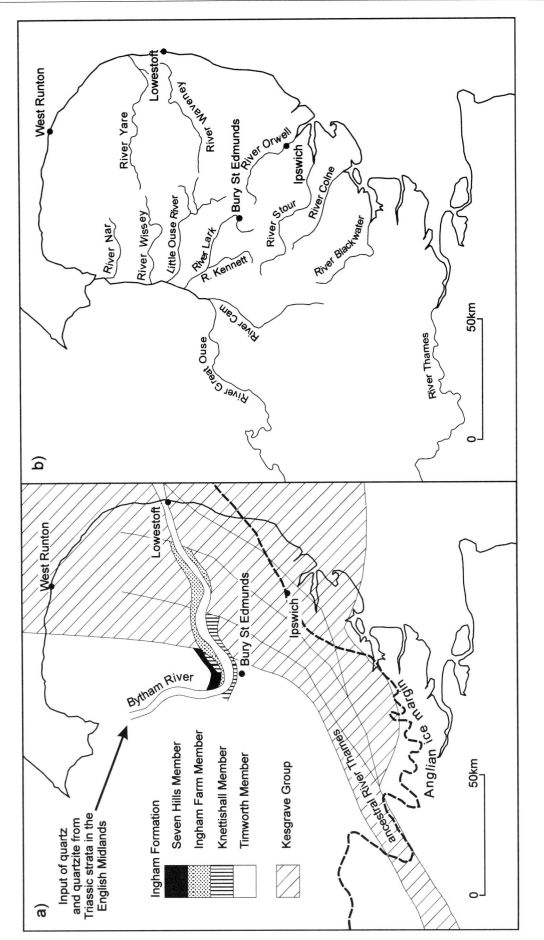

Figure. 7.1. Modern and palaeo-drainage of East Anglia. a) configuration of major river systems in East Anglia prior to the Anglian glaciation. Distribution of sediments of the ancestral river Thames after Whiteman (1992), distribution of quartz/quartzite rich sands and gravels of the Bytham River after Lewis (1993) and Rose (1994). Lithostratigraphic classification after Whiteman and Rose (1992) and Lewis (1993). Anglian ice limits after Perrin et al. (1979); b) modern drainage pattern in eastern England.

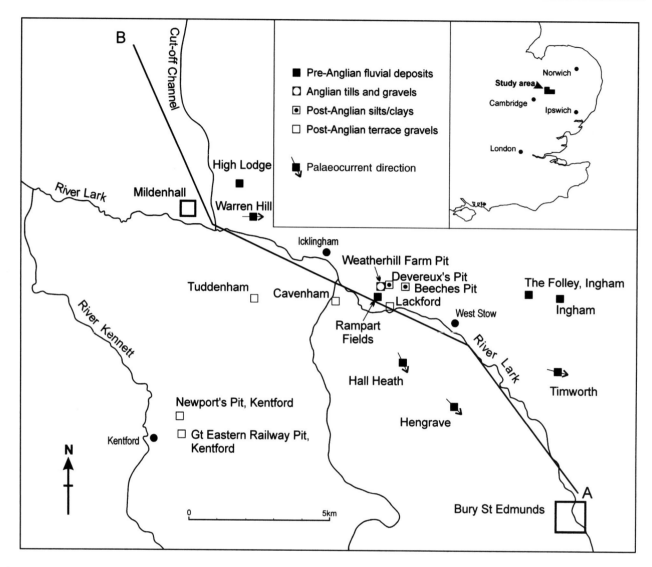

Figure. 7.2. The River Lark valley, showing location of sites discussed in the text.

it is in primary context, although it occurs within a rafted mass of sediment, and, importantly, it is associated with other environmental and biostratigraphical information. The other sites in the area of this age that have yielded artefacts do not offer the same quality of information. Warren Hill, just over 1km from High Lodge, has yielded a large number of handaxes, all of which are in a derived state, from the coarse gravel deposits (Wymer 1985; Bridgland *et al.* 1995). Despite the derived nature of this assemblage, the information raises a question concerning the 'taphonomic' factors that have lead to the apparent concentration of artefacts at this locality given the very high energy depositional environment with which they are associated.

A number of further sites also record some archaeological information, again in a derived context within gravel deposits. The gravels at Rampart Field have yielded a number of handaxes (Wymer 1985) and a flake, found during the recent investigations (Bridgland *et al.* 1995).

These gravels may form part of the same aggradation as similar quartz and quartzite rich gravels at Maidscross Hill, Lakenheath (TL 727825), which have also yielded artefacts (Flower 1869; Wymer 1985). These deposits have been considered to be part of the same river system (Rose 1987; Lewis 1993). In addition, a struck flake has been reported from Hengrave (Rose & Wymer 1994), which forms part of the higher level quartzose gravels in the Lark valley (Fig. 7.3). This would suggest an earlier age for this find, though some caution should be exercised as only a single flake has been recovered from this locality, and no other sites of similar age or geological context in the area have yielded any archaeology.

ANGLIAN DEPOSITS

The Anglian glaciation saw the most extensive coverage of the region by ice during the Pleistocene (Fig. 7.1) and

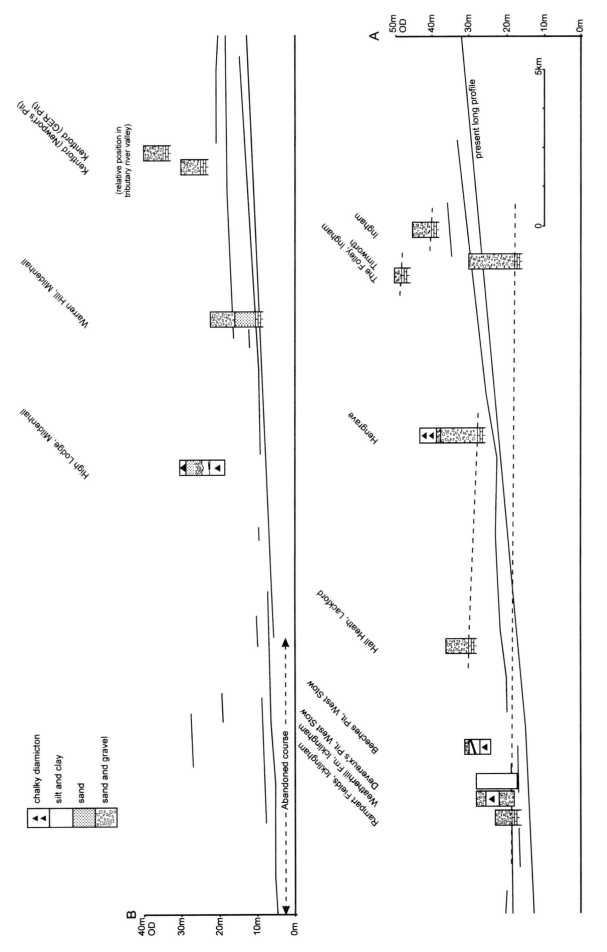

Figure. 7.3. Long profile of the River Lark, showing surface elevation of river terraces (after Clayton 1983 and Hawkins 1981) and schematic stratigraphy of selected sites discussed in the text. Dashed lines show slope of bedrock surface beneath the pre-Anglian, Ingham Formation draining from west to east.

significantly reorganised the drainage. The river from the Midlands was blocked by ice and the erosion of the low-lying Wash and Fen basin by ice traversing the soft Jurassic clays (Perrin *et al.* 1979) created a completely new drainage basin in this area. The Anglian sequence consists mainly of chalky Lowestoft till, together with glaciofluvial sands and gravels and fine-grained deposits. Till is wide-spread over the interfluve areas to the south and north of the River Lark, though there are also considerable areas where Chalk bedrock crops out at the surface adjacent to the river (Bristow 1990). Anglian deposits are well known from a number of localities (Bristow 1990). The Lark valley also contains a large drift-filled channel feature. This network of channels or tunnel valleys was probably excavated by sub-glacial meltwater during the Anglian glaciation (Woodland 1970) and is infilled with sands and gravels, till and fine-grained deposits. The geometry of the channel is highly variable and its long profile is irregular, with localised areas where rock head falls considerably below OD (Bristow 1990).

From an archaeological point of view, glaciogenic deposits are of little potential. However three sites of interest are considered briefly here. Weatherhill Farm Pit (TL 789715) (Fig. 7.2) displays a sequence of sands and gravels overlain by chalky till (Bridgland *et al.* 1995). The gravels are lithologically distinct from both the earlier Ingham-type gravels and later terrace deposits, as they contain a suite of lithologies including soft sandstone, limestone, derived Jurassic shell fragments, igneous rock types and *Rhaxella* chert, which together suggest a glacial origin. Artefacts are reported from this site (Wymer 1985), and a single piece was recovered from a solution feature in the top of the till when a section was cut in 1992 (Bridgland *et al.* 1995). No artefacts were recovered from the gravels during this work. In view of the scarcity of well-provenenced archaeological finds from glacial gravels in East Anglia (Wymer 1985), some doubt may be expressed concerning the records from this site. The known occurrence of artefacts within solution pockets in the till offers one possible explanation for the presence of artefacts in this sequence. A possible alternative explanation for the few handaxes from this site may be that the artefacts come from the eastern end of this pit, which is only *c.* 10m from the western end of the neighbouring Devereux's Pit (see below). It is possible that the younger deposits in the latter pit continue into Weatherhill Farm Pit and may be the source of the handaxes. This awaits further investigation.

The second candidate is the prolific site at Warren Hill from which many hundreds of handaxes have been re-covered (Wymer 1985). The deposits at this site have been interpreted as glacial outwash (Solomon 1933). However this view cannot easily be supported on clast lithological grounds as the gravels, despite their chalky nature, contain none of the distinctive erratic suite that is found at Weatherhill Farm Pit (Bridgland *et al.* 1995). At the adjacent site of High Lodge (Fig. 7.2), Anglian glaciofluvial gravels, which overlie the raft of fine-grained sediments which contain the High Lodge scraper industry (Lewis 1992), have yielded a number of handaxes, mainly of ovate and limande form (Ashton 1992). These are all in a secondary context, though it has been suggested, on the basis of their condition and proximity to the clayey-silts, that they are derived from the underlying deposits (McNabb & Ashton 1995). The gravels at Warren Hill and High Lodge have very different clast lithological characteristics, and do not form part of a single spread of gravels. The former may represent early Anglian gravels that formed prior to the incursion of ice into the district and the latter demonstrably formed during wastage of the ice sheet. Both may contain artefacts reworked from similar sources.

Glaciofluvial gravels, with no archaeological content, are known from a number of other localities (Fig. 7.2) including Hengrave (Rose & Wymer 1994), High Lodge (Lewis 1992) and Beeches Pit (TL 798719) (Bridgland *et al.* 1995). Gravels at the latter site probably represent a continuation of the glaciofluvial gravels at Weatherhill Farm Pit some 0.75km to the west (Fig. 7.2). The Geo-logical Survey memoir records a number of additional localities (Bristow 1990).

THE POST-ANGLIAN SEQUENCE

Following the Anglian glaciation, drainage along the Lark valley was reversed to flow in its present direction towards the Fens. The geology of the post-Anglian sequence is diverse, but is divisible broadly into i) a number of localised fine-grained sequences that have accumulated in hollows on the till surface and ii) the extensive spreads of sand and gravel that underlie a flight of terraces associated with successive phases of aggradation and incision by the River Lark.

The fine-grained sequences are represented at a number of sites; of particular note are Beeches Pit, West Stow, and Devereaux's Pit, Icklingham (TL 793720) (Fig. 7.2). Beeches Pit has been the subject of research for a number of years, as it has yielded a remarkable molluscan fauna from tufa deposits within the sequence (Kerney 1976; Preece *et al.* 1991), which includes species from diverse geographical locations such as the Pyrenees and the Canary Islands. Since 1990 the details of the geological sequence, vertebrate palaeontology and Palaeolithic archaeology have received attention. The sequence consists of till and outwash gravels, overlain by chalky slope deposits and tufaceous silts and clays. This is overlain by further fine-grained deposits containing abundant bone material and with considerable evidence for burning (Preece *et al.* 1991). The archaeology of the site is currently under detailed investigation and preliminary information appears in Gowlett (1997) and Andresen *et al.* (1997). The site is potentially of considerable importance as a number of pieces of information can be combined to relate the evidence for human occupation to the geological and environmental record. In addition age estimates have been

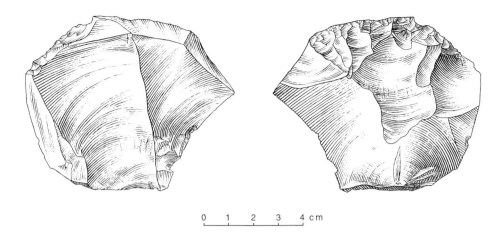

0   1   2   3   4 cm

Figure. 7.4. Artefact recovered from Devereux's Pit, Icklingham.

derived from amino acid geochronology, uranium-thorium dis-equilibrium and thermoluminescence dating techniques. An initial trial of TL dating of a piece of burnt flint yielded an age estimate of 471±51ka (BEP11) which, if confirmed by further analyses, would tend to support a correlation of this site with OIS 11.

Devereux's Pit, less than 1km west of Beeches Pit (Fig. 7.2), is another old brick pit; the remnants of the brick kiln are still visible adjacent to the pit. Initial field work (with DRB) has indicated that there is a sequence of clays, which are grey, calcareous and occasionally shelly in the lower part and oxidised and decalcified in the upper 3–4m. The deposits were proved to a depth in excess of 7m and it is likely that a thicker sequence is present in the centre of the pit. Limited archaeology is known from the site. A single handaxe is known to have come from the site (Wymer 1985). Sections cut in 1997 produced two artefacts from a location adjacent to the undisturbed section. Despite their insecure context they offer a hint of what may be present at the site. These artefacts are a flake tool in very fresh condition, which has been flaked invasively on the distal, ventral surface, and then finely retouched as a scraper along this same edge (Fig. 7.4), and a slightly stained core in a similar condition, worked by an episode of alternate platform technique, followed by parallel flaking from a single platform.

A flight of five terraces has been recognised associated with the River Lark (Bristow 1990; Hawkins 1981; Clayton 1983). The higher three of these are represented by very fragmentary remnants, whereas the lowest two terraces form extensive flat areas underlain by thick sequences of sand and gravels. The altitudinal distribution of the terrace surfaces (Fig. 7.3) indicates that the height separation on the lower terraces is minimal; the 1st terrace is only 1–2m above the present river, the 2nd terrace is some 5m above that. Fragments of the 3rd terrace lie some 10m above the river and 4th and 5th terrace fragments are approximately 14m and 22m above the river respectively. The clast lithology of the terraces is dominated by flint. Few of the

lithological constituents present in small quantities in the outwash, with the exception of *Rhaxella* chert, survive weathering or comminution as they are reworked into the terrace deposits. The first terrace deposits at Lackford contain some 82% flint (Hunt *et al.* 1991).

The distribution of the terrace deposits in this area indicates that the configuration of the river and its tributaries has changed throughout its development. The terrace distribution around Mildenhall indicates that for most of the period since the Anglian glaciation the River Lark flowed northwards along the line now taken by the artificial Cut-off Channel (Fig. 7.2). The course of the river changed to flow into the Fens immediately west of Mildenhall (Fig. 7.2). The River Kennett also appears to have switched its course, with terrace deposits suggesting a shorter route was utilised for some time between Kentford and Tuddenham (Fig. 7.2). The reasons for this change in the course of these rivers are unclear but probably occurred during the Late Devensian.

A number of archaeological finds are recorded from localities that are associated with the terraces of the River Lark (Wymer 1985). The majority of these are isolated find spots, with poor provenence. Even the extensive spreads of sand and gravel in the vicinity of Lackford (TL 8070), Tuddenham (TL 7471) and Cavenham (TL 7771) (Fig. 7.2) which have been dug for gravel over many years have yielded few artefacts (Wymer 1985). Those that have been found are of little use as they are derived, rolled and often of unsecure provenance.

One potentially significant site within the terrace sequence in terms of archaeology is that at Kentford (TL 7167), which is in the valley of the River Kennett, a south bank tributary of the River Lark (Fig. 7.2). Here, large spreads of sand and gravel some 4–5m in thickness have been dug, including areas of the 4th terrace and 2nd/3rd terrace remnants. Artefacts have been found over this area associated with both these terrace deposits (Wymer 1985). Two distinct artefact assemblages appear to be present. The first is associated with the 4th terrace at an altitude of *c.* 40m OD, from the old Great Eastern Railway pit (TL 718669) and consists of mainly cordate and ovate handaxes (Wymer 1985). The second assemblage comes from beneath a lower terrace (undifferentiated 2nd/3rd terrace) at a height of approximately 30m OD, from extensive gravel workings (TL 717675) and consists of a large number of flakes, ten handaxes, three cores and two sidescrapers, many of which are in a fresh condition (Wymer 1985). The latter assemblage was recovered from yellow silts at the base of the gravel sequence and appears to be in virtually primary context (Wymer 1985). No evidence of the use of Levallois technique has been found in these assemblages. The altitudinal position of these terrace deposits in relation to the terraces in the main valley (Fig. 7.3) may suggest that they predate the two lowest terraces (1st and 2nd terrace), which are considered to be Devensian in age on the basis of radiocarbon dating (Bristow 1990). The deposits at Kentford are thus probably of pre-Devensian age.

SUMMARY

Reinvestigation of a number of critical sites in this area over the last few years permits an examination of the stratigraphic context of Lower Palaeolithic archaeological assemblages in the area of the Lark valley.

The geological sequence in this area prior to the Anglian is characterised mainly by fluvial sands and gravels deposited by a large river with a catchment extending into the English Midlands supplying quartz and quartzite material in considerable quantities. These deposits are disposed into four distinct aggradations, each separated by some 10m of incision (Fig. 7.3). The river system developed through the Early and early Middle Pleistocene until it was obliterated by the Anglian glaciation. Drainage along the line of the Lark valley was in the opposite direction to that of the modern river at this time.

Archaeological information for the pre-Anglian period is known from a number of sites, of which one, High Lodge, contains artefacts in primary context and provides archaeological information of the highest quality. The other sites are sequences of sands and gravels and contain derived artefacts. However these provide important corroboration of the timing of the presence of humans in the British Isles prior to the Anglian glaciation (Roberts *et al.* 1995). The precise age of most of these sequences is, however, uncertain. The High Lodge clayey-silts probably represent a temperate phase immediately prior to the Anglian and may correlate with OIS 13. The gravels at Warren Hill are probably Early Anglian in age.

There is little archaeology associated with Anglian glacial and glaciofluvial deposits in this area or in East Anglia as a whole (Wymer 1985; 1988). A derived handaxe assemblage from gravels at High Lodge may represent the only archaeology from glaciofluvial deposits in this area. The reinterpretation of Warren Hill as pre- or early

Anglian fluvial deposits, removes the most prolific handaxe site in East Anglia from this category. However, precisely where Warren Hill fits into the sequence of deposits predating the Anglian glaciation remains uncertain.

Following the Anglian glaciation a completely new landscape was established. Drainage is characterised by small rivers forming a radial pattern around the low plateau of central East Anglia. Evidence for human activity during the temperate phase immediately following the Anglian glaciation is abundant. The site of Beeches Pit is of considerable importance, because of the quality of the geological, palaeontological and archaeological information from the site and also because multiple independent dating methods have been employed. This information suggests that the site dates to OIS 11 and further supports the emerging consensus that the underlying Anglian glacial sequence should be correlated with OIS 12 (Bowen *et al.* 1986).

The terrace sequence of the River Lark and its tributaries contains limited archaeology, much of which is derived and in a rolled condition. The lowest terraces (1st and 2nd terrace) are of Devensian (OIS 5d-2) age (Bristow 1990) and the archaeology that they contain is almost certainly derived from considerably older deposits. Important archaeological information, including material that has been moved only slightly from its original position, has been recovered from the gravels of the River Kennett around Kentford. This may provide evidence for human occupation during the later Middle Pleistocene. The absence of artefacts showing Levallois technique may be of significance, as it has been suggested that this first occurs in the UK during the latter part of OIS 8 (Wymer 1988; Bridgland 1996). However, the absence of Levallois technique in the small assemblage from this site does not preclude a younger age.

The Palaeolithic archaeological record from the Lark valley provides a large quantity of information that can be related to a well established geological sequence. Artefacts are scattered throughout the sequence in derived contexts, although a number of sites are of critical importance as they provide *in situ* assemblages and palaeoenvironmental information which allows a fuller reconstruction of the nature of the environment for human occupation during the Middle Pleistocene.

ACKNOWLEDGEMENTS

The author would like to acknowledge John Wymer for introducing him to a number of the sites discussed above and, with David Bridgland, for collaboration in many aspects of this work. Nick Debenham (QTLS) undertook the thermoluminescence dating at Beeches Pit. Nick Ashton commented on the artefacts from Devereux's Pit and Phil Dean illustrated the artefact shown in Fig. 7.4. Darrel Maddy and David Bridgland commented on an earlier draft of this paper. Grants from the Geologists' Association towards field work and from Cheltenham & Gloucester College of Higher Education for TL dating at Beeches Pit are gratefully acknowledged. Part of the work was undertaken while in receipt of a NERC training award.

REFERENCES

Andresen, S.A., Bell, D.A., Hallos, J. Pumphrey, T.R.J. & Gowlett, J.A.J. 1997. Approaches to the analysis of evidence from the Acheulian site of Beeches Pit, Suffolk, England. In A.Sinclair, E.Slater & J.Gowlett (eds), *Archaeological Sciences 1995*, 389–94. Oxford: Oxbow Books.

Ashton, N. 1992. The High Lodge flint industries. In N. Ashton, J. Cook, S.G. Lewis & J. Rose (eds), *High Lodge. Excavations by G. de G. Sieveking, 1962–68 and J. Cook, 1988*, 124–63. London: British Museum Press.

Ashton, N.M., Lewis, S.G. & Rose, J. 1992. Summary. In N. Ashton, J. Cook, S.G. Lewis & J. Rose (eds), *High Lodge. Excavations by G. de G. Sieveking, 1962–68 and J. Cook, 1988*, 169–79. London: British Museum Press.

Bowen, D.Q., Rose, J., McCabe, A.M. & Sutherland, D.G. 1986. Correlation of Quaternary glaciations in England, Ireland, Scotland and Wales. *Quaternary Science Reviews* 5, 299–340.

Bridgland, D.R. 1996. Quaternary river terrace deposits as a framework for the Lower Palaeolithic record. In C. Gamble & A.J. Lawson (eds), *The English Palaeolithic Reviewed*, 23–39. Salisbury: Trust for Wessex Archaeology.

Bridgland, D.R. & Lewis, S.G. 1991. Introduction to the Pleistocene geology and drainage history of the Lark valley. In S.G. Lewis, C.A. Whiteman & D.R. Bridgland (eds), *Central East Anglia and the Fen Basin. Field Guide*, 37–44. London: Quaternary Research Association.

Bridgland, D.R., Lewis, S.G. & Wymer, J.J. 1995. Middle Pleistocene stratigraphy and archaeology around Mildenhall and Icklingham, Suffolk: a report on a Geologists' Association field meeting, 27th June, 1992. *Proceedings of the Geologists' Association* 106, 57–69.

Bristow, C.R. 1990. Geology of the country around Bury St Edmunds. *Memoir of the British Geological Survey*, Sheet 189 (England and Wales), London: HMSO.

Clarke, M.R. & Auton, C.A. 1982. The Pleistocene history of the Norfolk-Suffolk borderlands. *Institute of Geological Sciences Report* 82(1), 23–9.

Clarke, M.R & Auton, C.A. 1984. Ingham Sand and Gravel. In P. Allen (ed.), *Field Guide to the Gipping and Waveney Valleys, Suffolk*, 71–2. Cambridge: Quaternary Research Association.

Clayton, A.R. 1983. The sand and gravel resources of the country between Mildenhall and Barrow, Suffolk: description of 1:25,000 sheets TL76, Tl77 and part of TL87. *Mineral Assessment Report* 123. London: Institute of Geological Sciences.

Flower, J.W. 1869. On some recent discoveries of flint implements of the drift in Norfolk and Suffolk, with observations on the theories accounting for their distribution. *Quarterly Journal of the Geological Society, London* 25, 449–60.

Gowlett, J.A.J. 1997. Beeches Pit. *Proceedings of the Suffolk Institute of Archaeology and History* 39(1), 100–103.

Hamblin, R.J.O. & Moorlock, B.S.P. 1995. The Kesgrave and Bytham Sand and Gravels of Eastern Suffolk. *Quaternary Newsletter* 77, 17–31.

Hawkins, M.P. 1981. The sand and gravel resources of the Bury St. Edmunds (Suffolk) area. Description of 1:25000 sheet TL86. *Mineral Assessment Report* 72. Keyworth: Institute of Geological Sciences.

Hunt, C.O., Lewis, S.G. & Wymer, J.J. (1991) Lackford, Suffolk. In S.G.Lewis, C.A.Whiteman & D.R.Bridgland (eds), *Central East Anglia and the Fen Basin Field Guide*. 85–92. London: Quaternary Research Association.

Kerney, M.P. 1976. Mollusca from an interglacial tufa in East Anglia, with the description of a new species of *Lyrodiscus Pilsbry* (Gastropoda: Zonitidae). *Journal of Conchology* 29, 47–50.

Lewis, S.G. 1992. High Lodge – stratigraphy and depositional environments. In N. Ashton, J. Cook, S.G. Lewis & J. Rose (eds), *High Lodge. Excavations by G. de G. Sieveking, 1962–68 and J. Cook, 1988*, 51–85. London: British Museum Press.

Lewis, S.G. 1993. *The Status of the Wolstonian Glaciation in the English Midlands and East Anglia*. Unpublished PhD Thesis, University of London.

Lewis, S.G & Bridgland, D.R. 1991. Ingham and Timworth, Suffolk. In S.G. Lewis, C.A. Whiteman & D.R. Bridgland (eds), *Central East Anglia and the Fen Basin Field Guide*. 71–83. London: Quaternary Research Association.

McNabb, J. & Ashton, N. 1995. Thoughtful flakers. *Cambridge Archaeological Journal* 5, 289–98.

Mottram, H.B. 1994. The geology of Hall Heath, Lackford. *Transactions of the Suffolk Naturalists' Society* 30, 48–9.

Perrin, R.M.S., Rose, J. & Davies, H. 1979. The distribution, variation and origins of pre-Devensian tills in eastern England. *Philosophical Transactions of the Royal Society of London* B287, 535–70.

Preece, R.C., Lewis, S.G., Wymer, J.J., Bridgland, D.R. & Parfitt, S. 1991. Beeches Pit, West Stow, Suffolk. In S.G. Lewis, C.A. Whiteman & D.R. Bridgland (eds), *Central East Anglia and the Fen Basin Field Guide*. 94–104. London: Quaternary Research Association.

Roberts, M.B., Gamble, C.S. & Bridgland, D.R. 1995. The earliest occupation of Europe: the British Isles. In W. Roebroeks & T. Van Kolfschoten (eds), *The Earliest Occupation of Europe. Proceedings of the European Science Foundataion Workshop at Tautavel (France), 1993*, 165–91. Leiden: University of Leiden.

Rose, J. 1987. The status of the Wolstonian glaciation in the British Quaternary. *Quaternary Newsletter* 53, 1–9.

Rose, J. 1994. Major river systems of central and southern Britain during the Early and Middle Pleistocene. *Terra Nova* 6, 435–43.

Rose, J. & Wymer, J.J. 1994. Record of a struck flake and the lithological composition of 'pre-glacial' river deposits at Hengrave, Suffolk, UK. *Proceedings of the Suffolk Institute of Archaeology and History* 38(2), 119–25.

Solomon, J.D. 1933. The implementiferous gravels of Warren Hill. *Journal of the Anthropological Institute* 63, 101–10.

Whiteman, C.A. 1992. The palaeogeography and correlation of pre-Anglian-Glaciation terraces of the River Thames in Essex and the London Basin. *Proceedings of the Geologists' Association*, 103, 37–56.

Whiteman, C.A. and Rose, J. 1992. Thames river sediments of the British Early and Middle Pleistocene. *Quaternary Science Reviews*, 11, 363–375.

Woodland, A.W. 1970. The buried tunnel-valleys of East Anglia. *Proceedings of the Yorkshire Geological Society* 37, 521–78.

Wymer, J.J. 1985. *The Palaeolithic Sites of East Anglia*. Norwich: Geo Books.

Wymer, J.J. 1988. Palaeolithic archaeology and the British Quaternary sequence. *Quaternary Science Reviews* 7, 79–97.

Wymer, J.J., Lewis, S.G. & Bridgland, D.R. 1991. Warren Hill, Mildenhall, Suffolk. In S.G. Lewis, C.A. Whiteman & D.R. Bridgland (eds), *Central East Anglia and the Fen Basin Field Guide*, 50–8. London: Quaternary Research Association.

8. Hoxne, Suffolk: Time Matters

Bruce G. Gladfelter

ABSTRACT

Without absolute dates from interglacial biozones at Hoxne, interpretation of data from the Upper Sequence assumes special significance for the correlation of other localities to Hoxne. The truncation of the interglacial pollen assemblage biozones sensu stricto *has allowed for varied palaeoenvironmental interpretations of the overlying Upper Sequence, and different correlations of it to other paratype localities and to oxygen isotope stages. Correlation must take into account implications for the interval of time represented by the gradation of the Upper Sequence, an interval that varies among the correlations that have been proposed by one order of magnitude.*

INTRODUCTION

When John Wymer conducted excavations of the Lower Palaeolithic on behalf of the University of Chicago, first at Clacton-on-Sea in 1969 (Singer *et al.* 1973) and then at Hoxne, begun in 1971 (Singer *et al.* 1993), it was thought that a Lower Palaeolithic presence in Britain first appeared during the Hoxnian interglacial. At the time, the Hoxnian was the penultimate interglacial, the Quaternary succession was anchored by the palynology of temperate periods, and the Hoxnian interglacial was followed in East Anglia by a glaciation. In the succeeding quarter-century, each of these interpretations has been revised significantly or rejected altogether. Now, concerns have addressed the nature of the transition from the Anglian glacial to the Hoxnian interglacial (e.g. Ashton *et al.* 1994a), and the nature of the post-interglacial sequence at Hoxne (e.g. Ehlers *et al.* 1991a). This commentary considers the gradational sequence at Hoxne from a temporal perspective as it may bear on these issues and on the British Lower Palaeolithic.

TIME AT HOXNE

Estimates of the length of the Hoxnian interglacial vary appreciably. Development of the temperate forest has been postulated to have encompassed as few as 20ky (West 1991) or as many as 50ky. (Turner 1970). Alternatively, depending upon the particular oxygen isotope stage (OIS) one prefers to adopt, the interglacial lasted either for 33ky (OIS 9) or 61ky (OIS 11). Unconformities and disconformities within the gradational sequence at Hoxne confound any effort to establish the duration of the interglacial.

Hiati and time

There are erosional disconformities between the interglacial sediments and the Upper Sequence and within the Upper Sequence (Table 8.1) (Gladfelter 1993). The durations of these hiati are of sufficient uncertainty that alternate chronostratigraphic reconstructions have been prepared.

Unconformity between Stratum D and the Upper Sequence. Stratum D is the Late-temperate stage IIIa at Hoxne, equivalent to the *Alnus-Corylus-Caprinus* biozone HoIIIa (West 1956). More recently an *Alnus-Pinus-Abies* association has been recovered from Stratum D (Mullenders 1993). The former pollen assemblage biozone from the margin of Lake Hoxne correlates with biozone HoIIIa at Marks Tey; the latter, which is from a deeper part of Lake Hoxne, is equivalent to biozone HoIIIb at Marks

Gladfelter (1993)	Comment	West (1956)
UPPER SEQUENCE		
Bed 9	Deposit that mantles the modern surface	Stratum A1
unconformity	Regional denudation during major hiatus	unconformity
Bed 8 Bed 7	Fluviatile sediments with fossil ice wedges (permafrost conditions)	Stratum A2
unconformity	Change in climatic conditions during major hiatus	
Bed 6 Bed 5	Fluviatile gravel (Bed 6) with derived artifacts interdigitated with flood plain silt (Bed 5) and artifacts of the Upper Industry: temperate conditions	unconformity
Bed 4	Chalky flint-gravel with "Middle Industry" at top; interdigitates with Stratum C	Stratum B
unconformity?	Interruption of aggradation	
Bed 3	Terminal lacustrine conditions: Lower Industry in bottom of Stratum C (Stratum C is Early-glacial, stage IV of West 1956)	Stratum C
Bed 2	Fluviatile sediments; lateral facies of bottom of Stratum C	
Bed 1		
unconformity	Phase of regional erosion after aggradation of Stratum D	unconformity
INTERGLACIAL SEQUENCE		
	Late-temperate (stage III of West 1956)	Stratum D
	Early-temperate (stage II of West 1956)	Stratum E
	Late-glacial (stage I of West 1956)	Stratum F
	Chalky boulder clay (Lowestoft Till)	Stratum G

Table 8.1. Sedimentary sequence at Hoxne, Suffolk

Tey. An erosional disconformity separates these lacustrine deposits of Stratum D from the overlying Upper Sequence. There are disconformities within the Stratum C – Bed 4 gradational complex that overlies Stratum D (e.g. Gladfelter 1993, fig. 2.4). However, these hiati are undoubtedly of short duration and it may not be inappropriate to consider them diastems.

Unconformity between Beds 6 and 7. The calibre and primary structure of the coarse gravel of Bed 6 and the sand and fine gravel of Bed 7 above it denote different regimes of fluviatile energy for each deposit. Fauna in Bed 6 connote a temperate environment; cryogenic features are preserved in Beds 6 and 7 but are penecontemporaneous only with Bed 7 and Bed 8 above it. The length of the hiatus between Beds 6 and 7 has not been established; it could be appreciable because different hydraulic regimes in the former and cryogenic structures in the latter signify a change in climate.

Unconformity between Beds 8 and 9. An angular disconformity separates Beds 8 and 9 (Fig. 8.1). Fine gravel, sand and silt in Beds 7 and 8 retain primary bedding structures of a low energy, fluvial regime. Bed 9, without bedding structure, overlies Bed 8, or Stratum C, or Lowestoft till where Bed 8 is missing. Bed 9 is widely thought to be a solifluced deposit, in which case it must have been derived from higher ground comprised of Lowestoft till that no longer is in the landscape, even though certain mineralogical properties of Bed 9 are unlike the Lowestoft chalky boulder clay (Perrin *et al.* 1973; but also see Gladfelter 1993). It is clearly post-Hoxnian in age and

presumably Wolstonian, but there are no contexts or contents that exclude the possibility that it is Devensian (see discussion in Gladfelter 1993, 62–6). Consequently, the duration of the hiatus between it and the underlying fluviatile deposits cannot be ascertained. The gap in time is appreciable, however, since during that interval the relief of the landscape became inverted; fluviatile deposits of the Upper Sequence infilled a valley but the sediment of Bed 9 mantles an interfluve.

TIME-BOUNDARIES AT HOXNE

The lower boundary of the Hoxnian interglacial begins at the base of Stratum E at Hoxne (stage II of West 1956), where the proportion of tree pollen, dominated by *Betula* and *Pinus*, first exceeds that of the non-tree pollen; Stratum E contains biozones HoI and HoII (Turner 1970).

The upper boundary of a temperate period occurs where the proportion of non-tree pollen again exceeds that of the tree pollen. This occurs at the end of stage IV, which is encompassed by Stratum C. Stage IV is not a biozone at Hoxne, but it is correlated with biozone HoIV at Marks Tey (Turner 1970, 402).

Glacial-interglacial Transition

The allostratigraphic contexts of Palaeolithic artifacts in the Lower Thames Valley, and at Clacton-on-Sea, suggested to Wymer (1985) that occupation of southern

Fig. 8.1. Upper Sequence, south face of Oakley Park Pit, Hoxne. The excavated surface in the foreground is comprised of the top of Bed 4. The coarse gravel of Bed 6 is a prominent stratum in the face of the baulk at the left. Ice wedge casts in Beds 7 and 8 can be seen at the right, under the telephone pole. A spade rests against the mechanically excavated face near the centre of the illustration. The unstratified deposit at the top of the sequence exposed in the centre, is 50 cm thick. Note that here Bed 9 comprises the surface of the upland plain.

Britain by hunter-gatherers and their prey occurred during a mild climatic phase of the waning Anglian glacial. Perhaps this was the time of aggradation of Stratum F at Hoxne. At Hoxne, the transition to the interglacial is thought to have directly succeeded upon the deposition of the Lowestoft till (West & Gibbard 1995). This interval of time is recorded by Stratum F, at most less than 50cm thick (Fig. 8.2) but the duration of this interval is not known.

The Late-glacial, stage I at Hoxne, is recorded by the contents of Stratum F (biozone lLo after Turner 1970). Near the edge of Lake Hoxne, it includes seeds, twigs, organic debris and clods of organic inclusions (West 1956). The oldest sediment of this deposit at this location contains abundant macrobotanical remains considered to indicate full glacial conditions (Turner 1968), and 74 taxa of aquatic coleoptera (Coope 1993). The insect remains include species indicative of both boreal and more southerly environments within a sample of sediment that was only 6cm thick. A rapid change in climate from glacial to interglacial conditions is indicated (Coope 1993). The pollen from Stratum F connotes climatic conditions away

from the edge of Lake Hoxne that were less rigorous than those of the Anglian full glacial (Mullenders 1993). Extrapolation of rates of sedimentation can indicate that the aggradation occurred during only one millennia, an estimate that is consistent with Coope's conclusion that rapid climatic change occurred at this time, or at most three millennia if the longest duration for the entire interglacial is assumed. The length of the interval would not have precluded people and game from having moved into the area; it was long enough to witness a brief, modest climatic amelioration and expansion of the pine-birch woodland (substage Ic). Whether or not hominid occupation of the landscape surrounding Lake Hoxne occurred at this time can only be surmised because there is no direct evidence for it.

Results of recent excavations in Suffolk 19 miles west of Hoxne, at Barnham East Farm (Ashton *et al.* 1994a; 1994b; 1995), also seem to indicate that there was a phase of warm conditions following the Anglian but that it was not the Hoxnian *sensu stricto*. This conclusion is based on D/L measurement for shells from sediment with temperate fauna that lies on Lowestoft till (OIS 12); the ratio of

Fig. 8.2. Lacustrine sediments, west face of Oakley Park Pit, Hoxne. This is the lower portion of Cutting XX of Wymer's excavations. It is adjacent to section 100 of West (1956). Chalky Boulder Clay is exposed at the bottom, overlain by about 50cm of Stratum F. The bulk of the sediment above Stratum F is Stratum E. The bottoms of two sampling columns (Monolith U) seen at the top of the illustration are in Stratum C. Sediment examined for coleoptera by Coope (1993) was obtained from this section.

0.3±0.015 equates with that from the Lower Loam at Swanscombe and corresponds to OIS 11 (Bowen, in Ashton *et al.* 1994a). Bowen believes that this evidence, as well as the D/L ratios from Swanscombe and from the Nar Valley (freshwater beds and marine clay) all with ratios equivalent to OIS 11, support the contention that this warm phase (i.e. OIS 11) and a cold stage (i.e. OIS 10) intervene between the Anglian (generally held to be OIS 12) and the Hoxnian (Stratum E at Hoxne equivalent to OIS 9). He concludes, therefore, that effectively there are two warm stages within the Hoxnian (*sensu lato*). West's interpretation of the palynology at Hoxne challenges this (West & Gibbard 1995) as does the conclusion that at Hoxne the interglacial directly succeeds the Anglian.

But West (West & Gibbard 1995, table 1) now allows the possibility that the correlations of East Anglian stages may be that the Hoxnian is OIS 11 or 9 and the Anglian could be OIS 12 or 10.

Interglacial-glacial Transition

There is a hiatus between Stratum D and Strata C and B, which are conformal units containing a mixture of cold and temperate floral and faunal elements, some of which are primary and some of which may not be. Which is which is contested. The length of the hiatus is not known but during it subaerial erosion occurred.

Bed 4, Stratum C and Stratum B all pertain to the same gradational unit of chalky gravel with flint and Jurassic fossils, and with thin or thick accretions of clay and silty or sandy clay. In all, as many as 5m of these deposits are found in the centre of Lake Hoxne. The Lower Industry at Hoxne is in the bottom of Stratum C, fossil vertebrates come from the bottom of Stratum C and the top of Bed 4 (Stuart *et al.* 1993), handaxes originally reported from Hoxne by Frere (1800) may have come from the top of Bed 4 on the opposite side of Lake Hoxne (Wymer's Middle Industry), and material from the bottom of Stratum C has yielded TL and ESR dates (Gladfelter *et al.* 1993). None of this information is from the Hoxnian interglacial, *sensu stricto*, but it cannot be proven or disproven that it is from sediments that are chronologically equivalent to biozone HoIV.

It now is clear that Statum C and its biological contents is a complicated phase of aggradation. The upper boundary of the interglacial stage cannot be considered to be fixed at this type locality, but still Hoxne is referred to as the type locality or stratotype site (West & Gibbard 1995). Indeed, the upper boundary is missing here (e.g. Turner 1989, 42) and at every other paratype site of this interglacial, except at Marks Tey. There the composite pollen diagram that includes biozone HoIV has been reconstructed from two boreholes that encompass biozones HoIIIa to eGl (now eWo) (Turner 1970).

All of the pollen profiles within the drainage basin of the River Waveney, and the rest of East Anglia as well, are truncated in pollen assemblage biozone HoIV, if not late in pollen assemblage biozone HoIII, indicating a period of regional landscape degradation during the last part of the interglacial (the Post-temperate stage), along with the onset of cooler environmental conditions. The length of this hiatus cannot be assessed. The hiatus in biozone HoIV at Marks Tey, during which time there was a drop in lake level and subaerial erosion, apparently is of a minor sort and it is not indicated on the composite pollen diagram of that site.

THE GEOMORPHOLOGIC TIME-PERSPECTIVE

The occurrence at Hoxne of a gradational sequence on a present-day interfluve has been observed by many. Indeed,

John Frere when first reporting the handaxes at Hoxne made elegant note of the peculiar situation of the deposits on the upland (Fig. 8.1). The inversion of upland-lowland components of the landscape post-dated Bed 8, the final fluviatile unit of the Upper Sequence. It pre-dated, or was penecontemporaneous with, Bed 9. What is more, this phase of deposition is of regional importance. The gradational sequences described for virtually every section exposed on interfluves of the Waveney drainage basin culminate with a deposit comparable to Bed 9. The deposit is variously called subsurface soil, trail, head, a chaotic mixture, decalcified head or perhaps in some cases made ground (discussion in Gladfelter 1993). When precisely in post-Hoxnian time widespread degradation of the Anglian till plain took place and when the surficial deposits were first in place are not known, other than that these changes can no longer be attributed to a Wolstonian glacier.

Sediments with Hoxnian biozones fill depressions in the surface of the Lowestoft till. With the disappearance of a Wolstonian ice sheet from the East Anglian Quaternary sequence, it follows that this surface has been available for colonization by vegetation for perhaps 400ky. Yet no palaeosol has been identified for this protracted time, unless one considers the Valley Farm (Rose & Allen 1977) and Barham (Rose *et al.* 1985) soils to be composite palaeosols where they are exposed at or near the surface, or one considers other soils at the surface today in East Anglia to be exhumed or relict palaeosols. Buried, post-Anglian, fossil pedogenesis has been interpreted, however, at Barnham East Farm (Ashton *et al.* 1994a). Except for discontinuous terraces in some East Anglian valleys, the aggradational counterparts of intervening phases of landscape instability are not recorded either. There are major gaps in our understanding of the geomorphic evolution of East Anglia in the Middle and Late Pleistocene and of the allostratigraphic succession, all of which deserve careful examination. Fluviatile members of the Upper Sequence demonstrate that in some cases the plateau gravels of the East Anglian till plain are post-Hoxnian in age.

THE ARCHEOLOGICAL TIME-PERSPECTIVE

John Wymer's comprehensive compilation and evaluation of the spatial distribution of Lower Palaeolithic artifacts in East Anglia shows a range of geomorphic and stratigraphic contexts for these materials (Wymer 1985; 1988; 1995). Lower Palaeolithic artifacts have been found sealed in deposits with pre-Anglian fauna and associated with Anglian stage sediments. There are, according to Wymer's inventory, more locations in East Anglia with Hoxnian biozones that do not have Palaeolithic artifacts than there are places where Palaeoliths are found directly associated with Hoxnian pollen. Indeed, 'the only Palaeolithic site in primary context that can definitely be dated to the Hoxnian stage, on the grounds of pollen analysis, is Clacton-on-Sea

(Freshwater Beds)' (Wymer 1985, 346). Interestingly, however, dozens of intra-Wolstonian Acheulian sites have been catalogued.

An important conclusion of Wymer's excavation at Hoxne is that the Lower Palaeolithic industries there are in deposits that cannot be allotted to Hoxnian biozones, and that the industries are therefore of post-Hoxnian age (Wymer 1983). He went on to propose that particular beds of the Upper Sequence may be assigned to different substages of the Wolstonian glacial – Beds 4 and 5 to an unnamed interstadial, and Bed 6 to a subsequent stadial (Wymer 1985). Further, he listed other Acheulian sites in East Anglia that could be temporally equivalent to these substages. The proposal for the beds at Hoxne was subsequently revised (Wymer *et al.* 1993), but for either version the interpretation would have significant ramifications, discussed in the next section.

DISCUSSION

There are very few sites where Lower Palaeolithic industries are in primary context: Boxgrove, Clacton-on-Sea, Barnham East Farm, Hoxne and Swanscombe Lower Loam (Wymer 1988, Table 1). Yet, it now can be said (Wymer 1988) that humans were present before the Anglian – the 'refined' Acheulian at Boxgrove and 'elegant scrapers' at High Lodge – and that the Acheulian and Clactonian people very likely co-existed in post-Anglian time (Ashton *et al.* 1994b). But only the Clactonian can be placed firmly within Hoxnian biozones, and the Acheulian is highly visible from late Hoxnian time through the Wolstonian. Acheulian hunter-gatherers invaded landscapes before and after the period of the temperate Hoxnian biozones but not during it, hence deforestation in biozone HoIIc cannot be shown to be anthropogenic. Subsequent temperate intervals may well lack a hominid presence as well (see Wymer 1988, table 2) so that it seems that since the Cromerian, Lower and Middle Palaeolithic hunter-gatherers roamed Britain during cooler periods. There is now evidence from elsewhere that Acheulian hunter-gatherers were able to subsist in cold environments (Waters *et al.* 1997).

Hoxne and chronology

Efforts to date the interglacial sediments are inconclusive (summary in Gladfelter *et al.* 1993). Bowen (in Gladfelter *et al.* 1993) has shown by D/L ratios that Stratum E and the base of the Upper Sequence (Stratum C-Bed 4) aggraded during the same oxygen isotope stage; aminoepimerization of four samples of *Valvata piscinalis* and *Pisidium* sp. from Stratum E have given comparable D/L ratios (Bowen, pers. comm.) that, in turn, are comparable to a ratio for shell from Stratum C (Bowen *et al.* 1989). These determinations correlate to OIS 9. Consequently, the disconformity between the alder-carr bog of Stratum

D, and Stratum C-Bed 4 of the Upper Sequence could not represent a protracted hiatus given that the duration of OIS 9 is only 36 ky (Imbrie *et al.* 1984).

The faunal assemblages from the bottom of Stratum C (megafauna) and the top of Bed 4 (microfauna) are both suggestive of a regional temperate forest; the megafaunal assemblage from Bed 5 is probably indicative of more open vegetation but the environmental implications of the fauna are difficult to interpret (Stuart *et al.* 1993). It has been proposed that the 'temperate' conditions indicated for Bed 5 signal a climatic amelioration after the cooler environmental conditions indicated in Stratum C – Bed 4. The 'cooler' conditions in Stratum C are based on botanical contents, while the temperate conditions in Stratum C and Bed 4 are inferred from faunal contents. Different taphonomies may pertain.

Nevertheless, several interpretations of the palaeoenvironmental significance of the Upper Sequence have been postulated. It has been suggested that Bed 5 signals a post-Hoxnian warm interval, indeed interstadial, following 'cooler' conditions during aggradation of Bed 4. The warm interval has been called the Dömnitzian (Gibbard &Turner 1988) and equated with the Wacken/Hoogeveen (Ehlers *et al.* 1991b, table 41). The Wacken/Dömnitzian, in turn, has been likened to a true interglacial, comparable to the Hoxnian or Ipswichian (Ehlers *et al.* 1991b, 493), which would further obfuscate palaeoenvironmental interpretations of Stratum C – Bed 4 at Hoxne. Wymer has referred to this period in Beds 4 and 5 as Wolstonian 1/2 (Wymer 1985, table 15) of OIS 9 and, in so doing, has correlated Beds 1–3 to OIS 10. Were these assignments to oxygen isotope stages to be appropriate, the alluviation of Beds 4 and 5, and Bed 6 with which Bed 5 interdigitates, would have occurred over a period of 59ky.

If the aminostratigraphy is adopted, the consequence at Hoxne is that the Palaeolithic industries there occur within the Hoxnian interglacial. The consequence for the Lower Palaeolithic is that Lower Palaeolithic industries at Clacton-on-Sea, Swanscombe and Barnham East Farm may be added to the expanding list of pre-Hoxnian sites in Britain.

At Hoxne, time matters

There are no absolute dates from the interglacial beds at Hoxne, unlike paratypes of the Holsteinian biostratigraphic correlative in Europe, to allow chronostratigraphic correlations. In addition, it is becoming increasingly apparent that biostratigraphic correlations and other correlations based on the evidence of a single discipline are equivocal and they can be insecure (Turner 1996).

Correlations of the Hoxnian with OIS 11 and the post Hoxnian deposits (the Upper Sequence) with OIS 10–6 (Wymer 1985) means that the entire Quaternary sequence preserved at Hoxne can span as many as 393ky! It is important to note that the sort of correlation one offers has significant ramifications for the respective temporal dimension into which the regional palaegeomorphic systems must fit.

At the time of the University of Chicago excavations, the Hoxnian was the penultimate interglacial (Mitchell *et al.* 1973). Since then, post-Hoxnian but pre-Ipswichian deposits with temperate flora or fauna have been alleged in East Anglia but none of the temperate phases or sites has as yet been accorded interglacial status or been formally designated as an interstadial (see Rose 1989). Consequently, at this point the Hoxnian is still the penultimate interglacial in Britain.

ACKNOWLEDGEMENTS

Collaboration over four seasons of field work at the Golf Course, Clacton-on-Sea, and at Hoxne was enhanced immensely by the collegiality of John Wymer and the companionship of John and Mollie. His and their generous and warm hospitality in Bury St Edmunds, Stowupland, Bildeston and Great Cressingham more than 20 years ago are pleasant remembrances, as are proper piano playing and my introduction to the campaign for real ale. That work was sponsored by several grants to Ronald Singer from the National Science Fourndation, the U. S. Public Health Service, the National Geographic Society and research refunds at the University of Chicago. The additional support and contribuitions of the Graduate Research Board and the Cartographic Laboratory, University of Illinois at Chicago, are acknowledged. I am grateful to the editors for the invitation to contribute to this festschrift and to Nick Ashton for his comments on a draft of this paper.

REFERENCES

Ashton, N.M., Bowen, D.Q., Holman, J.A., Hunt, C.O., Irving, B.G., Kemp, R.A., Lewis, S.G., McNabb, J., Parfitt, S. & Seddon, M.B. 1994a. Excavation at the Lower Palaeolithic site at East Farm, Barnham, Suffolk 1989–92. *Journal of the Geological Society, London* 151, 599–605.

Ashton, N.M., McNabb, J., Irving, B., Lewis, S. & Parfitt, S. 1994b. Contemporaneity of Clactonian and Acheulian flint industries at Barnham, Suffolk. *Antiquity* 68, 585–9.

Ashton, N.M., Bowen, D.Q. & Lewis, S.G. 1995. Discussion on excavations at the Lower Palaeolithic site at East Farm, Barnham, Suffolk, 1989–1992: reply. *Journal of the Geolgocial Society, London* 152, 571–4.

Bowen, D.Q., Hughes, S.K., Sykes, G.A. & Miller, G.H. 1989. Land-sea correlations in the Pleistocene based on isoleucine epimerization in non-marine molluscs. *Nature* 340, 49–51.

Coope, G.R. 1993. Late-Glacial (Anglian) and Late-Temperate (Hoxnian) Coleoptera. In R. Singer, B.G. Gladfelter & J.J. Wymer (eds), *The Lower Paleolithic Site at Hoxne, England*, 156–62. Chicago: University of Chicago Press.

Ehlers, J., Gibbard, P.L. & Rose, J. (eds) 1991a. *Glacial Deposits in Great Britain and Ireland*. Rotterdam: Balkema.

Ehlers, J., Gibbard, P. L. & Rose, J. 1991b. Glacial deposits of Britain and Europe: general overview. In J. Ehlers, P.L. Gibbard

& J. Rose (eds), *Glacial Deposits in Great Britain and Ireland*, 493–501. Rotterdam: Balkema.

Frere, J. 1800. Account of flint weapons discovered at Hoxne in Suffolk, in a letter to the Rev. John Brand, Secretary. *Archaeologia* 13, 204–5.

Gibbard, P.L. & Turner, C. 1988. In defence of the Wolstonian stage. *Quaternary Newsletter* 54, 9–14.

Gladfelter, B.G. 1993. The geostratigraphic context of the archeology. In R. Singer, B.G. Gladfelter & J.J. Wymer (eds), *The Lower Paleolithic Site at Hoxne, Hoxne, England*, 23–66. Chicago: University of Chicago Press.

Gladfelter, B.G., Wymer, J.J. & Singer, R. with contributions by S.G. Sheridan, H.P. Schwarcz & R. Grun. 1993. Dating the Deposits at Hoxne. In R. Singer, B.G. Gladfelter & J.J. Wymer (eds), *The Lower Paleolithic Site at Hoxne, England*, 207–17. Chicago: University of Chicago Press.

Imbrie, J., Hays, J.D., Martinson, D.G., McIntyre, A., Mix, A.C., Morley, J.J., Pisias, N.G., Prell, W.L. & Shackleton, N.J. 1984. The orbital theory of Pleistocene climate: support from a revised chronology of the marine ^{18}O record. In A. Berger, J. Imbrie, J.D. Hays, G. Kukla & B. Saltzman (eds), *Milankovitch and Climate*, part 1, 269–305. Dordrecht: D. Reidel.

Mitchell, G.F., Penny, L.F., Shotton, F.W. & West, R.G. 1973. *A Correlation of Quaternary Deposits in the British Isles.* London: Geological Society of London Special Report 4.

Mullenders, W.M. 1993. New palynological studies at Hoxne. In R. Singer, B.G. Gladfelter, & J.J. Wymer (eds), *The Lower Paleolithic Site at Hoxne, England*, 150–5. Chicago: University of Chicago Press.

Perrin, R.M.S., Davies, H. & Fysh, M.D. 1973. Lithology of the Chalky Boulder Clay. *Nature Physical Science* 245, 101–104.

Rose, J. 1989. Stadial type sections in the British Quaternary. In J. Rose & C. Schluchter (eds), *Quaternary Type Sections: Imagination or Reality?*, 44–67. Rotterdam: Balkema.

Rose, J. & Allen, P. 1977. Middle Pleistocene stratigraphy in southern East Anglia. *Journal of the Geological Society of London* 133, 83–102.

Rose, J., Boardman, A., Kemp, R.A. & Whiteman, C.A. 1985. Palaeosols and the interpretation of the British Quaternary stratigraphy. In K.S. Richards, R.R. Arnett & S. Ellis (eds), *Geomorphology and Soils*, 348–75. London: George Allen & Unwin.

Singer, R., Gladfelter, B.G. & Wymer, J.J. 1993. *The Lower Palaeolithic Site at Hoxne, England*. Chicago: University of Chicago Press.

Singer, R., Wymer, J.J., Gladfelter, B.G. & Wolf, R.G. 1973.

Excavation of the Clactonian Industry at the Golf Course, Clacton-on-Sea. *Proceedings of the Prehistoric Society* 39, 6–74.

Stuart, A.J., Wolff, R.G., Lister, A.M., Singer, R.K. & Egginton, J.J. 1993. Fossil vertebrates. In R.K. Singer, B.G. Gladfelter & J.J. Wymer (eds), *The Lower Paleolithic Site at Hoxne, England*, 163–206. Chicago: University of Chicago Press.

Turner, C. 1968 A Lowesoftian Late-glacial flora from the Pleistocene deposits at Hoxne, Suffolk. *New Phytologist* 67, 327–32.

Turner, C. 1970. The Middle Pleistocene deposits at Marks Tey, Essex. *Philosophical Transactions of the Royal Society of London* B257, 373–440.

Turner, C. 1989. Type sections and Quaternary deposits. In J. Rose & C. Schluchter (eds), *Quaternary Type Sections: Imagination or Reality?*, 41–4. Rotterdam: Balkema.

Turner, C. 1996. A brief survey of the early middle Pleistocene in Europe. In C. Turner (ed.), *The Early Middle Pleistocene in Europe*, 295–317. Rotterdam: Balkema.

Waters, M.R., Forman, S.L.K. & Pierson, J.M. 1997. Diring Yuriakh: a Lower Paleolithic site in Central Siberia, *Science* 275, 1281–4.

West, R.G. 1956. The Quaternary deposits at Hoxne, Suffolk. *Philosophical Transactions of the Royal Society of London* B239, 265–356.

West, R.G. 1991. *Pleistocene Palaeoecology of Central Norfolk.* Cambridge: Cambridge University Press.

West, R.G. & Gibbard, P. L. 1995. Discussion on the excavations at the Lower Palaeolithic site at East Farm, Barnham, Suffolk, 1989–1992. *Journal of the Geological Society, London* 152, 570–1.

Wymer, J.J. 1983. The Lower Palaeolithic Site at Hoxne. *Proceedings of the Suffolk Institute of Archaeology and History* 35, 169–89.

Wymer, J.J. 1985. *Palaeolithic Sites of East Anglia*. Norwich: Geo Books.

Wymer, J.J. 1988. Palaeolithic archaeology and the British Quaternary Sequence. *Quatenary Science Reviews* 7, 79–98.

Wymer, J.J. 1995 The contexts of Palaeoliths. In A.J. Schofield (ed.), *Lithics in Context: Suggestions for the Future Direction of Lithic Studies*, 45–51. London: Lithic Studies Society Occasional Paper 5.

Wymer, J.J., Gladfelter, B.G. & Singer, R. with a contribution by W.W.Mullenders 1993. The industries at Hoxne and the Lower Paleolithic of Britain. In R.K. Singer, B.G. Gladfelter & J.J. Wymer (eds), *The Lower Paleolithic Site at Hoxne, England*, 218–24. Chicago: University of Chicago press.

9. Unity and Diversity in the Early Stone Age

J. A. J. Gowlett

ABSTRACT

The Palaeolithic is unified by its basic technology, and perhaps no more. This, however is enough to give us a framework for testing similarity and diversity extending across the whole Pleistocene. Yet comparisons are rarely made systematically across the Lower Palaeolithic world, even though it is often seen as the most homogeneous part of the stone ages. Rather, as the discipline becomes more specialised, regional archaeologies tend to emerge, which look at problems in local terms. This paper argues the need to maintain an international inter-regional approach, and attempts to highlight some areas where this is beneficial.

From the origins of its study the Palaeolithic has become much bigger. The Abbé Breuil could survey it as one field (Breuil 1930). More recently figures such as Mary Leakey, Desmond Clark – and John Wymer – have been able to stand astride more than one field, perhaps as much at home with rock art as the Lower Palaeolithic, Syria as much as Angola, or rockshelters as much as open sites. With each generation, however, the effort becomes a greater strain. The change of scale which we are undergoing leads naturally to specialisation, even a tendency to form a series of clubs with little contact between them. This specialisation guarantees expertise, but it is also wasteful if it means that regional archaeologies do not make joint approaches to common problems, and do not intercompare their data. For the Lower Palaeolithic the problems remain different from those of later periods: archaeologists cannot each sit in a niche, confident that it can be treated in isolation – because our sampling is too poor for us to be confident of understanding diversity, and our knowledge of early cultural processes is too shallow for us to generalise from single regions and their sites, however rich these may be.

How great is the change of scale?

An obvious benchmark is Olduvai Bed I, where the trebling of perceived age to 1.8 million years caused faultlines through all succeeding periods (Evernden & Curtis 1965). Early signs of a readjustment can be seen in Glynn Isaac's paper of 1969 – now a generation ago (Isaac 1969; see also Isaac & Curtis 1974). We emphasise less that the scope of the Palaeolithic has at least doubled since this major readjustment. From the 1960s dates have expanded approximately as follows (Fig. 9.1):

Africa:	1.8 Ma >> 2.5 Ma
Middle East	0.7 Ma >> 1.6 Ma
Europe	0.5 Ma >> 1.0 Ma
Asia	0.5 Ma >> 1.6 Ma

Inevitably in the present state of knowledge, there are debates about the precise dates in each particular case, but the general picture is plain (Roche 1980; Bar-Yosef & Goren-Inbar 1993; Roebroeks & van Kolfschoten 1995; Swisher *et al.* 1994; Wanpo *et al.* 1995). Coupled with this expansion, new areas have been investigated, many more sites excavated and published, and there has been a much greater intensity of research.

We have to pick out and interpret this picture against the effects of history. Controlling ideas were often formed when the state of knowledge was much poorer. For example, the Movius line was drawn to mark the eastern limits of bifaces and Levallois technique, at a time when it was thought that early industries in Africa and Asia were of roughly similar age (Movius 1949). Then it became plain that the African Oldowan is far older than the best known chopper/chopping tool industries of eastern Asia; and indeed that the two are separated in time/space by the early Acheulean industries. Recent dates for early hominids in the Far East, however, establish the possibility of an early continuity between the Oldowan and the 'chopper/ chopping tool' industries, which might not differ from one another fundamentally if described in a common scheme (Schick & Zhuan 1993).

In this larger Palaeolithic, my principal question is 'What do we really want to know about variety?'

Variability was one of the great issue of Palaeolithic archaeology in the 1950s and 1960s, but now it seems *passé* (although currently favoured approaches to use of landscape touch on some of the same issues). It is perhaps time to enliven 'variability' by adopting evolutionary biology's terminology of diversity.

Is the position this: that now there are more interesting issues of adaptation and what we need from the artefacts is merely convenient synopses – simple descriptions that set the ground for progressing to other more topical problems? Or do we need to work hard at investigating, explicating, that variety as an essential precondition for gaining any deeper understanding of early hominid behaviour?

I would argue that the Palaeolithic can be seen from two fundamental viewpoints:

1) *purposive > evolutionary*: here the main purpose is to build the grand scenario of human evolution, to make a sweep through time, to pick out the developments in later periods. Individual sites and early periods are not really examined for their own sake.

2) *descriptive > ecological*: here every region, every site, every local phase is studied for its own value – as is usually the case in the study of recent periods. A similarly descriptive approach can be applied to any early period, and it is contributing to the appearance of regional Lower Palaeolithic archaeologies. For the workings of each such area to be understood in local terms, the approach has to be ecological, addressing relationships between variables in an environment – essentially without reference to what happened thousands of years earlier or later. The main problems with this approach are local gaps in continuity (*cf.* Stern 1994), and the vastness of the Palaeolithic. It might be that every Upper Palaeolithic in the world could be studied, millennium by millennium, but certainly not every Lower Palaeolithic. For the moment sampling is imposed by the twin forces of preservation and the availability of archaeologists.

Archaeologists are pulled both ways in relation to these approaches. Scholars in related fields may have little time for archaeological detail, and may omit it almost com-

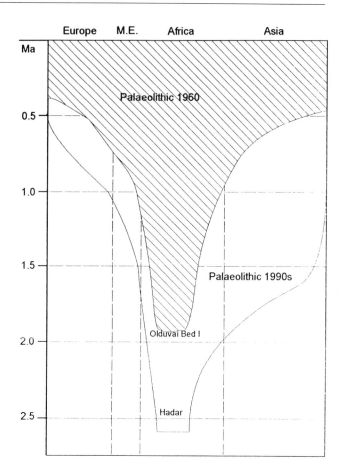

Figure 9.1: The expanding Palaeolithic.

pletely (e.g. Dunbar 1996; Deacon 1997; *cf.* Gowlett 1997). This paper takes as its basis that Palaeolithic variability in early times is insufficiently explained by theory, and also insufficiently explored. It is too little examined by current evolutionary arguments outside archaeology. I will try to illustrate the benefits of comparisons through discussion followed by some case-studies.

UNITY OR DIVERSITY?

Very different views have been expressed on such issues. For Lewis Binford, it is axiomatic that early hominid behaviour was 'culturally assisted' rather than fully cultural (e.g. Binford 1989). This would fit with the idea of an Acheulean that is essentially 'the same' in different continents, because the artefacts would be no more than simple intermediaries between humans and environment – providing some help in tackling immediate problems. If environments were profoundly different, but toolkits remained the same, this would be further testimony to a robust simplicity of adaptation. It would both demonstrate their limited importance in the past and imply their limited value for extracting information in the present. This view of sameness was also expressed by Bosinski (1982) who took the 'Lower Palaeolithic' as the period before the differentiation of finds into different industries (*Formengruppen*) of stone artefacts. If there are no culturally-determined differences in the Lower Palaeolithic then, he asserted, the material is open to world-wide discussion. Sites such as Zhoukoudian, Bilzingsleben and 'Ubeidiya were cited as examples.

The existence of variability was, however, fully recognised by Binford (e.g. 1972). It was merely interpreted in terms of functional variants, an approach also applied by J.D. Clark (e.g. Clark & Haynes 1970). Others would champion the importance of variability in a stylistic sense. Here it is useful to take note of the style/function debate which has been prominent in Americanist Palaeolithic archaeology. Although some argued that style and function were inherently separable, Sackett has argued that where there is a function to be met, there is generally a choice of artefact, which in itself amounts to style – passive style (Sackett 1982). Even using a flake rather than a chopper can be seen as an act of style. This argument is paralleled by Wrangham & Peterson (1996) in their recent analysis of the distinction between nature/nurture: they see the debate itself as misguided – the two cannot be disentwined.

Glynn Isaac carried out seminal work on the problem in looking at the Acheulean of Olorgesailie in Kenya (e.g. Isaac 1977). Here there were many different artefact assemblages of roughly similar age from a single site complex. Variations in proportions of choppers, scrapers, bifaces and flakes could be attributed to differences in the functions of individual sites – Desmond Clark's toolkits – but variations in hand-axe shape are not so easily explained in that way. The minor differences of shape and size probably have little bearing on function, yet the various hand-axe groups differed by much more than statistical probability. Arguably, then there is a style component in something like a modern sense. Isaac spoke of a drift in local craft traditions.

In a paper directly relevant to current issues, Isaac (1972) reviewed the problem of 'determinants' affecting artefacts, noting that each school stressed one factor in its models: there were the traditional or 'phylogenetic' models, and the 'activity variant models' But there was also – logically – a niche for a third school 'which advocates the physical properties of raw material as the primary determinant of variation'. This has become far more important since Isaac wrote. I argue that we can disentangle these factors of Lower Palaeolithic variation far more effectively by surveying a broad field, than by considering only the problems of one area.

THE HOMINID FIT

Recent interpretations of the fossil hominid record have found more and more species. Are these likely to coincide with archaeological traditions? Archaeology used to see parallel strands of separate toolkits made by distinct hominid lines (the phylogenetic model again). With his several traditions Bordes in this respect followed Breuil. In the 'lumping' phase of the 1950s and 1960s, the number of hominid species was minimised, and archaeological traditions were rationalised alongside these. Terms such as Chellean were finally abandoned and combined in the Acheulean (Bishop & Clark 1967, 897). The process was not always consistent: in Africa, the 'Hope Fountain' was assimilated into the Acheulean, but in Europe the Clactonian was not.

Since this phase most archaeologists have been reluctant to follow the idea of linking hominids and traditions. The reasons can be restated:

1) assemblage diversity within site complexes often matches that between regions
2) the same stone tool tradition is frequently found to be associated with more than one hominid
3) interpretations of hominids are based on very few specimens, are not consistent between scholars, and are fluid.

To get to grips with 'who made what' requires a return to the species and the specimens.

Early Homo

There are now at least four species of early Homo: *Homo habilis*, *Homo rudolfensis*, *Homo erectus* and *Homo ergaster*. Wood has placed early African specimens in *Homo ergaster* rather than *erectus* (Wood 1991; 1992). On the basis of cladistic analysis, he has suggested that *ergaster*, rather than *erectus* as seen in Asia, fits better as the ancestor of *Homo sapiens*. Not all scholars are convinced by this classification. Bilsborough (1992) has pointed out the intermixture of allegedly diagnostic characteristics. Rightmire (1990) emphasises the strong similarities between the Olduvai and the Asian specimens in the time-range 1.2–0.8mya. Before accepting any link through to *sapiens*, archaeologists can point to the lack of *ergaster* after 1.5mya, and the almost complete lack of classic *erectus* in Africa after 800kya (Fig. 9.2).

Homo sapiens

Although some writers (e.g. Bilsborough 1992; Bräuer 1989) see continuity between *erectus* and *sapiens* in Africa and Asia, a speciation event is envisaged by Rightmire (1990), who sees *erectus* as a long-lived stable species, then replaced by a more modern hominid. Although Tattersall (1986) emphasises regional variation in these successors – perhaps necessitating another array of species names (e.g. *rhodesiensis*) – Rightmire (1990; 1996) is inclined to see similarity between European and African specimens, even extending *Homo heidelbergensis* to include the Bodo specimen of Ethiopia. Stringer (e.g. 1981) has set out to find clear criteria for distinguishing

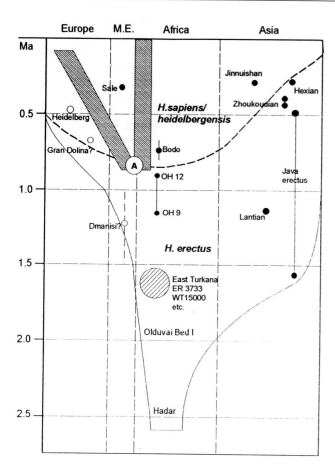

Figure 9.2: The hominid fit: the diagram shows how the huge extent of Homo erectus *in space and time is sustained by remarkably few sites with complete crania. (Sites with less complete remains shown with open circles; Middle Pleistocene dates are often uncertain). Crucial in Rightmire's (1996) view of a very early* Homo heidelbergensis *in Africa, is the dating of Bodo: the transition would have to come after OH12. The mtDNA data of Krings* et al. *(1997) suggest a divergence between Neanderthal ancestors and modern ancestors rooted deep in time (A), and apparently ruling out later Middle Pleistocene 're-placement scenarios'. Comparative approaches in archaeology may be able to test how different the technologies of the (apparently) diverging lineages became through this long timescale.*

erectus and *sapiens*, but emphasises that he is not talking about 'biological species' (Stringer 1992).

The idea that for a time *H. erectus* and *H. sapiens (/ heidelbergensis)* may have been separate, contemporary biological species which coexisted is strengthened by:

— approximate coexistence of Bodo and late *erectus* in China as at Zhoukoudian
— apparent temporal overlap between late *Homo erectus* (at Hexian) and *Homo sapiens* (at Chaohu and Jin-

nuishan) in China (Chen & Zhang 1991; Chen *et al.* 1994).

Recent DNA studies have helped enormously in building a perspective: not only do they show the Neanderthals as sufficiently divergent from modern humans to warrant a species designation, but they also suggest a long period of differentiation – perhaps 600kya (Krings *et al.* 1997). Although this figure could be incorrect, it tends to preclude the idea of regular waves of replacement in Europe. It makes rather unlikely the idea that an early *Homo erectus* population in Europe might have been replaced by an incoming archaic *sapiens/heidelbergensis* 400 – 500 kya. It thus seems to fit poorly with Rightmire's classification – unless we put his widespread *heidelbergensis* back to 700–800 kya, near the roots of diverging lines which then led to later African and /European hominids.

Consider then the transition from *erectus* in terms of dating: between Olduvai OH12 the latest classic *erectus* – and Bodo, there could be more than 200 ky – or, following Rightmire, hardly any time at all. Quite possibly, these absent hominids were making Acheulean bifaces, since these are abundant at both Olduvai Bed IV and Bodo. There are, however, other African Middle Pleistocene localities where bifaces are absent (e.g. the Losokweta industry at Chesowanja: Gowlett *et al.* 1981). Thus we have to weigh up archaeological variability on the one hand, and the possibility of a near-invisible speciation on the other.

This survey shows highly divergent opinions, and the need for archaeological variability to be assessed by archaeologists. Foley's (1987) attempt to link technological traditions and hominids has been discounted by Clark (1989) and again by Belfer-Cohen & Goren-Inbar (1994). Foley's indices measuring technological 'turnover' and 'diversity' are a useful stab at a problem (Foley 1996), but they depend on crucial assumptions about the durations of species and lithic traditions, and the approach has been unable so far to come to terms with the scale of variability within traditions.

AFRICAN ORIGINS TO EAST ASIA

As the Palaeolithic has grown, the domain of the Oldowan has waxed and waned. In East Africa, its timedepth has grown, but in north-west Africa the idea of its presence has been undercut (Raynal *et al.* 1995). In Israel, Ubeidiya, originally thought to represent Oldowan, is firmly within the Acheulean, and the status of possible older Yiron sites awaits confirmation (Ronen 1991). Older dates from Asia potentially extend the application of the Oldowan name to the earliest industries of Pakistan, China and Indonesia (e.g. Schick & Zhuan 1993; Wanpo *et al.* 1995). Here there is a case for a unified approach, since the diversity is largely uncharted.

In Africa, the suggestion that earlier industries would be simpler than the Oldowan of Olduvai has received some support from West Turkana (Kibunjia 1994), but has been checked by the discovery of abundant early artefacts from Hadar, apparently no simpler or less competently made than those of Olduvai Bed I (Harris 1983; work in progress).

THE ACHEULEAN WORLD

Over the last thirty years the Acheulean has become so vast that it is now beyond knowing for any individual. It is linked by its specific pattern of bifacial stone-working, but its domain is so poorly sampled and measured, that the extent of its diversity is not known. A simple notion of 'the biface' is projected across a million years, but the bifaces vary enormously in their contribution, and the space of this tradition could include many non-biface 'windows' – these might well go unremarked.

Statements about the sameness of the Acheulean often rest on assumption, so that studies outside Palaeolithic archaeology make generalisations which may be invalid. Even within archaeology, statements made about one region may not hold for another. These examples are intended to give documentation to some such points.

First, bifaces from far distant locations may sometimes be amazingly similar – in spite of raw material differences. A case in point is the obsidian bifaces from Kariandusi, aged about a million years, and the quartzite bifaces from Sidi Abderrahman Cunette, aged about 300–400 kya (Crompton and Gowlett 1997). Although these sites are about 5000km apart on the ground, and at least 500ky separated in time, the range of forms and standardisation are very similar (though the raw material is different). But, the Cunette bifaces differ greatly from those of the Sidi Abderrahman STIC site – nearby but older – and the Kariandusi obsidian bifaces differ clearly from the similarly aged localities with lava specimens (Wynn & Tierson 1990; Gowlett & Crompton 1994).

Other variability has been highlighted by the Leakey and Kleindienst typologies, emphasising the great variation in proportions of bifaces/heavy-duty tools/scrapers/debitage on sites that are close together. Olorgesailie, Isimila and Ubeidiya all have localities on which the heavy-duty material – choppers, polyhedrons, sub/spheroids – is far more abundant than hand-axes.

Thus it can seem surprising, from the outside, that the dichotomy of the Clactonian and Acheulean in Britain has caused 50 years of debate. Is the pattern perhaps slightly different? In Britain, the older generation of archaeologists tends to maintain the distinction between two traditions, whereas a younger generation argues that the Clactonian and Acheulean are two faces of one technology (Ashton *et al.* 1994; McNabb 1996; *pace* Mithen 1994; 1996). To Africanists, it has long seemed doubtful that there was a need for two named traditions – but they have puzzled equally over the Acheulean and Sangoan. It would be helpful to compare the diversity in East Africa and northwest Europe by the same criteria. The Kleindienst framework would seem able to encompass the Acheulean/Clactonian axis, but the scheme is not so easily applicable to Europe, where there are fewer clear 'site complexes', and where the approaches to using flint may have been significantly different from the African approaches to using lava: in Africa, there are usually eight to ten fairly distinct tool-categories (however subjectively assessed) – and in Lower Palaeolithic Europe that may not be so.

In recent papers Mithen (1994; 1996) has suggested a new explanation for the Clactonian/Acheulean separation, one proposing changes of adaptation by human populations to more closed and more open conditions of vegetation in different climatic phases: the Clactonian is interpreted as restricted to interglacial conditions, the Acheulean to predominate in colder periods. This was seen as a 'thoughtful' adjustment, mediated by adjustments in group size, which would affect the complexity of technology that could be 'carried'. This drew the response from McNabb & Ashton (1995) that the British chronology no longer supports a temporal separation of the Acheulean and Clactonian. There is indeed now good evidence of interglacial Acheulean (Ashton *et al.* 1994; Andresen *et al.* 1997), and little to support a clearly different environment for the Clactonian.

Even so, Mithen's ideas merit further testing. Some variables clearly did affect the stability of transmission of ideas. Explorations of possible social frameworks have been made (e.g. Isaac 1972; Steele 1994; 1996). It is not easy to see how the open country/closed country paradigm would work in the context of African environments. Much variability occurs very locally in small basins where there was probably a local transect from closed to more open vegetation. Mithen's idea, however invokes a chain of factors: palaeoenvironment, ecological 'problems', social consequences, learning modes and technological consequences. Do influences work through the chain in similar fashion on different sites? This is an attractive model in search of a suitable Middle Pleistocene home.

Such a discussion introduces ideas of social group size explored by Wobst (1974; see also Gamble 1998), and questions of the 'fit' of adaptation to landscape (Potts 1994; Peters & Blumenschine 1995; Tuffreau *et al.* 1997). A key factor affecting social transmission of ideas could be the proportion of the year in which resources would allow a large group to aggregate (facility of communication obviously also being relevant). The crucial point is that none of the worlds which we consider are entirely separate, so that African and European situations allow the transfer and reapplication of models.

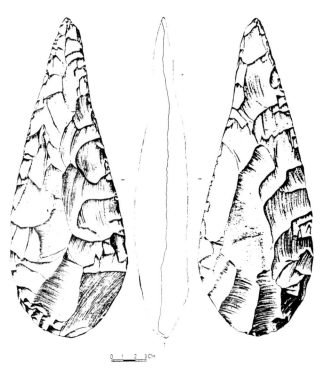

Figure 9.3: Large straight-edge biface from la Kamoa, after Cahen 1975.

STUDIES OF ARTEFACT FORM IN THE ACHEULEAN

Form studies have been with us for a long time. Isaac (1972) contrasted two approaches (see above), and sketched out a third – raw materials. This has now become very prominent. Some workers concentrate only on raw material and function. Yet the ultra-functional point of view has not led to a single solution, but rather contrasting interpretations of biface evidence.

Thus, in Britain, it has been argued that a major objective is to maximise length of cutting edge, making the ideal form of a biface an ovate (Ashton & McNabb 1994), and that more triangular forms are only adopted where raw material choice forces this (White 1995; Pitts & Roberts 1997).

In East Africa, Jones (1995) is inclined to believe that an ovate shape is the natural outcome of biface manufacture and use, but a curved edge is nevertheless seen as a disadvantage, since it offers only a short length of edge to be used at one time. Better is the long and generally straight edge available on a more triangular tool. But in Africa this shape is not the product of a poor raw material: it requires careful selection and shaping, usually of a fine-grained lava, as in specimens from La Kamoa (Cahen 1975, fig. 3), Kapthurin, or Chesowanja (Harris & Gowlett 1980).

The fixation of flint knappers is to find suitable nodules, because they are not dealing with bedrock. For African knappers, once a source was found, excellent lava or quartzite was plentiful, reliable and locally *cheap*. It is

just because preoccupations were different that inter-comparison is valuable.

MIDDLE PLEISTOCENE ECONOMY

In the matter of economy there has long been a creative tension between two ideas:

1) our very little evidence for human interventionism – active hunting – has to be taken as indicating that early hominids had very limited capabilities for exploiting environments, especially marginal ones
2) that if early humans made their way in temperate conditions at all, such abilities must have been present.

The scavenging debate in East Africa has provided one model. Carcases of large mammals are known, but in the absence of direct evidence for hunting, scavenging is taken to be a safer bet.

For long, Europe yielded little firmer evidence. Gamble's jest of the 'snow probe' summarised this intellectual discomfiture (Gamble 1986).

The picture has changed. The Schöningen spears (Thieme 1996) throw the Clacton and Lehringen specimens into perspective, forming a new pattern, in which the butchery evidence of Boxgrove and Aridos fits suggestively (Villa 1990; Pitts & Roberts 1997). In Africa, the butchery evidence from Olorgesailie may be slight, and has remained tendentious, but it is balanced by a strengthening of the evidence from Olduvai (Oliver 1994; Hill 1983), plus a series of single carcase/stone tool assemblage associations from other sites.

Together, this evidence allows a decisive shift from the idea of 'marginal scavengers' that seemed the safest proposition to many workers. Even so, there are not many sites in our pattern, and not all these are well-dated. Did humans in the three continents of Africa, Asia and Europe share similar capabilities of hunting and gathering at the beginning of the Middle Pleistocene 800 kya? If so, were these honed differently in different environments over hundreds of thousands of years?

It is tempting to shy from these questions, and to concentrate on the regional issues but artefact diversity is, I would argue, the only approach to some of the answers. We must, however, break down barriers of viewpoint as Gamble (1998) urges – and as has been the practice of past Palaeolithic generations. If we occasionally forget that one continent is relevant to another, the very evidence for the surge of modern humans around the globe should be sufficient reminder that it all joins up.

ACKNOWLEDGMENT

I am grateful to John Wymer for extending my knowledge and experience of the Palaeolithic on various occasions over the years; and especially for his indomitable good cheer in promoting our subject far and wide.

REFERENCES

Andresen, S. A., Bell, D. A., Hallos, J., Pumphrey, T. R. J. & Gowlett, J. A. J. 1997. Approaches to the analysis of evidence from the Acheulean site of Beeches Pit, Suffolk, England. In A. Sinclair, E. Slater, & J. Gowlett, (eds), 389–94. *Archaeological Sciences 1995*. Oxford: Oxbow Monographs No. 64.

Ashton, N. & McNabb, J. 1994. Bifaces in perspective. In: N.Ashton & A. David (eds), *Stories in Stone*, 182–191. London: Lithic Studies Society Occasional Paper 4.

Ashton, N.M.,Bowen, D.Q., Holman, J.A., Hunt, C.O., Irving, B.G., Kemp, R.A., Lewis, S.G., McNabb, J., Parfitt, S. & Seddon, M.B. 1994. Excavations at the Lower Palaeolithic site at East Farm, Barnham, Suffolk, 1989–92. *Journal of the Geological Society of London* 151, 599–605.

Bar-Yosef, O. & Goren-Inbar, N. 1993. *The Lithic Assemblages of the Site of Ubeidiya, Jordan Valley*. Jerusalem: Qedem 34.

Belfer-Cohen, A. & Goren-Inbar, N. 1994. Cognition and communication in the Levantine Lower Palaeolithic. *World Archaeology* 26(2), 144–57.

Bilsborough, A. 1992. *Human Evolution*. London: Blackie.

Binford, L.R. 1972. Contemporary model building: paradigms and the current state of palaeolitriic research. In D. L. Clarke (ed.) *Models in Archaeology*. 109–66. London: Methuen.

Binford, L.R. 1989. Isolating the transition to cultural adaptations: an organizational approach. In E. Trinkaus (ed.) *The Emergence of Modern Humans: Biocultural Adaptations in the later Pleistocene*. 18–41. Cambridge: Cambridge University Press.

Bishop, W.W. & Clark, J.D. (eds) 1967. *Background to Evolution in Africa*. Chicago: University of Chicago Press.

Bosinski, G. 1982. The transition Lower/Middle Palaeolithic in northwestern Germany. In A. Ronen (ed.) *The Transition from Lower to Middle Palaeolithic and the Origin of Modern Man. BAR International Series* 151, 165–75.

Bräuer, G. 1989. The evolution of modern humans: a comparison of the African and non-African evidence. In P. A. Mellars & C. B. Stringer (eds), *The Human Revolution*. 123–54. Edinburgh: Edinburgh University Press.

Breuil, H. 1930. Premières impressions de voyage sur la préhistoire Sud-Africaine. *L'Anthropologie* 40, 209–23.

Cahen, D. 1975. *Le Site Archéologique de la Kamoa (Région du Shaba, République du Zatre) de l'Age de la Pierre à l'Age du Fer*. Musée Royal de l'Afrique Centrale, Tervuren, Belgium. Annales. Série in 8ème Sciences Humaines 84.

Chen, Tiemei & Zhang, Yinyun 1991. Palaeolithic chronology and the possible coexistence of *Homo erectus* and *Homo sapiens* in China. *World Archaeology* 23(2), 147–54.

Chen, T., Quan, Y. & En, W. 1994. Antiquity of *Homo sapiens* in China. *Nature* 368, 55–6.

Clark, J.D. & Haynes, C.V. 1970. An elephant butchery site at Mwanganda's village, Karonga, Malawi, and its relevance for Palaeolithic archaeology. *World Archaeology* 1(3), 390–411.

Clark, G.A. 1989. Alternative models of Pleistocene biocultural evolution: a response to Foley. *Antiquity* 63, 153–62.

Crompton, R.H. & Gowlett, J.A.J. 1997. The Acheulean and the Sahara: allometric comparisons between North and East African sites. In A. Sinclair, E. Slater, & J. Gowlett, (eds),*Archaeological Sciences 1995*. Oxford: Oxbow Monographs No. 64.

Deacon, T. 1997. *The Symbolic Species: the Co-Evolution of Language and the Human Brain*. London: Allen Lane.

Dunbar, R. 1996.*Grooming, Gossip and the Evolution of Language*. London: Faber and Faber.

Evernden, J.F. & Curtis, G.H. 1965: Potassium-argon dating of late Cenozoic rocks in East Africa and Italy. *Current Anthropology* 6, 343–85.

Foley, R. 1987. Hominid species and stone-tool asemblages: how are they related? *Antiquity* 61, 380–92.

Foley, R. 1996. Measuring cognition in extinct hominids. In P. A. Mellars & K. Gibson (eds), *Modelling the Early Human Mind*, 57–65. Cambridge: McDonald Institute.

Gamble, C. S. 1986. *The Palaeolithic Settlement of Europe*. Cambridge: Cambridge University Press.

Gamble, C. 1998. Palaeolithic society and the release from proximity: a network approach to intimate relations. *World Archaeology* 29(3), 426–49.

Gowlett, J. A. J. 1997. Why the muddle in the middle matters: the language of comparative and direct in human evolution. In C. M. Barton & G. A. Clark (eds*), Darwin revisited: Evolutionary theory in archaeological explanation.* 49–65. Arizona: UAP/AAAS.

Gowlett, J. A. J. & Crompton, R. H. 1994. Kariandusi: Acheulean morphology and the question of allometry. *African Archaeological Review* 12, 1–40.

Gowlett, J. A. J., Harris, J. W. K., Walton, D. & Wood, B. A. 1981. Early archaeological sites, hominid remains and traces of fire from Chesowanja, Kenya. *Nature* 294, 125–9.

Harris, J.W.K. 1983. Cultural beginnings: Plio-Pleistocene archaeological occurrences from the Afar, Ethiopia. *African Archaeological Review* 1, 3–31.

Harris, J. W. K. & Gowlett, J. A. J. 1980. Evidence of early stone industries at Chesowanja, Kenya. In R. E. Leakey & B. A. Ogot (eds), *Proceedings of the 8th Panafrican Congress of Prehistory and Quaternary Studies, Nairobi, 1977*. 208–12. Nairobi: TILLMIAP.

Hill, A. 1983. Hippopotamus butchery by *Homo erectus* at Olduvai. *Journal of Archaeological Science* 10, 135–7.

Isaac, G. Ll. 1969. Studies of early culture in East Africa. *World Archaeology* 1(1),1–28.

Isaac, G. Ll . 1972. Early phases of human behaviour: models in Lower Palaeolithic archaeology. In: Clarke, D.L. (ed.), *Models in Archaeology*. 167–99. London: Methuen.

Isaac, G. Ll. 1977. *Olorgesailie: Archaeological Studies of a Middle Pleistocene Lake Bason in Kenya*. Chicago & London: University of Chicago Press.

Isaac, G. Ll. & Curtis, G. H. 1974. Age of Early Acheulian industries from the Peninj Group, Tanzania. *Nature* 249, 624–7.

Jones, P.R. 1995. Results of experimental work in relation to the stone industries of Olduvai Gorge. In M. D. Leakey & D. A. Roe (eds), *Olduvai Gorge, Vol. 5*. Cambridge: Cambridge University Press.

Kibunjia, M. 1994. Pliocene archaeological occurrences in the Lake Turkana Basin. *Journal of Human Evolution* 27, 159–71.

Krings, M., Stone, A., Schmitz, R.W., Krainitzki, H., Stoneking, M. & Pääbo, S. 1997. Neandertal DNA sequences and the origin of modern humans. *Cell* 90, 19–30.

Leakey, M. D. 1971. *Olduvai Gorge. Vol.III: Excavations in Beds I and II, 1960–1963*. Cambridge: Cambridge University Press.

McNabb, J. 1996. More from the cutting edge: bifaces from the Clactonian. *Antiquity* 70, 428–36.

McNabb, J. & Ashton, N. 1995. Thoughtful flakers. *Cambridge Archaeological Journal* 5, 289–301.

Mithen, S. 1994. Technology and society during the Middle Pleistocene. *Cambridge Archaeological Journal* 4, 3–33.

Mithen, S. 1996. Social learning and cultural tradition: interpreting early Palaeolithic technology. In J. Steele & S. Shennan (eds), *The Archaeology of Human Ancestry*, 207–29. London: Routledge.

Movius, H. 1949. The Lower Palaeolithic cultures of southern and eastern Asia. *Transactions of the American Philosophical Society* (NS) 38 (4) 329–420.

Oliver, J.S. 1994. Estimates of hominid and carnivore involvement in the FLK Zinjanthropus fossil assemblage: some socioecological implications. *Journal of Human Evolution* 27, 267–94.

Peters, C.R. & Blumenschine, R.J. 1995. Landscape perspectives on possible landuse patterns for Early Pleistocene hominids in the Olduvai Basin, Tanzania. *Journal of Human Evolution* 29, 321–62.

Pitts, M. & Roberts, M. 1997. *Fairweather Eden*. London: Century Books.

Potts, R. 1994. Variables versus models of early Pleistocene hominid land use. *Journal of Human Evolution* 27, 7–24.

Raynal, J.-P., Magoga, L., Sbihi-Alaoui, F.-Z. & Geraads, D. 1995. The earliest occupation of Atlantic Morocco: the Casablanca evidence. In W. Roebroeks & T. van Kolfschoten (eds), *The Earliest Occupation of Europe: Proceedings of the European Science Foundation Workshop at Tautavel (France), 1993. Analecta Praehistorica Leidensia 27*. Leiden: University of Leiden, 255–62.

Rightmire, G. P. 1990. *The Evolution of* Homo erectus. Cambridge: Cambridge University Press.

Rightmire, G. P. 1996. The human cranium from Bodo, Ethiopia: evidence for speciation in the Middle Pleistocene? *Journal of Human Evolution* 31, 21–39.

Roche, H. 1980. *Premiers Outils Taillés d'Afrique*. Paris: Société d'Ethnographie.

Roebroeks, W. & van Kolfschoten, T. (eds) 1995. *The Earliest Occupation of Europe: Proceedings of the European Science Foundation Workshop at Tautavel (France), 1993. Analecta Praehistorica Leidensia 27*. Leiden: University of Leiden.

Ronen, A. 1991. The Yiron-Gravel lithic assemblage: artefacts older than 2.4 My in Israel. *Archäologisches Korrespondenzblatt* 21, 159–64.

Sackett, J. R. 1982. Approaches to style in lithic archaeology. *Journal of Anthropological Archaeology* 1, 59–122.

Schick, K. & Zhuan, D. 1993. Early Paleolithic of China and eastern Asia. In J.D. Fleagle (ed.), *Evolutionary Anthropology*. Wiley-Liss 2(1), 22–35.

Steele, J. 1994. Communication networks and dispersal patterns in human evolution: a simple simulation model. *World Archaeology* 26(2), 126–43.

Steele, J. 1996. On predicting hominid group sizes. In J. Steele & S. Shennan (eds), *The Archaeology of Human Ancestry*. 230–52. London: Routledge.

Stern, N. 1994. The implications of time-averaging for reconstructing the land-use patterns of early tool-using hominids. *Journal of Human Evolution* 27, 89–105.

Stringer, C. B. 1981. The dating of European Middle Pleistocene hominids and the existence of *Homo erectus* in Europe. *Anthropologie (Brno)* 19, 3–14.

Stringer, C. B. 1992. Replacement, continuity and the origin of *Homo sapiens*. In G. Brauer & F. H. Smith (eds), *Continuity or Replacement*. 9–24. Rotterdam: Balkema.

Swisher, G.C., Curtis, G.H., Jacob, T., Getty, A.G., Suprijo, A. & Widiasmoro?. 1994. Age of the earliest known hominids in Java, Indonesia. *Science* 263, 1118–21.

Tattersall, I. 1986. Species recognition in human palaeontology. *Journal of Human Evolution* 15, 165–75.

Thieme, H. 1996. Altpaläolithische Wurfspeere aus Schöningen, Niedersachsen – ein Vorbericht. *Archäologisches Korrespondenzblatt* 26 (4), 377–93.

Tuffreau, A., Lamotte, A. & Marcy, J.-L. 1997. Land-use and site function in Acheulean complexes of the Somme Valley. *World Archaeology* 29(2), 225–241.

Villa, P. 1990. Torralba and Aridos: elephant exploitation in Middle Pleistocene Spain. *Journal of Human Evolution* 19, 299–309.

Wanpo, H., Ciochon, R., Yumin, G., Larick, R., Qiren, F., Schwarcz, H., Yonge, C., de Vos, J. & Rick, W. 1995. Early *Homo* and associated artefacts from Asia. *Nature* 378, 275–8.

White, M. J. 1995. Raw materials and biface variability in southern Britain: a preliminary examination. *Lithics* 15, 1–20.

Wood, B. A. 1991. *Koobi Fora Research Project, Vol. 4: Hominid Cranial Remains*. Oxford: Clarendon Press.

Wood, B. A. 1992. Origin and evolution of the genus *Homo*. *Nature* 355, 783–90.

Wobst, H. M. 1974. Boundary conditions for Palaeolithic social systems: a simulation approach. *American Antiquity* 39, 147–78.

Wrangham R. & Peterson, D. 1996. *The Demonic Males*. New York.

Wynn, T. & Tierson, F. 1990. Regional comparison of the shapes of later Acheulean handaxes. *American Anthropologist* 92, 73–84.

10. An Intuitive Sense ...

Nick Ashton and Phil Dean

After the successful completion of excavations at Hoxne in 1978, John Wymer, with a small team, undertook a two week trial excavation in July 1979 at the Lower Palaeolithic site of Barnham St Gregory, some 20 miles to the west (TL 809804). Previous work by Paterson (1937) in the early 1930s had put Barnham on the map, being only the second location (Swanscombe being the other) where Clactonian industries apparently lay beneath an Acheulian handaxe assemblage. The intentions of Wymer's fieldwork are not spelt out, but doubtless included study of the relationship between these two principal components of the British Lower Palaeolithic.

The two weeks fieldwork were dedicated to cutting a geological section and the detailed excavation of the archaeology on and within the gravel at the base. The location of the trench was thought to be roughly in the area of Paterson's excavation, but one also suspects that Wymer displayed, yet again, an intuitive sense of what was awaiting him in the ground.

Although the presence of an Acheulian industry was not established, it soon became apparent that a scatter of flint within the yellow silty sand on top of the gravel was of equal interest. As the large yellow-stained flakes in mint condition were excavated, refits were soon found. Eventually, 13 flakes in all were rejoined to a core, the whole forming one half of a large 'cannon-shot' nodule. The remainder of this paper describes these refits and the technology that they illustrate.

THE REFITTING GROUP

The group consists of 16 pieces, namely one core and 14 flakes (one broken in two, and one added since 1979). The flint was originally a large nodule, severely battered on the outside, and at some point had been split into two, probably naturally. The nodule was almost certainly obtained from the gravel, a lag at the edge of a slow-flowing river. The knapping consisted of one sequence of alternate platform flaking, whereby the first removal formed the platform for

the second set of removals, themselves forming the platform for a further removal in the original direction. This alternation between two directions of flaking continued so that the flaking migrated around part of the ridge created by the split in the nodule (Fig. 10.1a–d).

The sequence in detail consists initially of one missing flake that was removed in direction A, followed by three existing flakes and one missing flake in direction B (Wymer # 82 [+ 3-part of 82], 10, and 17). This was followed by a sequence of five existing and two missing flakes in direction A, removed from the platform created by the scar of flake 17 (Wymer # 6, 5, 7, missing, 11, 26, and missing). The core was turned and two missing flakes and one existing flake were removed in direction B (Wymer # 1). This was followed by a missing flake in direction A, flake 88 in direction B, and four existing and two missing in direction A (missing, Wymer # 8, 81, 9, missing, and 30).

The spatial distribution of the scatter suggests that there has been little movement since knapping, having been covered quickly by the yellow silty sand. The absence of at least eight flakes from the sequence deserves further attention. Although these might have been located in the areas adjacent to the Wymer trench, later excavation showed this not to be the case. None of the existing flakes show any evidence of retouch or use, but it is entirely plausible that at least some of the missing flakes were taken from the immediate area for use elsewhere. The final flake to be removed is particularly intriguing. This would have measured 12cm in length with two good cutting edges on the side. Unfortunately we can only speculate.

The rarity of refitting groups from the Lower Palaeolithic cannot be overemphasised, there being only four other sites with any quantity of refitting. It is also worth stating that this group from Barnham still stands as the most complete sequence of refitting flakes and a core from this period anywhere in Britain.

However, the value of refitting should not be measured by superlatives, but by the contribution it makes to the study of this period. It is now an unrivalled tool for the

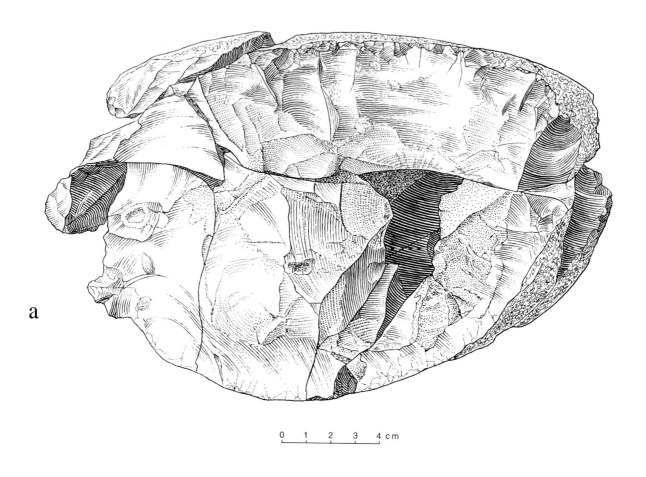

a

0   1   2   3   4 cm

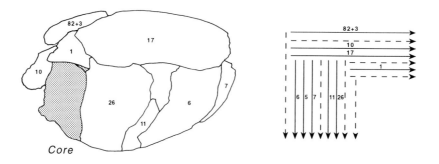

Figure. 10.1a–d. Refitting flakes and core from Group A. The schematic diagrams show the numbering of the flakes and the sequence in which they are removed.

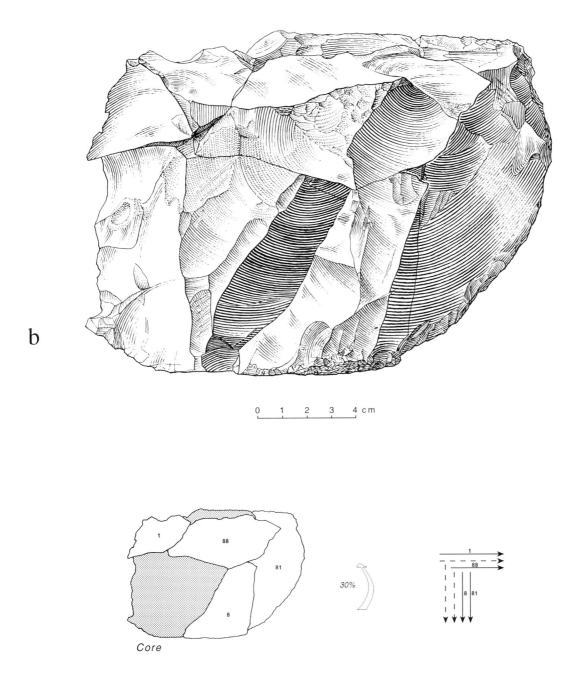

Figure. 10.1a–d. Refitting flakes and core from Group A. The schematic diagrams show the numbering of the flakes and the sequence in which they are removed.

c

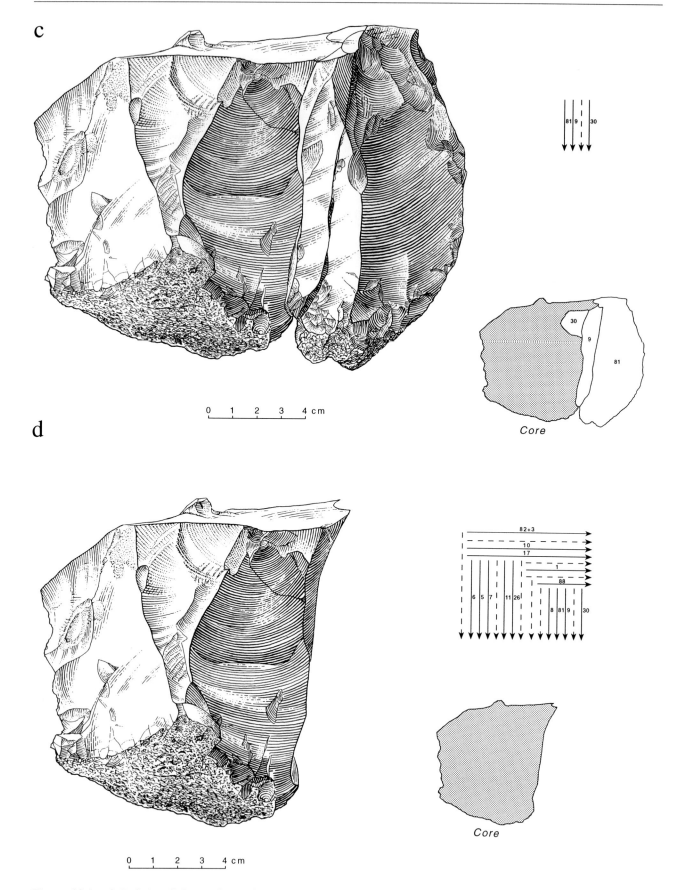

d

Figure 10.1a–d. Refitting flakes and core from Group A. The schematic diagrams show the numbering of the flakes and the sequence in which they are removed.

study of not only technology, but also of the post-depositional movement of artefacts. In circumstances where this can be demonstrated to have had minimal effect, the human movement of flint and the behaviour this reflects can be studied, now often described as high resolution archaeology (Gowlett 1997). At Barnham this amounts to the reconstruction of ten minutes of somebody's time, spent at the edge of a river, over some 400 kya. As such, it is a rare reflection of the individual we so commonly ignore (Gamble, this volume).

THE CONCLUSION

Due to other work committments no further excavation was undertaken by Wymer at Barnham. Details of the fieldwork were published (Wymer 1985), but it was not until March 1989 that I first saw the refitting group. There was only one way forward; with the blessing and unstinting support of John, fieldwork was started in the summer of that year and continued seasonally until 1994 (Ashton *et al.* 1994a; 1994b; in press). It was only John's initial fieldwork, his timely discovery of the refitting group, and continual enthusiasm, that ensured the success of the subsequent project.

REFERENCES

Ashton, N.M, Bowen, D.Q., Holman, J.A., Hunt, C.O., Irving, B.G., Kemp, R.A., Lewis, S.G., McNabb, J. Parfitt, S. & Seddon, M.B. 1994. Excavations at the Lower Palaeolithic site at East Farm, Barnham, Suffolk, 1989–92. *Journal of the Geological Society, London* 151, 599–605.

Ashton, N.M., Lewis, S.G. & Parfitt, S.A. (eds) in press.*Excavations at Barnham, 1989–94*. London: British Museum Occasional Paper No 125.

Ashton, N.M., McNabb, J., Irving, B.G., Lewis, S.G. and Parfitt, S. 1994. Contemporaneity of Clactonian and Acheulian flint industries at Barnham, Suffolk. *Antiquity* 68, 585–9.

Gowlett, J.A.J. 1997. High definition archaeology: ideas and evaluation. *World Archaeology* 29(2), 152–171.

Paterson, T.T. 1937. Studies on the Palaeolithic succession in England No 1, the Barnham sequence. *Proceedings of the Prehistoric Society* 3(1), 87–135.

Wymer, J.J. 1985. *Palaeolithic Sites of East Anglia*. Norwich: Geo Books.

11. An Interim Report of an Archaeological Watching Brief on Palaeolithic Deposits at Dunbridge, Hants

P. A. Harding

ABSTRACT

Gravel extraction at the prolific Palaeolithic site at Dunbridge, Hampshire has been the subject of a regular archaeological and geological watching brief which seeks to place these deposits in their correct regional context. The work has shown that the fluvial gravels, which incorporate bleached cryoturbated material in the upper parts, do not contain stratified industries as was formerly thought possible. Additional handaxes have been recovered, including one of probable Middle Palaeolithic date and a Levallois core, which suggest that the deposits probably correlate with Terraces 4 or 5 of the River Test at Romsey. The report concludes that a watching brief can provide a suitable response to gravel extraction of this sort.

INTRODUCTION

In 1987 Halls Aggregates (South Coast Limited) applied for planning permission to extract hoggin from land adjacent to the former gravel pits at Kimbridge Farm, Dunbridge, 5km north of Romsey, Hampshire, in the Test Valley. These pits, now a Site of Special Scientific Interest, produced the largest number of Palaeolithic handaxes known from Hampshire in the early 20th century. The published accounts of the stratigraphy (Dale 1912; 1918; White 1912) had described an upper 'white gravel' in which mint condition implements were present and a lower heavily stained gravel with rolled handaxes. This apparent superimposition of stratified industries in gravel deposits is rare and of great significance. The survival of implements in mint condition was confirmed by the discovery of a pointed handaxe in the talus during section cleaning by the Nature Conservancy Council as part of the Geological Conservation Review in 1986 (Bridgland & Harding 1987). This section, one of three examined in the old pits, was located *c*. 50m west of the application site.

The planning application coincided with a period of increased pressure by central Government on counties to meet demands for aggregates nationally, including gravels, as reserves became exhausted. Concurrently planning authorities were required to consider the preservation of valuable archaeological remains under PPG16 (Department of the Environment 1990). Palaeolithic sites are particularly at risk in such deposits and the Hampshire County Archaeological Officer recommended, in view of the apparent significance of the site, that the application be refused.

The Dunbridge planning inquiry was lengthy and the application was eventually resolved at Government level. A transect of machined test pits was dug to evaluate the deposits as a means of obtaining additional information on the potential of the site which could be used to determine the outcome of the application. The results, supplemented by the available borehole data, confirmed that the gravels were fluvial in origin and indicated that a lower, previously unrecorded, terrace lay to the east. A small number of implements was recovered which were all derived. Concern still remained amongst archaeologists for the future of the site and in view of the limited nature of the evaluation a Section 52 agreement was signed allowing a watching brief for recording the geological deposits and searching for additional implements to be undertaken.

The Southern Rivers Project was subsequently commissioned by English Heritage to provide an accurate database for future management of valuable Palaeolithic deposits. Its initial report (Wessex Archaeology 1993), which included the site at Dunbridge, reiterated the aims of the watching brief at Dunbridge as the need to place the deposits 'in their correct Quaternary context' (*ibid.* 92), particularly with relation to the gravels mapped by the BGS at Romsey. It also stressed the need to resolve the possibility that some implements were stratified, a question which remained unanswered following the evaluation.

THE WATCHING BRIEF

The extraction area (SU 321255) slopes for *c.* 19ha south east of the old Dunbridge pits from 47m OD to 36m OD. The original Section 52 agreement allowed for the pit to be monitored for one day a month which was undertaken as two half-day visits. At the time opinion varied as to whether this was sufficient. Quarrying of the Quaternary gravels has slowed since 1996 as Tertiary pebble beds have been exploited by the gravel company. The watching brief has therefore been modified in 1997, with the agreement of Hampshire County Council, to allow for one visit per month until such time as it is thought necessary to resume visits twice a month. Routine visits include the processing plant and the pit. The hoggin at Dunbridge has a clay matrix and artefacts are much easier to identify on the reject heap after material has been washed. This has the disadvantage that implements cannot be provenanced to specific areas of the pit, especially as material is routinely stockpiled, often for long periods of time, before it is washed.

Periodically the pit face is planned (Fig. 11.1) and the face profile drawn at scale to construct a composite record of the gravel. Areas of extraction are plotted routinely to note progress in the rates of quarrying. All visits are logged in a day book which reveal details of progress at the pit. Large orders for hoggin are noted, if they are known, to record the relocation of large amounts of material for future reference. Fortunately these orders do not destroy artefacts although large numbers are lost in the crusher.

RESULTS

Geology

An initial interim statement of the geological results of the watching brief was published (Bridgland & Harding 1993) after the first year. Sections were cleaned and logged and gravel samples were collected for future lithological analysis.

The survey of 1992 showed that up to 5m of well bedded sand and gravel were present in the north east corner of the

pit and that nowhere was this less than 1m in thickness towards the west. These deposits lay on a surface of Reading Beds at approximately 42 – 44m OD. Two elongated 'deeps' trending north east – south west formed the most notable features across the bedrock. They measured approximately 20 – 25m across and up to 6.5m deep at approximately 38m OD. The uppermost 2m of gravel were heavily contorted by the effects of cryoturbation (frost heaving) which had destroyed all traces of former bedding. Coincidental with this zone many of the individual flint pebbles were patinated and lay in a pale bleached clayey/loamy matrix which had resulted from the translocation of mineral salts in ground water and had given rise to the 'white' gravel described in the earlier reports. This was apparent as a cemented iron/manganese horizon above the ocreous gravel which could be traced across the entire pit. The report concluded that the bedded gravel represented a single terrace formation of the River Test, the 'Belbins Stage' of White (1912, 69) and was the equivalent to that which had produced so many implements in the former pits. It was unable to resolve whether the lower terrace identified by Collcutt in the evaluation represented the 'Mottisfont Stage' of White (1912, 69), which had been quarried by the Kimbridge Pits to the east, or was a previously unrecognised formation.

Subsequent surveys of the section have shown that the composition of the gravel is unaltered although it trends towards the south west along the line of the 'deeps' and thins. Approximately 100m south of the original logged section on the east side the Reading Beds outcrop at the surface (Fig. 11.1). Elsewhere on this side they are covered by a veneer of bleached cryoturbated gravel less than 1m thick which has incorporated the underlying Tertiary sands. The deposits on the west side, which now average only 1.2m thick, lie on a flat clay surface which also appears as lobes in the gravel. The 'deeps' remain as two distinct features 15m wide and 3m deep on the west and 40m wide and 4m deep on the east. They contain the only bedded material visible on the site and remnants of the iron/manganese horizon which is otherwise absent from the section. The bedded gravel included a large sarsen boulder towards the base which was probably rafted in with a block of frozen ice. This thinning of the deposits may indicate that the current extraction is approaching the edge of the terrace. The lower terrace identified in the evaluation has yet to be exposed so that its bench level, location and geology remain unresolved. No slack water deposits suitable for the preservation of environmental material are present on the site.

Archaeology

Since the project began 123 visits have produced 163 artefacts of which only 47 have been found at the pit, mostly as rainwashed pieces on the bund or in talus. The remaining finds have been recovered from the reject heap. No records were made of the freqencies of the first

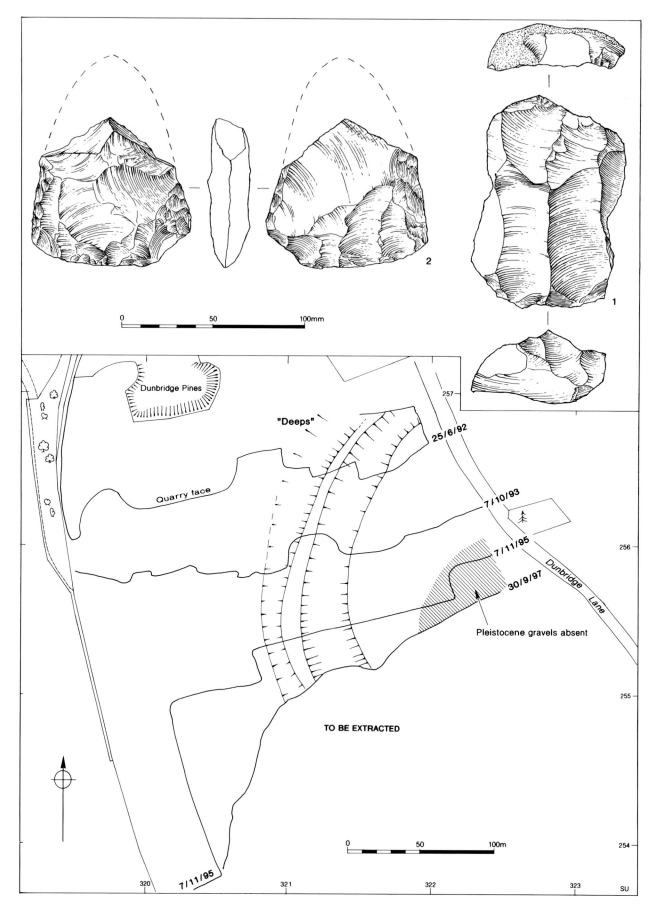

Figure 11.1.1. Levallois blade core: 2. Flat butted cordate handaxe; 3. Site plan showing location of recorded sections

	Handaxes	**Cores**	**Scrapers**	**Flakes**	**Misc.**	**Totals**
May 91-May 93	4	3		11		18
June 93-May 94	6	1	3	21	1	32
June 94-May 95	10	1		23		34
June 95-May 96	16	3		33		52
June 96-May 97	5	3		13	2	23
June 97-July 97	2	1		1		4
Total	**43**	**12**	**3**	**102**	**3**	**163**

Table 11.1: Artefact recovery from Dunbridge watching brief

discoveries. However, since June 1993, 145 artefacts have been recovered from 62 visits. The average recovery of 1.3 pieces per visit before October 1995 has now increased to over 2 pieces per visit. These figures, based on unbiased collection, indicate that considerable numbers of artefacts are still present in the Dunbridge Gravel. Annual interim summaries have been written and the progress of artefact recovery is tabulated above.

As early as July 1993 the number of unretouched flakes exceeded half the total formerly known from the Dunbridge pits (Roe 1968, 96). These are mainly large thick flakes removed during handaxe roughing out which are capable of surviving river transport. Handaxe thinning flakes, although present, are proportionally more scarce.

Roe (1981, 206) classified the Dunbridge handaxes as predominantly pointed forms with a few ovates. The handaxes from the watching brief, however, comprise roughly equal quantities of ovates, none with twisted profiles, and pointed implements. There are also occasional cleavers. Most handaxes are rolled or very rolled and are stained, some heavily, which confirms that they are derived and almost certainly come from the base of the gravels. Isolated pieces show rolling on one side which indicates that they have been exposed to the erosive force of the current and that they themselves have not been moved far. A small number of fresher, lightly stained pieces can be associated with the bleached cryoturbated gravel. The technology varies throughout from those made by crude hard hammer percussion to others which have been finished with a soft hammer. Most of the handaxes are undiagnostic, however the butt of a probable flat butted cordate ('*bout coupé*') (Fig. 11.1.2), which was found on the reject heap by a former plant manager, is chronologically significant. This type of handaxe is generally thought to correlate with Middle Palaeolithic activity and is the second handaxe of this type from Dunbridge (Roe 1981, 257).

Roe (1981, 206) noted the presence of Levallois material within the collection which he associated with the 'white' material from the upper bleached gravel. A Levallois opposed platform blade core (Fig. 11.1.1) has been found during the watching brief which has confirmed the presence of Levallois technology at the site. Both the handaxe fragment and the core are lightly stained and slightly rolled and probably came from within the bleached fluvial gravel. The remaining cores are undiagnostic.

DISCUSSION

The most recent descriptions of the geology (Bridgland & Harding 1987; 1993) were able to correlate the deposits with the earlier work of Dale (1912; 1918) and White (1912) and confirmed that the 'white' gravel was a leached deposit. Continued monitoring of the sections has confirmed that the gravels were all originally of fluvial origin, laid down under cold conditions in a fast flowing stream. The contour of the erosion surface has now become more apparent and has shown that the 'deeps' can be traced across the site to the south. The upper parts of the section, which comprise the 'white' leached gravel, continue to show the effects of modification by periglacial conditions. It is therefore extremely unlikely that *in situ* material remains at the site. Most but not all of the implements are very rolled and it is therefore likely that artefacts of differing periods are present with those of fresher appearance occurring nearer the surface.

No additional implements in mint condition have been found in the present working, although it is indisputable that these pieces were found in the old pits. They clearly represent handaxes which have suffered minimal movement since their abandonment. Isolated examples may have been rafted in with blocks of ice. However, collections of material may indicate occupation which occurred on the surface of the gravel after its deposition or at the least contemporary with it.

Although doubt has been expressed about the reliability of flat butted cordate ('*bout coupé*') handaxes as indicators of Middle Palaeolithic date (Coulson 1986), the associated Levallois core suggests that this date may be appropriate and confirm Roe's (1968; 1981) record of Middle Palaeolithic technology and associated handaxes from the gravels. Both pieces and the '*bout coupé*' in the British Museum are in a fresh condition. None of these pieces can be located precisely to the section. However, the consistency of the condition suggests that they have not moved as far as some of the other artefacts. The fact that they are not in mint condition suggests that they have been incorporated in the gravel rather than lying on the surface. It has been argued (Bridgland 1996, 29) that Levallois technology does not appear in the Thames Valley, where the terrace sequence is better understood, before OIS 8.

Although the detail of the site geology is now much clearer, some outstanding questions remain to be resolved, especially as the Quaternary deposits are thinning to the south. It is also not yet possible to relate the deposits and the material on a regional basis. This may be made easier when the lower terrace identified during the evaluation has been sampled, recorded and placed in its correct geological context. The British Geological Survey (Edwards *et al.* 1987) mapped nine terraces of the Test as far as the northern side of Romsey. This survey did not, however, extend as far as Dunbridge where the deposits have been mapped only as Valley Gravel and Sand (BGS 1975 Sheet 299). Estimates for the Dunbridge gravels generally agree that they probably correlate to Terrace 5 or 6 of the Test (Wessex Archaeology 1993, 88; Wymer 1996, 17) although no handaxes have been recorded from Terrace 6 (Wymer 1996, 17). However, it has also been suggested (Wessex Archaeology 1993, 92) that the Dunbridge gravels may equate with gravels of Terrace 4 in Romsey which produced large collections of handaxes. These gravels include Belbin's Pit which also included Levallois material.

The watching brief has produced constructive results with the mutual cooperation of the gravel company and the archaeologist. The final results may indicate whether the evaluation strategy provided sufficiently detailed data which was sufficient to interpret the site geology and its archaeology. The conclusions should suggest whether a more comprehensive survey might be more appropriate in the future. It is possible that more preliminary borehole data could be used although this should be collected by an engineer in collaboration with a Quaternary specialist.

This watching brief represents a formalisation of a strategy which has served Palaeolithic archaeology since the last century when enthusiastic antiquarians, such as Worthington Smith at Caddington and Treacher in the Thames Valley, visited and studied with the collaboration of the gravel diggers. It is essential that the terms of the watching brief are flexible so that visits can be modified to suit developments at the pit. Visits have been trimmed at Dunbridge to avoid unnecessary duplication, although in future they may be restored or increased to match developments. The work suggests that a watching brief provides an adequate, constructive response for retrieving data from sites of this type.

ACKNOWLEDGEMENTS

Thanks are extended to Halls Aggregates (South Coast Ltd.) for their cooperation throughout the watching brief especially to Rosemary Box (Estate Manager), Graham Osman (Plant Manager) and to the staff at the pit and processing plant. Acknowledgement is also due to David Hopkins (Hampshire County Council) for his continuing interest in the project.

REFERENCES

Bridgland, D.R. 1996. Quaternary river terrace deposits as a framework for the Lower Palaeolithic record. In C. Gamble & A.J. Lawson (eds), *The English Palaeolithic Reviewed*, 24–39. Salisbury: Trust For Wessex Archaeology.

Bridgland, D.R. & Harding, P.A. 1987. Palaeolithic sites in tributary valleys of the Solent River. In K.E. Barber (ed.), *Wessex and the Isle of Wight. Field Guide*, 45–57. Southampton: Quaternary Research Association.

Bridgland, D.R. & Harding P.A. 1993. Preliminary observations at the Kimbridge Farm Quarry, Dunbridge Hampshire: early results of a watching brief. *Quaternary Newsletter* 69, 1–9.

Coulson, S.D. 1986. The *bout coupé* handaxe as a typological mistake. In S.N. Collcutt (ed.), *The Palaeolithic of Britain and Its Nearest Neighbours: Recent Trends*, 53–54. Sheffield: Department of Archaeology & Prehistory, University of Sheffield.

Dale, W. 1912. On the implement-bearing gravel-beds of the lower valley of the Test. *Proceedings of the Society of Antiquaries, London*, Series 2, 24, 108–16.

Dale, W. 1918. Report as local secretary for Hampshire. *Proceedings of the Society of Antiquaries, London*, Series 2, 30, 20–32.

Department of the Environment, 1990. *Planning Policy Guidance: Archaeology and Planning,* (PPG 16). London: Department of the Environment.

Edwards, R.A. *et al.* 1987. *Applied Geological Mapping: Southampton area*. Research Report British Geological Survey No. IC50/87/2, Vol. 1.

Roe, D.A. 1968. *A Gazetteer of the British Lower and Middle Palaeolithic Sites*. London: Council for British Archaeology Research Report 8.

Roe, D.A. 1981. *The Lower and Middle Palaeolithic Periods in Britain*. London, Boston & Henley: Routledge and Kegan Paul.

Wessex Archaeology. 1993. *The Southern Rivers Palaeolithic Project Report No. 1 1991–1992. The Upper Thames Valley, the Kennet Valley and the Solent Drainage System*. Salisbury: Trust For Wessex Archaeology.

White, H.J.O. 1912. *The Geology of the Country around Winchester and Stockbridge*. Memoir of The Geological Survey.

Wymer, J.J. 1996. The English Rivers Palaeolithic Survey. In C.Gamble & A.J.Lawson (eds), *The English Palaeolithic Reviewed*. 7–23. Salisbury: Trust For Wessex Archaeology.

12. Observations on the Artefacts from the Breccia at Kent's Cavern

Jill Cook and Roger Jacobi

INTRODUCTION

During excavations directed by William Pengelly between 1868 and 1880, at least 103 flint and chert implements were recovered from recorded locations in the basal Breccia in Kent's Cavern, Devon (NGR SX 934641). These artefacts included handaxes which were then described as Acheulean and Chellean types (Evans 1897, 495) in recognition of their similarity to implements found in the Somme Valley. This established their relevance in the contemporary debate on the extent of human antiquity and, because they were stratified below remains of the lesser scimitar cat *Homotherium* (formerly *Machairodus*) *latidens*, their interest in this connection has not diminished. However, although cited in discussions on the age and character of the earliest artefacts in Britain (Campbell & Sampson 1971, 21–23; Roberts *et al.* 1995, 174–5; Roe 1981, 99–103; Wymer 1988, 85), the Breccia artefacts have never been the subject of analysis in their own right. To correct this and offer a preliminary re-evaluation of the material seemed an appropriate tribute to John Wymer whose vast knowledge of the Lower Palaeolithic, coupled with open-minded enthusiasm, has contributed so much to the subject.

THE BRECCIA ARTEFACTS

As a preliminary stage to this research, references to artefacts found in the Breccia were abstracted from Pengelly's reports to the British Association for the Advancement of Science. Eighty-three artefacts are mentioned in these publications. Forty-five of these have been found and examined for this paper with an additional 10 unpublished specimens which are numbered by Pengelly and referred to in his manuscript journals. Efforts to locate the remaining published and any further unpublished specimens are continuing so that the inventory (Table 12.1) can be completed in a future publication. The 55 pieces considered here form the largest sample considered to date (Campbell & Sampson 1971, 21; Lowe 1916, 81; Rogers 1956, 91–92; Roe 1968, 45; 1981, 97–103) and probably consists of about 50% of the material recovered. Table 12.1 gives details of the provenance, context and associations of the objects so far located. These have been abstracted from Pengelly's publications and manuscript journals. In three instances (6375, 6396 and 1/6411) the provenances, but not the context, given in Pengelly's journal differ from those he published. In these cases, the published account has been taken as correct. All of the labels on the objects have also been examined under an ultra-violet light source. This has shown up errors of attribution originating from curatorial work by E.H. Rogers in the 1950s and unfortunately perpetuated by Campbell and Sampson (1971). These have been noted in Table 12.1 with the published and archival references to each piece, as well as their present whereabouts and museum registration numbers.

DISTRIBUTION

As may be seen from Table 12.1, the Breccia artefacts were recovered from twelve widely separated areas throughout the cave system with a notable absence of finds in the areas behind the present entrances (Fig. 12.1). Furthermore, Pengelly's co-ordinates (Fig. 12.2), recently explained by Warren and Rose (1994), suggest that the finds were also dispersed horizontally and vertically through the Breccia. This shows that the artefacts did not occur in a single discrete assemblage. Consideration of their contexts and condition confirms this view and suggests that they probably derive from distinct sources outside the cave.

CONTEXT

The context of every Breccia piece located to date has been checked in Pengelly's published reports and journals (Table

Pengelly no.	Object	Provenance	KC Expl. J.	Year	Series	Deposit	Parallel	Level	Yard	Other material noted	BA Rpt.	Museum	Reg. no.	Previous attribution
6220	Flake	Underhay's	3,1242	1873	50	Breccia	3	2	3R	3 bear teeth, bone frags.	1874, 9	Liverpool	44.27.1208	
2/6221	Flake	Underhay's	3,1242	1873	50	Breccia	3	3	3R	3 bear teeth, flint core	1874, 9	Torquay		
6279	Flake	Underhay's	3,1256	1873	50	Breccia	14	2	2L	4 hyaena teeth, bone frags.	1874, 9	Torquay		
1/6797	Fragment	Labyrinth	3,1439	1876	65	Breccia	34	1	2L	Bones		Liverpool	44.27.1160	
1/6411	Handaxe	Clinnick's Gallery	3,1291	1874	52	Breccia	8	4	2R	Bear tooth, bone frags.	1874, 15	Torquay	A3964	
6427	Flake	Clinnick's Gallery	3,1296	1874	52	Breccia	16	4	2R	Bone frags.	1874, 15	NHM	E87	
6466	Flake	Clinnick's Gallery	3,1314	1874	53	Breccia	16	3	2R			BM	POA 180/6	
7316	Handaxe	Clinnick's Gallery	3,1615	1879	55	Breccia	22	3	1L		1879, 6–7	Torquay	A3963	
7317	Handaxe	Clinnick's Gallery	3,1616	1879	78	Breccia	1	2	2L		1879, 6–7	Torquay	A3965	
7189	Flake	High Chamber	3,1565	1878	51	Breccia	87	3	2R		1878, 6	Torquay		6378, Cave of Inscriptions
7207	Flake	High Chamber	3,1573	1878	51	Breccia	99	4	1L	Bear tooth	1879, 3	Liverpool	44.27.1206	
7220	Flake	High Chamber	3,1581	1878	51	Breccia	108	4	1L		1879, 3	Liverpool	44.27.1194	
7224	Flake	High Chamber	3,1582	1878	51	Breccia	111	4	2L		1879, 3–4	Torquay		6128, Long Arcade
7232	Flake	High Chamber	3,1584	1878	51	Breccia	115	3	1R		1879, 3–4	Torquay		5592, Wolf's Den
7260	Nodule	High Chamber	3,1592	1879	76	Breccia	3	4	1L			Torquay		
6375	Flake	Cave of Inscriptions	3,1278	1874	51	Breccia	13	4	2L		1874, 13	Torquay		
6396	Flake	Cave of Inscriptions	3,1286	1874	51	Breccia	22	1	2R		1874, 13	Liverpool	44.27.1207	
6550	Handaxe	Cave of Inscriptions	3,1356	1875	51	Breccia	36	2	2L		1875, 9	Torquay		6105, Long Arcade
6565	Handaxe	Cave of Inscriptions	3,1363	1875	51	Breccia	47	2	1R		1875, 9–10	BM	POA 180/5	
6581	Flake	Cave of Inscriptions	3,1371	1875	51	Breccia	57	2	3L		1875, 9, 10	Torquay		
7119	Chopper	Undervault	3,1536	1878	73	Cave-earth/Breccia	13	2	2R		1878, 4			
7021	Flake	Bear's Den	3,1491	1877	68	Breccia	25	2	1L			NHM	E135	
7040	Flake	Bear's Den	3,1495	1877	68	Breccia	30	1	4R		1877, 6	Torquay		
7059	Flake	Bear's Den	3,1499	1877	68	Breccia	33	2	1L		1877, 6	Torquay		
3991	Flake	Water Gallery	2,604	1869	11	Breccia	9	3	2R	3 bear teeth, bone frags.	1869,201–2	Torquay		6415, Long Arcade
5226	Flake	North Sally Port	2,675	1870	28	Cave-earth/Breccia	35	4	1R	1 horse tooth, 1 rhino tooth, bone frags.	1870, 26	Torquay		
1465	Flake	Gallery	1,219–20	18	1	Cave-earth/Breccia	79	1	2L			Torquay		
5900	Handaxe	Charcoal Cave	2,1123	1872	45	Breccia	14	3	1R		1872,44	BM	POA 180/2	
5903	Flake	Charcoal Cave	2,1124	1872	45	Breccia	16	2	1R		1872,44	BM	POA 180/1	

Pengelly no.	Object	Provenance	K. C. Expl. J.	Year	Series	Deposit	Parallel	Level	Yard	Other material noted	BA Rpt.	Museum	Reg. no.	Previous attribution
6022	Handaxe	Long Arcade	3,1169	1872	48	Breccia	39	2	2L		1873, 206	Torquay	A3957	
6025	Handaxe	Long Arcade	3,1173	1872	48	Breccia	48	1	1L		1873, 206	Torquay	A3959	
6029	Flake	Long Arcade	3,1174	1872	48	Cave-earth	51	2	1L	Fox tooth		Torquay	A2255	
6081	Handaxe	Long Arcade	3,1191	1873	48	Breccia	80	3	2L		1873, 206	NHM	E124	
6103	Handaxe	Long Arcade	3,1207	1873	48	Breccia	112	4	1L		1873, 206	Torquay	A3960	
6110	Flake	Long Arcade	3,1210	1873	48	Breccia	118	2	1L		1873, 207	BM	POA 180/8	
1/6115	Knapping frag.	Long Arcade	3,1212	1873	48	Breccia	120	1	1R			Torquay	A2468	
6128	Flake	Long Arcade	3,1216	1873	48	Breccia	124	1	2L		1873, 207	Torquay	A2481	
6129	Handaxe	Long Arcade	3,1216	1873	48	Breccia	124	4	2L		1873, 207	BM	POA 180/7	
6139	Core	Long Arcade	3,1218	1873	48	Breccia	127	3	1R		1873, 207	Torquay	A2480	7177, High Chamber
6174	Flake	Long Arcade	3,1231	1873	49	Breccia	1	2	11L	Bear tooth, bones	1873, 207	BM	POA 180/4	
6179	Flake	Long Arcade	3,1232	1873	49	Breccia	2	4	9L			Liverpool	44.27.1168	
6192	Flake	Long Arcade	3,1235	1873	49	Breccia	4	4	9L			Torquay	A2486	6466, Clinnick's Gallery
6204	Core	Long Arcade	3,1238	1873	49	Breccia	7	3	9L	Bone frags.		Torquay	A2472	
6291	Flake	Long Arcade	3,1259	1873	49	Breccia	9	4	1L			Torquay	A2490	
6292	Flake	Long Arcade	3,1259	1873	49	Breccia	9	4	4L			Torquay	A2488	
6324	Handaxe	Long Arcade	3,1266	1873	51	Cave-earth/Breccia	1	2	2R		1874, 5	NHM	E64	
6358	Biface	Long Arcade	3,1274	1874	51	Breccia	8	2	2L		1874, 6	NHM	E67	
6364	Flake	Long Arcade	3,1276	1874	51	Breccia	10	3	2L		1874, 6	Torquay	A2492	
7323	Handaxe	Deeper Excavation	3,1631	1879	48	Breccia	22	8	3L		1880, 66	Torquay	A3962	
2/7324	Flake	Deeper Excavation	3,1633	1880	48	Breccia	39	5	1R		1880, 66	Liverpool	44.27.1203	
7328	Handaxe	Deeper Excavation	3,1637	1880	48	Breccia	70	8	2L		1880, 66–7	BM	POA 180/8	
7333	Core	Deeper Excavation	3,1640	1880	48	Breccia	97	8	2L		1880, 67	BM	POA 180/9	
?	Biface	?										Torquay	A3961	7335, Long Arcade
7339	Handaxe	Deeper Excavation	3,1685	1880	49	Breccia	2	8	4L		1880, 67	BM	POA 180/10	
7340	Core	Deeper Excavation	3,1686	1880	49	Breccia	4	9	7L		1880, 67–8	BM	POA 180/11	

Table 12.1. Artefacts from the Kent's Cavern Breccia. K. C. Expl. J. = Kent's Cavern Exploration Journal, Torquay Museum. The British Association Reports (BA Rpt) are fully referenced in the bibliography under Pengelly.

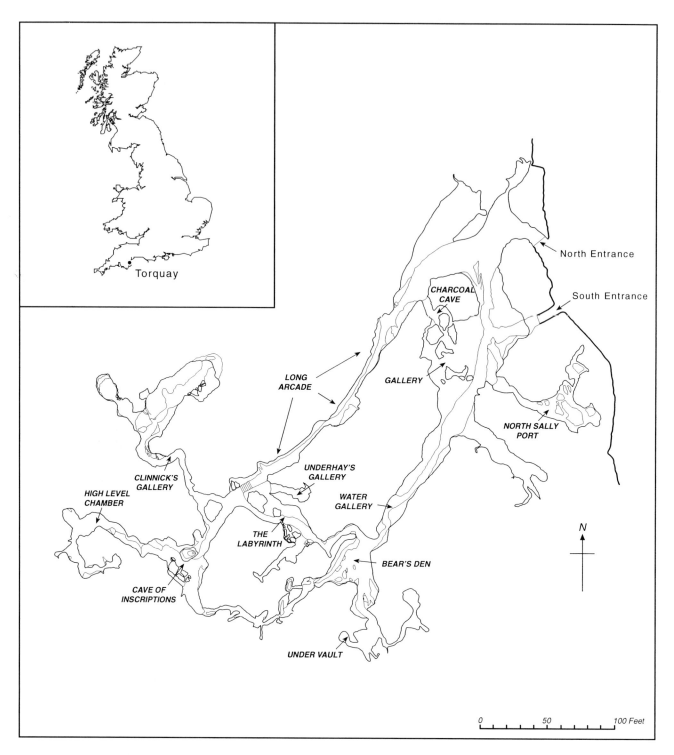

Figure 12.1. Plan of Kent's Cavern cave system.

12.1). This review showed that with the exception of the pieces from the Undervault, the North Sally Port and the Gallery where there was some disturbance of the deposits, all of the finds were recovered from *in situ* Breccia deposits (cf. Roe 1981, 98). Among the finds from the Long Arcade there are two pieces, 6029 and 6324, which have been noted as Breccia/Cave earth. Artefact 6324 was discovered at the junction of the Breccia and Cave-earth at a point where they were not separated by Crystalline Stalagmite (Pengelly 1874, 5). Although its cordiform shape and straight edges might be considered to distinguish it from other Breccia specimens, its altered condition is commensurate with it having come from that context. This latter point also applies to 6029 which Pengelly ascribes to

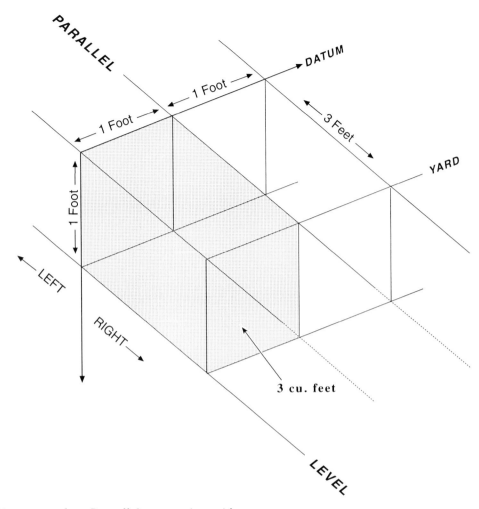

Figure 12.2. Diagram to show Pengelly's excavation grid system.

the Cave-earth in his journal but of which there is no published account. It may be noted, however, that fox remains and flint flakes were found in the area disturbed by MacEnery's earlier excavations (1825–29) where finds from the Cave-earth and the Breccia had become mixed together (Pengelly 1873, 204). One further piece, possibly from the Long Arcade and numbered 7335 in E. H. Rogers' handwriting, was not labelled by Pengelly and, as it does not correspond with either the journal or published (Pengelly 1880, 6) descriptions of this find, its provenance must be regarded as unknown, although its character and condition insinuate that it came from the Breccia.

CONDITION

All of the artefacts found in the Breccia are abraded. The degree of abrasion is probably uniform, although pieces from the Long Arcade, Underhay's Gallery and the North Sally Port appear to be more heavily modified than those from other areas. This impression is due to the profound

alteration of the flint and chert caused by the recrystallisation and dissolution of the interstitial chalcedony which cements a framework of silicified fossils and quartz aggregates (Curry 1963; Fairbairn & Robertson 1972; Dewolf 1977; Shepherd 1972). This process of decomposition produces a chalky appearance and texture which makes the edges and arêtes more susceptible to post-depositional and post-recovery deterioration and abrasion. Campbell and Sampson (1971, 19) suggest that this diagenetic alteration accounts entirely for the abraded appearance of the artefacts and conclude that they had not moved far from where they were abandoned. However, as the flint and chert pieces which have retained hard but patinated surfaces are also abraded it would seem that some transport must be assumed. The mechanical and thermal damage apparent on some of the handaxes, as well as the staining of the flint which was not commented on by Campbell and Sampson (*ibid.*) are also consistent with a history of redeposition.

The staining of the white patinated surfaces of all the artefacts is variable and may suggest that the pieces are derived from different sources. Flint objects from the Long Arcade exhibit a yellow-brown 'ferruginous tint' (Pengelly 1873, 204) quite distinct from the pinkish colour of the Breccia sediments. On some specimens (6204, 6022 and 6192) this is heavy and dark whilst on the remainder it is lighter, more yellow. However, two of the flint pieces (6110 and 7323) from the same area do not have this staining but are discoloured by patches of manganese deposition, whereas the chert specimens show reddish-brown staining taken up from the breccia sediments. The yellow-brown staining also occurs on the pieces found in the Cave of Inscriptions, the High Chamber and the Bear's Den. It does not occur on specimens from other areas which, with the exception of those from Clinnick's Gallery characterised by a heavy coating of manganese (Pengelly 1879, 7), are discoloured from the surrounding reddish-brown sediments. It is also absent from the artefacts found in the later deposits.

Whilst the abrasion and mechanical edge damage present on all the objects indicate that the entire collection was subject to transport, the variation in the staining suggests that some specimens took their colour following deposition in the cave, whereas others were derived from deposits in which they had been stained prior to re-deposition in the cave. The yellow-brown colour is typical of flint implements recovered from alluvial silts and gravels and is absent from the artefacts found in later deposits at Kent's Cavern. It implies that a number of the Breccia finds may be significantly older than the deposit itself, a point also noted by Garrod (1925, 118), Smith (1926, 71) and, more recently by Proctor (1994, 144), but discounted by Campbell and Sampson (1941, 19–20). The variation in the staining might also suggest different sources for the artefacts, a possibility consistent with the distribution of the finds through the cave system and Proctor's evidence (1994, 115–116) that the Breccia was deposited by at least two debris flows from sources outside via high level entrances now blocked.

THE HANDAXES

All of the 15 Breccia handaxes (Table 12.1) are thick forms with maximum breadth: thickness ratios of 1.6 to 2.1. Their shape is variable and appears to relate to the form and volume of the selected cobble of raw material as do the techniques used to manufacture them. These may be distinguished as trihedral and bifacial reduction sequences.

In the collections examined to date, three handaxes can be understood as products of trihedral reduction. Handaxe 7323 from the Long Arcade (Roe 1981, fig 4.4, 4) is made on a slab, the side of which has been reduced to provide an edge extending along most of its length. Part of the adjacent side has also been modified producing a pointed shape with about 50 and 75% of the respective faces covered with cortex. The steep-sided cross-section is irregularly hexagonal and the high-angled zig-zag edge

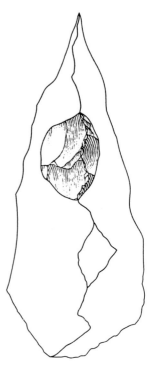

Figure 12.3. Characteristic shaping flake with broad facetted butt such as removed from high-angled edges of minimally flaked handaxe forms.

has been achieved by trifacial flaking with removals being detached from one side of the nodule to provide a striking platform for further detachments from both of its faces. Removals have also been made from the opposite side. The flat cortical butt has also been used as a fourth platform for removals along the long axis of one face. The flaking is not sequential. It has been done with a hard hammer and is restricted to the basic shaping of the piece with no thinning or finishing.

The two other handaxes made in this way are 7316 and 7317 from Clinnick's Gallery. Breccia obscures one side of the former (Roe 1981, fig. 4.4, 2) but it is still possible to see that the removal of flakes from the side of the piece has provided a platform for removals from their proximal and distal ends across both faces. The straight cleaver-like end has been produced by removals across the face rather than the more complex shaping and tranchet finishing found on true bifacial cleaver forms. By contrast, 7317 is a more pointed form on a globular cobble but it has also been produced by removing a series of flakes from one side and then utilising the distal ends of these removals as the platform for removals from the adjacent face whilst the third face has been reduced from the opposite edge. Both of these pieces retain large areas of cortex around their butts. Handaxe 7317 has a high-angled zig-zag edge whereas 7316 is irregular but slightly straighter.

The remaining 13 handaxes come from the Long Arcade, the Cave of Inscriptions and Charcoal Cave (Table 12.1). Although their forms vary, the bifacial technique used to make them is consistent. The variation in shape is determined by the form of the raw material. Whether the finished object is elongated with a broad straight or slightly rounded end, such as 6025, 7328 and 5900, globular with a more pointed tip like 6022, 6550, 6565 and 7339, broad and sub-rectangular as 6081 and 1/6411 or has a tear-drop or amygdaloid shape such as 6103, the knapping method is the same. The form of the raw material determines the finished shape and remains obvious. The cobbles are modified by the knapping rather than being transformed by it. As would be expected, all of the pieces retain some cortex most of which would be impossible to remove using the technique adopted. It involves adjusting the shape of the cobble by the removal of a relatively small number of flakes, less than twenty on most pieces. These are often detached simply from one face then the other, as for example on 5900, 6022 (Roe 1981, fig. 4.4, 3) and 7328. On each of these pieces a series of flakes has been detached around the ends of the cobbles modifying their domed surfaces. Flakes have then been removed across the opposite face from one edge before a series of small removals, usually step terminated, have been struck from the opposite side of this plane or less convex face. Occasionally, as on 6081, a protrusion in the centre of a face might be used as a second platform for the removal of one or two flakes, thereby helping to thin the piece. However, in general, no further thinning or finishing has been applied, but medium to high-angled edges are formed around most of the outline although cortex may be retained fortuitously on the butt (6022, 7328, 3624, 5900, 6559), the faces (6025), or in small patches interrupting the edge (6081). These edges tend to be irregular (Roe 1981, fig. 4.4, 7–9) because the point of impact selected in the process of hard hammer shaping was inset from the margin. In most cases, the edge continues around most (>75%) of the piece. This does not apply to the biface lacking a number which retains cortex around one side and end (*ibid.*, fig. 4.4, 1). Alternate bifacial flaking has been used to thin the opposite side of this globular cobble to an irregular edge in the manner often considered characteristic of a chopping tool. By contrast, the thinner spherical cobble on which 6324 was made has permitted the production of a regular straight edge around most of the piece resulting in a cordiform shape which only retains cortex around its broader end where it would be impossible to remove.

The only handaxe made on a flake is 6129 from the Long Arcade. The flake is a natural one resulting from a thermal fracture. Its plano-convex cross-section and fortuitous pointed shape have been modified by removals all round the upper surface and across the plane face just below the tip. It retains cortex on the apex of the steeply convex surface at the butt end.

THE DEBITAGE

The 30 flakes considered here are too few in number to constitute a significant sample but certain characteristics suggest that they derive from the type of reduction se-

quences used to produce the handaxes described above. They range from 25 to 122mm in size and 12 retain cortex on 50% or more of their dorsal surface areas. The largest flakes, 6292, 6375 and 6364, are preliminary shaping flakes struck to remove a protrusion on the outside of the nodule, a natural hole and a thermally fractured surface. The remainder appear to be handaxe shaping flakes some of which have clearly been detached from bifacial edges (fig. 12.3). These pieces have oblique butts which may be plain as in the case of 6396 or, dihedral or facetted like 6291, 7059, 2/7324 and 3991. Their dorsal surfaces may be cortical (6291), show two or three removals from the same platform (6029) or have a pointed form with a central dorsal arête along which the blow has been directed (6396, 7059). The high-angled, facetted, butt-like edge on 6128 suggests that it was removed from the side of a trihedral form. Some of these flakes have previously been mistaken for Mousterian or Levallois tools (Campbell & Sampson 1981, 19; Rogers 1956, 77).

None of the flakes show deliberate retouch. Artefacts 7059 and 7232 have what might be identified as small single and retouched notches respectively. Similarly, 6192, 5226 and 3991 could be taken for naturally backed knives.

Four of the pieces listed in Table 12.1 have been described tentatively as cores. They all come from the Long Arcade. Specimen 6139 is a cobble from which flakes have been removed from four platforms at different heights and from different directions. Pieces 6204, 7333 and 7340 are pebbles which have been reduced by the removal of flakes around one face from a single peripheral platform. The opposite surfaces retain cortex. In addition to these items, there is also a cobble of flint from the High Chamber (7260) which is naturally modified at one end and a quartzite cobble from the Undervault (7119). The latter has a series of deliberate percussion removals across one end and might be described as either a chopper or core.

Overall, the Breccia artefacts examined so far can all be considered to be the products of relatively simple reduction sequences (Fig. 12.4). The knapping techniques, the form of the handaxes and the character of the debitage all relate to the need to produce an edge on globular, elongated and spherical cobbles of flint. The source of this flint has not yet been investigated, but Pengelly (1873, 208) noted that the nodules 'appear to have been obtained from accumulations of supracretaceous flint-gravel, such as occur about four miles from the cavern'. Given the character of the flint this seems a reasonable hypothesis.

AGE

Over the last five years efforts have been made to obtain Uranium-series and ESR age estimates on speleothems within and overlying the Breccia (Proctor 1994; Proctor *et al.* in prep.). Although the results provide a minimum age for the deposit, the interpretation of its relative dating

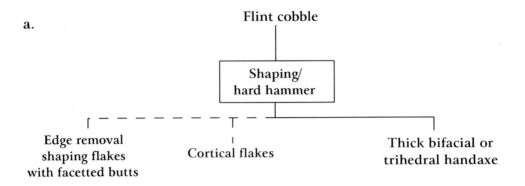

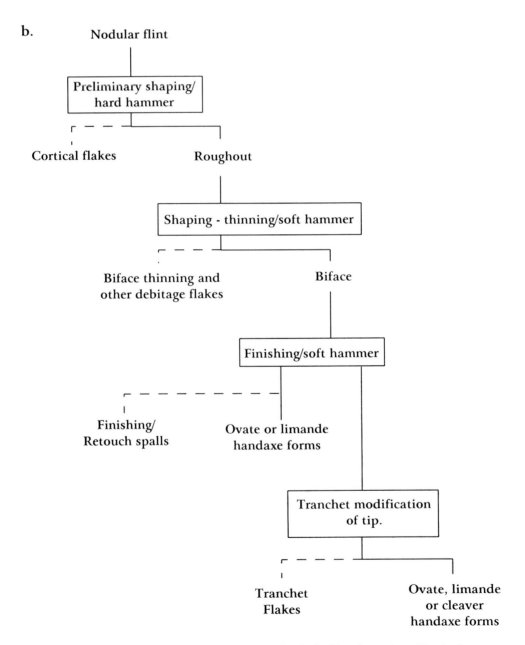

Figure 12.4. Reduction sequences for a. minimally flaked and trihedral handaxes from Kent's Cavern versus b. intensive bifacial reduction.

still depends on the faunal remains incorporated in it. However, as is often the case with material from old excavations, there have been misunderstandings, assumptions and circular arguments about this fauna.

Table 12.2 lists the mammalian species often attributed to the Breccia and considered diagnostic of its age. It shows that, of the species listed, only *Ursus deningeri*, *Panthera sp.*, a small canid, suggested to be fox, and *Microtus oeconomus* are certainly recorded from the Breccia. In addition, *Arvicola cantiana* and *Pitymys gregaloides*, identified by Hinton (1926), and *Microtus gregalis*, listed by Roberts *et al.* (1995, 175 table 3), have been attributed to the Breccia. However, the latter is referred to as an extinct pine vole (*ibid.*) and must be assumed to be a misprint for *Pitymys gregaloides*. Hinton's determinations (Table 12.2) have subsequently been quoted by Sutcliffe and Kowalski (1976) and Campbell and Sampson (1971) and both of these works have then been used as sources for further syntheses. However, a check on the specimens used by Hinton confirms that they were unstratified finds from the MacEnery collection. Their source is unknown and their attribution to the Breccia is no more than an assumption. The same assumption has caused over a century of confusion over the teeth of *Homotherium latidens* found in the cave (Alexander 1964; Dawkins 1874; Kennard 1945; Pengelly 1872a). The first specimens of this species found in Kent's Cavern were recovered by MacEnery in 1826 and described as *Ursus cultridens*. Owen (1846) re-identified them as remains of the sabre-tooth cat *Machairodus latidens* now known as the lesser scimitar cat *Homotherium latidens* (Kurtén 1968, 76–77). According to MacEnery's notes, written after the excavations and published posthumously (Pengelly 1869a), five canines and at least one incisor (Kennard 1945; Pengelly 1872a) of *Homotherium* were all found in the Wolf's Cave (Fig. 12.1) in 'diluvial mud' (Pengelly 1872b, 38) in a 'mixed assemblage of bones' (Pengelly 1869a, 369). These bones were 'heaped in incredible quantities' (*ibid.*, 294) and although most were shattered, 'many fine and delicate specimens, among which was *Ursus cultridens*, were found quite uninjured' (*ibid.*, 294) despite being 'gnawed at their base' (*ibid.*, 370). Working in the Wolf's Cave in 1872, Pengelly found that 'the deposit ... whether disturbed or undisturbed, was well-marked Cave-earth ... There were

no traces of the older deposits termed "Breccia" ... either *in situ* or redeposited ...' (Pengelly 1872b, 30). It might further be noted that the artefacts found in the Wolf's Cave include nothing which could be interpreted as derivative from the Breccia. All the finds are Late Pleistocene including Mousterian and Earlier and Later Upper Palaeolithic. Such evidence convinced Pengelly (*ibid.*) that the *Homotherium* teeth found by MacEnery must have come from the Cave-earth. His view was confirmed by the discovery of another *Homotherium* incisor from the first or uppermost foot level (Fig. 12.2) of the Cave-earth in the Long Arcade (Pengelly 1872b, 46). Further, he ruled out the possibility that the teeth could have been derived into that deposit from the Breccia on the basis that they showed no damage or abrasion consistent with re-deposition. They were not mineralised like specimens from the Breccia (cf. Dawkins 1874, 323) and the gnawing present on them was consistent with the Cave-earth finds but not those of the Breccia. These considerations remain to be checked, but it is clear that *Homotherium* cannot be taken as a reliable indicator of the age of the Breccia (cf. Campbell & Sampson 1971, 22; Dawkins 1874, 334; Roe 1981, 103). However, the occurrence of a machairodont cat with Late Pleistocene species in the Cave-earth is enigmatic given that, with one exception, other finds of this animal are from Cromerian contexts (Backhouse & Lydekker 1886; Bishop 1982; Boule 1901; Newton 1882; Stuart 1982). The exception is Robin Hood Cave, Creswell Crags, Derbyshire (Dawkins 1880, 186–187) and here, as at Kent's Cavern, the possibility that the fossil is a later human introduction to the site cannot be ruled out. In neither case have non-dental remains of the genus been found, and it is entirely possible that these attractive teeth were collected in Palaeolithic times and cached in dark recesses.

Of the remaining genera, the lion and fox specimens recorded from the Breccia by Pengelly (1875, 4–5, and 12 respectively) have not yet been located so the species are unknown. Both animals are also known in the Cave-earth (Pengelly 1874, 17). The bear remains which Pengelly noted throughout the Breccia have been identified as those of *Ursus deningeri* (M.J. Bishop, pers. comm.). This species has not been found in deposits post-dating the Anglian in Britain and is currently the only one which can be taken as providing a broad age estimate for the deposit.

Species	Context/Area	Record
Ursus deningeri	Breccia/throughout	Pengelly 1873, 205, *inter alia.* (*Ursus spelaeus*)
Panthera sp.	Breccia/Clinnick's Gallery	Pengelly 1875, 4–5. (*Felis spelaea*)
Canid	Breccia/The Alcove	Pengelly 1875, 12. (*Canis Vulpes*)
Homotherium latidens	Cave-earth/Wolf's Den and Long Arcade	Pengelly 1872a, 187. (*Machairodus latidens*)
Arvicola cantiana	Unstratified MacEnery collection	Kennard 1945, 185 citing Hinton unpublished. (*Arvicola greeni*)
Pitymys gregaloides	Unstratified MacEnery collection	Hinton 1926, 126–127, fig. 64.12.
Microtus oeconomus	Breccia	M. J. Bishop pers. comm.

Table 12.2. Fauna attributed to the Breccia.

Biometric analysis of a small sample of the Breccia bears by Bishop (pers. comm.) indicates that they are closely comparable to the bears from Westbury-sub-Mendip (Bishop 1982, 35–48) which differ biometrically from the form of *Ursus deningeri* found at West Runton (*ibid.*, 92). This variation and the character of the associated fauna at Westbury-sub-Mendip led Bishop to suggest that the latter site should be dated to a post-Cromerian but pre-Anglian temperate phase (*ibid.*, 92–96). Evidence in support of this view now seems strong (von Koenigswald & van Kolfschoten 1996, 218–20; Meijer & Preece 1996, 75–78; Stuart 1996, 20) and, given that the *U. deningeri* remains at Kent's Cavern are fresh, it would seem probable that the Breccia was emplaced in the later stages of this pre-Anglian phase. Finally, it might be noted that the bear remains found in the Cave-earth deposits have not yet been studied. This is unfortunate, since species' identification and biometric research might contribute fresh information on any re-working of Breccia age material into younger contexts.

DISCUSSION

The distribution, abrasion, mechanical damage and staining of the Breccia artefacts suggests that they were derived from alluvial deposits outside the cave and transported into it as part of the clast fraction of one or more debris flows. This is consistent with Proctor's (1994) analysis of the sediment which shows the Breccia to be a poorly sorted allochthonous deposit consisting of Devonian sandstone, siltstone, slate and vein quartz cobbles and pebbles in a dense clayey matrix (*ibid.*, 101). Limestone is rare (cf. Campbell & Sampson 1971, 9; Roe 1981, 97 table 8) ruling out autochthonous accumulation and the possibility that human activity occurred within the cave (Campbell & Sampson 1971, 23). As Proctor (1994, 115–116) notes, the debris flows must have moved into the cave via entrances above the High Level Chamber and the Bear's Den. These entrances, now blocked, once opened onto the overlying terrace which was probably the major source of the Breccia sediments as well as the artefacts. Given that the artefacts must have been made outside the cave and, judging by the ochreous staining on some of them, had perhaps even been buried in a gravel before the Breccia was emplaced, it is possible that they could date from an older phase of the Cromerian Complex than that infered for the Breccia on the evidence of the remains of *U. deningeri*.

Comparison of the Kent's Cavern handaxes with others from Boxgrove and High Lodge, which are considered to be pre-Anglian in age, reveals differences both in their form and technology. The reduction sequences (Fig. 12.4) used to produce the thick variable forms with zig-zag edges and large areas of cortex at Kent's Cavern involve fewer knapping actions than those employed to produce the thin ovate and limande handaxes with continuous straight edges which predominate at Boxgrove (Bergman *et al.* 1990;

Roberts 1986; Wenban-Smith 1989) and High Lodge (Ashton *et al.* 1992, 157–163). At the latter sites knapping continued beyond the basic roughing out of the shape to thinning and finishing which involved changes in hammer mode (Wenban-Smith 1989) and the use of tranchet technique (Roberts 1986). These actions are absent from the Kent's Cavern Breccia material. This absence may be explained by the fact that the Kent's Cavern pieces are made on cobbles of flint derived from secondary sources. These cobbles have been modified rather than transformed by flaking which, by its nature, prevented further more intensive reduction. This is consistent with White's (1995) analysis of later handaxe assemblages which suggests that the form and quality of the raw material are the main influences on handaxe morphology. However, it remains valid to ask whether there are other factors influencing morphological variation (*ibid.*, 14) and whether, given that the Kent's Cavern material might be older than Boxgrove, age might be a variable as suggested by Roe (1981, 99). Answering the latter question is difficult, given the paucity of handaxes which might be of similar age either in Britain (Roberts *et al.* 1995) or the near Continent (Tuffreau & Antoine 1995).

Thick, minimally flaked handaxes technologically similar to those found in the Kent's Cavern Breccia have been noted among the vast numbers of artefacts recovered from Farnham Terrace A, Surrey (Bury 1916; 1917; Oakley in Oakley *et al.* 1939; Roe 1981, 108–111), Warren Hill, Suffolk (Roe 1981, 111–115; Solomon 1933; Wymer *et al.*, 1991) and Fordwich, Kent (Dewey & Smith 1925; Roe 1981, 104–108). At Farnham and Warren Hill there is lithostratigraphic evidence to suggest that these may be derived in deposits of pre-Anglian age (Roe 1981, 108–111; Wymer *et al.* 1991). Roe (1981, 104–108) has also argued this possibility for Fordwich (cf. Ashmore 1981) and investigations in progress should clarify the age of the deposits there. However, the problem remains that the thick handaxes found at these sites are all derived and occur in secondary contexts with amygdaloid, ovate and limande forms which are now also known from pre-Anglian contexts as at Boxgrove. Consequently, distinguishing whether there is any age difference between the forms is currently impossible. However, at Warren Hill Solomon (1933, 107) noted that the heavily abraded thick, minimally flaked forms, which he called 'Chellean' (*ibid.*), are made on dark flint from the local Chalk geological unit, whereas the more intensively flaked forms were produced from Lincolnshire grey flint. It has been suggested that the latter was introduced by glacial processes, presumably during the Anglian. This led him to suggest that the former were older than the latter (*ibid.*). As there is also an unconfirmed record of *Archidiskodon meridionalis* (Andrews 1930), which is considered Cromerian *sensu stricto,* from this site, re-investigation of the finds and stratigraphy may well contribute to the problem of assessing whether age or raw material is the main feature of the minimally flaked handaxe forms. Meanwhile, Kent's

Cavern stands alone among British sites in having only such handaxes.

The situation in northern France is similar to that in Britain. As Tuffreau (1981, 173) notes the oldest industries of the high and middle terraces of the Somme are the least well known. In the first classification based on a stratigraphic framework (*ibid.*, 172) Commont (1910) distinguished the high terrace material as consisting of thick handaxes made by hard hammer technique which he referred to as 'Pré-Chelléen' whereas such forms derived into the gravels of the middle terrace were described as Chelléen. Breuil and Kelley (1954) re-named the high terrace material Abbevillian, a term which Bordes (1961, 83) subsequently used solely in a typological sense because thick minimally flaked bifaces may occur at any stage in the Lower Palaeolithic. However, Bordes (*ibid.*; 1968 52–54) also noted that at Abbeville, as at Kent's Cavern, d'Ault du Mesnil had found this and no other handaxe form in the lower part of the *marne blanche* which also contained a fauna (Auguste 1995, 45; Boule in Commont 1910) of pre-Mindel age. More recent chronostratigraphic research on the Carrière Carpentier Formation at Abbeville (Antoine, 1990, 129–131; 1993; Tuffreau & Antoine 1995, 149–150) confirms this, suggesting an age of OIS 16 to 15 for the deposits. However, Tuffreau (Antoine 1990, 130; Tuffreau & Antoine 1995, 150) has cast doubt on the context and character of du Mesnil's *marne blanche* material by noting that Commont recovered no artefacts from this deposit and that Breuil found only a limande above the *marne blanche* in the adjacent Carrière Léon, whilst at the Champs de Mars the more recent gravels (OIS 14 to 13, *ibid.*, 150) contained a derived mixture of thick, minimally flaked forms with more intensively flaked ovates and limandes. Given that Breuil (1939, 14) quoting Mesnil's notes states that there could be no doubt about the association of the handaxes with the fauna in the *marne blanche,* it would seem necessary to reappraise the latter's collections before dismissing it. If this was an assemblage without ovates and limandes, as reported (*ibid.*; Breuil & Koslowski 1931, 461; Bordes 1968, 52), then the technology could not be put down to the quality of the raw material which was the same as that used for the intensively flaked forms.

CONCLUSION

The handaxes from the Breccia at Kent's Cavern are thick, minimally flaked forms with areas of residual cortex and irregular edges. They were produced using a hard hammer technique of bifacial or, occasionally trihedral flaking. The flakes from the same deposit are the by-products of this technique. The absence of ovate and limande forms, as found in other pre-Anglian sites such as Boxgrove, may be due to the nature of the raw material. However, the possibility that they were derived into the Breccia from much older deposits might equally suggest that they

pre-date the more intensively flaked forms and that this may also account for the presence of similar handaxes in the mixed assemblages from such sites as Farnham and Warren Hill. Given the paucity of comparative material there cannot be any resolution of this problem at present, but the possible age of the Kent's Cavern pieces and perhaps that of the claimed material from the *marne blanche* at Abbeville should perhaps encourage us to review old finds from similarly ancient contexts and to search for new ones.

ACKNOWLEDGEMENTS

We are grateful to Dr M. J. Bishop, Curator of Torquay Museum, Robert Kruszynski of the Department of Palaeontology at The Natural History Museum and Mr R. Cowell at Liverpool Museum for allowing us access to the Kent's Cavern material in their care. We are further indebted to Dr Bishop and to Dr C. Proctor for the advice and information they shared with us based on their own research on the fauna, age and sediments of the site. Thanks are also due to Mr T. Clark who patiently typed the script and to Mr P. Dean who prepared Figures 12.1–12.3.

REFERENCES

Alexander, E. M. M. 1964. Father John MacEnery: scientist or charlatan. *Transactions of the Devonshire Association* 96, 113–46.

Andrews, H. 1930. On some fossil mammals of Western Suffolk. *Transactions of the Suffolk Naturalists Society* 1, 195–9.

Antoine, P. 1990. *Chronostratigraphie et Environnement du Paléolithique du Bassin de la Somme.* Lille: CERP.

Ashmore, A. M. 1981. The typology and age of the Fordwich handaxes. *Archaeologia Cantiana* 96, 83–117.

Ashton, N. M., Cook, J., Lewis, S. G. & Rose, J. 1992. *High Lodge. Excavations by G. de G. Sieveking, 1962–8, and J. Cook, 1988.* London: British Museum Press.

Auguste, P. 1995. Révision préliminaire des grands mammifères des gisements du Paléolithique inférieur et moyen de la vallée de la Somme. *Bulletin de la Société Préhistorique Française* 92 (2), 143–54.

Backhouse, J. & Lydekker, R. 1886. On a mandible of *Machairodus* from the Forest Bed. *Quarterly Journal of the Geological Society* 42, 309–12.

Bergman, C., Roberts, M. B., Collcutt, S. & Barlow, P. 1990. Refitting and spatial analysis of artefacts from Quarry 2 at the Middle Pleistocene Acheulian site of Boxgrove, West Sussex, England. In E. Cziesela, S. Eickhoff, N. Arts & D. Winter (eds), *The Big Puzzle. International Symposium on Refitting Stone Artefacts. Monrepos 1987. Studies in Modern Archaeology 1,* 265–81. Bonn: Holos.

Bishop, M. J. 1982. The mammal fauna of the early Middle Pleistocene cavern infill site of Westbury-sub-Mendip, Somerset. *Special Papers of the Palaeontological Association* 28, 1–108.

Bordes, F. 1961. *Typologie du Paléolithique Ancien et Moyen.* Bordeaux: Delmas.

Bordes, F. 1968. *The Old Stone Age.* (English Edition). London: Weidenfeld and Nicholson.

Boule, M. 1901. Revision des espèces européennes de *Machairodus*. *Bulletin de la Société Géologique de France* 1 (4th series), 551–73.

Breuil, H. 1939. Le vrai niveau de l'industrie abbevillienne de la Porte du Bois (Abbeville). *L'Anthropologie* 49, 13–34.

Breuil, H. & Kelley, H. 1954. Le paléolithique ancien. Abbevillien. Clactonien. Acheuléen. Levalloisien. *Bulletin de la Société Préhistorique Française* 51, 1–26.

Breuil, H. and Koslowski, L. 1931. Études de stratigraphie paléolithique dans le nord de la France, la Belgique et l'Angleterre. *L'Anthropologie* 41, 449–88.

Bury, H. 1916. The palaeoliths of Farnham. *Proceedings of the Geologists' Association* 27 (3), 151–92.

Bury, H. 1917. Some 'flat-faced' palaeoliths from Farnham. *Proceedings of the Prehistoric Society of East Anglia* 2 (3), 365–74.

Campbell, J. B. & Sampson, C. G. 1971. *A new analysis of Kent's Cavern, Devonshire, England*. University of Oregon Anthropological Papers 3.

Commont, V. 1910. Excursion de la Société géologique du Nord et de la Faculté des Sciences de Lille à Abbeville, le 11 juin 1910. *Annuelles de la Société Géologique du Nord* 39, 249–93.

Curry, D. 1963. On rotten flint pebbles in the Palaeogene of southern England. *Proceedings of the Geologists' Association* 74 (4), 457–60.

Dawkins, W. B. 1874. *Cave Hunting, Researches on the Evidence of Caves Respecting the Early Inhabitants of Europe*. London: Macmillan and Co.

Dawkins, W. B. 1880. *Early Man in Britain*. London: Macmillan and Co.

Dewey, H. & Smith, R. A. 1925. Flints from the Sturry gravels. *Archaeologia* 74, 117–36.

Dewolf, Y. 1977. Désilicification et silifications secondaires de certaines argiles à silex des marges occidentales du Bassin de Paris. *Compte Rendu des Academies des Sciences*, D 284, 725–8.

Evans, J. 1897. *The Ancient Stone Implements, Weapons and Ornaments of Great Britain* (2nd edition). London: Longmans.

Fairbairn, P. E. & Robertson, R. H. S. 1972. The decomposition of flint. *Scottish Journal of Science* 1 (3), 165–74.

Garrod, D. 1925. Le niveau inférieur de Kent's Cavern: une bréche à *Ursus spelaeus* avec outillage chelléan. *Bulletin de la Société Préhistorique Française* 22, 115–20.

Hinton, M. A. C. 1926. *Monograph on the Voles and Lemming (Microtinae), Living and Extinct. Vol. I*. London: British Museum (Natural History).

Koenigswald, W. Von & Kolfschoten, T. Van 1996. The *Mimomys – Arvicola* boundary and the enamel thickness quotient (SDQ) of *Arvicola* as stratigraphic markers in the Middle Pleistocene. In C. Turner (ed.), *The Early Middle Pleistocene in Europe*, 227–53. Rotterdam; Balkema.

Kennard, A. S. 1945. The early digs in Kent's Hole, Torquary and Mrs Cazalet. *Proceedings of the Geologists' Association* 56, 156–213.

Kurtén, B. 1968. *Pleistocene Mammals of Europe*. London: Weidenfeld and Nicholson.

Lowe, H. 1916. The stone implements from the Breccia of Kent's Cavern. *Journal Torquay Natural History Society* 2 (2), 80–7.

Meijer, T. & Preece, R. C. 1996. Malacological evidence relating to the stratigraphical position of the Cromerian. In C. Turner (ed.). *The Early Middle Pleistocene in Europe*, 53–82. Rotterdam: Balkema.

Newton, E. T. 1882. *The Vertebrata of the Forest Bed Series of Norfolk and Suffolk*. District Memoir of the Geological Survey, U. K.

Oakley, K. P., Rankine, W. F. & Lowther, A. W. G. 1939. *A Survey of the Prehistory of the Farnham District (Surrey)*. Guildford: Surrey Archaeological Society.

Pengelly, W. 1868. The Literature of Kent's Cavern, Torquay, prior to 1859. *Transactions of the Devonshire Association* 2 (2), 469–522.

Pengelly, W. 1869a. The Literature of Kent's Cavern. Part II. Including the whole of Rev. J. MacEnery's Manuscript. *Transactions of the Devonshire Association* 3, 191–482.

Pengelly, W. 1869b. Fifth report of the committee for exploring Kent's Cavern, Devonshire. *Report of the British Association for the Advancement of Science. 1869*, 189–208.

Pengelly, W. 1870. Sixth report of the committee for exploring Kent's Cavern, Devonshire. *Report of the British Association for the Advancement of Science. 1870*, 16–29.

Pengelly, W. 1871. Seventh Report of the committee for exploring Kent's Cavern, Devonshire. *Report of the British Association for the Advancement of Science 1871*, 1–14.

Pengelly, W. 1872a. Notes on *Machairodus latidens* found by Rev. J. MacEnery in Kent's Cavern. *Transactions of the Devonshire Association* 5, 165–179.

Pengelly, W. 1872b. Eighth report of the committee for exploring Kent's Cavern, Devonshire. *Report of the British Association for the Advancement of Science 1872*, 28–47.

Pengelly, W. 1873. Ninth report of the committee for exploring Kent's Cavern, Devonshire. *Report of the British Association for the Advancement of Science 1873*, 198–209.

Pengelly, W. 1874. Tenth report of the committee for exploring Kent's Cavern, Devonshire. *Report of the British Association for the Advancement of Science 1874*, 1–17.

Pengelly, W. 1875. Eleventh report of the committee for exploring Kent's Cavern, Devonshire. *Report of the British Association for the Advancement of Science 1875*, 1–13.

Pengelly, W. 1876. Twelfth report of the committee for exploring Kent's Cavern, Devonshire. *Report of the British Association for the Advancement of Science 1876*, 1–8.

Pengelly, W. 1877. Thirteenth report of the committee for exploring Kent's Cavern, Devonshire. *Report of the British Association for the Advancement of Science 1877*, 1–8.

Pengelly, W. 1878. Fourteenth report of the committee for exploring Kent's Cavern, Devonshire. *Report of the British Association for the Advancement of Science. 1878*, 1–7.

Pengelly, W. 1879. Fifteenth report of the committee appointed for the purpose of exploring Kent's Cavern, Devonshire. *Report of the British Association for the Advancement of Science. 1879*, 1–9.

Pengelly, W. 1880. Sixteenth and concluding report of the committee appointed for the purpose of exploring Kent's Cavern, Devonshire. *Report of the British Association for the Advancement of Science. 1880*, 1–7.

Proctor, C. J. 1994. *A British Pleistocene Chronology Based on U-series and ESR Dating of Speleothems*, 88–147. PhD thesis. University of Bristol.

Proctor, C. J., Berridge, P., Bishop, M. J., & Smart, P. In prep. Absolute age estimates for the Breccia in Kent's Cavern.

Roberts, M. B. 1986. Excavation of a Lower Palaeolithic site at Amey's Eartham Pit, Boxgrove, West Sussex: a preliminary report. *Proceedings of the Prehistoric Society* 52, 215–45.

Roberts, M. B., Gamble, C. S. & Bridgland, D. R. 1995. The earliest occupation of Europe: the British Isles. In W. Roebroeks & T. Van Kolfschoten (eds), *The Earliest Occupation of Europe*, 165–191, Leiden: University of Leiden.

Roe, D. A. 1968. *A Gazetteer of British Lower and Middle Palaeolithic sites*. CBA Research Report 8.

Roe, D. A. 1981. *The Lower and Middle Palaeolithic Periods in Britain*. London: Routledge and Kegan Paul.

Rogers, E. H. 1956. Stratification of the Cave Earth in Kent's Cavern. *Proceedings of the Devon Archaeological Exploration Society* 5, 68–92.

Shepherd, W. 1972. *Flint. Its Origins, Properties and Uses*. London: Faber and Faber.

Smith, R. A. 1926. *A Guide to the Antiquities of the Stone Age in the Department of British and Medieval Antiquities.* London: British Museum.

Solomon, J. D. 1933. The implementiferous gravels of Warren Hill. *Journal of the Royal Anthropological Institute of Great Britain and Ireland* 63, 101–10.

Stuart, A. J. 1982. *Pleistocene Vertebrates in the British Isles.* London: Longman.

Stuart, A. J. 1996. Vertebrate faunas from the early Middle Pleistocene of East Anglia. In C. Turner (ed.), *The Early Middle Pleistocene in Europe*, 9–24. Rotterdam: Balkema.

Sutcliffe, A. J. & Kowalski, K. 1976. Pleistocene rodents of the British Isles. *Bulletin of the British Museum Natural History (Geology)* 27 (2), 33–147.

Tuffreau, A. 1981. L'Acheuléen dans la France septentrionale. *L'Anthropologie* 19 (2), 171–83.

Tuffreau, A. & Antoine, P. 1995. The earliest occupation of Europe: continental Northwestern Europe. In W. Roebroeks & T. van Kolfschoten (eds.), *The Earliest Occupation of Europe*, 147–163. Leiden: University of Leiden.

Warren, C. N. & Rose, S. 1994. *William Pengelly's Spits, Yards and Prisms: the Forerunners of Modern Excavation Methods and Techniques in Archaeology.* Torquay: Torquay Natural History Society

Wenban-Smith, F. F. 1989. The use of canonical variates for determination of biface manufacturing technology at Boxgrove Lower Palaeolithic site and the behavioural implications of this technology. *Journal of Archaeological Science* 16 (1), 17–26.

White, M. J. 1995. Raw materials and biface variability in southern Britain: a preliminary examination. *Lithics* 15, 1–20.

Wymer, J. 1988. Palaeolithic archaeology and the British Quaternary sequence. *Quaternary Science Reviews* 7, 79–88.

Wymer, J., Lewis, S. G. & Bridgland, D. R. 1991. Warren Hill, Mildenhall, Suffolk (TL 744743). In S. G. Lewis, C. A. Whiteman & D. R. Bridgland (eds). *Central East Anglia and the Fen Basin. Field Guide*, 50–8. London: Quaternary Research Association.

13. Clactonian and Acheulian Industries in Britain: Their Chronology and Significance Reconsidered

Francis F. Wenban-Smith

ABSTRACT

This paper reviews the original recognition and current status of Clactonian industries in Britain. Recent challenges to their longstanding status as distinctive technological entities are rejected, and it is concluded that Clactonian industries with only a crude bifacial element characterise hominid lithic technology in at least the first part of the post-Anglian interglacial, and possibly the first part of the subsequent interglacial as well. The longstanding orthodoxy that Clactonian and Acheulian industries represent separate streams of hominid cultural tradition is, however, also rejected. Instead it is suggested that Acheulian industries, with their increased emphasis on well-formed handaxes used as portable tools, evolved directly from Clactonian industries in the face ultimately of the changing availability of raw material within the landscape.

INTRODUCTION

This volume in honour of John Wymer is a particularly appropriate place to reconsider the status of Clactonian and Acheulian industries in Britain. Wymer (1968; 1974; 1985; 1988) has played a central role in establishing as orthodoxy a framework of understanding for the British Lower Palaeolithic in which these industries are interpreted as the product of distinct cultural groups. In fact Wymer has directed geological and archaeological research, always followed by publication, at almost every Clactonian site in Britain, as well as some of the most important Acheulian ones (Table 13.1). Now is also a particularly appropriate time to reconsider this interpretation. Further Quaternary research has increased understanding of the chrono-stratigraphic framework of the Palaeolithic (Bridgland 1994), and recent archaeological work has on the one hand presented an alternative explanation of Clactonian and Acheulian industries (Mithen 1994), and on the other has challenged again, Ohel's (1979) uprising having been suppressed, the status of the Clactonian and Acheulian as distinct industries at all (McNabb 1992; Ashton *et al.* 1994). This paper

reviews the genesis of the orthodox identification and interpretation of Clactonian and Acheulian industries, and then considers the recently proposed alternatives.

THE ACHEULIAN AND THE CLACTONIAN ... CREATED

The analysis of lithic artefacts has been a fundamental part of Palaeolithic research since its beginning. The northwest European Palaeolithic was quickly divided by G. de Mortillet (1869; 1872) on the basis of perceived

Date	Site	Industry	Publications
1954	Little Thurrock	Clactonian	Wymer 1957
1955–60	Swanscombe	Clactonian/Acheulian	Wymer 1964
1969–70	Clacton	Clactonian	Singer *et al.* 1973
1971–74	Hoxne	Acheulian	Wymer 1983; Singer *et al.* 1993
1979	Clacton	Clactonian	Wymer 1985
1979	Barnham	Clactonian/Acheulian	Wymer 1985
1987	Clacton	Clactonian	Wymer 1988

Table 13.1. Fieldwork by John Wymer at key Clactonian and Acheulian sites

variations through time of manufacturing techniques and tool-types into stages, or epochs, purportedly reflecting the progress of prehistoric Man. De Mortillet's pioneering framework (1869) was based entirely on the caves and rock-shelters of southwest France, and began with the epoch of Le Moustier, or Mousterian, characterised by the prevalence of unifacially worked flake-tools, although associated with some bifacial core-tools (*coups-de-poing* or handaxes). He soon modified this framework (1872, 436), adding at the beginning an epoch of St Acheul, or Acheulian, characterised by large bifacial tools 'more or less almond-shaped', i.e. handaxes. In the last part of the 19th century de Mortillet recognised that collections from the lower terraces of rivers such as the Somme included both Acheulian handaxes and Mousterian flake tools. He therefore inserted a Chellean stage (when handaxes were the only tool) before the Acheulian, and changed the sense of Acheulian to being transitional between Chellean and Mousterian, hence including both handaxes and flake-tools. De Mortillet's work led to the widespread adoption by the end of the 19th century of a pan-European framework of Lower, Middle and Upper Palaeolithic periods, incorporating a linear sequence of development through these named cultural epochs identified by the presence, or combination of *instruments caractéristiques* (Fig. 13.1). Most assemblages containing nicer-looking handaxes included flake tools, although many of these would be dismissed as naturally retouched today, so the term Acheulian took strong root, and many assemblages were identified as Acheulian entirely from the handaxes. Chellean was used only for the stratigraphically earliest assemblages dominated by large and crude handaxes, such as from the high terrace of the Somme (Breuil & Koslowski 1931).

In the first part of the 20th century more controlled research led to a more detailed framework for the Pleistocene of northwest Europe incorporating four glacial-interglacial cycles (Penck & Brückner 1909) and better knowledge of the archaeological material contained in deposits of different periods. During this period of research contradictions in the existing linear developmental framework began to be exposed. Smith & Dewey (1913) recovered a large assemblage without handaxes consisting exclusively of cores and large flakes, some of them interpreted as retouched into tools, from the Lower Gravel at Swanscombe, stratified beneath levels (the Middle Gravels) containing Chellean and Early Acheulian types of handaxe; and Warren (1922) made a large collection of similar material from the Elephant Bed at Clacton-on-Sea between 1911 and 1916. The Clacton material was attributed by Breuil (in Warren 1922) to a Mesvinian industry, based on its similarity to material recovered from Mesvin in Belgium. Breuil subsequently divided the Belgian Mesvinian into early and later stages, and having retained the term Mesvinian for the later material suggested the term Clactonian for the earlier material from Clacton, Swanscombe and Mesvin after the site at Clacton-on-Sea (Warren 1926; Breuil 1926).

Breuil (1926; 1932) recognised that these Clactonian assemblages dated earlier than or contemporaneously with Chellean and Early Acheulian levels, contradicting the existing framework of cultural development whose unilinear trajectory dictated a decline through time in core-tool usage and a corresponding increase in flake-tool usage. Breuil also noted that during the climatic oscillations accompanying the Palaeolithic that i) the handaxe-dominated industries (Chellean to Acheulian) were associated with interglacial deposits, and ii) the core and flake industries were associated with cold climate deposits. Therefore Breuil re-wrote the Lower Palaeolithic as a story of the parallel and contemporaneous development of two separate industrial traditions practised by culturally separate human groups, one using predominantly bifacial technology in warmer conditions, and the other using exclusively core and flake tool technology in colder conditions. These groups moved north and south following climatic zones and their associated fauna in conjunction with the climatic oscillations of the Pleistocene, leading to the occasional superposition of interglacial Acheulian industries above late glacial or early interglacial Clactonian industries, for instance as at Swanscombe.

Breuil's (1932) definition of the Clactonian lithic industry specified that it was based on flakes and cores, and lacked symmetrical and bifacially flaked handaxes. The cores were worked in an *ad hoc* fashion, possibly by an anvil technique, to produce large flakes with wide striking platforms and a very open angle between the ventral surface and the striking platform. The resulting cores could be large or small, and ended up in a variety of shapes with differing degrees of reduction. The flakes were either left unretouched or made into crude scrapers with a minimum of retouch. The cores were sometimes slightly partially bifacially worked into tools, but never with any systematic idea suggesting the goal of a regular and symmetrical handaxe, such as found in Chellean and Acheulian industries.

Acheulian industries, in contrast, were characterised primarily by the presence of numerous well-made symmetrical handaxes. Breuil and Koslowski (1931; 1932; 1934) divided the Acheulian industrial tradition into seven stages, based on their assessment of changing handaxe shapes, although there is no discernible difference between their Stages I-V (Old and Middle Acheulian), and the basis of these stages seems to have been chronological order as inferred from geological context. All these stages include pointed and ovate forms, with and without features such as tranchet sharpening and worked butts. The Final Acheulian (stages VI-VII, or Micoquian) includes smaller, more finely pointed forms with concave sides and more cordiform shaped bifaces. It was recognised that flake-tools were an integral, although subsidiary, element of Acheulian industries. These were presumed to have been mostly made on debitage from handaxe manufacture, although it was recognised that some unstandardised core and flake technology was also practised.

CLASSEMENT DU QUATERNAIRE ANCIEN.

PALÉOLITHIQUE.	ÉPOQUES.	TECHNIQUE.	INSTRUMENTS CARACTÉRISTIQUES
FIN.	Tourassien,	Travail dégénéré : pierre et os.	Harpons plats à grandes barbelures, en corne de cerf. — Passage du paléolithique au néolithique.
SUPÉRIEUR.	Magdalénien.	Développement du travail de l'os.	Burins en silex. — Lames étroites et légères. — Développement des instruments en os et de l'art.
	Solutréen.	Pierre taillée par pression.	Pointes en feuille de laurier et à cran. — Apparition des grattoirs. — Apogée des instruments en pierre.
MOYEN.	Moustérien.	Pierre avec retouches (taille et retaille).	Pointes à main et racloirs. — Lames larges et épaisses. — Le tout taillé sur une seule face. — Disparition du coup de poing.
TRANSITION	Acheuléen.	Mélange.	Coups de poing de proportions plus légères, dimensions moindres, travail plus délicat, plus soigné, plus fini.
INFÉRIEUR.	Chelléen.	Percussion simple et directe.	Un seul instrument en pierre : le coup de poing, gros, lourd, taillé à grands éclats sur les deux faces.

Figure 13.1. Early division of the Palaeolithic into periods and epochs (de Mortillet, G. & A. 1900, 241).

... SUPPLIED

This framework was promptly supported by Paterson's work (1937) at Barnham in East Anglia. Paterson excavated a rolled assemblage of cores and flakes from within gravels associated with the Late Anglian or early Post-Anglian[1], and on the surface of these gravels he recovered a fresh condition assemblage with the same flake and core technology. The gravel surface was overlain by 20ft of brickearth which was grey at its base and contained several darker bands, and handaxes were recovered by Paterson from one of the dark bands three feet above the base of the brickearth. Paterson (1937, 91) used this evidence to suggest that 'subsequent to the occupation by flake-tool man ... Acheulian man lived in the area', duplicating the evidence from the Swanscombe sequence indicating the disappearance of Clactonian industries and their replacement by Acheulian industries in England during the post-Anglian interglacial.

Subsequent work at Little Thurrock (Wymer 1957), Clacton (Turner & Kerney 1971; Singer *et al.* 1973), Swanscombe (Ovey 1964; Conway *et al.* 1996) and Hoxne (Wymer 1974, 1983) further reinforced this framework. At Little Thurrock Wymer excavated a typical Clactonian assemblage from gravels abutting the Grays brickearth, and suggested a date in the Hoxnian a little later than the Swanscombe Lower Gravel. At Clacton Turner used pollen analysis to correlate the Freshwater Beds which were the source of Warren's Clactonian material with the early temperate phase of the Hoxnian (Ho. IIa–b), and Singer *et al.* recovered a sequence of derived Clactonian material underlying undisturbed Clactonian material from the golf-course site; the deposits producing this material were dated to the very late Anglian, or very early post-Anglian, ie. immediately before Warren's Freshwater Beds. At Swanscombe Wymer's excavations were focused on the Upper Middle Gravel, and led to the recovery of handaxe-dominated assemblages attributed by Wymer (1968) to the Middle Acheulian. Waechter's excavations recovered further and larger assemblages of Clactonian material from the Lower Gravel, and also recovered refitting Clactonian material from undisturbed horizons within the overlying Lower Loam, which divided the Lower Gravel from the Lower Middle Gravel, and which hitherto had been thought to be mostly sterile. Although Waechter only investigated a small amount of the Lower Middle Gravel, the assemblage of 145 artefacts included three handaxes, confirming to him its recognised Acheulian status. Finally, at Hoxne Wymer recovered a large fresh condition Acheulian assemblage, the Hoxne Lower Industry, with roughly equal numbers of flake cores and ovate/cordate handaxes. Wymer (1974) attributed this assemblage to the top of Statum D, and dated it on the basis of pollen evidence to the late temperate Hoxnian stage (Ho. III); a smaller assemblage from the top part of stratum E, also attributed by Wymer as Acheulian, was dated to the end of the early temperate Hoxnian stage (Ho. IIc).

The combination of these results led Wymer (1974) to argue for the exclusive presence in Britain of a hominid group sharing an inherited Clactonian lithic industrial tradition from the Late Anglian through to the middle of the early temperate Hoxnian stage (Ho. IIb). This group was then supplanted by another group with an Acheulian industrial tradition, which first appeared at Hoxne in the final early temperate Hoxnian stage (Ho. IIc), and at Swanscombe in the Lower Middle Gravels, attributed to the late temperate Hoxnian stage (Ho. III). The short time interval between the disappearance of Clactonian industries and the appearance of Acheulian ones led Wymer in 1974 to suggest these two groups may even have been briefly contemporary with each other in Britain during the latter part of the early temperate Hoxnian stage (Ho. IIc), with territorial infringements by Acheulians causing the demise of Clactonians. More recently, Wymer (1983) has re-appraised the earliest appearance of Acheulian industries at Hoxne to immediately after a stratigraphic hiatus in the Hoxne sequence towards the end of the late temperate stage Ho. III. This diminishes the argument for contemporaneity of Acheulian and Clactonian groups and territorial competition between them. Nonetheless, Wymer (1985; 1988) and Roe (1981) have subsequently re-iterated an essentially culture-historical interpretation (cf. Trigger 1989) for the differences between Clactonian and Acheulian assemblages i.e. that these are two different industrial traditions most probably representing separate streams of hominid cultural evolution.

... DENIED

This culture-historical orthodoxy for the post-Anglian presence of Clactonian and Acheulian industries has been subject to regular re-assessment since Wymer's (1974) synthesis. Ohel (1979), Mithen (1994), and McNabb and Ashton (McNabb 1992; McNabb & Ashton 1992; 1995; Ashton & McNabb 1994; Ashton *et al.* 1994) have all presented alternative interpretations of the archaeological evidence.

Ohel argued that both Clactonian and Acheulian industries were integral parts of a single sequence of reduction taking place in different parts of the landscape – Clactonian industries represented preliminary roughing-out of handaxes and Acheulian industries represented the later stages of manufacture and the abandoned tools themselves. While this idea was in tune with the contemporary theoretical ideas of the Binfords (1966; 1969) explaining spatial variation within the archaeological landscape as reflecting the spatial organisation of different activities, there were numerous practical flaws found in Ohel's argument. Among the most telling were the refitting evidence from Clactonian and Acheulian horizons at Swanscombe and Caddington respectively showing complete reduction sequences, and the lack of both handaxes and distinctive handaxe manufacturing debitage from the Lower Gravel at Swanscombe. This was a fluvial deposit containing a prolific Clactonian industry[2] gathered from a wide catchment area, and hence likely to include a good sample of the lithic technology being practised in different parts of the landscape (comments on Ohel 1979).

More recently, McNabb and Ashton have attacked the Clactonian and Acheulian orthodoxy from the opposite flank. They too reject Ohel's model that these industries represent complementary stages of the bifacial reduction sequence, but instead have suggested that the long-standing distinction between Clactonian and Acheulian industries is a misconception based on the inappropriate pigeon-holing into one or other industry of a fundamentally similar technological record whose main element of variability is the proportion of handaxes in assemblages. On the theoretical side, they have argued that Clactonian and Acheulian industries are the product of an out-dated epistemological framework inherited from the 19th century in which industries are identified by the presence or absence of a type-fossil, the handaxe, regardless of its prevalence and the range of non-bifacial techniques found in association. According to McNabb and Ashton, handaxes are one element of a flexible technological repertoire including both bifacial and non-bifacial knapping techniques, and the Clactonian is not a distinctive industry, but merely the non-handaxe end of a technological continuum of similar assemblages with varying proportions of handaxes. Factual evidence presented in support of this argument is i) typically Clactonian core and flake technology in many Acheulian industries, ii) handaxes and their distinctive manufacturing debitage in Clactonian industries, and iii) evidence of handaxe manufacture contemporary with the main *in situ* Clactonian horizon at Barnham.

The non-bifacial element of Acheulian industries is uncontroversial and was recognised both in the original definition of Acheulian industries and by the Abbé Breuil when he first distinguished Clactonian industries. The alleged presence of handaxes in Clactonian industries is more problematic. McNabb and Ashton have identified approximately twelve handaxes amongst the many thousands of artefacts comprising the British Clactonian industries. Firstly, the provenances of these handaxes are open to doubt. Only two have been recovered from controlled excavations, one from Little Thurrock (Conway 1995), and the other apparently from the Lower Gravel at Swanscombe, although doubts have been expressed about its provenance (Waechter 1969, 83; Newcomer 1979). Secondly, all bar two of the extant specimens are 'non-classic'[3], a term coined by Ashton and McNabb (1994) for core-tools with some bifacial flaking but lacking the imposition of preconceived shape and symmetry associated with more classic forms. The discovery of non-classic bifaces in Clactonian assemblages, leaving aside doubts over provenance, has been taken by McNabb and Ashton to support their suggestion. However, Breuil (1932) fully accepted crude bifacially flaked implements as part of Clactonian assemblages, and Wymer (1968, 336) identified six proto-handaxes 'deliberately made thinner or more pointed at one end' in a Clactonian assemblage from the Swanscombe Lower Gravel. Therefore, notwithstanding doubts over provenance, non-classic bifaces have long been accepted as a scarce element within Clactonian assemblages.

The only evidence for the association of classic handaxe manufacture with Clactonian industries is three unequivocal and two probable soft hammer thinning flakes in Marston's Lower Gravel collection from Rickson's Pit (Ashton & McNabb 1994, 185). These are more incompatible with the established orthodoxy for the constitution of a Clactonian assemblage, since their smoothly curved shape and numerous dorsal scars suggest classic Acheulian handaxe manufacture. It is possible i) that classic Acheulian handaxes were being manufactured contemporaneously with formation of the Lower Gravel, but have never been found, ii) that these flakes could have occasionally been produced during the manufacture of non-classic handaxes, or iii) that these flakes are intrusive in the Lower Gravel collection, and derive from the overlying Middle Gravels at Rickson's Pit which contain numerous classic handaxes and typical debitage. This seems more likely than that the only evidence of classic handaxe manufacture in the period represented by the Lower Gravel is a handful of distinctive flakes, considering the ease of recognition of handaxes, the amount of collecting and the large amount of distinctive debitage produced in the manufacutre of a single handaxe[4]. Although it is unsatisfactory to reject provenance selectively on typological or technological grounds, there comes a point when one has to face the reality that the old collections were mostly collected from talus slopes rather than controlled excavations, and one has to recognise the potential for these collections to contain erroneously provenanced material. Such anachronisms are only rarely highlighted since they are only recognised when they come into conflict with established orthodoxies, of which there are few in the Lower and Middle Palaeolithic. If such orthodoxies are to be overturned it should be on the basis of stratigraphically controlled excavated material rather than isolated specimens from old collections of uncertain integrity.

Recent fieldwork at Barnham (Ashton *et al.* 1994) involved excavation at several sites within an area of approximately one hectare. The work at the main site (Area I), previously investigated by Paterson and Wymer, confirmed the archaeological sequence established previously. A rich and refitting assemblage consisting of cores, flakes and flake tools was recovered from the base of a pale silt overlying a band of flint cobbles, interpreted as a lag gravel, which marked the top of a brown diamicton. This assemblage has to date been accepted as Clactonian. Most artefacts were found in the basal 10cm of the pale silt, with many also found embedded in the surface of the brown diamicton amongst the flint cobbles. No evidence of handaxe manufacture was found in association with the fresh Clactonian industry in Area I. The claim for contemporaneity with this industry of an Acheulian industry is based on the presence of handaxe manufacturing debitage from a site 50m away, Area IV(4), argued (*ibid.*) to come from a stratigraphically equivalent horizon. Lewis (pers. comm.) suggests that the burial of the cobble band in both Areas I and IV(4) relates to the infilling of the deep channel immediately to the north of these sites, which

took place during the the post-Anglian interglacial. What is of critical importance, and hardest to establish, is how much time could separate the deposition of archaeological material in Area I from that in Area IV(4). The cobble band may have been exposed over many thousands of years, and handaxe manufacturing debitage could easily have been deposited on the cobble band in Area IV(4) well after the Clactonian material in Area I. Therefore, the evidence from Barnham of handaxe manufacture at the same geological horizon as Clactonian material does not prove that the manufacturers of the Clactonian material in Area I were making handaxes elsewhere in the landscape.

From a more theoretical perspective, McNabb and Ashton's scenario would be compatible with the explanation of occasional *in situ* Clactonian industries contemporary with numerous *in situ* Acheulian industries. Given both bifacial and non-bifacial technology as part of a cultural repertoire, it is likely that all elements of this repertoire would not be deposited evenly around a landscape. However, given i) the mixing and transportation of material associated with its incorporation in a fluvial deposit such as the Freshwater Bed at Clacton or the Lower Gravel at Swanscombe, and ii) the large amount of distinctive debitage produced in the manufacture of a single handaxe, it seems inconceivable that if the makers of the prolific mixed and transported Clactonian assemblages from these deposits were in the habit of making classic handaxes, then more evidence of this would not have been recovered alongside the thousands of cores and flakes. Therefore we should accept that there was a period (or periods – see below) of the Lower Palaeolithic when the manufacture of classic handaxes was not part of the cultural repertoire, and that this is a real element of variability in the Lower Palaeolithic archaeological record, rather than a mirage imposed by a theoretical perspective inherited from the 19th century. Assemblages representing this non-handaxe repertoire have been labelled Clactonian. It remains, however, to reconsider the orthodox culture-historical interpretation of this variability.

... RECONSIDERED

Substantial transported Clactonian assemblages have been recovered from the sites of Barnham, Swanscombe, Clacton and Little Thurrock. For all these sites bar Little Thurrock, Bridgland's (1994) recent synthesis of the Quaternary of the Thames supports previous dating attributions, with the Clactonian material having come from deposits dating to the early Hoxnian, either Ho. I or Ho. II. In the late temperate phase of the Hoxnian, for instance at Hoxne and in the Lower Middle Gravel at Swanscombe, the industrial repertoire is more handaxe oriented, with the production of numerous classic forms, although retaining a significant core and flake element. It has also been recently proven that Acheulian industries dominated by classic handaxes were prevalent in southern England before the Anglian glaciation, probably in OIS 13 (Pitts & Roberts 1997).

This pattern of industrial variability has orthodoxly been interpreted as reflecting the incursions of different hominid groups with longstanding and separate cultural histories. This interpretation is implicitly based on an homogenous view of material culture, in which a hominid group is i) defined by characteristic artefacts, or type-fossils, and ii) is expected to have left representative examples wherever it went. These assumptions have been shown, originally by the Binfords (1966; 1969), to be unrealistically simplistic. However, it is inevitable that an infant hominid will acquire cultural practices from the previous generation, and there is evidence that techniques such as the production of thin and symmetrical bifaces are difficult to execute and most likely to flourish within the context of a sound framework of social learning (Mithen 1994). The issue to consider is how varied and how variably applied might the lithic technological practices of a network of hominids with a shared cultural background have been in space and time.

It was argued above that transported gravels might reasonably be expected to contain a valid sample of the lithic technological practices of a hominid group during the period of formation of the deposit, although *in situ* manifestations could be much more diverse. Therefore, if adjacent derived deposits could be shown to be i) contemporary at the scale of a hominid generation, and ii) to contain significantly contrasting lithic material culture, one could begin to consider the contemporaneous presence of different industrial traditions as suggested by Breuil and Wymer, although this does not seem to have been the case in southern England in the early Hoxnian. When one considers time, there is no reason to pre-suppose that vertical change in techonological practices, as observed in the geological record of a region, is more related to an incursion of a new group with a different industrial tradition than drift of cultural practices within the original group. In fact, when one reconciles the nature of the geological record, which probably preserves (even in transported contexts) archaeological data from relatively narrow bands of prehistoric time compared with the long periods when nothing is preserved, with the likelihood of drift within the cultural practices of a hominid group existing in an active and changing social and geographical environment, then quite sharp vertical changes in lithic technology become easily explained without the need to invoke an incursion by another group with different cultural practices. With respect to Clactonian and Acheulian industries, Clactonian industries already contain a bifacial element, so that all that is required to transform one into the other is a more intensive focus on the bifacial element, supported by a framework of mobility and social learning which solves the logistic problems of obtaining access to the soft-hammers necessary for thinning and finishing handaxes and enables the cultural transmission of the appropriate skills.

Mithen has suggested that the observed pattern of lithic technological change can be explained in relation to changing group-size and environment. There are several problems with this explanation, particularly the facts of Mithen's claimed association of Clactonian and Acheulian industries with wooded environments and open environments respectively, and the likely impact of particular environments on group-size and social learning frameworks (cf. Wenban-Smith 1995). An alternative explanation on similar grounds was proposed (*ibid.*) which explained the observed archaeological pattern as the fragmentation of stable groups under the stresses of living in a periglacial environment, and their re-establishment in more temperate conditions. However this explanation is similarly vulnerable to uncertainties about the association of technological practices with palaeo-environments, and the relationship between environment and social learning frameworks. A more viable alternative suggestion might be that flake and core technological strategies work well as an *ad hoc* technology, producing cutting tools on the spur of the moment. Such a technology would suffice for hominids in a flint-rich landscape, where appropriate raw material is never far away. Such landscapes would have been characteristic of the early temperate stages of postglacial periods, particularly the Hoxnian in south eastern England after the retreat of the Anglian ice, which would have left a landscape rich in coarse fluviatile and outwash gravels. However in a flint-poor landscape, with fluviatile gravels silting over and other sources becoming more vegetated, *ad hoc* technological strategies would have become increasingly inadequate. In these circumstances portable tools, carried in anticipation of possible use, would have been favoured. Current evidence from Middle Pleistocene sites such as Boxgrove Q1B (Pitts & Roberts 1997) and Olorgesaillie (Isaac 1977) shows that handaxes were habitually carried around the landscape before abandonment at certain locations for whatever reason. Therefore it is suggested here that the development of Acheulian industries in the Hoxnian in south eastern England is reflecting a drift in cultural practices over numerous generations of Archaic hominids from an *ad hoc* flake-and-core dominated lithic technology towards a more varied technology with a significant portable handaxe element in response to the changing availablity of raw material in the territory habitually exploited.

One issue which remains to be considered is a non culture-historical explanation for the Clactonian assemblage from Little Thurrock, which is neatly subsumed within Ohel's and McNabb and Ashton's scenarios, but which poses potential problems for other scenarios. The gravel containing this assemblage has recently been dated by Bridgland (1994) to early in OIS 10 (early Saalian), later than the Middle Gravels at Swanscombe. Previous workers (King & Oakley 1936; Wymer 1957) have used the Clactonian industry as an argument for correlating the gravel with Phase I of the Swanscombe sequence (the Lower Gravel and Lower Loam). Archaeological evidence aside, other workers have used biostratigraphic evidence to suggest correlation between the main Swanscombe sequence (Phase II – the Middle Gravels) and the Grays brickearths, under which the gravel containing the Clactonian material from Little Thurrock lies (Hinton 1926; Kerney 1959). However this requires the postulation of a special case of local erosion at Little Thurrock to a lower base than roughly contemporaneous deposits at nearby Swanscombe. Therefore there are a range of possibilities for explaining the Little Thurrock manifestation, other than Ohel's and McNabb and Ashton's. Firstly, one way or another, the Little Thurrock Clactonian assemblage dates to the early Hoxnian (OIS 11). This would mean either rejecting Bridgland's conclusions on the complex deposits in the Grays area, or postulating a complex scenario of erosion of the deposit originally containing the Clactonian assemblage and its re-incorporation into Saalian gravels. Secondly, the Clactonian industrial tradition could have been re-developed in conjunction with a similar cold climate flint-rich environment to that in which it first appeared. Considering the social investment and technological complexity in learning and maintaining a cultural tradition of handaxe manufacture, there would have to be adaptive pressure for handaxe based traditions to be maintained over long periods. In the absence of such pressure it is reasonable to suggest that simpler core and flake technologies would once again have sufficed, and that the significance of handaxe manufacture would have decreased.

CONCLUSIONS

It has been argued that, despite the theoretical inadequacies associated with the original creation of the Acheulian and the Clactonian as distinct industrial traditions, they nonetheless genuinely reflect real and significant patterning in the archaeological record, with Clactonian industries being exclusively present in south eastern England in the early part of the Hoxnian, before Acheulian industries become more prevalent in the later Hoxnian. The ideas that these industries reflect either integral parts of the same reduction sequence (Ohel 1979) or complementary parts of the same technological repertoire (McNabb 1992; Ashton *et al* 1994; McNabb & Ashton 1995) have both been rejected on the grounds of the lack of Acheulian bifacial technology in deposits containing Clactonian material formed over relatively long duration and from a wide catchment. The long-established orthodoxy that the Clactonian and the Acheulian are the industrial traditions of two separate groups has also been rejected in favour of an explanation which involves technological change within a hominid population network over a long period of time in response ultimately to changing raw material availability.

NOTES

1. Throughout this paper the main point of reference for dating is the Anglian glaciation, whose widespread till provides a straigraphic link both directly with East Anglian sites, and indirectly with Thames Valley sites by extrapolation of the relationship between the till and the Boyn Hill/Orsett Heath gravel at Hornchurch railway cutting. The immediate post-Anglian interglacial, represented in the Boyn Hill/Orsett Heath formation at Swanscombe, is referred to throughout this paper as the Hoxnian, notwithstanding doubts about whether the actual sequence at Hoxne is immediately post-Anglian (cf. Bridgland 1994).

2. The main collections (RA Smith, ex-Institute of Archaeology, Kennard, Leakey, Marston and Waechter) held by the British Museum contain between 2,500 and 3,000 artefacts from the Lower Gravel at Swanscombe and Rickson's Pit alone.

3. Four of Warren's specimens, collected off Clacton-on-Sea, cannot be relocated; Warren's description of three of these as 'rude' or 'pseudo-Chellean' suggest non-classic affinities, and the other is an unknown quantity.

4. Experimental work has shown that the manufacture of a handaxe produces between 50 and 100 pieces of debitage over 2cm maximum dimension, and that approximately 25% of this debitage is clearly identifiable as from bifacial production (Newcomer 1971; Wenban-Smith 1996).

REFERENCES

Ashton, N. & McNabb, J. 1994. Bifaces in perspective. In N.Ashton & A.David (eds), *Stories in Stone*, 182–191. London: Lithic Studies Society Occasional Paper No 4.

Ashton, N., McNabb, J., Irving, B., Lewis, S. & Parfitt, S. 1994. Contemporaneity of Clactonian and Acheulian flint industries at Barnham, Suffolk. *Antiquity* 68, 585–9.

Binford, L.R. & Binford, S.R. 1966. A preliminary analysis of functional variability in the Mousterian of Levallois facies. *American Anthropologist* 68(2), 238–95.

Binford, S.R. & Binford, L.R. 1969. Stone tools and human behaviour. *Scientific American* 220, 70–84.

Breuil, H. 1926. Palaeolithic industries from the beginning of the Rissian to the beginning of the Würmian glaciation. *Man* 116, 176–9.

Breuil, H. 1932. Les industries à éclats du paléolithique ancien: I. Le Clactonien. *Préhistoire* 1, 125–90.

Breuil, H. 1939. The Pleistocene succession in the Somme Valley. *Proceedings of the Prehistoric Society* 5, 33–8.

Breuil, H. & Koslowski, L. 1931. Etudes de stratigraphie paléolithique dans le nord de la France, la Belgique et l'Angleterre: la vallée de la Somme. *L'Anthropologie* 41, 449–88.

Breuil, H. & Koslowski, L. 1932. Etudes de stratigraphie paléolithique dans le nord de la France, la Belgique et l'Angleterre: V – Basse terrasse de la Somme. *L'Anthropologie* 42, 27–47, 291–314.

Breuil, H. & Koslowski, L. 1934. Etudes de stratigraphie paléolithique dans le nord de la France, la Belgique et l'Angleterre: La Belgique. *L'Anthropologie* 44, 249–90.

Bridgland, D.R. 1994. *Quaternary of the Thames*. London: Chapman & Hall, Geological Review Series 7.

Conway, B.W. 1995. Bifaces in a Clactonian context at Little Thurrock, Grays, Essex. *Lithics* 16, 41–6.

Conway, B.W., McNabb, J. & Ashton, N. (eds) 1996. *Excavations at Barnfield Pit, Swanscombe, 1968–72*. London: British Museum Occasional Paper 94

Hinton. M.A.C. 1926. The Pleistocene Mammalia of the British Isles and their bearing upon the date of the glacial period. *Proceedings of the Yorkshire Geological Society, New Series* 20, 325–48.

Isaac, G.L. 1977. *Olorgesaillie, Archaeological Studies of a Middle Pleistocene Lake Basin in Kenya*. London: University of Chicago Press.

Kerney, M.P. 1959. *Pleistocene Non-marine Mollusca of the English Interglacial Deposits*. Unpublished PhD thesis, University of London.

King, W.B.R. & Oakley, K.P. 1936. The Pleistocene succession in the Lower part of the Thames valley. *Proceedings of the Prehistoric Society* 1, 52–76.

McNabb, J. 1992. *The Clactonian: British Lower Palaeolithic Flint Technology in Biface and Non-biface Assemblages*. Unpublished PhD thesis, University of London.

McNabb, J. & Ashton, N.M. 1992. The cutting edge: bifaces in the Clactonian. *Lithics* 13, 4–10.

McNabb, J. & Ashton, N.M. 1995. Thoughtful flakers. *Antiquity* 5, 289–301.

Mithen, S. 1994. Technology and society during the Middle Pleistocene: hominid group size, social learning and industrial variability. *Cambridge Archaeological Journal* 4, 3–32.

de Mortillet, G. 1869. Essai d'une classification des cavernes et des stations sous abris. *Comptes Rendus de l'Academie de Science de Paris* 68, 553–5.

de Mortillet, G. 1872. Classification des ages de la Pierre. *Comptes Rendus: Congrés International d'Anthropologie et d'Archaéologie Préhistorique* (Bruxelles) 6, 432–44.

de Mortillet, G. & de Mortillet, A. 1900, 3rd edition. *Le Préhistorique Origine et Antiquité de l'Homme*. Paris: Reinwald.

Newcomer, M.H. 1971. Some quantitative experiments in hand-axe manufacture. *World Archaeology* 3, 85–94.

Newcomer, M.H. 1979. Comment. *Current Anthropology* 20, 717.

Ohel, M. 1979. The Clactonian: an independent complex or an integral part of the Acheulian. *Current Anthropology* 20, 685–726.

Ovey, C.D. (ed.) 1964. *The Swanscombe Skull: a Survey of Research on a Pleistocene Site*. London: Royal Anthropological Institute Occasional Paper 20.

Paterson, T.T. 1937. Studies in the Palaeolithic succession of England. No. 1: the Barnham sequence. *Proceedings of the Prehistoric Society* 3, 87–135.

Penck, A. & Brückner, E. 1909. *Die Alpen im Eiszeitalter*. Leipzig.

Pitts, M. & Roberts, M.B. 1997. *Fairweather Eden*. London: Century.

Roe, D.A. 1981. *The Lower and Middle Palaeolithic Periods in Britain*. London: Routledge & Kegan Paul.

Singer, R., Gladfelter, B.G. & Wymer, J.J. (eds) 1993. *The Lower Palaeolithic Site at Hoxne, England*. London: The University of Chicago Press.

Singer, R., Wymer, J.J., Gladfelter, B.G. & Wolff, R. 1973. Excavation of the Clactonian industry at the Golf Course, Clacton-on-Sea, Essex. *Proceedings of the Prehistoric Society* 39, 6–74.

Smith, R.A. & Dewey, H. 1913. Stratification at Swanscombe: report on excavations made on behalf of the British Museum and H.M. Geological Survey. *Archaeologia* 64, 177–204.

Trigger, B.G. 1989. *A History of Archaeological Thought*. Cambridge: Cambridge University Press.

Turner, C. & Kerney, M.P. 1971. A note on the age of the freshwater beds of the Clacton Channel. *Journal of the Geological Society of London* 127, 87–93.

Waechter, J. d'A. 1969. Swanscombe 1969. *Proceedings of the Royal Anthropological Institute of Great Britain and Ireland for 1969*, 83–5.

Warren, S.H. 1922. The Mesvinian industry of Clacton-on-Sea. *Proceedings of the Prehistoric Society of East Anglia* 3, 597–602.

Warren, S.H. 1926. The classification of the Lower Palaeolithic with especial reference to Essex. *Transactions of the South Eastern Union of Scientific Societies 1926*, 38–50.

Wenban-Smith, F.F. 1995. Another one bites the dust. *Lithics* 16, 99–108.

Wenban-Smith, F.F. 1996. *The Palaeolithic Archaeology of Baker's Hole: a Case Study for Focus in Lithic Analysis*. Unpublished PhD thesis, University of Southampton.

Wymer, J.J. 1957. A Clactonian flint industry at Little Thurrock, Grays, Essex. *Proceedings of the Geologists' Association* 68, 159–77.

Wymer, J.J. 1964. Excavations at Barnfield Pit, 1955–1960. In C.D.Ovey (ed.), *The Swanscombe Skull: a Survey of Research on a Pleistocene Site*, 19–60. London: Royal Anthropological Institute, Occasional Paper 20.

Wymer, J.J. 1968. *Lower Palaeolithic Archaeology in Britain as Represented by the Thames Valley*. London: John Baker.

Wymer, J.J. 1974. Clactonian and Acheulian industries in Britain-their chronology and significance. *Proceedings of the Geological Association* 85, 391–421.

Wymer, J.J. 1983. The Lower Palaeolithic site at Hoxne. *Proceedings of the Suffolk Institute of Archaeology and History* 35, 169–89.

Wymer, J.J. 1985. *Palaeolithic Sites of East Anglia*. Norwich: Geo Books.

Wymer, J.J. 1988. Palaeolithic archaeology and the British Quaternary sequence. *Quaternary Science Reviews* 7, 79–98.

14. Twisted Ovate Bifaces in the British Lower Palaeolithic: Some Observations and Implications

Mark J. White

ABSTRACT

This paper offers some observations on the mode of manufacture and occurrence of twisted ovate bifaces in the British Isles. It suggests that at a number of British sites twisted ovates represent a deliberately imposed form that, on the basis of the current evidence, seems to be temporally restricted to late OIS 11/early OIS 10. While the possibility of functional significance or resharpening cannot be discounted, the paper tentatively concludes that the practice of twisting the edges, for whatever purpose, might present evidence for relatively short-lived ('cultural') knapping traditions within biface making populations, who might have been predominantly right-handed.

INTRODUCTION

> *'This edge, however, is not in one plane, but considerably curved, so that when seen sideways it forms an ogee sweep...I have other implements ... with similarly curved edges, both from France and ... England, but whether this curvature was intentional, it is impossible to say. In some cases it is so marked that it can hardly be the result of accident, and the curve is, so far as I have observed, almost without exception Z, and not S. If not intentional, the form may be the result of all the blows by which the implement was finally chipped out, having been given on the one face, on one side, and on the opposite face on the other'*
> (Evans 1897, 558)

One hundred years after Evans penned these words the enigma surrounding twisted ovates remains as puzzling as ever. In one respect, this reflects the general problems still surrounding the significance of variations in biface form, but it also highlights the fact that favoured explanatory models, while probably capable of explaining large amounts of the extant variation, do not provide the whole picture. Twisted ovates are a good case in point.

In recent years many workers have argued that gross levels of biface variability, such as shape and apparent technological sophistication, largely reflect the dimensions and flaking potential of different raw materials (Jones 1979; Villa 1983; Isaac 1984; Ashton & McNabb 1994; White 1995; 1996; see also Evans 1863; Flower 1868). In Britain, such models have sought to explain Roe's (1968) pointed and ovate 'traditions', suggesting that this division relates to the nature of the flint resources used and their effects on human technological procedures (White 1995; 1996; Ashton & McNabb 1994). According to these models, well-worked ovates with all-round edges were preferentially produced wherever the local flint was large and robust enough to support intensive reduction procedures around the entire piece; while assemblages characterised by partially-edged, moderately worked pointed forms were the result of exploiting sources of smaller, narrower flint blanks that imposed restrictions on human technological actions regarding the location and extent of working. Both 'traditions' are thus seen not as the products of different biface making populations, but the same populations coping with the exigencies of a heterogeneous environment, using different resources in an adaptable, flexible manner.

Yet, while providing insights into large-scale variability, such models are ill-equipped to deal with small-scale, more idiosyncratic, phenomena such as twisted ovates. While the overall presence of twisted ovates, like ovate bifaces in general, might depend on adequate raw materials, under the tenets of these models, if it was possible to produce an ovate at all, it must also have been possible to produce the twisted variant. So the frequent occurrence of twists in some assemblages, but not in others, must be due to factors other than raw materials. This demonstrates that, even though raw materials may be a 'prime-mover', biface morphology is undoubtedly the result of several complex, interacting, superimposed factors. The key to a deeper understanding of biface variability lies in the relationships between these factors, and how each might contribute to the overall picture. This paper offers some observations on twisted ovates, along with some suggestions regarding their significance, which may prove useful in beginning this process.

METHODS OF MANUFACTURE

Twisted edges can have been produced accidentally, yet in many cases they are clearly the product of a distinct, definable knapping strategy – the 'classic twisted strategy' – reproduced so frequently in some assemblages that it surely must have been deliberate. This strategy involved the conceptual division of the implement into four quarters or arcs, with the working of each quarter occurring in a constant 'active zone'. This zone was located either near the knapper's fingers or wrist. The different quarters were brought into the active knapping zone via a series of rotations and inversions to arrive at differential working across the diagonal plane on each face (White & Pettitt 1996). In its classic format (Fig. 14.1) this strategy can be described thus:

1. the first quarter was held in the active zone and knapped
2. the piece was inverted, bringing the second quarter (the arc directly opposite 1, on the other face) into the active zone
3. the piece was rotated, bringing the third quarter (the arc diagonally opposite 2, on the same face) into the active zone
4. the piece was inverted, bringing the final quarter (the arc directly opposite 3, on the other face) into the active zone

The actual sequence of rotation and inversion was free to vary, the key to obtaining the twisted profile being differential reduction along the diagonal plane on each face. The twist could have been imposed upon a biface at any stage during the shaping or finishing phases of production, yet in many cases it is clearly the result of the final blows. To some extent the 'classic twisted strategy' may be classified as a finishing technique.

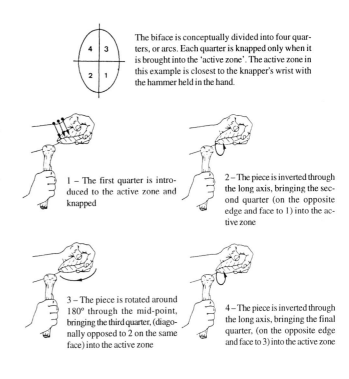

Figure 14.1. Proposed knapping technique for the manufacture of the classic twisted ovate.

To a large extent the production of a classic twisted profile depended upon working both the butt and the tip, and this is perhaps why they occur almost exclusively on the heavily worked, circumferentially-edged ovate forms. However, a twisted ovate may also have been obtained by preferentially working a single diagonal, and a single twisted edge may have sometimes resulted from more intensive working along a single quarter.

EVIDENCE OF HANDEDNESS?

As noted by Evans (1897) most twisted ovates exhibit a Z, rather than S, shaped profile. In a sample of 65 twisted ovates from 5 British sites, only 4 pieces exhibited an S-twist. This bias has implications for handedness in Middle Pleistocene hominids, although this is complicated by the fact that a Z-twist can be produced in either hand, depending on the position of the active zone (Fig. 14.2).

When creating a twisted ovate the knapper had two choices regarding the location of the active zone – it could have been the arc closest to the wrist (the wrist quarter), or that nearest the finger-tips (the finger quarter). Given

Toth's (1985a) observation that modern knappers tend to hold their hammer in their dominant hand to facilitate greater precision in direction and force (i.e. a right-handed knapper will hold their hammer in their right hand, the piece to be worked in their left), four cases can be described:

1. right handed knapper employing the 'wrist quarter' as the active zone- Z-twist
2. right-handed knapper employing the 'finger quarter' as the active zone- S-twist
3. left-handed knapper employing the 'wrist quarter' as the active zone- S-twist
4. left-handed knapper employing the 'finger quarter' as the active zone- Z-twist

The clear Z-twist bias in the archaeological record suggests that either 1 or 4 occurred most frequently among Middle Pleistocene hominids. Considered alone it is difficult to determine which situation is more likely, although the direction of removals and the relationship between adjacent flake scars may hold some clues (cf. Toth 1985a). Unfortunately, the data to examine this is unavailable at the present time. However, the primacy of right-handedness is perhaps to be favoured, given recent observations of cut-mark patterns on hominid teeth from Boxgrove and other European sites (Bermúdez *et al.* 1988; Selkirk 1997; Simon Parfitt pers. comm.) and other artefact studies which suggest a dominance of right-handed individuals during the Early and Middle Pleistocene (Toth 1985a; Cornford 1986; Bradley & Sampson 1986). The implications of such observations go far beyond bio-mechanics. Evidence for handedness suggests that the lateralisation present in the modern human brain, where the left hemisphere is dominant in nine out of ten individuals, is an archaic trait (Toth 1985a; Cornford 1986). The left hemisphere is also the centre for language, although the specific relationship between language, tool-use and handedness is still debated (see papers in Gibson & Ingold 1993; Toth 1985a), leaving the significance of such observations for language in Middle Pleistocene hominids unclear.

THE OCCURRENCE OF TWISTED OVATES: TECHNICAL TRADITIONS?

Twisted ovates occur in low or very low frequencies in many British biface assemblages. In such cases we might be justified in regarding them as the accidental replication of a 'twisted strategy' within a population that normally did not employ such techniques. In assemblages with major proportions of twisted ovates (Table 14.1), however, it seems more likely that they reflect the frequent transmission and use of a technique of manufacture designed to achieve twisted edges. Such assemblages pose the question: what was the significance of the twisted ovate for these hominid populations?

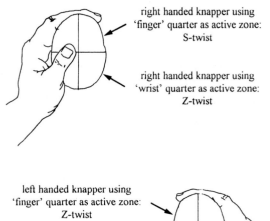

right handed knapper using 'finger' quarter as active zone: S-twist

right handed knapper using 'wrist' quarter as active zone: Z-twist

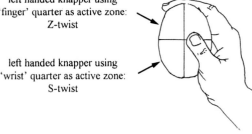

left handed knapper using 'finger' quarter as active zone: Z-twist

left handed knapper using 'wrist' quarter as active zone: S-twist

Figure 14.2. Zonal division of the twisted ovate showing how the use of different hands and different active zones may produce either a Z or an S twist.

1 – Ovate-dominated biface assemblages exhibiting high proportions of twisted ovates	
Bowman's Lodge, Kent	27–31%
Wansunt Pit, Kent	28%
Swanscombe, Kent: Barnfield Upper Loams	22%
Swanscombe, Kent: Rickson's Pit	at least 15%
Elveden, Suffolk	36–40%
Allington Hill, Cambridgeshire	46%
2 – Point-dominated biface assemblages showing high proportions of twisted bifaces in the ovate element	
Foxhall Road, Ipswich, Suffolk	40% (of ovate element only)
Hitchin Lake Beds, Hertfordshire	45% (of ovate element only)

Table 14.1. British Lower Palaeolithic sites exhibiting significant numbers of twisted ovates (data from Roe 1968, Wymer 1968 and personal observation. Ranges indicate differences in the observations of Roe and the author)

The geographical distribution of the sites listed in Table 14.1 is fairly widespread – the apparent concentration in the Lower Thames basin and East Anglia probably represents the more intensive research history in this area. However, perhaps of greater importance is the fact that, according to currently favoured dates, the human occupations represented by these assemblages all belong to the later phases of OIS 11 (Hoxnian Interglacial) or early OIS 10. (Bridgland 1994; Wymer 1985; Boreham & Gibbard 1995; Nick Ashton pers. comm.) These dates are based on lithostratigraphy and other independent dating techniques (not artefact typology), although Allington Hill is presently undated. Twisted ovates are virtually absent from pre-Hoxnian sites (belonging to OIS 12 and 13) such as High Lodge (Ashton *et al.* 1992), Boxgrove (Roberts *et al.* 1994), Caversham Ancient Channel (Wymer 1968) or Warren Hill (Roe 1968; Wymer *et al.* 1991), and do not, apparently, occur in any significant numbers in sites later than OIS 11/10 such as Purfleet, Stoke Newington, Wolvercote and Furze Platt (Roe 1968; Bridgland 1994). However in many of the currently dated later sites refined ovate bifaces in general are rare, which perhaps accounts for the absence of twisted ovates. Of course, the strength of a pattern based on so few good sites is always fragile and depends entirely upon the reliability of the suggested dates. Future revisions and new discoveries might well obliterate it.

In adjacent areas of Europe, notably northern France, this chronological patterning does not exist. Here twisted ovates occur in sites such as Cagny-La Garenne (OIS 12/11), Cagny-l'Epinette (OIS 10/9) and the famous *sable roux* at Rue de Cagny (OIS 8?) (Callow 1986; Tuffreau & Antoine 1995). Clearly, in France the twisted technique persisted over great lengths of time. But, if the British dating evidence survives future scrutiny, the apparent temporal patterning may provide precious insights into short term social trends, or traditions, in the earlier Palaeolithic.

For the sake of the argument, if we assume that this pattern is valid, several speculative scenarios might be suggested.

Continuity – the biface making hominids who colonised the 'British Peninsula' during the (later) Hoxnian came from restricted populations in which the twisted strategy was already an important part of the technological repertoire, twists eventually spreading throughout their known distribution as these original populations expanded into new areas, occurring frequently (not necessarily always) in the assemblages left by these hominids. This hypothesis has further implications regarding the geographical location of the ancestral populations and direction of colonisation.

Drift – Britain was colonised by various populations from adjacent areas of Europe with a diverse and flexible repertoire of biface making techniques. Partially isolated on this northwestern peninsula, virtually random effects on the dynamics of social transmission (see Mithen 1994; Steele & Shennan 1996) such as drift (Isaac 1972) or social distance (Mellars 1996) caused certain techniques to rise in importance. For a relatively short period during the later Hoxnian the classic twisted strategy became common among biface making populations in Britain, spreading over fairly long time scales through adjacent *'local hominid networks'* – local, spatially bounded structures which formed the arena for social, technological and subsistence behaviours and embraced only close kin and neighbours (Gamble 1993a; 1995; 1996a; 1996b) – eventually creating the impression of a regional tradition.

If Britain had become an island by the late Hoxnian (for opinions on this issue see Bridgland & d'Olier 1995; Gibbard 1995; Keen 1995; Meijer & Preece 1995; Stuart 1995), then such insularity could have easily contributed to either scenario, leading to the development of local 'technical traditions' (Mellars 1996), passed on through the social sphere purely by virtue of their frequency in previous generations, without any notions of normative stylistic/cultural preference. Following the subsequent cold stage (OIS 10), during which populations in Britain possibly became locally extinct or abandoned vast areas of the country (cf. Gamble 1993b; 1994), the same processes could have taken different routes, with twists never again assuming much importance. However, in the original parent populations, possibly including groups from areas around northern France, the technique persisted; either a continuous facet of certain groups or waxing and waning to assume importance during more than one period.

Both are nice *Just-So* stories, and probably ones we will never be able to test. Yet, they stress that concepts such as tradition, although often very difficult to access, might still be valuable in explaining some aspects of Lower Palaeolithic lithic variability. Considering the temporal resolution of our data, we might even argue that twists totally dominated production for a short period, eventually being replaced by untwisted forms to produce assemblages containing both types. Even if the apparent temporal patterning eventually proves illusory, twisted bifaces could still represent evidence for local technical traditions among particular groups (cf. Wymer 1991). With the improved resolution offered by the oxygen isotope sequence we may now begin to discern more patterning within the previously 'bewildering variety' (Roe 1981, 270) of Lower Palaeolithic assemblages.

EVIDENCE OF RESHARPENING?

While twisted ovates may be temporally restricted in the British Isles, suggesting that they might form a tradition of manufacture, we should not too readily abandon the quest for further explanations. The apparent patterning does not automatically imply *iconological style* (Chase & Dibble 1987), but may have a significance that underlines the social transmission of technological knowledge and the inextricable social nature of technical and functional acts (e.g. Ingold 1993; Gamble 1995). Patterns in the archaeological record which *prima facie* might purely suggest the presence of 'stylistically preferred forms' could conceal other levels of variation with further behavioural significance. Moreover, if the suggested pattern proves to be illusory, we must look elsewhere in order to explain twisted ovates. One vogue mechanism for variation in lithic tool forms is resharpening (commonly known as reduction) in which certain types of artefacts are seen as the later, resharpened expressions of other forms (Rolland & Dibble 1990; Dibble & Rolland 1992; McPherron 1994;

1996). A key stimulus behind resharpening is suggested to be raw material economising.

Taking the British evidence, the geology of the Kentish sites shows that during the relevant period of human occupation none were host to an immediate source of raw materials, and flints/roughouts/bifaces were probably imported to these locations from other adjacent areas of the landscape (White 1995; 1996). If 'Acheulean' hominids were practising resharpening, then these are precisely the conditions under which we might expect it to occur most frequently (Dibble 1991). The remaining sites in Table 14.1 all had access to an immediately available source of flint, although it is still possible to invoke reasons why economising might have been important. At Elveden, although two sources of flint existed, in the form of a Chalk riverbank and coarse solifluction gravel (Paterson & Fagg 1940), large, prime, unflawed nodules were probably at a premium at any given moment in time (Nick Ashton, pers. comm.) Similarly, while hominids at Hitchin and Foxhall Road had access to coarse gravel deposits, many of the available clasts seem to have been fairly small and suitable only for partially worked pointed forms, while large nodules, capable of supporting well-worked bifaces with an all-round edges, were relatively scarce.

If raw material economising, manifest as resharpening, was taking place at these sites, then the twisted ovate might represent a technique for reworking the more typical untwisted forms, perhaps allowing the rejuvenation of edges without detrimental alteration to the overall length of the biface or the bifacial edges. Such hypotheses are immediately amenable to testing through direct examination of the artefacts themselves. For the purposes of this paper, two basic preliminary tests can be proposed. If twisted ovates are resharpened variants of untwisted ovates then we might expect:

1. twisted ovates to display more flaking scars than untwisted ovates
2. if the twisted strategy concentrates on removing flakes from the margins of the biface, width might be expected to diminish more rapidly than length. Twisted ovates might therefore be more highly elongated than untwisted ovates.

Tables 14.2 and 14.3 present summary data for elongation and scar counts for twisted and untwisted ovates for five British sites. The results are ambiguous. While scar counts generally conform to the above prediction, elongation behaves as expected at only two sites, one of which (Bowman's Lodge) does not meet expectations for scar count. The differences in scar counts could simply show that twisted ovates require more finishing blows than untwisted forms, and reveal nothing about resharpening. However, it is premature to dismiss resharpening based on such a cursory examination, and more rigorous methodologies could be devised to test this notion further.

Site	Scar count	Elongation (B/L)	n
Bowman's Lodge	56	0.727	15
Elveden	58	0.610	23
Foxhall Road	51	0.679	16
Hitchin	50	0.597	12
Wansunt Pit	54	0.735	17

Table 14.2. Mean scar counts and elongation for untwisted ovates

Site	Scar count	Elongation (B/L)	n
Bowman's Lodge	56	0.658	9
Elveden	64	0.625	27
Foxhall Road	65	0.732	11
Hitchin	60	0.641	9
Wansunt Pit	60	0.703	9

Table 14.3. Mean scar counts and elongation for twisted ovates

DID TWISTED OVATES SERVE A UNIQUE FUNCTION?

Both Roe (1981) and Bosinski (1995) have postulated that twisted ovates might have served a different function to other biface forms, implying that their presence in some assemblages might reflect different activity facies. Such notions deserve full consideration, although proposing specific activities in the absence of use-wear analysis is a fairly fruitless exercise. Moreover, when considering biface function we must take into account the growing body of evidence, derived from use-wear, experimental and archaeological data (Jones 1980; 1981; Toth 1985b; Ashton & McNabb 1994; Mitchell & Gorman 1995; Mitchell 1996; cf. Villa 1990; Mussi 1995), that bifaces were primarily designed to assist in animal butchery. This is not to say that some forms did not serve auxiliary purposes, and indeed few data relate specifically to twisted implements, but envisaging precisely how a twist would radically alter the function of a biface is nonetheless difficult.

However, experiments conducted at the Institute of Archaeology, London, showed the twisted ovate to be an indifferent cutting tool, the twist hindering smooth operation, but theoretically more suited to long-term processing activities (Walter 1996 and pers. comm.). These experiments suggest, then, that twisted ovates were not used to cut or butcher, but to scrape, which raises the questions of why they possess long *sharp* edges and bifacial working. Could twists be a modified, re-worked form of the untwisted ovate designed to serve a new function (cf. Jelinek 1977) or is it simply that Middle Pleistocene hominids were far more adept at cutting with twisted bifaces than modern experimenters? If twists represent a specific mode of manufacture, could this have been accompanied by a specific rhythm of use? Use-wear analysis is required before we can take any of these suggestions further, but no extant assemblage appears to be of sufficient pristine freshness to facilitate successful micro-wear studies.

SOME TENTATIVE CONCLUSIONS

The available evidence suggests that twisted ovate bifaces in the British Lower Palaeolithic were temporally restricted, occurring frequently in sites dated to late OIS 11 to early OIS 10. This might indicate that twisted ovates represent a specific 'tradition of manufacture', the type of which has proved more elusive (even illusory) when dealing with larger, general variation in *shape and technological sophistication*. However, the evidence is admittedly meagre, and we should be hesitant to use twisted ovates as a temporal/cultural marker. Moreover, there is a real need to avoid making artificial divisions between the various factors which might account for biface variability and thereby rehearse the classic Bordes/Binford debate. They are not mutually exclusive and there are no reasons, for example, why a resharpening practice of twisting the edges should not be a temporally restricted technical tradition in Britain, why resharpening should not alter the function of a piece, or why twists should not be an isochrestic (Sackett 1982) or even functionally unique biface variant that was important in the body of social knowledge only during the late Hoxnian. In other words, there are no reasons why twisted bifaces could not at once be of technical, functional and social import. Indeed, that biface variability reflects the complex interaction of several forces, perhaps all working within the boundaries imposed by the prime-movers (raw material potential and human technological parameters), must be considered the only firm conclusion of this paper. Hopefully future research will come closer to resolving some of these issues.

ACKNOWLEDGEMENTS

Thanks to Nick Ashton, John McNabb and Paul Mellars for their comments on earlier drafts of this paper, and to Paul Pettitt for the original discussion in The Mitre, November 1994 that led to this paper.

REFERENCES

Ashton, N.M & McNabb, J. 1994. Bifaces in perspective. In N.M Ashton & A. David (eds), *Stories in Stone*, 182–91. London: Lithic Studies Society Occasional Paper 4.

Ashton, N.M., Cook, J., Lewis, S.G. & Rose, J. 1992. *High Lodge: Excavations by G. de G. Sieveking 1962–1968 and J. Cook 1988*. London: British Museum Press.

Bermúdez de Castro, J.M., Branage, T.G. & Jalvo, Y.F. 1988. Buccal striations on fossil human anterior teeth: evidence of handedness in the Middle and Early Upper Pleistoene. *Journal of Human Evolution* 17, 403–12

Boreham, S. & Gibbard, P.L. 1995. Middle Pleistocene Hoxnian stage interglacial deposits at Hitchin, Hertfordshire, England. *Proceedings of the Geologists' Association* 106, 259–70.

Bosinski, G. 1995. Stone artefacts of the European Lower Palaeolithic: a short note. In W. Roebroeks & T. Van Kolfschoten (eds), *The Earliest Occupation of Europe: Proceedings of the European Science Foundation Workshop at Tautavel (France), 1993*, 263–8. Leiden: University of Leiden.

Bradley, B.A. & Sampson, C.G. 1986. Analysis by replication of two Acheulian artefact assemblages. In G.N. Bailey & P. Callow (eds), *Stone Age Prehistory: Essays in Memory of Charles McBurney*, 29–44. Cambridge: Cambridge University Press.

Bridgland, D.R. 1994. *Quaternary of the Thames*. London: Chapman and Hall. Geological Conservation Review Series 7.

Bridgland, D.R. & D'Olier, B. 1995. The Pleistocene evolution of the Thames and Rhine drainage systems in the south North Sea basin. In R.C. Preece (ed.), *Island Britain: a Quaternary Perspective*, 27–45. London: Geological Society Special Publication 96.

Callow, P. 1986. A Comparison of British and French Acheulian bifaces. In S.N. Collcutt (ed.), *The Palaeolithic of Britain and its Nearest Neighbours: Recent Trends*, 3–7. Sheffield: Department of Archaeology & Prehistory, University of Sheffield.

Chase, P. & Dibble, H. 1987. Middle Palaeolithic symbolism: a review of the current evidence and interpretations. *Journal of Anthropological Archaeology* 6, 263–96

Cornford, J.M. 1986. Specialized resharpening techniques and evidence of handedness. In P. Callow & J.M. Cornford (eds), *La Cotte de St. Brelade 1961–1978: Excavations by C.B.M. McBurney*. Norwich: Geo Books.

Dibble, H. 1991. Local raw material exploitation and its effects on Lower and Middle Palaeolithic assemblage variability. In A. Montet-White & S. Holon (eds), *Raw Material Exploitation among Prehistoric Hunter-gatherers*, 33–46. Kansas: University of Kansas Publications in Anthropology 19.

Dibble, H. & Rolland, N. 1992. Beyond the Bordes Binford debate: a new synthesis of factors underlying assemblage variability in the Middle Palaeolithic of Western Europe. In H. Dibble & P.A. Mellars (eds), *The Middle Paleolithic: Adaptation, Behavior and Variability*, 1–28. Philadelphia: University Museum, University of Pennsylvania.

Evans, J. 1863. Account of some further discoveries of flint implements in the drift of the Continent and England. *Archaeologia* 39, 57–84.

Evans, J. 1897. *The Ancient Stone Implements, Weapons and Ornaments of Great Britain* (2nd Edition). London: Longmans Green.

Flower, J.W. 1868. On some flint implements lately found in the valley of the Little Ouse River at Thetford, Norfolk. *Quarterly Journal of the Geological Society of London* 23, 45–53

Gamble, C.S. 1993a. Exchange, foraging and local hominid networks. In C.Scarre & F.Healy (eds), *Trade and Exchange in Prehistoric Europe*, 35–44. Oxford: Oxbow Books.

Gamble, C.S. 1993b. *Timewalkers: The Prehistory of Global Colonisation*. Stroud: Alan Sutton.

Gamble, C.S. 1994. Personality most ancient. *British Archaeology* 1, 6.

Gamble, C.S. 1995. Lithics and social evolution. In A.J. Schofield (ed.), *Lithics in Context: Suggestions for the Future Direction of Lithic Studies*, 19–26. London: Lithics Studies Society Occasional Paper 5.

Gamble, C.S. 1996a. Hominid behaviour in the Middle Pleistocene: an English perspective. In C.S.Gamble & A.J. Lawson (eds), *The English Palaeolithic Reviewed*, 63–71. Salisbury: Trust For Wessex Archaeology.

Gamble, C.S. 1996b. Making tracks: hominid networks and the evolution of the social landscape. In J.Steele & S.Shennan (eds),

The Archaeology of Human Ancestry: Power, Sex and Tradition, 253–77. London: Routledge.

Gibbard, P.L. 1995. The formation of the Straits of Dover In R.C. Preece (ed.), *Island Britain: a Quaternary Perspective*, 15–26. London: Geological Society Special Publication 96.

Gibson, K.R. & Ingold, T. 1993 (eds), *Tools, Language and Cognition in Human Evolution*. Cambridge: Cambridge University Press.

Ingold, T. 1993. Tool use, sociality and intelligence. In K.R.Gibson & T. Ingold (eds), *Tools, Language and Cognition in Human Evolution*, 429–46. Cambridge: Cambridge University Press.

Isaac, G. 1972. Early phases in human behaviour: models in Lower Palaeolithic archaeology. In D.Clarke (ed.), *Models in Archaeology*, 167–99. London:Methuen.

Isaac, G. 1984. The archaeology of human origins: studies in the Lower Pleistocene in East Africa. In F.Wendorf & A.E.Close (eds), *Advances in World Archaeology* Vol. 3, 1–87. New York: Academic Press.

Jelinek, A. 1977. The Lower Palaeolithic: current evidence and interpretaion. *Annual Review of Anthropology* 6, 11–32

Jones, P. 1979. The effects of raw materials on biface manufacture. *Science* 204, 815–6.

Jones, P. 1980. Experimental butchery with modern stone tools and its relevance for Palaeolithic Archaeology. *World Archaeology* 12(2), 153–65.

Jones, P. 1981. Experimental implement manufacture and use: a case study from Olduvai Gorge, Tanzania. In J.Z.Young (ed.), *The Emergence of Man*, 189–95. Philosophical Transactions of the Royal Society of London 292.

Keen, D.H. 1995. Raised beaches and sea-levels in the English Channel in the Middle and Late Pleistocene: problems of interpretation and implications for the isolation of the British Isles. In R.C. Preece (ed.), *Island Britain: a Quaternary Perspective*, 63–74. London: Geological Society Special Publication 96.

McPherron, S.P. 1994. *A Reduction Model for Variability in Acheulian Biface Morphology*. Unpublished Ph.D. Dissertation, University of Pennsylvania.

McPherron, S.P. 1996. A Re-examination of the British biface data. *Lithics* 16, 47–63.

Meijer, T. & Preece, R.C. 1995. Malacological evidence relating to the insularity of the British Isles during the Quaternary. In R.C.Preece (ed.), *Island Britain: a Quaternary Perspective*, 89–110. London: Geological Society Special Publication 96.

Mellars, P.A. 1996. *The Neanderthal Legacy*. Princeton: University Press.

Mitchell, J.C. 1996. Studying biface butchery at Boxgrove: roe deer butchery with replica handaxes. *Lithics* 16, 64–9.

Mitchell, J.C. & Gorman, A. 1995. On the cutting edge: a report on a day meeting on lithic use-wear analysis. *Lithics* 15, 32–42.

Mithen, S.J. 1994. Technology and society during the Middle Pleistocene: hominid group size, social learning and industrial variation. *Cambridge Archaeological Journal* 4(1), 3–32.

Mussi, M. 1995. The earliest occupation of Europe: Italy. In W. Roebroeks & T. Van Kolfschoten (eds), *The Earliest Occupation of Europe: Proceedings of the European Science Foundation Workshop at Tautavel (France), 1993*, 27–50. Leiden: University of Leiden.

Paterson, T.T & Fagg, B.E.B. 1940. Studies in the Palaeolithic succession in England II: the Upper Brecklandian Acheul (Elveden). *Proceedings of the Prehistoric Society* 6, 1–29.

Roberts, M.B., Stringer, C.B. & Parfitt, S.A. 1994. A hominid tibia from Middle Pleistocene sediments at Boxgrove, U.K. *Nature* 369, 311–13

Roe, D.A. 1968. British Lower and Middle Palaeolithic handaxe groups. *Proceedings of the Prehistoric Society* 34, 1–82.

Roe, D.A. 1981. *The Lower and Middle Palaeolithic Periods in Britain*. London: Routledge and Kegan Paul.

Rolland, N. & Dibble, H. 1990. A new synthesis of Middle Paleolithic assemblage variability. *American Antiquity* 55(3) 480–99.

Sackett, J. 1982. Approaches to style in lithic technology. *Journal of Anthropological Archaeology* 1, 59–112.

Steele, J. & Shennan, S. 1996. Introduction. In J.Steele & S.Shennan (eds), *The Archaeology of Human Ancestry: Power, Sex, Tradition*, 1–41. London: Routledge.

Selkirk, A. 1997. Boxgrove. *Current Archaeology* 153, 323–33

Stuart, A.J. 1995. Insularity and Quaternary vertebrate faunas in Britain and Ireland. In R.C. Preece (ed.), *Island Britain: a Quaternary Perspective*, 111–25. London: Geological Society Special Publication 96.

Toth, N. 1985a. Archaeological evidence for preferential right-handedness in the Lower and Middle Pleistocene, and its possible implications. *Journal of Human Evolution* 14, 607–14.

Toth, N. 1985b. The Oldowan reassessed: a close look at early stone artefacts. *Journal of Archaeological Science* 12, 101–20.

Tuffreau, A. & Antoine, P. 1995. The earliest occupation of Europe: Continental Northwestern Europe. In W. Roebroeks & T. Van Kolfschoten (eds), *The Earliest Occupation of Europe: Proceedings of the European Science Foundation Workshop at Tautavel (France), 1993*, 147–63. Leiden: University of Leiden.

Villa, P. 1983. *Terra Amata and the Middle Pleistocene Archaeological Record of Southern France*. Berkley: University of California Publications in Anthropology No. 13.

Villa, P. 1990. Torralba and Aridos: elephant exploitation in Middle Pleistocene Spain. *Journal of Human Evolution* 19, 299–309.

Walter, D. 1996. *Twisted Bifaces: an Analysis of Intentionality and Functional Efficiency of Twisted Bifaces in the British Lower Palaeolithic*. Unpublished M.A dissertation, University of London.

White, M.J & Pettitt, P.B. 1996. Technology of Early Palaeolithic Western Europe: innovation, variability and a unified framework. *Lithics* 16, 27–40.

White, M.J. 1995. Raw materials and biface variability in southern Britain: a preliminary examination. *Lithics* 15, 1–20.

White, M.J. 1996. *Biface Variability and Human Behaviour: a Study from South-Eastern England*. Unpublished Ph.D Thesis, University of Cambridge.

Wymer, J.J. 1968. *Lower Palaeolithic Archaeology in Britain as Represented by the Thames Valley*. London: John Baker.

Wymer, J.J. 1985. *Palaeolithic Sites of East Anglia*. Norwich: Geo Books.

Wymer, J.J. 1991. The use of hand-axes for dating purposes. In S.G.Lewis, C.A.Whiteman & D.R. Bridgland (eds), *Central East Anglia and the Fen Basin*, 45–48. London: Quaternary Research Association Field Guide.

Wymer, J.J., Lewis, S.G. & Bridgland, D.R. 1991. Warren Hill, Mildenhall, Suffolk (TL 744743). In S.G.Lewis, C.A.Whiteman & D.R. Bridgland (eds), *Central East Anglia and the Fen Basin*, 50–8. London: Quaternary Research Association Field Guide.

15. Handaxes and Palaeolithic Individuals

Clive Gamble

Forty years ago Sir Grahame Clark made a strong case that 'the fact that prehistorians cannot identify individuals is no reason why they should ignore their existence' (1957, 248). This stricture has not been picked up with much enthusiasm in the Palaeolithic. Here the individual remains a twilight being lost in the long corridors of Pleistocene time. We are usually much happier when talking about the group, the species and even the techno-complex and the tradition. My aim in this paper is to point out that we continue to miss a great opportunity for Palaeolithic research if we persist in subscribing to this view. I want to take John Wymer's contribution to our subject as part of the evidence and celebrate, through an individual's contribution, the individuals we seek to understand in the remote past. This leads me to assess the capabilities of Pleistocene hominids in a rather different way than is popularly in vogue (Pitts & Roberts 1997; Roberts 1995).

PALAEOLITHIC INDIVIDUALS

It is common to find the view that studying the individual is an unpopular, if not impossible, goal in the Palaeolithic. A recent exchange makes the point. Mithen's studies of individual decision making (1990; 1993; 1994) have been criticised by Geoff Clark (1992) as unrealistic. The individual, according to Clark, cannot be adopted as an analytical unit in archaeology since only the accumulated results of group actions are preserved. 'The actions of individuals are forever likely to be beyond the resolution of the Palaeolithic...record (Clark 1992, 107)'. It is the group which persists rather than individuals. So, in Clark's view any attempt to analyse decision making by invoking individual psychology is doomed to failure. The proper perspective is one of group adaptation.

Mithen counters convincingly that

'It seems to me that a good explanation in archae-ology requires explicit reference to individual people going about their day to day business. They need to be explicitly attributed with knowledge of the world, a capacity to plan and make decisions, an ability to respond creatively and intelligently to the challenges of their social and physical environment. Without this, as in much of the group adaptationist archae-ology of the 1970s and 1980s, prehistoric people became swamped by the huge impersonal, mechan-istic forces such as "group selection" and "popu-lation pressure" (1993, 396)'.

The disagreement may be, as Mithen suggests (*op.cit.*) between proximate and ultimate explanations with an emphasis, respectively, on content as opposed to form when it comes to deciding what makes a good explanation. Clark clearly favours the latter, form based, approach. Mithen is also concerned with the decision rules that govern systems but which likewise enable individuals to express their capabilities to reach alternative solutions. Clark appears to deny this creativity. He sees the rules as paramount since this is how groups are constituted and perpetuated.

Mithen (*ibid.*, 394) echoes Shanks and Tilley's (1987, 210) view that we cannot screen the individual out of archaeological analysis. In this context it is worth re-membering how scientists build models of the world. They have successfully used such concepts as the unconscious, the gene, the atom or the molecule often long before they had the opportunity to observe them directly.

The distinction identified by Mithen between content and form seems to me crucial in our search for the Palaeolithic individual. It is not so much what we might, or might not find, but rather what capabilities we endow them with before the search begins. As Marshall Sahlins famously declared at the first Man the Hunter symposium in 1968:

'having equipped the hunter with bourgeois impulses and Palaeolithic tools, we judge his situation hope-less in advance (1968, 86).'

Sahlins was also describing a situation where a lifestyle was set by rules rather than created and worked out by individuals. It is as though individuals are hardwired to act in particular ways, pre-programmed to hunt, make tools and remain anonymous.

Of course this is not to deny that hominids lived, as we do, in wider groupings. The point is that those wider groupings are the result of negotiation, built from the bottom up by individuals, rather than pre-determined in some sort of top-down, genetic way. Admit this and there is much more creativity in the Palaeolithic than we are normally willing to own up to.

PRIMATES AS INDIVIDUALS

It seems strange that there is still resistance to the idea of Palaeolithic individuals when studies of the great apes are eager to identify their influence. Ever since Louis Leakey encouraged Jane Goodall to start her studies of the Gombe chimps we have come to learn about them as individuals. But we have not always followed through the implications of those demonstrable personalities. The reason for this appears to depend on our scientific culture and what is regards as a satisfying explanation.

For example, one aspect of primate individuality lies in the way they build bonds, their varying capacity for social life and their ability to grasp the fundamentals of a basic technology. Yes, some chimps are more intelligent than others, some more manipulating and malleable. They are highly individual in terms of their faces and characters. They create highly variable societies, albeit within the limits set by the resources available to them. These resources are their own bodies and the time they spend in interactions such as hugging, grooming, playing, parenting and fighting.

Asquith (1996) has drawn attention to the different primate research traditions in Japan and the West. The important point is that Japanese studies of macaques and other primates stem from a cultural rather than a biological approach. They started from a very different premise about the individual persona of an animal.

'Japanese researchers considered each individual of an entire species as a member of a society and as contributing to maintain the species society as a whole' (Asquith 1996, 248).

Even allowing for Goodall's named chimps, such as Flo, the Japanese went further by according variability to both the individual and to the groups to which they belonged. Such a view was not popular in the West since our scientific approach asks for objective criteria and measurement of such aspects as individuality or an animal's 'soul'. The approach which many favoured instead was to reserve the anthropomorphisation for the popular articles and use primate studies to examine concepts such as inclusive fitness and kin selection.

The parallels with the Mithen-Clark exchange are obvious. The Western view of primates was generally that once you had observed a single group, you knew the 'species-specific' behaviour for the entire taxon (Asquith 1996, 247). This assumption can be found in Palaeolithic expectations of, say, Neanderthal society or the world-wide capabilities of *Homo heidelbergensis*. By removing the individual from the equation all that remains to be discovered are the general rules governing behaviour. These can be applied to similar stone tools anywhere that they are found. All that has to be adjusted is the local ecology.

A PALAEOLITHIC DILEMMA

The Japanese approach which began in 1951 now seems to be carrying the day. As de Waal noted in his book *Chimpanzee Politics* (1982, 210):

'the influence on group processes does not always correspond to rank. It depends too on personality, age experience, and connections.'

Since this is the case we have a dilemma for the study of the Palaeolithic and its much favoured group approach. To date we have made more use in our interpretations of the observations of Chimpanzee tool making and tool using than we have about their political lives. We have no obvious counterpart in the Palaeolithic to the Japanese primate tradition to show us alternative scientific approaches. Yet, if we continue in our fixed view that the proper analytical units in the Palaeolithic are the group and not the individual, then we run the risk of de-humanising our ancestors, making them less capable as individuals than our modern primate cousins.

The answer to this line of argument will of course run as follows. Primates can be observed. We can see their facial reactions and we can watch them building their complex social lives. All we have in the Palaeolithic are stones and bones in various stages of preservation. We cannot see the faces of the people at Clacton or Klasies River Mouth. We often do not know much more about what they were doing than making stone tools and butchering animals. Moreover, if you compare the Masek beds at Olduvai, on the equator, with Swanscombe 6800km to the north, both of early Middle Pleistocene age (Conway *et al.* 1996; Leakey & Roe 1994; Wymer 1988), the overriding conclusion is how similar their archaeology looks. By comparison, the same transect through so many environmental zones 18,000 and 12,000 years ago produces a highly varied archaeology (Gamble & Soffer 1990; Soffer & Gamble 1990; Straus *et al.* 1996).

Here then is our problem. How do we begin to put the individual back into the Palaeolithic picture? How do we allow for their creativity in building societies but still account for the lack of variation in the archaeology of the Middle Pleistocene? Or do we abandon the task and instead just assert what must have happened through caricatures, not only of the remote past, but of any useful understanding of human behaviour (e.g. Roberts 1995)? To avoid that trap we need to understand handaxes.

'RUDE IMPLEMENTS AND ERRATIC FORMS'

John Wymer once wrote that 'the greatest enigma of lower Palaeolithic archaeology is the handaxe' (1982,102). These bifaces are enigmatic because they persist for over a million years and because their function remains obscure. Hodder, for example, has emphasised their enigmatic character by describing them as both celebrating and excluding the 'wild' (1990, 284). What he means is that such objects express the collision of natural and cultural worlds through human action. But this brings us no closer either to understanding them, in that western objective scientific sense as the products of groups, or to seeing them as representative of an alternative analytical unit, the individual. We are not much further advanced in interpreting these objects than a century ago when Worth-ington Smith described some of the artifacts from the Palaeolithic floor at Caddington as 'rude implements and erratic forms' (Smith 1894, 119).

But it was also Smith who gave us that first insight into what Roe has appropriately referred to as a precious moment in time (1981, 197). Smith refitted flakes at Caddington and elsewhere and famously reconstructed the core which was missing. The perfect freeze-frame image of individual activity.

MAKING HANDAXES

In a recent analysis White (1995) has made the case that the availability of raw material can explain part of the enigma. Following Roe's (1981) metrical demonstration that the British Lower Palaeolithic biface industries con-sisted of two groupings, composed of pointed (e.g. Stoke Newington) and ovate forms (e.g. Hoxne lower industry), White has examined the raw materials in such assem-blages. His findings are that pointed forms correlate with the use of river gravel flint which is generally of poorer flaking quality. The ovate industries are invariably found in close proximity, as at Slindon Park or Boxgrove, to a source of large sized nodules often in primary geological context.

Swanscombe (Table 15.1) provides an example of how the changing availability of raw material influenced biface shape. The pointed bifaces from the upper middle gravels were made on material derived from the layer below and now incorporated into a river beach. Above this level, in the upper loams, ovate bifaces were common at a time when the gravels had been covered by up to a metre of sand (Bridgland 1994). White suggests (1995,13) that with the loss of an immediate raw material source, higher quality raw material was carried in from a short distance away.

White concludes that the preferred biface was an ovate with the implication that maximising the circumferential edge was the knapper's goal. These implements were well designed for carcass butchery as revealed by experimental studies. Such a view runs counter to the notion that these hominids intended bifaces to look the way they do (Wynn 1993, 302). However, White's study also shows that their preferred procurement strategy was to use an immediate, rather than the best, source for raw material even if a short distance was involved. It seems they were quite prepared to settle for a pointed biface.

Here then is another example of form vs content. Handaxe shape was apparently determined by the rules of raw material, allied to a single functional goal – cutting meat – rather than the desires of the individual knapper. In the context of the British material White's scheme works well. It explains a good deal of the variation and makes a scientific explanation. But what if we step outside that tradition and return to the Middle Pleistocene of the Masek Beds in Olduvai Gorge? Roe's metrical analyses of the handaxes (1994) from sites in this unit and below in Beds III and IV produced overwhelming evidence, 17 out of 18 assemblages, for ovate bifaces. However, many of these are knapped on what to a flint reared, British Palaeolith would be regarded as poorer flaking material. For example, in the FLK site in the Masek Beds Leakey excavated a series of standardised, finely made ovate quartzite hand-axes (Leakey & Roe 1994, fig 6.3). Elsewhere basalts were used to make ovates.

Now, either we have seriously overplayed the im-portance of raw material or the African material is not as bad as it is sometimes portrayed. More studies of raw materials of the type undertaken by Jones (1994) at Olduvai would help us to choose. But there is of course an alternative. Rather than search for a rule, a simple function which explains the enigma of biface shape, why not treat the handaxe instead as a material expression of the person who made it? Bound by learned traditions they most

Depositional environment	Unit	Industry	Biface form
Land derived sediments	Upper gravel	Acheulian	
	Upper loam	Acheulian	Ovate
Aggrading stream deposits	Upper middle gravel	Acheulian*	Pointed
	Lower middle gravel		
Overbank deposits	Lower loam	Clactonian	
Aggrading river deposits	Lower gravel	Clactonian	

*Table 15.1. The Swanscombe sequence * = hominid skull horizon.*

certainly were, but at the same time they expressed through an every-day medium such as technology those essential differences that produced a rounded hominid-being in the Middle Pleistocene. In other words they had a social technology.

TACKING

John Wymer has of course excavated many of these well preserved localities and has made those inter-regional comparisons. He has also been the master of the regional survey – the Thames valley, the Mesolithic, East Anglia and most recently the Southern Rivers and the English Rivers Palaeolithic surveys. This exceptional breadth of experience is a model of how we go about doing Palaeolithic archaeology. Elsewhere (Gamble 1996, fig. 7.1). I have described this as an exercise in tacking between different scales and quality of data. This is how we learn about the past, how we build up a picture of what went on and how, intellectually, we bridge the gap between the *in-situ* flint scatter and the jumble of river-rolled material, the few minutes it took to knap a biface and the 70 ky during which they were incorporated into river terraces. I would now expand this metaphor. As we tack from the individual to the group, from the handaxe to the regional assemblage, with each going-about the material will become less enigmatic if we replace our own imposed mystery of the remote past with a more understandable view of how these early ancestors existed.

HOMINID CAPABILITIES

The key is social technology. Handaxes will always remain enigmatic if we only consider them as group artifacts or functional items. The characterisation of Middle Pleistocene people as tool assisted hominids (Binford 1989), although one I have previously subscribed to, now has to be recognised as unhelpful. In the same way, the excitement over the discovery of the Schöningen wooden spears (Dennell 1997) implies that we will know everything about these people so long as we recover their complete toolbox. Such views will only ever produce partial hominids. Handaxes will remain enigmatic because that is not how we know technology is used. The basic capability of all hominids is to be social.

This situation was revealed by Leroi-Gourhan thirty years ago in *Le Geste et la Parole* (translation 1993). He presented a concept of technology that was at the same time both social and technical. In other words the distinction between style and function was not needed. The separation of behaviour into such discrete analytical realms missed the essential point that people use artifacts as part of the performance of social life. Palaeolithic individuals created, as I discussed above, social life from the bottom-up rather than always conforming to rules imposed from the top-down. Artefacts helped structure the gatherings of hominids where interaction, the bedrock of social life, took place. They contributed to this social experience because artifacts were animated by gestures as individuals made, used and threw them away. They were part of the routines by which individuals were known and responded to in a social context.

From this perspective we see the enigma slipping away. But in its place is a methodological rather than conceptual void. For many years we have expected to interpret the Palaeolithic by discovering ever better preserved sites with clearer associations of stone, bones, plants and hominids. While such data are vital, as are the millions of rolled handaxes lying quietly in the terraces of the world, it is equally important that we begin to unlock those individual performances contained in the social technology. As John Wymer has shown us throughout his career that can only be done if we are willing to return an individual humanity to the study of the Palaeolithic. Equipped with his surveys, excavations and example we can certainly have a go.

REFERENCES

Asquith, P. J. 1996. Japanese science and western hegemonies, primatology and the limits set to questions. In L. Nader (ed.), *Naked Science: Anthropological Enquiry into Boundaries, Power, and Knowledge.* 239–256. New York: Routledge.

Binford, L. R. 1989. Isolating the transition to cultural adaptations, an organizational approach. In E.Trinkaus (ed.) *The Emergence of Modern Humans: Biocultural Adaptations in the Later Plesitocene.* 18–41. Cambridge: Cambridge University Press.

Bridgland, D. R. 1994. *Quaternary of the Thames.* 1st edition. London: Chapman and Hall.

Clark, G. A. 1992. A comment on Mithen's ecological interpretation of palaeolithic art. *Proceedings of the Prehistoric Society* 58, 107–9.

Clark, J. G. D. 1957. *Archaeology and Society* (3rd edition). London: Methuen.

Conway, B., McNabb, J. & Ashton, N. (eds) 1996. *Excavations at Barnfield Pit, Swanscombe, 1968–1972.* London: British Museum Occasional Paper 94.

Dennell, R. 1997. The world's oldest spears. *Nature* 385, 767–8.

Gamble, C. 1996. Hominid behaviour in the Middle Pleistocene; an English perspective. In C. S. Gamble & A. J. Lawson (eds), *The English Palaeolithic Reviewed.* 63–71. Salisbury: Trust for Wessex Archaeology.

Gamble, C. S. & Soffer, O. (eds) 1990. *The World at 18 000 BP. Volume 2 Low Latitudes.* London: Unwin Hyman.

Hodder, I. 1990. *The Domestication of Europe.* Oxford: Blackwell.

Jones, P. R. 1994. Results of experimental work in relation to the stone industries of Olduvai Gorge. In M. D. Leakey & D. A. Roe (eds), *Olduvai Gorge, Excavations in Beds III, IV and the Masek Beds, 1968–1971, vol. 5.* 254–98. Cambridge: Cambridge University Press.

Leakey, M. D. & Roe, D. A. (eds) 1994. *Olduvai Gorge, Excavations in Beds III, IV and the Masek Beds, 1968–71. Volume 5.* Cambridge: Cambridge University Press.

Leroi-Gourhan, A. 1993. *Gesture and Speech.* Cambridge: MIT Press.

Mithen, S. 1990. *Thoughtful Foragers.* Cambridge: Cambridge University Press.

Mithen, S. 1993. Individuals, groups and the Palaeolithic record, a reply to Clark. *Proceedings of the Prehistoric Society* 59, 393–8.

Mithen, S. 1994. Technology and society during the Middle Pleistocene: hominid group size, social learning and industrial variability. *Cambridge Archaeological Journal* 4, 3–32.

Pitts, M. & Roberts, M. 1997. *Fairweather Eden*. London: Century.

Roberts, M. B. 1995. Boxgrove man. *British Archaeology* 3, 10.

Roe, D. A. 1981. *The Lower and Middle Palaeolithic Periods in Britain*. London: Routledge & Kegan Paul.

Roe, D. A. 1994. A metrical analysis of selected sets of handaxes and cleavers from Olduvai Gorge. In M. D. Leakey & D. A. Roe (eds), *Olduvai Gorge, Excavations in Beds III, IV and the Masek Beds, 1968–1971, vol. 5*. 146–234. Cambridge: University Press.

Sahlins, M. 1968 Notes on the original affluent society (discussion) In R. B. Lee & I. Devore (eds), *Man the Hunter*. New York: Aldine de Gruyter.

Shanks, M., & C. Tilley. 1987. *Social Theory and Archaeology*. London: Polity.

Smith, W. G. 1894. *Man the Primeval Savage*. London: Stanford.

Soffer, O. & Gamble, C. S. (eds) 1990. *The World at 18 000BP. Volume 1 High Latitudes*. London: Unwin Hyman.

Straus, L. G., Eriksen, B.V., Erlandson, J.M. & Yesner, D.R. (eds) 1996. *Humans at the End of the Ice Age: the Archaeology of the Pleistocene-Holocene Transition*. New York: Plenum.

Waal, F. de 1982. *Chimpanzee Politics*. London: Johnathon Cape.

White, M. J. 1995. Raw materials and biface variability in southern Britain, a preliminary examination. *Lithics* 15, 1–20.

Wymer, J. J. 1982. *The Palaeolithic Age*. London: Croom Helm.

Wymer, J. J. 1988. Palaeolithic archaeology and the British Quaternary sequence. *Quaternary Science Reviews* 7, 79–98.

Wynn, T. 1993. Two developments in the mind of early *Homo*. *Journal of Anthropological Archaeology* 12, 299–322.

16. Southern Rivers

Katharine Scott

ABSTRACT

Anyone studying the prehistory of the Upper Thames region will appreciate the valuable contribution made by John Wymer in this area through a number of publications spanning 20 years. His excellent Southern Rivers Palaeolithic Project (Wymer 1993) includes a review of the archaeological evidence for human occupation of the Upper Thames Valley. During the Middle Pleistocene the River Thames meandered through my own excavation area at Stanton Harcourt near Oxford and thus, as I attempt to put my own research into perspective, I am much influenced by his ideas and his greater experience of Thames valley archaeology. However, his influence on my particular field of interest goes back much further via another southern river – almost the southernmost in Africa. As a result of his excavations at Klasies River, John Wymer quite inadvertently but very largely determined the course of my career. The purpose of this short paper is to outline some of the issues that interest me about the Palaeolithic of the Upper Thames and my excavations at Stanton Harcourt, many of which have their origins in those excavations at Klasies River.

I first encountered John Wymer in Cape Town 25 years ago in a large, dark shed that housed the vast African mammal collection of the South African Museum. It was not the most pleasant working environment as anyone who knows the waxy smell of recently boiled carcasses will testify, and there always seemed to be the soft crackling and rustling of insects busy discovering flesh or sinew that the preparator had missed. Beneath a rack of antelope skulls I had a desk in this dimly lit place where I worked happily for many weeks. My task, as research assistant to Richard Klein, was to help sort and identify the tens of thousands of bones that had been excavated a few years previously by John Wymer at Klasies River Mouth. This series of caves and rockshelters on the Tzitzikama Coast of South Africa is famous for the astonishing abundance and quality of its Middle Stone Age (MSA) and Late Stone Age (LSA) material. The Main Cave alone, with deposits reaching a depth of more than 20m, had produced hominid remains and more than a quarter of a million MSA artefacts

indicative of more or less continuous human presence at the site from about 120 to about 40kya. These artefacts and their cultural implications are now well-documented and illustrated (Singer & Wymer 1982) but to me, ten years before that publication, as I opened the carefully labelled packets of bones and teeth, signifying layer upon layer of prehistoric time, a new world had opened up. At that point I realised that my palaeontological, natural history and archaeological interests had found a direction.

There is an argument for saying that artefacts must be our primary source for understanding human behaviour because they are the result of conscious decision making and design whereas bones are merely the result of an instinctive need to eat whatever is most easily available. Klasies River Mouth illustrated for me that, if one had a very large number of bones spanning a very long time, it was not only possible to envisage an ancient landscape in the dusty piles of antelope, buffalo, tortoise and other animal remains, but it might be possible to document changes in the local environment and in the behaviour of people through time. Richard Klein's analyses (e.g. Klein 1976; 1978) of the Klasies River material were among the earliest that attempted to explain not simply what early people hunted or scavenged but why. He suggested, for example, that the prevalence of grazing vs browsing herbivores in different levels of the site indicated climatic and vegetational changes, and that the fluctuations in the presence or abundance of marine species (various molluscs, seals, etc.) signified the varying proximity of the coastline in response to world sea-level changes. Fascinating from the human perspective was the possible insight into early people's capabilities as, for example, they appeared to have selected the most vulnerable age groups among the biggest or potentially most dangerous prey species. Other authors might have placed a different interpretation on such a fauna but it is important to note that, until Wymer's excavations in 1966 and 1967, it would not have been possible to make such analyses. In fact, relatively little Palaeolithic excavation had been carried out at all in South Africa by 1966 and that which had been undertaken was primarily a quest for artefacts or human remains. Certainly, there had been no field work on such a scale nor carried out in such a controlled manner as at Klasies River.

I next came across John Wymer in Cambridge nearly 10 years later when I saw the fauna that he and his colleagues had excavated at Hoxne, and which was then in the process of being identified and analysed by Tony Stuart. Most of my archaeological experience at that time had been in caves and I had just embarked upon a study of faunas from caves in Britain, most of which were excavated in the last century. Those records and remains that had survived a century were in a lamentable state and I regarded the Hoxne material, so carefully packaged and labelled, with envy. The resultant monograph (Singer *et al.* 1993) speaks for the quality of the fieldwork.

Circumstances brought me to Oxfordshire, the archaeology of the Thames Valley and a reaquaintance with the work of John Wymer. My association with the Donald Baden-Powell Quaternary Research Centre, discussions with Derek Roe, and an introduction to R.J. 'Mac' MacRae served to focus my interest on the Upper Thames Valley. At first the future looked bleak: not a cave to be seen for a hundred miles! However, through Mac I became familiar with the numerous gravel pits of the area, some of which had yielded stone artefacts in abundance. Collections of bones and teeth from Oxfordshire gravel pits existed in several museums and in private collections but almost all without more than the vaguest information on their provenance. Wishing to discover whether there might be at least a broad temporal association between some of the artefacts and some animal species, I began the somewhat frustrating task of searching gravel stock piles for scattered faunal remains. In 1989 my attention was drawn to a mammoth tusk in Dix Pit near Stanton Harcourt. Mammoth tusks are often found in Oxfordshire gravel pits but the importance

of this one was that it was still *in situ* and was surrounded by other bones, teeth and freshwater molluscs. The deposit turned out to be a further exposure of an interglacial deposit reported by David Briggs and colleagues (1985) which they suggested to represent a hitherto undefined interglacial period about 200kya, subsequently equated with oxygen isotope stage 7 (Bowen *et al.* 1989). Thus began an excavation which I have directed since then (with the assistance of Christine Buckingham) and which has turned up more than 900 large vertebrate remains, a wealth of palaeoenvironmental material, and 23 artefacts. To the purist, the fact that these remains accumulated in an ancient river bed might be reason to claim that they have no real context and are therefore of little archaeological value. Indeed, a river bed consitutes a far from ideal archaeological site and it is true that the artefacts comprise a motley assemblage of handaxes and flakes ranging in condition from rolled to good, but the particular circumstances argue for special consideration of the value of the deposits at Stanton Harcourt. Firstly, the extraordinary range and preservation of plant and animal remains are providing detailed insight into the hitherto unknown climate and environment of the Upper Thames Valley a quarter of a million years ago. Secondly, there is compelling evidence from the excavations to claim a broad contemporaneity between the people who made the artefacts and the animal and plant remains among which they are found. Thirdly, despite its inadequacies, Stanton Harcourt represents the most knowledge we have ever had about the environment of Palaeolithic people in the region of the Upper Thames.

The importance of this last point may be illustrated with reference to Wymer's gazeteer of the Upper Thames (Wymer 1993). Although Palaeolithic material is known from more than 60 locations in the area, virtually nothing is known of the context of the finds nor of any association with plant and animal remains. The majority of the artefacts are handaxes found on spoil heaps at working quarries or picked up from the floors of deserted pits. Conditions for bone preservation in the Upper Thames region are generally good, so it must be assumed that the absence of faunal remains from all but a handful of the artefact locations reflects the single-mindedness of handaxe collectors over the years! But even at the few sites that are distinguished by having both artefacts and bones, other environmental information is remarkably scant. Undoubtedly, the most spectacular collection of artefacts in the Upper Thames region is from the mid-Pleistocene interglacial channel at Wolvercote. More than 100 artefacts (including many complete and broken handaxes) comprise the distinctive Wolvercote industry (Tyldesley 1986a; 1986b), yet all we know of the environment through the sparse faunal remains is that it was interglacial with sufficient grassland to support mammoth and horse. The association of fauna and 28 handaxes at Iffley is dubious in that the fauna includes two species not hitherto known in the same context: hippo, regarded as a warm-climate creature and the supposedly cold-adapted woolly rhinoceros. At Station Pit, Eynsham, the single handaxe came from a gravel unit overlying an interglacial deposit containing hippo but any possible temporal association is unclear. More promising are the deposits at Cassington, where lower gravels of probable early Devensian age contain abundant faunal remains indicative of a cool, partly wooded environment and upper gravels with fauna indicate a mid-Devensian colder environment. Very little controlled excavation has been possible at Cassington and most of some 2,000 animal remains as well as a number of artefacts were collected in the wake of quarrying activities and from spoil heaps (Hardaker & Scott in prep.).

One of the reasons why so little is known from the 60 or so artefact locations is because any site that predates the end of the Last Glaciation is likely to be buried under several metres of fluvial gravel and its discovery will probably depend upon the quarrying of that gravel. Quarrying is by necessity a violent method of excavation and the chances of finding bones and artefacts in their prehistoric context are rare. The excavation site at Stanton Harcourt is in such a quarry from which 6–8m of gravel had been removed and the pit deserted awaiting its further use as a waste disposal site. At the base of the pit, a metre or so of gravel had been left undisturbed in a wide linear depression in the Oxford Clay bedrock because it was deemed 'uneconomic'. Its poor quality, from a mining point of view, was due to the presence of tusks, bones, logs and other debris which had accumulated in the depression – an ancient river bed. From the point of view of a scientific excavation, a rare opportunity arose to follow the meandering of the ancient river (believed to be a former course of the Thames) across several acres. Although the excavation is not yet complete and all aspects of analysis are still in progress, preliminary accounts of the fieldwork and descriptions of artefacts discovered by the end of 1995 are given by Buckingham *et al.* (1996) and by Scott & Buckingham (1997). My own principal interest in the site is in the reconstruction of the prehistoric environment through the analysis of the large vertebrates against the background provided by the flora and other faunal remains. With each excavation season, the picture that emerges becomes more fascinating and more complex.

Although the density of bones per square metre is high, the list of large vertebrates is not extensive. Sutcliffe (1995) lists 12 large vertebrate species as characteristic members of OIS 7 faunas in Britain of which 8 are known from Stanton Harcourt: mammoth, straight-tusked elephant, bison, red deer, horse, bear, lion and hyaena. Other faunal remains include almost 100 species of insect, 40 species of mollusc (both aquatic and terrestrial), fish bones and scales, frogs and birds. Overall, the fauna presents a picture of a temperate environment with a climate slightly warmer than that of present day Britain. Although pollen is poorly preserved, other vegetation in the form of seeds, nuts and wood is copious and corroborates the faunal remains in describing fully interglacial conditions with deciduous woodland in the vicinity of the river. Significantly, the floral remains also indicate the presence of grassland and open-habitat plants. If that part of the interglacial represented at Stanton Harcourt offered a mosaic grassland/woodland habitat rather than the closed canopy forest conditions usually believed to characterise interglacial periods, then the archaeological implications are important. The evident scarcity of Palaeolithic artefacts from interglacial deposits in Britain has been taken to support the supposition and ethnographic observation that a forest environment is not (and presumably was not) ideal for hunter-gatherer groups (Currant 1986; Gamble 1987). More open territory therefore, such as seems to have been the case at Stanton Harcourt, with a mild climate and available water, meat, and plant food (including various berries and hazelnuts), offered a potentially ideal situation for people. We have a suitable environment and we have the artefacts, but is there a case for suggesting that the artefacts represent human activity in the vicinity of the river during some part of OIS 7? It might be argued that these tools and waste flakes, among many river pebbles, were borne in from older deposits elsewhere. Of this there is no evidence: there are no faunal or floral remains in the excavated deposits indicative of any earlier Quaternary stage, and few of the artefacts show the degree of battering that characterises the gravel matrix in which they were found. Indeed, a few, although they are not in the mint condition of those from Wolvercote or Boxgrove, would certainly come into Wymer's second category: 'fresh'. It is my view that, as the river meandered through the valley, occasionally flooding its banks, it incorporated bones, wood and artefacts that lay about on the land surface. The undamaged condition of many of the bones and teeth and of some of the artefacts suggests that, once in the water, they were moved virtually no distance from their original place of death or discard.

While making a case for the presence of people at Stanton Harcourt among the rest of the fauna, it is true that nothing can be said about the more direct association of the artefacts and the animal remains. The bones have yet to be examined for cut-marks and, in the absence of a land surface, we can say nothing about butchery or any other activities associated with human settlement. We can, however, make suggestions as to what life might have been like for people in the valley 200kya. We know, for example, that the local flint is of too poor quality for the manufacture of artefacts and undoubtedly early people knew that too and brought ready made tools with them from good flint sources some 20 miles downstream (MacRae 1988; Buckingham *et al.* 1996). We might suppose that one of the purposes for their visits upstream was a quest for food. There were edible berries and nuts to be gathered, and a variety of fish in the river (chub, roach and bream, to name a few). Horse, bison, and a small species of mammoth roamed the valley, while elephant and red deer browsed in the woodland nearby. Judging from the abundance of mammoth at the site (70% of the large vertebrate remains), mammoth was possibly the most common large animal in the area but elephant and bison remains are numerous too. Perhaps the people hunted on occasion but, given that a relationship of mutual avoidance has been observed among elephants and almost all people with such basic technology as sticks and stone tools (Haynes 1991), it seems improbable that hunting by humans accounted for the deaths of mammoths or elephants at Stanton Harcourt. Even bison, except the very young ones, might have posed a problem to hunters armed with so little. In any event, there is always meat available where large herds of herbivores congregate: natural mortality and hunting by large predators account for many deaths. At Stanton Harcourt there were brown bears and hyaenas, both of which may have played a role, but there was also an enormous species of lion. In my scenario, the humans moved cautiously in the wake of such predators, following the course of the river while exploring the valley. I can but hope that the final season of excavation might just reveal who they were!

In conclusion, I pay tribute to John Wymer for the significant influence his work has had on the archaeology of the Thames and, via Klasies River, also on my own career.

REFERENCES

Briggs, D. J., Coope, G. R. & Gilbertson, D. D. 1985. *The Chronology and Environmental Framework of Early Man in the Upper Thames Valley; a New Model.* BAR British Series 137. Oxford: British Archaeological Reports.

Bowen, D. Q., Hughes, S., Sykes, G. A. & Miller, G. H. 1989. Land-sea correlations in the Pleistocene, based on isoleucine epimerisation in non-marine molluscs. *Nature* 340, 49–51.

Buckingham, C. B., Roe, D. A. & Scott, K. 1986. A preliminary report on the Stanton Harcourt Channel deposits (Oxfordshire, England): geological context, vertebrate remains and Palaeolithic stone artefacts. *Journal of Quaternary Science* 11(5), 397–415.

Currant, A. P. 1986. Man and the Quaternary Interglacial Faunas of Britain. In S. N. Collcutt (ed.), *The Palaeolithic of Britain and its Nearest Neighbours: Recent Trends,* 50–52. Sheffield: University of Sheffield.

Gamble, C. 1987 Man the Shoveler. In O. Soffer (ed.), *The Pleistocene Old World,* 81–98. New York: Plenum.

Haynes, G. 1991. *Mammoths, Mastodonts and Elephants: Behaviour and the Fossil Record.* Cambridge: Cambridge University Press.

Klein, R.G. 1976. The mammalian fauna of the Klasies River Mouth sites, southern Cape Province, South Africa. *South African Archaeological Bulletin* 31, 75–98.

Klein, R.G. 1978. Stone age predation on large African bovids. *Journal of Archaeological Science* 5, 195–217.

MacRae, R. J. 1988. Belt, shoulder-bag or basket? An enquiry into handaxe transport and flint sources. *Lithics,* 9, 2–8.

Scott, K. & Buckingham, C. M. 1997. Quaternary fluvial deposits and palaeontology at Stanton Harcourt, Oxfordshire In S. G. Lewis & D. Maddy (eds), *The Quaternary of the South Midlands and the Welsh Marches,* 115–126. London: Quaternary Research Association Field Guide.

Singer, R. & Wymer, J.J. 1982. *The Middle Stone Age at Klasies River Mouth in South Africa.* Chicago: University of Chicago Press.

Singer, R., Gladfelter, B. G. & Wymer, J. J. 1993. *The Lower Palaeolithic Site at Hoxne, England.* Chicago: University of Chicago Press.

Sutcliffe, A. J. 1995. Insularity of the British Isles 250,000 – 30,000 years ago: the mammalian, including human, evidence. In R.C. Preece (ed.), *Island Britain: a Quaternary perspective,* 127–40. Geological Society Special Publication No 96.

Tyldesley, J. A. 1986a. *The Wolvercote Channel Handaxe Assemblage. A Comparative Study.* Oxford: British Archaeological Reports 153.

Tyldesley, J. A. 1986b. A re-assessment of the handaxe assemblage recovered from the Wolvercote Channel, Oxford. In S. Collcutt (ed.), *The Palaeolithic of Britain and its Nearest Neighbours,* 23–5. Sheffield: University of Sheffield.

Wymer, J. J. 1993. *The Southern Rivers Palaeolithic Project.* Salisbury: Report No.1 Wessex Archaeology.

17. Pleistocene Deposits and Archaeological Horizons in the Ariendorf Gravel Quarry, Lower Central Rhineland, Germany

Elaine Turner

ABSTRACT

In the Karl Schneider gravel quarry at Ariendorf, Middle Terrace gravels of the Rhine river are overlain by loessic cover deposits with intercalated palaeosols and layers of tephra. The gravel quarry is the type-site of the Ariendorf Interglacial, a warm phase dating to between 410–419 kya (OIS 11). Archaeological investigations in 1981–83 revealed three separate horizons of lithic artefacts with animal bones in the cover deposits. The fauna from the oldest horizon (Ariendorf 1) is a post-Holsteinian cold-stage fauna. Absolute dating of tephras stratified in the loess cover (⁴⁰Ar/³⁹Ar single crystal laser method) show that the second horizon (Ariendorf 2) was probably deposited during the main Saalian Glaciation (OIS 8) and the youngest archaeological horizon (Ariendorf 3) at the end of OIS 7 or during onsetting glacial conditions at the beginning of OIS 6.

LOCATION AND TOPOGRAPHY OF THE SITE

The Karl Schneider gravel quarry at Ariendorf is located in the Lower Central Rhineland of Germany, about 28km south of Bonn. The nearest towns are Bad Hönningen, about 1km to the south of the quarry, and Leubsdorf and Linz to the north. The site is named after the village of Ariendorf, which is located just north of the gravel pit at the confluence of the Ariendorf Stream and the Rhine (Fig. 17.1). Ariendorf is situated in the Rhenish Massif or Rhenish Shield, and sheer cliffs of Devonian slate form the side of the Rhine Valley between Bad Hönningen and Linz, upon which are gravels of the Rhine River terraces. The quarry is located on a small plateau of land known as 'Burgland' (Fig. 17.1) which is the southernmost tip of a levelled off Middle Terrace of the Rhine – the Leubsdorf Terrace – extending from Leubsdorf to Bad Hönningen between 120 and 140m OD, some 60m above the present-day valley floor.

STRATIGRAPHY, BIOSTRATIGRAPHY AND ABSOLUTE DATING

The deposits in the Ariendorf quarry were originally described by Karl Brunnacker (Brunnacker *et al.* 1975). At that time, three loessic beds (bed I, bed II and bed III) were observed above the fluvio-glacial sequence of the Leubsdorf Terrace. A warm phase, the 'Ariendorf Interglacial', was identified at the interface of the Leubsdorf Terrace and the cover deposits. A thick layer of calcium carbonate nodules at the top of bed I was interpreted as the remains (Cc horizon) of a truncated soil and, along with a reworked interglacial molluscan fauna at the base of bed II, was taken as representing evidence of interglacial deposits between beds I and II which had been subsequently eroded away. A thick palaeosol (*Parabraunerde*) at the top of bed II provided evidence of a younger interglacial phase. Tephras erupted by volcanoes in the East Eifel Volcanic Field, some 10km to the west of Ariendorf, were also observed in the loessic units.

The Ariendorf Interglacial was tentatively correlated with the Holsteinian, beds I and II with the Saalian, the palaeosol at the top of bed II with the Eemian and bed III with the Weichselian (Bosinski *et al.* 1983; Brunnacker 1975; Turner 1990a; 1990b; 1995). However, the subsequent identification of a new loess/palaeosol unit between the Ariendorf Interglacial sequence and bed I (Haesaerts 1990), the dating of tephra layers by the ⁴⁰Ar/³⁹Ar single

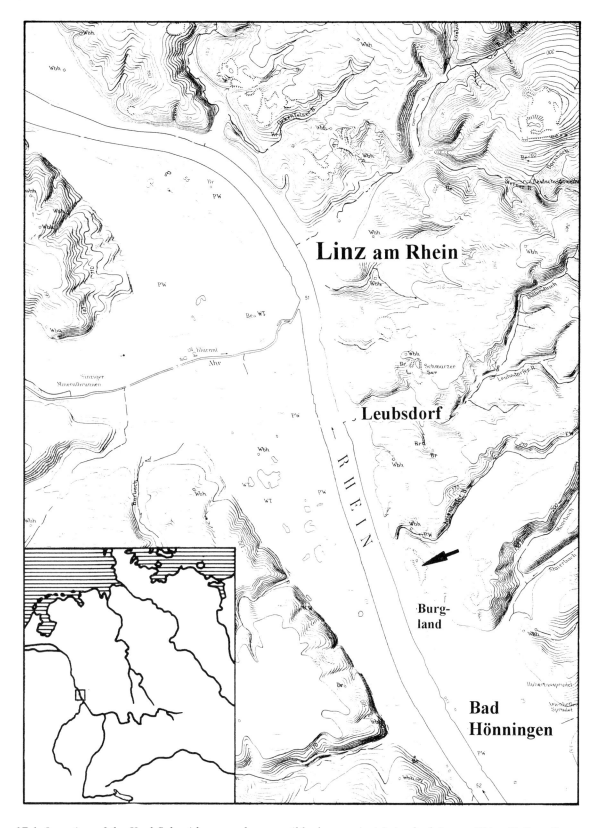

Figure 17.1. Location of the Karl Schneider gravel quarry (black arrow) at Ariendorf, Lower Rhine Valley, Germany.

crystal laser method (Bogaard & Schmincke 1990) and TL-dating of bed III (Frechen 1990), combined with mammalian biostratigraphy (Kolfschoten 1990a; 1990b) have led to a revision of some of the stratigraphical interpretations of the deposits in the quarry and the ages of the archaeological horizons (Fig. 17.2).

Fluvio-glacial sequence

The 30m thick gravels of the Leubsdorf Terrace lie unconformably on the Devonian slate bedrock and comprise cross-bedded sandy gravels with coarse gravels stratified above these (Hentzsch 1990). The oldest tephra at the site (ARI-DT1) is located in the coarse gravels and has a maximal age of about 490 kya (Bogaard & Schmincke 1990). Above the tephra, partially cryoturbated gravels, sands and hill-wash materials indicate that apart from

occasional periods of flooding, the main period of fluviatile activity had ceased. The fluviatile deposits end with a high flood loam.

Ariendorf Interglacial sequence

A series of weathered volcanic ashes and pumices is stratified above the fluvio-glacial sequence. The tephras show considerable synsedimentary loamification, representing a continuation of pedogenic processes already observed in the high flood loam. On the basis of this, Brunnacker assigned the tephras to the Ariendorf Interglacial, named after this site (Brunnacker *et al.* 1975). Imprints of leaves from deciduous trees were observed in the upper tephra deposits, but pollen was not recovered. Two of the tephras have been dated by Bogaard and Schmincke (1990). ARI-DT2 has a maximal age of 451 ±

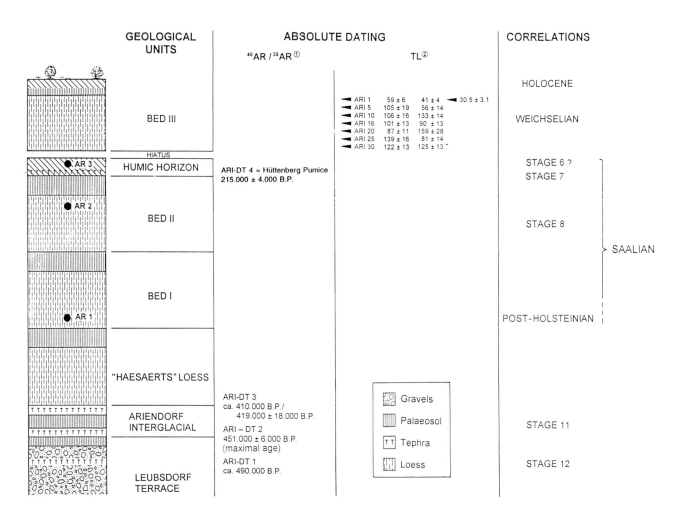

Figure 17.2. Schematical sequence of the Pleistocene deposits at Ariendorf, results of absolute dating and mammalian biostratigraphy, and correlations of the sequence to oxygen isotope stages and Pleistocene cold phases. [1]Dates obtained by the ⁴⁰Ar/³⁹Ar single crystal laser method are taken from Bogaard and Schmincke (1990). The date of 419 ±18 kya for the Ariendorf Interglacial sequence was obtained by the ⁴⁰Ar/³⁹Ar stepwise degassing method (Fuhrmann 1983; Lippolt et al. 1986). [2]TL-dates are taken from Boenigk and Frechen (in Turner et al. in press). AR 1–30 are samples dated by Frechen using the regeneration (first column) and additive (second column) methods. The single TL-date in the third column was sampled and dated by the regeneration method by Zöller (et al. 1988).

6 kya and ARI-DT3 dates to about 410 kya. One of the tephras, probably ARI-DT3, was also dated by the ^{40}Ar/^{39}Ar stepwise degassing method to 419 ± 18 kya (Fuhrmann 1983; Lippolt *et al.* 1986). A palaeosol (Parabraunerde) is stratified between the two dated tephras.

The cover series

In the current synthesis, the cover deposits at Ariendorf comprise four beds of loessic material ('Haesaerts' loess, bed I, bed II and bed III), two observable palaeosols (top of Haesaerts loess and top of bed II) and truncated interglacial deposits (top of bed I). A younger tephra (ARI-DT4) is located towards the base of a humic horizon stratified between the palaeosol of bed II and the loess of bed III. Its mineral content and chemical composition identify the tephra as a distal equivalent of the Hüttenberg pumice, which has been dated at its source in the Wehr volcano to around 215 ± 4 kya (Bogaard & Schmincke 1990). Dated samples of this pumice taken in Ariendorf have produced a similar age (Paul Bogaard, pers. comm., 1997). Two independent series of samples for TL dating were taken in the loessic beds (Boenigk & Frechen in Turner *et al.* in press; Frechen 1990; Zöller *et al.* 1988). TL dates from bed III show that the loess from the upper part of this unit was deposited during the Weichselian. Sampling for palaeomagnetism in the cover series showed

normal polarity with no evidence of Events (Schnepp in Turner *et al.* in press).

Biostratigraphy and palaeoenvironment of the faunas from the archaeological horizons

The oldest archaeological horizon, Ariendorf 1, is stratified at the base of bed I in lenses of local fluvial sediments (Sefkov in Turner *et al.* in press) which probably accumulated under low-energy conditions in a flood-plain environment. The large mammal fauna from this horizon (Table 17.1) is characteristic of those recorded in cold stage deposits in the region (Turner 1990a; 1991) and the dominance of larger herbivores, along with the presence of lemmings (*Dicrostonyx* sp. and *Lemmus lemmus*) and the lack of typical forest dwellers in the smaller mammal assemblage (Kolfschoten 1990a; 1990b; Kolfschoten in Turner *et al.* in press) indicates an open environment associated with cold, dry climatic conditions. The absence of smaller mammals typically found in Early Middle Pleistocene faunas and the SDQ-values (enamel differentiation quotient) of the arvicolid molars show that the Ariendorf 1 fauna dates to a cold stage younger than the Holsteinian, but older than the Belvédère Interglacial in the Netherlands, which is correlated with OIS 7 (Kolfschoten *ibid*). The larger mammals from this horizon, which include a large wolf comparable in size to recent

Ariendorf 1

Smaller mammals		*Larger mammals*	
Pygmy shrew	*Sorex* cf. *minutus*	Wolf	*Canis lupus* (1)
Mole	*Talpa* cf. *europaea*	Unidentified canid	*Canis* sp.
Long-tailed suslik	*Sphermophilus* cf. *undulatus*	Mammoth	*Mammuthus* sp. (1)
Hamster	*Cricetus cricetus* cf. *praeglacialis*	Horse	*Equus* sp. (2)
Arctic lemming	*Dicrostonyx* sp.	Woolly rhinoceros	*Coelodonta antiquitatis* (2)
Norway lemming	*Lemmus lemmus*	Red deer	*Cervus elaphus* (1)
Water vole	*Arvicola terrestris* ssp. A.	Large bovid	*Bos* sp. or *Bison* sp. (2/3)
Short-tailed vole	*Microtus arvalis*		
Common vole	*Microtus agrestis*		
Narrow-skulled vole	*Microtus gregalis*		
Root vole	*Microtus oeconomus*		

Ariendorf 2

Smaller mammals		*Larger mammals*	
Water vole	*Arvicola terrestris* ssp. B.	Wolf	*Canis lupus* (1)
		Mammoth	*Mammuthus trogontherii-primigenius* (1)
		Horse	*Equus* sp. (2/3)
		Woolly rhinoceros	*Coelodonta antiquitatis* (2)
		Red deer (coronate)	*Cervus elaphus elaphus* (2)
		Extinct bison	*Bison priscus* (2)

Ariendorf 3

excavated site in humic horizon:		unstratified remains from humic horizon:	
Red deer	*Cervus elaphus* (1)	Bear	*Ursus* sp. (*Ursus spelaeus* after Poplin in Brunnacker 1975)
		Mammoth	*Mammuthus primigenius*
		Horse	*Equus* sp.
		Woolly rhinoceros	*Coeleodonta antiquitatis*
		Red deer	*Cervus elaphus*
		Large Bovid	*Bos* sp. or *Bison* sp.

Table. 17.1. List of smaller and larger mammals from the Ariendorf 1–3 horizons. Identification of smaller mammals by Thijs van Kolfschoten and larger mammals by Elaine Turner. List taken from Turner et al. *in press. Numbers in parentheses are minimum numbers of indiviuals (MNI) for the larger mammals.*

Canis lupus and the presence of woolly rhinoceros, also indicate a post-Holsteinian age for the fauna.

The main archaeological horizon, Ariendorf 2, is located in the upper part of bed II, in a true loess facies deposited under periglacial conditions (Sefkov in Turner *et al.* in press). A cold molluscan fauna, dominated by *Pupilla muscorum*, was also recovered in this part of bed II. The larger mammal fauna (Table 17.1) is similar to the one from Ariendorf 1, indicating a predominantly open environment with herbaceous vegetation and cold climatic conditions. The arvicolid molars from Ariendorf 2 are more advanced than those from Ariendorf 1, and comparable SDQ-values have been recorded on arvicolid molars from pre-Eemian (=Saalian) faunas (Kolfschoten 1990a; 1990b; Kolfschoten in Turner *et al.* in press).

The youngest archaeological horizon, Ariendorf 3, is located in the humic horizon just above the Hüttenberg tephra. The mammalian fauna from Ariendorf 3 is similar in composition to the cold stage faunas of Ariendorf 1 and 2 (Table 17.1) and a molluscan fauna in the humic horizon also indicates fluctuating phases of cool and damp, and cool and very dry conditions during the accumulation of this deposit. The presence of *Chondrula tridens*, a reduction in the total number of molluscan species and a high proportion of *Pupilla muscorum* in the uppermost humic levels, mark onsetting glacial conditions (Brunnacker *et al.*1975).

EARLY HUMANS AT ARIENDORF

Ariendorf 1

Rescue excavations totalling some 110m² recovered only a thin scatter of 126 lithic artefacts, five large blocks of stone which may have been transported to the site, 192 larger vertebrate remains and a few remains from smaller mammals from this horizon. The lithic artefacts (Figs 17.3–17.5) are made of locally and regionally-occurring raw materials, and the assemblage is dominated by varieties of quartz (45.2%) and siliceous slate (43.6%), with low quantities of quartzites (9.5%) and single pieces of river flint and of radiolarite, all of which are in a fresh condition.

The assemblage mainly consists of debitage, including flakes of all sizes and many pieces of angular debris. Cortical flakes indicating primary debitage, and flakes with cortical platforms produced during later sequences of reduction were present, as were flakes which had been finely retouched (Fig. 17.4). One elongated quartz flake of almost blade-like appearance, and the distal end of a second, similar quartz artefact (Fig. 17.3b and 17.d), show that early humans at Ariendorf were quite capable of working this difficult material well. Closely distributed pieces of debitage were refitted onto a small siliceous slate core, proving that this raw material had also been worked at the site (Fig. 17.4).

Little information could be gleaned about the interaction of humans with the faunal remains. Cut marks were

not observed on the bones as their surfaces were too poorly preserved, and although some bones had been broken in the fresh state only one of these, a shaft fragment from the humerus of a horse, had an impact notch which could have been produced by hammerstone-wielding humans. Although early humans may have modified horse bones at Ariendorf 1, the way in which they procured horse remains is unclear, as is their interaction with the few remains of the other species at this site.

Ariendorf 2

The second archaeological horizon is stratified in bed II, in loess deposits about 50cm below the thick palaeosol formed on the top of this bed. Excavations revealed concentrations of animal remains associated with a small assemblage of lithic artefacts totalling only 37 pieces. Early humans continued to use the same spectrum of raw materials for their lithic artefacts at Ariendorf 2, and as at Ariendorf 1 the assemblage consisted mainly of flake material (including some cortical flakes), angular debris and a core. An unworked quartzite block and a hammerstone complete the lithic inventory. Conjoining flakes show that some material was worked at the site (Fig. 17.6).

Although the bones of larger mammals were better preserved than those in the older assemblage, cut marks were not observed and only one bone, a humerus from woolly rhinoceros may have been smashed open by humans to obtain marrow. Thus, the role of humans in the accumulation and modification of this faunal assemblage is just as difficult to establish as in the older horizon. This horizon also featured a D-shaped, shallow hollow, in which some faunal remains, especially those of a young mammoth, and artefacts were deposited. Originally interpreted as the remains of a dwelling structure (Bosinski *et al.* 1983), a recent detailed study of this feature has shown that it is more likely to be of non-anthropogenic origin, possibly a tree fall hollow (Turner in Turner *et al.* in press).

Ariendorf 3

Little is known about Ariendorf 3; faunal remains (Table 17.1) were collected from the humic horizon during quarrying and a small test-pit was excavated into this horizon in 1982. Only a few finds – bones and an antler frontlet from a red deer and two lithic artefacts – were recovered from the excavated site. Bones and two Levallois flakes made from a type of greywacke (Fig. 17.7) were collected from quarried spoil heaps.

DISCUSSION AND CORRELATION

The oldest tephra at the site is stratified in the Leubsdorf Terrace and has been dated to about 490 kya (Fig. 17.2). The date is a maximum age, and gravel deposition prob-

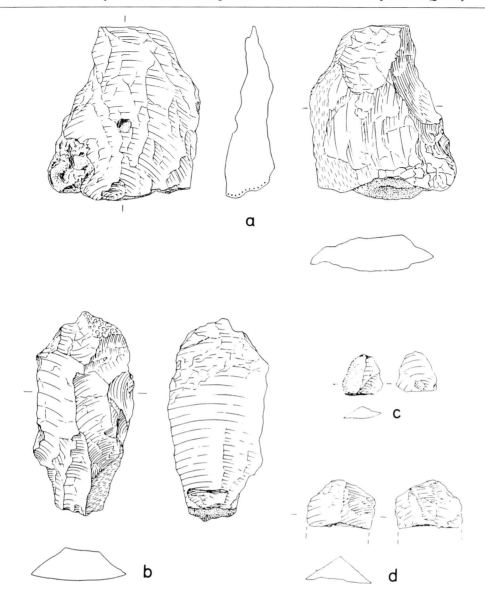

Figure 17.3. Ariendorf 1: quartz artefacts. a: large flake with cortex on striking platform; b: elongated flake; c: flake; d: distal end of an elongated flake. Scale 2:3.

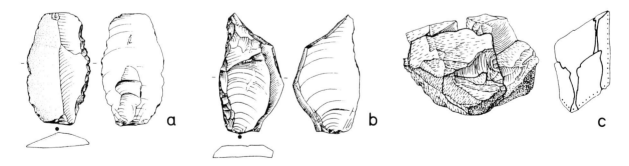

Figure 17.4. Ariendorf 1: siliceous slate artefacts. a and b: flakes with retouch; c: small core with refitting flakes and angular debris. Scale 2:3.

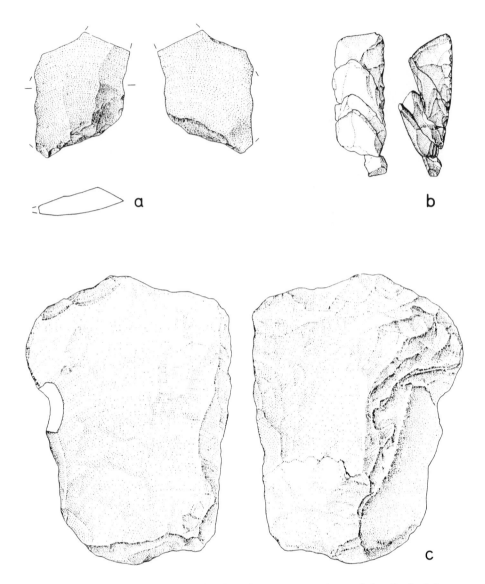

Figure 17.5. Ariendorf 1: quartzite artefacts. a: flake; b: side-scraper; c: large flake. Scale 2.3.

ably took place earlier, during OIS 12. Tephras in the Ariendorf Interglacial sequence date this warm phase to between 419–410 kya, but not older than 451 kya (maximum age for lower tephra). According to these dates a correlation with OIS 11 is likely for this warm phase. The Hüttenberg tephra in the humic horizon dates to around 215 kya, placing the eruption of this tephra into OIS 7. If the palaeosol at the top of bed II is also attributed to OIS 7 and the Ariendorf Interglacial is equated with OIS 11, it is necessary at Ariendorf to accomodate three loessic beds (Haesaerts loess, beds I and II), one observable interglacial palaeosol (top of Haesaerts loess) and truncated deposits representing a second interglacial phase (top of bed I) into OIS 10–8. The only fixed point in the lower part of the loessic series is bed I. This unit cannot be definitely attributed to a particular cold stage, but based on the biostrati-

graphical evidence, the fauna from Ariendorf 1 must be younger than the Holsteinian.

Regardless of its exact age, Ariendorf 1 is important as it provides evidence of the presence of hominids in northern Europe during a relatively early 'cold period' (Roebroeks *et al.* 1992). The fauna from Ariendorf 1 also represents early evidence of an Eurasian faunal complex, termed the *Mammuthus-Coelodonta* complex, a faunal complex which during the Upper Pleistocene combined the most distinctly cold-adapted species of larger mammals ever encountered during the Pleistocene in Eurasia (Kahlke 1994).

TL dates taken in bed III at Ariendorf show that the upper part of the loess overlying the humic horizon was deposited during the Weichselian. The age of the Hüttenberg tephra and TL dates for bed III thus indicate that a climatic cycle is missing between the humic deposit and the loess of the youngest unit in the cover series at

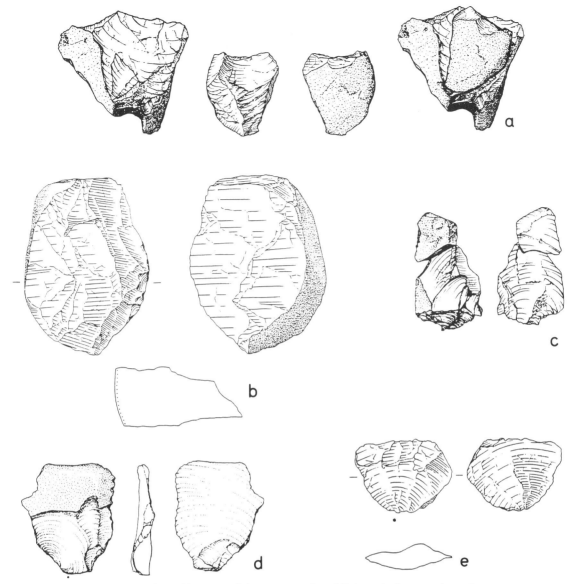

Figure 17.6. Ariendorf 2: a (refitted) and b quartz debitage; c: refitted flakes of siliceous slate; d: quartzite cortex flake; e: quartz flake. Scale 2:3.

Ariendorf. The revised stratigraphy of the site shows that the archaeological horizon Ariendorf 2, was probably deposited during the Saalian Glaciation in OIS 8. The 'cold' character of the fauna from Ariendorf 3 and climatic evidence from the molluscan assemblage in the humic horizon suggests deposition during a cool phase at the end of OIS 7 or during onsetting glacial conditions at the beginning of OIS 6.

In earlier publications, the Ariendorf Interglacial was tentatively correlated with the Holstein Interglacial. Pollen sequences resembling the Holsteinian are however unknown from the Rhineland, and in fact only one pollen sequence from a Middle Pleistocene interglacial has been identified so far. This sequence was recorded at Kärlich, a clay-pit situated in the Neuwied Basin some 20km to the south of Ariendorf (Gaudzinski *et al.* 1996). The eponymous Kärlich Interglacial, is characterized by two distinct phases, a well-developed predominantly *Quercus mixtum* phase (Kärlich I) followed by a phase in which *Carpinus* and *Abies* dominate (Kärlich II) (Bittmann 1995), which is typical of warm stages of the Cromer Complex (Zagwijn 1992). The Brockentuff tephra, dated to 396 ± 20 kya (Bogaard & Schmincke 1990) separates the two interglacial phases at Kärlich. The absolute dates thus place both the Kärlich and the Ariendorf Interglacials into OIS 11. However, the Kärlich pollen sequence does not resemble the Holsteinian (*sensu stricto*) and most likely corresponds to the second optimum of the Rhume Interglacial of Bilshausen (Lower Saxony, Germany) (Bittmann & Müller 1996), which is overlain by Elsterian deposits. On present evidence, the Kärlich and Ariendorf Interglacials can be regarded as chronologically equivalent. The Kärlich Interglacial probably represents a warm phase between the youngest interglacial of the Cromer Complex (Cromer IV)

Figure 17.7. Ariendorf 3: greywacke Levallois flakes. Scale 2:3.

and the Holsteinian (Gaudzinski *et al.* 1996) and the same age can be postulated for the Ariendorf Interglacial.

ACKNOWLEDGEMENTS

The author would like to thank M. Street for useful criticism of the manuscript and last-minute corrections.

REFERENCES

Bittmann, F. 1995. Vegetationsgeschichtliche Untersuchungen an mittel- und jungpleistozänen Ablagerungen des Neuwieder Beckens (Mittelrhein). *Jahrbuch des Römisch-Germanischen Zentralmuseums Mainz* 38, 135–403.

Bittmann, F. & Müller, H. 1996. The Kärlich Interglacial site and its correlation with the Bilshausen sequence. In C. Turner (ed.), *The Early Middle Pleistocene in Europe*, 187–93. Rotterdam: Balkema.

Bogaard, P.V.D. & Schmincke, H.-U. 1990. Die Entwicklungsgeschichte des Mittelrheinraumes und die Eruptionsgeschichte des Osteifel-Vulkanfeldes. In W. Schirmer (ed.), *Rheingeschichte zwischen Mosel und Maas,* 166–90. Hannover: deuqua-Führer 1.

Bosinski, G., Brunnacker, K. & Turner, E. 1983. Ein Siedlungsbefund des Frühen Mittelpaläolithikums von Ariendorf, Kr. Neuwied. *Archäologisches Korrespondenzblatt* 13(2), 157–69.

Brunnacker, K. 1975. The mid-Pleistocene of the Rhine Basin. In K.W. Butzer & G. L. Isaac (eds), *After the Australopithecines,* 189–224. The Hague, Paris: Mouton.

Brunacker, K., Löhr, H., Boenigk, W., Puisségur, J.J. & Poplin, F. 1975. Quartär-Aufschlüsse bei Ariendorf am unteren Mittelrhein. *Mainzer Naturwiss Archiv* 14, 93–141.

Frechen, M. 1990. TL-Datierungen in Ariendorf. In W. Schirmer (ed.), *Rheingeschichte zwischen Mosel und Maas,* 114–7. Hannover: deuqua Führer 1

Fuhrmann, U. 1983. *Kalium-Argon-Untersuchungen an neogenen Vulkaniten des Rheinischen Schildes.* Dissertation University Heidelberg.

Gaudzinski, S., Bittmann, F., Boenigk, W., Frechen, M. & Kolfschoten, T. van. 1996. Palaeoecology and Archaeology of the

Kärlich-Seeufer Open-Air Site (Middle Pleistocene) in the Central Rhineland, Germany. *Quaternary Research* 46, 319–34.

Haesaerts, P. 1990. Stratigraphical approach to the Pleistocene deposits of the Schneider quarry at Ariendorf (Middle Rhine, Germany). In W. Schirmer (ed.), *Rheingeschichte zwischen Mosel und Maas*, 112–14. Hannover: deuqua Führer 1.

Hentzsch, B. 1990. Die Mittelterrasse bei Ariendorf. In W. Schirmer (ed.), *Rheingeschichte zwischen Mosel und Maas*, 110–11. Hannover: deuqua-Führer 1.

Kahlke, R.-D. 1994. *Die Entstehungs-, Entwicklungs- und Verbreitungsgeschichte des oberpleistozänen Mammuthus-Coelodonta Faunen-komplexes in Eurasia (Großsäuger)*. Abhandlungen Senckenbergiana naturforschung Gesellschaft, 546.

Kolfschoten, T. van. 1990a. The evolution of the mammal fauna in the Netherlands and the middle Rhine Area (Western Germany) during the late Middle Pleistocene. *Mededelingen Rijks Geologische Dienst* 43(3), 1–69.

Kolfschoten, T. van. 1990b. Die Kleinsäuger von Ariendorf. In W. Schirmer (ed.), *Rheingeschichte zwischen Mosel und Maas.* 117–20. Hannover: deuqua-Führer 1.

Lippolt, H.J., Fuhrmann, U. & Hradetzky, H. 1986. $^{40}Ar/^{39}Ar$ age determinations on sanidines of the Eifel volcanic field (Federal Republic of Germany): Constraints on age and duration of a Middle Pleistocene cold period. *Chemical Geology (Isotope Geoscience Sections)* 59, 197–204.

Roebroeks, W., Conard, N.J. & Kolfschoten, T. van. 1992. Dense forests, cold steppes and the Palaeolithic settlement of northern Europe. *Current Anthropology* 33, 551–86.

Turner, E. 1990a. The excavations in the Karl Schneider Quarry, Ariendorf. In W. Schirmer (ed.), *Rheingeschichte zwischen Mosel und Maas*, 121–4. Hannover: deuqua-Führer 1.

Turner, E. 1990b. Middle and Late Pleistocene Macrofaunas of the Neuwied Basin Region (Rhineland Palatinate) of West Germany. *Jahrbuch des Römisch-Germanischen Zentralmuseums Mainz* 37(1), 135–403.

Turner, E. 1991. Pleistocene Stratigraphy and Vertebrate Faunas from the Neuwied Basin region of Western Germany. *Cranium* 8(1), 21–34.

Turner, E. 1995. Ariendorf. In G. Bosinski, M. Street & M. Baales (eds), *The Palaeolithic and Mesolithic of the Rhineland*. In W. Schirmer (ed.), Quaternary field trips in Central Europe, vol. 2, 15, 934–7.

Turner, E., Boenigk, W., Frechen, M., Kolfschoten, T. van, Schnepp, E., Sefkov, E. & Steensma, K. In press. Ariendorf. Quaternary deposits and Palaeolithic excavations in the Karl Schneider gravel pit. *Jahrbuch des Römisch-Germanischen Zentralmuseums Mainz*.

Zagwijn, W.H. 1992. The beginning of the Ice Age in Europe and its major subdivision. *Quaternary Science Reviews* 11, 583–92.

Zöller, L., Wagner, G. A. & Stremme, H. E. 1988. Thermolumineszenz-Datierung an Löss-Paläoboden-Sequenzen von Nieder,- Mittel- und Oberrhein. *Chemical Geology (Isotope Geosciences Section)* 73, 39–62.

18. Discoidal Core Technology in the Palaeolithic at Oldbury, Kent

Jill Cook and Roger Jacobi

ABSTRACT

The research presented here results from curatorial work on the Harrison collection from Oldbury, Kent (TQ 59/56) held by the British Museum. It reveals that there have been misunderstandings of both the collection and the site. A review of the material in relation to published and archival sources suggests that the main excavation from which a large number of the artefacts were recovered was probably not the source of the handaxes and flake tools so often cited. Analysis of the debitage assemblage from this excavation reveals a distinctive discoidal technology which is described for the first time in a British context.

BACKGROUND

In August 1890, Benjamin Harrison, village grocer of Ightham, Kent, began excavating on and below the north east talus slope of Oldbury Hill in search of what he called 'Rockshelter' implements. Harrison had used the term 'Rockshelter' in a typological sense since a visit to the British Museum Christy Collection in 1872[1] when he perceived that the artefacts he was finding on the slopes of Oldbury Hill showed similarities to the handaxes and flake tools from the French rockshelters excavated by Edouard Lartet and Henry Christy (1875). Further, he recognised that they differed from the implements of the 'River Drift' period (Evans 1872, 477) that he had found in the deposits of the Shode Valley. A field trip to Ightham in 1889, organised by the Geologists' Association (Topley 1891), persuaded geologists and archaeologists such as Professor Sir Joseph Prestwich, F. C. J. Spurrell and John Allen Brown that Harrison's collection from Oldbury and the promising rock overhang warranted further investigation. A grant of £25 was arranged to finance excavation[2]. Only £15 was spent and, judging by the brevity of Harrison's subsequent (1892) report to the British Association, as well as Prestwich's rather reserved comments (1892), it

would seem that the excavation was regarded as disappointing both in terms of the character of the artefacts and the nature of the site. The former included few handaxes or flake tools of the kind Harrison considered as of 'Rockshelter' type which had justified the British Association grant. Further, the locality below the rock overhang did not preserve a stratified accumulation of deposits such as had been found in south west France. In sending material excavated and collected through the project to the British Museum, Harrison felt it necessary to supplement the finds with 'Rockshelter' types from his own, earlier collecting[3]. Evans (1897, 608) was certainly not persuaded by the distinctive character of the artefacts, mentioning Oldbury in a single brief sentence in the enlarged chapter on River Drift material in the second edition of *Ancient Stone Implements*. This suggests that he continued to regard all handaxes as part of his River Drift period and that the Oldbury finds failed to make him any less sceptical of the validity of the term Mousterian and its chrono-stratigraphic distinctiveness as proposed for such 'Rockshelter' material by Gabriel de Mortillet (1869; 1872; Evans 1897, 528). Thus, it was left to later workers to establish Oldbury as a rare British example of a rockshelter with 'specimens practically identical with Le Moustier' (Smith 1926, 77),

	Mesolithic/Neolithic Flint	**Pottery**	**Other**
Box 1	1 bladelet fragment; 6 flakes	3 sherds (indet)	2 unmodified flint pebbles (exotic)
Box 2	6 flakes		1 unmodified piece of chalk (exotic)
Box 3	4 bladelet fragments; 7 flakes	5 sherds (indet)	2 unmodified flint pebbles (exotic) 6 charcoal fragments

Table 18.1. Initial excavation finds.

as Mousterian (Mellars 1974, 64–65) and, more specifically Mousterian of Acheulean Tradition (Collins & Collins 1970; Coulson 1990; Roe 1981, 182). Although these researchers have vindicated Harrison's belief in the typological and chronological distinctiveness of his finds, the sources, nature and significance of the material have not been precisely established and the following review aims to contribute to this area.

THE COLLECTION

In the initial stages of this research, the material acquired by the British Museum from Harrison in 1893 was laid out and sorted by its condition, technological and typological characteristics. Prior to this procedure the collection appeared mixed and of limited archaeological value. However, the sorting produced eight groups of finds which relate to Harrison's descriptions of his fieldwork in published and archival sources, as well as to his opinions, influenced by Prestwich and the Christy Collection, about the age of the material. These groups are described below.

1. Initial excavation finds

The items summarised in Table 18.1 were deposited and have been curated in three cotton boxes marked consecutively:

> 'From C. (= Cave) Brief works Aug. 4 1890. First inset surface. Box no. 1. Neolithic'; 'Box no. 2 August 14 Oldbury – top surface. Neolithic' and, Box 3, 'August 21. Thursday. Dunn, E R Harrison, Head top surface, Neolithic'.

These annotations, the sketch inside the lid of the third box (Fig. 18.1) and the postscript of a letter[4] from Harrison to Charles Hercules Read, assistant in the Department of British and Mediaeval Antiquities at the time of the Oldbury acquisition, indicate that this was the material found when Harrison cleared areas parallel to, then below the rock face (Harrison 1892, 353). A contemporary photograph[5] shows this area (Fig. 18.2). Harrison evidently hoped that the sandstone overhang protected an accumulation of deposits or, perhaps, the mouth of a cave, but soon found that the rock was 'near the surface, and forming merely a shoulder under the surface soil' (*ibid.* 353). There being no rockshelter analogous to those known from France, Harrison turned his attention to other areas of the

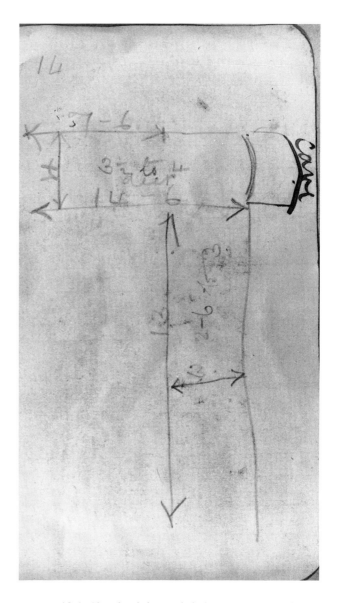

Figure 18.1. Sketch of the rockshelter excavation drawn by Harrison (BM, PRBA QS Archive).

slope. This was not appreciated by R.A. Smith who, in interpreting the material following Bennett (1907, 41) created the rockshelter site, albeit weathered away, which Harrison had hoped for but never claimed to have found (Smith 1911, 68; PRBA QS archives Harrison/Oldbury file items 20, 21). Smith's interpretation has lingered on in the literature (Gardiner 1990, 40), but it is now possible to state that the area immediately below the rock overhang produced only Mesolithic and later prehistoric finds (Table 18.1). This material provides an additional record of Holocene rockshelter use in the Weald (*ibid.* 42).

2. Oldbury slope finds

There are five artefacts in the collection which have paper labels provenancing them to Oldbury slope. Four of these are Neolithic flakes one of which shows substantial re-working of an older piece, whilst another has a naturally modified dorsal surface. Three out of these four are also marked 1890, the fourth is noted as *'from the cave slope'*. These labels suggest that the specimens might have come from the rocky area below the overhang excavation (Harrison 1892, 354). The fifth piece is a previously un-published Palaeolithic triangular biface, much abraded and badly damaged at or prior to the time of its discovery. Its condition is indeed commensurate with it having been found on a slope which had been used as a source of stone for road metalling in the 1840s. The accounts of rock breaking and removal, recorded by Harrison from local[6] and personal sources (E. Harrison 1933, 67), must be reckoned as a major cause of disturbance and damage in this area.

3. Oldbury East finds

In a letter to Read[7], Harrison records that, in addition to the excavated artefacts, he had sent some surface flakes to the Museum, most of which he had marked *'Oldbury East'* or *'E'*. This reference, the clear marking of the artefacts and mention of Oldbury East by Spurrell (1883, 11) suggest that the 40 Palaeolithic debitage flakes and three natural fragments in the British Museum come from a discrete area and should not be counted as part of find group 7 described below. All of the material is abraded and shows the edge damage and random staining typical of surface finds. The discoveries recorded by Spurrell (*ibid.*) are of four small bifaces for which he saw counter-parts among the implements from Le Moustier.

4. Post Palaeolithic finds

There are 81 pieces in this group, all of which show the patination, abrasion, edge-damage and random iron stain-ing indicative of surface finds. With the exception of four semi-circular or 'thumbnail' scrapers, the material consists of debitage which is mostly Neolithic but also includes a Mesolithic adze sharpening flake marked *'Oldbury, Igh-tham'* (93.3–23.25) previously described as a Palaeolithic biface fragment (Coulson 1990, fig. 9.7).

5. Natural pieces

All but one of the 31 pieces in this group are flint so, although naturally modified, they are exotic to this sand-stone hillside. The exceptional fragment may be Oldbury

Figure 18.2. Oldbury rockshelter (1893).

chert. None of the pieces bears any resemblance to those which Harrison regarded as much older artefacts and refered to as Eoliths (cf. Coulson 1990, 335).

6. Abraded Middle Palaeolithic artefacts

This group includes 68 objects, several of which have come to typify the Oldbury Middle Palaeolithic in the literature. However, both the abraded condition and the marking of these artefacts suggest that they are the 'Rock-shelter' or Middle Palaeolithic specimens which Harrison collected from the hillslope prior to the excavations. Three of these pieces, including 93.3–23.12 have remnants of stamp edge labels such as have been used on the Oldbury East pieces but their surfaces have been lost and their original marking is uncertain. Another, 93.3–23.13, has a label fragment similar to those on the Oldbury slope specimens. Of the remaining artefacts 11 are marked *'Oldbury Ightham'* in a hand other than Harrison's. Among these, five pieces (93.3–23.6, 10, 14, 17 and 18) have numbers written by Harrison which, although deliberately erased, show up in ultra-violet light. These suggest that they were taken from Harrison's own collection and had originally been numbered for his own catalogue (Cook & Jacobi 1994). Unfortunately, although diligent about recording his finds, Harrison was in the habit of re-numbering pieces and creating new catalogues for col-lections which he gave away or, more often, sold to museums or individuals. As his original catalogues have not been found in the known archive collections, no additional information about the re-marked pieces has been ascertained. The material in this group is listed in Tables 18.2 and 18.3 and then described.

Comparison of the biface inventory in Table 18.2 with the types recorded by Coulson (1990, 337) reveals differences in the identifications which can be attributed to the fact that the pieces are not standard forms and have also been badly damaged. Coulson's analysis (*ibid.*) was based on the altered outlines. Consequently, the irregular forms of two metrically triangular pieces (Bordes 1961, 71: 93.2–23.3 and 7) have been described as sub-triangular by Coulson (1990, 337). The marked convexity of the edges of these objects, as well as 93.2–23.4 and the sub-triangular specimens (Table 18.3), as expressed by results of >0.9 for the ratio of mid-length breadth : maximum breadth, is a notable characteristic of the triangular and sub-triangular pieces which are also all made on flakes and weighted along the longitudinal mid-line, decreasing in thickness from the middle towards both ends. On each example the edge extends around the entire outline of the tool so that the butt forms a straight or slightly convex third side which, on 93.2–23.4 and 7, is neatened and thinned by retouch on the inverse face of the original flake blank. For Tyldesley (1987, 64), 93.2–23.4 is a *bout coupé* form but there would not appear to any reason for separating it from the other similar bifaces discussed here.

The discoid bifaces (Table 18.2) are distinctive and true to type (Bordes 1961, 76). Two additional possible discoids, 93.2–23.10 and 18, identified by Coulson (1990, 337) both show considerable ancient and some sub-recent damage. Allowing for this, these pieces are perhaps more aptly re-classified as cordiforms.

The two remaining pieces, 93.2–23.8 and 15, are difficult to classify except as atypical. Both are bifacially modified flakes. 93.2–23.8 has a sub-rectangular form and is modified by direct small scalar marginal retouch on one of its long edges whereas the opposite side has been altered by a single inverse removal along its entire length. The latter led Coulson (*ibid.* 337) to suggest that this piece could be a thinned back side scraper. Here, it is listed with the bifaces as is 93.2–23.15 which resembles a small cordiform, although its alternate flaking and skewed cross-section defy certain classification. A flake thermally detached from a biface surface completes an inventory which might be said to be indicative of derivation from a Middle Palaeolithic source.

The flake tools (Table 18.3) are few in number and individually difficult to classify. Comparison of the inventory with the flake tool identifications given by Coulson (*ibid.* 335–337) shows variations which result entirely from the equivocal nature of the pieces. All are altered by ancient and sub-recent edge damage and breaks. The side scrapers show no consistent pattern of blank choice or retouch. The latter tends to be scalar or sub-parallel, semi-invasive and limited in extent. The notch (Table 18.3) is a retouched example but is interrupted by an ancient break, whereas the denticulate is almost certainly the result of accidental damage along the transverse edge of the flake. Although useless for defining the age and affinities of this part of the collection, the rather impoverished flake tool inventory

Type	Registration no.	No.
Triangular	93.3–23.3,4,7	3
Sub-triangular	93.3–23.9,11	2
Cordiform	93.3–23.5,10,18	3
Discoid	93.3–23.16,17	2
Miscellaneous	93.3–23.8	1
Partial	93.3–23.15	1
Flake from biface	93.3–23.31	1

Table 18.2. Group 6 bifaces.

Type	Registration nos.	No.
Single side scrapers	93.3–23.6	2
Side scraper fragments		2
Convergent side scrapers	93.3–23.12,14	2
Naturally backed knife		1
Notch	93.3–23.13	1
Denticulates	93.3–23.13	1
Miscellaneous		1
Retouched fragment		1
Debitage flakes		22

Table 18.3. Group 6 flake tools and debitage.

might be a reflection of raw materials influencing and determining a distinctive technology and the availability of suitable blanks.

7. Mixed and naturally modified Palaeolithic material

This group is distinguished by the fact that all of the 77 artefacts have been abraded, scratched and altered by natural, mechanical and/or thermal fractures suggesting they were derived from a talus or debris flow. The mixture of classifiable material (Table 18.4) supports such derivation. The group includes a Lower Palaeolithic biface of limande form (93.3–23.1) which is notably larger and has a distinctive condition from the cordiform and sub-triangular bifaces described below in Group 7. There are also two thermal flakes (93.3–23.2 & 20) which appear to have sprung from the surfaces of large biface forms and a broken and thermally altered fragment with bifacial modification. Artefacts in a similarly altered condition were also recovered from the Collins' excavation at Oldbury (Collins & Collins 1970) and include a biface fragment (P1971.7–3.129) from layer 2 area IX previously described and illustratred as a damaged cordiform (*ibid.*, fig. 5.9) but more probably part of an older, larger limande form. The only other diagnostic piece in this group is a medial fragment of a blade struck from an opposed platform core, possibly Upper Palaeolithic. Seven flakes are modified by edge damage resembling retouch and this includes a piece (93.3–23.19) identified by Coulson (1990, 937) as a side scraper – denticulate. However, the denticulate retouch invades the older patinated surface of the piece and prob-

Objects	Registration nos.	No.
Limande biface	93.3–23.1	1
Thermal flakes from bifaces	93.3–23.2 & 20	2
Bifacially modified fragment		1
Edge modified flakes	93.3–23.19,21,23,24,27,33,34	7
Debitage fragments		62
Blade fragment	93.3–23.29	1

Table 18.4. Inventory of group 7 pieces.

Type	No.
Side scraper fragment	1
Double side scrapers	2
Convergent convex sidescraper fragment	1
Transverse scraper fragment	1
Notches	3
Denticulate	1
Fragment with inverse retouch	1
Thin alternately retouched	1
Miscellaneous minimally retouched	8
Biface fragments	3

Table 18.5. Group 8 tools.

ably results from post-depositional mechanical damage. This mixture of artefacts (Table 18.4) and their condition suggests that these pieces were derived in a colluvium, talus or debris flow and should be separated from those in groups 7 and 8.

8. Fresh excavated finds.

In their descriptions of the Oldbury excavations both Harrison and Prestwich record that to overcome the difficulties caused by large boulders and trees, the site of the work was moved to 'the bold projecting spur below Mount Pleasant lying about fifty yards south east of the former digging' (Harrison 1892, 354), 'lower down the hill where the ground was undisturbed' (Prestwich 1892, 652). Digging over an area of some nine to ten rods (*c.* 7–8m²) numerous flakes were recovered 'some of these so minute that it seemed as if the place of the actual workshop had been lighted on' (Harrison 1892, 354). This description seems to fit the material in this group which consists of tools and debitage (Table 18.5) distinguished from the rest of the collection on the basis of their fresh condition and distinct characteristics. None of this material was marked by Harrison, nor was it individually numbered within the 93.3–23 registration by R.A.Smith, who presumably regarded it simply as debitage.

Although this part of the collection does not include any complete bifaces, the presence of three small biface fragments and biface thinning flakes (Table 18.6) indicate that bifaces were part of the toolmaking repertoire. However, the nature of the bifaces cannot be interpreted from the surviving remnants and the character of the flake tools (Table 18.5) is similarly equivocal. There are only five scrapers, three of which are broken fragments. These exhibit semi-invasive scalar retouch, although the modification on the possible transverse example is limited in extent and may not be deliberate. Of the two complete double side scrapers one has irregular edges and the other is made on a thermally detached flake which also has a thermal flake scar on its dorsal surface. Random percussion removals are present on the inverse face of this piece but their significance is difficult to interpret. Of the notches, only one is a clearly deliberate 'Clactonian' form. The denticulate has a bold, inversely retouched edge on the side of a short, thick flake which retains >50% cortex on its dorsal face. The remainder of the flake tools consist of minimally retouched pieces which fall within Bordes' non-diagnostic

Type	No.
Biface thinning flakes	25
Chordal flakes (pseudo-Levallois points & core edge removal flakes)	36
Debitage flakes (including centripetal flakes)	136
Debitage flake fragments	75
Retouch flakes	10
Shatter fragments	14
Cores	5
Upper Palaeolithic blade	1

Table 18.6. Group 8 debitage.

categories 42–49 and 62. As in the case of group 6, the flake tool inventory is not helpful in respect of the age and affinities of the collection but the debitage is more informative. As shown in Table 18.6, it includes biface thinning flakes (Fig. 18.7) indicating that handaxes were at least modified in the vicinity of the excavated area, although no complete forms can confidently be provenanced to this locality. By contrast, the remainder of the debitage is indicative of discoidal core reduction, a technology which has not previously been described from a British site. Indeed, its significance has only recently been recognised in the French literature (Boëda 1993, 392; Locht *et al.* 1994, 20).

As Boëda (*ibid.*) has shown, discoidal technique is a deliberate and patterned method of allowing the removal of many flakes of varied but predetermined form. These flakes are removed from around the intersecting edge (*charnière*) between two asymmetrical convex surfaces (*ibid.* 392, fig. 1.1). This sinuous edge forms the line of the striking platform (Fig. 18.3) which changes throughout the reduction sequence as each removal detaches part of it, being directed at an angle through it towards the opposite convex surface. The axis of removal thus crosses the intersection of the convex core surfaces (Fig. 18.3). Boëda (*ibid.*) refers to this as the intersecting plane of detachment (*plan sécant*) and contrasts it with the method used in Levallois technique which involves removals parallel to the line of intersection between the two core surfaces (*ibid.*, fig 1.4). The discoidal core may be reduced in three different ways: by detaching flakes first from around one face then around the other, by removing each flake alternately, or by using one face solely as the striking platform

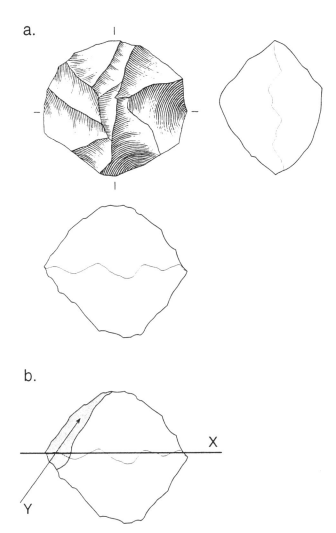

X Plane of detachment (plan sécant)

Y Axis of removal

Figure 18.3. Diagrams to show: a, plan-view and cross-sections of discoidal core and b, the method of flake removal (from Boëda 1993).

for removals from the opposite surface. The flakes may be removed in a centripetal direction with the axis of removal passing through the centre of the convex face (Fig. 18.4), or the axis may be offset (*ibid.* 397, fig. 6). This produces two distinct categories of flakes refered to as *centripetal* and *chordal* respectively (Fig. 18.4). Both of these flake types are present in the excavated group 8 material of the 1893 Oldbury collection.

Table 18.6 shows that there are 36 chordal flakes from Oldbury. Within this category, Boëda (*ibid.* 397) distinguishes two types of flake: pseudo-Levallois points and core edge removal flakes (*éclats débordants*). Locht and Swinnen (1994, 90) suggest that the former tend to have only one arête which connects the point to the detached

core edge remnant, whereas the latter have at least two arêtes and their sharp edge is parallel or sub-parallel to a 'backed' side formed by the core edge remnant. However, Bordes' description of pseudo-Levallois points (1961, 29) seems to incorporate both forms of chordal flakes and this reflects the difficulty of separating Boëda's types in practice. The problem is not helped by the use of the term 'point' as pseudo-Levallois flakes are not always clearly or symmetrically pointed, although Depaepe *et al.* (1994) note that these are generally more triangular whereas the core edge removal flakes have a rectangular shape. Within the Oldbury excavated group there are pieces which can be differentiated as pseudo-Levallois points (Fig. 18.5) but with many more pieces the distinction is at best arbitrary, a problem also noted by Locht and Swinnen (1994, 91) in respect of the Beauvais assemblage. Consequently, all of the offset flakes are recorded here under the heading of chordal pieces.

The remaining Oldbury debitage (Table 18.6) includes centripetal flakes. Again Boëda (1993, 397) distinguishes between short broad and four-sided forms which have proved difficult to separate in this study. However, as Table 18.7 suggests, 57% of the measurable Group 8 debitage does have the short, broad character typical of centripetal flakes, the majority of undamaged flakes being broader than, or as wide as, they are long. This form is caused by the convexity of the core surface which limits the extension of force from the knapper's blow (*ibid.* 397, fig. 6).

The majority of flakes exhibit an intersecting dorsal scar pattern and plain butts or unprepared proximal ends showing only a point of percussion (Table 18.8). These characteristics are also consistent with the use of discoidal technology. Furthermore, the presence of prominent cones of percussion and their occasional replacement by Janus flake scars, as well as conspicuous fissuring on ventral surfaces, spontaneous flakes and flake scars (Newcomer 1975) and shatter fragments all testify to the direct hard hammer percussion used for this technique (Boëda 1993, 395).

As may be seen from the number of observations recorded as indeterminate in Table 18.8, this part of the Oldbury collection, although fresh, shows considerable ancient mechanical damage much of which probably occurred during or shortly after knapping. This is probably due to the poor quality of the flint combined with the hard hammer flaking mode. The source of the flint is unknown, but exotic to Oldbury, and the low proportion of flakes (6% or 8 pieces) retaining more than 50% cortex compared with 62% lacking cortex suggests that the primary stage of core reduction was carried out elsewhere.

Five previously unrecognised cores (*cf.* Coulson 1990, 351) also confirm the presence of discoidal technology. They include two almost exhausted discoid cores and a plunged centripetal flake which has been detached from the apex of a discoid core. The remaining pieces are more informal, including a re-cycled fragment from which two

a. Direction of removal

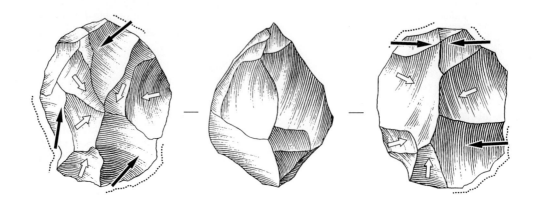

→ Chordal

⇨ Centripetal

......⸍ Length of core edge detached

b. Chordal flakes

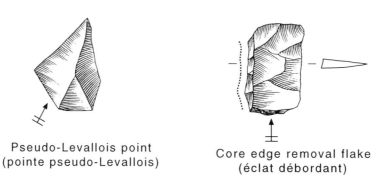

Pseudo-Levallois point
(pointe pseudo-Levallois)

Core edge removal flake
(éclat débordant)

c. Centripetal flakes

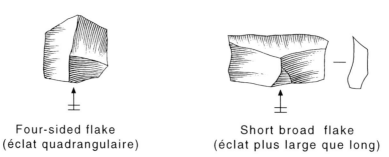

Four-sided flake
(éclat quadrangulaire)

Short broad flake
(éclat plus large que long)

Figure 18.4. Diagrams to show: a, the direction of removal for chordal and centripetal flakes; b, the form of chordal and c, centripetal flakes (from Boëda 1993).

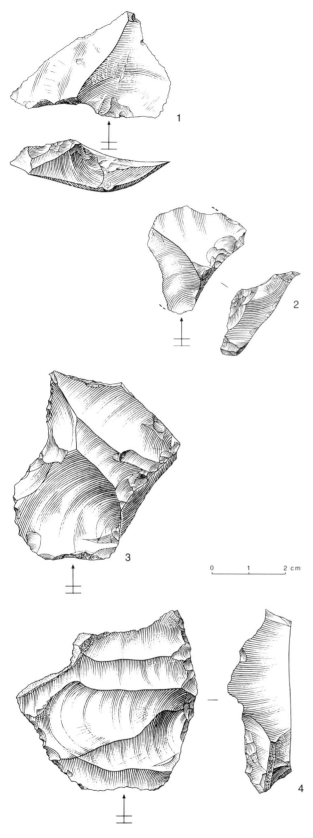

Length:breadth	no.	%
Indet	71	52.0
<1	37	27.2
1.1–1.49	21	15.4
1.5–2.0	6	4.4
>2	1	0.7
$\bar{x} = 1.1$ $\sigma = 0.3$		

Table 18.7. Length:breadth ratios for group 8 debitage flakes.

flakes have been removed from a single platform and a cobble split possibly on an anvil with flakes removed from two platforms at different heights.

Overall, the fresh material, presumed to come from the excavation below Mount Pleasant (Harrison 1892, 354), indicates some biface manufacture and the presence of discoidal technology. The latter may be regarded as Middle Palaeolithic, although it is not certainly indicative of age. The absence of flake tools from this part of the collection is notable. The source of the single Upper Palaeolithic blade (Table 18.6) is unknown.

INTERPRETATION

Re-sorting the 1893 Oldbury collection suggests that Harrison's accounts of his finds, both in the published report (1892) and his unpublished notes, are actually quite reliable, although assumptions about the author's competence and what an English rockshelter assemblage ought to be like have cast doubt on their accuracy. Table 18.9 summarises their interpretation.

As described above, Harrison began his excavations at a point on the Oldbury slope where there had been a cave or rockshelter within living memory[8]. He found only a few Mesolithic and Neolithic finds in this area (Table 18.1) and so began to dig on the slope below the rockshelter where he recovered a small number of artefacts (group 2) from remnants of colluvium which had survived the effects of quarrying around and below large boulders (Harrison 1892, 354). The scarcity of finds, the disturbance caused by quarrying and the difficulty of working around the blocks then influenced the decision to move his diggers to the slope below Mount Pleasant, a prominent rock outcrop labelled as such in Collins and Collins (1970, 154, fig. 2) where he dug a large area and found a considerable number of flakes *in situ* at a depth varying from 2½ to 3 feet (75–90cm). His description of the undisturbed flakes fits the material discussed here in group 8 which consists of the products of discoidal core technology, a few non-diagnostic flake tools (Table 18.5) and some biface thinning flakes (Table 18.6). Given that Harrison records that he also found 'finely fashioned Palaeolithic implements' in this area (Harrison 1892, 354), it is probable that the material separated here into group 7 and, perhaps, group 5, may have come from the deposits overlying the *in situ* flakes.

Figure 18.5. Chordal flakes from Oldbury. 1–2, pseudo-Levallois points; 3–4, core edge removal flakes.

Dorsal scar pattern	%	Butt type	%	Termination	%
Indeterminate	5.9	Indeterminate	36.8	Indeterminate	41.9
No scars	2.9	Not pre-formed	10.3	Normal	36.0
1 scar	5.9	Plain	33.8	Hinged	15.4
Intersecting	68.4	Dihedral	4.4	Step	5.9
Same platform simple	14.0	Facetted	14.7	Plunged	0.7
Same platform convergent	2.9				

Table 18.8. Group 8. Debitage flake characteristics.

Group	Provenance	Context	Character
8	Excavation below Mt. Pleasant	*in situ* on top of gravelly wash	Flakes produced by discoidal core technique. Some evidence of biface manufacture
7	Uncertain. Possibly from excavation below Mt. Pleasant	Derived in superficial deposits	Mixed Palaeolithic artefacts. Naturally modified
6	Uncertain	Derived in superficial deposits	Bifaces and flake tools
5	Uncertain	Derived in superficial deposits	Natural pieces
4	Uncertain	Surface finds	Mesolithic and Neolithic
3	Oldbury East	Surface finds	Palaeolithic debitage flakes
2	Oldbury slope	Superficial deposits below 'Rockshelter'	Biface and Neolithic
1	Rockshelter	Superficial deposit	Mesolithic and Neolithic

Table 18.9. Summary of Harrison's Oldbury Collection.

They are certainly similar to those found in the superficial deposit recorded by Collins and Collins (1970) in their more recent excavations near to Harrison's site and the condition of the material is commensurate with having been found in a colluvium. Further support for this interpretation has been found in a draft of Harrison's published report.[9]

In the printed account of the Mount Pleasant excavation Harrison (1892, 354) describes the discovery of the *in situ* flakes and then in the next or seventh paragraph goes on to give the total number of artefacts found 'at this spot'. However, the draft of the report reveals a printing error which has been misleading. The seventh paragraph should have been printed as the penultimate paragraph and, following the account of the flakes in the sixth paragraph, the report should have continued with the description of the stratigraphy printed in the subsequent eighth paragraph. Positioned according to the draft version the stratigraphy noted in the next printed eighth paragraph is clearly that found on the Mount Pleasant site, whereas the flake and tool totals given in the seventh paragraph which far exceed those sorted into the present groups 7 and 8, in fact refer to all the finds from the Oldbury slopes. A further misprint occurs in the description of the Mount Pleasant stratigraphy. Having recorded the depth of the finds, Harrison states in his draft that they 'lay at the base, immediately overlying a gravelly wash'. This was changed by the printer to read 'at the base of, or immediately overlying a gravelly wash'. Whilst the latter description suggests that some confusion existed either in the deposits or the author's mind, the

unaltered version indicates that the stratigraphy observed by Harrison was like that recorded by Collins and Collins (1970, 156–7). In these more recent excavations, artefacts were recovered above a sterile basal brown stony deposit overlain by 10–100cm of sediments. Both the context of the artefacts and the thickness of the superfical deposit are therefore commensurate with those noted by Harrison and it might further be observed that, although not recognised in the published report (*ibid.*), fresh flakes from discoidal cores are present in the more recent Oldbury collection together with abraded and mixed material like that in group 7.

The remaining artefacts listed in groups 3, 4 and 6 are surface finds from Oldbury generally. Those in group 3 come from the site of Oldbury East (Spurrell 1883, 11), whilst the material in groups 4 and 6 may have been spread more widely. Edward Harrison (1933, 149) noted that his father linked 'the white implements with the rockshelters' and found 'that although these tools might be picked up on many fields in the Ightham district, they seemed to have a particular association with Oldbury as they occurred in far greater numbers there than elsewhere'. Given this record and the evidence for the re-marking of some specimens, it seems probable that the group 6 bifaces and flake tools regarded for so long as being characteristic of a Mousterian of Acheulean Tradition assemblage from the Oldbury Rockshelter are in fact selected surface finds from a wide area. This should not be read as an attempt to dissemble by Harrison. He made no such specific claims for his finds and it is clear from Evans' brief dismissal of the site (1897,

608) that the expectation of *in situ* deposits below a rockshelter had not been met.

AGE

There is currently no means of estimating the age of the Oldbury artefacts. No faunal remains have been found in the deposits. Those reported by Shackley (1977, 334, table 1, 337) were in fact recovered from the Ightham Fissures in the Hythe Beds south east of Oldbury between Borough Green and Basted (Abbott 1894; Dines *et al.* 1969, 139). Collins and Collins (1970, 158) suggest that the age of the sterile basal brown stony deposit, Harrison's 'gravelly wash', must be early Devensian on the basis of the typology of the bifaces and flake tools in the superficial deposit. However, as these were all derived and included a fragment of a Lower Palaeolithic handaxe, these objects cannot be regarded as providing a reliable *terminus ante quem.* The recognition that Harrison's *in situ* assemblage consists mainly of material produced by discoidal technology does not improve matters. This technique does not seem to be chronologically specific, appearing both before and during the last glaciation (see below). Consequently, the age of the Oldbury deposits must be regarded as unknown.

DISCUSSION

Although small caves and rockshelters certainly exist at Oldbury (Reeve 1982), the re-interpretation of Harrison's finds suggests that none of the archaeological material, except that in group 1, can be said to have come from a rockshelter. The bifaces and flake tools which have come to characterise the Mousterian of Acheulean Tradition at Oldbury all occur in secondary contexts on the slopes where they may, or may not, have been derived from deposits originally protected by a rock overhang before they 'slipped down from above' (Harrison 1892, 354). Similarly, it is currently impossible to determine whether the Mount Pleasant *in situ* material (group 8) was always an open site as now. All that it is possible to say is that the prominent feature of Oldbury Hill attracted human groups to its protective slopes.

The recognition of the discoidal core technology at Oldbury adds a new dimension to its general relevance. Previous descriptions of the tools have focussed either on the bifaces as typologically distinct indicators of the British Mousterian (Roe 1981, 182–3, 261; Shackley 1977, 333; Tyldesley 1987, 64) or the flake tools (Coulson 1990). The former can certainly be distinguished from the larger Lower Palaeolithic pointed handaxes found in the gravels of the nearby Shode Valley. This may suggest that the differing forms are chronologically separate and it also implies that the source of nodular flint utilised for the larger handaxe forms was not available to the makers of the Oldbury bifaces. By contrast, the flake tools (Table 18.3) are not certainly diagnostic of the Mousterian, nor would they be regarded as unusual in an older assemblage. Given that mixing has occurred in the slope deposits, it seems unwise to justify dating the small bifaces as Mousterian on the basis of the flake tools (cf. Coulson 1990, 351). However, both biface thinning flakes and a few flake tools have been found amongst the fresh excavated material (group 8) from below Mount Pleasant, most of which can be attributed to discoidal core technology. Fifteen of the biface flakes show remnants of retouch on the dorsal face edge of the butt (Fig. 18.7). This characteristic has also been noted on flakes in the debitage from Little Paxton, Huntingdonshire, where triangular and sub-triangular bifaces similar to those from Oldbury have been found (Paterson & Tebbutt 1947, 42–43, fig. 5). On this basis it can be suggested that the manufacture of bifaces and the use of discoidal core technology were contemporary at Oldbury.

The association of biface manufacture and discoidal core technology has also been noted by the authors in the collections from the Hyaena Den, Wookey Hole, Somerset, Uphill, Somerset and Robin Hood Cave and Church Hole, Creswell Crags, Derbyshire/ Nottinghamshire (Fig. 18.6). These occurrences are thought to be Middle Devensian and, although this dating remains to be proved, it is possible that these sites, with Oldbury, reflect a variant of the Mousterian in Britain which may differ from that seen at Kent's Cavern. At the latter site, the bifaces include larger triangular and cordiform types. The flake tools are distinctive and there is some evidence for the use of Levallois technique which is absent from Oldbury (cf. Roe 1968, 18; Shackley 1977, 334 table 1) and the other sites at which discoidal technology has been noted. The latter is absent from Kent's Cavern. Such variation suggests that prepared core techniques were adapted to the raw materials available. At Kent's Cavern the knappers utilised large pieces of evenly textured local chert from which they could produce Levallois flakes and blanks suitable for the production of flake tools, whereas at Oldbury, the cobbles of flint from secondary sources carried to site, perhaps in a partially reduced state judging by the paucity of cortical debitage flakes, were perhaps more suited to discoidal technique. This may also have applied at Robin Hood Cave and Church Hole where discoidal technique has been used to reduce local quartzite cobbles. A similar picture has been noted at Mauran, Haute Garonne, France (Jaubert 1993) where quartzite has been used for heavy duty tools and discoidal technique, whilst flint has been used for the manufacture of flake tools. Such variation reflects what Boëda (1993, 403) describes as the coherent systems of exploitation which distinguish Levallois and discoidal techniques.

Like Levallois technique, discoidal technology may not be specific to a particular chronological period. At Mauran it occurs within a Late Middle Palaeolithic Denticulate Mousterian assemblage, which may be contemporaneous with OIS 3 (Jaubert 1993, 328). The dating of the assemblage from Beauvais, Oise, France is less certain. The lithostratigraphic evidence suggests the site was occupied

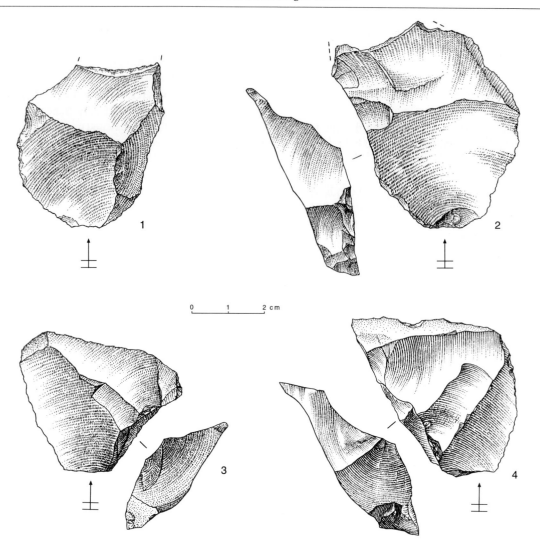

Figure 18.6. 1, Quartzite core edge removal flake from Church Hole (Christy Colln. 8008); 2, quartzite core edge removal flake Robin Hood Cave (Christy Colln. 7985); 3, pseudo-Levallois point from Robin Hood Cave (Christy Colln.); 4, chert core edge removal flake from Hyaena Den, Wookey Hole (HD 1990, D26, 5).

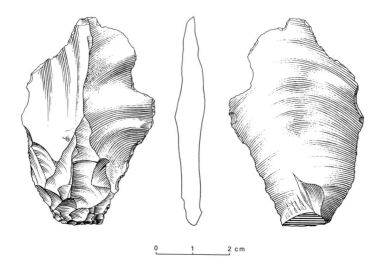

Figure 18.7. Biface thinning flake from Oldbury (1893.3–23.28).

in a cold dry steppe phase during the second part of the Saalian, attributed to OIS 6 (Locht & Swinnen 1994, 89). On faunal grounds, however, the site is considered more likely to date from OIS 4, in the early Weichselian. At Biache-Saint-Vaast, Pas-de-Calais, France, Boëda (1988, 194–195) has identified possible, but uncertain, evidence of discoidal technology in a small sample amongst the material from level IIA, thought to date from OIS 7. The British sites have been dated on the basis of particular handaxe types which Shackley (1977, 333) has described as a 'chronological and typological datum line for the arrival of Mousterian man in Britain' and which Roe (1981, 252) has placed during 'the close of the Ipswichian and the earlier parts of the Devensian'. However, Coulson (1986) has questioned the typological basis of this model and the problem requires some reconsideration.

In his metrical study of British handaxes Roe (1968) found that the bifaces from Oldbury clustered as 'more pointed ovates' in Group VI (*ibid.*, 63). To account for particular variations this group was then subdivided. In this process, the Oldbury bifaces were placed in Sub-Group D (*ibid.* 70) with those from Great Pan Farm, Isle of Wight, to distinguish the presence of the *bout coupé* type. Roe (*ibid.*, 18) introduced this term to distinguish pieces with flat butts and convex sides. He noted 'a number' of such pieces in the Oldbury Collection (*ibid.*, 18) although Tyldesley (1987, 64) identified only one. However, as should already have become apparent, the samples used by these authors and by Collins and Collins (1970) lack any context beyond wishful attribution deriving from Harrison's use of the term 'rockshelter'. As noted above, this term was used in a typological rather than a topographic sense.

Using a typological (Bordes 1961) rather than a metrical approach, the present authors, like Coulson (1986), have found that bifaces from the Oldbury area and other *bout coupé* finds listed by Roe (1981, 254–267) and Tyldesley (1987) are cordiform, triangular, sub-triangular and sub-rectangular forms (Jacobi & Cook in prep.). It is also notable that the ratio of mid-length breadth: maximum breadth is always > 0.9, expressing the marked convexity of their edges which, when plotted against length: length to point of maximum breadth (Bordes 1961, fig. 7), places them to the right of the diagram in contrast to triangular and sub-triangular forms with straight sides which do not seem to occur in this country. The significance of this is still being researched and it remains to be proved whether these handaxes can be used to identify the Mousterian in Britain. The same is true of the discoidal technology described in this paper. As the latter is known in both Saalian and Weichselian contexts on the continent, it is now crucial to investigate its chronology in this country to establish whether it is a marker of the Devensian Mousterian, or whether it has a longer history.

CONCLUSION

Overall, the project vindicates Harrison's account of his work at Oldbury. It has also allowed the first identification of discoidal core technology which clearly occurs at other British sites. The research also shows the value of some old collections, however hopeless they might seem at first sight, a fact well known and advocated by John Wymer to whom this paper is offered.

ACKNOWLEDGEMENTS

We wish to express our thanks to Ms C. Mason and Mr R. Stutely of Maidstone Museum and Art Gallery for providing access to Harrison archives. Dr D. Roe, Dr. J. Wymer and Dr P. Pettitt helped us with information and encouragement. We are also indebted to Mr T. Clark for typing the manuscript and Mr P. Dean for drawing the figures.

NOTES

1. Harrison notebook, British Museum (BM) PRBA QS archive, Harrison/Oldbury item 1.
2. *Benjamin Harrison Notebook Volume 8*. Maidstone Museum and Art Gallery.
3. Letter dated 29 June 1893 from Harrison to C. H. Read. BM PRBA QS archive Harrison/Oldbury item 5.
4. Letter dated 1893 from Harrison to C. H. Read. BM PRBA QS archive Harrison/Oldbury item 6.
5. BM PRBA QS archive Harrison/Oldbury item 13.
6. Transcripts of B. Harrison's notes by E. Harrison. *Records' Book Series J.* 152–154. Maidstone Museum and Art Gallery.
7. *ibid.* note 4.
8. *ibid.* note 6, 153.
9. Extracts from the unpublished appendices to E. Harrison (1928). The Natural History Museum, Palaeontology Library, J. N. Carreck archive.

REFERENCES

Abbott, W. J. L. 1894. The ossiferous fissures in the valley of the Shode, near Ightham, Kent. *Quarterly Journal of the Geological Society* 50(2), 171–87.

Bennett, F. J. 1907. *Ightham: the Story of a Kentish Village and its Surroundings*. Letchworth: Garden City Press.

Boëda, É. 1988. Analyse technologique du débitage du niveau IIA. In A. Tuffreau & J. Sommé (eds), Le gisement paléolithique moyen de Biache-Saint-Vaast (Pas-de-Calais). Volume 1. Stratigraphie, Environnement, Études archéologiques (Ière partie). *Mémoires de la Sociéte Préhistorique Française* 21, 185–214.

Boëda, É. 1993. Le débitage discoïde et le débitage Levallois récurrent centripète. *Bulletin de la Société Préhistorique Française* 90(6), 392–404.

Bordes, F. 1961. *Typologie du Paléolithique Ancien et Moyen*. Bordeaux: Delmas.

Cook, J. & Jacobi, R. 1994. Where are they now? *Past* 18, 9.

Collins, D. & Collins, A. 1970. Cultural evidence from Oldbury. *Bulletin of the Institute of Archaeology* 8–9, 151–76.

Coulson, S. D. 1986. The *bout coupé* as a typological mistake. In S. N. Collcutt (ed.), *The Palaeolithic of Britain and its Nearest Neighbours*, 53–4. Sheffield: University of Sheffield.

Coulson, S. D. 1990. *Middle Palaeolithic Industries of Great Britain.* Bonn: Holos.

Depaepe, P., Locht, J-L. & Swinnen, C. 1994. Pointes pseudo-Levallois et éclats débordants sur le site de Beauvais (Oise, France). *Notae Praehistoricae* 14, 25–8.

Dines, H. G., Buchan, S. and Bristow, C. R. 1969. *Geology of the Country around Sevenoaks and Tonbridge.* London: HMSO.

Evans, J. 1872. *The Ancient Stone Implements, Weapons and Ornaments, of Great Britain.* (1st edn) London: Longmans, Green, Reader & Dyer.

Evans, J. 1897. *The Ancient Stone Implements, Weapons and Ornaments, of Great Britain.* (2nd edn, rev.). London: Longmans, Green & Co.

Gardiner, M. 1990. The archaeology of the Weald – a survey and a review. *Sussex Archaeological Collections* 128, 33–53.

Harrison, B. 1892. Report of the committee appointed to carry on excavations at Oldbury Hill near Ightham. *Report of the Sixty-First Meeting of the British Association for the Advancement of Science, Cardiff* 1891, 353–4.

Harrison, E. 1933. Oldbury Hill, Ightham. *Archaeologia Cantiana* 45, 142–61.

Jaubert, J. 1993. Le gisement paléolithique moyen de Mauran (Haute-Garonne): techno-économie des industries lithiques. *Bulletin de la Société Préhistorique Française* 90(5), 328–35.

Lartet, E. & Christy, H. 1875. *Reliquiae Aquitanicae.* London: Williams & Norgate.

Locht, J-C. & Swinnen, C. 1994. Le débitage discoïde du gisement de Beauvais (Oise): aspects de la chaîne opératoire au travers de quelques remontages. *Paléo* 6, 89–104.

Locht, J. L, Swinnen, C., Antoine, P., Patou-Mathis, M., Auguste, P., Mathys, P. & Depaepe, P. 1994. Le gisement de Beauvais: deux occupations du Paléolithique moyen durant une phase pléniglaciaire. *Notae Praehistoricae* 13, 15–20.

Mellars, P. A. 1974. The Palaeolithic and Mesolithic. In C. Renfrew (ed.), *British Prehistory: a New Outline,* 41–99. London: Duckworth.

Mortillet, G. de 1869. Essai d'une classification des cavernes et des stations sous abri, fondée sur les produits de l'industrie humaine. *Matériaux pour l'Histoire de l'Homme* 5(3), 172–9.

Mortillet, G. de 1872. Classification des âges de la pierre. *Congrès International d'Anthropologie et d'Archéologie Préhistoriques. Compte Rendu de la 6e Session, Bruxelles, 1872,* 432–59.

Newcomer, M. H. 1975. Spontaneous retouch. *Staringia* 3, 62–4.

Paterson, T. T. & Tebbutt, C. F. 1947. Studies in the Palaeolithic succession in England, No. III: Palaeoliths from St. Neots, Huntingdonshire. *Proceedings of the Prehistoric Society* 13, 37–46.

Prestwich, J. 1892. Preliminary notes on the excavations at Oldbury Hill. *Report of the Sixty-First Meeting of the British Association for the Advancement of Science. Cardiff, 1891.* 651–2.

Reeve, T. 1982. Oldbury Rock Shelters. Natural caves in sandstone at Ightham, Kent. *Caves and Caving* 16, 27.

Roe, D. A. 1968. British Lower and Middle Palaeolithic handaxe groups. *Proceedings of the Prehistoric Society* 34, 1–82.

Roe, D. A. 1981. *The Lower and Middle Palaeolithic Periods in Britain.* London: Routledge & Kegan Paul.

Shackley, M. L. 1977. The *bout coupé* handaxe as a typological marker for British Mousterian industries. In R.V.S. Wright (ed.), *Stone Tools as Cultural Markers,* 332–9. Canberra: AIAS.

Smith, R. A. 1911. *A Guide to Antiquities of the Stone Age in the Department of British and Mediaeval Antiquities* (2nd edn). London: British Museum.

Smith, R. A. 1926. *A Guide to Antiquities of the Stone Age in the Department of British and Mediaeval Antiquities* (3rd edn). London: British Museum.

Spurrell, F. C. J. 1883. Palaeolithic Implements found in west Kent. *Archaeologia Cantiana* 15, 89–103.

Topley, W. 1891. Excursion to Ightham (Kent). *Proceedings of the Geologists' Association* 11, 66–7.

Tyldesley, J. A. 1987. *The Bout Coupé Handaxe. A Typological Problem.* Oxford: British Archaeological Reports, British Series.

19. The Archaeology of Distance: Perspectives from the Welsh Palaeolithic

Stephen Aldhouse-Green

ABSTRACT

The aim of the present paper is to offer an overview and interpretation of Palaeolithic research and discoveries in Wales over the past three decades. A review of discoveries focuses both on the evidence for the pattern of settlement provided by stray finds and on the results of recent and ongoing excavation. Lower Palaeolithic stray finds are distributed along the littoral zone of South Wales, probably relics of a once more extensive distribution destroyed by glacial advance. The remarkable preservation of coeval deposits at Pontnewydd Cave in North Wales is testimony to the once wider distribution. An interim analysis of finds from the New Entrance of Pontnewydd Cave is presented and is suggestive of the possibility of two discrete phases of occupation, centred on c. 225 and 175 kya respectively. The existence of a Mousterian, or earlier, phase at Paviland Cave is now attested. Analysis of the distribution of Late Upper Palaeolithic sites and finds shows occupation limited to the margins of the Welsh upland massif and this may represent an original Upper Palaeolithic distribution pattern.

Consideration, from a Welsh perspective, is given to the question of whether hunter-gatherer populations are likely to have become established on the mainland of the British peninsula for significant periods of time. The concept of the 'archaeology of distance' is introduced as a means of interrogating the evidence: its sub-themes include colonisation, the impact of the presence or absence of indigenous groups on incoming people, communication, and culture loss.

INTRODUCTION

It is now 20 years since the commencement of the 'Palaeolithic settlement of Wales' research project. Excavation began in 1978 at Pontnewydd Cave in the Elwy Valley of Denbighshire in North Wales, where work has also taken place at the cave-sites of Cefn and Cae Gronw. In South Wales, excavations have been completed at the Pembrokeshire sites of Hoyles Mouth and Little Hoyle, and the 1960s excavations of Charles McBurney and John Clegg at Coygan Cave have been published. The current focus of activity lies with a definitive study of the predominantly Early Upper Palaeolithic site of Paviland Cave, Gower, and the broadly contemporary sites of Ffynnon Beuno and Cae Gwyn in the Vale of Clwyd. In addition, I have been involved with the publication of finds of Lower Palaeolithic age from the southern Welsh littoral, and with a few discoveries of artefacts of probable Upper Palaeolithic age from the area of the Welsh Marches.

John Wymer has been a stalwart supporter throughout the period of my research. His visit to Pontnewydd Cave at an early stage of the investigation is still fondly remembered and John has played a vital continuing role as a grant referee. More recently, he has contributed directly to the project through his completion of the *Welsh Lower Palaeolithic Survey*, produced in parallel with his *English Rivers Palaeolithic Survey*.

THE EARLIER PALAEOLITHIC

Stray finds

Stray finds of Earlier Palaeolithic age are limited to the southern coastal region and immediate hinterland of South Wales. The distribution (Green & Walker 1991) most likely reflects area that remained ice-free during the Welsh glaciations of the later Pleistocene, in that all of those finds, which can plausibly be accepted as losses or discards of Pleistocene age, lie south of the known limit of Devensian ice. By implication, the distribution also suggests that the less well known boundary of the OIS 6 glaciation must have lain to the north of the findspots (Campbell & Bowen 1989, 16).

The finds (Aldhouse-Green 1993; Green 1989) have recently been reviewed by Wymer (1996). The contexts of a few suggest the possibility that they may be modern discards: for example, a handaxe of Broom Chert from the make-up of a railway embankment at Rhiwbina, Cardiff, and a handaxe found lying on waste ground at Blaenafon in Monmouthshire. Other findspots are less problematic: these include a handaxe in mint condition found in the valley of the Afon Marlais near Narberth; a handaxe from the beach at Rhosili, Gower, below a cliff composed of Devensian head (Green 1981), and a handaxe from Penylan in Cardiff, made of local quartzite (Lacaille 1954). Also from the Cardiff area is a handaxe from Lavernock (Fig. 19.1). The discovery was actually made in 1940 and, so, was the first such stray find to be recorded from Wales; however, the likelihood of its being a genuine Palaeolithic loss was discounted at the time and it remained unpublished. The handaxe is of typological interest in that its rounded tip and crudely squared-off base resemble so-called *bout coupé* handaxes dated to c. 50 kya (Aldhouse-Green *et al.* 1995). However, its thickness and the lack of fine retouch on its base indicate that it cannot be considered as a classic example of the type.

The most important discoveries are those from the gravels of the River Severn. Finds from Sudbrook, all rolled, include four handaxes, a core and flake, and a Levallois flake and flake-blade. Their context is a re-worked gravel deposit and, in consequence, the age of the palaeoliths cannot reliably be inferred. However, the handaxe from the nearby site of Sedbury Cliff has almost certainly been eroded from Terrace 4 deposits of the River Severn and is therefore likely, given its correlation with the Bushley Green terrace of the main Severn sequence (Maddy *et al.* 1991; G. W. Green 1992), to be of pre-Ipswichian age.

Sites

There are only three sites which can be attributed with confidence to the Lower/Middle Palaeolithic: Pontnewydd,

Paviland and Coygan. Of these, Pontnewydd Cave may actually contain two discrete episodes of occupation. Paviland Cave, with handaxe and discoidal cores (Swainston 1997) can now be seen to represent a further site; it could, however, be as recent as 50 kya or as old as the Middle Pleistocene. The results of recent survey and excavation (Aldhouse-Green in press) would, however, favour a Devensian age and, so, a Mousterian attribution. Coygan Cave – a Mousterian site with classic *bout coupé* handaxes and dated within the range *c.* 60–40 kya – has recently been the subject of definitive publication and will not be further considered here (Aldhouse-Green *et al.* 1995).

The discoveries from the Main Cave at Pontnewydd Cave, and its stratigraphic sequence (Table 19.1), are now relatively well known: Green (1984) presents the definitive study, updated by Green (1988), Green *et al.* (1989), Aldhouse-Green (1995) and Aldhouse-Green *et al.* (1996). The site was excavated from 1978–1995 and work on the final monograph is now in progress.

The Lower/Upper Sands & Gravels were emplaced by debris flow action, perhaps at a time when the entrance of the cave lay some distance from its present location. It is even possible (William Jones, pers. comm.) that these deposits predate the local formation of the Elwy Valley and belong to a time when the cave was part of an extensive karstic system. These deposits contain no artefacts, bones or, even, speleothems other than interstitial calcite. However, they are full of cobbles of volcanic rocks and also contain small amounts of natural flint, mostly as small subangular gravel. Study of the petrology of the Pont-newydd artefacts (Bevins 1984) has shown that these raw materials precisely mirror those used for the stone tools recovered from overlying layers (Green 1988). It may be, therefore, that the availability of raw materials at Pont-newydd – in part, at least – led to its becoming a cyclically reoccupied or 'persistent place' (*sensu* Barton *et al.* 1995, 109–11), whereby it became a focus for repeated behaviour or behaviours of particular kinds.

The site, and its immediate surroundings, had much to offer. It was a potential source of raw materials for stone tool manufacture. It lay adjacent to, or above, a river which would have provided a water supply both for humans and for prey animals. The river valley would not only have been a route likely to have been used by herbivores, but

Layer	Layer Code	Mode of Emplacement	Estimated Age of Emplacement
Laminated Travertine	LT	*in situ* stalagmite	Holocene
Upper Clays & Sands	UCS	fluvial	Late Glacial/Holocene
Upper Breccia	UB	debris flow	25–15 kya
Silt beds	Sb	fluvial	80–15 kya
Stalagmite lithozone	Sl	*in situ* stalagmite	225–80 kya
Lower Breccia	LB	debris flow	*c.* 225 kya
Intermediate complex	Ic	debris flow	250–225 kya
Upper Sands & Gravels	USG	debris flow	pre-250 kya
Lower Sands & Gravels	LSG	debris flow	pre-250 kya

Table 19.1. Pontnewydd: the Main Cave. Stratigraphic succession.

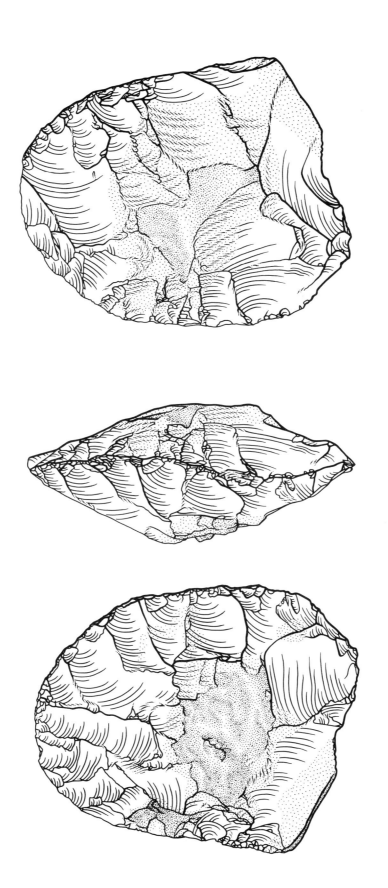

Figure 19.1. The Lavernock handaxe. The artefact is of mottled brown flint. National Museums and Galleries of Wales accession number 89.40H. Drawing by Jackie Chadwick.

also probably had sources of raw material exposed in eroded river banks and elsewhere, and caves to provide shelter along parts of its margins. The cave itself was both a shelter and a landmark, a place easily identified in the contemporary landscape, and so a readily identifiable goal as an overnight stop, rendezvous or quarry site. As a camp site, the rock walls offered shelter from the wind and the recovery of numerous burnt artefacts shows that actual encampment was accompanied by the lighting of fires. It is worth remembering, too, if the occupation was in proximity to a glacial phase, that wind speeds would have been much higher than those obtaining under temperate conditions and that night cold would have contrasted strongly with summer daytime temperatures. Perhaps, too, the cave was a place of mystery or fear or, even, just a convenient place to dispose of the dead. If the origin of the numerous human skeletons unearthed in the Sima de los Huesos at Atapuerca in northern Spain is truly anthropogenic (Arsuaga *et al.* 993, 534), then one may envisage caves or swallets as places for such disposal of the dead long before the appearance of anatomically modern humans.

A cave like Pontnewydd clearly could have had multiple functions and these may well have varied over time. The archaeological evidence from the Main Cave comes from the two layers immediately above the Upper Sands & Gravels, namely the Intermediate complex and the Lower Breccia. The Intermediate complex has an interglacial fauna and the few artefacts which have come from the uppermost level of that complex may plausibly be regarded as intrusive. The layer primarily associated with the archaeological industry is the Lower Breccia debris flow and here, jumbled together – stratified but *ex situ* – are artefacts and associated food and other modified bones, and derived carnivore accumulations. Their age is known within the limits of the Uranium-series and thermoluminescence dating methods and is given a *terminus ante quem* by determinations on a stalagmitic floor formed on the surface of the Lower Breccia yielding statistically consistent ages of 215 ± 36 kya (Schwarcz 1984, 91–92) and 224+41/-31 kya (Ivanovich *et al.* 1984). Dates probably contemporary with the occupation are, however, provided by thermoluminescence determinations on burnt flint artefacts from the Main Cave respectively of 200 ± 25 kya and 269 ± 37 kya, neither statistically distinguishable from the other. An estimated age of *c.* 225 kya for the human presence at the Main Cave would, therefore, seem reasonable.

Some 40m from the Main Cave, excavations between 1987–95 revealed a New Entrance buried under up to 6m of scree and solifluction deposits. This entrance has proved to contain a sequence of debris flows relatively rich in artefacts and fauna, and with one securely stratified hominid tooth. Sedimentological analysis indicates that the sources of the flows in both the Main Cave and the New Entrance lie outside of their respective entrances. Thus, it is clear that substantial occupation has taken place

Principal Artefact Types	Main Cave No.	%	New Entrance No.	%
Handaxes	32	13.5	2	1.8
Choppers/Chopping Tools	2	0.8	2	1.8
Discoidal cores	12	5.1	5	4.4
Levallois cores	18	7.6	1	0.9
Miscellaneous cores	26	11.0	22	19.3
Levallois flakes, blades, points	36	15.2	26	22.8
Side-scrapers	22	9.3	16	14.0
Notches/denticulates	6	2.5	6	5.3
Other retouched artefacts	8	3.4	7	6.1
Naturally backed knives	9	3.8	2	1.8
Pseudo-tools	66	27.8	25	21.9
totals	237		114	

Table 19.2. Pontnewydd Cave. Artefacts from the Main Cave (excavations 1978–1983) and New Entrance compared.

outside at least these two entrances. Excavation has now revealed virtually the full sequence of deposits and the account here supersedes that in Aldhouse-Green (1995, 39, 45, fig. 3), where it was suggested that an *in situ* stalagmitic floor of *c.* 130 kya had been located. It is now clear that this 'floor' must be re-interpreted as no more than a derived stalagmitic clast.

The principal artefact-bearing layer of the New Entrance consists of a Limestone Scree unit emplaced by debris flow action. In origin, this layer – or, rather, complex of layers – seems to have been an external scree where artefacts had possibly accumulated during the scree-formation process. This unit is sedimentologically quite different from the Lower Breccia bed of the Main Cave and seems to have been a 'stored' deposit, emplaced long after its formation, along the lines of the model so presciently described by Collcutt (1984, 53).

Final study of the Pontnewydd artefacts as a whole is at an early stage, but it is possible here to offer a very tentative comparative analysis of the New Entrance artefacts (Table 19.2) with that already published from the Main Cave (Green 1984). Looking at the main categories only, the New Entrance figures reveal the presence of only two handaxes (both heavily rolled), an incidence of only 2% compared with 14% in the Main Cave. Both sites display relatively high frequencies of side-scrapers and Levallois debitage, but the higher values come from the New Entrance. 'Pseudo-tools', genuine artefacts modified by pressure in debris flow action or earlier cryoturbation, figure prominently in both analyses. Thermoluminescence dating of burnt flint from the New Entrance by Nicholas Debenham has produced ages of 214 ± 21 kya, 173 ± 20 kya and 179 ± 22 kya. The latter two ages, whilst statistically indistinguishable from the earliest result of 214 kya and the Main Cave determinations, nonetheless suggest the possibility of a younger age for an element of the New Entrance assemblage. The reasons for the differing statistical compositions of the two assemblages have yet to be assessed in detail. Nonetheless, the impression at this stage is that, in the New Entrance, we may be dealing with a somewhat younger industry wherein handaxes formed a very minor component and in which the products of Levallois technology and side-scrapers were dominant.

THE UPPER PALAEOLITHIC

Distribution

In the Early Upper Palaeolithic, finds are attested only from cave sites. This probably relates more to the near total glaciation of Wales during the Devensian glacial maximum than to the contemporary distribution of settlement. The occurrence of caves only in the Carboniferous Limestone of Wales, and the location of outcrops only in the very south and north of the country, mean that the distribution inevitably appears polarised. To those sites previously known may now probably be added Pontnewydd Cave, where unpublished study by Ruth Charles has identified humanly-made cut marks on fauna recovered from the Upper Breccia and of Upper Breccia preservation type (Currant 1984). Fauna from the Upper Breccia has now been dated in the range 35–25 kya (Hedges *et al.* 1987, 291; Hedges *et al.* 1996, 391–92). The cut-marked fauna itself, however, remains to be dated; an Upper Palaeolithic age seems likely but a Mousterian date remains a possibility. No unequivocal Mousterian or Upper Palaeolithic artefacts, which might relate to this occupation, have yet been identified from the Upper Breccia. Turning to South Wales, recent re-evaluation by David (1990, 20–22) has cast doubt on the interpretation of finds from Long Hole and Nottle Tor as Early Upper Palaeolithic and reassessment of those sites is clearly needed. Sites certainly of Early Upper Palaeolithic age are few in number, being limited to Ffynnon Beuno and Cae Gwyn in the North and to Paviland and Hoyle's Mouth (Aldhouse-Green 1996c) (with the probable addition of Cat Hole) in the South. One should, however, mention King Arthur's Cave on the English side of the River Wye.

Late Upper Palaeolithic sites are far more numerous, over 20 in number, although most sites have fewer than half a dozen finds. In contrast with the Early Upper Palaeolithic, both open and cave sites are known. If these sites reflect the original pattern (if not the density) of settlement, it can be seen that such settlement was truly limited to the northern and southern littorals of Wales, as in the Early Upper Palaeolithic, but with a scattering of sites along the Welsh Marches. In other words, the sites have a broadly lowland distribution around the margins of the Welsh upland massif.

Sequence and dating

The Welsh cultural sequence contains most of the key elements seen elsewhere in the British Upper Palaeolithic but remains largely unsupported by stratigraphic or chronometric dating evidence. The relationship of leaf points to

the Aurignacian remains enigmatic. Radiometric dating suggests that they may appear before the Aurignacian in Britain; indeed, their abraded and *concassé* appearance at Paviland marks them out as potentially earlier and is in contrast with the other Early Upper Palaeolithic elements present (Jacobi 1980, 30). However, the argument as to whether leaf points pre-date the Aurignacian would seem to be of relevance only to Britain for, in Belgium, they appear at Trou Magrite in both the lower and upper Aurignacian levels, dated respectively to c. 38 and 34–30 kya (Otte and Straus 1995, 229–30). Again, at Couvin, a leaf point has been dated to as early as 46,820 ± 3290 BP (Lv-1559). Whatever their separate origins, it seems plausible to argue that the co-occurrence of typical leaf points and Aurignacian types at such a seemingly remote site as Ffynnon Beuno may suggest that they were or became part of the equipment of an Aurignacian hunter in western Britain as also at sites in Belgium.

The new study of Paviland currently underway (Aldhouse-Green 1996b; Aldhouse-Green in press) has embraced a significant dating programme of artefacts and fauna from that site. The results (Aldhouse-Green & Pettitt forthcoming) may serve to clarify some of the current issues in dating the phases of Upper Palaeolithic settlement in Britain.

A recent reassessment of the British Late Upper Palaeolithic (Barton & Roberts 1996) has suggested that two phases can be detected here, a 'Creswellian' with characteristic Cheddar points dating c. 12.5–12 kya and a Final Palaeolithic c. 12–10 kya with penknife points. New Late Glacial dates from Hoyles Mouth (Table 19.3) – but on unmodified bone – are consistent with David's (1991) comparison of the assemblage from that site to the Creswellian of Gough's Cave (Jacobi 1986a; 1991).

THE ARCHAEOLOGY OF DISTANCE

Isolation

A theme recurring in any reference to the site of Pontnewydd is its remoteness in relation not only to the British distribution of earlier Palaeolithic sites but to Europe as a whole (Tattersall 1995, 84). The British perspective on Ice Age settlement has tended to involve seeing Britain in all periods of the Palaeolithic as 'the Ultima Thule of ... Europe, a north-west cape, remote

ref. no.	species	determination
HM 2023	bear	12 220 ± 130 (OxA-6230)
HM 1120	horse	12 110 ± 150 BP (OxA-6225)
HM 2336	bear	12 010 ± 110 BP (OxA-6229)
HM 2422	collared lemming	11 860 ± 110 (OxA-6228)

Table 19.3. Hoyles Mouth. Lateglacial radiocarbon dates on unmodified bone. All samples from excavations 1986–1995.

and inhospitable' (Garrod 1926, 191; Roe 1981, 279) with a small population, composed of hunting groups, present during milder phases only or, even, visiting largely on a seasonal basis from basecamps on what is now the Continental mainland.

We can now see that Wales was settled, whether sporadically or not, during a number of separate phases over the last quarter of a million years. First, evidenced at Pontnewydd certainly *c*. 225 and possibly *c*.175 kya, are two phases of occupation which may correlate with temperate climatic phases marked by stalagmitic growth. The Severn Levels palaeoliths may belong here also. Mousterian occupation *c*. 50 kya is attested certainly at Coygan; probably at Paviland; possibly at Lavernock, if the typological comparison of the handaxe with the *bout coupé* type is valid; and, just possibly, at Pontnewydd. The timing of occupation during the Early Upper Palaeolithic remains to be verified by chronometric dating but the conventional view is one of settlement from *c*. 35 kya or earlier, with a possible hiatus in occupation from *c*. 23–13 kya, followed by successive Creswellian and Final Palaeolithic occupations.

Undoubtedly, over the last 500 kya, settlement of the British peninsula has been discontinuous with climate, vegetation and sea level among the key environmental determining factors, influencing both the motivation for and possibility of human movement. Incomers would have been few in total number, as must also any indigenous population. Interactions of interest to us as archaeologists will particularly include those where incoming groups arrived to find a landscape devoid of human population or one peopled by hominids of another species, perhaps Neanderthals, with whom communication of all kinds may have presented an especial difficulty. In this context, Zubrow's model (1989, 216) is relevant with its picture of a landscape so empty that one Neanderthal could perhaps walk for two weeks without meeting another. It is interesting, therefore, to characterise both such potential hominid interactions and the evidence for settlement, whether continuous, sporadic or seasonal. In the earliest Palaeolithic phase, the limited range of material culture offers little opportunity of distinguishing differing cultural origins outside Britain or of identifying long term *in situ* culture change suggestive of continuous settlement. The growing Welsh evidence suggests, however, a picture of settlement which was possibly far more extensive than hitherto supposed, with all its implications for settlement also of the English Midlands (MacRae & Moloney 1988). We must extend our interpretation beyond that of a happy-go-lucky people camping by the rivers and using the resources to hand. Rather, we should see the pattern of settlement as primarily resource-driven with the needs of food/water, raw materials, shelter and landmarks all being important factors. It is striking that, where finds occur away from resource-rich places (and even some of these Lower Palaeolithic 'concentrations' may not be sites at all but, rather, lag gravels or hydraulic accumulations), they are

generally single finds interpreted as hunting expedition losses (Keeley 1993, 137).

From the range of Mousterian industries recognized in France, only the Mousterian of Acheulian Tradition (MTA) is unambiguously identifiable in Britain (but cf. Cook & Jacobi on Oldbury, this volume). Although a perennial subject for debate, it would seem that the French MTA represents a chronological horizon – rather than simply a task-specific toolkit – falling within the range 55–41 kya (Mellars 1986; 1996, 183–90). The early phase, which has a higher frequency of handaxes and dating *c*. 55–48 kya, probably offers the most likely horizon for the arrival of Mousterian groups in Britain (Aldhouse-Green *et al.* 1995, 77), a period coinciding with the presence of Middle Devensian 'Coygan' faunas (Currant & Jacobi 1997) characterised by the presence of a number of large herbivores. The first Neanderthals to colonise the British peninsula would apparently have come into an empty landscape, without human competition but devoid equally of the possibility of mutual support. In spite of the evidence for abundant game, the scanty evidence of the MTA in Britain suggests that it was a 'bridge too far' or, in Roe's words 'impoverished, short-lived and .....insignificant by Continental standards' (Roe 1981, 252).

By contrast, it is an open question as to whether Britain had any indigenous population when people of Aurignacian culture arrived. If Neanderthals were still present, it is more than possible that the differing ancestry of the two groups (Ward & Stringer 1997) meant that Aurignacians shared no common language, perhaps could not interbreed, and indeed possessed such differing cognitive skills that possibilities of meaningful communication were very limited. The ultimate disappearance of Neanderthals and their replacement by anatomically modern humans in western Europe is perhaps sufficient testimony of their inability to form just such an effective symbiotic relationship. In consequence of this the Aurignacians may have entered an environment that was not only remote but lacked also the possibility of building support networks through exchange of prestige and everyday goods, marriage alliances etc. That such groups were few in number is attested by the relative paucity of the British archaeological record. With this paucity its interest grows, however, for the identification and interpretation of the evidence of a society at the margin of its range presents a particular challenge. The variety of activity is diminished in comparison with the Continent: art is absent, bonework is rare, although the presence of burins may imply the latter's manufacture. It may be that the appearance of leaf points at Paviland and at other Aurignacian sites may simply arise from the need to replace an item of equipment – the Aurignacian bone point – that was no longer manufactured. Even the apparently post-Aurignacian ceremonial burial at Paviland lacks the range of adornment identified at some Continental sites such as Sunghir or the Grotta delle Arene Candide. This one burial may reflect Continental tradition but elaborately adorned vestments are clearly missing – perhaps not part of the equipment of a colonising group and not manufactured by a group whose low numbers may imply either a lack of skilled craftsmen, or the lack of a social context for such activity in a 'remote and inhospitable' environment. I suspect that there are two influences here, working in parallel: the small size of the colonising groups and isolation from their ultimate point of origin. Such isolation may have had the specific effect of culture loss, as seen in the case of the polar Eskimo or the Tasmanians (Malaurie 1976; Jones 1977; Mussi 1990, 138–40). This may explain the fact that radiometric dates from British Aurignacian sites seem generally to fall younger than would be predicted on the basis of Continental analogy. We may here be seeing isolated and, indeed, fully separated groups surviving in a landscape largely devoid of fellow humans (at least ones capable of social interaction) with cultural traditions and equipment progressively diminishing in range and refinement.

Territorial range

The substantive nature of some Lower Palaeolithic settlements in Britain and the overall wealth of finds of that period suggest that, for periods at least, Britain was thoroughly suitable for sustained settlement by early hunter-gatherers. It may be of course that we are looking at this from the wrong perspective. Britain viewed from Wales looks very different from Britain viewed from London, as present day politicians sometimes find out to their cost. The size of hunter-gatherer territories is dependent upon geographic variation in resources, particularly game (Gamble 1986, 48, 53), and we should expect to see differences in Neanderthal and anatomically modern human land use and subsistence strategies (e.g. Stiner 1994, 380). Much of the territorial data assembled as part of modern hunter-gatherer studies is probably of primary relevance only to the Upper Palaeolithic.

Jacobi's interpretation (1986b) of the peopling of Upper Palaeolithic Britain is in keeping with a hypothesis of hunters ranging widely across the mammoth steppe of mainland Europe to the westernmost extremity of Britain. In these circumstances, groups of quite different geographical and cultural origin could have left material traces in Britain – perhaps producing, through their co-mingling, unique assemblages. The result would be an archaeological record in which a straightforward archaeological sequence was replaced by 'unexpected punctuations'. We may enquire here, however, what were the stimuli to this long distance roving? Scott (1986) has criticised the theory of long distance human migration specifically to follow the movement of herds of game. More recently, Burch (1991) has defined a 'herd following' strategy as essentially a repositioning of hunters from winter breeding areas to summer ranges rather than involving simple pursuit of a specific migrating herd. Recent European Upper Palaeolithic studies have, however, produced some conflicting

views on the issue of the degree of mobility of hunters (Straus & Otte 1995; Burke 1995, 71; Newell & Constandse-Westermann 1996).

John Campbell's analysis (1977, 32) of hunter-gatherer territory sizes suggested that the diameter of lifetime territories seldom exceeded values of 100–200 km, areas respectively of *c.* 7,500–30,000 km^2. He suggested a figure of no more than 50 km in respect of annual territories, an area of 2,000 km^2. Recent analysis of several North American hunter-gatherer societies living in areas comparable to Lower Palaeolithic Europe (Newell & Constandse-Westermann 1996) suggests that typical annual territories exploited by groups dependent upon open country resources may range between 2,500 and 5,500 km^2, areas with diameters of between 60 and 85 kilometres respectively. By contrast, societies exploiting forest mammals occupied territories up to 28,000 km^2. Social territories on this scale are probably relevant archaeologically only to the Final Palaeolithic and Mesolithic periods.

It may be appropriate here to quote some distances: London is 130 km from Calais; Paviland is 250 km and Pontnewydd 400 km from the nearest points on the French coast. Given the likely diameters of annual territories even among the mobile hunter-gatherers of the Upper Palaeolithic, it would seem appropriate to think of the then British peninsula or cape not as an area available for seasonal extension of territory but, rather, as an area whose population would have been relatively static. If, as seems sometimes to have been the case, hunters did not move with the seasons but instead employed differing seasonal strategies (Burke 1995, 77), we must clearly give thought as to the processes actually involved in the long distance communication and exchange processes that clearly took place among Upper Palaeolithic groups. It may be that, as in later prehistoric societies, the processes of exchange involved the movement of comparatively few people. We must remember, too, that we are not dealing with a landscape hostile to faunal presence except during the very height of the glaciations. British Pleistocene faunas show climate-related change but, during the cold stages, populations of game animals and carnivores seem to have been present almost continuously and would have provided the relatively small number of hunters with an adequate or, indeed, abundant food supply. The implication is obvious: climatic change may, at times, have driven hunter-gatherer populations out of the British Isles or have led to their local extinction but, for most of the time, hunter-gatherer groups of viable size that became established on the British peninsula could have remained permanently.

ACKNOWLEDGMENTS

I am pleased to express my thanks both to my many colleagues in the Palaeolithic Settlement of Wales Research Project who have made its undertaking such a pleasure; to colleagues in Cadw and the Countryside

Council for Wales who have responsibility for the sites discussed and who have been such a ready source of help and advice. My especial gratitude goes to the landowners, without whose ready consent to excavate, this paper could never have been written. The Lavernock handaxe was drawn by Jackie Chadwick of the National Museums and Galleries of Wales. Above all, I must express my thanks to Derek Roe not only for reading this paper through in draft – and thereby removing many infelicities of expression – but also for his many years of support as grant referee, as member of the Archaeology Committee of the National Museums and Galleries of Wales, and as a regular visitor to the excavations.

REFERENCES

Aldhouse-Green, S.H.R. 1993. Lithic Finds. In S. Godbold & R.C. Turner (eds) *Second Severn Crossing. Archaeological Response: phase 1 – the Intertidal Zone in Wales*, 45–47. Cardiff: Cadw.

Aldhouse-Green, S. H. R. 1995. Pontnewydd Cave, Wales; a later Middle Pleistocene hominid and archaeological site: a review of stratigraphy, dating, taphonomy and interpretation. In J. M. Bermudez., J. L. Arsuaga & E. Carbonell (eds) *Human Evolution in Europe and the Atapuerca Evidence*. 37–55. Junta de Castilla y León.

Aldhouse-Green, S. H. R. 1996b. Paviland Cave and the 'Red Lady' – new research. In S.H.R. Aldhouse-Green (ed.) *Explaining the Unexplainable: Art, Ritual and Death in Prehistory*, 6–7. Cardiff: National Museums and Galleries of Wales.

Aldhouse-Green, S. 1996c. Hoyle's Mouth and Little Hoyle caves. *Archaeology in Wales* 36, 70–71.

Aldhouse-Green, S. H. R. in press. The Paviland research project: the field assessment. *Archaeology in Wales* 37 (1997)

Aldhouse-Green, S. H. R., Scott, K., Schwarcz, H., Grün, R., Housley, R., Rae, A., Bevins, R. & Redknap, M. 1995. Coygan Cave, Laugharne, south Wales – a Mousterian site and hyaena den: a report on the University of Cambridge excavations. *Proceedings of the Prehistoric Society* 61, 37–79.

Aldhouse-Green, S., Pettitt, P. B. & Stringer, C. 1996. Holocene humans at Pontnewydd and Cae Gronw caves. *Antiquity* 70, 444–7.

Aldhouse-Green, S. & Pettitt, P. forthcoming. Paviland Cave: contextualising the 'Red Lady'. *Antiquity* 72 (December 1998).

Arsuaga, J-L., Martinez, I., Gracia, A., Carretero, J-M. and Carbonell, E. 1993. Three human skulls from the Sima de los Huesos Middle Pleistocene site in Sierra de Arapuerca, Spain. *Native 362*, 534–37.

Barton, R. N. E., Berridge, P. J., Walker, M. J. C. & Bevins, R. E. 1995. Persistent places in the Welsh Mesolithic: an example from the Black Mountain upland of South Wales. *Proceedings of the Prehistoric Society* 61, 81–116.

Barton, R. N. E & Roberts, A. 1996. Reviewing the British Late Upper Palaeolithic: new evidence for chronological patterning in the Lateglacial record. *Oxford Journal of Archaeology* 15, 245–65.

Bevins, R. E. B. 1984. Petrological investigations. In H. S. Green, 1984, *Pontnewydd Cave: a Lower Palaeolithic Hominid Site in Wales*. 193–198. Cardiff: National Museum of Wales.

Burch, E. S. 1991. Herd following reconsidered. *Current Anthropology* 32, 439–45.

Burke, A. M. 1995. *Prey Movements and Settlement Patterns during the Upper Palaeolithic in Southwestern France*. Oxford: British Archaeological Reports, International Series 619.

Campbell, J. B. 1997. *The Upper Palaeolithic of Britain*. Oxford: Clarendon Press.

Campbell, S. & Bowen, D. Q. 1989. *Geological Conservation Review: Quaternary of Wales*. Peterborough: Nature Conservancy Council.

Collcutt, S. N. 1984. The sediments. In Green, H. S. 1984, 31–76.

Currant, A. P. 1984. The mammalian remains. In H. S. Green, 1984, 171–80. *Pontnewydd Cave: a Lower Palaeolithic Hominid Site in Wales*. Cardiff: National Museum of Wales.

Currant, A. & Jacobi, R. 1997. Vertebrate faunas from the British Late Pleistocene and the chronology of human settlement. *Quaternary Newsletter* 82, 1–8.

David, A. 1990. *Palaeolithic and Mesolithic Settlement in Wales with Special Reference to Dyfed*. Unpublished Ph. D. thesis, University of Lancaster.

David, A. 1991. Late Glacial archaeological residues from Wales: a selection. In N. Barton, A. J. Roberts & D. A. Roe (eds), *The Late Glacial in North-West Europe: Human Adaptation and Environmental Change at the End of the Pleistocene*, 141–59. London: Council for British Archaeology Research Report no. 77.

Gamble, C. 1986. *The Palaeolithic Settlement of Europe*. Cambridge: Cambridge University Press.

Garrod, D. A. E 1926. *The Upper Palaeolithic Age in Britain*. Oxford: Clarendon Press.

Green, G. W. 1992. Bristol and Gloucester region. *British Regional Geology*. London: H.M.S.O.

Green, H. S. 1981. A Palaeolithic flint handaxe from Rhosili, Gower. *Bulletin of the Board of Celtic Studies* 29, 337–9.

Green, H. S. 1984. *Pontnewydd Cave: a Lower Palaeolithic Hominid Site in Wales*. Cardiff: National Museum of Wales.

Green, H. S. 1988. Pontnewydd Cave: the selection of raw materials for artefact-manufacture and the question of natural damage. In R. J. MacRae & N. Maloney (eds), *Non-Flint Stone Tools and the Palaeolithic Occupation of Britain*. 223–232. Oxford: British Archaeological Reports British Series, 189.

Green, H. S. 1989. Some recent archaeological and faunal discoveries from the Severn Levels. *Bulletin of the Board of Celtic Studies* 36, 187–99.

Green, H. S. Bevins, R. E., Bull, P. A., Currant, A. P., Debenham, N., Embleton, C., Ivanovich, M., Livingston, H., Rae, A. M., Schwarcz, H. P. & Stringer, C. B. 1989. Le site acheuléen de la Grotte de Pontnewydd, Pays de Galles: géomorphologie, stratigraphie, chronologie, faune, hominidés fossiles, géologie et industrie lithique dans le contexte paléoécologique. *L'Anthropologie 93*, 15–52.

Green, H. S. & Walker, E. A. 1991. *Ice Age Hunters. Neanderthals and Early Modern Hunters in Wales*. Cardiff: National Museum of Wales.

Hedges, R. E. M., Housley, R. A., Law, I. A., Perry, C. & Gowlett, J. A. J. 1987. Radiocarbon dates from the Oxford AMS system: Archaeometry datelist 6. *Archaeometry* 29, 289–306.

Hedges, R. E. M., Pettitt, P. B., Ramsey, C. B. & Van Klinken, G. J. 1996. Radiocarbon dates from the Oxford AMS system: Archaeometry datelist 22. *Archaeometry* 38, 391–415.

Ivanovich, M., Rae, A. M. B. & Wilkins, M. A. 1984. Brief report on dating the *in situ* stalagmitic floor found in the East Passage in 1982. In H. S. Green, 1984, *Pontnewydd Cave: a Lower Palaeolithic Hominid Site in Wales*. 98–99. Cardiff: National Museum of Wales.

Jacobi, R. M. 1980. The Upper Palaeolithic of Britain with special reference to Wales. In J. A. Taylor (ed.) *Culture and Environment in Prehistoric Wales*, 15–100. Oxford: British Archaeological Reports British series 76.

Jacobi, R. M. 1986a. The Lateglacial archaeology of Gough's Cave at Cheddar. In S. N. Collcutt, (ed.) *The Palaeolithic of Britain and its Nearest Neighbours: Recent Trends*, 75–79. Sheffield: University of Sheffield.

Jacobi, R.M. 1986b. The contents of Dr Harley's showcase. In S. N. Collcutt (ed.) *The Palaeolithic of Britain and its Nearest Neighbours: Recent Trends,* 62–68. Sheffield: University of Sheffield.

Jacobi, R. M. 1991. The Creswellian, Creswell and Cheddar. In N. Barton, A. J. Roberts, & D. A. Roe (eds) *The Late Glacial in North-West Europe,* 128–140. London: Council for British Archaeology, Research Report no. 77.

Jones, R. 1977. The Tasmanian paradox. In R.V.S. Wright (ed.), *Stone Tools as Cultural Markers,* 189–204. New Jersey: Humanities Press.

Keeley, L. H. 1993. The utilization of lithic artefacts. In R. Singer, B.G. Gladfelter & J. J. Wymer (eds) *The Palaeolithic Site at Hoxne, England,* 129–49. Chicago: University of Chicago Press.

Lacaille, A. D. 1954. A handaxe from Penylan, Cardiff. *Antiquaries Journal* 34, 64–67.

McBurney, C.B.M. 1965. The Old Stone Age in Wales. In I. Ll. Foster & G. E. Daniel, (eds) *Prehistoric and Early Wales,* 17–34. London: Routledge and Kegan Paul.

Maddy, D., Keen, D. H., Bridgland, D. R. & Green, C. P. 1991. A revised model for the Pleistocene development of the River Avon, Warwickshire. *Journal of the Geological Society* 148, 473–84.

MacRae, R. J. & Moloney, N. (eds) 1988. *Non-Flint Stone Tools and the Palaeolithic Occupation of Britain.* Oxford: British Archaeological Reports British Series, 189.

Malaurie, J. 1976. *Les Derniers Rois de Thulé.* Paris: Plon.

Mellars, P.A. 1986. A new chronology for the French Mousterian period. *Nature* 322, 410–11.

Mellars, P. 1996. *The Neanderthal Legacy.* Princeton: University Press.

Mussi, M. 1990. Continuity and Change in Italy at the Last Glacial Maximum. In O. Soffer & C. Gamble (eds), *The World at 18 000 BP. Volume One. High Latitudes,* 126–47. London: Unwin Hyman.

Newell, R. R. & Constandse-Werstermann, T. S. 1996. The use of ethnographic analyses for researching Late Palaeolithic settlement systems, settlement patterns and land use in the Northwest European Plain. *World Archaeology* 27, 372–88.

Otte, M. & Straus, L. G. 1995. *Le Trou Magrite: Fouilles 1991–1992. Résurrection d'un Site Classique en Wallonie.* (ERAUL 69). Liège: Université de Liège.

Roe, D. A. 1981. *The Lower and Middle Palaeolithic Periods in Britain.* London: Routledge and Kegan Paul.

Schwarcz, H. P. 1984. Uranium-series dating and stable isotope analyses of calcite deposits. In H. S. Green, 1984 *Pontnewydd Cave: a Lower Palaeolithic Hominid Site in Wales.* 88–97. Cardiff: National Museum of Wales.

Scott, K. 1986. Man in Britain in the Late Devensian: evidence from Ossom's Cave. In D. A. Roe (ed.), *Studies in the Upper Palaeolithic of Britain and Northwest Europe,* 63–87. Oxford: British Archaeological Reports International Series, 296.

Stiner, M. C. 1994. *Honor Among Thieves: a Zooarchaeological Study of Neanderthal Ecology.* Princeton: University Press.

Straus, L. & Otte, M. 1995. Stone Age Wallonia. *Currrent Anthropology* 36, 851–54.

Swainston, S. 1997. Palaeolithic typology and Paviland Cave. *Lithics* 17/18, 82–83.

Tattersall, I. 1995. *The Last Neanderthal.* New York: Macmillan.

Ward, R. & Stringer, C. 1997. A molecular handle on the Neanderthals. *Nature* 388, 225–26.

Wymer, J. J. 1996. *The Welsh Lower Palaeolithic Survey. A Supplement to the English Rivers Palaeolithic Survey.* Salisbury: Wessex Archaeology.

Zubrow, E. 1989. The demographic modelling of Neanderthal extinction. In P. A. Mellars and C. B. Stringer (eds) *The Human Revolution,* 212–31. Edinburgh: Edinburgh University Press.

20. Pushing Out the Boat for an Irish Palaeolithic

Peter C. Woodman

ABSTRACT

The history of the search for Palaeolithic deposits and artefacts in Ireland is reviewed; the likely nature of any evidence for a human presence in Ireland and the locations where it might survive are discussed, first for the Lower Palaeolithic, then for the Middle and Upper Palaeolithic. The chronology and extent of human occupation of adjacent parts of west Britain and the restricted survival of deposits in which corresponding evidence might be preserved in Ireland together suggest that such evidence could exist in so far under-researched areas and formations. In the Middle and Upper Palaeolithic the successful colonisation of Ireland by mammals makes human colonisation all the more likely. Steps towards finding the evidence for it are outlined.

INTRODUCTION

The history of the search for an Irish Palaeolithic shows that attitudes have swung from a determination to find evidence for a Palaeolithic, and not surprisingly finding indications of its presence, to, at the other extreme, a series of attitudes which underpin an assumption that Ireland was pre-ordained never to have a Palaeolithic settlement. Unfortunately, as will be shown below, uncritical and often hopelessly optimistic reliance on certain sites or the discovery of certain objects which were claimed to be of Palaeolithic age helped reinforce the more commonly held prejudice that Ireland did not have a Palaeolithic occupation and that the matter was beyond discussion.

There is, as yet, no unequivocal evidence for a Palaeolithic but there is always the possibility that Irish archaeology has either overlooked evidence for its presence or else has not looked in the right places. However, this is not simply a question of success if a Palaeolithic can be found and failure if evidence continues to be absent. One of the most important questions which should be asked is 'Why is there no evidence for any human presence in Ireland before the Holocene?' In examining this question from that particular perspective, not only must the potential of Ireland be considered, as well as the nature of the division of Ireland from Britain, but certain aspects of the British Palaeolithic may need to be looked at in a different light. It should of course be remembered that Ireland is virtually unique in being a large island which is adjacent to an area occupied during the Palaeolithic and which had the potential for a Palaeolithic settlement although none has been found. At one extreme there are offshore islands of the same size, such as Japan or Tasmania, where at any of the glacial maxima, but in particular the last, the sea level was sufficiently low that it was possible to walk to these areas. Therefore it is not surprising that they show traces of pre-Holocene settlement. Perhaps other parallels are the Mediterranean islands which, in the case of Cyprus or Sardinia, *appear* to lack settlement before the beginning of the Holocene but where suggestions that earlier settlement took place are now being considered.

'The Palaeolithic' is of course a long and very complex period and only those in countries with no or virtually no Palaeolithic settlement would ever consider it an entity. In fact, even in Britain no-one would consider themselves comfortable researching all aspects of the Palaeolithic, therefore it is proposed that this paper look only at the earlier parts of the Palaeolithic period from an Irish perspective.

This paper will look at the problems associated with the period before the last glacial maximum, a period of time which would usually be presumed to be much too early to have any reasonable chance that human settlement took place in Ireland. However, in spite of the lack of evidence, the possibility that human communities may have reached Ireland should not be totally dismissed. Even within the period pre-dating the Late Glacial Maximum there are two very different types of problems:

1. those associated with attempts to find an Irish Lower Palaeolithic;
2. those associated with attempts to find an Irish Middle or Early Upper Palaeolithic.

As was noted by Woodman *et al.* (1997), questions associated with the fauna of the Late Glacial period in Ireland could to some extent be seen as an extension to the problems associated with the Holocene colonisation of Ireland. In the same manner the question of the Late Glacial human occupation of Ireland can be seen as an investigation of whether the known Early Holocene human occupation of Ireland could be stretched back into the Late Glacial or seen as a series of intermittent attempts to colonise Ireland leading to a successful colonisation in the early Holocene. This is of course a very small window of 2.5ka whereas the period before the Last Glacial Maximum (18–20kya) presents an entirely different set of problems based on a period of up to 500kya in which length of time and opportunity for human settlement are to be balanced against the chances of survival of evidence.

AN IRISH LOWER PALAEOLITHIC

To some extent time should be on the side of a Lower Palaeolithic occupation of Ireland. However, as will be discussed below, deposits which pre-date the last glacial maximum are comparatively rare in Ireland. On the optimistic side there is the fact that Britain has evidence of numerous phases of human occupation some of which, such as Boxgrove (Roberts *et al.* 1994), could date back to over 500kya, i.e. there is evidence of human occupation during OIS 7, 9, 11 and 13 – if not earlier. Therefore on a number of occasions an area close to Ireland was occupied, and this included on at least one occasion an area within sight of Ireland, i.e. North Wales.

It cannot be emphasised too strongly that there is a qualitative difference between the Irish situation and the absence of Palaeolithic artefacts in certain deposits like the Cromerian Forest beds where, as Roebroeks (1996) noted, J. Reid Moir 'assembled an impressive negative data set that is still extremely relevant for correct scientific research'. In this case, or in the search of European deposits such as the Teglen clay pits in the Netherlands,

the issue was whether even earlier evidence of human settlement could be found in northwest Europe, while in Ireland the issue is whether a known Lower Palaeolithic settlement could be extended westwards to Ireland.

Claims for a Lower Palaeolithic in Ireland

The numerous false dawns in the search for an Irish Palaeolithic have tended to dampen any enthusiasm for a fresh search – particularly for a Lower Palaeolithic. At the beginning of the twentieth century William Knowles was still arguing for an exceptional antiquity for his 'older series of flint implements' found in what had become accepted as Holocene deposits (Knowles 1914). Knowles had earlier even argued that some tools were so crude that they must be older than anything else found in Europe (Knowles 1883) and he maintained on typological grounds that it was possible to argue for an Irish Palaeolithic when all other Quaternary evidence pointed to his artefacts being later (see Woodman 1978). Similarly there were the handaxe-like picks which we now know are Holocene Later Mesolithic artefacts (Woodman 1978) (Fig. 20.1:3, 4). This was a common error which was made by a number of nineteenth-century collectors.

Ireland fortunately has never suffered from the problems of regions such as Limburg in the Netherlands where early stage roughouts of Neolithic polished flint axes were mistakenly identified as Lower Palaeolithic handaxes (Stappert 1981). Again in Denmark, Johansen and Stappert (1996) have concluded that with one exception all the putative Lower and Middle Palaeolithic handaxes are in fact much later in age.

In the 1920s the Reid Moir/Warren debate on human antiquity in East Anglia flowed over into Ireland. Burchell claimed to have identified numerous crude tools in glacial deposits in Co. Antrim (Burchell 1931) and also brought to the attention of the world the so-called Irish Mousterian of Rosses Point (Woodman forthcoming). In this case a series of simple limestone flakes were recovered from below a scree of limestone slabs at the edge of the intertidal beach at Rosses Point, Co. Sligo. Burchell and Reid Moir claimed that certain pieces were either side scrapers or handaxes (they are in fact natural). In order for this material to survive the last glacial period the authors claimed that it had been protected in a cave during the last glacial and that the cave then collapsed. In reality many of the surviving pieces, such as Figure 20.2, are struck, but there is nothing about the assemblage to suggest that it is Mousterian. However suggestions by Macalister that the material was entirely natural was an equally extreme reaction to this assemblage and again helped create the perception that the question of an Irish Palaeolithic was not even a serious one.[1]

Genuine handaxes have occasionally been found in Ireland, but there is a reasonable chance that they found their way there in recent centuries. The Dun Aenghusa axe (Murphy 1977) was found in a gryke in the flat limestone

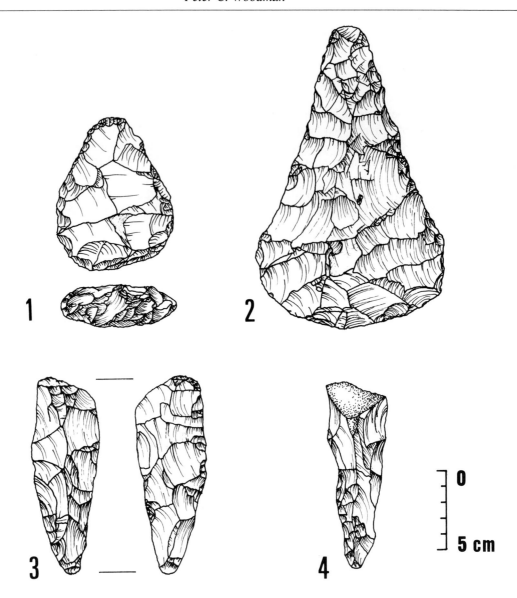

Figure 20.1. 1 handaxe from Dun Aenghus, Co. Clare (after Murphy 1977). 2 handaxe from Coolalisheen townland, Araglin valley, Co. Cork (after Woodman & Griffiths 1988). 3 trihedral pick from Coleraine, Co. Derry (after Woodman 1978). 4 trihedral pick from the river Bann, Cos Antrim and Derry (after Woodman 1978).

plateau at Dun Aenghusa fort on the Aran Islands (Fig. 20.1:1). It is a genuine handaxe but it is difficult to see how a heavily water-rolled specimen typical of so many from the southern English river valleys, such as the Thames, could at some point during the Pleistocene come to be deposited on top of this limestone plateau. The other axe from County Cork was found 60cm down in a garden (never a good indication of a genuine location for an antiquity) overlooking the Araglin river (Fig. 20.1:2; Woodman & Griffiths 1988). This particularly fine specimen is made from a type of flint which resembles that used to make handaxes which can be found in Hampshire (A. ApSimon & D.R. Roe, pers. comm.), and given the circumstances of its discovery it is unlikely that the Araglin

handaxe is an indication of an Irish Lower Palaeolithic.

The one object which could be regarded as somewhat more genuine is the flake from Mell, Co. Louth (Mitchell & Sieveking 1972). Mitchell felt that this large flake could be Clactonian. McCabe (1987) and others have argued that the deposits in this area are mostly glacio-marine and date to the Last Glacial Maximum in OIS 3. Most authors would suggest that the Clactonian cannot be found in deposits which post-date OIS 9 (Bridgland 1994), i.e. 300ky earlier than the Mell deposits. Therefore it is impossible to judge whether or not the Mell flake is a product of activity in Ireland or a chance inclusion in deposits which eventually ended up in Ireland at a very much later date.

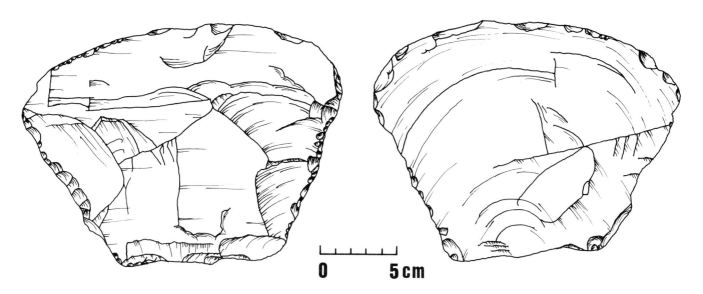

Figure 20.2. Limestone flake from Rosses Point, Co. Sligo.

The Potential for an Irish Lower Palaeolithic

The absence of any consensus on the relative or absolute age of a series of interglacial deposits and Pleistocene wave-cut platforms complicated any search for an Irish Palaeolithic. Even before the adoption of the isotope chronology there was a growing lack of confidence in the Mitchell *et al.* (1973) sequence of Quaternary deposits for Ireland, and in particular the correlation of the British and Irish sequences (Table 20.1). As there was no firm stratigraphic sequence at Gort, Warren (1985) in particular had expressed reservations about the Gortian/Hoxnian correlation and suggested that the Gortian deposits could equally be attributed to an Irish equivalent of the Ipswichian, i.e. last interglacial. McCabe (1987) has gone even further and suggested that the glacio-marine Ballycroneen till found on the south coast of Ireland, which had been associated with the Munsterian, was in fact a product of an extension of the Midlandian ice sheets at the last glacial maximum (Coxon & Waldren 1995; Woodman *et al.* 1997). While there is no consensus as to the precise age of many Quaternary deposits, there is some agreement that many of the Irish Pleistocene deposits are much younger than had been presumed. A possible chronological sequence based on Coxon & Waldren (1995) is provided in Table 20.2.

As Ireland has been totally glaciated quite late in the Middle Pleistocene and extensively glaciated during the Upper Pleistocene, there are not convenient river terraces, as in the case of the Thames Valley, or equivalent sequences, as in East Anglia, which provide a chronological framework or convenient deposits which would contain objects. Some of the deposits which have survived and are accessible on the south coast are glacio-marine in origin, e.g. the Ballycroneen till. These are less likely to produce evidence of human settlement.

Britain		Ireland
Devensian	Glacial	Midlandian
Ipswichian	Interglacial	?
Wolstonian	Glacial	Munsterian
Hoxnian	Interglacial	Gortian
Anglian	Glacial	?

Table 20.1. Pleistocene correlation between Britain and Ireland (Mitchell et al. *1973).*

Britain		Ireland
Devensian Cold Stage	5d–2 122–10,000 (Glacial)	Midlandian
Ipswichian Interglacial	5e 128–122,000 *Interglacial*	Screen Hills Interglacial
Cold Stage	6 186–128,000 Glacial	Munsterian ? (Glacial)
Minchin Hole	7 245–186,000 *Interglacial*	?
Cold Stage	8 303–245,000 Glacial	?
Hoxnian	9 339–303,000 *Interglacial*	Gortian Interglacial?

Table 20.2. Pleistocene correlation between Britain and Ireland (based on OIS, after Coxon & Waldren 1995).

So far the discussion may appear particularly negative, and it is important to retain a healthy scepticism of any finds which appear to indicate occupation which is thought to be earlier than is usually accepted. However, there is a potential optimistic side to the discussion. As already noted, Britain was occupied during at least four interglacials during the Middle Pleistocene, therefore from an Irish perspective the extent of each of these phases of occupation and the capacity of these communities to spread to western Britain are of crucial importance.

Of course, while these occupations took place throughout a period of 500ky, the actual time periods in which there was a human presence in Britain is quite limited. Even if some caution is being expressed as to the concept proposed by Gamble that human settlement only took place in the transitional phases between full glacial and interglacial (Gamble 1986; Roebroeks *et al.* 1993) there is no doubt that occupation took place during limited periods of time.

While Gamble (1986) had also proposed a model which suggested that Lower Palaeolithic communities relied extensively on scavenging, the evidence of the punch mark suggesting the spearing of horse as well as the butchering of rhino at Boxgrove (Pitts & Roberts 1997) and the spears from Schöningen suggest a more active approach to hunting (Thieme 1997). Again the proposition that the *Homo heidelbergensis* from Boxgrove was a powerful, robust individual suggests that these peoples would have been capable of exploring much of Britain and perhaps attempt more difficult barriers such as the Irish Sea. Gamble (1996) has recently provided an eloquent argument that the level of debate and the types of question considered in the English Lower Palaeolithic have been constrained by an unwarranted minimalist expectation for the available data. He has suggested that a series of behavioural questions need to be asked.

'The behavioural questions which need answering in the period between 130kya and one million years ago are simple. What exactly could these hominids do? How varied were their solutions to the many different types of ecological settings that they inhabited ... Were they hard wired for survival or did they adapt through the interface of culture.'

The potential for a Middle Pleistocene/Lower Palaeolithic occupation of Ireland surely must be one of those questions.

Obviously it is impossible to speculate on who could cross the Irish Sea basin, which would have existed as a stretch of open water of varying width, but it is interesting that caves in Wales and others in south-west England have produced handaxes in areas where less extensive mid-Pleistocene river valley gravels would not act as traps for artefacts (Wymer 1996). In fact the handaxes from caves probably provide an indication of a much more extensive Lower Palaeolithic presence in western regions than is usually presumed. In addition, while the axes from Kent's

Cavern could date to OIS 11 or 13, it would appear that handaxes from Three Holes Cave in the Torbryan Valley in Devon (Roberts 1996), and Pontnewydd in Clwyd, Wales (Green 1984), both date to OIS 7 (Fig. 20.3). Green and Walker (1991) have noted that several stray handaxes can be identified from beyond the ice limits on the south coast of Wales. These again may date to OIS 7 (see also Aldhouse-Green, this volume).

As it is highly probable that numerous reglaciations of Ireland have removed any traces of early interglacials, then it is more than likely that the only hope for survival of deposits and traces of human settlement would be OIS 5 and 7. Although Coxon and Waldren (1995) have

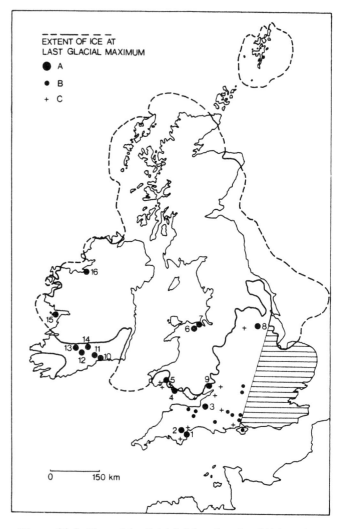

Figure 20.3. Map of the British Isles showing (A) location of key sites referred to in the text, (B) bout coupé handaxes, and (C) location of earlier Upper Palaeolithic findspots. Shaded area denotes region of more extensive occurrence of handaxes.

1 Kent's Cavern, 2 Torbryan valley caves, 3 Hyaena Den, 4 Paviland Cave, 5 Coygan Cave, 6 Pontnewydd Cave, 7 Cae Gwynn and Ffynnon Beuno caves, 8 Creswell Crags, 9 King Arthur's Cave, 10 Shandon Cave, 11 Ballynamintra Cave, 12 Foley Cave, 13 Castlepook Cave, 14 Coolalisheen, 15 Dun Aenghus, 16 Rosses Point.

suggested that the Gortian deposits in general should be associated with OIS 9 or 11 and, as noted earlier, some OIS 5 (Ipswichian) deposits are beginning to be identified, e.g. Screen Hills moraine (McCabe & Coxon 1993), there are in Ireland so far no convincing traces of OIS 7 deposits. There is a certain irony that, while the OIS 5e deposits (an 'Irish Ipswichian') are for the first time now beginning to be identified, there is a growing realisation that during OIS 5e Britain may have been an island which lacked a significant Palaeolithic presence. In fact, as is becoming apparent in the search for human settlement elsewhere in Europe, during OIS 5e the absence of certain types of deposits or the existence of phases of erosion will reduce the chances of survival of traces of human activity (Pettitt, pers. comm).

In contrast OIS 7 should have some potential. At the moment, as noted by Coxon and Waldren (1995), there is no clear idea as to which deposits in Ireland would belong to OIS 7. This is further complicated by the fact that there are no known Irish faunal assemblages from either OIS 5 or 7. In fact, as will be discussed in more detail below, only one of the samples of bone from the Quaternary Fauna Project produced a date beyond the limit of ^{14}C dating, i.e. older than 45kya. The Aghnadarragh fauna of mammoth and musk ox (McCabe *et al.* 1987), which is associated with deposits which have been radiocarbon dated to 48kya or earlier in age, could be earlier than the indications of the ^{14}C dates. Sutcliffe (1995) has noted that the musk ox occurs only in OIS 6 in Britain, therefore the Aghnadarragh fauna could contain a residue which pre-dates the Upper Pleistocene. The only occurrence of straight-tusked elephant in Ireland comes from a river behind the house of one of Ireland's leading natural historians who lived in Holywood, Co. Down, at the turn of the century (Doughty, pers. comm.)! Other occasional finds, such as the mammoth from Belturbet, Co. Cavan (Woodman *et al.* 1997), could be residual elements of a much older fauna, but it is striking that there is nothing known from the Irish caves which could date to earlier than OIS 3. This absence of convenient traps for artefacts, i.e. caves, which existed prior to OIS 3 and of early river terraces like those of southeastern England reduces the chances of finding any Lower Palaeolithic in Ireland. As noted earlier, much of the Welsh material comes from an area beyond the ice limits and has therefore survived total obliteration.

In spite of these problems it is possible that if, in OIS 7, hominids populated the west of England and Wales then they could have crossed over to Ireland. The tendency in Ireland to look for flint artefacts could have created a perceptual barrier to its discovery. If, by a date early in the Middle Pleistocene, the various glaciations had eroded away the Cretaceous Chalk with flint from much of the southern part of Ireland then, aside from some coastal beach flint which might have been present along the east and part of the south coast, flint would not have been easily available for artefact manufacture. Of course, as has been shown from Ferriter's Cove, a range of other material could have been used, in fact chipped Mesolithic core tools were made at that site from rhyolite and volcanic tuff (Woodman & O'Brien 1993). In certain regions of Britain alternative sources were used; the Derbyshire handaxes made from quartzite (Roe 1981), the handaxes from Coygan cave in South Wales made from rhyolite (Aldhouse-Green *et al.* 1995), and the Pontnewydd handaxes made from a range of igneous rocks illustrate this possibility (Green 1984).

The discovery of Lower Palaeolithic artefacts at Saint Colomban in the Carnac area of Brittany shows that Palaeolithic material can be found in regions where it had hitherto been undetected. This material supplements the occasional handaxe found in Brittany but consists of a series of small quartz and flint flakes which, without a context, would be unrecognisable as being of Lower Palaeolithic age (Tuffreau & Antoine 1995).

On the basis of evidence from later periods it would be more reasonable to presume that as a flora managed to establish itself in Ireland at various points throughout the Middle Pleistocene (Coxon & Waldren 1995) and, as will be discussed below, a significant mammalian fauna can be shown to have successfully colonised Ireland during the Upper Pleistocene, there is a slight but very real possibility that an Irish extension to the Lower Palaeolithic of Western Europe could be absent due to destruction of evidence rather than a simple case of absence. If, as suggested by Keen (1995), the Dover straits were breached in the Middle Pleistocene and Britain was totally isolated in both OIS 5 and 7 as well as possibly 9, then during OIS 7 either a movement of humans, dryshod, into Britain took place during a very narrow window of time when the climate had improved but the sea level had not risen, or else a boat or raft journey was required. Would it not be reasonable to assume that there is a chance that during one of the two very significant temperate phases in OIS 7, i.e. 7a and 7c, these peoples could also have crossed the Irish Sea basin? There is a potential contradiction in that it would seem to be acceptable that animals such as red deer would have been able to swim to islands such as Jersey during the interglacials (Lister 1995) while at the same time it was assumed that the human settlement of Jersey would only take place during OIS 7 at a point in time when there would have been a land connection to the island (Callow & Cornford 1986).

In summary, as Gamble (1996) has noted, an early hominid presence in Ireland is the type of issue which allows a debate on the potential of early/archaic forms of *Homo sapiens*!

AN UPPER PLEISTOCENE HUMAN OCCUPATION OF IRELAND

While the suggestion that Ireland could have been occupied during OIS 7 may be regarded as a flight of fancy for which there is little supporting evidence, the possibility that Ireland might be occupied during the Upper Pleistocene and in particular during OIS 3 is of a different order of magnitude. At the moment, Ireland must be considered to be anomalous without any known human occupation between 65 and 20kya.

There is a small but significant Mousterian presence in the West of Britain, i.e. Kent's Cavern, Wookey Hole, Coygan Cave and King Arthur's Cave, and numerous Earlier Upper Palaeolithic sites are known from the Mendips, South Wales and the Severn Valley as well as the two sites of Cae Gwyn and Fynnon Beunno in the Clwyd Valley in North Wales (Fig. 20.3). In the case of the Mousterian assemblages Coulson was inclined to consider them as Ipswichian or Early Devensian in date (Coulson 1990). Currant and Jacobi (1997) suggest that they may be somewhat later in date, after the commencement of OIS 3, i.e. after 65kya. On the basis of dates quoted by Currant and Jacobi for their Coygan phase there may be very little if any chronological gap between the Mousterian and the Earlier Upper Palaeolithic assemblages in these regions and elsewhere in Britain. Therefore there may have been a consistent though not necessarily continuous occupation of western Britain throughout a large portion of OIS 3, i.e. 65–25kya.

In 1986 Woodman noted that, associated with Castlepook Cave in particular, there appeared to be a rich Mid-Midlandian fauna in Ireland and that the question as to whether humans also reached the island of Ireland should be considered. There was therefore a chance that some pre-Last Glacial Maximum traces of settlement might be found, in that a small portion of the south of Ireland had remained unglaciated throughout the Midlandian (Fig. 20.3). The absence of any known Middle or Early Upper Palaeolithic material could be explained by:

1. the fact that most Irish caves were low-lying fissures which were unsuitable for human settlement;
2. the virtual lack of research on Stone Age archaeology in many parts of this region, e.g. the Mesolithic in Munster has only been identified just over 10 years ago;
3. the expectation that traces of Palaeolithic settlement would be much more difficult to find and therefore there was little point in looking for it.

Recent research on both sides of the Irish Sea, facilitated by the availability of the Oxford University Radiocarbon Accelerator Unit, has tended to reinforce the proposition that Ireland could have been occupied during the period immediately prior to the Last Glacial Maximum. In both cases OIS 3 is characterised by a comparatively rich and diverse mammalian fauna (Table 20.3).

It is interesting to note Currant and Jacobi's (1997) interpretation of their Coygan type faunal assemblage.

'Human populations appear to return to Britain in association with a vertebrate fauna including *Mammuthus primigenius*, *Coelodonta antiquitatis*, *Equus ferus* and *Crocuta crocuta*. Coygan Cave, Laugh-

arne, Dyfed is chosen here as the defining locality for this assemblage . . . Although this is the classic cold-stage fauna of older literature, this assemblage is actually quite difficult to interpret in terms of its environmental signal. It has a much higher species diversity than the Banwell-type fauna and is particularly rich in large mammalian herbivores. This is suggestive of a very productive environment, in many ways more akin to interglacial conditions. It seems to us highly unlikely that this fauna can be indicative of anything other than OIS 3 and we have found nothing to contradict this interpretation. It has often been noticed that OIS 3 is something of an anomaly in the context of the longer Quaternary sequence and has many of the characteristics of a series of rapidly superimposed interstadials (e.g. Woillard & Mook, 1982).'

As was noted in Woodman *et al.* (1997) some of the differences between contemporaneous faunal lists from Britain and Ireland can be explained by different research priorities. Thus the absence of hare and the two species of lemming from Britain is due to the Irish project's desire to date a range of faunal remains rather than human activity. It is also important to remember that the human presence in Britain is rarely indicated through the occurrence of skeletal remains. In fact the two earliest ^{14}C-dated human presences referred to by Currant and Jacobi (1997) are evidenced by cut-marked animal bones. Currant and Jacobi (1997) envisage this fauna colonising Britain at one time as a group, and by implication have suggested that the human recolonising of Britain took place at the same time.

The Irish fauna would appear to be a substantial subset of the Coygan type fauna. However, the Irish interpretation (Woodman *et al.* 1997) is of a gradual accumulation of species over a period of time, beginning with many of the most cold-adapted species occurring at Castlepook Cave

	Britain	Ireland
Homo sp (human)	P	?
Canis lupus (wolf)	P	P
Vulpes vulpes (red fox)	P	P?
Alopex lagopus (arctic fox)	P	P
Crocuta crocuta (spotted hyena)	P	P
Ursus arctos (brown bear)	P	P
Mammuthus primigenius (woolly mammoth)	P	P
Coelodonta antiquitatis (woolly rhinoceros)	P	A
Equus ferus (wild horse)	P	P
Megaloceros giganteus (giant deer)	P	P
Cervus elaphus (red deer)	P	P
Rangifer tarandus (reindeer)	P	P
Bison priscus (bison)	P	A
Lepus timidus (hare – Irish/Arctic?)	P?	P
Lemmus lemmus (Norwegian lemming)	P?	P
Dicrostonyx torquatus (Arctic lemming)	P?	P

Table 20.3. Faunal List.
P = Present, P? = probably present but not ^{14}C-dated, A = absent, ? = possibly present but no evidence.

between 40 and 30kya and with the addition of what might be regarded as more temperate elements at Shandon and Ballynamintra in the period 30–26kya (Fig. 20.4). Given that Ireland is one island further out than Britain, it is possible that the two models may not be incompatible. However one of the most surprising differences between the two faunal assemblages is that the most adaptable mammal is not present in Ireland, i.e. humans.

Throughout a period of more than 20ky it is probable that there was no continuous human presence in the west of Britain but it is still possible to document numerous episodes in which human groups lived in Wales. It would seem remarkable that, on each occasion, the eastern edge of the Irish Sea basin represented the limit of human settlement. Shackleton (1987) has suggested that the sea level was significantly lower during OIS 3 but it is presumed that in the case of the Irish Sea there was still a significant stretch of water. However, irrespective of its extent, the sea should not have been a barrier in itself. The rich and diverse range of species which managed to reach Ireland during OIS 3 shows that the Irish Sea was not an insurmountable obstacle. In fact, as a result of the Quaternary Faunas Project, it has been suggested that in general too much attention has been paid to how Ireland was colonised by various species, i.e. by landbridge or by other means, yet the nature of the environment in Ireland at any time, i.e. its suitability for the survival of the species, might be of greater importance. In this case there is a general recognition that much of OIS 3 is made up of short-lived phases of cool and cold climate, some of which, such as the Hollymount stage in Ireland, would have been comparatively temperate and that some sparse tree cover would have developed (Coxon 1993). Throughout this stage, however, the climate would never have been categorised as glacial, and this again is reflected in the range of species which were able to survive in Britain and Ireland.

Obviously the ultimate counter-argument to a human presence in Ireland in OIS 3 is the simple fact that nothing has been found. However, as noted earlier, the fact that the discovery of a Mesolithic in the southern third of Ireland took place only just over a decade ago illustrates the lack of research on this part of the Stone Age in the one area where traces of a Palaeolithic might survive. This has been shown from the location of the southern Irish end moraine, and the fact that the four cave faunas which date to OIS 3 come from south of the moraine shows that the greatest chance of discovering OIS 3 traces of human settlement comes from a region where there is little tradition of research. The fact that less than 30 stray finds of stone arrowheads from the Neolithic and Bronze Age are known from the three south-western counties (Woodman & Scannell 1993) illustrates the impoverished nature of the database (there are more arrowheads from the Lough Gur excavations of S.P. Ó Ríordáin than are stray/chance finds from this region!).

In that context, there are probably only three distinctive artefact types which, if found by themselves, might be

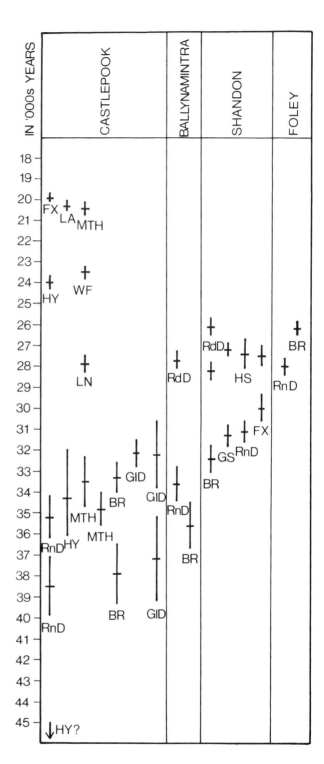

Figure 20.4. Chronological chart of ^{14}C-dated faunal remains from before the Last Glacial Maximum.
BR brown bear, FX Arctic fox, GID giant deer, GS goose, HR hare, HY hyaena, LA Arctic lemming, LN Norwegian lemming, MTH mammoth, RdD red deer, RnD reindeer.

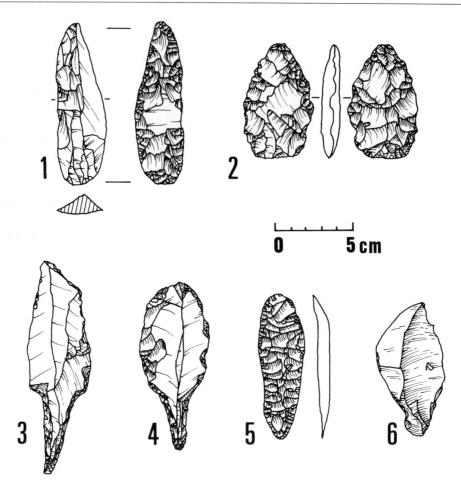

Figure 20.5. 1–2 leaf points from Kent's Cavern (after Campbell 1977), 3 tanged point from Pinhole Cave (after Campbell 1977), 4 tanged point from Ipswich (after Campbell 1977), 5 Irish Neolithic elongated plano-convex knife, 6 later Mesolithic tanged point, from Newferry, Co. Antrim (after Woodman 1977).

recognisable as belonging to either a Middle Palaeolithic or an earlier Upper Palaeolithic. These are the *bout coupé* handaxes of the Mousterian, e.g. from Coygan Cave, many of the early leaf points, e.g. from Kent's Cavern (Fig. 20.5:1), and possibly the tanged points, also present at Kent's Cavern (Fig. 20.5:3), which would be different from Irish Later Mesolithic forms. However, as noted by Woodman (1993) in the Komsa culture of Finnmark, there can be a tendency to take particularly distinctive examples of an artefact type and present them as typical or normal, while many assemblages actually lack these extreme forms of 'type fossils'. Some of the Irish Later Mesolithic tanged points and those of the Earlier Upper Palaeolithic are not dissimilar (note Fig. 20.5:6 from Zone 6 at Newferry and the Ipswich example Fig. 20.5:4). Again there are many examples of leaf points, such as Fig. 20.5:2, which out of context would not immediately be recognised as being of Earlier Upper Palaeolithic date and could be mistaken for Irish Neolithic elongated plano-convex forms (Fig. 20.5:5) or laurel leaf forms. Similarly some of the small *bout coupé* handaxes would, out of context in an area such as Ireland, be presumed to be something else. Much of the rest of the retouched tools could easily, if found as

individual items, be assumed to belong to either the Irish Later Mesolithic or more likely the Neolithic period; forms such as side scrapers have, for example, been found in Irish Neolithic assemblages. Again many of the artefacts in MTA assemblages could exist in other much later technologies. Stappert (1982) has described a Middle Palaeolithic assemblage from the eastern part of the Netherlands at Mander. Here, because of the discovery of a handaxe, a careful field survey eventually produced 24 other finds which might be assigned to the Middle Palaeolithic, but this was in addition to several hundred pieces of presumably Neolithic age. Without the handaxe this small Middle Palaeolithic component would not have been recognised. In Ireland, with the use of a pseudo-Levallois technology and the use of faceted platforms in the Neolithic, it is possible that small assemblages of Middle Palaeolithic age could be masked by later material.

Obviously the danger is in a return to the identification of a Palaeolithic through the use of individual artefacts which might be of a Palaeolithic type. It is too easy to allow subjective pressures to sway judgements as to the age of individual artefacts or in some cases assemblages. In Ireland a classic example was the desire of Burchell and Reid Moir to ascribe an assemblage at Rosses Point in Co. Sligo to the Mousterian. As noted above, in this instance perfectly good flakes were given lesser significance than natural pieces of stone which were thought to be Mousterian side scrapers or handaxes (Woodman forthcoming).

Not surprisingly no surface assemblages of the relevant age have been found in Ireland and it is of interest that a similar situation exists in Wales where virtually all OIS 3 Palaeolithic finds have come from caves. As noted earlier, only four cave faunal assemblages of this period have been found (Woodman *et al.* 1997). Castlepook is a fissure system, whose entrance, where settlement may have taken place, has never been found. Foley Cave, on the side of a gorge on the Awbeg river, contained deposits washed in at the time of the Last Glacial Maximum. Meltwater from the Midlandian ice sheets, which lay further north, would have washed material into the cave. Ballynamintra Cave contained very little pre-Late Glacial Maximum fauna, and that was in a derived context in shattered blocks of stalagmite (layer 4). The most interesting example is the large cave at Shandon where it is possible that complete or articulated portions of animals were uncovered below the collapsed roof of a large cavern. Unfortunately this was the first of the modern cave excavations, i.e. in the 1850s, and as the entrance area was exposed during quarrying for a road, it is uncertain if any traces of human settlement had been present. M. McCarthy (pers. comm.) has examined a selection of bones from Castlepook and Shandon in the hope of identifying human cut-marks but so far only traces of animal gnawing have been found.

While animals may have found an opportunity to migrate to Ireland during OIS 3, human settlement might have required more conscious decisions. Traditionally Britain is seen as an area of marginal settlement during the Palaeolithic and therefore regions such as Wales are presumed to be extremely marginal. If this is an accurate reflection of OIS 3 settlement in Britain then Ireland was simply an island too far. However if the few cave finds in Wales and southwest England are an indication of more extensive settlement of the region during OIS 3, then a possible, if limited, extension of settlement to Ireland should be considered.

The extensive OIS 3 mammalian fauna in Ireland shows that the Irish Sea, presumably reduced in width, was not an insurmountable barrier. Human communities would, of course, have made more choices and perhaps the greatest imponderable is whether there was a marine component within Upper Palaeolithic economies. Obviously the fact that worldwide sea levels were significantly lower during OIS 3 has created a situation where many of the coastal Welsh cave sites, such as Paviland, would have overlooked what was almost an extension to the Severn Valley rather than the Bristol Channel, and therefore the absence of a marine component in the economy is not surprising. However, in northern Spain at La Riera (Strauss & Clark 1986) in the period prior to the Late Glacial Maximum marine resources occurred on site. At that time period the lowering of the sea level had not caused the coastline to move significantly away from its present location. In general around Britain and Ireland, due to radical changes to the shape of the coastline it would not be possible to observe whether there was a marine component in the diet and any coastal settlement would be buried below sea level.

At a later date the Early Holocene colonisation of Norway and adjacent parts of Sweden prior to 9kya must have required a movement across an open water channel where middle Sweden now exists, and the sea would have been the vector to extend settlement up to and across the Norwegian Arctic. In contrast, the movement into the high Arctic islands of Baffin Island and on to Greenland only took place after 5kya when a highly specialised technology suitable for that region had been developed. It is unlikely that the colonisation of Ireland at this date would have required such a highly specialised marine-based economy as exists in the Canadian Arctic. Instead some knowledge of the sea and its resources would have been sufficient. In this case, if equipment used primarily on the coast was curated and cached, we would not be very aware of its existence. However a OIS 3 human presence in Ireland could be used to infer that at this period there were groups of people who made some if not a significant use of marine resources.

CONCLUSION

The search for a Palaeolithic in Ireland has been hindered by some uncritical attempts to claim its discovery. These attempts were particularly common in the earlier part of the twentieth century. However, it should be remembered that 'The absence of evidence is not evidence of absence'! While it is extremely unlikely that any traces of a Lower Palaeolithic will ever be discovered in Ireland it is just possible that the reasons for this lack of discovery are the destructive power of several ice sheets rather than a genuine absence of a human presence.

In contrast the apparent absence of either a Middle or Earlier Upper Palaeolithic presence is much more anomalous. Given the combination of a clear human presence on numerous occasions in OIS 3 in parts of Western Britain and the extensive mammalian fauna which found its way to Ireland at the same date, then a OIS 3 human presence should be expected in Ireland. While a chance find might firm up this possible presence, it is probable, as with research on the Mesolithic of the province of Munster, that a more pro-active approach will be required. Only an assemblage, preferably in a sealed context, will provide an adequate indication of pre-Holocene settlement in Ireland.

SUMMARY

In 1984, at the end of the Post Glacial Colonisation conference in Cork (Sleeman *et al.* 1984), a series of research priorities was suggested, some of which have been addressed. In the case of a search for a Palaeolithic presence in Ireland there is a need for a carefully constructed research strategy which would need to be sufficiently pro-active so as to encourage a rigorous examination of the topic without creating an uncritical rush to accept any indications of a Palaeolithic.

A new research initiative will include the first priority laid down at the 1984 Cork conference.

1. 'High priority should be given to an organised and inter-disciplinary search for suitable repositories of faunal and floral information of Late Midlandian and postglacial age; such as caves, lake basins, inter-drumlin areas, turloughs and swallow holes. Particular reference should be given to southern areas which may have remained unglaciated during the last cold stage.' This priority could be simply extended back in time to cover the whole of the Upper Pleistocene.

2. A search for caves and/or rockshelters in locations where human occupation would seem probable and where entrance areas have survived reasonably intact.

3. Based on research in others parts of Europe, some consideration should be given to the type of landscapes which would have attracted a range of fauna in OIS 3 and in the southern areas left unglaciated at the time of the Last Glacial Maximum a search for traces of settlement should begin.

4. Although the relevant material is quite limited the few lithic assemblages from Munster should be scrutinised to see if any residual Palaeolithic material had survived.

ACKNOWLEDGEMENTS

I would like to thank Dr Nyree Finlay for her useful comments on an early draft of this paper and suggestions as to how it could be improved. The final version and opinions are, however, the responsibility of the author. Ms Bríd Kirby produced the drawings.

NOTE

1. There is at the moment an interestingly parallel debate taking place in Finland where the media have highlighted claims that a Palaeolithic assemblage has survived intact in a cave near Karisoki where it is claimed that a coarse stone tool assemblage dates to at least 74kya!

REFERENCES

Aldhouse-Green, S., Scott, K., Schwarz, H., Grun, R., Housley, R., Rae, A., Bevins, R. & Redknap, M. 1995. Coygan Cave, South Wales, a Mousterian site and hyaena den: a report on the University of Cambridge excavations. *Proceedings of the Prehistoric Society* 61, 37–80.

Bridgland, D.R. 1994. Dating of Lower Palaeolithic industries within the framework of the Lower Thames terrace sequence. In N. Ashton & A. David (eds), *Stories in Stone*, 28–40. London: Lithic Studies Society Occasional Paper 4.

Burchell, J.P.T. 1931. Early Neanthropic man and his relation to the Ice Age. *Proceedings of the Prehistoric Society of East Anglia* 6, 253–303.

Callow, P. & Cornford, J.M. 1986. *La Cotte de St Brelade 1961–1978. Excavations by C.B.M. McBurney*. Norwich: Geo Books.

Campbell, J. 1977. *The Upper Palaeolithic of Britain*. Oxford: Clarendon Press.

Coulson, S.D. 1990. *Middle Palaeolithic Industries of Great Britain*. Bonn: Studies in Modern Archaeology 4.

Coxon, P. 1993. Irish Pleistocene biostratigraphy. *Irish Journal of Earth Sciences* 12, 83–105.

Coxon, P., & Waldren, 1995. The floristic record of Ireland's Pleistocene temperate stages. In R.C. Preece (ed.), *Island Britain: a Quaternary Perspective*, 243–68. London: Geological Society Special Publication 96.

Currant, A., & Jacobi, R. 1997. Vertebrate faunas of the British Late Pleistocene. *Quaternary Newsletter* 82, 1–8.

Gamble, C. 1986. *The Palaeolithic Settlement of Europe*. Cambridge: Cambridge University Press.

Gamble, C.S. 1996. Hominid behaviour in the Middle Pleistocene; an English perspective. In C. Gamble & A.J. Lawson (eds), *The English Palaeolithic Reviewed. Papers from a Day Conference Held at the Society of Antiquaries of London 28 October 1994*, 63–72. Salisbury: Wessex Archaeology.

Green, H.S. 1984. *Pontnewydd Cave. A Lower Palaeolithic Hominid Site in Wales*. Cardiff: National Museum of Wales.

Green, H.S. & Walker, E. 1991. *Ice Age Hunters: Neanderthals and Early Modern Hunters in Wales*. Cardiff: National Museum of Wales.

Johansen, L. & Stappert, D. 1996. Handaxes from Denmark. Neanderthal tools or 'vicious flints'?, *Palaeohistoria* 37/38, 1–28.

Keen, D.H. 1995. Raised beaches and sea levels in the English Channel in the Middle and Late Pleistocene: problems of interpretation and implications for the isolation of the British Isles. In R.C. Preece (ed.), *Island Britain: a Quaternary Perspective*, 63–72. London: Geological Society Special Publication 96.

Knowles, W.J. 1883. On the antiquity of man in Ireland. Southport: *Report of the British Association for the Advancement of Science*, 562.

Knowles, W.J. 1914. The antiquity of man in Ireland, being an account of the older series of Irish flint implements. *Journal of the Royal Anthropological Institute* 44, 83–121.

Lister, A., 1995. Sea levels and evolution of island endemics. The dwarf red deer of Jersey. In R.C. Preece (ed.), *Island Britain: a Quaternary Perspective*, 151–72. London: Geological Society Special Publication No. 96.

McCabe, M. 1987. Quaternary deposits and glacial stratigraphy in Ireland. *Quaternary Science Reviews* 6, 259–99.

McCabe, M., Coope, R.J., Gennard, D.E. & Doughty, P. 1987. Freshwater organic deposits and stratified sediments between Early and Late Midlandian (Devensian) till sheets, at Aghnadarragh, Co. Antrim, Northern Ireland. *Journal of Quaternary Science* 2, 11–33.

McCabe, M. & Coxon, P. 1993. A *Carpinus*-dominated interglacial peat fall within glaciomarine delta sediments, Blackwater, Co. Wexford: evidence for part of the last interglacial cycle? *Proceedings of the Geologists' Association* 114, 201–7.

Mitchell, G.F., Penny, L.F., Shotton, F.W. & West, R.G. 1973. *A Correlation of Quaternary Deposits in the British Isles*. London: Geological Society of London Special Report 4.

Mitchell, G.F. & Sieveking, G. de G. 1972. Flint flake, probably of Palaeolithic age from Mell townland, near Drogheda, Co. Louth,

Ireland. *Journal of the Royal Society of Antiquaries of Ireland* 102(2), 174–7.

Murphy, B. 1977. A handaxe from Dun Aenghus, Inishmore, Aran Islands, Co. Galway. *Proceedings of the Royal Irish Academy*, 77, 257–59.

Pitts, M. & Roberts, M. 1997. *Fairweather Eden*. London: Century Books.

Roberts, A. 1996. Evidence for Late Pleistocene and Early Holocene human activity and environmental change from the Torbryan Valley, South Devon. In D.J. Charman, R.M. Newnham & D.G. Groot (eds), *Devon and East Cornwall Field Guide*, 168–224. London: Quaternary Research Association.

Roberts, M.B., Stringer, C.B. & Parfitt, S.A. 1994. A hominid tibia from Middle Pleistocene sediments at Boxgrove, UK. *Nature* 369, 311–13.

Roe, D.A., 1981. *The Lower and Middle Palaeolithic Periods in Britain*. London: Routledge & Keegan Paul.

Roebroeks, W. 1996. The English Palaeolithic record: absence of evidence, evidence of absence and the first occupation of Europe. In C. Gamble & A.J. Lawson (eds), *The English Palaeolithic Reviewed. Papers from a Day Conference Held at the Society of Antiquaries of London 28 October 1994*, 57–63. Salisbury: Wessex Archaeology.

Roebroeks, W., Conard, N.J. & van Kolfschoten, T. 1993. Dense forests, cold steppes and Palaeolithic settlement of Northern Europe. *Current Anthropology* 33, 551–86.

Shackleton, N.J., 1987. Oxygen isotopes, ice volume and sea level. *Quaternary Science Reviews* 6, 183–90.

Sleeman, D.P., Devoy, R.J. & Woodman, P.C., 1984. *Proceedings of the Postglacial Colonisation Conference, University College Cork, 15–16 October 1983*. Dublin: Occasional Publication of the Irish Biogeographical Society 1.

Stappert, D., 1981. Handaxes in Southern Limburg (the Netherlands) – how old? In F.H.G. Engelen (ed.), *Third International Symposium on Flint, Maastricht 1979* (Staringia 6). 107–113. Herleen.

Stappert, D. 1982. A Middle Palaeolithic artifact scatter, and a few younger finds from near Mander N.W. of Ootmarsum. *Palaeohistoria*, 1–34.

Strauss, L.G. & Clark, G.A., 1986. La Riera cave, *Stone Age Hunter Gatherer Adaptions in Northern Spain*. Arizona State University Anthropological Research Papers 36.

Sutcliffe, A.J., 1995. Insularity of the British Isles 250,000–30,000 years ago: the mammalian, including human, evidence. In R.C.

Preece (ed.), *Island Britain: a Quaternary Perspective*, 127–41. London: Geological Society Special Publication 96.

Thieme, H., 1997. Lower Palaeolithic hunting weapons from Schöningen, Germany – the oldest spears in the world. *Past 26*, 7–8.

Tuffreau, A. & Antoine, P. 1995. The earliest occupation of Europe: continental north-western Europe. In W. Roebroeks & T. van Kolfschoten (eds), *The Earliest Occupation of Europe*, 147–64. Leiden: Analecta Praehistorica Leidensia 27.

Warren, W.P. 1985. Stratigraphy. In K.J. Edwards & W.P. Warren (eds), *The Quaternary History of Ireland*, 39–65. London: Academic Press.

Woillard, G.M. & Mook, W., 1982. Carbon 14 dates at Grand Pile: correlation of land and sea chronologies. *Science* 215, 159–61.

Woodman, P.C., 1977. Excavations at Newferry, Co. Antrim. *Proceedings of the Prehistoric Society* 43, 155–200.

Woodman, P.C. 1978. *The Mesolithic in Ireland*. Oxford: British Archaeological Reports, British Series 58.

Woodman, P.C., 1986. Why not an Irish Upper Palaeolithic? In D. Roe (ed.), *Studies in the Upper Palaeolithic of Britain and North-West Europe*, 43–55. Oxford: British Archaeological Reports International Series 296.

Woodman, P.C., 1993. The Komsa culture. *Acta Archaeologica* 63, 57–76.

Woodman, P.C., forthcoming. Rosses Point revisited. *Antiquity* 72 no. 277 pages to follow.

Woodman, P.C., & Griffiths, D.A. 1988. The archaeological importance of flint sources in Munster. *Journal of the Cork Historical and Archaeological Society* 93, 66–72.

Woodman, P.C., McCarthy, M. & Monaghan, N. 1997. The Irish Quaternary Fauna Project. *Quaternary Science Reviews* 16, 129–59.

Woodman, P.C. & O'Brien, M. 1993. Excavations at Ferriter's Cove, Co. Kerry: an interim statement. In E. Shee Twohig & M. Ronayne (eds), *Past Perceptions*, 25–34. Cork: Cork University Press.

Woodman, P.C. & Scannell, M. 1993. A context for the Lough Gur lithics. In E. Shee Twohig & M. Ronayne (eds), *Past Perceptions*, 53–62. Cork: Cork University Press.

Wymer, J., 1996. The English Rivers Palaeolithic Survey. In C. Gamble & A.J. Lawson (eds), *The English Palaeolithic Reviewed. Papers from a Day Conference Held at the Society of Antiquaries of London 28 October 1994*, 7–22. Salisbury: Wessex Archaeology.

21. Long Blade Technology and the Question of British Late Pleistocene/Early Holocene Lithic Assemblages

Nick Barton

ABSTRACT

Flint assemblages consisting entirely or almost entirely of blade and flake debitage are notoriously difficult to classify in terms of age and cultural affiliation. A case in point concerns artefact assemblages characterized by long blades (>12cm in length) believed to date to the latest Pleistocene/earliest Holocene in Britain but which contain few if any diagnostic tool types. Since they cannot easily be fitted into either of the existing Palaeolithic or Mesolithic typological frameworks they have in the past been designated 'long blade' assemblages (Wymer & Rose 1976; Wymer & Robins 1994; Barton 1986a; 1991). Up to the present this term has been useful in a purely descriptive sense but, as will be argued below, a more specific definition is now required if such assemblages are to be recognized as having chronological/cultural significance in their own right.

INTRODUCTION: THE NATURE OF THE PROBLEM

Nearly a century ago the French prehistorian Victor Commont, excavating in the 'Champ Magnier' near the village of Belloy-sur-Somme, unearthed a lithic industry of Upper Palaeolithic aspect, with extremely large flakes and blades but containing few other readily identifiable features. Amongst the artefacts were long flakes with edge damage developed along their lateral margins, which he referred to as 'éclats à écrasements latéraux' (Commont 1913). The significance of these finds was further enhanced by the fact that the industry lay stratigraphically above another Upper Palaeolithic assemblage containing 'becs' (large borers) which we would now recognize as Late Magdalenian (Fagnart 1993, 390). Following the recent work of Jean-Pierre Fagnart, attention has been drawn to a number of other sites in northern France which share the characteristics of the upper industry at Belloy (Fagnart 1992). He has proposed that they are sufficiently distinctive to group them together under the term 'industries à pièces mâchurées' or 'bruised (blade) industries'

(Fagnart 1992) or simply as 'Belloisian' (Fagnart 1997, 63).

In Britain, artefacts belonging to a 'long blade industry' and believed to occupy an intermediate position between the Upper Palaeolithic and Mesolithic were first described by John Wymer in his publication on rescue excavations at the Devil's Wood Pit, Sproughton (Wymer & Rose 1976). Although not cited directly, a number of 'bruised flakes and blades' were also recognized in the assemblage (Barton 1986a; 1986b). The present author subsequently identified various findspots in southern Britain where bruised pieces were found in association with flakes and blades longer than 12cm (Barton 1989). In addition to parallels with the Belloy-type assemblages, comparisons were also made with Final Upper Palaeolithic (Ahrensburgian) tanged point industries of the Eggstedt-Stellmoor group in northern Germany (Barton 1989, 270). Amongst the leading characteristics of this group of assemblages was the presence of 'large' and 'giant' blades (12–15 and 15cm long respectively), including bruised examples (Taute 1968, figs 80–81). As a result the long blade assemblages with bruised pieces were seen as belonging to a wider north European Final Upper Palaeolithic tradition (Barton 1989).

The question of the dating of bruised blade assemblages in Britain and northern Europe (France and Germany) has been comprehensively reviewed in the literature (Barton 1991; Fagnart 1993; Cook & Jacobi 1994). Amongst the very few radiocarbon dates so far available from Britain are those from Three Ways Wharf (Uxbridge, Greater London). Here two AMS dates of 10,270±100 BP (OxA-1788) and 10,010±120 BP (OxA-1902), were obtained on individual horse bones within a scatter of long and bruised blades (Lewis 1991; Hedges *et al.* 1990). The dates compare closely with those from the 'Ahrensburgian' level at Stellmoor (Fischer & Tauber 1986) and overlap substantially with radiocarbon determinations on horse from the upper industry at Belloy-sur-Somme (Fagnart 1993, 142). Although this part of the radiocarbon record is often in itself difficult to interpret because of the known 'plateau effect' (Becker & Kromer 1991), it is significant that new OSL (optically stimulated luminescence) measurements from Avington VI, Berkshire, show that sediments enclosing a bruised blade assemblage have an average age of about 10,200 years (Barton *et al.* 1998).

Despite the apparent consistency which is beginning to emerge in respect of the chronological evidence, many long blade finds derive from surface collected material and cannot in themselves be dated. In these cases there may be a hidden assumption that the size criterion alone (blades larger than 12cm) is enough to justify classifying them within the same Final Upper Palaeolithic tradition. This line of reasoning is almost certainly erroneous. For example it excludes the fact that large flakes and blades are not solely restricted to the European Final Upper Palaeolithic: they can occur in the Middle Palaeolithic (Heinzelin & Haesaerts 1983; Tuffreau 1984), the early Upper Palaeolithic (Bordes 1966; 1968; 1970), the Late Upper Palaeolithic (Brézillon 1977), the Mesolithic (Bille-Henriksen 1976; Andersen 1973; 1978) and even the Neolithic (Louwe Kooijmans 1981).

Given the potential hazards of classification, it seems appropriate to reaffirm the main characteristics of the Final Upper Palaeolithic 'bruised blade' assemblages.

CHARACTERISTICS OF FINAL UPPER PALAEOLITHIC 'BRUISED BLADE' ASSEMBLAGES

British assemblages of this type tend to have the following features in common:

i) The presence of flakes or blades 12cm or more in length. In fact such assemblages normally contain a range of blade sizes, varying from a maximum of over 25cm to the smallest around 4–5cm . Blades of intermediate size (10–12cm) seem to show the greatest care in their production: they are often parallel-sided, with one or two central ridges and are straight in profile. Bladelets may form a significant component of some assemblages (Dumont 1997).

ii) The presence of bruised blades or flakes. These are typified by invasive scalar retouch and distinct battering-damage (bruising) along their edges (Fig. 21.1). The damage is often observed on stouter pieces, with a thick or triangular cross-section, as in the case of crested blades. The function of these tools has been the subject of vigorous debate. Various authors have demonstrated experimentally that the heavily invasive edge-damage can be caused by chopping through organic materials such as hardwood, bone or antler (Bordes 1967; 1969; Barton 1986b). Recently, however, there has been a counter-suggestion that they made equally effective tools for honing or shaping soft sandstone hammers (Fagnart 1993; Bodu *et al.* 1997; Fagnart & Plisson 1997).

iii) A dominance of blade debitage. The *chaîne opératoire* (reduction sequence) is fully represented in nearly all of its stages, except usually that of retouched tool production. This excludes the bruised blades, which are believed to be entirely the result of use damage rather than intentional retouch.

iv) High quality raw material is frequently available within a few hundred metres of the sites.

v) The blade cores usually include a high proportion of opposed platform types, and individual cores may display crested backing. Unlike other Upper Palaeolithic industries, however, detachment of blades did not take place preferentially from one end. Instead the striking platforms functioned independently with blades being removed either in short series or alternately from either end of the core (Fig. 21.2). Typically, the front of the core is relatively straight or only slightly convex in profile. An additional feature of these assemblages is that the smaller blades may be made on flake cores.

vi) The knapping technique relied heavily on softer stone hammers made of sandstone, altered quartzite or materials of comparable density. Amongst the diagnostic features of the blades (Fig. 21.3) are narrow butts, flattish bulbs, a bulbar scar which originates at or near the butt, many small fissures radiating out from the point of percussion, visible percussion rings emanating from the butt end, and slight lipping between the butt and bulb. The butts are also generally heavily abraded. Many of the larger knapping products end in hinge terminations. In combination, such features can generally be used to infer soft stone percussion (Barton 1997, 18), although no such hammer types have yet been found in a British context. There is also a tendency for some overlap to exist with the attributes produced by antler hammers.

Deliberately omitted from the above criteria are the small retouched tools. The reason for this is that they are

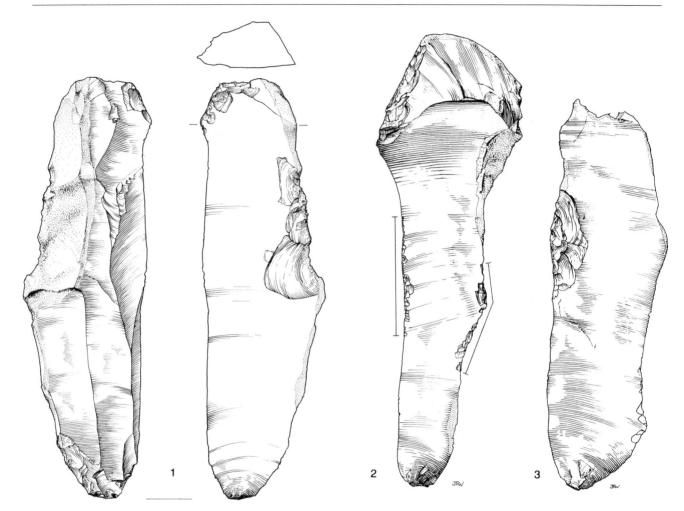

Figure 21.1. Bruised blades from Gatehampton Farm, Oxfordshire (Barton 1995). 1–2 on thick plunging blades detached from opposed platform cores, 3 non-cortical blade. (All to scale, blade on left is 159mm long).

generally rare and, in any case, vary a great deal from assemblage to assemblage. As a rule of thumb, however, the small tool component can include broad non-geometric microliths (simple obliquely blunted points, sometimes with additional basal retouch) as well as small, slender, backed pieces. Evidence for the use of the microburin technique is very restricted. Of potential chronological relevance also is the fact that there are so far no excavated instances where bruised blades have been found associated with thick curve-backed pieces, typical of Final Upper Palaeolithic 'Federmesser' industries (Barton & Roberts 1996).

Adopting the new criteria, it is now possible to identify some 28 findspots in southern Britain as belonging to the Final Upper Palaeolithic 'bruised blade' grouping (Fig. 21.4). Excluded from this list, for the moment, are 'long blade' sites which do not contain bruised artefacts, and are lacking in some or all of the stated characteristics. Amongst them is the discrete assemblage of surface-collected artefacts from Crown Acres, Berkshire (Anon 1963), which includes a large curve-backed blade and other tools of 'Federmesser' appearance (Barton 1986a, fig. 2.7).

'BRUISED BLADE' ASSEMBLAGES AND THE QUESTION OF INTER-ASSEMBLAGE VARIABILITY

On present evidence, only the long blade assemblages with bruised pieces can be attributed with certainty to the latest Pleistocene/early Holocene periods. Nevertheless there are good intuitive grounds for suspecting the contemporary existence of other lithic assemblages of this age, even if positive proof is currently lacking.

The reasons for believing this are twofold: to begin with, there is little doubt that the 'bruised blade' sites served as knapping locations where blades were manufactured. Despite disagreement over the function of the bruised artefacts, neither of the present interpretations conflicts with the idea that provisioning activity took place and that *some* of the blades (and probably bladelets) were removed for use elsewhere, either as finished tools or raw blanks (Barton 1986a, 283). Clearly, an important priority for future work will be to establish which types of blades, bladelets or finished tools were extracted from such sites and whether or not these form recognisable components

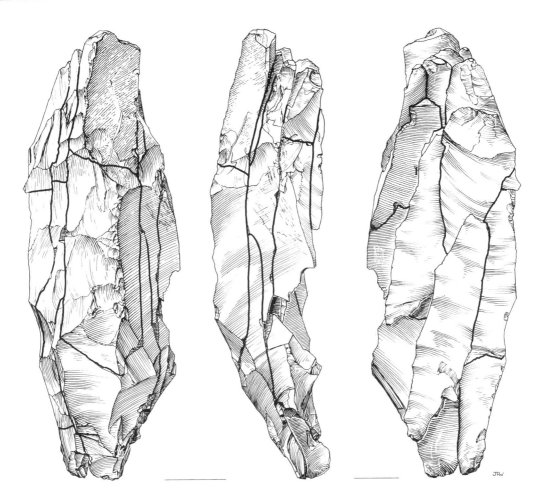

Figure 21.2. Refitted blade reduction sequence from Gatehampton Farm, Oxfordshire, showing alternate blade removals from either end of the core (maximum length of the core is 170mm).

in other assemblages. Work in progress by Sabrina Dumont of Paris University on the undisturbed lithic scatters at Avington VI might help answer this question (cf. Dumont 1997).

Secondly, drawing upon evidence from the Final Upper Palaeolithic of northern Germany, it is apparent that considerable variation exists from assemblage to assemblage within the Ahrensburgian Complex. According to Taute, six sub-groups can be listed (1968, 312–13) based on chronological, typological and morphometric indicators. Amongst his proposals were that three early Ahrensburgian groups could be distinguished from three younger Ahrensburgian groups according to the presence of more advanced microlithic forms, such as triangles. He also suggested that long-bladed and small-bladed industries existed side by side in both early and late phases. Finally, although all of his sub-groups contained Ahrensburgian tanged points, other small tool components, such as broad non-geometric microliths, were present and sometimes even heavily outnumbered the tanged forms. While details of the integrity and dating of specific Ahrensburgian assemblages remain to be established, it nevertheless raises the intriguing

possibility that an analogous degree of inter-assemblage variability could be present in the contemporary British archaeological record.

Although many of the precise archaeological details of this period are still lacking it is nevertheless interesting that small tanged points, typologically identical to those found in the Ahrensburgian, have been recovered from Avington VI (Berkshire), Risby Warren (Humberside), Tayfen Road, Bury St Edmunds (Suffolk) and Doniford Cliff (Somerset) (Barton 1991). So far the only definite association with a 'bruised blade' assemblage is at Avington VI (Barton & Froom 1986, fig. 20.1). Elsewhere, artefact collections of potentially contemporary age are characterized by long blades but without bruised artefacts. One such example is the collection from the King's Site, Mildenhall (Suffolk) which, in addition to long blades, contains a small tool component of broad triangles and other microliths that can be exactly paralleled in younger Ahrensburgian assemblages of the Diddersee-Lavesum sub-group (Taute 1968, fig. 20; Jöris & Thissen 1995, fig. 121). Finally, it may be no coincidence that various Ahrensburgian assemblages from northern Germany, dom-

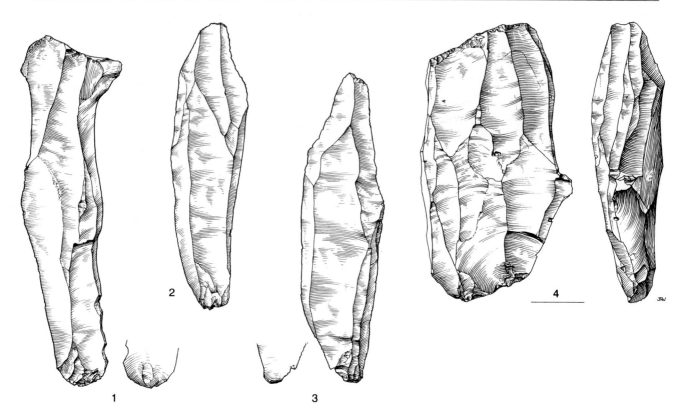

Figure 21.3. Long blade and core debitage from Gatehampton Farm, Oxfordshire. 1–3 blades from opposed platform cores, 4 Opposed platform core. Features diagnostic of soft stone hammer percussion are visible on no. 1. (All to scale, core on right is 106mm long).

inated by broad, non-geometric microliths and relatively long, well-made blades, bear striking resemblances to collections attributed to the earliest Mesolithic of eastern Britain e.g. Kelling Heath (Sainty 1925). Indeed, perhaps we should not be overly surprised if the two traditions prove to be intimately connected given the geographic proximity of the two areas at the southern end of the dry North Sea Plain and the ecologically similar conditions shared by them at the end of the Pleistocene.

CONCLUSION

While the presumption is that the British 'long blade' assemblages form a western extension of a major Ahrensburgian social territory (Barton 1989, 270) and are therefore Late Glacial/early Postglacial in age, much clearer guidelines are needed in describing lithic collections of this type. For the moment, only the bruised blade assemblages, which form a coherent group and have clear affinities with French Belloy-type and north German early Ahrensburgian industries, can confidently be assigned to this period.

ACKNOWLEDGEMENTS

The author would like to thank Jeff Wallis for his illus-

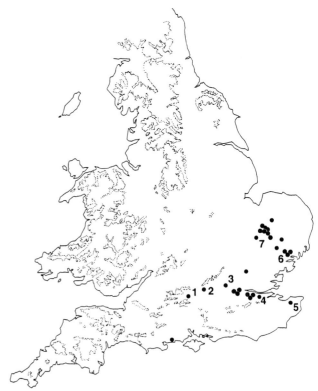

Figure 21.4. Distribution of Final Upper Palaeolithic bruised blade assemblages.

1 Avington VI, 2 Gatehampton Farm, 3 Three Ways Wharf, Uxbridge, 4 Springhead (Lower Floor), 5 Riverdale, Canterbury, 6 Sproughton, 7 Swaffham Prior.

trations of the Gatehampton Farm artefacts, which were made available by the Oxford Archaeological Unit. Gerry Black, School of Social Sciences, Oxford Brookes University, is acknowledged for her help in producing Figure 4. Jean-Pierre Fagnart and Sabrina Dumont are also thanked for their comments on an earlier draft of this paper.

BIBLIOGRAPHY

Andersen, S.H. 1973. Ringkloster. En jysk inlandsboplads med Ertebøllekultur. *Kuml* 1973–4, 11–108.
Andersen, S.H. 1978. Aggersund. En Ertebølleboplads ved Limfjorden. *Kuml* 7–56.
Anon 1963. Archaeological notes from Reading Museum. *Berkshire Archaeological Journal* 61, 98.
Barton, R.N.E. 1986a. *A Study of Selected British and European Flint Assemblages of Late Devensian and Early Flandrian Age.* Unpublished DPhil thesis, University of Oxford.
Barton, R.N.E. 1986b. Experiments with long blades from Sproughton, near Ipswich, Suffolk. In D.A. Roe (ed.), *Studies in the Upper Palaeolithic of Britain and Northwest Europe*, 129–41. Oxford: British Archaeological Reports, International Series 296.
Barton, R.N.E. 1989. Long blade technology in Southern Britain. In C. Bonsall (ed.), *The Mesolithic in Europe*, 264–71. Edinburgh: John Donald.
Barton, N. 1991. Technological innovation and continuity at the end of the Pleistocene in Britain. In N. Barton, A.J. Roberts, & D.A. Roe (eds), *The Late Glacial in North-west Europe: Human Adaptation and Environmental Change at the End of the Pleistocene*, 234–45. London: Council for British Archaeology Research Report 77.
Barton, R.N.E. 1995. The long blade assemblage. In T.G. Allen, *Lithics and Landscape: Archaeological Discoveries on the Thames Water Pipeline at Gatehampton Farm, Goring, Oxfordshire 1985–92*, 54–64. Thames Valley Landscapes Monograph No. 7. Oxford: Oxford University Committee for Archaeology.
Barton, N. 1997. Stone Age Britain. London: Batsford.
Barton, R.N.E. & Froom, F.R. 1986. The long blade assemblage from Avington VI, Berkshire. In S.N. Collcutt (ed.), *The Palaeolithic of Britain and its Nearest Neighbours: Recent Trends*, 80–4. Sheffield: University of Sheffield Department of Archaeology & Prehistory.
Barton, R.N.E. & Roberts, A.J. 1996. Reviewing the British late Upper Palaeolithic: new evidence for chronological patterning in the Late Glacial record. *Oxford Journal of Archaeology* 15(3), 245–65.
Barton, R.N.E., Antoine, P., Dumont, S. & Hall, S. 1998. New OSL dates from the Late Glacial archaeological site of Avington VI, Kennet Valley, Berkshire. *Quaternary Newsletter* 85, 21–31.
Becker, B. & Kromer, B. 1991. Dendrochronology and radiocarbon calibration of the early Holocene. In N. Barton, A.J. Roberts & D.A. Roe (eds), *The Late Glacial in North-west Europe: Human Adaptation and Environmental Change at the end of the Pleistocene*, 22–24. London: Council for British Archaeology Research Report 77.
Bille-Henriksen, B. 1976. *Svaerdborg I*. Copenhagen: Arkaeologiske Studier 3.
Bodu, P., Hantaï, A. & Valentin, B. 1997. La Long Blade Technology au sud du Bassin Parisien: découvertes récentes. In J.-P. Fagnart & A. Thévenin (eds), *Le Tardiglaciaire en Europe du Nord-Ouest. Actes du 119ème Congrès National des Sociétés Historiques et Scientifiques*, 211–22. Paris: Editions CTHS.
Bordes, F. 1966. Informations Archéologiques. Circonscription d'Aquitaine. *Gallia Préhistoire* 9(2), 533–43.

Bordes, F. 1967. Considérations sur la typologie et les techniques dans le Paléolithique. *Quartär* 18, 25–55.
Bordes, F. 1968. Informations Archéologiques. Circonscription d'Aquitaine. *Gallia Préhistoire* 11(2), 456–7.
Bordes, F. 1969. Bruised blades and flakes in the Upper Perigordian at Corbiac, Dordogne, France. In A.K. Ghosh (ed.), *Perspectives in Palaeoanthropology*, 135–138. Calcutta.
Bordes, F. 1970. Réflexions sur l'outil au Paléolithique. *Bulletin de la Société Préhistorique Française* 67(7), 199–202.
Brézillon, M.N. 1977. *La Dénomination des Objets de Pierre Taillée.* 2nd Edition. Paris: CNRS.
Commont, V. 1913. Les hommes contemporains du renne dans la vallée de la Somme. *Mémoires de la Société des Antiquaires de Picardie* 37, 207–646.
Cook, J. & Jacobi, R. 1994. A reindeer antler or 'Lyngby' axe from Northamptonshire and its context in the British Late Glacial. *Proceedings of the Prehistoric Society* 60, 75–84.
Dumont, S. 1997. Nouvelles recherches sur la transition tardiglaciaire-préboréal dans le Sud et l'Est de l'Angleterre. In J.-P. Fagnart & A. Thévenin (eds), *Le Tardiglaciaire en Europe du Nord-Ouest. Actes du 119ème Congrès National des Sociétés Historiques et Scientifiques*, 517–27. Paris: Editions CTHS.
Fagnart, J.-P. 1992. Nouvelles observations sur le gisement paléolithique supérieur de Belloy-sur-Somme (Somme). *Gallia Préhistoire* 34, 57–83.
Fagnart, J.-P. 1993. *Le Paléolithique Supérieur Récent et Final du Nord de la France dans son Cadre Paléoclimatique.* Unpublished doctorat de l'Université. Université des Sciences et Technologies de Lille, France.
Fagnart, J.-P. 1997. Paléohistoire du bassin de la Somme à la fin des temps glaciaires. In J.-P. Fagnart & A. Thévenin (eds), *Le Tardiglaciaire en Europe du Nord-Ouest. Actes du 119ème Congrès National des Sociétés Historiques et Scientifiques*, 55–78. Paris: Editions CTHS.
Fagnart, J.-P. & Plisson, H. 1997. Fonction des pièces mâchurées du Paléolithique final du bassin de la Somme: caractères tracéologiques et données contextuelles. In J.-P. Fagnart & A. Thévenin (eds), *Le Tardiglaciaire en Europe du Nord-Ouest. Actes du 119ème Congrès National des Sociétés Historiques et Scientifiques*, 95–106. Paris: Editions CTHS.
Fischer, A. & Tauber, H. 1986. New C-14 datings of Late Palaeolithic cultures from northwestern Europe. *Journal of Danish Archaeology* 5, 7–13.
Hedges, R.E.M., Housley, R.A., Bronk, C.R. & van Klinken, G.J. 1990. Radiocarbon dates from the Oxford AMS system: Archaeometry datelist 11. *Archaeometry* 32(2), 211–37.
Heinzelin, J. de & Haesaerts, P. 1983. Un cas de débitage laminaire au Paléolithique ancien: Croix l'Abbé à Saint-Valery-sur-Somme. *Gallia Préhistoire* 26, 189–201.
Jöris, O. & Thissen, J. 1995. Ubäch-Palenberg. In G. Bosinski, M. Street, & M. Baales: The Palaeolithic and Mesolithic of the Rhineland, 957–61. In W. Schirmer (ed.), *Quaternary Field Trips in Central Europe Vol. 2*. München: Verlag Dr Friedrich Pfeil.
Lewis, J. 1991. A Late Glacial and early Postglacial site at Three Ways Wharf, Uxbridge, London: interim report. In N. Barton, A.J. Roberts & D.A. Roe (eds), *The Late Glacial in North-West Europe: Human Adaptation and Environmental Change at the End of the Pleistocene*, 246–55. London: Council for British Archaeology Research Report 77.
Louwe-Kooijmans, L.P. 1981. Rijckholt-type flint and the Michelsberg culture in the Dutch river district. In F.H.G. Engelen (ed.), *Third International Symposium on Flint: Staringia 6*. 105–6. Heerlen: Nederlandse Geologische Vereiniging.
Sainty, J.E. 1924. A flaking site on Kelling Heath, Norfolk. *Proceedings of the Prehistoric Society of East Anglia* 4(2), 165–76.
Taute, W. 1968. *Die Stielspitzen-gruppen im Nördlichen Mitteleuropa.* Köln Graz: Böhlau Verlag.

Tuffreau, A. 1984. Le débitage des lames dans le Paléolithique inférieur et moyen de la France septentrionale. In J. Tixier, M.-L. Inizan & H. Roche (eds), *Préhistoire de la Pierre Taillée 2: Economie du Débitage Laminaire*. Valbonne: CREP.

Wymer, J.J. & Robins, P.A. 1994. A long blade flint industry beneath Boreal peat at Titchwell, Norfolk. *Norfolk Archaeology* 42(1), 13–37.

Wymer, J.J. & Rose, J. 1976. A long blade industry from Sproughton, Suffolk and the date of the buried channel deposits at Sproughton. *East Anglian Archaeology* 3, 1–10.

22. A Preboreal Lithic Assemblage from the Lower Rhineland Site of Bedburg-Königshoven, Germany

Martin Street

ABSTRACT

The lithic assemblage from a Preboreal Mesolithic site in the Lower Rhineland, Bedburg-Königshoven, is described. The lithic material, which had been discarded into a body of water, was probably used for butchering the large mammals whose remains form the main category of finds at the site. Details of the raw material, technology and typology are presented and it is argued that the assemblage shows broad affinities with the English Early Mesolithic tradition.

INTRODUCTION

The site of Bedburg-Königshoven was discovered in late 1987 at the centre of the Garzweiler open-cast lignite mine, in the valley of the River Erft some 20km southeast of Mönchengladbach (Street 1989a). Although the Erft valley has been greatly changed by mining and the archaeological site was cut through on two sides by quarry faces and partially truncated vertically, it was established that it had originally been situated at the northern end of the silted-up channel of a former meander of the Erft. Terrestrial sediments in which the main settlement area had lain had already been destroyed and only limnic sediments and younger peat deposits from silting-up of the oxbow lake were preserved. Here, bones found eroding out of a calcareous gyttja below the basal peat layer were identified as fragments of skull and shoulder blades of aurochs (*Bos primigenius*) and most of the antlers and skull of a red deer (*Cervus elaphus*). The latter specimen, modified by two holes pierced through the parietal bones, and a second, similarly modified skull recovered by excavation, can be compared with frontlets of similar date from Star Carr (Clark 1954; Street 1989a; 1991).

The most common category of material comprises bones of several species of large mammal butchered by man (Street 1990; 1993), including bones of domestic dog (Street 1989b), with which were found just under 200 artefacts, mainly struck flint, but also grinding and hammerstones and bone tools. The recovered material shows a relatively diffuse distribution over the site, but is definitely more concentrated closer to the shoreline. Larger finds, such as the skulls of aurochs or the antler frontlets, were all found at about the same distance from the ancient river bank (Fig. 22.1). On several occasions artefacts were found lying close together. Since the artefacts were manufactured from different raw materials it is not possible to interpret these clusters as the remains of *in situ* knapping scatters. In some areas of the excavation the density of material was much higher than elsewhere. An example is the area 84/105 and 84/106 at the west of the site, where it was possible to recover a concentration of smaller material such as bones of roe deer and beaver, flint bladelets, and a microlith (Fig. 22.1).

The incomplete nature of the assemblage adversely affects the conjoining of recovered material, but it was nevertheless possible to identify artefacts from the same piece of raw material separated by as much as 15m. Three conjoined pieces of flint from a frost-damaged nodule found 10m apart and conjoining bone fragments found more than 10m apart underline the unity of the assem-

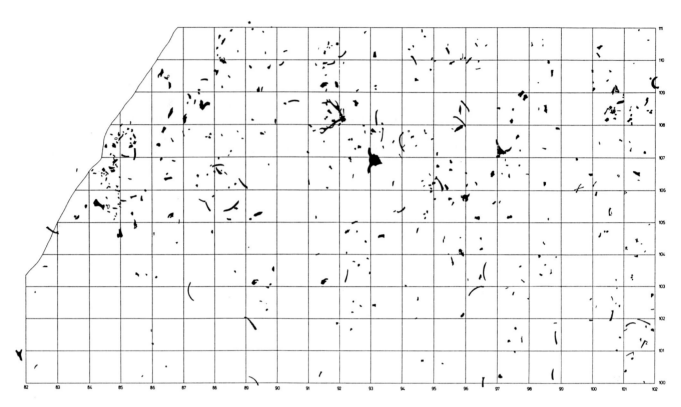

Figure 22.1. Location of the main concentration of bones and lithics at Bedburg-Königshoven, parallel to the ancient river bank at the north of the site (top of plan). Recognisable are a frontlet of red deer and several skulls and ribs of aurochs, and a denser concentration of smaller material at the extreme west (left) of the site.

Lab. No.	Site designation/co-ordinate		Height O.D. (m)	¹⁴C age BP	Material
KN-4006	Sample 12	93/105	52.00 – 52.10	8010±75	peat
KN-4005	Sample 11	93/105	51.90–52.00	9060±85	wood (birch)
KN-4003	Sample 9	93/105	51.70–51.80	9310±80	wood indet.
KN-4001	Sample 7	93/105	51.50–51.60	9690±85	reed peat
KN-3999	Sample 5	100/107	C1 (**AH**)	9780±100	wood indet.
KN-3998	Sample 4	101/103	C1 (**AH**)	9600±100	wood indet.
KN-3997	Sample 3	83/106–85/110	D	10,010±85	wood indet.
KN-3996	Sample 2	83/106–85/110	D	10,070±95	wood indet.
KN-3995	Sample 1	80/100	above terrace gravel	10,270±90	wood indet.
KN-4135		90/108–2		9740±100	aurochs bone
KN-4136		96/108–1		10,020±100	aurochs bone
KN-4139		87/108–2		10,140±100	aurochs bone
KN-4137		96/105–2		10,290±100	aurochs bone
KN-4138		93/106–2		10,670±100	aurochs bone

*Table 22.1. Radiocarbon dates on wood, peat and bone from Bedburg-Königshoven (**AH** = archaeological horizon)*

blage over the excavated area. At least some of the distribution patterns mirror human activities rather than post-settlement erosion, and the material can be shown convincingly to result from disposal of waste into deeper water.

By far the greatest part of the archaeological material was found in the upper part of a gyttja sealed by reed swamp peat, both deposits being dated by pollen analysis to the Preboreal (Behling 1988). Conventional radiocarbon samples date a series of samples of wood and peat from the base of an underlying Dryas 3 floodloam to the top of a Boreal peat below Atlantic tufa bands (Table 22.1). Two results from the gyttja deposit (KN-3998, -3999) date the context of the archaeological assemblage (Street *et al.* 1994). Samples of aurochs bone gave appreciably older results, and it is unclear if this might be due to contamination by the hard water effect or to what extent the known plateaux in the early Holocene radiocarbon record could be responsible.

THE LITHIC ASSEMBLAGE

The greater part of the lithic assemblage originally present at the site was not recovered. At more completely preserved Mesolithic sites in comparable waterside situations the concentration of lithic material is located on the drier land of the actual settlement, while bones survive in limnic sediments adjacent to this (e.g. Henriksen 1976, 36–37). At Bedburg the major part of the lithic assemblage would have been situated on the raised ground north of the surviving section of the site and not in the area investigated, which is characterized by faunal material representing discarded butchering waste.

Raw Materials

With few exceptions, the artefacts were manufactured from several different varieties of flint, the nodules of which were worked in the immediate area of the site. Among other lithic materials are a fine-grained quartzite and two varieties of *Kieselschiefer* (lydite). The assemblage of less than 200 artefacts probably represents more than 15 raw material groups.

The flint is derived for the most part from Pleistocene gravels of the River Meuse and often has the rolled surface typical of gravel flint. Flint-bearing gravels mainly occur west of the River Rur, 25km to the southwest, although flint is also found sporadically in gravels closer to the site. Only rarely represented (six artefacts) is *Maasei* ('Meuse egg') flint. This material is found locally in the form of heavily rolled pebbles with a typical bluish-black mottled cortex, and occurs primarily in marine beach deposits of Miocene age. Banks of these pebbles can be observed in deposits revealed by lignite mining, and are also often exposed and reworked by Pleistocene fluviatile activity. This raw material is the one most commonly used in the Mesolithic assemblages of the region (Arora 1979, 20 – but see also Heinen 1990, 17). The low proportion of this material at Bedburg is probably because the small *Maasei* pebbles did not allow the manufacture of the larger blades found at the site.

A few flint artefacts with fresh chalk cortex suggest flint was obtained from primary sources in Cretaceous formations west of Aachen, some 50km from the site. This cannot be established with certainty and these pieces are not classed separately from the main group of Meuse gravel flint. Fifteen artefacts with a translucent glassy appearance are made of 'Baltic' flint from moraine deposits of the Saale glaciation, which are located in the Ruhr region some 30km to the northeast and near Krefeld, the same distance to the north. The absence of a further raw material commonly found in Mesolithic assemblages in the region, the fine-grained Wommersom quartzite, is probably chronologically determined since this material of Belgian origin only occurs in quantity on later Mesolithic sites (Gendel 1984).

Kieselschiefer (lydite), which is represented by only five artefacts (Fig. 22.4:10, 11), could be obtained from local Pleistocene gravel deposits. This is also true of fine-grained Tertiary quartzite. The only artefact of this material, a core, has a calcareous encrustation covering a flake scar on the base of the piece. Such encrustations do not otherwise occur on the Bedburg artefacts, but are common on artefacts from sites within loess. The encrustation is interrupted by flake scars formed by working the core into its present form and it is possible that the piece in fact represents reutilization of an artefact collected from an older context.

In summary, most lithic material was obtained within a radius of some 30km around the site, with a smaller amount probably brought in from distances of over 50km. There is a clear preference for better quality, but not immediately local materials. The absolute dominance of Meuse gravel flint is reflected both in the number of artefacts and total weight of recovered material (Table 22.2). In the case of flakes the Meuse gravel flint forms 95.8% of the assemblage by number of artefacts, or 94.3% by weight. Locally available Tertiary *Maasei* flint forms only 2.8% or 2.5% of the assemblage, and 'Baltic' flint is represented by only 1.4% or 3.2%. Lydite and Tertiary quartzite are not represented as flakes. The representation of other technological forms/raw materials is shown in Table 22.2.

	Meuse flint		*Maasei* flint		Baltic flint		Lydite		Quartzite		Indet.		Totals	
	No	Wt	No	Wt	No	Wt	No	Wt	No	Wt	No	Wt	No	Wt
Flakes	68	609g	2	16g	1	21g	-	-	-	-	-	-	71	646g
Blades	44	298g	1	2g	9	82g	2	6g	-	-	-	-	56	388g
Bladelets	20	22g	-	-	3	3g	1	1g	-	-	-	-	24	26g
Cores	9	1344g	1	36g	1	14g	2	46g	1	198g	1	13g	15	1641g
Chunks	10	299g	1	8g	-	-	-	-	-	-	-	-	11	307g
Splinters	16	16g	1	1g	1	1g	-	-	-	-	1	1g	19	19g
Totals	167	2578g	6	63g	15	121g	5	53g	1	198g	2	14g	196	3027g
%	85.2	85.1	3.06	2.08	7.65	4.0	2.56	1.75	0.51	6.54	1.02	0.46		

Table 22.2. Representation of raw material and technological groups at Bedburg-Königshoven

Technology

Primary production of artefacts at the site is shown by fifteen cores and the high proportion of cortex flakes. With the exception of bladelets and splinters < 1 cm, more than 50% of each category of artefact is represented by pieces with cortex, whether calculated by number of pieces or by weight. A large proportion of the worked-out cores and all 'chunks' still bear cortex, reflecting the relatively small size and irregular character of the flint nodules brought to the site. The recovered cores are mainly bladelet cores, leaving open the question whether the larger blades of the assemblage were in fact produced on-site. Cores can have one or more flake removal surfaces, and in some cases have been worked by systematic bipolar reduction. One core is of Tertiary quartzite and two are of lydite, one a regular disc core. One very small core is of an undetermined chert. Although 'Baltic' flint is represented by only a single small core (Fig. 22.4:1), primary working of this material at the site is also demonstrated by a large core-rejuvenation flake. All remaining cores are Meuse flint; one of these is a simple core on a *Maasei* nodule, the others Meuse gravel flint.

Flint-working technology at the site shows a definite bias towards the production of laminar forms (flakes with parallel or sub-parallel edges, whose length/breadth ratio exceeds 2:1). Bladelets (breadth ≤ 1 cm) occur alongside much larger regular blades (breadth > 1 cm). Despite the small size of the assemblage, it seems possible to recognise some differentiation in the use of raw materials, specifically an increased proportional representation of blades of 'Baltic' flint. Although Meuse gravel flint remains the most important raw material, the small assemblage of 'Baltic' flint makes up 16.1% (by number) of the laminar debitage or 21.1% (by weight), possibly reflecting a selection for this better quality material. Expressed another way, laminar forms contribute 48.5% to the total number of flakes and blades of Meuse gravel flint, while in the case of 'Baltic' flint the figure rises to 86% (Fig. 22.2a).

Blades and bladelets were made both by carefully controlled (soft?) percussion, with resultant small (in some cases punctiform) striking platforms and diffuse bulbs of percussion, and by less controlled (hard?) direct percussion, leaving broad striking platforms and clear bulbs, often with an *éraillure* flake scar. Striking platforms sometimes show careful dorsal reduction. Several crested blades show core preparation, although the crested blades were not necessarily manufactured as a preliminary to blade preparation in the sense of Brézillon's (1968) '*lame à crête double*', but may simply represent the transverse removal of a blade to renew a striking platform. These '*lames à crête simples*' (Fig. 22.4:15) are possibly functionally equivalent to the core-rejuvenation flakes also present in the assemblage.

Although relatively long and well-made blades are a striking part of the assemblage, these forms do not dominate the lamellar debitage. Many of the laminar forms are broken, but the length of 33 intact pieces was measured (Fig. 22.2b). Well over half (57.5%) of the laminar debitage is between 40 and 60mm in length, with only isolated specimens above this. Blades of 'Baltic' flint tend to fall at the higher end of the range compared with equivalent debitage of Meuse gravel flint, a trend emphasised by consideration of broken blades of 'Baltic' flint, which are in some cases clearly from very long blades (Fig. 22.4:15–16).

Retouched Pieces

Although only three simple oblique points and five scrapers can be assigned to formal typological groups, many other pieces have retouch which is probably due to deliberate modification. Burins are not present and although some thick bladelets can be typologically described as burin spalls, it is unclear whether they really indicate the presence of burins.

Three simple oblique-retouched microlithic points made on narrow bladelets of Meuse gravel flint are typical for early Mesolithic assemblages (Fig. 22.4:2–4). Two points were found relatively close together in the denser concentration of material at the west of the site (Fig. 22.3). It is questionable whether they might originally have been hafted together. No geometric microlithic forms were recovered.

The scrapers are varied in form (Fig. 22.4:5–8), comprising three short convex end scrapers, a large convex flake scraper and a straight-edged side scraper (Fig. 22.4:5), which is the only certainly thermally altered artefact in the assemblage, revealing changes in colour and several 'potlid fractures'. An end scraper of 'Baltic' flint is made on the thick terminal end of a short blade with prepared striking platform, and has been steeply retouched to form an irregular 'nosed' working edge (Fig. 22.4:8). Of the other scrapers of Meuse gravel flint, one is made on a large and flat flake with rolled chalk cortex (Fig. 22.4:7). The flake edge opposite the striking platform is retouched over a length of 48mm to a convex scraper edge, interrupted by a natural fault in the material. The terminal end of a short broken blade of black flint has been retouched to a regular convex scraper edge (Fig. 22.4:6). Both lateral edges are retouched basally, one dorsally and one ventrally, over a length of 20–25mm, possibly suggesting that the piece was hafted.

In view of the low number of artefacts, even eight typologically definable tools represent a relatively large proportion (4.1%) of the lithic assemblage. This is increased by including retouched pieces which cannot be classified typologically, among which are thick flakes and chunks with abrupt edge retouch and a truncated blade the striking platform of which has been removed by steep end retouch (Fig. 22.4:19). Regular, fine retouch along the edges of several artefacts is possibly more than just edge damage (Fig. 22.4:10). Several cores with carefully retouched striking platforms are of a type often described as

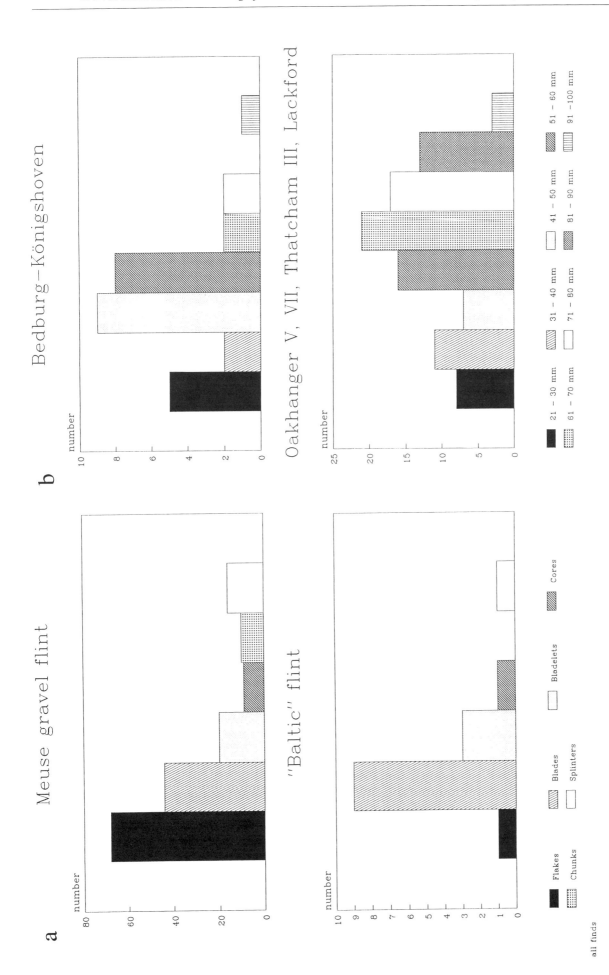

Figure 22.2. a) Differing proportions of the technological groups made of Meuse gravel flint and 'Baltic' moraine flint at Bedburg-Königshoven (all artefacts). b) Length of intact laminar debitage at Bedburg-Königshoven (all raw materials) compared with a sample of laminar debitage from English Early Mesolithic sites (measurements by the author).

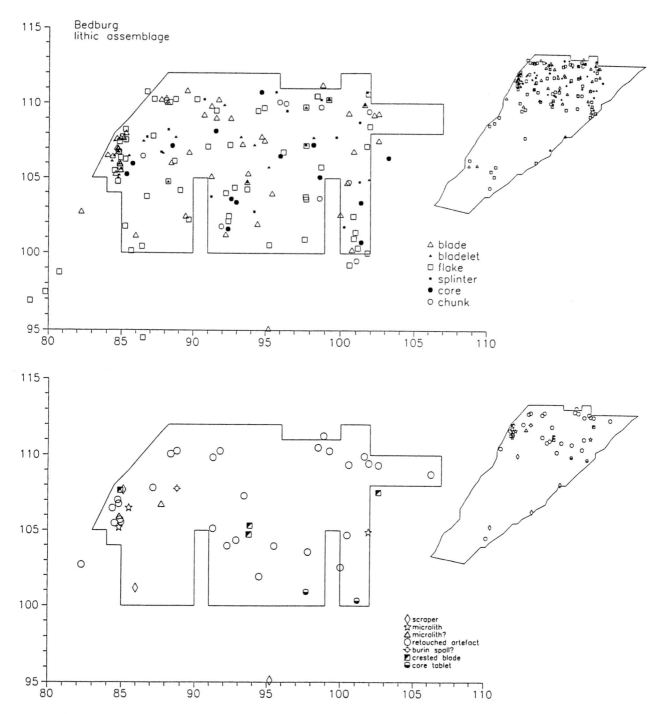

Figure 22.3. Plot of the spatial distribution of debitage and artefact types at Bedburg-Königshoven.

core scrapers (*Kernschaber*), although the retouch might be explained purely as preparation of the core. One polygonal core of lydite has pronounced edge battering which may be due to subsequent use as a hammerstone, but could equally derive from attempts to work the core after the angle of the striking platform had ceased to be suitable. The largest flint artefact is a coarsely struck nodule weighing 805g, modified by the removal of a few large flakes to give a roughly triangular cross section. The tip was finely retouched to a point. The piece might

represent the first stage in preparation of a core from which crested blades would have been removed, or could have served as a heavy-duty 'pick' as its form might suggest. Rounding of the tip of the piece might support the latter interpretation.

In summary, of the 196 artefacts excavated at Bedburg, 40 show some form of retouch. This figure excludes pieces on which the retouch is probably caused by post-depositional (e.g. excavation) damage, and possibly approximates to the proportion of artefacts retouched intentionally

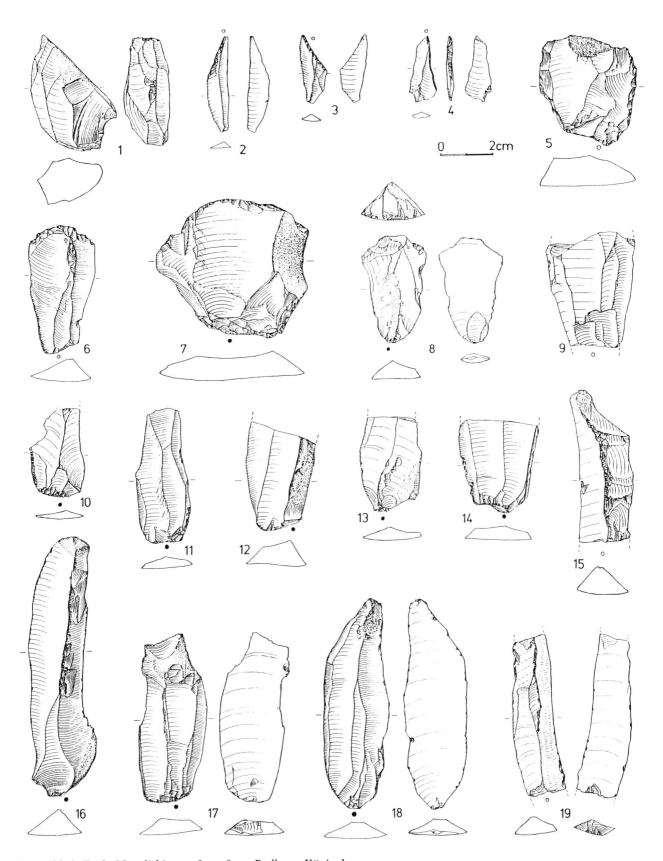

Figure 22.4. Early Mesolithic artefacts from Bedburg-Königshoven:
1 – bladelet core of 'Baltic' flint; 2–4 – oblique microlithic points of Meuse gravel flint; 5 – side scraper of Meuse gravel flint; 6–8 – end scrapers
on blades and a flake (6, 7 – Meuse gravel flint; 8 – 'Baltic' flint); 9–19 – intact and broken blades (10, 11 – lydite; 12–14, 17–19 – Meuse gravel
flint; 15, 16 'Baltic' flint)

or during use. A total of some 20% retouched finds might seem exceptionally high, but consideration of the processes leading to the formation of the assemblage places it in perspective. Only 19 splinters of microdebitage <1cm x 1cm were present within the excavated area, which reflects the fact that there is only a small amount of retouch waste to inflate the total number of artefacts.

If we accept the premise that the excavated area of limnic sediments represents a peripheral zone of the site rather than the main settlement area (Fig. 22.1), a large number of unmodified 'waste' artefacts should not be expected. Rather we should seek the explanation for the presence of any artefacts at all within this area. One possibility is that the investigated area can be interpreted as a variation on Binford's (1983) model of a 'toss zone', and that the distribution of the finds reflects deliberate disposal of items of waste. It is interesting that four of the five scrapers were found at an appreciable distance from the bank (Fig. 22.3). Were the standardised (and more intensively handled?) tools thrown further out into the water than *ad hoc* modified flakes and blades used in butchering, or did they float, because they were in a wooden haft?

Evidence for intensive butchering activities at the site (Street 1990) suggests that the majority of the artefacts, made from a wide range of raw materials, were deliberately selected from the debitage in order to carry out butchering activities, which in some cases demonstrably occurred close to the water's edge. There would be no need for flakes and blades used in butchering to show any common features, beyond selection for a certain size and stability, or any formal standardisation of retouch, although improvised modfication would be common, as would edge damage caused by the activity itself. A late glacial aurochs kill-site near to Berlin, Potsdam-Schlaatz (Gustavs 1987), shows the association of a limited number of selected, unmodified blades with a single episode of butchering. Serial butchery of several animals might be expected to create an assemblage such as that found at Bedburg.

CULTURAL AFFINITIES OF THE ASSEMBLAGE

The component of large and well made laminar debitage in the Bedburg assemblage finds no direct parallels in Mesolithic assemblages previously known in the Lower Rhineland, which are often surface collections primarily characterized by their microlithic component. An initial interpretation (before the Preboreal age of the site had been confirmed) was therefore that the Bedburg assemblage could represent a transitional tradition linking the Final Palaeolithic and the Early Mesolithic. The author was, however, subsequently able to examine lithic assemblages from a number of English early Postglacial sites, including Star Carr (Clark 1954), the East Anglian sites Lackford Heath (Todd n.d.; Dumont 1997), Kelling Heath (Sainty 1924; 1925; 1927; Dumont 1997) and Great

Melton (Wymer & Robins 1995) and several further sites from the south of England including Thatcham III (Wymer 1962), Broxbourne (Reynier 1997), Oakhanger V and VII (Rankine 1952; Rankine *et al.* 1960) and Iping Common (Keef *et al.* 1965). Technological and morphological similarities with Bedburg were apparent and the lengths of a sample of English Early Mesolithic blades measured by the author are actually higher than those of the Bedburg specimens (Fig. 22.2b).

More comprehensive metrical data for certain English assemblages, which were subsequently kindly provided by John Wymer, removed any doubt that, technologically, the Bedburg assemblage represents a perfectly 'normal' facies of the northern European Early Mesolithic, similar to many assemblages of the English Early Mesolithic. It should be stressed that since the low number of artefacts, and particularly of microlithic armatures, precludes any typological classification of the Bedburg assemblage, the English Early Mesolithic sites have simply been grouped together. This should not obscure the fact that these larger assemblages are in fact subdivided by several workers on typological grounds into regional/chronological groups at a far higher level of resolution than can be described in the context of the present paper. (e.g. Jacobi 1978; Reynier 1997; Reynier this volume).

Various explanations can be found for the differences between Bedburg and other early Mesolithic assemblages in the Lower Rhineland. These might be chronological, if Bedburg – unambiguously dated to the Preboreal – represents a somewhat older and hitherto unknown facies of the Rhineland Mesolithic. On the other hand, the special nature of the Bedburg lithic material – overall low number of artefacts and bias towards larger, unmodified artefacts used in butchering – should not be overlooked, and functional considerations might determine the character of the assemblage.

It might be borne in mind that if an assemblage of Bedburg type, with a component of relatively large and well-made blades, were to be found without clear evidence for a postglacial context, it would probably automatically be described as 'Palaeolithic'. By contrast, the Mesolithic surface collections of the region are, to a large extent, 'self-defined' by their microlithic component. It is thus quite possible for poor reliability of context and definitions based on circular arguments to combine in perpetuating a preconceived 'hiatus' between laminar Lateglacial and microlithic Postglacial technologies. In fact, the evidence at Bedburg for the continuance of good blade production, and for the survival of relatively extended and selective systems of lithic raw material procurement well into the Preboreal, tends rather to suggest a basic continuity between Palaeolithic and Mesolithic traditions in the Lower Rhineland.

Clearly, a final resolution of the problem of hiatus or continuity of technological tradition can only be provided by the analysis of further series of lithic assemblages from secure contexts, which are unfortunately rare in the Lower

Rhineland. This problem of hiatus/continuity is, of course, not specific to the Rhineland. That even the analysis of a larger amount of material from several sites with good context can still leave room for ambiguity, is suggested by recent studies of English assemblages dated close to the Pleistocene-Holocene transition. Although arguments can be found for continuity between Final Palaeolithic and Early Mesolithic assemblages (Barton this volume), analytical results can also be interpreted as revealing significant differences in the technology of the 'Long Blade' and Early Mesolithic traditions (Dumont 1997).

REFERENCES

Arora, S. K. 1979. Mesolithische Rohstoffversorgung im westlichen Deutschland. *Rheinische Ausgrabungen* 19, 1–51.

Behling, H. 1988. *Vegetationsgeschichtliche Untersuchungen an dem mesolithischen Fundplatz Bedburg in dem Braunkohlentagebau Garzweiler*. Diplomal thesis, Göttingen.

Binford, L. R. 1983. *In Pursuit of the Past: Decoding the Archaeological Record*. New York: Thames & Hudson.

Brézillon, M. 1968. *La Dénomination des Objets de Pierre Taillée. IVe Supplément à Gallia Préhistoire*. Paris: C.N.R.S.

Clark, J. G. D. 1954. *Excavations at Star Carr*. Cambridge: Cambridge University Press.

Dumont, S. 1997. Nouvelles recherches sur la transition tardiglaciaire-préboréal dans le Sud et l'Est de l'Angleterre. In J.-P. Fagnart & A. Thévenin (eds), Le *Tardiglaciaire en Europe du Nord-Ouest. Actes du 119ème Congrès National des Sociétés Historiques et Scientifiques*, 517–27. Paris: Editions CTHS.

Gendel, P. A. 1984. *Mesolithic Social Territories in Northwestern Europe*. Oxford: British Archaeological Reports International Series S218.

Gustavs, S. 1987. Das Ur-Skelett von Potsdam-Schlaatz. Der archäologische Befund. *Veröffentlichungen des Museums für Ur- und Frühgeschichte Potsdam* 21, 3–31.

Heinen, M. 1990. Der spätpaläolithisch-mesolithische Oberflächenfundplatz 'Ueddinger Broich', Gemeinde Korschenbroich, Kreis Neuss. *Archäologisches Korrespondenzblatt* 19, 11–24.

Henriksen, B.B. 1976. *Svaerdborg I, Excavations 1943–44. A Settlement of the Maglemose Culture*. Arkaeologisk Studier Volume III.

Jacobi, R.M. 1978. Northern England in the eighth millenium bc: an essay. In P. Mellars (ed.), *The Early Postglacial Settlement of Northern Europe*, 295–332. London: Duckworth.

Keef, P. A., Wymer, J. J. & Dimbleby, G. W. 1965. A Mesolithic site on Iping Common, Sussex, England. *Proceedings of the Prehistoric Society* 31, 85–92.

Rankine, W.F. 1952. A Mesolithic chipping floor at the Warren, Oakhanger, Selborne, Hants. *Proceedings of the Prehistoric Society* 18, 21–35.

Rankine, W. F., Rankine, W. M. & Dimbleby, G. W. 1960. Further excavations at a Mesolithic site at Oakhanger, Selborne, Hants. *Proceedings of the Prehistoric Society* 26, 246–62.

Reynier, M. J. 1997. Radiocarbon dating of Early Mesolithic stone technologies from Great Britain. In J.-P. Fagnart & A. Thévenin (eds), Le *Tardiglaciaire en Europe du Nord-Ouest. Fin du Paléolithique supérieur et début du Mésolithique. Actes du 119e Congrès National des Sociétés Historiques et Scientifiques*, 529–42. Paris: Editions CTHS.

Sainty, J. E. 1924. A flaking site on Kelling Heath, Norfolk. *Proceedings of the Prehistoric Society of East Anglia* 4(2), 165–76.

Sainty, J. E. 1925. Further notes on the flaking site on Kelling Heath, Norfolk. *Proceedings of the Prehistoric Society of East Anglia* 5(1), 56–61.

Sainty, J. E. 1927. The Kelling flaking site. *Proceedings of the Prehistoric Society of East Anglia* 5(3), 283–5.

Street, M. 1989a. *Jäger und Schamanen. Bedburg-Königshoven – Ein Wohnplatz am Niederrhein vor 10 000 Jahren*. Römisch-Germanisches Zentralmuseum, Mainz: RGZM.

Street, M. 1989b. Ein frühmesolithischer Hund und Hundeverbiß an Knochen vom Fundplatz Bedburg-Königshoven, Niederrhein. *Archäologische Informationen* 12, 203–15.

Street, M. 1990. Butchering activities at the early Mesolithic site Bedburg-Königshoven, Rhineland, F.R.G. *Cranium* 7, 25–43.

Street, M. 1991. Bedburg-Königshoven: A Pre-Boreal Mesolithic Site in the Lower Rhineland (Germany). In N. Barton, A.J. Roberts & D.A. Roe (eds), *The Late Glacial in North-West Europe: Human Adaptation and Environmental Change at the End of the Pleistocene*, 256–70. London: Council for British Archaeology Research Report 77.

Street, M. 1993. *Analysis of Late Palaeolithic and Mesolithic Faunal Assemblages in the Northern Rhineland, Germany*. Unpublished Ph.D. thesis, University of Birmingham.

Street, M., Baales, M. & Weninger, B. 1994. Absolute Chronologie des späten Paläolithikums und Frühmesolithikums im nördlichen Rheinland. *Archäologisches Korrespondenzblatt* 24, 1–28.

Todd, K.R.U. n.d. *A Mesolithic Settlement on Lackford Heath*. Unpublished manuscript, British Museum.

Wymer, J. J. 1962. Excavations at the Maglemosian sites at Thatcham, Berkshire. *Proceedings of the Prehistoric Society* 28, 329–61.

Wymer, J.J. & Robins, P.A. 1995. A Mesolithic site at Great Melton. *Norfolk Archaeology* 42(2), 125–47.

23. Early Mesolithic Settlement in England and Wales: Some Preliminary Observations

Michael John Reynier

ABSTRACT

This paper presents settlement data for a selection of Early Mesolithic sites in England and Wales. Data concerning distribution, altitude and location were collected for 89 Early Mesolithic assemblages, 61 of which were classified into one of three Early Mesolithic assemblage-types. Analysis of the results demonstrated that by the end of the Early Mesolithic period the whole of England and Wales had been settled by human groups using Early Mesolithic technology, although there is a belt of low density settlement across central England and Wales. Each of the three Early Mesolithic assemblage-types appears to have developed a distinct settlement pattern, and it has been suggested that each pattern may correspond to a different settlement strategy.

INTRODUCTION

Arguably the most important piece of work John Wymer has produced in connection with the Mesolithic period is the *Gazetteer of Mesolithic Sites in England and Wales* (1977). Indeed, there are few students of the Mesolithic who do not regularly refer to it in their everyday research. However, only a handful of researchers have chosen the Gazetteer as a primary source, using it as the database from which to examine large-scale patterns in the distribution of Mesolithic sites in Britain (cf. Mellars & Reinhardt 1978; Mellars & Haynes 1986). This essay hopes to contribute to this area of research by examining three key aspects of the distribution of Early Mesolithic sites in England and Wales, namely: their distribution, altitude and location. However, unlike existing studies, which have usually examined the differences in settlement between Early and Later Mesolithic sites, the basic unit of analysis in the present study are three distinct stone assemblage-types found *within* the Early Mesolithic.[1]

EARLY MESOLITHIC ASSEMBLAGE-TYPES

For a number of years researchers have been aware of three types of stone assemblage in the Early Mesolithic

period (*c.* 9.7 kya BP to *c.* 8.7 kya BP). These assemblage-types are named after the sites at which they were first recognized: the 'Star Carr' type; the 'Deepcar' type and the 'Horsham' type. Other assemblage-types are known to fall in or close to the Early Mesolithic time-frame and there may, of course, be further ones which remain to be identified. However, at present these three assemblage-types represent the sum of our knowledge concerning wholly Early Mesolithic stone technologies in England and Wales. The fundamental distinction between the 'Star Carr', 'Deepcar' and 'Horsham' assemblage-types lies in their microlith populations. Definitions of these have been presented in detail elsewhere (Reynier 1997; 1998); the following points serve as a summary:

1) The 'Star Carr' type microlith assemblage is dominated by broad obliquely truncated points, with isosceles triangles and trapezoids the only other microlith forms present in any notable frequency.

2) The 'Deepcar' type microlith assemblage is characterized by long, slender partially-backed points which can equal obliquely truncated points in frequency, although more often they remain subdominant. Isosceles triangles and trapezoids are rare, but still represented by a few examples. New in this type of assem-

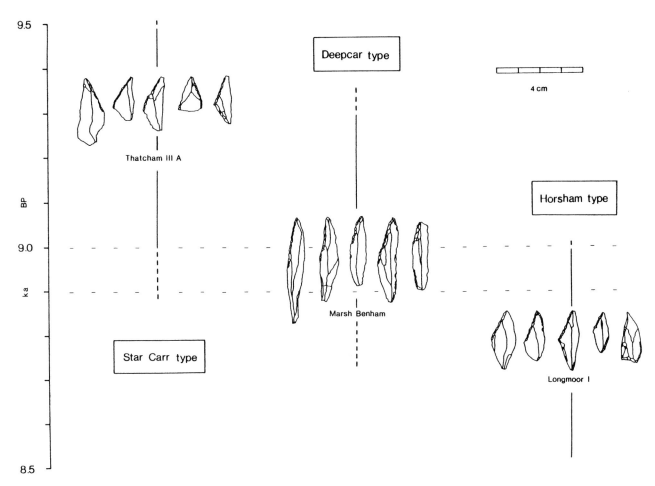

Figure 23.1. Suggested sequence of microlith assemblages for southeast England. The diagram shows the early appearance of 'Star Carr' type assemblages, followed by 'Deepcar' type assemblages and then 'Horsham' type assemblages. The dashed lines indicate the point at which all three Early Mesolithic assemblage-types appear to be contemporary.

blage are the occasional backed point and, in some assemblages, basally modified points.

3) The 'Horsham' type microlith assemblage has a diverse array of microlith forms. Usually dominant are short, squat obliquely truncated points. Partially-backed points are extremely rare or absent. In addition there are various geometric forms, such as small isosceles triangles and rhomboids. However, the characteristic microlith form is the hollow-based point which in some assemblages can outnumber oblique points.

Recent research has suggested that these three Early Mesolithic assemblage-types may follow a general chronological sequence (Reynier 1997). The situation is confused by the existence of at least three radiocarbon compressions during the Early Holocene. These plateaux in the radiocarbon record make absolute chronology for the Early Mesolithic virtually impossible. However, a *relative* sequence can be suggested using the plateaux as benchmarks. The maximum plateau distortion is 400 calendar years (Becker & Kromer 1991, 24), therefore if the Early

Holocene is divided into 400-year blocks of time (10.0–9.6 ky BP, 9.6–9.2 ky BP, etc.), dates that fall in the first block will be older than those that fall in the next block, and so on, despite the compression (Fig. 23.1). On this evidence the 'Star Carr' type assemblage appears first in Britain around *c.* 9.7 ky BP. The 'Deepcar' type assemblage does not appear until after *c.* 9.4 ky BP, while the earliest dates for the 'Horsham' type assemblage are shortly after *c.* 9.0 ky BP. New radiocarbon dates and the calibration of existing ones may alter this framework. If this sequence is correct, however, an important aspect of it is that, once present in Britain, each assemblage-type persists, so that at *c.* 9.0 ky BP all three appear to be contemporary.

THE EARLY MESOLITHIC SETTLEMENT DATABASE

Given this current understanding of Early Mesolithic typo-chronology in Britain, it would be interesting to examine how these assemblage-types are distributed within the landscape. Specifically: are these assemblage-types located randomly within the landscape or is patterning observable between or within them? To answer these questions a database of published Early Mesolithic assemblages from England and Wales was compiled.[2] The initial database consisted of 89 assemblages. However, selection of sites for further analysis was restricted to those with: 1) a total of ten microliths or more and 2) a minimum of admixture. These criteria were intended to ensure that each assemblage could be correctly assigned to one of the three Early Mesolithic assemblage-types. When it was not possible to do this with absolute confidence the site was dropped from the analysis.

The effective database (those sites selected for further analysis) consisted of 61 Early Mesolithic sites (Table 23.1). It must be emphasised that this database is *not* intended to represent the entirety of Early Mesolithic settlement in England and Wales. For instance not all published Early Mesolithic sites will have been included, while other well-known sites remain to be published. Therefore this database is considered a *sample* of Early Mesolithic settlement. The position of selected sites was taken as the National Grid References given in the *Gazetteer of Mesolithic Sites* (Wymer 1977), while altitude and location were obtained from 1:50,000 Ordnance Survey maps. Altitudes were read off from the nearest contour to the site, while the location was determined by taking a *c.* 1km² area around the site and assigning it to one of nine typical locales (Fig. 23.4b).

DISTRIBUTION

The distribution of Early Mesolithic sites across England and Wales was analysed in two parts. Firstly, the overall distribution was studied with a view to gaining a general impression of Early Mesolithic settlement and flagging regions of potential bias. Secondly, the distribution of each of the known Early Mesolithic assemblage-types was examined in isolation, in order to build a more detailed picture of contemporary settlement.

General distribution

In Figure 23.2 each open square represents one Early Mesolithic assemblage. It is apparent that Early Mesolithic settlement encompassed most areas of England and Wales. Even comparatively remote locations such as Anglesey and the south-west tips of Wales and Cornwall possess good evidence of Early Mesolithic activity. There are, however, several regions with little or no recorded evidence of Early Mesolithic settlement. Principally, these are central England (i.e. parts of Cambridgeshire, Northamptonshire, Leicestershire, Warwickshire, Gloucestershire and Herefordshire) and central Wales (i.e. Powys). Smaller blank spots exist in parts of Cumbria, lowland north-east England, Devon, Kent and Wiltshire. The apparent cluster of Early Mesolithic sites in southeast England is an artefact of research bias, both past and present.

The presence of blank spots does not mean that Early Mesolithic material is absent. In certain cases Early Mesolithic assemblages were too small or too mixed to be selected for analysis, while in others the material has not been published or otherwise made available. Most blank spots, however, seem to be best explained by physical geography. Those in central Wales and in parts of Cumbria, Devon and Wiltshire correspond closely to the major areas of upland in these regions, respectively parts of the Cambrian Mountains, the Cumbrian Mountains, Dartmoor, Exmoor and Salisbury Plain. Given the density of Early Mesolithic settlement around the margins of these blank spots, it seems improbable that such areas were not at least partly exploited during this period; indeed, stray Early Mesolithic finds have been recorded in most of them. Nevertheless, the possibility that upland regions were used more ephemerally than their lowland counterparts ought not to be discounted.

There remain three blank spots on Figure 23.2 which are not upland regions: central England, Kent and lowland northeast England. The apparent dearth of Early Mesolithic assemblages here is intriguing. All three are low-lying regions which, although prone to colluvial action, are also the focus of major ground disruption in the form of urbanization and agriculture. Such activities would be expected to unearth a number of stone assemblages purely by chance. Furthermore, lowland regions are generally more accessible to local and amateur researchers who may be expected, on average, to locate at least one major site per county. On both grounds, there ought to be a random sample of sites from these areas.

Either these lowland blank spots represent genuine disruptions of Early Mesolithic settlement, or there is some other form of research bias operating. In favour of the latter argument archaeologists in all three areas report that at least some Early Mesolithic material has been mixed in with later prehistoric assemblages and remains to be properly identified and separated. Field walking is also producing more Mesolithic material. However, it is worth observing that these finds are more often Later Mesolithic in age, or mixed, while definitive Early Mesolithic assemblages remain rare.

Distribution of assemblage-types

In Figure 23.3 only those assemblages that could be *positively* identified down to assemblage-type level are plotted. The assemblages have been coded so that all known Early Mesolithic assemblage-types can be displayed on one map. The patterns which emerge are discussed in turn, according to their suggested chronological sequence (see above).

1) *'Star Carr' type assemblages* (closed circles). These are low in number and restricted to northern England

Site No.	Site Name	Assemblage type	Altitude (m OD)	Location	References
1	Aller Farm	3	80	3	Berridge 1985
2	Beeding Wood	3	119	6	Clark 1934
3	Bourne Hill	3	75	3	Standing collection
4	Brigham	2	15	2	Manby 1966
5	Broxbourne 102	2	25	2	Warren *et al.* 1934
6	Broxbourne 104	1	30	2	Unpublished
7	Daylight Rock	1	20	8	David 1990
8	Deepcar	2	150	3	Radley & Mellars 1964
9	Denham	2	45	2	Lacaille 1963
10	Downton	2	42	2	Higgs 1959
11	Dozmary Pool	2	275	4	Jacobi 1979
12	Fairbourne Court	3	100	3	Jacobi 1982
13	Flixton 1	1	20	2	Moore 1950
14	Great Melton	2	40	2	Wymer & Robins 1995
15	Greenham Dairy Farm	2	70	2	Sheridan *et al.*1967
16	Greenway Farm	2	48	2	Norman 1975
17	Ham Fields	3	3	2	Lacaille 1966
18	Hengistbury Head	2	30	8	Barton 1992
19	High Beach	2	70	3	Jacobi *et al.* 1978
20	Iping Common	2	50	3	Jacobi collection
21	Iwerne Minster	2	160	3	Summers 1941
22	Kelling Heath	2	60	4	Sainty 1924
23	Kettlebury 103	3	95	4	Unpublished
24	Kettlebury II	3	90	4	Rankine 1949
25	Lackford Heath	2	15	2	Jacobi 1984
26	Lominot 3	2	450	6	Stonehouse 1992
27	Longmoor 1	3	88	4	Unpublished
28	Marsh Benham	2	82	2	Unpublished
29	Mickleden 3	2	445	4	Radley & Marshall 1965
30	Misterton Carr 1	2	8	2	Buckland & Dolby 1973
31	Moor Farm	2	25	2	Ames 1993
32	Nab Water	2	400	3	Gilks 1994
33	New Plantation, Tubney	2	95	4	Bradley & Hey 1993
34	Newhouse Farm	3	60	4	Standing collection
35	Oakhanger 5/7	2	85	4	Rankine 1952; 1960
36	Pike Lowe	2	465	6	Radley & Marshall 1965
37	Pointed Stone 2	1	400	6	Unpublished
38	Pointed Stone 3	1	400	6	Unpublished
39	Pule Hill Base	2	361	4	Stonehouse 1992
40	Reigate Heath	2	70	3	Unpublished
41	Sandstone, Iver	2	31	2	Lacaille 1963
42	Shapwick	2	10	2	Wainwright 1960
43	Sheffields Hill	2	75	3	Armstrong 1931
44	St Catherine's Hill	3	65	3	Gabel 1976
45	Stanstead Abbotts	2	30	2	Davies *et al.* 1980–2
46	Star Carr	1	20	2	Clark 1954
47	Telegraph Cottage	2	220	6	Berridge 1985
48	Thatcham IIIa	1	70	2	Unpublished
49	Thatcham IIIb	2	70	2	Wymer 1962
50	Towler Hill	2	150	2	Coggins *et al.* 1989
51	Turnpike	1	375	4	Stonehouse 1992
52	Uxbridge C	2	31	2	Lewis 1991
53	Warcock Hill North	2	375	4	Buckley 1924
54	Warcock Hill South	1	374	4	Buckley 1924
55	Waun Fignen Felen 8	1	485	4	Barton *et al.* 1995
56	Wawcott 15	2	80	2	Froom 1972
57	Wawcott 30	2	80	2	Froom *et al.* 1994
58	Waystone Edge 1	2	420	6	Stonehouse 1982
59	West Heath	2	60	2	Clark 1932
60	White Colne	2	30	2	Layard 1927
61	Winfrith Heath	2	52	4	Palmer & Dimbleby 1979

Table 23.1. Selected Early Mesolithic settlement data. Source: Mesosett
Assemblage-type: 1 'Star Carr' type, 2 'Deepcar' type, 3 'Horsham' type. *Location:* 1 river/lake bank, 2 valley floor, 3 valley side, 4 plateau, 5 ridge, 6 hillcrown, 7 hill summit, 8 cliff top, 9 coastal plain.

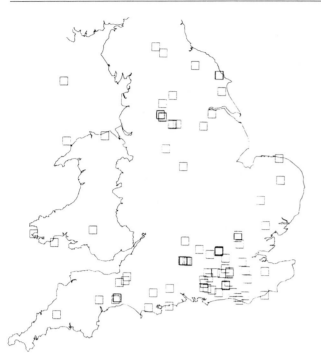

Figure 23.2. Distribution of selected Early Mesolithic sites in England and Wales. The map includes any assemblage with a substantial Early Mesolithic element within it, as well as typologically pure assemblages. Note the low density of sites across central England and Wales.

Figure 23.3. Distribution of classified Early Mesolithic sites in England and Wales. The map shows only those assemblages that could be positively assigned to one of the three Early Mesolithic assemblage-types: 'Star Carr' type assemblages (solid circles); 'Deepcar' type assemblages (open squares) and 'Horsham' type assemblages (solid triangles).

and Wales. To date, only two assemblages have been identified outside these areas: the patinated assemblage from Thatcham III in Berkshire and the assemblage from Broxbourne 104 in Hertfordshire (both Reynier in prep.). Whether these are outliers from the main distribution or indicate a broader pattern of settlement is not at present known. However, it is notable that 'Star Carr' type assemblages are more frequent in northern England and Wales than elsewhere.

2) *'Deepcar' type assemblages* (open squares). The immediate impression is that these are more numerous than any other Early Mesolithic assemblage-type. In fact, they outnumber both 'Star Carr' and 'Horsham' type assemblages by a ratio of nearly 4:1, representing *c.* 67% of all classified Early Mesolithic assemblages in the analysis. They currently tend to form two distinct clusters, one in southern and the other in northern England. This distribution is most likely an effect of the research bias noted above for central England, although the possibility of two populations of 'Deepcar' type assemblages cannot be discounted.

3) *'Horsham' type assemblages* (closed triangles). These assemblages are restricted to south-east England and correlate closely with the Wealden area, by which term they are alternatively known (Jacobi 1978, 21). Nevertheless, isolated examples of basally modified

points can be found outside the south-east in a small number of assemblages, e.g. Crandons Cross in Devon (Berridge 1985) or Cass ny Hawin on the Isle of Man (Woodman 1987). However, these occurrences are considered to reflect secondary influence through exchange or the drifting of ideas and/or people, rather than primary 'Horsham' settlement.

There is, then, some evidence of geographical patterning in the distribution of the three Early Mesolithic assemblage-types, with 'Star Carr' type assemblages restricted chiefly to northern England, 'Horsham' type assemblages restricted to south-east England, and 'Deepcar' type assemblages appearing in both regions.

SITUATION

In order to learn more about the specific choices that may have influenced Early Mesolithic settlement patterns, particularly in regard to the three main assemblage-types, two aspects of settlement situation were selected for further analysis. These aspects were altitude and location.

Altitude (Fig 23.4a)

Among most Early Mesolithic sites there was a unimodal

altitude distribution indicating a preference for low-lying locales. Indeed, *c.* 70% of 'Deepcar' type and 90% of 'Horsham' type assemblages were found to occur below the 100m contour. However, the 'Star Carr' type assemblages displayed a more balanced altitude distribution. Only 50% of 'Star Carr' type assemblages were situated below the 100m contour, the remainder occurring between 300m and 500m OD.

These data suggest that both 'Deepcar' and 'Horsham'

type assemblages are primarily placed at low altitudes. The 'Horsham' type assemblages are the most restricted in this respect with no sites above 200m OD. However, the 'Deepcar' type assemblages exhibit more flexibility in altitude with small numbers of sites also found between 100 and 500m OD. The 'Star Carr' type assemblages are unique in that they are more commonly found in two altitude bands: those sites below 100m (50%) and those sites above 300m OD (50%).

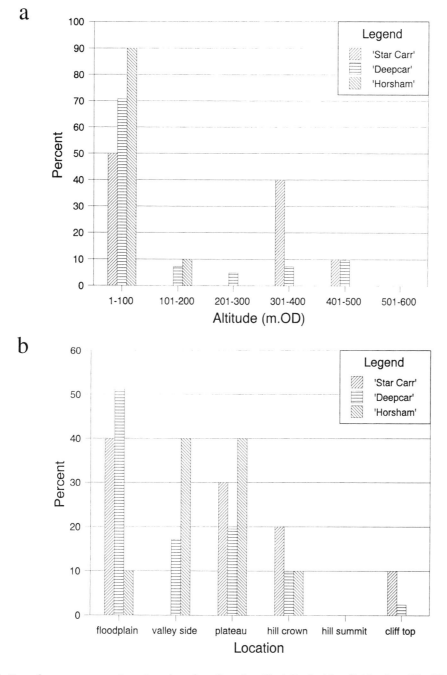

Figure 23.4. Bar charts representing situation data for classified Early Mesolithic sites (N=61) belonging to the 'Star Carr', 'Deepcar' and 'Horsham' assemblage-types from England and Wales: A) Altitude; B) Location. Source: Table 23.1.

An obvious explanation for the increased number of 'Star Carr' type assemblages at high altitudes is again physical geography. 'Star Carr' assemblages are concentrated across northern England and into southwest Wales – both regions dominated by land over 300m OD. It is reasonable to assume that at least a portion of this higher land will have been exploited, even if the general preference was for lower lying land. In south-east England, where the land is generally below 300m OD, the option to exploit higher land was not available. Consequently the 'Horsham' type assemblages, which are concentrated in the southeast, appear restricted in altitude.

Location (Fig 23.4b)

A distinct location pattern emerged for those assemblage-types found to favour low altitudes (all of the 'Horsham' type assemblages, most of the 'Deepcar' type assemblages and half of the 'Star Carr' type assemblages). Both the 'Deepcar' type assemblages and the lowland 'Star Carr' type assemblages were located on the floodplains of major river valleys (40% and *c.* 50% respectively). However, the 'Horsham' type assemblages were primarily located on valley sides and the lowland plateaux in between valleys (40% each). Very few 'Horsham' type assemblages were located on major valley floodplains (10%).

In the case of those assemblage-types found at high altitudes (50% of the 'Star Carr' type assemblages and a small number of 'Deepcar' type assemblages), the favoured locations were upland plateaux (30% and 19% respectively). A lesser proportion of these assemblage-types occurred on hill crowns (20% and 10% respectively), while none of those sites selected occurred on hill summits. Interestingly, 'Star Carr' type assemblages were the only Early Mesolithic assemblage-type to display notable near-coastal preferences, with *c.* 10% of assemblages in the analysis occurring close to the present coastline (cliff top).

In summary, 'Star Carr' type assemblages commonly occupy two areas: lowland river valleys and upland plateaux. In contrast, 'Deepcar' type assemblages are seen to be predominantly situated in lowland river valleys with only a small number of sites located on hills, while 'Horsham' type assemblages are situated on valley sides and lowland plateaux.

DISCUSSION

Before discussing these results in more detail it is necessary to re-state three limitations of the database. Firstly, the data used here are a *sample* of Early Mesolithic sites – not a complete schedule. Therefore the database is likely to possess bias. Secondly, the selection of positively identified and largely uncontaminated assemblages for the analysis has reduced the sample of 'Star Carr' and 'Horsham' type assemblages to 11 and 10 respectively. Sample sizes of this order are easily biased by outliers. Examination of the

raw data for each analysis indicated that the selected Horsham assemblages possessed no outliers. However, the selected 'Star Carr' type assemblages displayed considerable variation in certain analyses. Thirdly, any analysis of Early Mesolithic settlement patterns must allow for the fact than a large portion of the landscape has been inundated by Early Flandrian rises in sea level and that the surviving British landscape is itself a sample of what was formerly a much larger territory. Given these limitations the observations made below should be considered as preliminary statements only.

General settlement patterns

It is clear that most regions of England and Wales were occupied at some point during the Early Mesolithic period. Settlement extends from the east coast to the west coast, as far, at least, as Anglesey, and from the southern tip of Cornwall to the northern valleys of Northumberland. Indeed it is only in Scotland and Ireland that no record currently exists of assemblages that can be directly related to those assemblage-types present during the Early Mesolithic in England and Wales. In Ireland the earliest Mesolithic assemblages appear to date to *c.* 9.0 ky BP and are characterized by a different suite of microlith and tool forms (Woodman 1978). A similar situation exists in Scotland (Wickham-Jones 1994) although parts of some assemblages, as at Glenbatrick Waterhole I on the Isle of Jura and possibly some of Morton A in Fife, possess microlith elements that would not be out of place in England and Wales (Jacobi 1982b; Myers 1988). So while elements of Early Mesolithic settlement in England and Wales may conceivably have reached parts of Scotland, they do not appear to have crossed the Irish Sea.

Within England and Wales one region that appears to be consistently poorly represented with Early Mesolithic sites is the English and Welsh central belt – an area that includes the modern counties of Cambridgeshire, Northamptonshire, Warwickshire, Hereford and Worcester and Powys. In this central belt a marked 'faint site' pattern is observable (Figs 23.2, 23.3), with Early Mesolithic sites rarer than in the surrounding regions. Two potential sources of error may account for this phenomenon: preservation and recovery biases – where Early Mesolithic sites formerly existed but have not been preserved or found, or 'dark settlement' – where the presence of an unrecognized assemblage-type distorts the distribution of identified assemblages, giving the appearance of blank spots on the distribution map.

Unfortunately, preservation and recovery biases can never be discounted altogether. However, the point has been made that if Early Mesolithic settlement *did* exist in the central belt of England and Wales one might reasonably expect a random sample of it to have been unearthed during the course of this century purely by chance. Of course one may look to the surface geology of the region as a likely source of influence. However the English Midlands are dominated by industry, urbanization and agriculture, where ground disruption is certain to have been maximized which, if anything, increases the likelihood of finding archaeological sites. Indeed, throughout the central 'faint site' belt Early Mesolithic artefacts do occur as stray finds, but there are still no definitive Early Mesolithic sites, although more substantial elements may be mixed up with later flintwork.

Alternatively, it may be that the central 'faint site' belt was occupied by a fourth Early Mesolithic assemblage-type (so-called 'dark settlement'). If so, a likely candidate is the 'Honey Hill' assemblage-type. The typological details of this assemblage-type have been outlined elsewhere (Saville 1981). The small number of 'Honey Hill' type assemblages currently recognized (*c.* 15) are restricted to central England, in particular Cambridgeshire, Lincolnshire, Northamptonshire and Warwickshire – precisely the area of the 'faint site' belt. Futhermore, 'Honey Hill' type assemblages do not correspond directly to any of the three main Early Mesolithic assemblage-types discussed here, and thus are not represented in the present database. They do in fact share a number of typological elements with the 'Deepcar' and 'Horsham' assemblage-types, although other elements of the 'Honey Hill' type inventory resemble more closely Later Mesolithic assemblages. This raises the possibility that 'Honey Hill' type assemblages are either a mixture of Early and Later Mesolithic material, or that they date to a transitional period between the two.

The precise age of the 'Honey Hill' type assemblages is difficult to assess since no radiometric dates are available. Saville, although generally favouring a Later Mesolithic affinity, observed certain similarities between 'Honey Hill' and 'Horsham' type assemblages (namely the presence of basally-worked points) and suggested an age for 'Honey Hill' type assemblages sometime after *c.* 9.0 ky BP (Saville 1981, 59). If so, this would place them towards the end of the Early Mesolithic time-frame and would still leave the central belt available for settlement for most of the period. More recently, it has been tentatively suggested, on purely typological grounds, that the 'Honey Hill' type assemblage may date close to *c.* 8.5 ky BP, or younger (Reynier 1998). If this proves to be the case then the 'Honey Hill' assemblages would lie outside the Early Mesolithic time-frame altogether, consequently leaving the central belt poorly settled *throughout* the period. In either case the influence of 'Honey Hill' type assemblages as a dark settlement effect on the Early Mesolithic settlement pattern would be greatly reduced.

Specific Settlement Strategies

Figure 23.3, showing only those assemblages in the analysis that could be positively identified to one of the three main Early Mesolithic assemblage-types, suggested that they each occupied relatively well defined regions. This distribution pattern, together with the altitude and

location data, allows some tentative observations to be made on specific Early Mesolithic settlement strategies.

On the basis of our current understanding 'true' Mesolithic settlement begins shortly after *c.* 9.7 ky BP with groups using a 'Star Carr' type technology (Reynier 1997). This settlement, on the evidence presented here, appears to be largely restricted to northern and western England and Wales. At present two southerly outliers are known: Broxbourne 104 in Hertfordshire and the patinated series from Thatcham III in Berkshire. These two southern outliers indicate that a more extensive distribution of the 'Star Carr' assemblage-type may remain to be established in southern England, although its low frequency in this heavily researched region remains notable.

The altitude and location of the selected 'Star Carr' assemblages suggests a bimodal pattern with both lowland river valley locations and upland hill crown locations favoured almost equally. This might suggest two different human groups, one lowland- and one upland-based, although a more traditional interpretation would be the movement of a single population between the upland and lowland zones (cf. Clark 1972). The apparent concentration of 'Star Carr' type sites in northern and western England is, if correct, intriguing. It is likely that in the first half of the tenth millennium these regions remained relatively lightly wooded compared with southern and eastern England, and it is conceivable that this may have influenced resource distribution and hence human economic strategies. However, the possibility that further 'Star Carr' type sites remain to be identified outside the core region ought not to be discounted at this early stage.

Around *c.* 9.3 ky BP the first 'Deepcar' type assemblages appear and within a matter of a few hundred years have spread across most regions of England and Wales (Reynier 1997) with the possible exception of the central belt 'faint site' zone observed above. The radiocarbon chronology for the 'Deepcar' assemblages, although better than for other Early Mesolithic assemblage-types, is still poor. Indeed, there are no reliable dates for 'Deepcar' assemblages from northern England, which makes it difficult to estimate spread rates or examine possible sources. What is apparent, however, is that the floors of major river valleys exerted a strong influence on human groups using 'Deepcar' type technology. The correlation between 'Deepcar' assemblages and major valleys is so strong, in fact, (*c.* 70% of 'Deepcar' type assemblages) that it is difficult to avoid the conclusion that the 'Deepcar' settlement pattern is a specific adaptation to this particular locale.

If the 'Deepcar' assemblage-type does indeed represent a predominantly valley-based settlement strategy, how such a settlement system may have operated and why it evolved become paramount questions. At this early stage one can only speculate. However, between *c.* 9.5 and 9.0 ky BP southern England, in particular, was dominated by heavy pine forest, and it is certainly conceivable that in this type of environment major river valleys afforded considerable advantages to human groups in terms of movement and dietary breadth. The fact that 'Deepcar' type groups spread across the whole of England and Wales relatively rapidly may be related to this phenomenon, or alternatively may suggest an increase in population after *c.* 9.4 ky BP.

After *c.* 9.0 ky BP the first 'Horsham' type assemblages appear in Britain (Reynier 1997). These assemblages are concentrated almost exclusively in south-east England and, although isolated examples of hollow-based points have been recorded from sites outside this core area, in these cases the associated assemblages were not considered to be of 'Horsham' type. More detailed analysis appears to indicate that human groups using 'Horsham' type technology markedly preferred low-lying valley side, and in particular plateaux locales. This may represent a shift in settlement emphasis away from the major river valley floors towards the interior. If this assumption is correct the significance of such a shift in settlement strategy, and ultimately economy, in the Early Mesolithic ought to be examined in more detail. One may, for instance, speculate that such a shift corresponds reasonably closely to the onset of more open mixed forest in southern England, perhaps allowing easier access through the interior regions for both humans and resources. Again, the apparent regional territoriality of 'Horsham' type groups may signify a general reduction in human group mobility. Both observations argue for a marked shift in settlement strategy after *c.* 9.0 ky BP.

CONCLUSIONS

Providing that one acknowledges the potential effects of research biases such as sampling errors, dark settlement effects and changes in the land:sea ratio, it is considered likely that the general patterns observed above are a reasonably accurate reflection of known Early Mesolithic settlement in Britain. The following observations can be made:

1) Most areas of England and Wales were settled by the end of the Early Mesolithic.
2) There is a markedly low frequency of known Early Mesolithic assemblages in central England and Wales. The precise cause of this is at present unclear.
3) 'Star Carr' type assemblages are concentrated in northern and western Britain; 'Horsham' type assemblages appear restricted to south-east England; 'Deepcar' assemblages appear in both regions.
4) Each assemblage-type may have operated a different settlement strategy, with 'Star Carr' groups employing a bimodal lowland/upland strategy, 'Deepcar' groups developing a mobile river valley-based strategy and 'Horsham' groups maintaining a more static strategy.

At present these observations must remain tentative and further discoveries may, of course, alter the picture. It is hoped that in the future the results presented here can be tested and improved as the databases are expanded. However, the ultimate goal of learning how such patterning arose and what they may mean in terms of human society is still some way off.

ACKNOWLEDGEMENTS

I am greatly indebted to Nick Ashton (British Museum), Frances Healy, and Alison Roberts (Ashmolean Museum) for their comments on earlier versions of the text. The data were collected during a doctoral research project based at the University of Nottingham, and in this respect I acknowledge the encouragement and assistance of Roger Jacobi and Hamish Forbes (University of Nottingham). Thanks too to the staff of the Cripps Computing Centre and Doug.

For my brother, Mark.

NOTES

1. Although this paper specifically deals with settlement as defined by struck stone assemblages, there is evidence throughout England and Wales of Early Mesolithic settlement that is not linked to definable lithic assemblages (i.e. unassociated ^{14}C dates, organic remains or environmental disturbance). These data are not considered here, but later analyses ought to take this type of settlement evidence into consideration.
2. Scotland and Ireland were not included because no conclusive evidence of any of the three assemblage-types under examination has been identified from these regions.

REFERENCES

Ames, R.E. 1993. A Mesolithic assemblage from Moor Farm, Holyport, near Maidenhead. *Berkshire Archaeological Journal* 74 [for 1991–93], 1–8.

Armstrong, A.L. 1931. A late Upper Aurignacian site in north Lincolnshire. *Proceedings of the Prehistoric Society of East Anglia* 6, 335–9.

Barton, R.N.E. 1992. *Hengistbury Head, Dorset. Volume 2: The Late Upper Palaeolithic and Early Mesolithic Sites.* Oxford University Committee for Archaeology Monograph, 34, *vide* 201–61.

Barton, R.N.E., Berridge, P.J., Walker, M.J.C & Bevins, R.E. 1995. Persistent places in the Mesolithic landscape: an example from the Black Mountain uplands of south Wales. *Proceedings of the Prehistoric Society* 61, 81–116.

Becker, B. & Kromer, B. 1991. Dendrochronology and radiocarbon calibration of the early Holocene. In R.N.E. Barton, A.J. Roberts & D.A. Roe (eds), *The Late Glacial in North-west Europe: Human Adaptation and Environmental Change at the End of the Pleistocene*, 22–24. London: Council for British Archaeology Research Report 77.

Berridge, P.J. 1985. Mesolithic sites in the Yarty valley. *Proceedings of the Devonshire Archaeological Society* 43, 1–21.

Bradley, P. & Hey, G. 1993. A Mesolithic site at New Plantation, Fyfield and Tubney, Oxfordshire. *Oxoniensia* 58, 1–26.

Buckland, P.C. & Dolby, M.J. 1973. Mesolithic and later material from Misterton Carr, Notts – an interim report. *Transactions of* the *Thoroton Society of Nottinghamshire* 77, 5–33.

Buckley, F. 1924. *A Microlithic Industry of the Pennine Chain. Related to the Tardenois of Belgium.* Privately printed.

Clark, J.G.D. 1932. A microlithic flaking site at West Heath, W. Harting. *Sussex Archaeological Collections* 73, 145–55.

Clark, J.G.D. 1934. The classification of a microlithic culture: The Tardenoisian of Horsham. *Archaeological Journal* 90, 52–77.

Clark, J.G.D. 1954. *Excavations at Star Carr.* Cambridge: Cambridge University Press.

Clark, J.G.D. 1972. *Star Carr: A Case Study in Bioarchaeology.* Module in Anthropology, 10. Reading, Mass., USA: Addison-Wesley.

Coggins, D., Laurie, T. & Young, R. 1989. The late Upper Palaeolithic and Mesolithic of the northern Pennine dales in the light of recent fieldwork. In C Bonsall (ed.), *The Mesolithic in Europe: Papers Presented at the Third International Symposium*, 164–74. Edinburgh: John Donald.

David, A. 1990. *Palaeolithic and Mesolithic Settlement in Wales, with Special Reference to Dyfed.* University of Lancaster: unpublished doctoral thesis.

Davies, A.G., Gibson, A.V.B. & Ashdown, R.R. 1980–2. A Mesolithic site at Stanstead Abbots, Hertfordshire. *Hertfordshire Archaeology* 8, 1–10.

Froom, F.R. 1972. Some Mesolithic sites in south-west Berkshire. *Berkshire Archaeological Journal* 66, 11–22.

Froom, R., Cook, J., Debenham, N. & Ambers, J. 1994. Wawcott XXX: An interim report on a Mesolithic site in Berkshire. In N. Ashton & A. David (eds), *Stories in Stone*, 206–12. London: Lithics Studies Society Occasional Paper 4.

Gabel, G. 1976. St Catherine's Hill: a Mesolithic site near Guildford. *Surrey Archaeological Society Research Volume* 3, 77–101.

Gilks, J.A. 1994. Earlier Mesolithic sites at Nab Water, Oxenhope Moor, West Yorkshire. *Yorkshire Archaeological Journal* 66, 1–19.

Higgs, E. 1959. Excavations at a Mesolithic site at Downton, near Salisbury, Wiltshire. *Proceedings of the Prehistoric Society* 25, 209–32.

Jacobi, R.M. 1978. The Mesolithic of Sussex. In P.L. Drewett (ed.), *Archaeology in Sussex to AD 1500*, 15–22. London: Council for British Archaeology Research Report 29.

Jacobi, R.M. 1979. Early Flandrian hunters in the south-west. *Proceedings of the Devon Archaeological Society* (Special Issue) 37, 48–93.

Jacobi, R.M. 1982. Later hunters in Kent: Tasmania and the earliest Neolithic. In P.E Leach (ed.), *Archaeology in Kent to AD 1500*, 12–24. London: Council for British Archaeology Research Report 48.

Jacobi, R.M. 1982b. When did Man come to Scotland? *Mesolithic Miscellany* 3(2), 8–9.

Jacobi, R.M. 1984. The Mesolithic of northern East Anglia and contemporary territories. In C. Barringer (ed.), *Aspects of East Anglian Pre-History (Twenty Years after Rainbird Clarke)*, 43–76. Norwich: Geo Books.

Jacobi, R.M., Martingell, H.E. & Huggins, P.J. 1978. A Mesolithic industry from Hill Wood, High Beach, Epping Forest. *Essex Archaeology and History* 10, 206–19.

Lacaille, A.D. 1963. Mesolithic industries beside Colne waters in Iver and Denham, Buckinghamshire. *Records of Buckinghamshire* 17(3), 143–81.

Lacaille, A.D. 1966. Mesolithic facies in the transpontine fringes. *Surrey Archaeological Collections* 63, 1–43.

Layard, N.F. 1927. A late Palaeolithic settlement in the Colne Valley, Essex. *Antiquaries Journal* V, 500–14.

Lewis, J. 1991. A Late Glacial and early Postglacial site at Three Ways Wharf, Uxbridge, England: Interim report. In N. Barton, A.J. Roberts & D.A. Roe (eds), *The Late Glacial in North-West Europe: Human Adaptation and Environmental Change at the*

End of the Pleistocene, 246–55. London: Council for British Archaeology Research Report 77

Manby, T.G. 1966. Creswellian site at Brigham, east Yorkshire. *Antiquaries Journal* 46, 211–28.

Mellars, P.A & Haynes, M. 1986. Mesolithic exploitation of sandy areas: towards the testing of some hypotheses. In G.N. Bailey & P. Callow (eds), *Stone Age Prehistory: Studies in the Memory of Charles McBurney*, 69–76. Cambridge: Cambridge University Press.

Mellars, P.A. & Reinhardt, S.C. 1978. Patterns of Mesolithic land-use in southern England: a geological perspective. In P.A. Mellars (ed.), *The Early Postglacial Settlement of Northern Europe*, 243–93. London: Duckworth.

Moore, J.W. 1950. Mesolithic sites in the neighbourhood of Flixton, north-east Yorkshire. *Proceedings of the Prehistoric Society* 16, 101–8.

Myers, A.M. 1988. Scotland inside and outside of the British mainland Mesolithic. *Scottish Archaeological Review* 5(1 & 2), 23–29.

Norman, C. 1975. Four Mesolithic assemblages from west Somerset. *Proceedings of the Somerset Archaeological and Natural History Society* 119, 26–37.

Palmer, S.W. & Dimbleby, G.W. 1979. A Mesolithic habitation site on Winfrith Heath, Dorset. *Proceedings of the Dorset Natural History and Archaeological Society* 101, 27–50.

Radley, J. & Marshall, G. 1965. Maglemosian sites in the Pennines. *Yorkshire Archaeological Journal* 41, 394–402.

Radley, J. & Mellars, P.A. 1964. A Mesolithic structure at Deepcar, Yorkshire, and the affinities of its associated flint industries. *Proceedings of the Prehistoric Society* 30, 1–24.

Rankine, W.F. 1949. *A Mesolithic Survey of the West Surrey Greensand.* Guildford: Research Papers of the Surrey Archaeological Society 2.

Rankine, W.F. 1952. A Mesolithic chipping floor at The Warren, Oakhanger, Selbourne, Hants. *Proceedings of the Prehistoric Society* 18, 21–35.

Rankine, W.F, Rankine, W.M. & Dimbleby, G.W. 1960. Further excavations at a Mesolithic site at Oakhanger, Selbourne, Hants. *Proceedings of the Prehistoric Society* 26, 246–62.

Reynier, M.J. 1997. Radiocarbon dating of Early Mesolithic stone technologies from Great Britain. In J.-P. Fagnart & A. Thevénin (eds), *Le Tardiglaciaire en Europe du Nord-Ouest*, 529–42. Paris: Editions du CTHS.

Reynier, M.J. 1998. *Aspects of the Early Mesolithic Period in Britain with Particular Reference to South-East England.* University of Nottingham: Unpublished doctoral thesis.

Sainty, J.E. 1924. A flaking site on Kelling Heath, Norfolk. *Proceedings of the Prehistoric Society of East Anglia* 4(2), 165–76.

Saville, A. 1981. Mesolithic industries in central England: an exploratory investigation using microlith typology. *Archaeological Journal* 138, 49–71.

Sheridan, R., Sheridan, D. & Hassell, P. 1967. Rescue excavation of a Mesolithic site at Greenham Dairy Farm, Newbury, 1963. *Transactions of the Newbury and District Field Club* 11(4), 66–73.

Stonehouse, W.P.B. 1982. Mesolithic sites on the Pennine watershed. *Greater Manchester Archaeological Journal* 3 [1987–1988], 5–17.

Stonehouse, W.P.B. 1992. Two Early Mesolithic sites in the central Pennines. *Yorkshire Archaeological Journal* 64, 1–15.

Summers, P.G. 1941. A Mesolithic site near Iwerne Minster, Dorset. *Proceedings of the Prehistoric Society* 7, 145–46.

Wainwright, G.J. 1960. Three microlithic industries from south-west England and their affinities. *Proceedings of the Prehistoric Society* 26, 193–201.

Warren, S. H., Clark, J.G.D., Godwin, H., Godwin, M.E. & Macfadyen, W.A. 1934. An early Mesolithic site at Broxbourne sealed under Boreal peat. *Journal of the Royal Anthropological Institute* 64, 101–28.

Wickham-Jones, C. 1994. *Scotland's First Settlers*. London: Batsford/Historic Scotland.

Woodman, P.C. 1978. *The Mesolithic in Ireland: Hunter-Gatherers in an Insular Environment*. Oxford: British Archaeological Reports British Series 58.

Woodman, P.C. 1987. Excavations at Cass ny Hawin, a Manx Mesolithic site, and the position of the Manx microlithic industries. *Proceedings of the Prehistoric Society* 53, 1–22.

Wymer, J.J. 1962. Excavations at the Maglemosian sites at Thatcham, Berkshire, England. *Proceedings of the Prehistoric Society* 28, 329–61.

Wymer, J.J. 1977. *Gazetteer of Mesolithic Sites in England and Wales*. London: Council for British Archaeology Research Report 20.

Wymer, J.J. & Robins. P.A. 1995. A Mesolithic site at Great Melton. *Norfolk Archaeology* 42(2), 125–47.

24. Early Mesolithic Mastic: Radiocarbon Dating and Analysis of Organic Residues from Thatcham III, Star Carr and Lackford Heath

Alison Roberts, Nick Barton and John Evans

ABSTRACT

Three rare examples of mastic recovered from Early Mesolithic sites in England were submitted for both AMS radiocarbon dating and scientific analysis to determine their composition. The dates provide independent confirmation of the early chronological position of such assemblages. The identifiable mastics appear to be admixtures of birch resin and other substances. The dates thus also provide direct dates on the Mesolithic use of this type of mastic.

INTRODUCTION

In 1962 John Wymer reported the discovery of a flake with some adhering organic material, presumed to be resin, and a small piece of the same substance at the Early Mesolithic site of Thatcham III, Berkshire (1962, 353). This was only the second recorded occurrence of such material from the Mesolithic in Britain, the first having being described a decade before from Star Carr, North Yorkshire (Clark 1954). An earlier find of mastic from Lackford Heath, Suffolk, in 1947 was unpublished (Todd n.d.). These three cases still remain the only substantial instances of Mesolithic mastic to be found in Britain, and were all unambiguously associated with Early Mesolithic flint assemblages.[1]

In this paper we present results of the scientific analysis of these resin samples[2] as well as three direct AMS radiocarbon dates. Although a relatively large number of radiocarbon determinations now exist for the Early Mesolithic in England, the value of many of them may be questioned due to doubtful archaeological association, large error brackets, or a combination of these and other interpretational factors (Barton 1992; Jacobi 1994). In the case of the mastic samples no such objections can be raised; they are all unequivocally linked to archaeological assemblages. When calibrated,[3] the dates seem to support a revised chronological succession for the British Early Mesolithic proposed by Michael Reynier (1997; 1998).

THE EARLY MESOLITHIC PERIOD IN BRITAIN

In Britain there are few records of multi-stratified Meso-lithic sites. Hence much of the understanding of the Meso-lithic internal chronology and its development is based on the comparison of radiocarbon dates and correlation of biostratigraphic sequences. The question of typological divisions within the Early Mesolithic of England was first addressed by Roger Jacobi in his doctoral thesis (1975). At that time he recognised three major typological group-ings in the British Early Mesolithic, represented by assem-blages from Star Carr, Deepcar, and Horsham (Jacobi 1975; 1978; Pitts & Jacobi 1979). He saw the major division as being between two 'Maglemosian' assemblage types ('Star Carr' and 'Deepcar') and the 'Horsham' industries of southeastern England with their distinctive basally retouched microliths ('Horsham points'). The separate nature of the 'Horsham' industries has since been confirmed, as has evidence of their slightly later dating in the Early Mesolithic period (Reynier 1994). 'Star Carr' microlith assemblages are characterised by the presence of broad oblique points, isosceles triangles and trapezoids. 'Deepcar' assemblages are dominated by narrower oblique point and partially-backed microliths with additional leading edge retouch (Radley & Mellars 1964; Jacobi 1975, 1978; Reynier 1997, 1998). A dating within the mid 10th millennium BP was proposed for both assemblage types (Jacobi 1978; Switzur & Jacobi 1979). Preliminary work by Michael Reynier (which incorporates the radiocarbon results cited here) indicates that a chronological division between the two assemblage types may be demonstrable, with 'Deepcar' assemblages occurring slightly later in time than 'Star Carr' ones (1997).

SITES AND SAMPLES

Thatcham III, Berkshire

OxA-2848. Resin adhering to unretouched flake (Reading Museum 213.62/717). 9200±90 BP

Site III is the most prolific of the complex of Thatcham sites investigated between 1958 and 1961 (Wymer 1962). It is also generally assumed to be one of the oldest (Jacobi 1975). The two often-quoted conventional radiocarbon dates (Q-658 10,030±170 BP; Q-659 10,365±170 BP; Godwin & Willis 1964) have been interpreted as evidence that Mesolithic settlement commenced close to the end of the last glaciation, making it the potentially earliest Mesolithic site in northern Europe. The dates, however, are equivocal. They both come from bulked charcoal samples from two hearths and the possibility exists that organic material of different ages has been amalgamated. Other attempts to provide radiocarbon dates for this site have proved unsuccessful due to problems of low collagen levels in bone and antler (i.e. OxA-1201 5100±350 BP; OxA-940 6550±130 BP; Hedges *et al.* 1988).

The site lies on the edge of a low gravel terrace overlooking a reed swamp near the river Kennet. It produced large quantities of flint artefacts in association with well-preserved faunal remains and a bone and antler industry which included several simple unbarbed points (Wymer 1962, fig. 13). The Mesolithic finds were located in a silty clay, sealed by algal marl and peat (Churchill 1962, fig. 2). Although the flint assemblage has been accepted as being homogeneous, recent work by Michael Reynier suggests that there are two spatially distinct artefact scatters of differing types and surface conditions (Reynier 1998).

The flint flake with organic material adhering to its surface (no. 379, cutting E3, transect 8, layer IV) came from the main artefact horizon and from the same layer as the two oldest conventional radiocarbon dates. It was found next to a small concentration of nine oblique points

on the northwest side of a burnt patch of sediment, separate from both of the dated hearths (Wymer pers. comm.). The context and location of the artefact, combined with its surface condition indicates that it is part of Reynier's 'unpatinated series'. This forms the major assemblage present at the site, and Reynier considers it to be an assemblage of 'Deepcar' type (1998).

The mastic is located on the dorsal surface of the flake (Fig. 24.1). The position of the mastic and the thickness of the artefact offer few clues as to the original use of the flake, although its provenance next to a burnt patch may suggest softening of the resin occurred nearby. The fact that it is not a formal (retouched) tool warns against assuming that all unretouched items should be regarded as discarded waste. However, it is possible that the presence of the mastic on this flake might be accidental rather than deliberate.

Star Carr, North Yorkshire

OxA-2343. Resin 'cake' (Cambridge University Museum of Archaeology and Ethnology). 9350±90 BP

Star Carr, investigated by J.G.D. Clark between 1949 and 1951, lies on the former shore of the glacial Lake Pickering on a low hillock which extended into the lake basin. Pollen and lithological analysis show that in the early Holocene there was a natural hydroseral progression from open water to reedswamp and fen carr conditions. At the time of the earliest Mesolithic occupation, believed

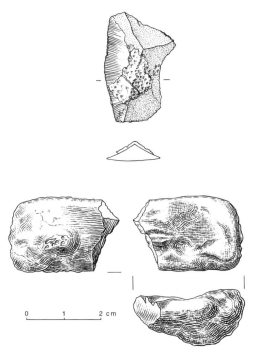

Figure 24.1. Objects discussed in the text.
Top: *unretouched flake with adhering mastic from Thatcham III, Berkshire.* Bottom: *small block of mastic from Lackford Heath, Suffolk. Illustrations by Phil Dean.*

to have been around 9600 BP (Cloutman & Smith 1988, 37; Day & Mellars 1994), fen had largely replaced the reedswamp. The occupation layer investigated by Clark (1954), lies within a series of detrital muds underlying peat (Cloutman & Smith 1988, fig. 3). Near the old shoreline the muds contained a 'single layer of (birch) trunks or branches some 100–150mm diameter lying roughly parallel to the shoreline' (*ibid.*, 39). This was interpreted as the remains of an occupation platform since it contained axe-felled wood (Clark 1954, 2) and was associated with artefacts.

The site yielded over 16,000 flints and a rich Mesolithic bone and antler industry, which included 191 barbed points. Amongst the retouched flint tools were non-geometric microliths (oblique points, isosceles triangles), burins, end-scrapers, piercers and transversely-sharpened axes (Clark 1954, 96). It is the type-site for Early Mesolithic assemblages of 'Star Carr' type. Remains of resin were found adhering to one of the microliths (an elongate triangle) and on the tangs of two barbed antler points (Clark 1954, 102, 127). The resin, which was part of the original mounting agent, was located on the retouched edge of the microlith (Clark 1954, pl. XX, F). In addition to these finds, several small, flat cakes of the same substance were found during the 1951 excavations. The composition of the cakes was identified by Dr Hey of the Natural History Museum as either 'a much oxidised wood pitch or a natural resin such as is found in lignite' (Clark 1954, 167). The former interpretation was favoured by Clark in view of the known ethnographic uses of birch pitch and the predominance of birch in the contemporary landscape.[4]

The subject of the age of the occupation at the site has received much attention in recent years (Switsur & Jacobi 1975, 33; Cloutman & Smith 1988, 42; Mellars 1990; Day & Mellars 1994). The traditionally cited dates of 9557±210 BP (Q-14; Godwin & Willis 1959) and 9488±350 BP (C 353; Arnold & Libby 1951) were both on bulked charcoal samples, and do not necessarily date the occupation of the site. At the time of the excavations no conventional dating was undertaken on any of the organic objects from the archaeological site as they were considered too valuable. Radiocarbon dating of this material, even by AMS, would now be problematic as the conservation technique involved impregnating the objects with PVC under vacuum (Clark 1954, pl. III). The newly dated sample is a small fragment from the interior of one of the resin cakes, where only the immediate surface of the cake had been treated in this manner.

Although recent palaeoenvironmental work in the area of the Clark excavations seems to show that human occupation in the Vale of Pickering may have started as early as 9600 BP (Day & Mellars 1994), the resin date provides a clear association with the archaeology.

Lackford Heath, Suffolk

OxA-2342. Resin block (British Museum 1950.7–1). 9240±110 BP

The Mesolithic site at Lackford Heath, located on a sandy gravel ridge near the west bank of the river Lark, was discovered and excavated by Commander and Mrs K.R.U. Todd during the summer of 1947. The site stratigraphy which they reported was as follows: turf 1 inch; sandy humus 5 inches; heathery peat 1 inch; windblown sand 9 inches; archaeological horizon 6 inches. The archaeological layer was located on, and in one place slightly dug into, the underlying gravels. Although the results of their excavations were not published, a manuscript by Commander Todd describing this work survives at the British Museum (Todd n.d.). Many details from the manuscript and a description of the surviving assemblage are included in Roger Jacobi's summary of the Mesolithic of East Anglia (1984, 47–52). It is interesting to note that J.G.D. Clark had considered re-excavating the site before Star Carr came to his attention (Clark 1949, 54–55).

The archaeological horizon at Lackford Heath was described by the excavator as an 'occupation floor of black sand thickly packed with flints' (Todd n.d., 2). The floor ranged from 4 to 6 inches in depth, was *c*. 21 inches from the surface, and covered a discrete area *c*. 7 feet in diameter. Commander Todd believed that the feature delimited a lean-to shelter with a curved back (*ibid.*, 3). A large hearth (2 feet x 1.75 feet) was identified within the layer and in a position which corresponded with the entrance of his shelter. Two small apparently burnt areas at the 'back of the hut' were interpreted as subsidiary hearths (*ibid*). More than 5000 flint artefacts were reported from the black sand, of which *c*. 500 were retained and are now in the British Museum. The surviving collection is a homogeneous Early Mesolithic assemblage of 'Deepcar' type. The only post-Early Mesolithic artefacts found during the excavation (two microliths of geometric form and two pottery fragments) were found in the blown sand deposit which overlay the 'floor'. No such items were found in the 'floor' itself.

A small block of mastic (*c*. 3cm x 2cm x 1cm) was discovered in the archaeological horizon 'from outside the hut entrance' (Fig. 24.1). Although its exact location was not recorded, the 'implementiferous layer' did not extend much beyond the 'entrance' and therefore it seems highly likely that the mastic originated from close to the large hearth which dominated this area. The surface of the block seems to contain indentations which superficially could be mistaken for the human chew marks found on similar resins from Mesolithic sites elsewhere in northern Europe (e.g. Bang-Andersen 1989, fig. 6, from the Setesdal mountains, Norway). In this case, however, they are more likely to have been created naturally when the mastic was formed into a block. The radiocarbon determination provides the first dating evidence for this site.

RADIOCARBON RESULTS

Uncalibrated, these three radiocarbon dates are remarkably similar and at face value could be construed as evidence for the contemporary existence of different assemblage types in the Early Mesolithic of Britain. When they are calibrated, however, a possible division emerges. The Lackford Heath and Thatcham III dates appear unaffected by the plateaux in the early Holocene radiocarbon chronology (Becker & Kromer 1991). By contrast, the Star Carr date is affected by the plateau at $c.$ 9500 BP. Although this consideration could be insignificant within the calculated age ranges of the dates, it is more likely to indicate that the Star Carr sample is older than the other two (Fig. 24.2). In this respect, it is worth noting that the Thatcham and Lackford Heath samples were associated with 'Deepcar' type Early Mesolithic flint assemblages, and the Star Carr sample with the eponymous 'Star Carr' type assemblage.

METHODOLOGY AND RESULTS OF MASTIC ANALYSIS

Although the presence of mastic in archaeological deposits has been noted for at least a century (e.g. in the Alpine lake villages; Lee 1866), appropriate techniques for their analysis have been slow to develop. Mastic, resins, and other organic residues tend to occur archaeologically in very small quantities and are often partially carbonized. Consequently, traditional organic analytical techniques have not been sensitive enough to obtain useful data about their composition. Recent developments in chromatography, both thin-layer and instrumental methods, can now provide the archaeochemist with tools to investigate the nature of these organic residues. In addition, similar developments in spectroscopy have made it possible to investigate as little as a few milligrams of material.

Initially the mastic samples (maximum 2mg subsamples of the archaeological material) were examined by infrared spectroscopy to investigate the possible presence of chemical, organic substances. Where positive results were obtained the sample was subjected to sequential extraction with a Soxhlet apparatus using solvents of different polarities, namely hexane, chloroform and 2-propanol. Each extraction took three hours and the resultant extracts were then concentrated and again examined by infrared spectroscopy which enabled an appropriate gas chromatographic procedure to be applied. Unfortunately the levels of most substances present were insufficiently low, making certain identification difficult. The results are presented in Table 24.1. The Thatcham sample was also examined for the presence of any identifiable organic material or pollen by an ISI 60A scanning electron microscope at the Natural History Museum. No such debris was seen and the analysis was not repeated for the other samples.

In addition, differential infrared spectroscopy was applied to the two most promising samples: those from Star Carr and Lackford Heath. Infrared spectra are usually obtained using a double beam instrument. One beam takes the sample disc and the second one the reference disc (usually potassium bromide). In the case of complex mixtures it is possible to insert a suspected component into the reference beam and thus 'remove' its spectrum from that of the sample, thus simplifying the resulting spectrum and hence making it easier to interpret. In the present study by careful selection of suspected components it has been possible to obtain a relatively detailed understanding of the deposits (see Fig. 24.3 for differential IR analysis of Star Carr mastic).

There are several problems involved in utilising modern methods of organic residue analysis: the extent to which individual components of an organic residue can be separated by extraction and then identified; the possibility of exchange of chemical substances between the material and its depositional environment; and the effect of decomposition processes on the organic materials. The first problem can be overcome by using a range of solvents of varying polarities, starting with a non-polar solvent such as hexane. Not only is extraction practically complete using this method, but as each solvent extracts a particular group of compounds subsequent identification is facilitated. The remaining difficulty in this area is that many of the isolated components occur in very small amounts and can only be identified to a general origin. This is the case with the resin identified on the Thatcham sample and the lipid in the mastic from Lackford Heath.

The problem of exchange with the environment appears not to be as serious as was first feared (Evans & Elbeih 1984). Moreover, other studies have suggested that possible contamination can occur (Condamin $et\ al.$ 1976), and as exchange may be dependent on age and/or ground conditions, it is generally recommended that related soil samples are also analysed. As the mastic samples were all found on excavations which took place 30–40 years ago, suitable soil samples were not available. However, none of the mastic samples appears to have been affected by exchange with the environment.

Unfortunately, little hard data exist about decomposition processes, but experience indicates that the problem is less significant than originally supposed. For charred residues, it appears that material becomes trapped in vesicles produced by the very act of charring. The tough, inert carbon walls of the vesicles then protect the residue from further degradation by heat, bacterial attack, oxidation and other degenerative processes. It is probable that resins have a certain amount of anti-bacterial protection, and/or that the admixture of clay could inhibit bacterial reactions. In this respect, is interesting to note that the two most useful samples were those that contained a proportion of clay (Star Carr and Lackford Heath), although they were from very different depositional environments.

THE USE OF MASTIC DURING THE EARLY MESOLITHIC

The widespread use of birch bark and its by-products is well attested in the north European Mesolithic record (Clark 1952, 207–12; Clark 1975, 127–128; Gramsch & Kloss 1989, 322; Bokelmann *et al.* 1981). In addition to wood and bark artefacts, the glue-like properties of birch resin enabled microliths and barbed antler points to be fixed into wooden and antler shafts (Mathiassen 1937; Petersson 1951; Clark 1954).

Despite plentiful evidence for its use in the past little information exists on how it was prepared and extracted in the Mesolithic. Over 40 years ago, Grahame Clark speculated that the resin (*Birkenteer*) may first have been noticed by Mesolithic people as a result of using rolls of birch bark as torches. His idea being that the heat of the lighted torches would cause beads of resin to exude from the layers of bark (Clark 1952; 1954). It is known that temperatures of greater than 80°C and an anaerobic environment for heating are required in order to extract the resin, but the method by which this was accomplished during the Mesolithic is still unknown (Aveling 1997, 6). However, rather than suggesting a complex distillation process involving sealed containers, perhaps it is possible that rolls of bark were simply heated in the manner described by Clark. Once heated, the composition of the rolls themselves should produce the correct conditions for extracting the tar from the inner coils of the bark. This view would be supported by the find of such resin adhering to one of the numerous rolls of birch bark found at the Early Mesolithic site of Friesack, Germany (Gramsch & Kloss 1989, 322) although the method of mixing-in other compounds remains to be demonstrated.

According to the present analysis, the mastic in the three samples studied consists of a combination of resin (birch where identifiable), clay and at least one other ingredient, possibly a lipid and/or beeswax. Such mixtures are well-known in the ethnographic record (Keeley 1982); the addition of binding agents minimizes fragmentation of the resin through crystallisation (*ibid.*). The proportion of clay to resin in the identifiable mastic was *c.* 30%. This is too high to be explained by simple environmental contamination and therefore must have been deliberately added. Unfortunately the amounts involved are insufficient to conduct any provenancing work on the clays.

The combined subjects of hafting and tool function are beyond the scope of this paper. However, it should be noted

that, of the sites discussed here, Star Carr has definite evidence that microliths were hafted using resin. Elsewhere, evidence for hafting can probably be adduced from patterns of differential burning on microliths (Berridge & Roberts 1986, 17, fig. 4.1) and distribution of pedogenic iron staining (Dumont 1985, 68–70). Based on published archaeological examples and the highly standardized shapes of Early Mesolithic microlith types it seems reasonable to deduce that they were mainly used as projectile tips and side armatures. Nevertheless, this may not hold true for all forms of microliths. For example archaeological evidence from the Later Mesolithic demonstrates uses in knives and tool handles that were clearly not designed as projectiles (e.g. Lozovski 1996, fig. 27). The presence of mastic on the flake from Thatcham III, also reminds us that hafting was not necessarily restricted to microliths. If correctly interpreted, it might suggest for example that resin was used to insert unretouched flakes into plant grating boards (Clarke 1976, fig. 2;

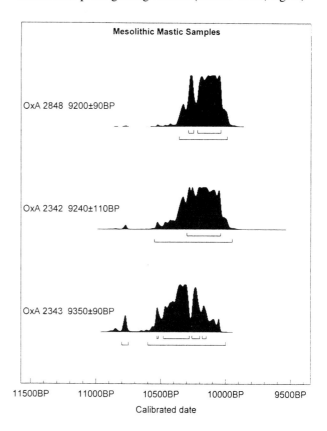

Site	Lab. No.	BP	Calibrated at 68.2% confidence	Calibrated at 95.4% confidence
Thatcham III	OxA-2848	9200±90	10290 BP (0.15) 10250 BP 10220 BP (0.85) 10040 BP	10360 BP (1.00) 9990 BP
Lackford Heath	OxA-2342	9240±110	10300 BP (1.00) 10040 BP	10550 BP (1.00) 9950 BP
Star Carr	OxA-2343	9350±90	10530 BP (0.01) 10520 BP 10480 BP (0.71) 10280 BP 10260 BP (0.22) 10200 BP 10180 BP (0.05) 10150 BP	10800 BP (0.03) 10750 BP 10600 BP (0.97) 10000 BP

Figure 24.2. Calibration results of AMS radiocarbon dates on Mesolithic mastic samples. Calibrated by the program OxCal 2.18 (Bronk Ramsey 1995).

Mowat 1989) or perhaps even shredders for flaying birch bark fibres.

Finally, the presence of mastic 'cakes' and birch bark rolls, and perhaps the utilized pebbles, at Star Carr implies that the mastic was probably being manufactured there. This kind of activity may only very rarely become archaeologically visible. In our opinion it is also unlikely that mastic would have been produced entirely from raw ingredients each time it was needed. Both the Star Carr 'cakes' and the small block from Lackford Heath reveal how this material could have been stored and transported. Routine use of mastic would probably have involved softening the prepared cakes (or the mastic already employed in hafts) by re-heating in order to make it more malleable. This conjecture could partly explain the association of broken microliths and other tools around hearths of this age.

ACKNOWLEDGEMENTS

We would like to thank Mr Leslie Cram (Reading Museum), Dr Pat Carter (Cambridge University Museum of Archaeology and Ethnology), and the British Museum for allowing the work to take place on their objects; and the Oxford Radiocarbon Accelerator Unit for providing the three accelerator dates. Figure 24.1 is by Phil Dean. Thanks are also due to Henry Kenny (University of Pennsylvania) for bringing alternate methods for analysing the composition of these mastics to our attention. [5]

NOTES

1. A possible trace of mastic on a Later Mesolithic microlith from Seamer Carr, North Yorkshire (A. David, this volume) is not considered here.
2. A fourth sample, that of an oblique point microlith from the Early Mesolithic site of Oakhanger VII (Hampshire) with suspected mastic adhering, was also submitted for analysis. It was an inorganic concretion.
3. In accordance with international convention, all radiocarbon dates quoted in the text are in uncalibrated years before the present (BP), with the 'present' set at AD 1950, and the radiocarbon ages based on the Libby half-life for radiocarbon of 5570 years (Stuiver & Kra 1986). All dates were calibrated by the use of the program OxCal 2.18 (Bronk Ramsey 1995). The calibration dataset used The present authors are aware that the exact fluctuations in this curve are still somewhat uncertain and may change slightly in the future.
4. Clark also considered the possibility that two utilised pebbles 'smeared with a dark resinous substance' might have been used in the manufacture of birch pitch (1949, 57). The hypothesis was apparently abandoned after Professor E. Vogt reported that the black substance was unidentifiable, and that the Star Carr pebbles lacked the evidence of heating at one which characterised similar examples from Neolithic sites in Switzerland which could be demonstrated to have been used in this manner (*ibid.*). The present authors, however, would not rule out some connection between these pebbles and the manufacture and/or use of birch-based mastic at the site.

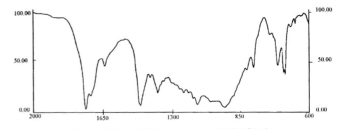

Spectrum of Original Mixture as Found on Star Carr Sample

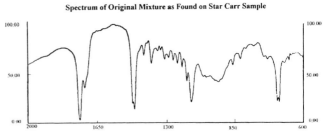

Differential Spectrum of Star Carr Residue vs Resin and Clay

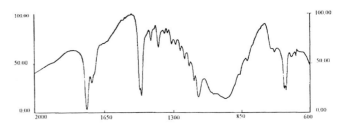

Differential Spectrum of Star Carr Residue vs Birch Resin

Figure 24.3. Differential infrared spectroscopy results for Star Carr samples.

Site	Methods	Conclusion
Star Carr	DIR, GC	Traces of a resinous substance detected, probably birch resin admixed with clay and possible beeswax
Thatcham III	IR, GC	Traces of probable resin, not further identified
Lackford Heath	DIR, GC	Traces of birch resin, lipid (fat?) and clay
Oakhanger VII	IR, GC	No obvious organic substances detected

Table 24.1. Results of the mastic analysis
DIR = differential infrared spectroscopy; IR = infrared spectroscopy; GC = gas chromatography (Perkin Elmer 781 infrared spectrometer; PE gas chromatograph with FID detector)

5. Mr Kenny submitted a sub-sample of the Star Carr mastic for preliminary analyses by FT-IR/Ramen microscopy in conjunction with his program investigating the organic residues on stone tools from the Epi-Palaeolithic site of Ali Tappeh, Iran. The analyses were undertaken by Dr P.H. Turner of Bruker Spectrospin, Ltd. and showed extremely promising results for this technique. Although a full range of reference material could not be tested in this preliminary work, the technique did identify the presence of beeswax in the mixture, and eliminated pine resin. The technique can work on small samples of archaeological material without the need to first prepare potassium bromide discs, and has the potential to be able to work on material still adhering to archaeological objects (subject to the size of the microscope chamber). This is clearly a technique which has

much potential for future work on archaeological organic residues.

REFERENCES

Arnold, J.R. & Libby, W.F. 1951. Radiocarbon dates. *Science* 113, 111–20.

Aveling, E. 1997. Chew, chew, that ancient chewing gum. *British Archaeology* 21, 6.

Bang-Andersen, S. 1989. Mesolithic adaptations in the southern Norwegian Highlands. In C. Bonsall (ed.), *The Mesolithic in Europe*, 338–50. Edinburgh: John Donald.

Barton, R.N.E. 1992. *Hengistbury Head, Dorset. Volume 2: The Late Upper Palaeolithic and Early Mesolithic Sites.* Oxford: Oxford University Committee for Archaeology Monograph 34.

Becker, B. & Kromer, B. 1991. Dendrochronology and radiocarbon calibration of the early Holocene. In R.N.E. Barton, A.J. Roberts & D.A. Roe (eds), *The Late Glacial in North-west Europe: Human Adaptation and Environmental Change at the End of the Pleistocene*, 22–24. London: Council for British Archaeology Research Report 77.

Berridge, P. & Roberts, A. 1986. The Mesolithic period in Cornwall. *Cornish Archaeology* 25, 7–34.

Bokelmann, K., Averdieck, F.R. & Wilkomm, H. 1981. Duvensee Wohnplatz 8, Neue Aspekte zur Sammelwirtschaft im frühen Mesolithikum. *Offa* 38, 21–40.

Bronk Ramsey, C. 1995. Radiocarbon calibration and analysis of stratigraphy: the OxCal program. *Radiocarbon* 37(2), 425–30.

Churchill, D.M. 1962. The stratigraphy of the Mesolithic sites III & V at Thatcham, Berkshire, England. *Proceedings of the Prehistoric Society* 28, 362–70.

Clark, J.G.D. 1949. A preliminary report on excavations at Star Carr, Seamer, Yorkshire. *Proceedings of the Prehistoric Society* 15, 52–69.

Clark, J.G.D. 1952. *Prehistoric Europe: the Economic Basis.* London: Methuen.

Clark, J.G.D. 1954. *Excavations at Star Carr Mesolithic Site at Seamer, near Scarborough, Yorkshire.* Cambridge: Cambridge University Press.

Clark, J. G. D. 1975. *The Earlier Stone Age Settlement of Scandinavia.* Cambridge: Cambridge University Press.

Clarke, D.L. 1976. Mesolithic Europe: the economic basis. In G. Sieveking, I.H. Longworth & K.E. Wilson (eds), *Problems in Economic and Social Archaeology*, 449–481. London: Duckworth.

Cloutman, E.W. & Smith, A.G. 1988. Palaeoenvironments in the Vale of Pickering. Part 3: environmental history at Star Carr. *Proceedings of the Prehistoric Society* 54, 37–58.

Condamin, J., Formenti, F., Metais, M.O., Michel, M. & Blond, P. 1976. The application of gas chromatography to the tracing of oil in ancient amphorae. *Archaeometry* 18(2), 195–201.

Day, S.P. & Mellars, P.A. 1994. 'Absolute' dating of Mesolithic human activity at Star Carr, Yorkshire: new palaeoecological studies and identification of the 9600 BP radiocarbon 'plateau'. *Proceedings of the Prehistoric Society* 60, 417–22.

Dumont, J.V. 1985. A preliminary report on the Mount Sandel microwear study. In P.C. Woodman, *Excavations at Mount Sandel 1973–77*, 61–70. Belfast: Northern Ireland Archaeological Monographs 2.

Evans, J. & Elbeih, S.M. 1984. Medieval food residues from Exeter. In J.P. Allan, *Medieval and Post Medieval Finds from Exeter, 1971–1980*, 37–39. Exeter: Exeter Archaeological Reports 3.

Godwin, H. & Willis, E.H. 1959. Cambridge University Natural Radiocarbon Measurements I. *Radiocarbon* 1, 63–75.

Godwin, H. & Willis, E.H. 1964. Cambridge University Natural Radiocarbon Measurements VI. *Radiocarbon* 6, 116–37.

Gramsch, B. & Kloss, K. 1989. Excavations near Friesack: an Early Mesolithic marshland site in the northern plain of central Europe. In C. Bonsall (ed.), *The Mesolithic in Europe*, 313–24. Edinburgh: John Donald.

Hedges, R.E.M., Housley, R.A., Law, I.A., Perry, C. & Hendy, E. 1988. Radiocarbon dates from the Oxford AMS system Archaeometry datelist 8. *Archaeometry* 30(2), 291–305.

Jacobi, R.M. 1975. *Aspects of the Postglacial Archaeology of England and Wales.* Unpublished PhD thesis, University of Cambridge.

Jacobi, R.M. 1978. Northern England in the eighth millennium bc: an essay. In P.A. Mellars (ed.), *The Early Postglacial Settlement of Northern Europe*, 295–332. London: Duckworth.

Jacobi, R. 1984. The Mesolithic of northern East Anglia and contemporary territories. In C. Barringer (ed.), *Aspects of East Anglian Prehistory (Twenty Years after Rainbird Clarke)*, 43–76. Norwich: Geo Books.

Jacobi, R. 1994. Mesolithic radiocarbon dates: a first review of some recent results. In N. Ashton & A. David (eds), *Stories in Stone*, 192–98. London: Lithic Studies Society Occasional Paper 4.

Keeley, L. 1982. Hafting and retooling: effects on the archaeological record. *American Antiquity* 47, 798–809.

Lee, J.E. 1866. *The Lake Dwellings of Switzerland and Other Parts of Europe.*

Lozovski, V.M. 1996. *Zamostje 2: The Last Prehistoric Hunter-fishers of the Russian Plain.* Belgium: Editions de CEDARC.

Matthiessen, T. 1937. Gudenna-Kulturen. En mesolitisk inlandsbebyggelse i Jylland. *Aarb ger* 1–186.

Mellars, P. 1990. A major 'plateau' in the radiocarbon timescale at c. 9650 b.p.: the evidence from Star Carr (North Yorkshire). *Antiquity* 64, 836–41.

Mowat, L. 1989. *Cassava and Chicha: Bread and Beer of the Amazonian Indians.* Princes Risborough: Shire Publications.

Petersson, M. 1951. Microlithen als Pfeilspitzen. Ein Fund aus dem Lilla Loshult Moor, Ksp. Loshult, Skåne. *Meddelanden fran Lunds Universitets Historika Museums* 123–37.

Pitts, M.W. & Jacobi, R.M. 1979. Some aspects of change in flaked stone industries of the Mesolithic & Neolithic in southern Britain. *Journal of Archaeological Science* 6(2), 163–77.

Radley, J. & Mellars, P.A. 1964. A Mesolithic structure at Deepcar, Yorkshire, and the affinities of its associated flint industries. *Proceedings of the Prehistoric Society* 30, 1–24.

Reynier, M. 1994. A stylistic analysis of ten Early Mesolithic sites in south-east England. In N. Ashton & A. David (eds), *Stories in Stone*, 199–205. London: Lithic Studies Society Occasional Paper 4.

Reynier, M. J. 1997. Radiocarbon dating of Early Mesolithic stone technologies from Great Britain. In J.-P. Fagnart & A. Thévenin (eds), *Le Tardiglaciaire en Europe du Nord-Ouest. Fin du Paléolithique supérieur et début du Mésolithique. Actes du 119e Congrès National des Sociétés Historiques et Scientifiques*, 529–42. Paris: Editions CTHS.

Reynier, M.J. 1998. *Aspects of the Early Mesolithic Period in Britain with Particular Reference to South-east England.* Unpublished Ph.D. thesis, University of Nottingham.

Stuiver, M. & Kra, R.R. (eds) 1986. Calibration issue, Proceedings of the 12th International Radiocarbon Conference, 1985. *Radiocarbon* 28 (2B) 805–1030.

Stuiver, M., Long, A. & Kra, R.S. (eds) 1993. Calibration issue. *Radiocarbon* 35(1)

Switsur, V.R. & Jacobi, R.M. 1975. Radiocarbon dates for the Pennine Mesolithic. *Nature* 256, 32–34.

Switsur, V.R. & Jacobi, R.M. 1979. A radiocarbon chronology for the Early Postglacial stone industries of England and Wales. In

R. Berger & H.E. Suess (eds), *Radiocarbon Dating: Proceedings of the Ninth International Conference, 1976,* 41–68. Berkley: University of California Press.

Todd, K.R.U. n.d. *A Mesolithic Settlement on Lackford Heath.* Unpublished manuscript, British Museum.

Wymer, J.J. 1962. Excavations of the Maglemosian sites at Thatcham, Berkshire, England. *Proceedings of the Prehistoric Society* 28, 329–61.

25. The Methods used to Produce a Complete Harpoon

John Lord

ABSTRACT

The methods and materials used to make a harpoon with a head modelled on Obanian forms are described, together with the processes of making hog gut and nettle fibre cordage.

INTRODUCTION

A harpoon, made by hand using natural materials that would have been available during the Mesolithic period, was commissioned by Kilmartin House Centre for Archaeology and Landscape Interpretation, Argyll, Scotland. The finished weapon was to be robust enough to be used for hunting seal. The harpoon point was based on the Obanian examples described by John Wymer in *Mesolithic Britain* (1991, 31, 52).

This account does not contain precise measurements, weights and timings, due to the variable factors encountered when using natural materials, but is intended to provide a description of useful techniques, as well as some futile ones.

THE HARPOON

A complete red deer antler was chosen, one that would yield a strip from the beam measuring approximately 140mm x 25mm. After soaking the antler in water for two weeks, a series of flint burins was produced, some of which would score a 70° groove and others a 30° groove. Work on the antler commenced by using the 70° burins to score two grooves 30mm apart for a distance of 180mm. The 30° burins were brought into use after the 70° burins had scored to a depth of 2mm, and work continued until

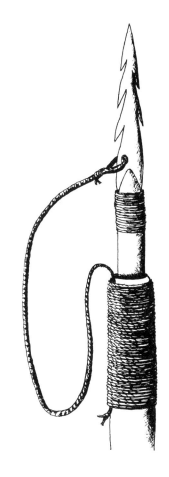

Figure 25.1. The completed harpoon

the spongy tissue was revealed. Grooving with hand-held burins takes its toll on the thumb and fingers over a period of three to four hours, it is therefore worth considering the use of hafted burins, making a two-handed operation possible. The cross-cuts to link the parallel grooves were made using a hafted blade which had been bifacially retouched to resemble a crude saw blade. Frequent re-touching of the blade made this a speedy and efficient 15-minute operation. The separation of the splinter from the main beam was prolonged by mistakenly assuming that a series of flint wedges hammered into the spongy tissue would loosen it. The wedges that did not shatter with the hammering became firmly wedged in compressed spongy tissue. After twenty minutes wasted and many more passed in deep thought, work was resumed by hammering a series of severed antler points into the spongy tissue (Fig. 25.2). The elasticity and the fast taper of the points led to the success of this method, the only hindrance was in getting by the flint embedded in the beam from the previous operation.

The bulk of the spongy tissue which clung to the splinter was removed by abrading with bifacially-prepared flints. Honing and thinning the splinter with blades and scrapers to gain the correct proportions for a harpoon blank proved to be tedious. Fast and efficient results were obtained by drawing the splinter across the facets of a large flake core, facets that presented an angle of 90° or slightly more (Fig. 25.3).

This process consumed another three to four hours. The outline of the harpoon was scored onto the blank with a burin. Bow-drilled holes were then bored at the rear and base of each barb as well as a bow-drilled hole for the attachment of cordage (Fig. 25.4).

A series of serrated flint blades were used to cut behind each barb to a depth of 1mm, followed by carving to the base of the saw cut, using a series of sharp unretouched blades, thus forming the front of the barb below. This process was repeated over and over until contact had been made with all the bow-drilled holes. The finishing touches to the harpoon point were achieved by carving with blades, burins and scrapers.

THE HARPOON HAFT

A suitable section of ash sapling, 240mm long and 35mm in diameter, was bow-drilled through the diameter 40mm from one end. Backed flint blades were hammered into the end of the haft in order to create two splits down to the top of the bow-drilled hole. This allowed a section of timber to be removed which left a notch in the end of the haft measuring 40mm x 35mm x 8mm. The haft was carved to a fine taper with hafted blades and finally honed on a sandstone slab. The harpoon point was fitted to the haft and the complete length of the notch was whipped tightly with a single strand of twisted hog gut (Fig. 25.1). The whole joint assembly was coated with a mixture of pine

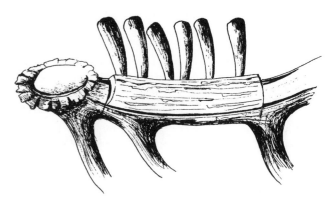

Figure 25.2. Removing a splinter of antler by driving in tine tips

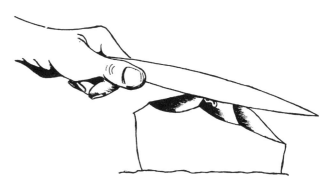

Figure 25.3. Thinning the harpoon head on a flint core

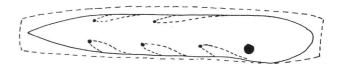

Figure 25.4. The outline of the harpoon head marked on the splinter, with small holes drilled at the base of each barb and a larger hole drilled for the line

resin and beeswax, after which the joint was rotated in heat which allowed the resin mixture to flow, thus forming a smooth watertight seal.

THE MAIN HARPOON SHAFT

The shaft was made from the main stem of a young pine tree. The section used was 2m long and the end destined to be the socket was 50mm in diameter. Two slits down to a drilled hole were made by hammering in backed flint blades, the same technique as was used on the point haft. After the removal of the central timber section, blades were used in 'spokeshave' fashion to form a tapering notch, to match the taper of the point haft. The point haft was then fitted to the main shaft and the full length of the notch was whipped, not over-tightly, with 4-ply stinging nettle fibre cordage. The whipping also secured the link cord between the pin and main shaft (Fig. 25.1). The link cord was made of 8-ply nettle fibre and was long enough to allow the complete removal of the point haft from the socket. The whipping was coated with resin and beeswax and sealed with the aid of additional heat. The tapering point haft was then finely tuned to fit the socket so that when fully inserted it was stable but not jammed. The point haft could be pulled free with one sharp tug. When this condition has been achieved, the point haft and the inside of the shaft socket were coated with animal fat for lubrication. The thrusting grip on the harpoon shaft was made by whipping on a strip of twisted ox rawhide. If required, this whipping arrangement could also be used to secure a main line cordage.

NOTES ON CORDAGE

Hog gut

The hog gut cordage was prepared by cleaning lengths of small intestine of hog. While still wet, one end of a length was secured to a post and the other to a crank-shaped piece of timber. While keeping the gut under tension, many twists were introduced with the aid of the timber crank. When sufficiently twisted, the crank end of the gut was secured to another post while still keeping the whole length under tension. This arrangement was maintained until the gut had dried out thoroughly, after which it was coiled and stored. Gut makes no attempt to untwist when in a dry condition. One single strand of gut makes a neat strong whipping, and after sealing with resin and beeswax, it is fine for joints that are to remain permanently fixed. Gut proved to be of no use for the link or main cordage of the harpoon because the gut became soft and elastic when wet, unlike the joints which were protected by the waterproof resin. Gut may be braided or plied in order to increase strength if necessary.

Nettle fibre

The useful fibres of the stinging nettle are contained in the outer skin of the main stem of the plant and they need to be collected when the plants are fully grown but still green. Cut the nettle at ground level and remove all growth from the main stem. The stem can be quite easily split open down its whole length, rather like opening a pod. Once opened out flat, the woody centre can be snapped and peeled from the outer skin. The actual fibres can be twisted from the outer skins and used for fine work like the preparation of the fishing hook linkages. If the skins are not to be used immediately, they can be dried and stored. They become flexible again in seconds if soaked in water.

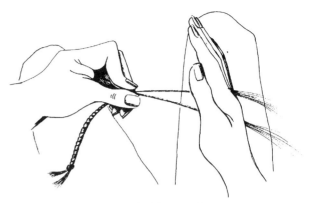

Figure 25.5. Making nettle fibre cordage

To ply nettle fibre into a useful 2-ply cordage, take two outer skins and knot them together at one end. Separate each skin into several strands; the structure of the plant will clearly indicate where this should be done. Hold the knot firmly and lay the two stranded skins across a thigh, not necessarily your own, about 35mm apart. Roll both bunches of fibres on the thigh using the free hand until they appear to be equally well twisted. Keeping the fibres clamped down with the rolling hand, let go of the knot and the two sets of fibres will automatically braid together. With the hand that was holding the knot, re-grip the fibres where the braiding ceased, grip firmly and repeat the rolling operation (Fig. 25.5). Each time after rolling the fibre, release grip on the braided end and watch the braided section grow. Fresh fibres will need to be introduced approximately 70mm before the end of those already in use. Continue until there is sufficient length or cordage. It will aid control if the hand, thigh and fibres are all kept damp during the braiding operation. To produce a 4-ply cordage, knot together two lengths of 2-ply and while firmly holding the knot, roll the braided lengths on the thigh causing them to untwist until four separate groups of fibre appear to lay parallel. Slowly release grip on the knot and watch the four strands integrate to become a section of 4-ply cordage. In order to gain differing strengths of cord, the integration of plies may be continued, 4-ply plus 4-ply to give an 8-ply. Intermediate strengths may be obtained by the integration of differing plies, a 4-ply plus an 8-ply to make a 12-ply for example. To preserve cordage of any kind it will help to drive out any residual water. The application of natural oil or fat will remove water and maintain flexibility.

REFERENCE

Wymer, J.J. 1991. *Mesolithic Britain*. Princes Risborough: Shire Publications.

26. Two Assemblages of Later Mesolithic Microliths from Seamer Carr, North Yorkshire: Fact and Fancy

A. David

ABSTRACT

A find of two groups of later Mesolithic microliths recovered from Boreal peat at Seamer Carr, North Yorkshire, is described. Despite detailed study it has not been possible to conclude with certainty what these particular flints were used for. It remains a strong possibility that they were once component parts of projectiles.

INTRODUCTION

The purpose of this brief account is to place on record, so far as is possible, the details of finds in 1983 and 1984 of two discrete groups of later Mesolithic microliths from peat at Seamer Carr, North Yorkshire, England. These discoveries were first described and illustrated by the author in a lecture to the Palaeolithic-Mesolithic day meeting held at the University of Sheffield in January 1986. Since then, their formal publication has been postponed pending inclusion within the full publication of the the Seamer Carr excavations of 1977–85 (Schadla-Hall *et al.* in prep). Details of these particular finds have nonetheless entered the literature (e.g. Cloutman 1988b; Myers 1989; Bergman 1993; Barton *et al.* 1995) and the rumour of a preserved Mesolithic 'arrow', the first from the UK, has given rise to rather more optimism than the modest finds and their analysis can actually justify. The invitation to contribute to this volume of papers provides an opportunity to set the record straight.

It is perhaps appropriate, too, that such a contribution, modest though it is, should join others in honouring John Wymer whose own much greater contributions to Mesolithic and later prehistoric studies ought not to be too overshadowed by his stature in Palaeolithic scholarship.

Although this account necessarily focuses down upon a highly particular and very limited set of data, it is of course obvious that the broader study of backed bladelets, and the ramifying implications that can be drawn there from, has had – and will continue to have – great influence on perceptions of hunter-gatherer behaviour. For better or worse, the microlith is still popularly perceived in Britain as 'a diagnostic hallmark of the period' (Wymer 1991, 27), a type-fossil of the Mesolithic, the two terms being as good as synonymous with one another. Whilst outmoded in some quarters, the equation of microliths with hunting is still strong, although only slightly better founded than the more extenuated theoretical superstructures which deal with chronology, social territories, stylistic evolution, gender, social and economic transition and so on. But, despite the endeavours of microwear analysts and experimental archaeologists, the elementary issue of function for such a morphologically diverse grouping of artefacts has not been much illuminated. This surely remains one of the most aggravating areas of ignorance in British prehistory.

Such a subject deserves more space, time and new research than is within the grasp of this author, so it must suffice here firstly just to describe these particular finds from Seamer Carr, and their context, and then to add some concluding comments.

CIRCUMSTANCES OF DISCOVERY

The two groups of microliths were found by chance during the 1983 and 1984 excavation seasons at Site K (TA 034820) at Seamer Carr, near Scarborough, North Yorkshire. Excavations here and at other locations along the edge of the former Late Glacial Lake Pickering, have concentrated on prospecting for and recording early Holocene and Late Glacial lithic scatters (Schadla-Hall 1987a; 1987b). These tend to lie at or near the interface between the mineral substrate and the overlying muds and peats that infilled the lake basin during the early Holocene (Cloutman 1988a). Site K was located by test pits and, on wider excavation (of some 1800m²), was shown to include numerous Late Glacial lithic artefacts, and a hearth. This earlier level was overlain by and intermingled with an extensive aggregation of nucleated scatters of early Holocene lithic material, also associated with hearths and pits (Schadla-Hall 1987a; Schadla-hall *et al.* in prep.). Since later prehistoric lithic and ceramic finds had been made on nearby higher ground, the possibility of stray finds in the higher levels of the peat was not discounted, although removal of these on such a large scale precluded detailed examination.

Indeed, one group of microliths (Group 2) was found in 1984 on a machined peat surface that had been exposed since the previous year and was in use as a general thoroughfare during the excavation, thus becoming very dried out and crumbly. Microliths were first recognised lying about on this surface within an area of approximately 1m². This was then trowelled over and the remainder of the assemblage recovered (locations and plans in archive). Although none of the microliths was recovered *in situ*, it remains a fair assumption that they represent an associated grouping and that they were embedded in the peat at a level approximately 30–45cm from its base (F. Wenban-Smith pers. comm.).

The other group (Group 1) was noticed in 1983 in the edge of a machine trench cut through the peat. The digging of the trench had disturbed the flints, removing an unknown number, leaving several dislodged and four visible still *in situ*. The surviving group occurred over a depth of 10cm, between 42cm and 52cm from the modern root mat, and the flints all pointed slightly downwards. The sediment profile consisted of coarse detritus mud overlying a woody fen peat (containing the flints) below which was a reed-swamp deposit of greenish peat containing *Phragmites* and other species of reeds (Cloutman 1988b, fig. 4b, 28–30; Cloutman pers. comm.).

The possibility that the microliths in Group 1 might be physically linked with traces of organic artefactual material was recognised and therefore it was decided to remove the assemblage and its surrounding peat *en bloc*. Beforehand, samples were taken for pollen analysis at 1cm intervals from 11cm below the present surface to the peat/mineral interface (pollen site K5: Cloutman 1988a, 28–30). The samples were taken from a cleaned section which included the flint assemblage. A 2cm thick sample adjacent to the flints was removed for radiocarbon dating. Aluminium sheeting was then inserted edgeways into the baulk of the trench, from the top and in from the side, to remove a block measuring approximately 30cm x 20cm x 15cm.

Once in the laboratory, the block was X-rayed and the resulting radiographs identified the presence of additional flints. Micro-exavation was then able gently to strip away the peaty matrix and expose a total of nine flints *in situ* (Figs 26.1, 26.2). They lay seemingly not at random, but (with the exception of an outlier) in two somewhat irregular and contorted alignments. At least some appeared to be placed in opposing pairs with their retouched edges tending to be aligned against decayed fragments of wood. Whilst the latter might indeed be the remains of some sort of original support for the flints, such evidence is highly tentative. The wood fragments were too small and degraded to provide evidence of deliberate modification and the flints themselves were not observed to be inset in any way, nor were traces of adhering organic matter observed (see below).

The better preserved fragment of wood (9cm x 1.5cm max.) was identified as of either *Populus* sp (poplar) or *Salix* sp (willow) (J. Watson pers. comm.). As such it was different from other woody components of the peat which were mostly *Corylus* sp (hazel). Apart from a slice still preserved on a microscope slide, the remainder of the piece was submitted for radiocarbon dating. The resulting determination (Walker & Otlet 1988), based on assay of only 11mg of carbon (Walker pers. comm.), provides a calibrated (Pearson *et al.* 1993; two sigma) result of 7540–6670 cal BC (HAR-6498; 8210±150 BP). This compares with a determination from the peat sample at the same level of 7260–6600 cal BC (HAR-5789; 8020±90 BP). These dates are statistically indistinguishable (Ward & Wilson 1978) and are also consistent with pollen evidence which indicates a Boreal vegetational assemblage (Godwin Zone VI).

The palaeobotanical evidence suggests that the flint assemblage lay in rich fen, fringing land dominated by hazel (Cloutman 1988a, fig 4b; pers. comm.). The flints lay broadly within the pollen assemblage phase A (*ibid.*), although the interpretation of this phase states that there is no good evidence for human interference with the vegetation cover at this time. The most common local trees were probably birch and pine, with willow occupying wetter areas. Elm and oak on the dryer ground may have completed the woodland flora. Higher in the pollen profile (phase B, a little after *c.* 7000 cal BC) there is evidence for a drier bog surface, and the presence of *Rumex* and Chenopodiaceae pollen and *Pteridium* spores is suggestive of disturbance by human or animal agency. Cloutman notes the possibility that, if the flints were contemporary with this disturbance, then (if they were part of a composite instrument) they might might have been thrust into the slightly older deposits.

In terms of raw material, the microliths of Group 2 are indistinguishable from those of Group 1. Typologically, though, the contrast between them is very marked: in Group 2 the predominant type is the 'micro-scalene triangle', 15 of which may be so described; one is too fragmentary to classify; and the last is a straight-backed lanceolate piece (Fig. 26.3).

MICROSCOPIC ANALYSIS (EMILY MOSS)

All the microliths from Groups 1 and 2 were examined by Emily Moss for microscopic traces of wear. She reported (pers. comm. January 1986) as follows:

The condition of all of the microliths is extremely fresh macroscopically and microscopically. A soil sample taken from the upper peat (5005) had a pH value of 1.5. The acidity of the soil seems to have had no visible effect on the flint surface at magnifications of up to 560x.

Of the 34 flints, nine have no microscopic traces at all. All of the others have traces which are so weakly developed that it was impossible to say whether they are the result of use, handling, or, less likely, trampling. There are no macroscopic or microscopic impact fractures, which usually signal projectile use.

The traces can be divided into several types:

Micro-rounding: 7 cases, any of which could have resulted from manufacture or from use.
Linear markings, parallel or perpendicular to the edge: 16 cases, one of them associated with micro-rounding and four with minor surface abrasion. None of the linear markings are well developed.
General surface abrasion: 2 pieces have minor surface abrasion in the form of weakly developed polish and striations.
Localised polish and striations: 2 pieces have lightly developed polish and striations at the tip and on both dorsal and ventral surfaces, possibly indicative of a drilling motion.

The ambiguity of the traces is due to the small size of the artefacts. Manufacturing traces can be more highly developed on microliths than on larger tools because more of the surface area is handled and there is more pressure applied per unit of surface area during retouch. In addition, it is likely that the microliths were braced against a hard material to hold them steady during retouching. Use wear traces tend to be less highly developed on small objects than on larger ones because the amount of pressure applied per edge area during work tends to be less (drills being an exception). Experimentally, microlithic points used as arrow tips tend to sustain impact traces which are much more lightly developed than those on heavier, larger arrowheads. The distribution of the traces on the microliths from Seamer Carr is like that on the backed bladelets from Pincevent (Moss 1983, ch. 7) and also like that on bladelets from Oldholtwolde (Moss 1988), but the Seamer

Carr traces are not so well developed. Significantly they do not seem to be random, as from trampling, but they tend to be either horizontal or vertical to the long axis of the tool. They could be use wear traces, but manufacturing traces cannot be ruled out. One of the microliths with localised traces (Group 1, no 12) has a point which is particularly suitable for small-scale drilling, as to make an eye in a bone needle. The polish and striations correspond well with this function, but they are not well enough developed for firm conclusions to be drawn.

The microliths from the peat block (832976) do not have any linear markings, only general abrasion (two pieces) and micro-rounding (three pieces).

For the reasons stated, microliths may be particularly prone to have ambiguous traces. There are also several conditions in which flint tools may be used without sustaining wear traces (Moss 1988). The 34 microltihs do not display definite use wear traces, but they may have been used.

ORGANIC RESIDUE ANALYSIS

In a further attempt to derive clues about these finds, the flints from both groups were submitted to John Evans (Department of Environmental Sciences, University of East London) for organic residue analysis. Although no adhering matter had been detectable during the preceding microscopic examinations it was nonetheless felt that such analysis might indicate traces, at the molecular level, of surviving organic residues such as mastics or poisons.

Each flint was tested, initially by using infrared spectroscopy. Only one positive result was obtained, from a scalene triangle in Group 2, the infrared spectra suggesting the presence of a complex mixture of wax and resin. Differential infrared studies strongly indicated the wax to be beeswax and the resin to be of *Pinus* origin. Further analysis using gas chromatographic (GC) techniques supported this conclusion. The same microlith also gave traces of protein but the levels were too low for identification. However, high performance liquid chromatography (HPLC) revealed traces of glutamic acid and glycine – although these two acids, being very common in proteins, are consequently undiagnostic.

DISCUSSION

Balancing assumption and inference with the factual record, these findings can be baldly summed up as follows: two separate groups of late Mesolithic microliths, one predominantly of scalene shapes, the other predominantly of rod shapes, were found in Boreal peat at Seamer Carr. No other contemporary lithic artefacts were present with them. Only one group was found partially *in situ*: highly degraded wood fragments of poplar or willow lay adjacent to some of the microliths but there is no secure evidence, save their suggestive arrangement, of any functional association between the two materials. Microscopic analysis and organic residue analysis of the microliths of both groups was inconclusive.

Despite such meagre direct evidence, the spatial isolation of the two groups, their similar raw material and their separate typological integrities, suggest strongly that these finds represent the loss either of two or more composite tools, or the loss or deposition of caches of microliths, with or without an organic component.

To take speculation any further seems inevitably to devolve discussion towards the case for microliths as components of hunting gear — a time-worn area explored by countless previous authors and which this one has no space (or wish) to rehearse in any detail. As for so many other archaeological constructs, perception of microlith function has fluctuated. The dominant theme has always been an equation between the Mesolithic, microliths and hunting, expressed in its most direct form, for instance, when the period ('epipalaeolithic') is described as that of the Bowmen (Rozoy 1989). Another extreme is the forceful proposition from David Clarke (1976) that microliths may have had a role in the processing of vegetable foods. There are other theories.

The poverty of direct evidence for microliths as hunting gear from the British Isles contrasts vividly with abundant instances from the European mainland (e.g. Clark 1975; Fischer 1989). From a British perspective it is no wonder then that every scrap of evidence is marshalled, however slight (e.g. Myers 1989). Much of recent conjecture is fuelled by experimentation and analysis of impact damage and micro-traces on microliths. As a result of this, opinions are now more open-minded, sticking firmly both to the certainty that at least some microlith types were used in composite hunting weapons, and acknowledging also the clear possibility of a much wider range of functions relating to craft activities, such as drilling, and food processing (e.g. Dumont 1987; Mithen & Finlayson 1991; Grace 1992; Mithen 1994; Finlayson & Mithen 1997).

The Seamer microliths, for want of any sustainable evidence to the contrary, were considered in terms of their possible use as components of arrows. Experimental reconstructions (e.g. Fig. 26.4) by Chris Bergman confirm that triangular and rod microliths can be mounted on wooden shafts and function effectively as arrows. Triangular microliths can be positioned to serve as barbs, and rod microliths can serve either as points or, when set laterally, as barbs or cutting edges. It may be worth noting that microliths can be attached securely to a shaft without being inset within grooves (but excessive resin can cause drag); also, a sharpened wooden tip to the shaft (fire hardened if necessary) is often as capable of penetration as a flint-tipped point. Such observations tally well with traditional expectations, and the possibility that some form of hunting projectiles are represented cannot easily be dismissed. The Seamer microliths do not exhibit the type of edge damage observed on the flints used on the experi-

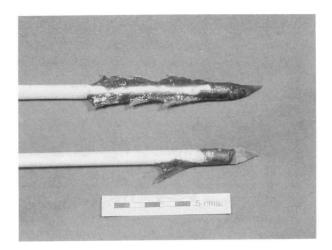

Figure 26.4. Reconstruction of arrowhead (made by Chrisptopher Bergman), illustrating possible use of scalene triangular microliths. The mastic is made of pine resin mixed with beeswax.

mental arrows shot into a target, and it is of course possible that they represent a 'miss' or hunting loss. A problem which was not tested experimentally was the reproduction and use of a full set of 16 or 17 microliths on a single shaft (as speculatively reconstructed in Figures 26.5 and 26.6). It is not clear how such combinations would affect the draw of the bow, or the balance and aerodynamics of an arrow.

It may or may not be justifiable to hang so much interpretational endeavour on these diminutive flints, ubiquitous, perhaps, merely because of their indestructible material. However, given the lack of adequate organic preservation on British sites, the focus on microliths is unlikely to diminish. One may hope that chance finds of relevant artefacts or artefact assemblages lying, as many of them must, in isolated and at arbitrary locations in the landscape, will continue to be made. The discoveries at Seamer illustrate that such finds, isolated and imperfectly preserved though these ones were, nevertheless offer analytical potential. As such finds rely substantially on the quirks of survival and chance observation, research must also continue to be directed to the location and excavation of sites where organic preservation can allow a view of the entire material record.

ACKNOWLEDGEMENTS

Tim Schadla-Hall directed the Seamer Carr Project and I am grateful for his permission to write about these findings in advance of the full publication of twenty years research in the Vale of Pickering. In addition, many other people have been involved in the recovery and examination of these particular flints. The sharp eyes of Paul Lane picked out the microliths of Group 1, whilst Francis Wenban-

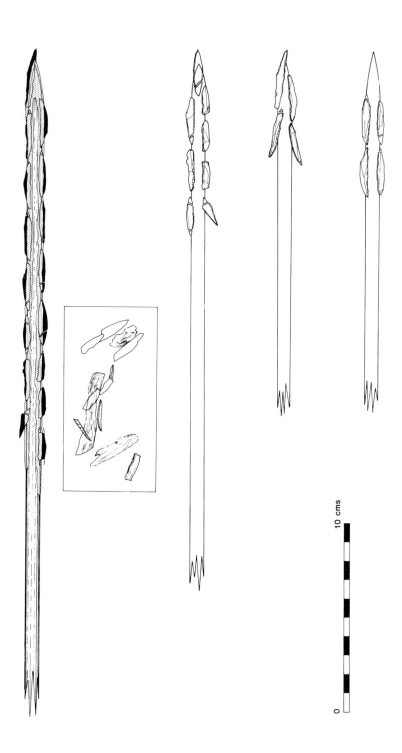

Figure 26.5. Possible reconstructions of Group 1 microliths if interpreted as an arrow or harpoon

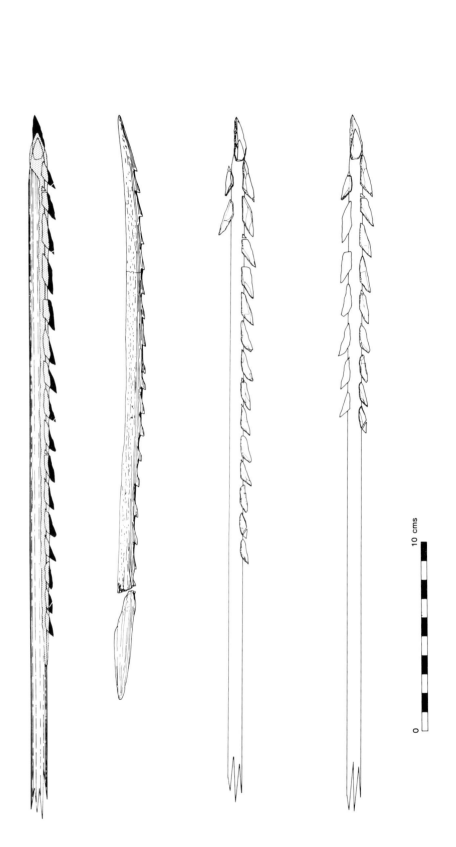

Figure 26.6. Possible reconstruction of Group 2 microliths if interpreted as an arrow or harpoon, compared with an early Mesolithic antler point from Star Carr (Clark 1954: fig 51, P11)

Smith spotted Group 2 which was recovered and recorded by Peter Cardwell. Edward Cloutman took samples at the Group 1 findspot, was responsible for the subsequent pollen analysis, and later made his field notes available. The radiocarbon dates were provided by Jill Walker, then at AERE Harwell. The removal of the peat block was Jacqui Watson's idea and it was she who undertook the X-radiography, subsequent excavation, and wood identification. Emily Moss found time amongst her other research to make the microscopic examinations of the microliths and John Evans kindly undertook analysis for traces of organic remains. Christopher Bergman was a special source of inspiration and ingenuity regarding archery and made experimental reconstructions of arrow shafts armed with microliths. All these individuals deserve thanks, as do the Mesolithic specialists, archer-antiquaries and others with whom it has been possible to share discussion of these finds over the last fourteen years.

REFERENCES

Barton, R. N. E., Berridge, P. J., Walker, M. J. C. & Bevins, R. E. 1995. Persistent places in the Mesolithic landscape: an example from the Black Mountain uplands of south Wales. *Proceedings of the Prehistoric Society* 61, 81–116.

Bergman, C. 1993. The development of the bow in western Europe: a technological and functional perspective. In G. L. Peterkin, H. M. Bricker & P. Mellars (eds), *Hunting and Animal Exploitation in the Later Palaeolithic and Mesolithic of Eurasia,* 95–105. Washington: Archaeological Papers of the American Anthropological Association 4.

Clark, J. G. D. 1954. *Excavations at Star Carr, an Early Mesolithic site at Seamer near Scarborough, Yorkshire.* Cambridge: Cambridge University Press.

Clark, J. G. D. 1975. *The Earlier Stone Age Settlement of Scandinavia.* Cambridge: Cambridge University Press.

Clarke, D. 1976. Mesolithic Europe: the economic basis. In G. de G. Sieveking (ed.), *Problems in Economic and Social Anthropology,* 449–81. London: Duckworth.

Cloutman, E. 1988a. Palaeoenvironments in the Vale of Pickering. Part I: stratigraphy and palaeogeography of Seamer Carr, Star Carr and Flixton Carr. *Proceedings of the Prehistoric Society* 54, 1–20.

Cloutman, E. 1988b. Palaeoenvironments in the Vale of Pickering. Part 2: environmental history at Seamer Carr. *Proceedings of the Prehistoric Society* 54, 21–36.

Dumont, J. 1987. Mesolithic microwear research in northwest Europe. In P. Rowley-Conwy, M. Zvelebil, & H. P. Blankholm (eds), *Mesolithic Northwest Europe: Recent Trends,* 46–54. Sheffield: Department of Archaeology and Prehistory, University of Sheffield.

Finlayson, B. & Mithen, S. 1997. The microwear and morphology of microliths from Gleann Mor. In H. Knecht (ed.), *Projectile Technology,* 107–29. New York: Plenum.

Fischer, A. 1989. Hunting with flint tipped arrows: results and experiences from practical experiments. In C. Bonsall (ed.), *The Mesolithic In Europe,* 29–39. Edinburgh: John Donald.

Grace, R. 1992. Use wear analysis. In F. Healy, M. Heaton & S. Lobb, Excavations of a Mesolithic site at Thatcham, Berkshire. *Proceedings of the Prehistoric Society* 58, 53–63.

Henson, D. 1985. The flint resources of Yorkshire and the east Midlands. *Lithics* 6, 2–9.

Mithen, S. J. 1994. The Mesolithic Age. In B. Cunliffe (ed.), *The Oxford Illustrated Prehistory of Europe,* 79–135. Oxford: Oxford University Press.

Mithen, S. J. & Finlayson, B. 1991. Red deer hunters on Colonsay? The implications of Staosnaig for the interpretation of the Oronsay middens. *Proceedings of the Prehistoric Society* 57(2), 1–8.

Moss, E. H. 1983. *The Functional Analysis of Flint Implements: Pincevent and Pont D'Ambon: Two Case Studies from the French Final Palaeolithic.* Oxford: British Archaeological Reports, International Series 177.

Moss, E. H. 1988, Techno-functional studies of the Hamburgian from Oldeholtwolde, Friesland, the Netherlands. In M. Otte (ed.), *De la Loire à l'Oder: Les Civilisations du Paléolithique Final dans le Nord-ouest Européen,* 399–426. Oxford: British Archaeological Reports, International Series 444.

Myers, A. 1989. Reliable and maintainable technological strategies in the Mesolithic of mainland Britain. In R. Torrence (ed.), *Time, Energy and Stone Tools,* 78–91. Cambridge: New Directions In Archaeology Series, Cambridge University Press.

Pearson, G. W., Becker, B. B. & Qua, F. 1993. High precision ^{14}C measurement of German and Irish oaks to show the natural ^{14}C variations from 7890 to 5000 BC. *Radiocarbon* 35(1), 93–104.

Rozoy, J-G. 1989. The revolution of the Bowmen in Europe. In C. Bonsall (ed.), *The Mesolithic In Europe.* Edinburgh: John Donald.

Schadla-Hall, R. T. 1987a. Recent investigations of the early Mesolithic landscape and settlement in the Vale of Pickering, North Yorkshire. In P. Rowley-Conwy, M. Zvelebil & H. P. Blankholm (eds), *Mesolithic Northwest Europe: Recent Trends,* 46–54. Sheffield: Department of Archaeology and Prehistory, University of Sheffield.

Schadla-Hall, R. T. 1987b. Early man in the eastern Vale of Pickering. In S. Ellis (ed.), *East Yorkshire Field Guide,* 22–30. Cambridge: Quaternary Research Association.

Schadla-Hall, T. *et al.* (in prep.), Star Carr in Context: archaeological and environmental investigations in the Vale of Pickering (North Yorkshire) 1976–1996.

Walker, A. J., & Otlet, R. L. 1988. Harwell radiocarbon measurements VI, *Radiocarbon* 30, 297–317.

Ward, G. K., & Wilson, S. R. 1978. Procedures for comparing and combining radiocarbon age determinations: a critique. *Archaeometry* 20, 19–31.

Wymer, J. 1991. *Mesolithic Britain.* Princes Risborough: Shire Publications Ltd.

27. Mesolithic Sites at Two Mile Bottom, near Thetford, Norfolk

Peter Robins

ABSTRACT

The history of earlier surface collections of Later Mesolithic material from Two Mile Bottom and its environs is surveyed. Preliminary results from recent excavations, which have yielded undisturbed Later Mesolithic industries, are presented and discussed.

THE LOCATION OF TWO MILE BOTTOM

Downstream of Thetford, the Little Ouse River flows on a northerly course for about 4km before turning westwards towards Brandon. Ordnance Survey maps show Two Mile Bottom as located on the north bank of the river, after its westerly turn, lying between the river and the railway line from Thetford to Brandon, which runs parallel to the river in this area. It is clear from the archaeological literature, however, that the term 'Two Mile Bottom' has been applied to a much more extensive area, more than 3km in length, between the railway line and the river, and extending from St Helen's Well in the west to Chisley Vale in the south, including a factory site, often referred to as the 'Two Mile Bottom Works'. Figure 27.1 shows the relationship between these named sites and also the locations of archaeological sites and findspots relevant to the following discussion. These latter are indicated by the Norfolk Sites and Monuments Record numbers (SMR).

The development of the factory site up to the present day is also relevant to the present paper: the initial factory, 'Fison's Vitriol and Manure Works' (SMR 6531), was located close to the river bank and was served by a railway spur from the main line; the construction of this spur revealed the presence of a Roman pottery kiln (5730; Frere & Clarke 1942). Subsequent changes of use and expansion of the site for the production of building blocks resulted in the dumping of large quantities of inorganic waste on the area immediately to the north of the factory site. Most recently, redevelopment of the site for the installation of a power station, involving expansion into the dump area, has resulted in an archaeological evaluation and subsequent excavation of the land surface formerly covered by the dump.

EARLY WORK BY F. N. HAWARD AND H. DIXON HEWITT

The prehistoric archaeological potential of the area was first given prominence by F. N. Haward in his publication 'A workshop site of primitive culture at Two-Mile-Bottom, Thetford' in the initial volume of the recently formed Prehistoric Society of East Anglia (Haward 1914). Haward describes his collecting on this site as follows: 'In 1904, the site (which is of sandy loam) was ploughed up for the first time for many years and for some six years I searched it three or four times a year, which resulted in the discovery, *in a very small area*, [my italics] of a very complete and interesting series of small worked flint implements'. Haward recognised, *inter alia*, the presence of blades and blade cores, together with 'small pointed implements' (straight backed microliths or rods) and 'arrow tips' (obliquely backed microliths), which were illustrated in

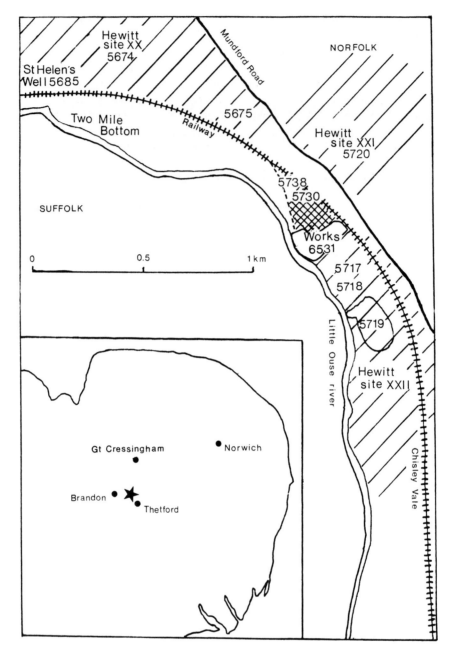

Figure 27.1. Location of sites in the Two Mile Bottom area. Hatching shows the probable extent of Hewitt's 'Sites'. Cross hatching shows the area recently under investigation.

his paper and subsequently redrawn for illustration by J.G.D. Clark in *The Mesolithic Age in Britain* (1932). Haward appears to have continued collecting on the site after the appearance of his publication and was joined in 1912 by H. Dixon Hewitt, who designated the area Site XXII. However it is clear from his notebooks and artefact labels that Hewitt was collecting over a wide area, from the southern edge of the factory site down to Chisley Vale (Fig. 27.1), and that the term 'Site' referred to an extensive area which at that time was either breck or ploughland. Hewitt was, however, aware of the more restricted area (SMR 5719) from which Haward had collected his pub-

lished material, and Norwich Castle Museum possesses three photographs, taken by Hewitt in 1934, on which the 'main site' is indicated. Hewitt also collected extensively to the north of the factory site, in areas shown on Figure 27.1, which he designated Sites XX (5674) and XXI (5720). His Site XX is defined in his own words as 'that part of the parish (of Thetford St Peter) next the Santon boundary: it is bounded by the main Mundford-Thetford road, the aforesaid Santon boundary bank, the Great Eastern Railway and a short imaginary line drawn from the G.E.R. [Great Eastern Railway] to the main road through the keeper's lodge beyond Two Mile Bottom'. It is nevertheless clear from labels that some Site XX artefacts came from well to the west of this defined area. Hewitt also collected from an area to the east and north of the main Mundford-Thetford road (his Site XXI; Hewitt 1915), but neither of these collections contains any diagnostic components that could be assigned to the Mesolithic except for a few items from the vicinity of St Helen's Well (5685), to which Hewitt refers as Sub-Site XX* 'owing to peculiarities of the implements found there'. There is no evidence that either Haward or Hewitt collected from the area bounded by the railway and the river, north of the factory site, which is the original Two Mile Bottom of the OS maps.

Most of Hewitt's collection from Site XXII was transferred to Haward in 1922, and the combined collections have become dispersed among several museums, with main concentrations at the University Museum of Archaeology and Ethnology, Cambridge and the Castle Museum, Norwich and lesser amounts in Birmingham and the British Museum (Wymer 1977). No general description of these later collections has ever been published, but Jacobi (1984) has classified 79 and illustrated 50 microliths from the Norwich and Cambridge collections, including several of those illustrated by Haward (1914) and Clark (1932). Jacobi firmly assigns the microliths to the Later Mesolithic. He also notes that the collections contain many artefacts that could be Neolithic but which could not logically be separated from those which may be associated with the microliths. Hewitt collected small quantities of Neolithic pottery (e.g. Healy 1984, fig. 5.5:P35, fig. 5.9:P44, both from Hewitt's site XX).

MORE RECENT WORK IN THE TWO MILE BOTTOM AREA

Since the Haward/Hewitt era other collectors have worked in the general area and entries in the Sites and Monuments Record show that, as well as Roman and later artefacts, prehistoric flintwork, together with sparse prehistoric pottery and metalwork finds, confirm use of the neighbourhood from the Mesolithic to the Iron Age. Mesolithic finds are generally confined to the immediate vicinity of the river, with records from St Helen's Well (5685), R.R. Clarke's site (5738), A.T. Phoenix's site (5718), H. Tyrell Green's site (5675) and T.R. English's site (5717). Clarke's small collection includes a single, rather thick, lanceolate point as the only microlith: Tyrell Green's collection is not described in detail in the SMR and is not available for study. As can be seen from Figure 27.1, these two last are closest to the recent excavation site.

Elsewhere on Hewitt's Sites XX and XXI collections have been made by, *inter alios*, W.G. Clarke, J. and V. Lord, E. Rogers and D. G. Woollestone, but again no artefacts that can confidently be assigned to the Mesolithic are included.

Haward's original 'main site' (5719), part of which is now occupied by an Anglia Water installation, has been

the subject of a brief test pitting evaluation by Wymer (1986) and a slightly more extensive examination, included a gridded surface collection and excavation of an interrupted trench on the river bank (Wymer 1988). The surface collection yielded indications of Mesolithic occupation in the form of two broken microliths, but the trench failed to find any related land surface and only revealed modern disturbance.

Whilst most of the area covered by Figure 27.1 is now part of Thetford Forest and is under plantation, a small area of land to the northwest of the factory site and its waste dump is still open meadow and may well have been disturbed only by former ploughing. This land slopes gently from the northeast to the river bank: the latter may well have been disturbed by dredging. Expectations of a similar relatively undisturbed land surface beneath the factory dump site led the Norfolk Archaeological Unit (NAU) to undertake an evaluation in 1995 (directed by Trevor Ashwin) prior to redevelopment. This evaluation required the removal of 2m or more of modern overburden in a series of trenches totalling some 300m in length. Because of safety restraints only a small total area of basal deposits could be exposed for examination. Despite some deep modern disturbances, the trenches confirmed the presence of much undisturbed land surface from which Romano-British sherds and worked flints were recovered: a few undated features, cut into the natural sand, were also encountered. The worked flint, mainly knapping debitage, included one broken microlith fragment and evidence of an industry based on small blade production.

Following the evaluation, NAU mounted a larger scale excavation under the direction of Sarah Bates, involving the removal of overburden from two large areas previously sampled by the evaluation trenches, and totalling approximately 2800m². A full report on these excavations, which exposed Romano-British pottery kilns as well as the Later Mesolithic occupation to be described below, is in preparation.

Mesolithic features

In a concentrated area of about 40m² at the extreme southeastern edge of the excavation site, close to the boundary fence of the existing factory, stripping of overburden and topsoil revealed a group of rather irregular and indistinct patches of a marginally darker colour than the fine yellow stone-free sand that formed the natural subsoil: this latter is probably of aeolian origin and when dry is extremely loose and friable. These patches clearly contained quantities of worked flint, and on excavation three proved to be the fills of shallow, irregular hollows, while the rest were shown to be disconnected areas of a thin layer. Of the hollows, one (Feature 108) contained a large assemblage of Mesolithic flintwork while the other two (Features 311 and 499) yielded smaller groups of clearly Mesolithic artefacts.

Feature 108. 108 proved to be an irregular oval hollow with gently sloping sides, measuring 3.0 by 1.5m and with a surviving depth of 0.20m. It has been suggested that it may be a tree-throw hollow. Hand excavation and sieving of the contents yielded 4554 worked flints, together with 149 shatter pieces, a number of small burnt fragments of flint and a central mass of larger burnt flints, some of more than 100mm in maximum dimension, which is interpreted as a central hearth. No organic remains or traces of internal features were found, which is unsurprising given the loose and friable nature of the natural sand; samples of the fill of the hollow and of the deposit surrounding the presumed hearth have been assessed (Fryer & Murphy 1997), but plant macrofossils were extremely rare, apart from hazelnut shells and heavily charred material. A single indeterminate cereal grain was probably a contaminant from overlying Roman deposits.

The Industry from 108. Table 27.1 summarises the categories of artefacts recovered from 108: it is noteworthy that almost two-thirds are spalls and microblades of less than 20mm maximum dimension, indicating the primary nature of the deposit and suggesting that it was a working hollow. This assemblage represents 73% of the total of flint artefacts found in the entire excavation area.

None of the 16 microliths is complete; the predominating type is a narrow, straight-backed form seldom exceeding 3mm in width (Fig. 27.2:1–12) with a single scalene triangle (Fig. 27.2:13). The few other classifiable artefacts include a notched blade (Fig. 27.2:30), a serrated blade (Fig. 27.2:28), a possible borer and four burins. Of these last, one is a dihedral burin prepared on a crested flake (Fig. 27.2:31) while the other three are of the 'core-burin' type (one being made on a core tablet, Fig. 27.2:29) which can be considered alternatively as micro-blade cores on thick flakes, a function that is credible in an industry that appears to concentrate on the production of micro-blades and the use of them as blanks for the production of very small microliths. Apart from these formal tools the assemblage includes 221 miscellaneous retouched or utilised pieces on which the retouch is usually extremely fine and where wear is manifested only as a visible loss of sharpness on the blade or flake edge. In view of the apparently undisturbed nature of the fill of 108, it seems likely that such wear is due to the casual use of unmodified flakes prior to their discard. A striking absence from the assemblage is the scraper. None was found in any of the Mesolithic features, while in the total of worked flint from the whole area of excavation (*c.* 6000 pieces) only one poorly characterised end scraper was recognised, in a derived context and remote from the area of Mesolithic activity. The predominant raw material of the industry was a greyish-black nodular flint with a thick white or greyish white cortex, of a similar type to that mined at a later date from the nearby Grime's Graves. However, some of the raw material was clearly frost-damaged and therefore probably surface-collected: the presence of many shatter

			Features			
	108	**139**	**311**	**313**	**345**	**499**
Microliths	16	1	5	1	1	7
Burins	1					1
Serrated flakes	1					
Borers	1					
Notched pieces	1					
Misc. retouched/utilised	227			2		28
Cores	22			3		2
'Core burins'	3					
Core fragments & trimmings	50			7		2
Blades	215			41		69
Flakes	1029	2	22	281		110
Spalls & microblades	2988		14	222		200
TOTALS	4554	3	41	557	1	419

Table 27.1. Features containing microliths

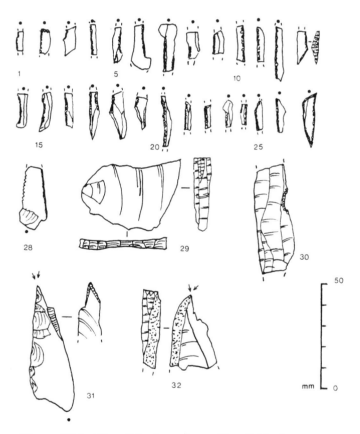

Figure 27.2. Microliths from Later Mesolithic features: Feature 108: 1–13; Feature 499: 14–19; Feature 311: 20–24; Layer 313: 25. Microliths from derived contexts: 26, 27. Other artefacts: Feature 108, serrated blade: 28, 'core burin' on core tablet: 29, notched blade: 30, dihedral burin: 31; Feature 499, dihedral burin: 32.

pieces and of fractured core fragments attests to its rather fragile nature. Among the intact cores, small single-platform pyramidal forms predominate (*c.*50% of all cores), while core tablets, crested flakes and core face and edge rejuvenating flakes are all present among the core trimmings.

Feature 499. Situated less than a metre to the northwest of Feature 108, Feature 499 was another, but smaller, shallow depression, the fill of which contained only 341 pieces of worked flint and 7 shatter pieces; this assemblage included six microliths and a burin – none of the microliths was complete but the group proved to be different in character from that in 108. While three of the microliths can be classified as straight-backed (Fig. 27.2:14–16) a fourth, also straight-backed, has additional retouch on the leading edge (Fig. 27.2:17). The point of the last is broken, but it closely resembles that illustrated by Jacobi (1984, Fig. 4.7:39) from the Haward/Hewitt site. Two further incomplete microliths (Fig 27.2:18,19) are small obliquely-backed points of the type common there (Jacobi 1984, fig. 4.7, table 4.3). The burin is dihedral, made on a flake fragment (Fig. 27.2:32).

Feature 311. Feature 311 was a further shallow, ill-defined hollow a little to the north of Feature 499. Its fill yielded only 41 pieces of worked flint, of which five were incomplete microliths, four being straight-backed bladelet segments (Fig. 27.2:20–23), while the fifth was the distal tip of a bladelet with backing along one edge and on part of the other (Fig. 27.2:24). The presence of several sherds in this fill is indicative of disturbance.

Layer 313. Approximately 5m north of Feature 108 a thin diffuse layer with evidence of worked flint was sampled: although no definable feature was encountered, the 557 worked flints recovered included one microlith, an incomplete scalene triangle (Fig. 27.2:25). The assemblage also included blades, blade cores and core trimmings.

Microliths from Other Contexts. Two further microliths were recovered from derived contexts not far from the main concentration of Mesolithic features. Figure 27.2:26 is a fragment of a straight-backed microlith with a trace of retouch on the opposing edge from the fill of a Romano-British pottery kiln, while Figure 27.2:27 is a lanceolate point from an undated posthole. This latter microlith is paralleled by examples from the Haward/Hewitt site illustrated by Jacobi (1984, fig. 4.7) and by unpublished examples from Clarke's site (5738) and Phoenix's site (5718).

seem to belong to the same industrial tradition, with the production of narrow, straight-backed microliths as a main objective. The virtual absence of any other tool type in the assemblages perhaps suggests a short-term occupation with a narrow non-domestic focus, such as a hunting party renewing its armaments. Feature 108, with its central hearth, might suggest a 'living hollow', though the high concentration of sharp flint debitage would preclude it being a comfortable one; a better interpretation might be a 'cold weather working hollow'.

Within the microlith group from Feature 108 are two examples (Fig. 27.2:6 and 7) of unfinished straight-backed microliths which have a club-shaped remnant of the bladelet blank attached at one end, perhaps a 'handle' to assist in holding the microlith during the backing operation. The presence of these, and the complete absence of microburins from the two assemblages, suggest that straight-backed microliths were prepared directly from complete bladelets. A further example of a microlith with a 'handle' is in the Hewitt collection at the University Museum in Cambridge, and is labelled as coming from a 'sandpit at the extreme north end of Site XXII', i.e. separated from the present excavation only by the modern factory site. I am indebted to Dr Jacobi for supplying information and a drawing of this artefact and two other associated straight-backed microliths.

The specialisation in Features 108 and 311 towards production of straight-backed microliths is paralleled at the Hampshire site of Oakhanger III. This site has been described only briefly by Rankine (1952), but was noted as unique among the Oakhanger group for its concentration on the exclusive production of rod-like microliths, of which more than fifty were recorded. In contrast to the present assemblages, however, it also comprised larger tool types, including 'gravers, *scrapers* [my italics] and saws'. I am again indebted to Dr Jacobi for supplying drawings of a number of the Oakhanger III microliths, now in the British Museum, which clearly show the close resemblance to those from Features 108 and 311. A separation can be made, on typological grounds, between the concentration on production of narrow straight-backed microliths in Features 108 and 311, and perhaps at another putative site just to the south of the factory site, and the more mixed, but predominantly small, obliquely-backed types from the Haward/Hewitt site farther to the south, for which Feature 499 serves as an excavated example to the north of the factory site. In the absence of any stratigraphic evidence or datable material, there is no certainty that any temporal succession can be deduced from these typological differences, and the possibility remains that a specialist end-user demand is responsible for the concentration of production on a single microlith form.

ASSOCIATIONS AND CONCLUSIONS

Based on the microliths alone, as the main developed class of artefact in the assemblages, Features 108 and 311 would

ACKNOWLEDGEMENTS

Thanks are due to the Principal Field Archaeologist, Brian Ayers, and the Project Director, Sarah Bates, of the

Norfolk Archaeological Unit, for making available records and artefacts prior to the more general publication of the excavation results, and to Roger Jacobi for helpful discussion. Sarah Bates, who excavated the Mesolithic features with the author, also assisted in the sorting and classification of the artefacts. The latter, after further study, will be deposited in the Castle Museum, Norwich.

REFERENCES

Clark, J.G.D. 1932. *The Mesolithic Age in Britain*. Cambridge: Cambridge University Press.

Frere, S. & Clarke, R. 1942. The Romano-British village at Needham, Norfolk. *Norfolk Archaeology* 28, 213–5

Fryer, V. & Murphy, P. 1997. *Charred Plant Macrofossils and Other Remains from Two Mile Bottom, Thetford, Norfolk (5738 THD): an Assessment*. Report to the Norfolk Archaeological Unit.

Haward, F.N. 1914. A workshop of primitive culture at Two-Mile-Bottom. *Proceedings of the Prehistoric Society of East Anglia* 1, 461–67.

Healy, F. 1984. Farming and field monuments: the Neolithic in Norfolk. In C. Barringer (ed.), *Aspects of East Anglian Pre-history (Twenty Years after Rainbird Clarke)*, 77–140. Norwich: Geo Books.

Hewitt, H.D. 1915. A Neolithic site near Thetford. *Proceedings of the Prehistoric Society of East Anglia* 2, 42–45.

Jacobi, R. 1984. The Mesolithic of northern East Anglia and contemporary territories. In C. Barringer (ed.), *Aspects of East Anglian Pre-History (Twenty Years after Rainbird Clarke)*, 43–76. Norwich: Geo Books.

Rankine, W.F. 1952. A Mesolithic chipping floor at the Warren, Oakhanger, Selborne, Hants. *Proceedings of the Prehistoric Society* 18, 21–35.

Wymer, J.J. 1977. *Gazetteer of Mesolithic Sites in England and Wales*. London: Council for British Archaeology Research Report 20.

Wymer, J.J. 1986. Untitled internal report to the Norfolk Archaeological Unit. SMR 5719/c2.

Wymer, J.J. 1988. Untitled internal report to the Norfolk Archaeological Unit. SMR 5719/c3-c5.

28. Studying the Mesolithic Period in Scotland: A Bibliographic Gazetteer

Alan Saville

ABSTRACT

After an introductory section concerning the omission of Scotland from the Council for British Archaeology's 1977 Mesolithic Gazetteer, and reflections on some of the problems and potential of studying the artefact record of the Mesolithic period in Scotland, this paper provides a regional index to the bibliographic sources.

INTRODUCTION

One of John Wymer's less well-known roles, undeservedly so, was as Honorary Secretary in the late 1960s and early 1970s of the Mesolithic Sub-Committee of the Council for British Archaeology's former Palaeolithic and Mesolithic Research Committee. From this resulted the considerable achievement of the edited volume *Gazetteer of Mesolithic Sites in England and Wales* (Wymer 1977a).

Coverage of Ireland and Scotland was omitted from the *Mesolithic Gazetteer*. With characteristic generosity, John noted in the publication that the inclusion of both countries had simply 'not been possible' (Wymer 1977a, vii). In fact there were specific grounds for omitting Ireland. Eire was excluded because some senior Irish prehistorians persisted in the view – common in the 1950s (Evans & Jope 1952, 75; Raftery 1951, 59) and still reflected in the 1970s (Herity & Eogan 1977) – that there was little or no definite evidence for Mesolithic occupation. The error of this view was shortly to become obvious (Ryan 1980; Woodman 1989a), but at the time the Sub-Committee began its work, it was sufficiently entrenched to create organizational difficulties. As for Northern Ireland, it emerged (CBA 1970, 28) that survey work on the Mesolithic period was already under way locally as postgraduate research, and the resulting publication of the thesis did indeed include a gazetteer (Woodman 1978).

The case with Scotland was different, however, since the original and continuing plan of the Sub-Committee was that the Scottish material should be included, and its non-appearance in the volume represents the only significant shortcoming of the project.

What exactly went wrong? It is not possible to pinpoint any single cause. The local organizer for Scotland was the late R.B.K. Stevenson, Keeper at the National Museum of Antiquities in Edinburgh. He did receive batches of the specially produced index cards from the CBA in London, and he duly circulated them to other museums and to individuals. The Minutes of the meeting of the Mesolithic Sub-Committee on 16 April 1970 record that 'Mr Stevenson has circulated cards to most of the people actively engaged in work connected with the Survey'. Some 26 completed cards are in the National Museums of Scotland (NMS) and correspondence on file suggests that others may have been finished, but these were either not returned or are otherwise not now traceable.

Of the 26 cards available, five relate to artefacts in Dundee Museum, three to the late John Mercer's sites on the Isle of Jura, and one to the 'midden' beneath the Glecknabae cairn on the Isle of Bute (Bryce 1904, 42). The remainder were compiled by Mr J.W. Elliot and concern finds from surface sites in Roxburghshire and Selkirkshire in his own and other private collections. The sites include the well-known and very prolific Tweedside locations of

PARISH	COUNCIL FOR BRITISH ARCHAEOLOGY MESOLITHIC SURVEY		
	COUNTY	NAME and/or LOCATION OF SITE	NAT. GRID REFERENCE Qualify by G (General) E (Estimate) or A (Accurate)
Selkirk	Selkirk	Howden. West of Motte.	NT 458268

NATURE OF SITE	COLLECTION or SOURCE OF INFORMATION	COMPILER OF CARD
Brow of hill	J.B. Mason Collection J.W. Elliot "	J.W. Elliot

CATEGORIES OF ARTIFACTS (actual or estimated numbers)

Tranchet axes or adzes	Other axes or adzes	Axe sharpening flakes	Picks	Pebble maceheads	Micro and blade cores	Blades and flakes unretouched	Blade and flake tools other than microliths			Microliths	Micro-burins	Bone or antler artifacts	Other artifacts	Several lumps of unworked
							Scrapers	Gravers	Others					
Nil	Nil	Nil	Nil	Nil	10	5	8	Nil	20 approx.	3 known. (pitchstone)	Nil	Nil	5 rough cores	(Several lumps of unworked pitchstone.)

Please put additional notes, if any, on reverse of card

Figure 28.1. An example of the data card used for the compilation of the CBA's Mesolithic Gazetteer. *This is one of the cards for findspots in the Scottish Borders completed by Mr J.W. Elliot.*

Dryburgh, Rink Farm, and Springwood Park, and most of them were included in Mulholland's (1970) article on the Mesolithic period in the Tweed Valley. The card for one of the locations not listed by Mulholland is illustrated here (Fig. 28.1), principally to show the details of the survey pro forma used to gather data for the *Gazetteer*.

The Scottish cards obviously came in very slowly; in a letter dated 18 May 1971 to John Coles, the Sub-Committee's collaborator for Scotland, R.B.K. Stevenson complains that only four had so far been returned (NMS correspondence file), whereas coverage of England and Wales was by that stage well advanced.

The Mesolithic Sub-Committee's Minutes of 27 October 1971 record that for Scotland:

This region was far behind the other regions and the Hon. Secretary had received no cards other than a few of Scottish material in English Museums. The difficulties were appreciated: Mr Stevenson needed assistance and the area was large. It was suggested that the Hon. Secretary should seek the advice of Prof. S. Piggott.

Whether the late Stuart Piggott, then the Abercromby Professor of Prehistoric Archaeology at Edinburgh University, was consulted is not known, but the next Minutes of the Sub-Committee for 22 November 1972

report tersely that 'Scotland remained a problem'. In the final Minutes of 29 November 1973, Scotland is not mentioned at all.

This lack of progress with Scotland by the Sub-Committee is echoed in the Annual Reports of the Council for British Archaeology. That for 1972 records: 'This gazetteer of Mesolithic sites was originally envisaged as covering the three countries in a single volume but it may be necessary to publish England and Wales first, and a subsequent volume for Scotland' (CBA 1972, 44). Thereafter the Reports make no reference to Scotland.

One can speculate that a major difficulty was the absence of anyone in Scotland at the time able to become the driving force. The obvious candidate, John Coles, was by then in Cambridge and at the crucial period was committed among other things to the publication of his work at Morton (Coles 1971). R.B.K. Stevenson was a renowned polymath (O'Connor & Clarke 1983), but he was not a Mesolithic specialist and would have been reliant upon local help, in a context where in many parts of Scotland there was neither the interest nor the expertise to undertake completion of the index cards. The concentration of resources in the Central Belt is a well-recognized bias on many aspects of archaeological study in Scotland (cf. Barclay 1992, 106–7; Woodman 1989b, 5–6) and the absence, for the most part, of regional foci for information gathering at the time the *Gazetteer* was being compiled must have been a hindrance to Stevenson.

Another factor may have been that the Mesolithic objects in the national collections in Edinburgh, the major repository of archaeological material from Scotland, were not easy to isolate. Labyrinthine storage and classification systems hampered, if not in practice prevented, ready access (Burnett 1991; Clarke 1991). The alpha-numeric cataloguing of the collections was begun long before 'Mesolithic' was in regular use as an archaeological term (Anon 1892) and the catalogued collections are not organized in such a way as to include a comprehensive 'Mesolithic' category. The Oban caves material is catalogued under HL..; the Oronsay shell midden finds are HP..; while ABA.., the category for 'microlithic (pigmy) implements', has never been consistently applied, since it includes many other artefact types apart from microliths and is cut across by other designations for lithic finds catalogued by region, for example BME.. for Lanarkshire or BMJ.. for Jura. Other Mesolithic site assemblages may have their own designations; thus the Morton Farm, Fife, excavation assemblage is BNA...

This cataloguing complexity would certainly have made the task of identifying the Mesolithic finds a daunting one in the days of index cards and typescript inventories and would for Stevenson have been a major stumbling block, both practically and psychologically. How could a Scottish section of the *Gazetteer* be produced without the national collections being included; how could the national collections be included without the necessary resources?

As for the uncatalogued material then in the National Museum of Antiquities of Scotland, the letter from Stevenson to Coles of 18 May 1971 already quoted is unguardedly frank:

> I had hoped that we should by now at least have got some uncatalogued collections well started for registration and incidentally inclusion in the Survey. But other things have kept getting in the way and at the present rate it will be several years before our holdings can possibly be included.

The sentiment expressed here will have a resonance for anyone with museum experience.

MESOLITHIC DATA

Whatever the cause of the omission of Scotland from the CBA Survey, there has remained an absence of codified data for Mesolithic Scotland, a situation lamented by Woodman (1989b, 24), who urged the need for 'a definitive gazetteer including all known Mesolithic sites and descriptions of the range of artefacts found at each site'. This would, as in the case of the CBA Sub-Committee's work, involve a search of all museum and private collections with lithic items, in order to extract the information on those objects regarded as diagnostic (Wymer 1977a, ix, fig.2).

Such a database is an ideal still to be aspired to, but current postgraduate research at Glasgow University, sponsored by Historic Scotland, will create a wide-ranging record of prehistoric lithic scatters in Scotland and may well form a foundation for this. One would not now envisage any database being published in the same way as the 1977 *Gazetteer*; one intended outcome of the Historic Scotland-sponsored work is for a database of lithic scatters to be incorporated into the National Monuments Record of Scotland (Gordon Barclay pers.comm.).

This database, like the *Mesolithic Gazetteer* itself, will of course present users with problems of reliability and verification as far as the identification of Mesolithic artefacts is concerned. This is not a simple matter when depending on artefact typology for ascription to period. After all, it is not unknown for lithic analysts to disagree on the precise characterization and diagnostic value of an artefact. Thus, when dealing with reports of discoveries of Mesolithic tools, especially by non-specialists, a degree of scepticism is advisable. This applies in particular to the annual publication *Discovery and Excavation in Scotland*, the editors of which cannot do other than accept reports of finds largely as submitted, but it also applies in general, especially when descriptions are unaccompanied by illustrations.

Numerous cases of items misidentified as Mesolithic lurk in the older (and not so old) literature and can trap the unwary. It is very frustrating that commentators continue to recycle old notifications of Mesolithic finds as genuine, without making any attempt to examine critically the actual objects (e.g. Hunt 1987). Obsessive pursuit of obscure published references to Mesolithic and/or microlithic flints – misleading examples quoted by some recent researchers include MacDonald & Laing (1975, 149) and Robertson (1964, 154) – is of no value for Mesolithic studies unless the flints themselves are examined and reassessed. A rare example of self-correction in the literature was provided by Truckell, whose initial report of Mesolithic 'limpet-hammers' and flint-knapping tools, from the excavation at Chippermore Farm, Wigtownshire (Truckell 1954, 175), was superseded by his reclassification of them as Iron Age or later (Truckell 1962, 45).

Normally one would feel the greatest confidence in accepting as Mesolithic those descriptions which refer to the presence of the most diagnostic items – microliths and microburins – and, as far as an actual 'site' is concerned, preferably in quantities which at least reach double figures. Even so, often has been the disappointment on finally getting to see a collector's prized batch of microliths to discover they are no such thing. When faced with even less specific terminology – and relatively recent reports have examples of 'microlithic tendencies', 'microliths of a very advanced type', 'debased Mesolithic type', and 'Larnian' – the alarm bells ring, and one surely suspects a misprint or a misunderstanding in the description of one site in the north west as having 'a total of 6017 microliths' (quoted *passim* from descriptions in *Discovery and Excavation in Scotland*).

Perhaps the main contribution of the *Gazetteer* at the time it was published was finally to give the lie to the notion of limited, patchy Mesolithic settlement in England and Wales. The famous map published by the late Grahame Clark as the frontispiece to his 1932 book, *The Mesolithic Age in Britain*, though it was never intended as a distribution map, seemed to support the existence of several Mesolithic-free tracts of country. The *Gazetteer*, though hugely biased by such factors as the differentially distributed work of collectors and the regionally disparate availability of ploughland for field searches, did show there was Mesolithic material from virtually every part. The only county to have not even a single entry was Merionethshire (though Montgomeryshire only just found a place in the *Gazetteer*, with one microlith from the mound of a barrow: Wymer 1977a, 203). Thus the *Gazetteer* provided the documentation for Jacobi's (1973, fig. 5) hypothesis that the whole of England and Wales was colonized by the end of the Mesolithic period.

The omission of Scotland from the *Gazetteer* meant that here the Mesolithic-free tracts continued without correction, as Woodman (1989b) found when he came to compile his overview. Even excluding the more mountainous zones, however, any Scottish gazetteer based on existing records would inevitably be patchy, because of the inaccessibility of so much potential field evidence due to peat cover, afforestation, pasture, etc. Coastal locations have predominated in the older literature because of the ease of collecting from sand-dune areas such as Culbin, Luce, Shewalton, and Tentsmuir (Lacaille 1954, 275). Of other local factors, the absence in the recent past of interested collectors (perhaps also the case in Merionethshire?) must be the explanation for so few known Mesolithic finds from certain areas, for example Angus or the Isle of Skye.

Certainly the perception of the Scottish Mesolithic as primarily coastal (cf. Simmons 1996, 158) was countered by the evidence for inland, upland Mesolithic activity in the south west (Edwards *et al.* 1983). This picture is now being echoed by recent fieldwork in South Lanarkshire (Ward 1995), but only because of the chance opportunities for observation provided by low water-levels in a reservoir where water has artificially eroded the peat cover. Elsewhere in the upland, forestry ploughing or drainage work occasionally might provide the circumstances to find Mesolithic evidence, which would only otherwise be detectable by large-scale test-pitting.

The work required to produce the data for the CBA's *Gazetteer* was itself a springboard for or an adjunct to several subsequent publications which helped to fill the gaps in the regional coverage of Mesolithic research in England and Wales (e.g. Jacobi 1980; Saville 1981). This was putting the raw data into a context, something which

John Wymer (1977b) saw as important; the Gazetteer was never meant to be an end in itself but a tool for enabling further research.

This stimulus towards more detailed publication of the listed data was one of the outcomes Jacobi (1979) hoped for from the *Gazetteer*, and a similar incentive would have been welcome in Scotland. Jacobi's other hope, that the information would guide the policy of future research on the Mesolithic, was perhaps optimistic, and does not appear to have happened much in England and Wales outside his own personal research programme, or that which he supervised (e.g. David 1990), though the *Gazetteer*'s data were used in other innovative ways (Care 1979; Mellars & Haynes 1986; Mellars & Reinhardt 1978; Smith & Openshaw 1990).

Paradoxically, there have in Scotland, irrespective of the lack of a database, been several targeted research operations with a Mesolithic period focus, as on Oronsay (Mellars 1987); on Colonsay and Islay (Mithen & Lake 1996); on Jura (Mercer 1979a; Searight 1984); in the Forth Valley (Sloan 1984b; 1985b; 1986); and around Oban (Macklin & Rumsby 1991; Macklin *et al.* 1992).

Woodman's (1989b) rather bleak view of Scottish Mesolithic studies appears now, after a decade of new work and discoveries, to be overly pessimistic. It is true that researchers have continued to find traces of Late Glacial or immediately postglacial human presence elusive, but for the later Mesolithic period, from *c.* 8500 BP, the increased evidence allows a reasonably full picture to be painted (Saville forthcoming). This improvement is reflected by the number of 1990s publications on the Mesolithic in Scotland (see below), though it will take well into the next millennium for all the 1990s fieldwork discoveries and research to reach definitive publication. That one can be so optimistic is in large part because organizations and funding bodies, in particular Historic Scotland, have begun to take seriously the problems and potential of the Mesolithic period (Barclay 1995; 1997). The serendipity factor of developer-funded archaeology, now on the increase in Scotland, is also becoming important in bringing Mesolithic material to light (e.g. Dalland 1996; Pollard 1993).

However, it is also not too much of a generalization to say that, with the exception of the late John Mercer, much of the recent thinking and writing about the Mesolithic in Scotland have downplayed artefacts in favour of economy and environment. This approach was exemplified by the publication resulting from the Oronsay project (Mellars 1987) and reflects the huge influence on Mesolithic studies in Britain of the 'Cambridge school' of economic prehistory (Trigger 1989, 264–70). The late Grahame Clark was surely throwing out both baby and bathwater when he turned against artefact studies (Clark 1972), a field in which he himself initially had excelled (e.g. Clark 1934). Though entirely understandable in the context of contemporary developments in prehistoric archaeology (cf. Rowley-Conwy 1994), with hindsight the emphasis on ecological, economic, and social approaches can be seen to have somewhat hampered Mesolithic studies, in the sense of deterring publication of purely lithic evidence.

Since in so many cases it is the lithic evidence which alone survives, the prehistorian is duty bound to make the most of this residue. There is a diversity within the artefact record from Mesolithic Scotland which has not been allowed to emerge with any clarity because of the restricted documentation of the material. Since Lacaille's (1954) overview there have, for example, been very few illustrations of Scottish microliths published to an acceptable standard, yet the importance of making the diagnostic data available in this way cannot be over-emphasized. Just as the animal and human remains, and the antler and bone artefacts, surviving in museum collections are now making previously unforeseen impacts on Mesolithic period research (Bonsall *et al.* 1995; Day 1996; Kitchener & Bonsall 1997), so will the existing lithic artefact record for the Scottish Mesolithic period, once carefully analysed and published, be able to make its proper contribution.

THE BIBLIOGRAPHIC GAZETTEER

Undoubtedly one of the main ways in which the *Mesolithic Gazetteer* has proved of lasting value is that it provides an easy quarry for the available published information on the Mesolithic in any part of England and Wales. Searching for publications on the Mesolithic in Scotland has always been less of a problem than in England, because of the fewer publication outlets and because there are already several published overviews with their own bibliographies. Even so it is still an arduous task, which the present writer has undertaken as part of his own research (Saville forthcoming). As a contribution to this *Festschrift* it seems an appropriate way to acknowledge the Mesolithic element of John Wymer's *oeuvre* by providing a bibliographic gazetteer for the Mesolithic period in Scotland.

A pragmatic approach has been taken to the geographical subdivisions used and the following list of references starts in the north with Orkney, moves to the islands off the west coast (in alphabetical order), then proceeds from north to south through the mainland. Not all the overlaps between coverage of regions or islands are cross-referenced in the list; each citation is given at the most relevant point.

Shetland and the whole of the Western Isles (Outer Hebrides), including St Kilda, are not represented because they have as yet produced no diagnostic finds, though there is considerable debate about the possible anthropogenic indicators in the palaeoenvironmental evidence from these locations (Brayshay & Edwards 1996; Edwards 1996a; Edwards & Mithen 1995; Tipping 1994; 1996). The flint core-tool from Fair Isle (Cumming 1946), situated between Orkney and Shetland, though presumably Mesolithic, must on present evidence be regarded as a 'sport'

(Saville 1994b), pending any other indications of pre-Neolithic presence on the island (Hunter 1996).

The list concentrates on references to 'sites' and artefactual evidence rather than any palaeoenvironmental aspects such as pollen analyses or shoreline studies. Sites – growing in number – where excavations have produced charcoals from which Mesolithic age radiocarbon dates have been obtained, but where indicators of Mesolithic culture are apparently absent (e.g. Carter 1993; CFA 1994; Johnston 1991), have not been included.

Restricted use has been made of older entries in *Discovery and Excavation in Scotland* for the reasons alluded to above; more recent entries have been included, pending any fuller publication elsewhere, and these demonstrate the increased number of Mesolithic discoveries occurring. However, it can be noted that, over the period 1955–1996, entries in *Discovery and Excavation in Scotland* claiming Mesolithic findspots total approximately 90 (excluding all sites and finds for which references are included below). Sixty of these 90 potential Mesolithic findspots are in the former counties of Ayr, Kirkcudbright, and Wigtown in the south west, and reflect the activities of particular local collectors.

Essentially, the references in this bibliography relate to the later Mesolithic period, from *c.* 8500 BP onwards. Industries characterized by narrow-blade, geometric microlith components have now been dated to this period at a recently-excavated site on the east coast in Fife (Dalland 1996; Denison 1997; Wickham-Jones pers. comm.) as well as in the west on the island of Rum (Wickham-Jones 1990b). Any earlier activity in Scotland remains a matter of speculation (Jacobi 1982; Morrison 1982a; Morrison & Bonsall 1989; Price 1982) and this speculation is not fully referenced here (see Saville forthcoming for a detailed discussion).

The high number of references for Jura and Oronsay reflects the concentration of fieldwork there in the 1960s and 1970s, and the same is true for Colonsay and Islay in the 1980s and 1990s; the entries for the central region are swollen by the presence of Morton, Fife, and the debates about its artefacts and palaeoenvironmental evidence, and by Sloan's work on the enigmatic Forth Valley middens; while the south west entries reflect in part the existence of a strong local society with its own journal in Dumfriesshire and Galloway.

Perhaps the most noteworthy contrasts with these areas where research has been focused are: the south east, which has some of the most prolific Mesolithic surface sites in Scotland, yet hardly any post-war publications, apart from the important but now rather dated treatment by Mulholland (1970); the north east, where Mesolithic research arguably has been traumatized by the as yet unfulfilled promise of the Nethermills site on the Dee (Kenworthy 1980; 1981); and the large islands of Mull and Skye, both (but especially the former) very under-researched for early prehistory, though known from largely unpublished information to have Mesolithic flint assemblages. Regionalized studies based on these areas would be an obvious way forward for Mesolithic research.

It will be apparent that the nature of virtually all work published thus far on the Mesolithic period in Scotland is normative description or overview. As the database expands one can predict the growth of scientific applications (e.g. Lake *et al.* 1998) and, as research trends developed for the later prehistoric periods are progressively applied to earlier periods, an increase in theoretical interpretations (e.g. Pollard 1996).

No bibliography such as this can ever be complete and it will, like the *Mesolithic Gazetteer*, inevitably be out-of-date before it appears in print. Nevertheless, it is hoped (in combination with Saville forthcoming), that it will be a useful research tool for future studies of the Mesolithic period in Scotland. The writer would welcome information on any omissions of relevant pre-1996 references, however obscure.

Orkney
Hunter 1986; Lacaille 1935; Livens 1956; Rendall 1937; Richards 1985; Richards 1986; Saville 1996a; Wickham-Jones 1990a

Arran
Affleck *et al.* 1988; Allen & Edwards 1987; Gorman *et al.* 1995; Haggarty 1991; Robinson 1983a; Robinson 1983b

Bute
Cormack 1985; Cormack 1986; McFadzean 1985

Coll
Ritchie *et al.* 1978

Colonsay
Mithen 1989; Mithen 1995; Mithen & Finlayson 1991; Mithen & Lake 1996

Iona
RCAHMS 1982

Islay
Burgess 1976; Finlayson *et al.* 1996; Mithen 1990; Mithen 1993; Mithen 1995; Mithen 1997; Mithen & Lake 1996; Mithen *et al.* 1992; McCullagh 1989; Newall 1962; Newall 1963; RCAHMS 1984

Jura
Bonsall 1988; Mercer 1968; Mercer 1970a; Mercer 1970b; Mercer 1971; Mercer 1972; Mercer 1974a; Mercer 1974b; Mercer 1979a; Mercer 1980; Mercer 1981; Mercer & Searight 1986; RCAHMS 1984; Searight 1984; Searight 1990; Searight 1993

Mull
RCAHMS 1980

Oronsay
Anderson 1898; Bishop 1914; Bonsall 1996; Bonsall 1997; Grieve 1885; Grieve 1923; Jardine 1977; Jardine & Jardine 1978; Jardine & Jardine 1983; MacKie 1972; Mellars 1977; Mellars 1978; Mellars 1981; Mellars 1987; Mellars & Payne 1971; Mellars & Wilkinson 1980; RCAHMS 1984; Wickham-Jones *et al.* 1982

Risga
Foxon 1991; Pollard *et al.* 1996

Rum
Wickham-Jones 1989; Wickham-Jones 1990b; Wickham-Jones & Pollock 1985

Skye
Armit 1996a; Lacaille 1954; Saville & Miket 1994a; Saville & Miket 1994b

Tiree
Livens 1956; MacKie 1963

Ulva
Bonsall *et al.* 1991; Bonsall *et al.* 1992; Bonsall *et al.* 1994; Russell *et al.* 1995

North Mainland (Caithness, Sutherland, Ross & Cromarty, Inverness-shire, Nairn, Moray)
Davidson 1947; Davidson & Henshall 1991; Henshall 1982; Lacaille 1944; Lacaille 1951; Myers & Gourlay 1991; Saville 1993; Walker n.d.; Wickham-Jones & Firth 1990a; Wickham-Jones & Firth 1990b; Wordsworth 1985

North east Mainland (Aberdeenshire, Banffshire, Kincardine, Angus)
Baird & Finlayson 1994; Boyd & Kenworthy 1992; Childe 1943; Dalwood 1987; Dawson *et al.* 1990; Hawke-Smith 1980; Kenworthy 1980; Kenworthy 1981; Kenworthy 1982; Lacaille 1944; Paterson 1912; Paterson 1913; Paterson 1929; Paterson & Lacaille 1936; Shepherd 1987

Central Mainland (Clackmannanshire, Renfrewshire, West Lothian, Midlothian, Lanarkshire, Perthshire, Fife, Kinross, Stirlingshire, Dunbartonshire)
Alexander 1996; Anon 1971; Anon 1972; Ashmore & Hall 1996; Bonsall 1988; Bonsall *et al.* 1995; Candow 1989; Clark 1947; Clarke 1989; Clarke & Wickham-Jones 1988; Coles 1971; Coles 1983b; Dalland 1996; Davidson *et al.* 1949; Dean 1993; Deith 1983; Deith 1986; Deith 1989; Denison 1997; Hanson 1987; Hoy 1988; Lacaille 1944; McFadzean 1984; MacKie 1972; Myers 1988; RCAHMS 1963; RCAHMS 1978; Reed 1995; Rideout 1996; Saville 1996b; Sloan 1982; Sloan 1984a; Sloan 1984b; Sloan 1985a; Sloan 1985b; Sloan 1986; Sloan 1987; Sloan 1993; Sloan & Murray 1980; Turner 1889; Ward 1995; Woodman 1988

Argyll (mainland)
Anderson 1895; Anderson 1898; Bonsall 1996; Bonsall 1997; Bonsall & Sutherland 1992; Bonsall *et al.* 1993; Bonsall *et al.* 1995; Clark 1956; Coles 1983a; Connock 1990; Connock *et al.* 1992; Gray 1975; Macklin & Rumsby 1991; Macklin *et al.* 1992; Mercer 1979b; Pollard 1990; RCAHMS 1971; RCAHMS 1975; RCAHMS 1980; RCAHMS 1988; Ritchie 1997; Saville & Hallén 1994; Turner 1895

South west Mainland (Ayrshire, Dumfriesshire, Kirkcudbrightshire, Wigtownshire)
Affleck 1983; Affleck 1986; Bain 1995; Chapman 1988; Coles 1963; Coles 1966; Cormack 1964; Cormack 1970; Cormack 1982; Cormack 1983; Cormack 1995; Cormack & Coles 1968; Cowie 1996; Edgar 1939; Edwards 1996b; Edwards *et al.* 1983; Finlayson 1990b; Hughes 1988; Hughes 1991; Jardine & Morrison 1976; Lacaille 1930; Lacaille 1931; Lacaille 1939; Lacaille 1945; Lacaille 1948; Livens 1957; McCallien &

Lacaille 1941; McFadzean 1984; Mackenzie 1995; Masters 1981; Morrison 1981; Morrison 1982b; Morrison 1996; Murray 1991; Pollard 1993; RCAHMS 1997; Truckell 1954; Truckell 1957; Truckell 1962

South east Mainland (Berwickshire, East Lothian, Roxburghshire, Selkirkshire, Peeblesshire)
Anon 1956; Callander 1927; Childe 1942; Corrie 1916; Corrie 1920; Cowie *et al.* 1986; Cree 1923; Dent & McDonald 1997; Innes & Shennan 1991; Mason 1927; Mason 1931; Mulholland 1970

The National Level
For national and supra-regional surveys of the Mesolithic period in Scotland, at various levels, and for studies of some particular Mesolithic aspects, see the following. Lacaille (1954) and Woodman (1989b) are highlighted, the former because it is still the major summary and key to the earlier literature, the latter because it is the most significant recent overview.

Armit 1996b; Atkinson 1962; Bonsall 1996; Bonsall 1997; Bonsall & Smith 1990; Breuil 1922; Childe 1935; Clark 1932; Clark 1956; Edwards 1989; Edwards 1990; Edwards & Ralston 1984; Finlayson 1990a; Finlayson 1995; Finlayson & Edwards 1997; Hunt 1987; Kenworthy 1975; Kinnes 1985; Lacaille 1937; Lacaille 1942; **Lacaille 1954**; Morrison 1980; Morrison & Bonsall 1989; Mountain 1979; Movius 1942; Movius 1953; Murray 1994; Reynolds 1983; Ritchie & Ritchie 1972; Ritchie & Ritchie 1981; Saville 1994a; Saville forthcoming; Scott 1966; Sloan 1993; Smith 1989; Smith 1992; Smith & Bonsall 1991; Wickham-Jones 1994; Woodman 1978; **Woodman 1989b**

ACKNOWLEDGEMENTS

As ever, I am indebted to colleagues in the library of the National Museums of Scotland for their ready assistance. In contributing an article to this volume it is a very great pleasure to acknowledge the inspiration provided over many years by John Wymer's scholarship and his enthusiasm for all things lithic.

REFERENCES

Affleck, T.L. 1983. Smittons (Carsphairn parish): enclosure, Mesolithic flints. In E.V.W. Proudfoot (ed.), *Discovery and Excavation in Scotland 1983*, 5–6. Edinburgh: Council for British Archaeology (Scotland).

Affleck, T.L. 1986. Excavation at Starr, Loch Doon 1985. *Glasgow Archaeological Society Bulletin* 22, 10–21.

Affleck, T.L., Edwards, K., & Clarke, A. 1988. Archaeological and palynological studies at the Mesolithic pitchstone and flint site of Auchareoch, Isle of Arran. *Proceedings of the Society of Antiquaries of Scotland* 118, 37–59.

Alexander, D. 1996. Sites and artefacts: the prehistory of Renfrewshire. In D. Alexander (ed.), *Prehistoric Renfrewshire: Papers in Honour of Frank Newall*, 5–22. Edinburgh: Renfrewshire Local History Forum.

Allen, C. & Edwards, K.J. 1987. The distribution of lithic materials of possible Mesolithic age on the Isle of Arran. *Glasgow Archaeological Journal* 14, 19–24.

Anderson, J. 1895. Notice of a cave recently discovered at Oban, containing human remains, and a refuse-heap of shells and bones

of animals, and stone and bone implements. *Proceedings of the Society of Antiquaries of Scotland* 29 [for 1894–95], 211–30.

Anderson, J. 1898. Notes on the contents of a small cave or rock-shelter at Druimvargie, Oban; and of three shell-mounds in Oronsay. *Proceedings of the Society of Antiquaries of Scotland* 32 [for 1897–98], 298–313.

Anon. 1892. *Catalogue of the National Museum of Antiquities of Scotland.* Edinburgh: Society of Antiquaries of Scotland.

Anon. 1956. Donations to and purchases for the museum, 1955–6. *Proceedings of the Society of Antiquaries of Scotland* 89 [for 1955–56] 458–63.

Anon. 1971. Donations to and purchases for the museum, 1970–71. *Proceedings of the Society of Antiquaries of Scotland* 103 [for 1970–71] 242–5.

Anon. 1972. Donations to and purchases for the museum, 1971–2. *Proceedings of the Society of Antiquaries of Scotland* 104 [for 1971–72] 316–19.

Armit, I. 1996a. *The Archaeology of Skye and the Western Isles.* Edinburgh: Edinburgh University Press.

Armit, I. 1996b. The transition to agriculture: Scotland. In T. Pollard & A. Morrison (eds), *The Early Prehistory of Scotland*, 280–90. Edinburgh: Edinburgh University Press.

Ashmore, P.J. & Hall, D. 1996. Shell midden at Braehead, Alloa. *Forth Naturalist and Historian* 20, 123–9.

Atkinson, R.J.C. 1962. Fishermen and farmers. In S. Piggott (ed.), *The Prehistoric Peoples of Scotland*, 1–38. London: Routledge & Kegan Paul.

Bain, S. 1995. Barmore Moss (Kirkcowan parish): lithic scatter. In C.E. Batey (ed.), *Discovery and Excavation in Scotland 1995*, 22. Edinburgh: Council for Scottish Archaeology.

Baird, D. & Finlayson, B. 1994. A Mesolithic and later flint scatter at Little Gight, Grampian Region. *Proceedings of the Society of Antiquaries of Scotland* 124, 95–101.

Barclay, G.J. 1992. The Scottish gravels: a neglected resource? In M. Fulford & E. Nicols (eds), *Developing Landscapes of Lowland Britain*, 106–24. London: Society of Antiquaries of London, Occasional Paper 14.

Barclay, G.J. 1993. The excavation of pit circles at Romancamp Gate, Fochabers, Moray, 1990. *Proceedings of the Society of Antiquaries of Scotland* 123, 255–68.

Barclay, G.J. 1995. What's new in Scottish prehistory? *Scottish Archaeological Review* 9/10, 3–14.

Barclay, G.J. 1997. *State-funded 'Rescue' Archaeology in Scotland: Past, Present and Future.* Edinburgh: Historic Scotland, Occasional Paper 2.

Bishop, A.H. 1914. An Oransay shell-mound — a Scottish pre-Neolithic site. *Proceedings of the Society of Antiquaries of Scotland* 48 [for 1913–14], 52–108.

Bonsall, C. 1988. Morton and Lussa Wood, the case for early Flandrian settlement of Scotland: comment on Myers. *Scottish Archaeological Review* 5, 30–3.

Bonsall, C. 1996. The 'Obanian problem': coastal adaptation in the Mesolithic of western Scotland. In T. Pollard & A. Morrison (eds), *The Early Prehistory of Scotland*, 183–97. Edinburgh: Edinburgh University Press.

Bonsall, C. 1997. Coastal adaptation in the Mesolithic of Argyll: rethinking the 'Obanian' problem. In J.D.G. Ritchie (ed.), *The Archaeology of Argyll*, 25–37. Edinburgh: Edinburgh University Press.

Bonsall, C., Robinson, M.R., Payton, R., & Macklin, M.G. 1993. Lón Mór (Kilmore & Kilbride parish): Mesolithic site, post-ring structure. In C.E. Batey (ed.), *Discovery and Excavation in Scotland 1993*, 76. Edinburgh: Council for Scottish Archaeology.

Bonsall, C. & Smith, C. 1990. Bone and antler technology in the British Late Upper Palaeolithic and Mesolithic: the impact of accelerator dating. In P.M. Vermeersch & P. van Peer (eds),

Contributions to the Mesolithic in Europe, 359–68. Leuven: Leuven University Press.

Bonsall, C. & Sutherland, D.G. 1992. The Oban caves. In M.J.C. Walker, J.M. Gray & J.J. Lowe (eds), *The South West Scottish Highlands: Field Guide*, 115–21. Cambridge: Quaternary Research Association.

Bonsall, C., Sutherland, D. & Lawson, T. 1991. Excavations in Ulva Cave, western Scotland 1987: a preliminary report. *Mesolithic Miscellany* 12(2), 18–23.

Bonsall, C., Sutherland, D., Lawson, T. & Russell, N. 1992. Excavations in Ulva Cave, western Scotland 1989: a preliminary report. *Mesolithic Miscellany* 13(1), 7–13.

Bonsall, C., Sutherland, D.G., Russell, N.J., Coles, G., Paul, C.R.C., Huntley, J.P. & Lawson, T.J. 1994. Excavations in Ulva Cave, western Scotland 1990–91: a preliminary report. *Mesolithic Miscellany* 15(1), 8–21.

Bonsall, C., Tolan-Smith, C. & Saville, A. 1995. Direct dating of Mesolithic antler and bone artifacts from Great Britain: new results for bevelled tools and red deer antler mattocks. *Mesolithic Miscellany* 16(1), 2–10.

Boyd, W.E. & Kenworthy, J.B. 1992. The use of wood as a natural resource at a Scottish Mesolithic site. *Glasgow Archaeological Journal* 17 [for 1991–92], 11–23.

Brayshay, B. & Edwards, K. 1996. Late-glacial and Holocene vegetational history of South Uist and Barra. In D. Gilbertson, M. Kent, & J. Grattan (eds), *The Outer Hebrides: the Last 14,000 years*, 13–26. Sheffield: Sheffield Academic Press.

Breuil, H. 1922. Observations on the pre-Neolithic industries of Scotland. *Proceedings of the Society of Antiquaries of Scotland* 56 [for 1921–22], 261–81.

Bryce, T.H. 1904. On the cairns and tumuli of the Island of Bute: a record of explorations during the season of 1903. *Proceedings of the Society of Antiquaries of Scotland* 38 [for 1903–04], 17–81.

Burgess, C. 1976. An early Bronze Age settlement at Kilellan Farm, Islay, Argyll. In C. Burgess and R. Miket (eds), *Settlement and Economy in the Third and Second Millennia B.C.*, 181–207. Oxford: British Archaeological Reports, British Series 33.

Burnett, J. 1991. Collections, information and computers in the National Museums of Scotland. *Proceedings of the Society of Antiquaries of Scotland* 121, 5–16.

Callander, J.G. 1927. A collection of Tardenoisian implements from Berwickshire. *Proceedings of the Society of Antiquaries of Scotland* 61 [for 1926–27], 318–27.

Candow, R. 1989. *Prehistoric Morton*. Dundee: Privately printed.

Care, V. 1979. The production and distribution of Mesolithic axes in southern England. *Proceedings of the Prehistoric Society* 45, 93–102.

Carter, S. 1993. Tulloch Wood, Forres, Moray: the survey and dating of a fragment of prehistoric landscape. *Proceedings of the Society of Antiquaries of Scotland* 123, 215–33.

CBA (Council for British Archaeology). 1970. *Report No. 20 for the Year Ended 30 June 1970*. London: CBA.

CBA (Council for British Archaeology). 1972. *Report No. 22 for the Year Ended 30 June 1972*. London: CBA.

CFA (Centre for Field Archaeology). 1994. Spurryhillock (Fetteresso parish): Mesolithic pit and Neolithic pit with pottery. In C.E. Batey & M. King (eds), *Discovery and Excavation in Scotland 1994*, 28. Edinburgh: Council for Scottish Archaeology.

Chapman, R. 1988. Mesolithic to Neolithic in the Firth of Clyde: some comments. *Scottish Archaeological Review* 5, 56–8.

Childe, V.G. 1935. *The Prehistory of Scotland*. London: Kegan Paul, Trench, Trubner & Co.

Childe, V.G. 1942. Rare flint in Hawick Museum. *Transactions of the Hawick Archaeological Society* [for 1942], 31.

Childe, V.G. 1943. The prehistoric archaeology of north east Scotland. In J.F. Tocher (ed.), *The Book of Buchan*, 62–80. Aberdeen: The Buchan Club.

Clark, J.G.D. 1932. *The Mesolithic Age in Britain*. Cambridge: Cambridge University Press.

Clark, J.G.D. 1934. The classification of a microlithic culture: the Tardenoisian of Horsham. *Archaeological Journal* 90, 52–77.

Clark, J.G.D. 1947. Whales as an economic factor in prehistoric Europe. *Antiquity* 21, 84–104.

Clark, J.G.D. 1956. Notes on the Obanian with special reference to antler- and bone-work. *Proceedings of the Society of Antiquaries of Scotland* 89 [for 1955–56], 91–106.

Clark, J.G.D. 1972. The archaeology of Stone Age settlement. *Ulster Journal of Archaeology* 35, 3–16.

Clarke, A. 1989. Corse Law, Carnwath, Lanarkshire: a lithic scatter. *Proceedings of the Society of Antiquaries of Scotland* 119, 43–54.

Clarke, A. & Wickham-Jones, C.R. 1988. The ghost of Morton revisited: comment on Myers. *Scottish Archaeological Review* 5, 35–7.

Clarke, D.V. 1991. Managing output rather than input? The implications of computerising the National Museums of Scotland's archaeological information. In W.S. Hanson & E.A. Slater (eds), *Scottish Archaeology: New Perceptions*, 218–28. Aberdeen: Aberdeen University Press.

Coles, J.M. 1963. New aspects of the Mesolithic settlement of south west Scotland. *Transactions of the Dumfriesshire & Galloway Natural History & Antiquarian Society* 41 [for 1962–63], 67–98.

Coles, J.M. 1966. A 'Bann point' from Dumfriesshire. *Transactions of the Dumfriesshire & Galloway Natural History & Antiquarian Society* 43, 147.

Coles, J.M. 1971. The early settlement of Scotland: excavations at Morton, Fife. *Proceedings of the Prehistoric Society* 37(2), 284–366.

Coles, J.M. 1983a. Excavations at Kilmelfort Cave, Argyll. *Proceedings of the Society of Antiquaries of Scotland* 113, 11–21.

Coles, J.M. 1983b. Morton revisited. In A. O'Connor & D.V. Clarke (eds), *From the Stone Age to the 'Forty-Five*, 9–18. Edinburgh: John Donald.

Connock, K.D. 1990. A shell midden at Carding Mill Bay, Oban. *Scottish Archaeological Review* 7, 74–6.

Connock, K.D., Finlayson, B. & Mills, C.M. 1992. Excavation of a shell midden site at Carding Mill Bay near Oban, Scotland. *Glasgow Archaeological Journal* 17, 25–38.

Cormack, W.F. 1964. Daltonhook, Dumfriesshire. In M.E.C. Stewart (ed.), *Discovery and Excavation in Scotland 1964*, 25–6. Edinburgh: Scottish Regional Group, Council for British Archaeology.

Cormack, W.F. 1970. A Mesolithic site at Barsalloch, Wigtownshire. *Transactions of the Dumfriesshire & Galloway Natural History & Antiquarian Society* 47, 63–80.

Cormack, W.F. 1982. Sheddock (Whithorn parish): midden and Mesolithic site. In E.V.W. Proudfoot (ed.), *Discovery and Excavation in Scotland 1982*, 9. Edinburgh: Council for British Archaeology (Scotland).

Cormack, W.F. 1983. A flint blade from Redkirk Point, Dumfriesshire. *Transactions of the Dumfriesshire & Galloway Natural History & Antiquarian Society* 58, 92.

Cormack, W.F. 1985. A note on Mesolithic sites in Bute. *Transactions of the Buteshire Natural History Society* 22, 6.

Cormack, W.F. 1986. Little Kilchattan (Kingarth parish): Mesolithic site. In E.V.W. & B.E. Proudfoot (eds), *Discovery and Excavation in Scotland 1986*, 26. Edinburgh: Council for British Archaeology, Scotland.

Cormack, W.F. 1995. Barhobble, Mochrum: excavation of a forgotten church site in Galloway. *Transactions of the Dum-*

friesshire & Galloway Natural History & Antiquarian Society 70, 5–106.

Cormack, W.F. and Coles, J.M. 1968. A Mesolithic site at Low Clone, Wigtownshire. *Transactions of the Dumfriesshire & Galloway Natural History & Antiquarian Society* 45, 44–72.

Corrie, J.M. 1916. Notes on some stone and flint implements found near Dryburgh, in the parish of Mertoun, Berwickshire. *Proceedings of the Society of Antiquaries of Scotland* 50 [for 1915–16], 307–13.

Corrie, J.M. 1920. Pigmy flint implements found in Roxburghshire and Berwickshire. *Transactions of the Hawick Archaeological Society* 13–16.

Cowie, T.G. 1996. Torrs Warren, Luce Sands, Galloway: a report on archaeological and palaeoecological investigations undertaken in 1977 and 1979. *Transactions of the Dumfriesshire & Galloway Natural History & Antiquarian Society* 71, 11–105.

Cowie, T.G., Wickham-Jones, C.R., & Knox, R. 1986. Manor Bridge and Peebles: lithic scatters. In E.V.W. & B.E. Proudfoot (eds), *Discovery and excavation in Scotland 1986*, 49. Edinburgh: The Council for British Archaeology, Scotland.

Cree, J.E. 1923. Account of the excavations on Traprain Law during the summer of 1922. *Proceedings of the Society of Antiquaries of Scotland* 57 [for 1922–23] 180–226.

Cumming, G.A. 1946. Flint core axe found on Fair Isle, Shetland. *Proceedings of the Society of Antiquaries of Scotland* 80 [for 1945–46], 146–8.

Dalland, M. 1996. Craighead Golf Course, Balcomie, Fife Ness (Crail parish): Mesolithic shelter, Neolithic/Bronze Age pits, Iron Age and Dane's Dyke. In R. Turner (ed.), *Discovery and Excavation in Scotland 1996*, 46–7. Edinburgh: Council for Scottish Archaeology.

Dalwood, H. 1987. Mesolithic occupation at Castlehill of Stachan, Kincardine and Deeside. *Proceedings of the Society of Antiquaries of Scotland* 117, 353.

David, A. 1990. *Palaeolithic and Mesolithic Settlement in Wales, with Special Reference to Dyfed.* Unpublished PhD thesis, University of Lancaster.

Davidson, J.L. & Henderson, A.S. 1991. *The Chambered Cairns of Caithness.* Edinburgh: Edinburgh University Press.

Davidson, J.M. 1947. A stone flaking site at Burghead, Morayshire. *Transactions of the Glasgow Archaeological Society* 11, 28–30.

Davidson, J.M., Phemister, J. & Lacaille, A.D. 1949. A Stone Age site at Woodend Loch, near Coatbridge. *Proceedings of the Society of Antiquaries of Scotland* 83 [for 1948–49], 77–98.

Dawson, A.G., Smith, D.E. & Long, D. 1990. Evidence for a tsunami from a Mesolithic site in Inverness, Scotland. *Journal of Archaeological Science* 17, 509–12.

Day, S.P. 1996. Dogs, deer and diet at Star Carr: a reconsideration of C-isotope evidence from Early Mesolithic dog remains from the Vale of Pickering, Yorkshire, England. *Journal of Archaeological Science* 23, 783–7.

Dean, V. 1993. Cramond Roman fort (City parish of Edinburgh): Mesolithic deposits, post-medieval demolition, possible kiln. In C.E. Batey (ed.), *Discovery and Excavation in Scotland 1993*, 59. Edinburgh: Council for Scottish Archaeology.

Deith, M.R. 1983. Molluscan calendars: the use of growth-line analysis to establish seasonality of shellfish collection at the Mesolithic site of Morton, Fife. *Journal of Archaeological Science* 10, 423–40.

Deith, M.R. 1986. Subsistence strategies at a Mesolithic camp site: evidence from stable isotope analyses of shells. *Journal of Archaeological Science* 13, 61–78.

Deith, M.R. 1989. Clams and salmonberries: interpreting seasonality data from shells. In C. Bonsall (ed.), *The Mesolithic in Europe*, 73–9. Edinburgh: John Donald.

Denison, S. 1997. Oldest occupation site in east Scotland. *British Archaeology* 28 [October 1997], 5.

Dent, J. & McDonald, R. (eds). 1997. *Early Settlers in the Borders.* Newton St Boswells: Scottish Borders Council.

Edgar, W. 1939. A Tardenoisian site at Ballantrae, Ayrshire. *Transactions of the Glasgow Archaeological Society* 9(3), 184–8.

Edwards, K.J. 1989. Meso-Neolithic vegetational impacts in Scotland and beyond: palynological considerations. In C. Bonsall (ed.), *The Mesolithic in Europe*, 143–55. Edinburgh: John Donald.

Edwards, K.J. 1990. Fire and the Scottish Mesolithic: evidence from microscopic charcoal. In P.M. Vermeersch & P. Van Peer (eds), *Contributions to the Mesolithic in Europe*, 71–9. Leuven: Leuven University Press.

Edwards, K.J. 1996a. A Mesolithic of the Western and Northern Isles of Scotland? Evidence from pollen and charcoal. In T. Pollard & A. Morrison (eds), *The Early Prehistory of Scotland*, 23–38. Edinburgh: Edinburgh University Press.

Edwards, K.J. 1996b. The contribution of Tom Affleck to the study of the Mesolithic of southwest Scotland. In T. Pollard & A. Morrison (eds), *The Early Prehistory of Scotland*, 108–22. Edinburgh: Edinburgh University Press.

Edwards, K.J., Ansell, M. & Carter, B.A. 1983. New Mesolithic sites in south west Scotland and their importance as indicators of inland penetration. *Transactions of the Dumfriesshire & Galloway Natural History & Antiquarian Society* 58, 9–15.

Edwards, K.J. & Mithen, S. 1995. The colonization of the Hebridean Islands of western Scotland: evidence from the palynological records. *World Archaeology* 26(3), 348–65.

Edwards, K.J. & Ralston, I. 1984. Postglacial hunter-gatherers and vegetational history in Scotland. *Proceedings of the Society of Antiquaries of Scotland* 114, 15–34.

Evans, E.E. & Jope, E.M. 1952. Prehistoric: Mesolithic, Neolithic, and Bronze Ages. In E. Jones (ed.), *Belfast in its Regional Setting*, 75–87. Belfast: British Association for the Advancement of Science.

Finlayson, B. 1990a. Lithic exploitation during the Mesolithic in Scotland. *Scottish Archaeological Review* 7, 41–57.

Finlayson, B. 1990b. The function of microliths: evidence from Smittons and Starr, SW Scotland. *Mesolithic Miscellany* 11(1), 2–6.

Finlayson, B. 1995. Complexity in the Mesolithic of the western Scottish seaboard. In A. Fischer (ed.), *Man and Sea in the Mesolithic*, 261–4. Oxford: Oxbow Monograph 53.

Finlayson, B. & Edwards, K.J. 1997. The Mesolithic. In K.J. Edwards & I.B.M. Ralston (eds), *Scotland: Environment and Archaeology, 8000 BC-AD 1000*, 109–25. Chichester: John Wiley & Sons.

Finlayson, B., Finlay, N. & Mithen, S. 1996. Mesolithic chipped stone assemblages: descriptive and analytical procedures used by the Southern Hebrides Mesolithic Project. In T. Pollard & A. Morrison (eds), *The Early Prehistory of Scotland*, 252–66.

Foxon, A.D. 1991. *Bone, Antler, Tooth and Horn Technology and Utilisation in Prehistoric Scotland.* Unpublished PhD thesis, Department of Archaeology, University of Glasgow.

Gorman, F., Murray, B. & Lambie, E. 1995. Kildonan and Machrie, Arran (Kilmory parish): Mesolithic sites. In C.E. Batey (ed.), *Discovery and Excavation in Scotland 1995*, 72. Edinburgh: Council for Scottish Archaeology.

Gray, D.M.R. 1975. Flints from Acharn, Morvern, Argyll. In Ritchie *et al.* 1975, 27–30.

Grieve, S. 1885. *The Great Auk, or Garefowl: its History, Archaeology, and Remains.* London: Thomas C. Jack.

Grieve, S. 1923. *The Book of Colonsay and Oronsay.* Edinburgh: Oliver & Boyd.

Haggarty, A. 1991. Machrie Moor, Arran: recent excavations at two stone circles. *Proceedings of the Society of Antiquaries of Scotland* 121, 51–94.

Hanson, W.S. 1987. Elginhaugh (Dalkeith parish): Roman fort and prehistoric settlement. In E.V.W. & B.E. Proudfoot (eds),

Discovery and Excavation in Scotland 1987, 31–2. Edinburgh: Council for British Archaeology in Scotland.

Hawke-Smith, C.F. 1980. Two Mesolithic sites near Newburgh, Aberdeenshire. *Proceedings of the Society of Antiquaries of Scotland* 110 [for 1978–80], 497–502.

Henshall, A.S. 1982. The distant past. In D. Omand (ed.), *The Sutherland Book*, 135–45. Golspie: The Northern Times.

Herity, M. & Eogan, G. 1977. *Ireland in Prehistory*. London: Routledge & Kegan Paul.

Hoy, C. 1988. Cramond: flints. In E.V.W. Proudfoot (ed.), *Discovery and Excavation in Scotland 1988*, 18. Edinburgh: Council for Scottish Archaeology.

Hughes, I. 1988. Megaliths: space, time and the landscape — a view from the Clyde. *Scottish Archaeological Review* 5, 41–56.

Hughes, I. 1991. Solway and Clyde: some comments. *Scottish Archaeological Review* 8, 33–4.

Hunt, D. 1987. *Early Farming Communities In Scotland: Aspects of Economy And Settlement 4500–1250 B.C.* Oxford: British Archaeological Reports, British Series 159.

Hunter, J.R. 1986. *Rescue Excavations on the Brough of Birsay 1974–82*. Edinburgh: Society of Antiquaries of Scotland, Monograph 4.

Hunter, J.R. 1996. *Fair Isle: the Archaeology of an Island Community*. Edinburgh: National Trust for Scotland/HMSO.

Innes, J.B. & Shennan, I. 1991. Palynology of archaeological and mire sediments from Dod, Borders Region, Scotland. *Archaeological Journal* 148, 1–45.

Jacobi, R.M. 1973. Aspects of the 'Mesolithic Age' in Great Britain. In S.K. Kozlowski (ed.), *The Mesolithic in Europe*, 237–65. Warsaw: Warsaw University Press.

Jacobi, R.M. 1979. Review of J.J. Wymer (ed.), 'Gazetteer of Mesolithic sites in England and Wales'. *Antiquity* 53, 63.

Jacobi, R.M. 1980. The early Holocene settlements of Wales. In J.A. Taylor (ed.), *Culture and Environment in Prehistoric Wales*, 131–206. Oxford: British Archaeological Reports, British Series 76.

Jacobi, R.M. 1982. When did man come to Scotland? *Mesolithic Miscellany* 3(2), 8–9.

Jardine, W.G. 1977. Location and age of Mesolithic coastal occupation sites on Oronsay, Inner Hebrides. *Nature* 267, 138–40.

Jardine, W.G. & Jardine, D.C. 1978. A Mesolithic barbed point from Cnoc Sligeach, Isle of Oronsay, Argyll. *Proceedings of the Society of Antiquaries of Scotland* 109 [for 1977–78], 352–5.

Jardine, W.G. & Jardine, D.C. 1983. Minor excavations and small finds at three Mesolithic sites, Isle of Oronsay, Argyll. *Proceedings of the Society of Antiquaries of Scotland* 113, 22–34.

Jardine, W.G. & Morrison, A. 1976. The archaeological significance of Holocene coastal deposits in south western Scotland. In D.A. Davidson & M.L. Shackley (eds), *Geoarchaeology: Earth Science and the Past*, 175–95. London: Duckworth.

Johnston, D.A. 1991. Biggar Common (Biggar parish): round cairns, long mound, surface scatter. In C.E. Batey & J. Ball (eds), *Discovery and Excavation in Scotland 1991*, 65. Edinburgh: Council for Scottish Archaeology.

Kenworthy, J.B. 1975. The prehistory of north east Scotland. In A.M.D. Gemmell (ed.), *Quaternary Studies in North east Scotland*, 74–81. Aberdeen: Department of Geography, University of Aberdeen.

Kenworthy, J.B. 1980. Banchory, Nethermills Farm, Crathes, Grampian Region: Mesolithic flint scatter. *Proceedings of the Prehistoric Society* 46, 364.

Kenworthy, J.B. 1981. *Excavation of a Mesolithic Settlement Site at Nethermills Farm, Crathes, near Banchory, Grampian, 1978–80: Interim Statement*. Duplicated report; unpublished.

Kenworthy, J.B. 1982. The flint. In J.C. Murray (ed.), *Excavations in the Medieval Burgh of Aberdeen 1973–81*, 200–15. Edinburgh: Society of Antiquaries of Scotland, Monograph 2.

Kinnes, I. 1985. Circumstance not context: the Neolithic of Scotland as seen from outside. *Proceedings of the Society of Antiquaries of Scotland* 115, 15–57.

Kitchener, A.C. & Bonsall, C. 1997. AMS radiocarbon dates for some extinct Scottish mammals. *Quaternary Newsletter* 83, 1–11.

Lacaille, A.D. 1930. Mesolithic implements from Ayrshire. *Proceedings of the Society of Antiquaries of Scotland* 64 [for 1929–30], 34–48.

Lacaille, A.D. 1931. Silex tardenoisiens de Shewalton (Comté d'Ayr), Ecosse. *Bulletin de la Société Préhistorique Française* 28, 301–12.

Lacaille, A.D. 1935. The small flint knives of Orkney. *Proceedings of the Society of Antiquaries of Scotland* 69 [for 1934–35], 251–64.

Lacaille, A.D. 1937. The microlithic industries of Scotland. *Transactions of the Glasgow Archaeological Society* 9, 56–74.

Lacaille, A.D. 1939. A barbed point of deer-antler from Shewalton, Ayrshire. *Proceedings of the Society of Antiquaries of Scotland* 73 [for 1938–39], 48–50.

Lacaille, A.D. 1942. Scottish micro-burins. *Proceedings of the Society of Antiquaries of Scotland* 76 [for 1941–42], 103–19.

Lacaille, A.D. 1944. Unrecorded microliths from Tentsmuir, Deeside, and Culbin. *Proceedings of the Society of Antiquaries of Scotland* 78 [for 1943–44], 5–16.

Lacaille, A.D. 1945. The stone industries associated with the raised beach at Ballantrae. *Proceedings of the Society of Antiquaries of Scotland* 79 [for 1944–45], 81–106.

Lacaille, A.D. 1948. The Stone Age background of Scotland. *Transactions of the Dumfriesshire & Galloway Natural History & Antiquarian Society* 26 [for 1947–48], 9–40.

Lacaille, A.D. 1951. A stone industry from Morar, Inverness-shire; its Obanian (Mesolithic) and later affinities. *Archaeologia* 94, 103–39.

Lacaille, A.D. 1954. *The Stone Age in Scotland*. London: Oxford University Press (for the Wellcome Historical Medical Museum).

Lake, M.W., Woodman, P.E. & Mithen, S.J. 1998. Tailoring GIS software for archaeological applications: an example concerning viewshed analysis. *Journal of Archaeological Science* 25, 27–38.

Livens, R.G. 1956. Three tanged flint points from Scotland. *Proceedings of the Society of Antiquaries of Scotland* 89 [for 1955–56], 438–43.

Livens, R.G. 1957. Excavations at Terally (Wigtownshire), 1956. *Transactions of the Dumfriesshire & Galloway Natural History & Antiquarian Society* 35 [for 1956–57], 85–102.

McCallien, W.J. & Lacaille, A.D. 1941. The Campbeltown raised beach and its contained stone industry. *Proceedings of the Society of Antiquaries of Scotland* 75 [for 1940–41], 55–92.

McCullagh, R. 1989. Excavation at Newton, Islay. *Glasgow Archaeological Journal* 15, 23–51.

MacDonald, A.D.S. & Laing, L.R. 1975. Excavations at Lochmaben Castle, Dumfriesshire. *Proceedings of the Society of Antiquaries of Scotland* 106 [for 1974–75], 124–57.

McFadzean, H. 1984. A venture into Scottish prehistory. *Scottish Archaeological Gazette* 6, 7–9.

McFadzean, H. 1985. A prehistoric chipping-floor of agates on the hills of south Bute. *Transactions of the Buteshire Natural History Society* 22, 33–8.

Mackenzie, J.R. 1995. 73–75 Irish Street, Dumfries: urban Medieval and Mesolithic. In C.E. Batey (ed.), *Discovery and Excavation in Scotland 1995*, 19. Edinburgh: Council for Scottish Archaeology.

MacKie, E.W. 1963. A dwelling site of the earlier Iron Age at Balevullin, Tiree, excavated in 1912 by A. Henderson Bishop. *Proceedings of the Society of Antiquaries of Scotland* 96 [for 1962–63], 155–83.

MacKie, E.W. 1972. Radiocarbon dates for two Mesolithic shell heaps and a Neolithic axe factory in Scotland. *Proceedings of the Prehistoric Society* 38, 412–16.

Macklin, M.G. & Rumsby, B.T. 1991. *Geomorphological Survey of Caves And Rockshelters In The Oban District, Scotland: Report To Historic Scotland.* Unpublished report: Historic Scotland, Edinburgh.

Macklin, M.G., Rumsby, B.T., Bonsall, C., Rhodes, A.N. & Robinson, M. 1992. Archaeological conservation in Oban, western Scotland. In C. Stevens, J.E. Gordon, C.P. Green & M.G. Macklin (eds), *Conserving Our Landscape*, 168–75. Crewe: English Nature/Scottish Natural Heritage.

Mason, J.B. 1927. Notes on flint and other implements found near Selkirk. *Proceedings of the Society of Antiquaries of Scotland* 61 [for 1926–27], 111–15.

Mason, W.D. 1931. Prehistoric man at Tweed Bridge, Selkirk. *Proceedings of the Society of Antiquaries of Scotland* 65 [for 1930–31], 414–17.

Masters, L. 1981. A Mesolithic hearth at Redkirk Point, Gretna, Annandale and Eskdale District. *Transactions of the Dumfriesshire & Galloway Natural History & Antiquarian Society* 56, 111–4.

Mellars, P.A. 1977. Excavation and economic analysis of Mesolithic shell-middens on the island of Oronsay (Hebrides). In L.M. Thoms (ed.), *Early Man In The Scottish Landscape*, 43–61. Edinburgh: Edinburgh University Press (=*Scottish Archaeological Forum* 9).

Mellars, P.A. 1978. Excavation and economic analysis of Mesolithic shell middens on the island of Oronsay (Inner Hebrides). In P.A. Mellars (ed.), *The Early Postglacial Settlement of Northern Europe: An Ecological Perspective*, 371–96. London: Duckworth.

Mellars, P.A. 1981. Cnoc Coig, Druim Harstell and Cnoc Riach: problems of the identification and location of shell middens on Oronsay. *Proceedings of the Society of Antiquaries of Scotland* 111, 516–18.

Mellars, P.A. 1987. *Excavations on Oronsay: Prehistoric Human Ecology on a Small Island.* Edinburgh: Edinburgh University Press.

Mellars, P.A. & Haynes, M. 1986. Mesolithic exploitation of sandy areas: towards the testing of some hypotheses. In G.N. Bailey & P. Callow (eds), *Stone Age Prehistory: Studies In Memory of Charles McBurney*, 69–76. Cambridge: Cambridge University Press.

Mellars, P.A. & Payne, S. 1971. The excavation of two Mesolithic shell middens on the island of Oronsay (Inner Hebrides). *Nature* 231, 397–8.

Mellars, P.A. & Reinhardt, S.C. 1978. Patterns of Mesolithic land-use in southern England: a geological perspective. In P.A. Mellars (ed.), *The Early Postglacial Settlement of Northern Europe: an Ecological Perspective*, 243–93. London: Duckworth.

Mellars, P.A. & Wilkinson, M.R. 1980. Fish otoliths as indicators of seasonality in prehistoric shell middens: the evidence from Oronsay (Inner Hebrides). *Proceedings of the Prehistoric Society* 46, 19–44.

Mercer, J. 1968. Stone tools from a washing-limit deposit of the highest post-glacial transgression, Lealt Bay, Isle of Jura. *Proceedings of the Society of Antiquaries of Scotland* 100 [for 1967–68], 1–46.

Mercer, J. 1970a. Flint tools from the present tidal zone, Lussa Bay, Isle of Jura, Argyll. *Proceedings of the Society of Antiquaries of Scotland* 102 [for 1969–70], 1–30.

Mercer, J. 1970b. The microlithic succession in N. Jura, Argyll, W. Scotland. *Quaternaria* 13, 177–85.

Mercer, J. 1971. A regression-time stone-workers' camp, 33ft OD, Lussa River, Isle of Jura. *Proceedings of the Society of Antiquaries of Scotland* 103 [for 1970–71], 1–32.

Mercer, J. 1972. Microlithic and Bronze Age camps, 75–26ft OD, N Carn, Isle of Jura. *Proceedings of the Society of Antiquaries of Scotland* 104 [for 1971–72], 1–22.

Mercer, J. 1974a. Glenbatrick Waterhole, a microlithic site on the Isle of Jura. *Proceedings of the Society of Antiquaries of Scotland* 105 [for 1973–74], 9–32.

Mercer, J. 1974b. New C14 dates from the Isle of Jura, Argyll. *Antiquity* 189, 65–6.

Mercer, J. 1979a. The Palaeolithic and Mesolithic occupation of the Isle of Jura. *Almogaren: Jahrbuch des Institutum Canarium und der Gisaf* 9–10 [for 1978–79], 347–67.

Mercer, J. 1979b. Barr River, a microlithic site in Morvern, Argyll. *Glasgow Archaeological Journal* 6, 1–4.

Mercer, J. 1980. Lussa Wood 1: the Late-Glacial and early Post-Glacial occupation of Jura. *Proceedings of the Society of Antiquaries of Scotland* 110 [for 1978–80], 1–32.

Mercer, J. 1981. The Palaeolithic and Mesolithic occupation of the Isle of Jura. *The Kist* (Magazine of the Natural History & Antiquarian Society of Mid-Argyll) 22, 15–18.

Mercer, J. & Searight, S. 1986. Glengarrisdale: confirmation of Jura's third microlithic phase. *Proceedings of the Society of Antiquaries of Scotland* 116, 41–55.

Mithen, S.J. 1989. New evidence for Mesolithic settlement on Colonsay. *Proceedings of the Society of Antiquaries of Scotland* 119, 33–41.

Mithen, S.J. 1990. Gleann Mor: a Mesolithic site on Islay. *Current Archaeology* 119, 376–7.

Mithen, S.J. 1993. Islay and Coulerach: Mesolithic settlement. In C.E. Batey (ed.), *Discovery and Excavation in Scotland 1993*, 68–9. Edinburgh: Council for Scottish Archaeology.

Mithen, S.J. 1995. Mesolithic settlement and raw material availability in the southern Hebrides. In A. Fischer (ed.), *Man and Sea in the Mesolithic*, 265–72. Oxford: Oxbow Monograph 53.

Mithen, S.J. 1997. The Southern Hebrides Mesolithic project. In A.G. Dawson & S. Dawson (eds), *Quaternary of Islay and Jura*, 60–5. Cambridge: Quaternary Research Association.

Mithen, S.J. & Finlayson, B. 1991. Red deer hunters on Colonsay? The implications of Staosnaig for the interpretation of the Oronsay middens. *Proceedings of the Prehistoric Society* 57(2), 1–8.

Mithen, S.J, Finlayson, B., Finlay, N. & Lake, M. 1992. Excavations at Bolsay Farm, a Mesolithic Settlement on Islay. *Cambridge Archaeological Journal* 2(2), 242–53.

Mithen, S.J. & Lake, M. 1996. The southern Hebrides Mesolithic project. In T. Pollard & A. Morrison (eds), *The Early Prehistory of Scotland*, 123–51. Edinburgh: Edinburgh University Press.

Morrison, A. 1980. *Early Man in Britain and Ireland.* London: Croom Helm.

Morrison, A. 1981. The coastal Mesolithic in south west Scotland. In B. Gramsch (ed.), *Mesolithikum in Europa*, 441–50. Berlin: VEB Deutscher Verlag der Wissenschaften.

Morrison, A. 1982a. Man in the early Scottish environment: comment on Price. *Scottish Archaeological Review* 1(2), 73–7.

Morrison, A. 1982b. The Mesolithic period in south west Scotland: a review of the evidence. *Glasgow Archaeological Journal* 9, 1–14.

Morrison, A. 1996. John Smith and the earlier prehistory of Ayrshire. In D. Reid (ed.), *John Smith of Dalry: Geologist, Antiquarian and Natural Historian. Part 2: Archaeology and Natural History*, 11–33. Darvel: Ayrshire Archaeological & Natural History Society (Ayrshire Monographs No. 17).

Morrison, A. & Bonsall, C. 1989. The early post-glacial settlement of Scotland: a review. In C. Bonsall (ed.), *The Mesolithic in Europe*, 134–42. Edinburgh: John Donald.

Morrison, A. & Hughes, I. 1989. *The Stone Ages in Ayrshire*. Darvel: Ayrshire Archaeological & Natural History Society.

Mountain, M.-J. 1979. The later Mesolithic of Britain: Scotland and Ireland. In J.V.S. Megaw & D.D.A. Simpson (eds), *Introduction to British Prehistory*, 60–71. Leicester: Leicester University Press.

Movius, H.L., Jr 1942. *The Irish Stone Age*. Cambridge: Cambridge University Press.

Movius, H.L., Jr 1953. Curran Point, Larne, County Antrim: the type site of the Irish Mesolithic. *Proceedings of the Royal Irish Academy* C 56, 1–195.

Mulholland, H. 1970. The microlithic industries of the Tweed Valley. *Transactions of the Dumfriesshire & Galloway Natural History & Antiquarian Society* 47, 81–110.

Murray, J. 1991. Megaliths again — a view from the Solway. *Scottish Archaeological Review* 8, 26–32.

Murray, J. 1994. *The Role of Monuments In The Neolithic of The South of Scotland*. Unpublished PhD thesis, University of Edinburgh.

Myers, A.M. 1988. Scotland inside and outside of the British mainland Mesolithic. *Scottish Archaeological Review* 5, 23–9.

Myers, A.M. & Gourlay, R.B. 1991. Muirtown, Inverness: preliminary investigation of a shell midden. *Proceedings of the Society of Antiquaries of Scotland* 121, 17–25.

Newall, F. 1962. Mesolithic occupation of Gleann Mor and the Port Charlotte area. In M.E.C. Stewart (ed.), *Discovery and Excavation in Scotland 1962*, 12–13. Edinburgh: Scottish Regional Group, Council for British Archaeology.

Newall, F. 1963. Mesolithic occupation of Gleann Mor. In M.E.C. Stewart (ed.), *Discovery and Excavation in Scotland 1963*, 18. Edinburgh: Scottish Regional Group, Council for British Archaeology.

O'Connor, A. & Clarke, D.V. (eds). 1983. *From the Stone Age to the 'Forty-Five: Studies Presented to R.B.K. Stevenson*. Edinburgh: John Donald.

Paterson, H.M.L. 1912. Pigmy flints in the Dee Valley. *Report of the British Association*, 605–6.

Paterson, H.M.L. 1913. Pygmy flints in the Dee Valley. *Man*, 103–5.

Paterson, H.M.L. 1929. Pygmy flints. *The Deeside Field* 4, 64–6.

Paterson, H.M.L. & Lacaille, A.D. 1936. Banchory microliths. *Proceedings of the Society of Antiquaries of Scotland* 70 [for 1935–36], 419–34.

Pollard, T. 1990. Down through the ages: a review of the Oban cave deposits. *Scottish Archaeological Review* 7, 58–74.

Pollard, T. 1993. Kirkhill Farm (Johnstone parish): Mesolithic flint scatter with associated structures and burnt mound. In C.E. Batey (ed.), *Discovery and Excavation in Scotland 1993*, 15. Edinburgh: Council for Scottish Archaeology.

Pollard, T. 1996. Time and tide: coastal environments, cosmology and ritual practice in early prehistoric Scotland. In T. Pollard & A. Morrison (eds), *The Early Prehistory of Scotland*, 198–210. Edinburgh: Edinburgh University Press.

Pollard, T., Atkinson, J. & Banks, I. 1996. 'It is the technical side of the work which is my stumbling block': a shell midden site on Risga reconsidered. In T. Pollard & A. Morrison (eds), *The Early Prehistory of Scotland*, 165–82. Edinburgh: Edinburgh University Press.

Price, R.J. 1982. The magnitude and relative frequency of late Quaternary environmental changes in Scotland: implications for human occupation. *Scottish Archaeological Review* 1(2), 61–72.

Raftery, J. 1951. *Prehistoric Ireland*. London: Batsford.

RCAHMS (Royal Commission on the Ancient & Historical Monuments of Scotland). 1963. *Stirlingshire, an Inventory of The Ancient Monuments. Vol.1*. Edinburgh: HMSO.

RCAHMS (Royal Commission on the Ancient & Historical Monuments of Scotland). 1971. *Argyll: an Inventory of the Ancient Monuments. Vol. 1: Kintyre*. Edinburgh: HMSO.

RCAHMS (Royal Commission on the Ancient & Historical Monuments of Scotland). 1975. *Argyll: an Inventory of the Ancient Monuments. Vol. 2: Lorn*. Edinburgh: HMSO.

RCAHMS (Royal Commission on the Ancient & Historical Monuments of Scotland). 1978. *Lanarkshire: an Inventory of the Prehistoric and Roman Monuments*. Edinburgh: HMSO.

RCAHMS (Royal Commission on the Ancient & Historical Monuments of Scotland). 1980. *Argyll: an Inventory of the Monuments. Vol. 3: Mull, Tiree, Coll & Northern Argyll*. Edinburgh: HMSO.

RCAHMS (Royal Commission on the Ancient & Historical Monuments of Scotland). 1982. *Argyll: an Inventory of the Monuments. Vol. 4: Iona*. Edinburgh: HMSO.

RCAHMS (Royal Commission on the Ancient & Historical Monuments of Scotland). 1984. *Argyll: an Inventory of the Monuments. Vol. 5: Islay, Jura, Colonsay & Oronsay*. Edinburgh: HMSO.

RCAHMS (Royal Commission on the Ancient & Historical Monuments of Scotland). 1988. *Argyll: an Inventory of the Monuments. Vol. 6: mid Argyll & Cowal*. Edinburgh: HMSO.

RCAHMS (Royal Commission on the Ancient & Historical Monuments of Scotland). 1997. *Eastern Dumfriesshire: an Archaeological Landscape*. Edinburgh: The Stationery Office.

Reed, D. 1995. Cramond Roman fort (City parish of Edinburgh): Mesolithic features, artefacts. In C.E. Batey (ed.), *Discovery and Excavation in Scotland 1995*, 53. Edinburgh: Council for Scottish Archaeology.

Rendall, R. 1937. The South Ettit flint industries. *Proceedings of the Orkney Antiquarian Society* 14, 45–56.

Reynolds, T.E.G. 1983. *Form, Function, and Technology: a Test Case of Limpet Scoops*. Unpublished BA dissertation, University of Cambridge.

Richards, C. 1985. *Orkney Survey Project: Interim Report 1984*. Glasgow: University of Glasgow, Department of Archaeology.

Richards, C. 1986. Seatter Farm 1 (Stromness parish) flint scatters. In E.V.W. & B.E. Proudfoot (eds), *Discovery and Excavation in Scotland 1986*, 22. Edinburgh: Council for British Archaeology, Scotland.

Rideout, J.S. 1996. Excavation of a promontory fort and a palisaded homestead at Lower Greenyards, Bannockburn, Stirling, 1982–5. *Proceedings of the Society of Antiquaries of Scotland* 126, 199–269.

Ritchie, J.N.G. 1997. Early settlement in Argyll: Mesolithic evidence. In J.N.G. Ritchie (ed.), *The Archaeology of Argyll*, 38–44. Edinburgh: Edinburgh University Press.

Ritchie, J.N.G., Crawford, J., Close-Brooks, J., Lane, A.M. & Wickham-Jones, C.R. 1978. Recent work on Coll and Skye. *Proceedings of the Society of Antiquaries of Scotland* 109 [for 1977–78], 75–103.

Ritchie, J.N.G. & Ritchie, A. 1972. *Regional Archaeologies: Edinburgh and South east Scotland*. London: Heinemann Educational Books.

Ritchie, J.N.G. & Ritchie, A. 1981. *Scotland: Archaeology and Early History*. London: Thames & Hudson.

Ritchie, J.N.G., Thornber, I., Lynch, F., & Marshall, D.N. 1975. Small cairns in Argyll: some recent work. *Proceedings of the Society of Antiquaries of Scotland* 106 [for 1974–75], 15–38.

Robertson, A.S. 1964. *The Roman Fort at Castledykes*. Edinburgh: Oliver & Boyd.

Robinson, D. 1983a. Possible Mesolithic activity in the west of Arran: evidence from peat deposits. *Glasgow Archaeological Journal* 10, 1–11.

Robinson, D. 1983b. Prehistoric man and the environment on the west of Arran, Scotland. In B. Proudfoot (ed.), *Site, Environment and Economy*, 57–9. Oxford: British Archaeological Reports, International Series 173.

Rowley-Conwy, P. 1994. Palaeolithic and Mesolithic: from culture to behaviour. In B. Vyner (ed.), *Building on the Past: Papers Celebrating 150 Years of the Royal Archaeological Institute*, 75–89. London: Royal Archaeological Institute.

Russell, N.J., Bonsall, C. & Sutherland, D.G. 1995. The exploitation of marine molluscs in the Mesolithic of western Scotland: evidence from Ulva Cave, Inner Hebrides. In A. Fischer (ed.), *Man and Sea in the Mesolithic*, 273–88. Oxford: Oxbow Books, Monograph 53.

Ryan, M. 1980. An early Mesolithic site in the Irish Midlands. *Antiquity* 54, 46–7.

Saville, A. 1981. Mesolithic industries in central England: an exploratory investigation using microlith typology. *Archaeological Journal* 138, 49–71.

Saville, A. 1993. Report on the flint tools recovered at Romancamp Gate. In Barclay 1993, 262–3.

Saville, A. 1994a. Exploitation of lithic resources for stone tools in earlier prehistoric Scotland. In N. Ashton & A. David (eds), *Stories in Stone*, 57–70. London: Lithic Studies Society, Occasional Paper 4.

Saville, A. 1994b. A possible Mesolithic stone axehead from Scotland. *Lithics* 15, 25–8.

Saville, A. 1996a. Lacaille, microliths, and the Mesolithic of Orkney. In T. Pollard & A. Morrison (eds), *The Early Prehistory of Scotland*, 213–24. Edinburgh: Edinburgh University Press.

Saville, A. 1996b. Foreshore W of Blackness Bay: Mesolithic barbed point. In R. Turner (ed.), *Discovery and Excavation in Scotland 1996*, 41. Edinburgh: Council for Scottish Archaeology.

Saville, A. forthcoming. Mesolithic Scotland. In R.J. Mercer (ed.), *The Archaeology of Scotland*. Edinburgh: Edinburgh University Press.

Saville, A. & Hallén, Y. 1994. The 'Obanian Iron Age': human remains from the Oban cave sites, Argyll, Scotland. *Antiquity* 68, 715–23.

Saville, A. & Miket, R. 1994a. An Corran rock-shelter, Skye: a major new Mesolithic site. *Past* 18, 9–10.

Saville, A. & Miket, R. 1994b. An Corran, Staffin, Skye (Kilmuir parish): rock-shelter. In C.E. Batey & M. King (eds), *Discovery and Excavation in Scotland 1994*, 40–1. Edinburgh: Council for Scottish Archaeology.

Scott, J.G. 1966. *Regional Archaeologies: South West Scotland*. London: Heinemann Educational Books.

Searight, S. 1984. The Mesolithic on Jura. *Current Archaeology* 90, 209–14.

Searight, S. 1990. Mesolithic activity at Carn Southern raised beach, Isle of Jura. *Proceedings of the Society of Antiquaries of Scotland* 120, 7–16.

Searight, S. 1993. Lussa Bay, Isle of Jura, Argyll: a note on additional tools. *Proceedings of the Society of Antiquaries of Scotland* 123, 1–8.

Shepherd, I.A.G. 1987. The early peoples. In D. Ormand (ed.), *The Grampian Book*, 119–30. Golspie: The Northern Times.

Simmons, I.G. 1996. *The Environmental Impact of Later Mesolithic Cultures: the Creation of Moorland Landscape in England and Wales*. Edinburgh: Edinburgh University Press.

Sloan, D. 1982. Nether Kinneil. *Current Archaeology* 84, 13–15.

Sloan, D. 1984a. Shell middens and chronology in Scotland. *Scottish Archaeological Forum* 3(2), 73–9.

Sloan, D. 1984b. A research design for the Forth Valley. *Scottish Archaeological Gazette* 6, 9–13.

Sloan, D. 1985a. Falkirk District: shell middens. In E.V.W. Proudfoot (ed.), *Discovery and Excavation in Scotland 1985*, 5–8. Edinburgh: Council for British Archaeology, Scotland.

Sloan, D. 1985b. Fieldwork in the Forth Valley, 1984–85. *Scottish Archaeological Gazette*. 9, 6–8.

Sloan, 1986. Shell middens of Scotland. *Popular Archaeology* 7(1), 10–15.

Sloan, 1987. The shell mounds mystery. *The Scots Magazine* 127(4), 383–9.

Sloan, D. 1993. *Sample, Site and System: Shell Midden Economies in Scotland, 6000–4000 BP*. Unpublished DPhil thesis, University of Cambridge.

Sloan, D. & Murray, J.F. 1980. Nether Kinneil, Falkirk District, Central Region, NS958880, shell midden. *Proceedings of the Prehistoric Society* 46, 364–5.

Smith, C. 1989. British antler mattocks. In C. Bonsall (ed.), *The Mesolithic in Europe*, 272–83. Edinburgh: John Donald.

Smith, C. 1992. *Late Stone Age Hunters of the British Isles*. London: Routledge.

Smith, C. & Bonsall, C. 1991. Late Upper Palaeolithic and Mesolithic chronology: points of interest from recent research. In N. Barton, A.J. Roberts & D.A. Roe (eds), *The Late Glacial in North West Europe: Human Adaptation and Environmental Change at the End of the Pleistocene*, 208–12. London: Council for British Archaeology, Research Report 77.

Smith, C. & Openshaw, S. 1990. Mapping the Mesolithic. In P.M. Vermeersch & P. van Peer (eds), *Contributions to the Mesolithic in Europe*, 17–22. Leuven: Leuven University Press.

Tipping, R. 1994. The form and fate of Scotland's woodlands. *Proceedings of the Society of Antiquaries of Scotland* 124, 1–54.

Tipping, R. 1996. Microscopic charcoal records, inferred human activity, and climate change in the Mesolithic of northernmost Scotland. In T. Pollard & A. Morrison (eds), *The Early Prehistory of Scotland*, 39–61. Edinburgh: Edinburgh University Press.

Trigger, B.G. 1989. *A History of Archaeological Thought*. Cambridge: Cambridge University Press.

Truckell, A.E. 1954. Recent Museum acquistions – 1955. *Transactions of the Dumfriesshire & Galloway Natural History & Antiquarian Society* 32 [for 1953–54], 172–7.

Truckell, A.E. 1957. Finds at Twiglees. *Transactions of the Dumfriesshire & Galloway Natural History & Antiquarian Society* 35 [for 1956–57], 140.

Truckell, A.E. 1962. The Mesolithic in Dumfries and Galloway: recent developments. *Transactions of the Dumfriesshire & Galloway Natural History & Antiquarian Society* 40 [for 1961–62], 43–7.

Turner, W. 1889. On implements of stag's horn associated with whales' skeletons found in the Carse of Stirling. *Report of the British Association*, 789–91.

Turner, W. 1895. On human and animal remains found in caves at Oban, Argyllshire. *Proceedings of the Society of Antiquaries of Scotland* 29 [for 1894–95], 410–38.

Walker, M. n.d. *Archaeological Excavation of a Microlithic Assemblage at Shieldaig, Wester Ross, Scotland, 24/iii/73 – 6/iv/73: Preliminary Report*. Unpublished duplicated report: copy in the National Monuments Record of Scotland, Edinburgh.

Ward, T. 1995. Daer reservoir (Crawford parish): bastle house, cairns, find-spots, Mesolithic knapping site. In C.E. Batey (ed.), *Discovery and Excavation in Scotland 1995*, 87. Edinburgh: Council for Scottish Archaeology.

Wickham-Jones, C.R. 1989. Recent work on the island of Rhum, Scotland. In C. Bonsall (ed.), *The Mesolithic in Europe*, 156–63. Edinburgh: John Donald.

Wickham-Jones, C.R. 1990a. Orkney Islands: survey of Mesolithic sites. In E.V.W. & B.E. Proudfoot (eds), *Discovery and Excavation in Scotland 1990*, 44. Edinburgh: Council for Scottish Archaeology.

Wickham-Jones, C.R. 1990b. *Rhum, Mesolithic and Later Sites at Kinloch: Excavations 1984–86*. Edinburgh: Society of Antiquaries of Scotland, Monograph 7.

Wickham-Jones, C.R. 1994. *Scotland's First Settlers*. London: Batsford/Historic Scotland.

Wickham-Jones, C.R., Brown, M.M., Cowie, T.G., Gallagher, D.B. & Ritchie, J.N.G. 1982. Excavations at Druim Arstail, Oronsay, 1911–12. *Glasgow Archaeological Journal* 9, 18–30.

Wickham-Jones, C.R. & Firth, C. 1990a. Mesolithic survey: Caithness. In E.V.W. & B.E. Proudfoot (eds), *Discovery and Excavation in Scotland 1990*, 22. Edinburgh: Council for Scottish Archaeology.

Wickham-Jones, C.R. & Firth, C. 1990b. Baile Mhargait, Invernaver (Farr parish): scatter of Mesolithic stone tools. In E.V.W. & B.E. Proudfoot (eds), *Discovery and Excavation in Scotland 1990*, 28. Edinburgh: Council for Scottish Archaeology.

Wickham-Jones, C.R. & Pollock, D. 1985. Excavations at Farm Fields, Kinloch, Rhum 1984–85: a preliminary report. *Glasgow Archaeological Journal* 12, 19–29.

Woodman, P.C. 1978. *The Mesolithic in Ireland*. Oxford: British Archaeological Reports, British Series 58.

Woodman, P.C. 1988. Comment on Myers. *Scottish Archaeological Review* 5, 34–5.

Woodman, P.C. 1989a. The Mesolithic of Munster: a preliminary assessment. In C. Bonsall (ed.), *The Mesolithic in Europe*, 116–24. Edinburgh: John Donald.

Woodman, P.C. 1989b. A review of the Scottish Mesolithic: a plea for normality! *Proceedings of the Society of Antiquaries of Scotland* 119, 1–32.

Wordsworth, J. 1985. The excavation of a Mesolithic horizon at 13–24 Castle Street, Inverness. *Proceedings of the Society of Antiquaries of Scotland* 115, 89–103.

Wymer, J.J. (ed.). 1977a. *Gazetteer of Mesolithic Sites in England and Wales (with a Gazetteer of Upper Palaeolithic sites in England and Wales Edited by C.J. Bonsall)*. London: Geo Abstracts and the Council for British Archaeology, Research Report 20.

Wymer, J.J. 1977b. Foreword. In S. Palmer, *Mesolithic Cultures of Britain*, 7–8. Poole: The Dolphin Press.

29. The Surface of the Breckland

Frances Healy

ABSTRACT

The Later Neolithic and Bronze Age occupation of the Breckland is discussed in the context of the use of its exceptional flint resources within and around the region.

INTRODUCTION

Flint has been one of the most enduringly exploited resources of the Breckland of southwest Norfolk and northwest Suffolk, through the region's many physical transformations, down to the gunflint industry of the recent past (Skertchly 1879). While flint is almost ubiquitous in East Anglia, that of the Breckland is exceptional in quality, abundance and size. The west-to-east dip of the East Anglian Chalk has meant that beds containing high quality flint have long been close to the surface of the area. In addition the local gravels consist almost entirely of flint and the tills are flint-rich. To the east, on the other hand, later zones of flint-bearing Chalk became covered by a succession of Pleistocene deposits which rendered them increasingly less accessible. To the west lie older Chalk zones containing progressively less, smaller and poorer flint, the western limit of regularly flint-bearing Chalk lying *c* 8km west of Grime's Graves (Healy 1991c, fig. 4.1). To the west again are the flintless clays and sandstones which eroded to form the Fenland basin.

The use of Breckland flint in the Pleistocene is seen at a wealth of Palaeolithic sites in the area (Wymer 1985, 102–42), including Barnham (Ashton & Dean this volume). Late Glacial sites are also known (Wymer 1971; Jacobi 1984, fig. 4.2). Frequent Mesolithic sites (Jacobi 1984, 47–69), like Lackford Heath, Suffolk (Roberts *et al.* this volume), and Two Mile Bottom, Thetford, Norfolk (Robins this

volume), lie within in a spread of dispersed contemporary finds. The Early Neolithic is similarly represented by a scatter of sites and artefacts. Lithics of these periods are, however, swamped by the mass of struck flint discarded in the area from the Middle and Late Neolithic onwards. Substantial flint industries were generated throughout the third and second millennia cal BC, at least up to the time of the Late Bronze/Early Iron Age settlement at West Harling, Norfolk (Clark & Fell 1953). The smith who cast bronze palstaves from the moulds found at Harling (Wymer 1987) would have been a flint-user.

COLLECTING IN ANOTHER ERA

'It may be recalled that in 1905 Messers W.G. Clarke and W.A. Dutt measured off a rod of land on the Inkerman Breck, Santon, . . . and taking the number of chips, flakes and implements lying in this plot as a basis, found that an average square mile would yield, on the surface, 2,764,800 implements and 13,209,600 worked flints.' (Clarke & Hewitt 1914, 432).

Lithics of the third and second millennia cal BC would have made up the bulk of the 15 million-odd total in this early exercise in quantitative archaeology (based on a <1% sample with no explicit consideration of its representativeness). In the first quarter of this century the antiquarian enthusiasm of the founders of the Prehistoric Society of

East Anglia coincided with the last decades in which much of the coversands which characterize the Breckland were still heath, where sandblows and numberless rabbits combined to provide optimal collecting conditions, enhanced by further ground-breaking during the expansion of the coniferous plantations which now mantle the region. These circumstances, in which the collections described by Peter Robins (this volume) were made, now survive in restricted zones, notably the Stanford military training area, and obtain elsewhere only during intervals between felling and replanting.

W.G. Clarke describes a Breckland almost unrecognisable today, 'the tawny bents that border the winding cart tracks in the sand seem as though they must be the product of a thousand years; the heathland road on which one may wander for mile after mile through parish after parish without seeing any human being, seems as though its only fitting user would be a skin-clad Neolithic hunter with his flint-tipped arrows' (1925, 34). His experiences in this environment mirrored those of any collector or field walker, 'Neolithic implements . . . may be found on the surface of heaths (where rabbits and moles turn them out), brecks and arable fields. I have found them in every parish in Breckland . . . Yet it must not be assumed that implements occur in all parts of these parishes. Stations are usually limited in area . . . . Even on arable sites that are well-known as settlements the condition of the soil is an important factor in the discovery of implements. When newly ploughed the flints are hidden in the loose sand, and it is only after rains have consolidated the soil that there is any real opportunity of a search being rewarded with success . . . In some of the finest examples the flint is translucent and butter-scotch in colour. No source of the raw material is known.' (1925, 179–81).

High yields were commonplace, reflected in the Reverend Nightingale's summary of his collection from Beechamwell, 'Above 3,000 worked flints have been found in an area of half a square mile, of which one-third were considered worth preservation. These included 500 scrapers, 50 arrowheads and points, 47 axes (these were found scattered over a much larger area), 40 spear and javelin heads, very many knives, awls, borers, saws and "fabricators" ' (1913).

These activities were the context of the excavations at Grime's Graves, begun in 1914 under the direction of Harold Peake (Clarke 1915), and continued by A.L. Armstrong up to the outbreak of World War II. In the mid-twentieth century fieldwork tended to focus on barrow excavation, the salvage of a Late Neolithic living site at Honington, Suffolk, being an almost accidental exception (Fell 1951).

THE LAST FEW DECADES

Excavations at Grime's Graves under the aegis of the Department of the Environment in 1971–2 (Mercer 1981)

were followed by the British Museum's 1972–6 research programme. In the surrounding area, collecting has continued when enthusiasm and opportunity have coincided. At the same time, excavations like those of the Iron Age complex at Fison Way, Thetford, Norfolk, a Late Iron Age enclosure at Barnham, Suffolk, a Saxon settlement at West Stow, Suffolk, and a Saxon and medieval site at Middle Harling, Norfolk, have provided snapshots of the Neolithic and Bronze Age archaeology in and below the topsoil.

Such excavations have shown that Late Neolithic and Bronze Age subsoil features were extremely rare, as they had been at Honington, while contemporary struck flint was near-ubiquitous (Gregory 1991, fig. 6; Martin 1993, 10–11, 14–16; West 1990, 5–10, fig. 44; Rogerson 1995, figs 7, 26). They have generated samples of contemporary lithics which are in relatively fresh condition, making assessment of raw material sources easier than for the often heavily corticated surface material. They have also provided collections which are far less selective than the Reverend Nightingale's or, for example, that of R.F. Parrott, who paid farmworkers for the artefacts they brought him on a scale which ran from 1d or 2d for a scraper to up to 2s 6d for an arrowhead. To the west of the Breckland the wasting peat fen and its skirtland have been the subject of extensive fieldwalking survey (Silvester 1991), following decades of selective collection (Healy 1996).

THE BRECKLAND IN THE LATER NEOLITHIC AND BRONZE AGE

By *c.* 3,000 cal BC the area had long been covered by mixed deciduous forest, broken by short-lived clearings, like those in which flint mine shafts were sunk at Grime's Graves (Bennett 1983; Evans 1981, 106–7). By the Early Bronze Age there were open, probably grazed, areas on calcareous slope soils (the most water-retentive facets of an over-drained area), where clearance and cultivation are likely to have been concentrated (Legge 1981; Murphy 1984). The heaths of historical times seem to have developed as a consequence of intensified cultivation during the Iron Age (Bennett 1983; Murphy 1991).

Large raw material size is a distinguishing mark of collections from many parts of the Breckland, seen in mean cores weights like some of those in Table 29.1. Variation in weight across the area reflects variation in immediately available raw material. The surface nodules at Harling, to the east (Fig. 29.1) are generally smaller than their equivalents closer to Grime's Graves. The cores in a Late Bronze or Early Iron Age collection from London Road, Thetford, for example, weigh up to 215g (Gardiner 1993, 456). With large size goes an 'industrial' aspect. A Levallois-like technique was used not only to produce blanks for transverse arrowheads, a widespread contemporary practice, but much larger flakes, some of which served as blanks for discoidal knives or even axeheads.

	Site/assemblage	Main flint type	Distance from Grime's Graves (km)	Mean weight of complete cores (g)	Sources
Grime's Graves	Grime's Graves, 1971, trenches 3 & 4, layer 3. Late Neolithic	Freshly mined floorstone	-	372	Saville 1981, 35-6
	Grime's Graves 1972 shaft. Middle Bronze Age 'midden' in top of silted mine shaft	Floorstone and wallstone retrieved from Neolithic spoil	-	305	Saville 1981, 20
	Grime's Graves shaft X Middle Bronze Age 'midden' in top of silted mine shaft	Floorstone and wallstone retrieved from Neolithic spoil	-	340	Herne 1991, table 11
Elsewhere in Breckland	Fengate Farm, Weeting-with-Broomhill, unstratified and redeposited, mainly Late Neolithic and Bronze Age	Surface	4.5	322	
	Middle Harling, pits with Fengate Ware, Middle Neolithic	Surface	18	168	Healy 1995, table 4
	Middle Harling, pits with Grooved Ware, Late Neolithic	Surface	18	68	" "
Beyond Breckland	Blackdyke Farm, Hockwold-cum-Wilton, Beaker/Early Bronze Age living sites	Surface	12.5	35	Healy 1996, table 6
	Spong Hill, North Elmham, feature groups B and D, Early Neolithic	Glacial outwash gravel	35	69	Healy 1988, figs 33–34
	Redgate Hill, Hunstanton, pits with Grooved Ware, Late Neolithic	Beach pebbles	50	109	Healy *et al.* 1993, table 23

Table 29.1. Mean core weights from Grime's Graves and collections from within and beyond the Breckland

Both of the last were made in the region. Massive, often broken, flaked discoidal knives can be found in the surface collections, among them several from Santon, Lynford, in the Halls and Warburton collections (Norwich Castle Museum accession numbers 84.924 and 153.929). The form, whether ground or not, has one of its maximum concentrations in the Breckland (Clark 1928; Healy 1980, vol. 1, 287, 306). An attempt to examine the distribution of different classes of flint and stone axeheads across Norfolk, excluding those found on known mine and quarry sites, showed that flaked implements, with no trace of grinding, are commonest in the northern part of the Breckland, where they were almost twice as frequent as in the county as a whole (Healy 1984, fig. 5.12). On an even more local level, flaked axeheads are commoner in the Breckland and ground ones commoner on the adjacent fen edge; the same is true of discoidal knives (Healy 1996, figs 39–40).

Several aspects of Breckland surface material are represented in the small collection illustrated in Figures 2 and 3, from the excavation of a Romano-British site on a farm which was once the home of the collector R.W. Parrott (Gregory 1996). These include large size (Table 29.1), Levallois-like technique (no. 1), implements calling for large, sound flakes as blanks (nos 3, 4, 7); and the use of a variety of flints, dominated by nodular chalk flint, often weathered (Appendix; cf. Gardiner 1993, 456). Nos 2 and 3 are made on fresh, dark flint. Nos 1 and 6 must have come from a variety of secondary sources. Nos 4 and 7 are made of the translucent, butterscotch-coloured flint noted

by Clarke more than 70 years ago. Its sources remain unknown, but the relatively fresh, unabraded cortex of some of it suggests collection from tills rather than gravels. It is widespread in collections from the Breckland and fen edge (Healy 1991b, 125, fig. 68), where its apparent selection for arrowhead manufacture at Hurst Fen (Clark & Higgs 1960, fig. 9) does not seem to be replicated on other sites.

Manufacture of heavy core tools can be seen at sites like the 'floor' investigated by Sturge in old OS field 307 at Icklingham, Suffolk, at a location compatible with quarrying in the side of the Lark valley, where a mass of knapping debris was found under blown sand on the rotted surface of the Chalk. The surviving collection includes Levallois-like cores, flaked axes, an irregular heavy biface and hammerstones, as well as a flake from a ground implement and flake tools such as scrapers and serrated pieces (British Museum, unregistered, labelled '307 floor'). Charcoal was also present, possibly in recognisable hearths (Sturge 1913). Sturge concluded that the industry was Neolithic, though of unusual aspect. Reginald Smith saw it as Palaeolithic, complete with hand-axes (1931, 6–10, cat. nos 42–54), a reverberation from the debate over the age of Grime's Graves and other flint mines. This 'floor' was probably the context of a Fengate Ware assemblage (Piggott 1931, fig. 17; 1954, pl. X:2), which is registered as excavated from Icklingham OS field 307 in 1913 by Dr W.A. Sturge, with a reference to his 1913 report (British Museum 1914, 2–12).

One feature of Breckland surface collections is the

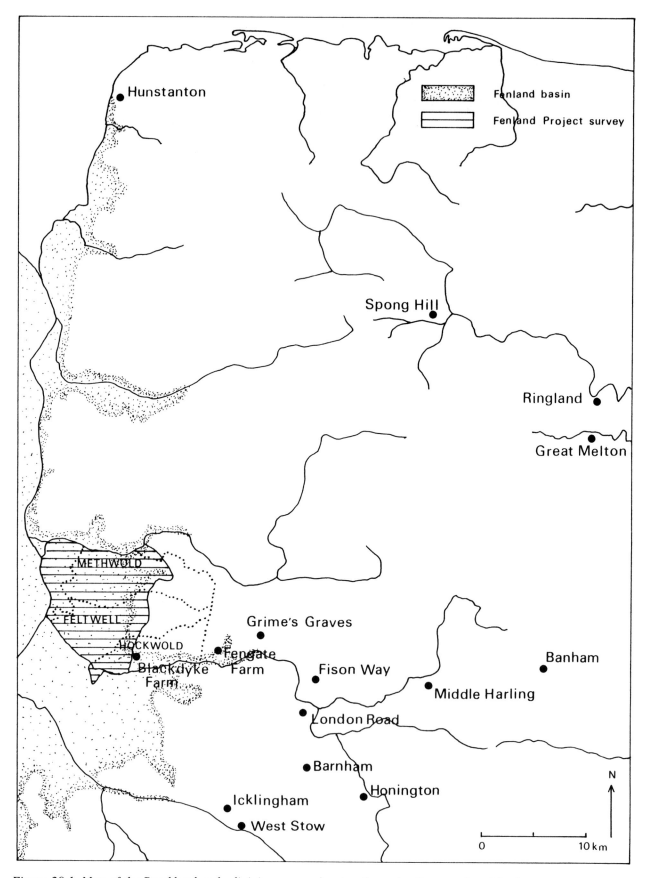

Figure 29.1. Map of the Breckland and adjoining areas, showing the main sites mentioned in the text.

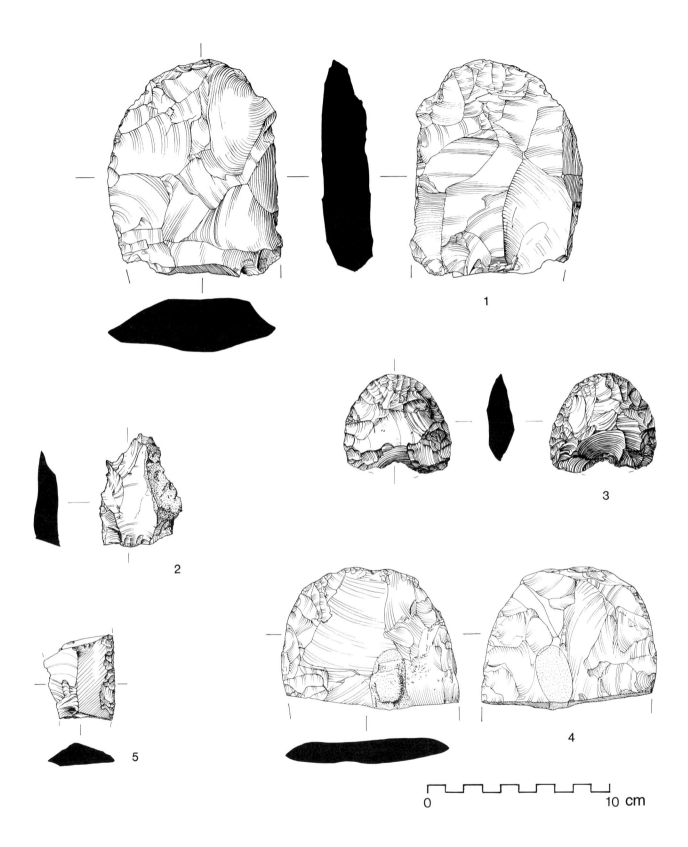

Figure 29.2. Flint artefacts from Fengate Farm, Weeting, drawn by Hoste Spalding and John Hostler. Particulars in Appendix. Scale 1:2.

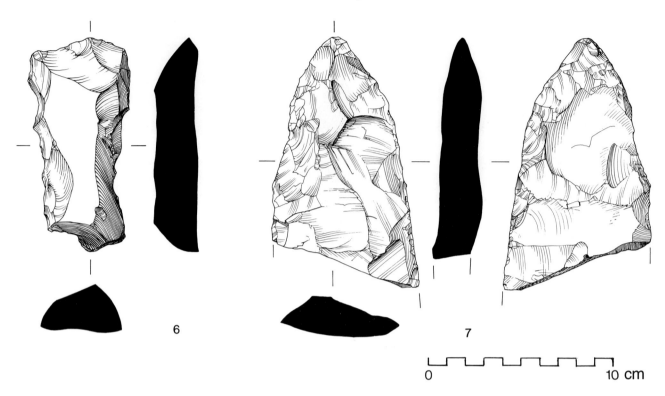

Figure 29.3. Flint artefacts from Fengate Farm, Weeting, drawn by Hoste Spalding and John Hostler. Particulars in Appendix. Scale 1:2.

presence of a group of core tools seldom found in stratified contexts, but recurrent on sites and in areas where extraction at whatever level (grubbing/quarrying/mining) and primary knapping were significant, and where the balance of evidence is for a Late Neolithic date. Of the group, only picks have an obvious extractive function and only irregular bifaces and flaked or roughout axes are likely to be unfinished artefacts. The remainder are apparently finished implements best known from collectors' cabinets, like waisted core tools (e.g. Piggott 1954, fig. 44:6), tranchet tools of triangular or trapezoid outline with a narrow butt and a wide distal cutting edge formed by a tranchet blow (e.g. Evans 1897, 69, fig. 14; Piggott 1954, fig. 44:1), and tribrachs – three-armed functional conundrums, the best-known of which is illustrated by Evans (1897, 77, fig. 25A).

The recurrence of such forms in 'heavy' industries has long been recognised within East Anglia and beyond, and the techno-typological cluster has, give or take a type or two, had a succession of labels: the 'Cissbury types' of the high collecting period (Clarke 1909, 223–6 – although his plates (1913, pls LXXV–lXXIX) show that the term could embrace almost anything chunky), Piggott's heavy 'secondary Neolithic' flint industry (1954, 279, fig. 44), and Gardiner's group 11 (1987, 65). Clarke knew of 'Cissbury-type' implements from almost every Breckland parish (1925, 8), and waisted core tools, tranchet tools, tribrachs and indeterminate bifaces are to be found, for

example, in collections made in Cranwich by him and by Newham, Halls and Haward (Norwich Castle Museum 32.926, 114.950, 83.24, 558.974).

Imperfect indices combine to suggest that, by the Late Neolithic, areas of the Breckland formed a zone of dispersed settlement in which flint nodules of large size and often high quality were collected and/or extracted from a variety of more-or-less superficial sources and a range of implements was made, including those calling for big, relatively sound blanks, some of them being finished by grinding elsewhere. The picture is a similar one to that painted for the Clay-with-Flints in Cranborne Chase, Dorset (Gardiner 1991, 60–64).

But in the midst of this extensive 'industrial' activity was the more intensive focus of Grime's Graves. Available information derives from the investigation of a small and anything-but-random fraction of many hectares of mining, quarrying and flint working. As far as can be seen, the mines were worked in the second half of the third millennium cal BC by users of Grooved Ware who exploited a localised seam of high quality semi-tabular flint, the floorstone, by sinking shafts with radiating galleries where it was deepest and by a variety of other methods when it was closer to the surface. The most recent of several estimates suggests that one of the deeper mines, with a ramified gallery system, could have been worked by an initial team of at least 14, with reduced numbers during the extraction of flint from the galleries, over a period of 90-odd days,

Site/assemblage	Distance from Grime's Graves (km)	Total struck flint	Pieces with floorstone-like cortex	Sources
Fengate Farm, Weeting-with-Broomhill, unstratified and redeposited, mainly Later Neolithic and Bronze Age	4.5	80	4 5%	
Fison Way, Thetford, almost all unstratified and redeposited, mainly Later Neolithic and Bronze Age	6.5	1481	9 0.6%	Healy 1991a, 143–4
Middle Harling, pits with Fengate Ware, Middle Neolithic	18	928	-	Healy 1995, 32–33
Middle Harling, pits with Grooved Ware, Late Neolithic	18	2005	1 0.05%	" "
Middle Harling, unstratified and redeposited, mainly Later Neolithic	18	1811	-	" "
Fenland Survey, Mesolithic to Bronze Age collections	10–20	15,512	72* 0.5%	Healy 1991b, 121, 126

* almost all from predominantly Later Neolithic and/or Bronze Age collections

Table 29.2. Collections including flint with floorstone-like cortex

during which some 53 tonnes of floorstone could have been extracted (Longworth & Varndell 1996, 82–6). This takes no account of the less regularly-occurring nodular flint (topstone, wallstone, etc.) in the overlying Chalk beds through which the shaft was sunk. Close to 18,000 tonnes could have been extracted from the whole of the slight Chalk hill where floorstone occurs regularly, disregarding the less predictable output of shallower, more disturbed flint deposits in other parts of the complex (*ibid.* 89).

Implements made on the site included discoidal knives, like Fig. 29.2:3–4, (Smith 1915, fig. 74; Saville 1981, figs 50–51: F129–F131) and axeheads, some of them made on flakes, of triangular outline and plano-convex section, like Fig. 29.3:7, (Smith 1915, figs 26, 36, 54; Saville 1981, figs 43–45). These were sporadic on the site but produced in some numbers on one 'floor' (Richardson 1920). Picks and indeterminate bifaces occur, and Levallois-like cores may reflect the manufacture of chisel and oblique arrowheads, both known from the site, as well as that of discoidal knives, some of which were made on large Levalloisoid flakes. Also present are the quickly-made flake tools of contemporary settlements (the debris of temporary occupation?). Blade cores and blades, often of large size, in mining period contexts cannot relate to the manufacture of any of these. A strikingly low proportion of cores on one Late Neolithic knapping floor suggests that cores themselves might have been removed, although the area excavated was small (Saville 1981, 69). Saville, not surprisingly, concluded that the mining period industry was a multi-product one in which axes were relatively unimportant (1981, 67–72).

Also present in small numbers are the rarer heavy 'secondary Neolithic' artefacts: tranchet tools (e.g. Saville 1981, fig. 40: F104), at least one waisted core tool (Smith

1915, fig. 59 – from a 'floor' sandwiched between two layers of chalk rubble upcast from mining), and two tribrachs, both surface finds, one found 'among a general scatter of flakes and partly worked tools of Neolithic type, about 50 yards outside the main complex of pits' (Lampert 1963) and another in the Cambridge University Museum of Archaeology and Ethnology (A.1908).

All Grime's Grave's flint is predominantly black and clear with relatively few inclusions. Floorstone is distinctive, characterised by an exceptionally thick, cream-coloured cortex. The rarity of such cortex among the flint naturally occurring on the surface of the region could make it a rough guide to the dispersal of mined floorstone. Floorstone-like cortex is, however, very scarce in industries from the surrounding area (Table 29.2). Even those probably contemporary with the working of Grime's Graves, like that from the Grooved Ware pits at Middle Harling, were made on weathered surface flint, just like the Late Mesolithic industry from Two Mile Bottom, Thetford (Robins this volume), or, for that matter, the pre-Anglian industry of High Lodge (Ashton *et al.* 1992, 137; Lewis this volume). Unless floorstone was little used in the immediate locality, it must have been transported without cortex, as dressed nodules, cores, blanks, preforms, finished implements or all of these. This in turn makes macroscopic identification even more of a guessing game, since any non-cortical artefact of sound, black flint *might* have been made of flint mined at Grime's Graves, but none need have been.

Relation to the Fen Edge

At about the time that mining began at Grime's Graves the Fenland to the west underwent a marine incursion, bringing salt marsh conditions close to the fen margin and reducing the accessibility of patchy gravel and till flint sources on the floor of the basin (Waller 1994, 118–155). Late Neolithic and Bronze Age collections from occupied hillocks of the fen edge contain a correspondingly higher proportion of chalk flint, brought from the immediate upland, than their predecessors. Most of this consists of small, weathered nodules and fragments, which seem to have been transported largely in nodular form over distances of up to 10 or 12km, in the course of the exploitation of territories that spanned upland and fen. Good quality non-cortical black flint is, however, also present. Furthermore, predominantly Late Neolithic collections, i.e. those broadly contemporary with the working of Grime's Graves, show an increase in the frequency of non-cortical flakes to roughly 10% above their previous level, an increase which is not sustained in subsequent Beaker and Bronze Age industries and which may relate to the import of flint without cortex and/or of larger nodules or slabs of raw material than were used before or afterwards. Another new feature of the Late Neolithic collections is an approximately twofold increase in the frequency of retouched forms, a change which is not reversed in the denser post-transgression Beaker and Bronze Age occupation (Healy 1991b, figs 65, 66, 68).

Axeheads

Triangular-outlined flake axeheads, one of the axehead forms made at Grime's Graves were also produced elsewhere in the Breckland, as at Weeting (Fig. 29.3:7) and Icklingham (Smith 1931: cat. no. 49). They are readily recognisable, yet there are none among the axeheads in the Fenland Project collections (Healy 1991b, 126), and only one (from Feltwell but otherwise unprovenanced; Cambridge University Museum of Archaeology and Ethnology 1898.95) among the far more numerous flint axeheads examined during a review of previous finds from the area (Healy 1996). Furthermore, the form seems nationally rare. It does not figure in Pitts' survey of British flint and stone axeheads, not even among the infrequent, exceptional forms which he singles out for mention (1996). Unless asymmetrical section and near-pointed butt were regularly transformed during grinding, the type seems to have been truly scarce beyond its immediate areas of manufacture. That such features would not necessarily have been obscured is shown by a partly-ground example from Swaffham (Healy 1984, fig. 5.8: F5).

A disturbed hoard from Banham, beyond the Breckland to the east, includes Late Neolithic forms like an edge-ground discoidal knife and a stone macehead, but neither of the two flint axes in it approximates to this type (Gurney 1990, fig. 2). No illustration has been published of the five flint axeheads found with a stone axehead and a discoidal knife in a hoard at Great Baddow, Chelmsford, Essex (Pitts 1996, 356).

Indeed, triangular-outlined flake axeheads seem almost confined to the Breckland and to small-scale industrial sites elsewhere, like Great Melton in the Yare valley and Ringland in the Wensum Valley (Healy 1984, fig. 5.8: F3, F4; Clarke & Halls 1918; Clarke 1918) and Beaker living sites in field 69 at Edingthorpe, Bacton, in northeast Norfolk, where massive debitage suggests localised exploitation of till flint in one part of an area settled from the Earlier Neolithic into the Bronze Age (Healy 1980, vol 2, 371–6). At Great Melton and Ringland flake axes are accompanied by heavy 'secondary Neolithic' core tools like picks, tranchet tools, and a waisted core tool (Norwich Castle Museum: Halls, W.G. Clarke and Cockerill collections). The whole group may have had a functional relation to quarry and workshop sites, although that function can only be guessed at. One possibility is a specialised use in making wooden or other organic quarrying equipment.

In and around the Breckland, many axeheads are made from flints which *could not* have been mined at Grime's Graves, and which at the same time stand out from the collections in which they occur. A fragmentary ground axe and another flaked down into a miniature form from West Stow are both of pale grey flint (Pieksma & Gardiner 1990, 49–50). Mottled pale grey flint is the material of a ground axe from Fison Way (Healy 1991a, 145–7) and of fragments of others found on Beaker/Early Bronze Age sites at Blackdyke Farm, Hockwold-cum-Wilton (Healy 1996, fig. 49: L62; fig. 53: L103). Three of the ground axes and most of the 12 flakes from ground implements in the Fenland project collections are of orange flint, often with matt, cortical inclusions like Figure 29.2: 4. Two of the remaining axeheads and two of the remaining flakes are of heavily mottled flints. The remainder are unassignably corticated. Even at Grime's Graves, one fragmentary flaked axehead seems to be of a flint alien to the site (Saville 1981, 52–3). The exceptional flint of some axeheads may have been selected from local tills. Others may have been imports, like some of the stone axes found in the area, including two of southwestern origin from mining period contexts at Grime's Graves itself (Clough & Green 1972, 133).

The record of the surrounding area thus seems to confirm Saville's conclusion that axeheads were an unimportant product at Grime's Graves, and suggests that the British Museum's flint analysis programme, for all its problems and limitations, may have been correct here too (Craddock *et al.* 1983).

Discoidal Knives

Dark, sound flint which *could* have been mined at Grime's Graves is more easily recognised in the form of discoidal knives. Instances include Figure 29.2:3, as well as edge-ground examples from West Stow (Pieksma & Gardiner 1990, 51, fig. 41:47) and Feltwell (Healy 1996, fig. 57: L123). Also from Feltwell is a 190mm long single-piece sickle, of dark flint, retaining floorstone-like cortex (Healy 1996, fig. 58:L130). There is a fragmentary ground implement, probably a chisel, of dark, floorstone-like flint from

Methwold (Healy 1991b, 126). Objects like these suggest that any or all of the elaborately worked flint artefacts of the Late Neolithic may have been made on floorstone, which would have been admirably suited to their manufacture.

POSTSCRIPT

The balance of evidence is that mining at Grime's Graves had ceased by the end of the third millennium cal BC, and that there was a lull of as much as a thousand years until the Neolithic spoil heaps were scavenged in the course of extensive Middle Bronze Age occupation. It is, however, possible that the flint already brought to the surface was being used throughout. A deposit of 209kg of fresh, sharp knapping debris of Bronze Age technology, most of it of re-used flint other than floorstone, was found near the top of the mineshaft excavated in 1971, *beneath* layers containing Middle Bronze Age pottery (Mercer 1981, 20; Saville 1981, 13–15). The single sherd from the deposit, described as Middle Bronze Age in the excavation report, is identified in the pottery report as of Early Bronze Age fabric, probably from a Food Vessel or Collared Urn (Longworth 1981, 39, fig. 23:P6). There are in total 40 sherds from collared vessels and 63 body sherds of Early Bronze Age fabric from mine tops and superficial contexts at the site (Longworth *et al.* 1988, 23–4, fig. 7), as well as a handful of Beaker (*ibid.* 12).

This was the period of dense post-transgression occupation on the fen edge *c.* 12km to the west, where some, but by no means all, fine artefacts, like barbed and tanged arrowheads, flint daggers, and scale-flaked and planoconvex knives, were made of black flint. Two surface finds of scale-flaked knives of Early Bronze Age type with floorstone-like cortex from this zone (Healy 1991b, 126) enhance the possibility of collection of Grime's Graves flint in this period, as does the presence of the odd artefact of similar material in industries excavated from Beaker/Early Bronze Age sites (e.g. Healy 1996, fig. 53: L101).

This episode of fen edge settlement was marked by an upsurge in cereal cultivation (Waller 1994, 154; Martin & Murphy 1988, 356–7), reflected by numerous flint and stone saddle querns from the occupied zone (Healy 1996, fig. 43). One Feltwell collector, Frank Curtis, had so many that he used them to build the kerb of his garden pond. Flint saddle querns were made from large slabs of flint, the surfaces of which were dressed by pounding with hammerstones to make them abrasive. Once broken or disused they provided substantial amounts of raw material for knapping. Even small fragments are recognisable by the combination of a battered surface with the gloss formed on the highest points as they were worn down by grinding grain with a stone rubber, as on fragments from the Middle Bronze Age occupation of Grime's Graves (Herne 1991, 52, figs 31–2). Floorstone would have been particularly suitable for this purpose, providing adequate size and a relatively flat surface. On the fen edge reworked fragments seem to be concentrated in Early Bronze Age industries, as at Mildenhall Fen (Clark 1936, 44) and Hockwold-cum-Wilton (Healy 1996, 179). Their presence in industries largely made on the small, weathered nodules of the immediate upland, points strongly to the import of querns or the blocks or nodules from which they were made from the Breckland, in a continuation of the 'industrial' use of the area, if not actually of Grime's Graves, through the Early Bronze Age.

SUMMARY AND CONCLUSIONS

The scarcity of flint with floorstone-like cortex in the area around Grime's Graves, even in industries likely to have overlapped with mining and quarrying there, indicates that flint was normally removed from the site in a decorticated state. The balance of evidence suggests that this may have been done at any or all of the subsequent stages of the reduction sequence. In the Late Neolithic a common range of flintworking techniques and finished artefacts characterised Grime's Graves and the surrounding Breckland. It is possible to see the deep, galleried mines as one end of a spectrum which extended through the various extraction methods used in those parts of Grime's Graves where the floorstone was close to the surface, small-scale quarrying and grubbing elsewhere, and selective collection from particular deposits to apparently indiscriminate use of the nearest available surface flint. The same finished artefacts were made on both floorstone and other flints at Grime's Graves and entirely on other flints beyond the site. The salient different lies in the time and labour expended to win the raw material from deep, galleried shafts.

Why was so much time, labour and skill invested in the extraction, at some risk, of material for products which could have been made on flint from superficial sources? The properties of mined flint may have been preferred in knapping and in use. Floorstone may have had something of the aesthetic appeal which, in all subjectivity, it has today. Material extracted at considerable cost, and perhaps of restricted availability, may have been valued above its functional qualities. Low-intensity working, with blocks of unknapped floorstone remaining on working floors and in shaft backfills would be compatible with this (Longworth & Varndell 1996, 90). Use for artefacts like discoidal knives, in which craftsmanship goes beyond functional needs, suggests that the material itself may have contributed to value of elaborate implements.

ACKNOWLEDGEMENTS

The opportunity is gladly taken to thank John Wymer for advice, support and encouragement over the last twenty years. Thanks are also extended to the Field Archaeology Division of the Norfolk Museums Service and to the late

Tony Gregory for the opportunity to publish the Fengate Farm, Weeting, material and for Figures 1 and 2. Roger Mercer, Alan Saville and Gillian Varndell have all kindly commented on an earlier version of the text.

REFERENCES

Ashton, N.M., Cook, J., Lewis, S.G. & Rose, J. 1992. *High Lodge. Excavations by G. de G. Sieveking, 1962–8 and J. Cook, 1988.* London: British Museum Press.

Bennett, K.D. 1983. Devensian, Late Glacial and Flandrian vegetation history at Hockham Mere, Norfolk, England. *New Phytologist* 95, 457–87.

Clark, J.G.D. 1928. Discoidal polished flint knives – their typology and distribution. *Proceedings of the Prehistoric Society of East Anglia* 6, 40–54.

Clark, J.G.D. 1936. Report on a Late Bronze Age site in Mildenhall Fen, W Suffolk. *Antiquaries' Journal* 6, 29–50.

Clark, J.G.D. & Fell, C.I. 1953. The Early Iron Age site of Micklemoor Hill, West Harling, Norfolk, and its pottery. *Proceedings of the Prehistoric Society* 29, 50–98.

Clark, J.G.D. & Higgs, E.S. 1960. Flint industry. In Clark, J.G.D., Excavations at the Neolithic site at Hurst Fen, Mildenhall, Suffolk (1954, 1957 and 1958). *Proceedings of the Prehistoric Society* 26, 214–26.

Clarke, W.G. 1909. The classification of Norfolk flint implements. *Transactions of the Norfolk and Norwich Naturalists' Society* 8, 215–30.

Clarke, W.G. 1913. Norfolk implements of Palaeolithic 'cave' type. *Proceedings of the Prehistoric Society of East Anglia* 1(3), 338–45.

Clarke, W.G. 1915 (ed.). *Report on the Excavations at Grime's Graves, Weeting, Norfolk, March–May 1914.* London: Prehistoric Society of East Anglia.

Clarke, W.G. 1918. A prehistoric flint pit at Ringland. *Proceedings of the Prehistoric Society of East Anglia* 2, 148–151.

Clarke, W.G. 1925. *In Breckland Wilds.* London: Robert Scott.

Clarke, W.G. & Halls, H.H. 1918. A Cissbury type station at Great Melton. *Proceedings of the Prehistoric Society of East Anglia* 2, 374–80.

Clarke, W.G. & Hewitt, H.D. 1914. An early Norfolk trackway: the Drove Road. *Proceedings of the Prehistoric Society of East Anglia* 1, 427–34.

Clough, T.H.McK. & Green, B. 1972. The petrological identification of stone implements from East Anglia. *Proceedings of the Prehistoric Society* 38, 108–55.

Craddock, P.T., Cowell, M.R., Leese, M.N. & Hughes, M.J. 1983. The trace element composition of polished flint axes as an indicator of source. *Archaeometry* 25, 135–63.

Evans, J. 1897. *The Ancient Stone Implements, Weapons and Ornaments of Great Britain.* Second edition. London: Longmans, Green and Co.

Evans, J.G. 1981. Sub-fossil land snail faunas from Grime's Graves and other Neolithic flint mines. In R.J. Mercer, *Grimes Graves, Norfolk, Excavations 1971–72: Volume I,* 104–111. Department of the Environment Archaeological Reports 11. London: Her Majesty's Stationery Office.

Fell, C.I. 1951. A Late Bronze Age urnfield and Grooved Ware occupation at Honington, Suffolk. *Proceedings of the Cambridge Antiquarian Society* 45, 30–43.

Gardiner, J. 1987. Tales of the unexpected: approaches to the assessment and interpretation of museum flint collections. In A. G. Brown & M.R. Edmonds (eds), *Lithic Analysis and Later British Prehistory,* 49–63. Oxford: British Archaeo-

logical Reports British Series 162.

Gardiner, J. 1991. The [Late Neolithic] flint industries of the study area. In J.C. Barrett, R. Bradley & M. Green, *Landscape, Monuments and Society. The Prehistory of Cranborne Chase,* 59–69. Cambridge: Cambridge University Press.

Gardiner, J. 1993. The flint assemblage. In J.A. Davies, Excavation of an Iron Age pit group at London Road, Thetford. *Norfolk Archaeology* 41(4), 456–9.

Gregory, T. 1991. *Excavations in Thetford, 1980–1982, Fison Way,* 143–7, 148–54, 188. Gressenhall: East Anglian Archaeology 53.

Gregory, T. 1996. *A Romano-British Farmyard at Weeting, Norfolk.* East Anglian Archaeology Occasional Paper 1.

Gurney, D. 1990. Archaeological finds in Norfolk 1989. *Norfolk Archaeology* 41(1), 96–106.

Healy, F., 1980. *The Neolithic in Norfolk.* Unpublished Ph. D. thesis, University of London.

Healy, F. 1984. Farming and field monuments: the Neolithic in Norfolk. In C. Barringer (ed.), *Aspects of East Anglian Pre-history (Twenty Years after Rainbird Clarke),* 77–140. Norwich: Geo Books.

Healy, F., 1988. *The Anglo-Saxon Cemetery at Spong Hill, North Elmham: Occupation during the Seventh to Second Millennia BC.* Gressenhall: East Anglian Archaeology Report 39.

Healy, F.1991a. Lithic material; Pre-Iron Age pottery; Pre-Iron Age activity. In T. Gregory, *Excavations in Thetford, 1980–1982, Fison Way,* 143–7, 148–54, 188. Gressenhall: East Anglian Archaeology 53.

Healy, F. 1991b. Appendix 1. Lithics and pre-Iron Age pottery. In R. J. Silvester, *The Fenland Project Number 4: the Wissey Embayment and the Fen Causeway, Norfolk,* 116–39. Gressenhall: East Anglian Archaeology Report 52.

Healy, F. 1991c. The hunting of the floorstone. In A.J. Schofield (ed.), *Interpreting Artefact Scatters: Contributions to Ploughzone Archaeology,* 29–37. Oxford: Oxbow Monograph 4.

Healy, F. 1995. Prehistoric material. In A. Rogerson, *A Late Neolithic, Saxon and Medieval Site at Middle Harling, Norfolk,* 32–46. Gressenhall: East Anglian Archaeology Report 74.

Healy, F. 1996. *The Fenland Project, Number 11: the Wissey Embayment: Evidence for Pre-Iron Age Occupation Accumulated prior to the Fenland Project.* Gressenhall: East Anglian Archaeology Report 78.

Healy, F., Cleal, R.M.J. & Kinnes, I. 1993. Excavations on Redgate Hill, Hunstanton, 1970 and 1971. In R. Bradley, P. Chowne, R.M.J. Cleal, F. Healy & I. Kinnes, *Excavations on Redgate Hill, Hunstanton, Norfolk, and at Tattershall Thorpe, Lincolnshire,* 1–77. Gressenhall: East Anglian Archaeology 57.

Herne, A. 1991. The flint assemblage. In I. Longworth, A. Herne, G. Varndell & S. Needham, *Shaft X: Bronze Age Flint, Chalk and Metal Working. Excavations at Grime's Graves Norfolk 1972–1976. Fasicule 3,* 21–93. London: British Museum Press.

Jacobi, R. 1984. The Mesolithic of northern East Anglia and contemporary territories. In C. Barringer (ed.) *Aspects of East Anglian Pre-History (Twenty Years after Rainbird Clarke),* 43–76. Norwich: Geo Books.

Lampert, R.J. 1963. Grime's Graves: an unusual flint implement, *Norfolk Archaeology* 33(2), 236–7.

Legge, A.J. 1981. The agricultural economy. In R. J. Mercer, *Grimes Graves, Norfolk, Excavations 1971–72: Volume 1,* 79–103. Department of the Environment Archaeological Reports 11. London: Her Majesty's Stationery Office.

Longworth, I.H. 1981. Neolithic and Bronze Age Pottery. In R. J. Mercer, *Grimes Graves, Norfolk, Excavations 1971–72: Volume 1,* 39–59. Department of the Environment Archaeological Reports 11. London: Her Majesty's Stationery Office.

Longworth, I.H., Ellison, A. & Rigby, V. 1988. *Excavations at Grime's Graves 1972–1976. Fasicule 2. The Neolithic, Bronze Age and Later Pottery.* London: British Museum Press.

Longworth, I. & Varndell, G. 1996. *Excavations at Grime's Graves Norfolk 1972–1976. Fasicule 5. Mining in the Deeper Mines.* London: British Museum Press.

Martin, E. 1993. *Settlements on Hill-tops: Seven Prehistoric Sites in Suffolk.* Ipswich: East Anglian Archaeology 65.

Martin, E. A. & Murphy, P. 1988. West Row Fen, Suffolk: a Bronze Age fen-edge settlement site. *Antiquity* 62(235), 353–8.

Mercer, R.J. 1981. *Grimes Graves, Norfolk, Excavations 1971–72: Volume I.* Department of the Environment Archaeological Reports 11. London: Her Majesty's Stationery Office.

Murphy, P. 1984. Prehistoric environments and economies. In C. Barringer (ed.) *Aspects of East Anglian Pre-History (Twenty Years after Rainbird Clarke)*, 13–30. Norwich: Geo Books.

Murphy, P. 1991. Plant remains and the environment. In T. Gregory, *Excavations in Thetford, 1980–1982, Fison Way*, 175–81. Gressenhall: East Anglian Archaeology 53. .

Nightingale, R.C. 1913. The Stone Age in Beechamwell. *Proceedings of the Prehistoric Society of East Anglia* 1(3), 320–1.

Pieksma, E.J. & Gardiner, J. 1990. The prehistoric flint and stone. In S. West, *West Stow, Suffolk: the Prehistoric and Romano-British Occupations*, 46–59. Bury St Edmunds: East Anglian Archaeology Report 48.

Piggott, S., 1931. The Neolithic pottery of the British Isles. *Archaeological Journal* 88, 67–158

Piggott, S., 1954. *Neolithic Cultures of the British Isles.* Cambridge: Cambridge University Press

Pitts, M. 1996. The stone axe in Neolithic Britain. *Proceedings of the Prehistoric Society* 61, 311–71.

Richardson, D. 1920. A new celt-making floor at Grime's Graves. *Proceedings of the Prehistoric Society of East Anglia* 3(2), 243–58.

Rogerson, A. 1995. *A Late Neolithic, Saxon and Medieval Site at Middle Harling, Norfolk.* Gressenhall: East Anglian Archaeology Report 74.

Saville, A. 1981. *Grimes Graves, Norfolk, Excavations 1971–72: Volume II the Flint Assemblage.* Department of the Environment Archaeological Reports 11. London: Her Majesty's Stationery Office.

Silvester, R.J. 1991. *The Fenland Project Number 4: the Wissey Embayment and the Fen Causeway, Norfolk.* Gressenhall: East Anglian Archaeology Report 52.

Skertchly, S.B.J. 1879. *On the Manufacture of Gun-flints, the Methods of Excavating for Flint, the Age of Palaeolithic Man, and the Connexion between Neolithic Art and the Gun-flint Trade.* Memoirs of the Geological Survey. London: Her Majesty's Stationery Office.

Smith, R.A. 1915. The flint implements. In W.G. Clarke (ed.), *Report on the Excavations at Grime's Graves, Weeting, Norfolk, March–May 1914*, 147–207. London: Prehistoric Society of East Anglia.

Smith, R.A. 1931. *The Sturge Collection. An Illustrated Selection of Flints from Britain Bequeathed in 1919 by W. Allen Sturge, M.V.O., M.D., F.R.C.P.* London: Trustees of the British Museum.

Sturge, W.A. 1913. Postscript. *Proceedings of the Prehistoric Society of East Anglia* 1(3), 292–6.

Waller, M. 1994. *The Fenland Project Number 4: Flandrian Environmental Change in Fenland.* Gressenhall: East Anglian Archaeology Report 70.

West, S. 1990. *West Stow, Suffolk: the Prehistoric and Romano-British Occupations.* Ipswich: East Anglian Archaeology Report 48.

Wymer, J.J. 1971. A possible Late Upper Palaeolithic site at Cranwich, Norfolk. *Norfolk Archaeology* 35(2), 259–63.

Wymer, J.J. 1985. *Palaeolithic Sites of East Anglia.* Norwich: Geo Books.

Wymer, J.J. 1987. A pair of bronze palstave moulds from Harling. *Norfolk Archaeology* 40(1), 122–6.

APPENDIX. Catalogue of flint artefacts from Fengate Farm, Weeting-with-Broomhill (SMR 5636/c2; TL 7780 8782) illustrated in Figures 2 and 3.

The collection comprises 8 cores, 1 fragment of irregular waste, 1 core rejuvenation flake, 47 flakes, 4 blades, 7 scrapers, 2 borers, 3 knives, 1 rod (i.e. Fig. 29.2, no. 6, a heavy, 'fabricator'-like implement as defined by Saville (1981, 10), rather than a rod microlith), 1 axe fragment, 1 fragment of gunflint-making waste and 4 miscellaneous retouched pieces, all found during the excavation of a Romano-British site (Gregory 1996).

1. Levallois-like core, perhaps on a flake. Mottled, banded grey flint with many inclusions. Slight ferruginous patina.
2. Piercer. Fresh, dark flint with pitted cortex.
3. Flaked discoidal knife, damaged. Homogenous dark flint. One face slightly corticated.
4. Flaked discoidal knife, fragmentary. Mottled orange-grey flint with inclusions, notably a granular, cortex-like mass running from one face to the other, along which the object seems to have broken during manufacture. Slight cortication on one face.
5. Knife, fragmentary. Dark grey flint
6. Rod. Made on a fragment retaining heavily corticated, thermally fractured surfaces on both faces. Light secondary cortication on retouched areas.
7. Flaked axe, fragmentary. Orange-grey flint, heavily corticated. Plano-convex section suggests manufacture on a flake.

John Wymer, A Bibliography

It would be virtually impossible to compile a complete record of such a prolific output. Every attempt has been made to make this list as full as possible (excluding book reviews), but omissions are inevitable. It is hoped that they will be forgiven.

1956

Palaeoliths from gravel of the ancient channel between Caversham and Henley at Highlands near Henley. *Proceedings of the Prehistoric Society* 4, 29–36.

1957

A Clactonian industry at Little Thurrock, Grays, Essex. *Proceedings of the Geologists' Association* 68, 159–77.

1958

Excavations at Thatcham, Berks, 1958. *Transactions of the Newbury and District Field Club* 10(4), 31–48.

Localised battering on handaxes. *Archaeological Newsletter* 6(6), 139.

Further work at Swanscombe, Kent. *Archaeological Newsletter* 6(8), 190–1.

Archaeological notes from Reading Museum. *Berkshire Archaeological Journal* 56, 54–9.

Long Lane, Whitley. *Berkshire Archaeological Journal* 56, 60–62.

1959

Excavations on the Mesolithic site at Thatcham: interim report *Berkshire Archaeological Journal* 57, 1–24.

Archaeological notes from Reading Museum. *Berkshire Archaeological Journal* 57, 121–24.

1960

Excavations at Thatcham, Berks (second interim report). *Transactions of the Newbury and District Field Club* 11(1), 12–19.

Archaeological notes from Reading Museum. *Berkshire Archaeological Journal* 58, 52–54.

1961

The Lower Palaeolithic succession in the Thames Valley and the date of the ancient channel between Caversham and Henley. *Proceedings of the Prehistoric Society* 27, 1–27.

The discovery of a gold torc at Moulsford. *Berkshire Archaeological Journal* 59, 36–7.

Palaeolithic flint hand-axe. In M.A. Cotton, Robin Hood's Arbour and rectilinear enclosures in Berkshire. *Berkshire Archaeological Journal* 59, 9–10.

Work at Swanscombe 1960. *Archaeological Newsletter* 7(2), 32–33.

Archaeological notes from Reading Museum. *Berkshire Archaeological Journal* 59, 58–61.

1962

Excavations at the Maglemosian sites at Thatcham, Berkshire, England. *Proceedings of the Prehistoric Society* 28, 329–61.

Archaeological notes from Reading Museum. *Berkshire Archaeological Journal* 60, 114–20.

1963

Excavations at Thatcham. Final report. *Transactions of the Newbury and District Field Club* 11(2), 41–52.

1964

Excavations at Barnfield Pit, 1955–60. In C.D. Ovey (ed.), *The Swanscombe Skull: a Survey of Research at a Pleistocene Site*, 19–61. London: Royal Anthropological Institute Occasional Paper 20.

Report on the flints. In J. Moss-Eccardt, Excavations at Wibury Hill, an Iron Age hill-fort near Letchworth, Herts, 1959. *Bedfordshire Archaeological Journal* 2, 44–45.

Archaeological notes from Reading Museum. *Berkshire Archaeological Journal* 61, 96–109

Smith. I.F. & Wymer, J.J. The Treacher collection of prehistoric artefacts from Marlow. *Records of Buckinghamshire* 17 (4), 286–300.

1965

Appendix: worked flints from Westward Ho! (1961–2). In D.M. Churchill, The kitchen midden site at Westward Ho!, Devon, England: ecology, age, and relation to changes in land and sea level. *Proceedings of the Prehistoric Society* 31, 83–84.

Keef, P.A., Wymer, J.J. & Dimbleby, G.W. A Mesolithic site on Iping Common, Sussex, England. *Proceedings of the Prehistoric Society* 31, 85–92.

1966

Excavations of the Lambourn long barrow, 1964. *Berkshire Archaeological Journal* 62 [for 1965–6], 1–16.

Archaeological notes from Reading Museum. *Berkshire Archaeological Journal* 62 [for 1965–6], 70–76.

1968

Lower Palaeolithic Archaeology in Britain as Represented by the Upper Thames Valley. London: John Baker.

Appendix A. Flint and stone artefacts. In J. H. Money, Excavations in the Iron Age hill-fort at High Rocks, near Tunbridge Wells, 1957–1961. *Sussex Archaeological Collections* 106, 186–7.

Singer, R. & Wymer, J. J. 1968. Archaeological investigations at the Saldanha Skull site in South Africa. *South African Archaeological Bulletin* 23, 63–74.

1970

Radiocarbon date for the Lambourn long barrow. *Antiquity* 44(174), 144.

Mesolithic dwellings in Britain. *Ago* 1(3), 22–26

Wymer, J. & Singer, R. The first season of excavation at Clacton-on-Sea, Essex, England: a brief report. *World Archaeology* 2(1), 12–16.

1971

A possible late upper Palaeolithic site at Cranwich, Norfolk. *Norfolk Archaeology* 35(2), 259–63.

1972

Note on a hand-axe found at Mortimer. *Berkshire Archaeological Journal* 66 [for 1971–2], 7–9.

Flint collecting and the distribution of Palaeolithic and Mesolithic sites. In E. Fowler (ed.), *Field Survey in British Archaeology*, 26–28. London: Council for British Archaeology.

1973

Singer, R., Wymer, J.J. & Gladfelter, B.G. Radiocarbon dates from the interglacial deposits at Hoxne, England, *Journal of Geology* 81, 508–9.

Singer, R., Wymer, J.J., Gladfelter, B.G. & Wolff, R. Excavation of the Clactonian industry at the golf course, Clacton-on-Sea, Essex. *Proceedings of the Prehistoric Society* 39, 6–74.

1974

Clactonian and Acheulian industries in Britain: their chronology and significance. *Proceedings of the Geologists' Association* 85, 391–421.

1975

Two barbed points from Devil's Wood Pit, Sproughton. Ipswich: *East Anglian Archaeology Report* 1, 1–4.

Appendix B. Flints. In J. H. Money, Excavations in the two Iron Age hill-forts on Castle Hill, Capel, near Tonbridge, 1965 and 1969–71. *Archaeologia Cantiana* 91, 81–5.

Wymer, J.J., Jacobi. R.M. & Rose, J. Late Devensian and early Flandrian barbed points from Sproughton, Suffolk. *Proceedings of the Prehistoric Society* 41, 25–41.

1976

A long blade industry from Sproughton, Suffolk. Ipswich: *East Archaeology Report* 3, 1–10.

A hand axe from Witham, Essex. In R.T. Brookes & A.H. Stokes,

Excavations at Witham Lodge, Essex, 1972. *Essex Journal* 10(4) [for 1975–6], 123–8.

Highlands Farm Pit, Rotherfield Peppard (Caversham ancient channel). In D.A. Roe (ed.), *Field Guide to the Oxford Region*, 48–49. Quaternary Research Association.

The interpretation of Palaeolithic cultural and faunal material found in Pleistocene sediments. In D.A. Davidson & M. Shackley (eds), *Geoarchaeology: Earth Science and the Past*, 327–34. London: Duckworth.

A chert hand-axe from Chard, Somerset. *Proceedings of the Somerset Archaeological and Natural History Society* 120, 101–3.

Singer, R. & Wymer, J.J. The sequence of Acheulian industries at Hoxne, Suffolk. In J. Combier (ed.), *L'Evolution de l'Acheuléen en Europe, Colloque X*, 14–30. Nice: ninth congress of the International Union of Prehistoric and Protohistoric Sciences.

1977

Gazetteer of Mesolithic Sites in England and Wales. London: Council for British Archaeology Research Report 20.

The archaeology of man in the British Quaternary. In F.W. Shotton (ed.), *British Quaternary Studies, Recent Advances*, 93–106.

Worked flints; Notes on other Mesolithic material in the Scole district. In A. Rogerson, Excavations at Scole, 1973, 152–4. Gressenhall: *East Anglian Archaeology* 5.

Sulhamstead. In E.R.Shepherd-Thorn & J.J.Wymer (eds), *South-east England and the Thames Valley. X INQUA Congress Excursion Guide A5*, 11–2. Norwich: Geo Abstracts.

Savernake. In E.R.Shepherd-Thorn & J.J.Wymer (eds), *South-east England and the Thames Valley. X INQUA Congress Excursion Guide A5*, 12–4. Norwich: Geo Abstracts.

Theale and Englefield. In E.R.Shepherd-Thorn & J.J.Wymer (eds), *South-east England and the Thames Valley. X INQUA Congress Excursion Guide A5*, 15–6. Norwich: Geo Abstracts.

Highlands Farm, Rotherfield Peppard. In E.R.Shepherd-Thorn & J.J.Wymer (eds), *South-east England and the Thames Valley. X INQUA Congress Excursion Guide A5*, 24–8. Norwich: Geo Abstracts.

Remenham. In E.R.Shepherd-Thorn & J.J.Wymer (eds), *South-east England and the Thames Valley. X INQUA Congress Excursion Guide A5*, 28–9. Norwich: Geo Abstracts.

Winter Hill. In E.R.Shepherd-Thorn & J.J.Wymer (eds), *South-east England and the Thames Valley. X INQUA Congress Excursion Guide A5*, 29–30. Norwich: Geo Abstracts.

Furze Platt. In E.R.Shepherd-Thorn & J.J.Wymer (eds), *South-east England and the Thames Valley. X INQUA Congress Excursion Guide A5*, 30–4. Norwich: Geo Abstracts.

Taplow. In E.R.Shepherd-Thorn & J.J.Wymer (eds), *South-east England and the Thames Valley. X INQUA Congress Excursion Guide A5*, 34–5. Norwich: Geo Abstracts.

Langley. In E.R.Shepherd-Thorn & J.J.Wymer (eds), *South-east England and the Thames Valley. X INQUA Congress Excursion Guide A5*, 35–7. Norwich: Geo Abstracts.

Shepherd-Thorn, E.R. & Wymer, J.J. Introduction. In E.R.Shepherd-Thorn & J.J.Wymer (eds), *South-east England and the Thames Valley. X INQUA Congress Excursion Guide A5*, 7–11. Norwich: Geo Abstracts.

Wymer, J.J. & Straw, A. Handaxes from beneath glacial till at Welton-le-Wold, Lincolnshire, and the distribution of palaeoliths in Britain. *Proceedings of the Prehistoric Society* 43, 355–60.

1978

Pre-Roman period. In P. Arthur & K. Whitehouse, Report on excavations at Fulham Palace moat, 1972–73. *Transactions of the London and Middlesex Archaeological Society* 29, 50–52.

Rose, J., Allen, P. & Wymer, J.J. Weekend field meeting in south-east Suffolk. *Proceedings of the Geological Association* 89, 81–90.

Singer, R. & Wymer, J.J. A hand-ax from northwest Iran: the question of human movement between Africa and Asia in the Lower Paleolithic period. In L. Freeman (ed.) *Views of the Past*, 13–27. Chicago: Mouton.

1979

Comment on G. P. Rightmire, Implications of Border Cave skeletal remains for Later Pleistocene human evolution. *Current Anthropology* 20(1), 32–33.

Comment on M. Y. Ohel, The Clactonian. An independent complex or an integral part of the Acheulean? *Current Anthropology* 20(4), 719.

1980

The Palaeolithic of Essex. In D.G. Buckley (ed.), *Archaeology in Essex to AD 1500*, 8–11. London: Council for British Archaeology Research Report 34.

The excavation of the Acheulian site at Gaddesdon Row. *Bedfordshire Archaeological Journal* 14, 2–4.

1981

The Palaeolithc. In I.G. Simmons & M. Tooley (eds), *The Environment in British Prehistory*, 49–81. London: Duckworth.

The status of the Clactonian industry. *Lithics* 2, 2–5.

Comment on B. Hayden, Research and development in the Stone Age: technological transitions among hunter-gatherers. *Current Anthropology* 22(5), 539–40.

1982

The Palaeolithic Age. London: Croom Helm.

The Palaeolithic period in Kent. In P.E. Leach (ed.), *Archaeology of Kent to AD 1500*, 8–11. London: Council for British Archaeology Research Report 48.

Singer, R. & Wymer, J.J. *The Middle Stone Age at Klasies River Mouth in South Africa.* Chicago: University of Chicago Press.

Singer, R., Wolff, R., Gladfelter, B.G. & Wymer, J.J. Pleistocene *Macaca* from Hoxne, Suffolk, England. *Folia Primatologica* 37, 141–52.

1983

The Lower Palaeolithic site at Hoxne. *Proceedings of the Suffolk Institute of Archaeology and History* 35 (3), 169–89.

Gibbard, P.L. & Wymer, J.J. Highlands Farm. In J.Rose (ed.), *Diversion of the Thames. Field Guide*, 69–76. Cambridge: Quaternary Research Association.

1984

East Anglian Palaeolithic sites and their settings. In C. Barringer (ed.), *Aspects of East Anglian Prehistory (Twenty Years after Rainbird Clarke)*, 31–42. Norwich: Geo Books.

1985

Palaeolithic Sites of East Anglia. Norwich: Geo Books.

Early man in Britain – time and change. *Modern Geology* 9, 261–72.

The archaeology of Barnfield Pit. In K.L. Duff (ed.), *The Story of Swanscombe Man*, 20–27. Kent County Council and Nature Conservancy Council.

1986

Overview: recent trends in British Palaeolithic studies. In S.N. Collcutt (ed.), *The Palaeolithic of Britain and its Nearest Neighbours: Recent Trends*, 103–6. Sheffield: Department of Archaeology and Prehistory, University of Sheffield.

Comment on A.T. Bunn & E.M. Kroll, Systematic butchery by Plio/Pleistocene hominids at Olduvai Gorge, Tanzania. *Current Anthropology* 27(5), 447–8.

Early Iron Age pottery and a triangular loom weight from Redgate Hill, Hunstanton. *Norfolk Archaeology* 39(3), 286–96.

A further Neolithic pit on Bunker's Hill, Witton. *Norfolk Archaeology* 39(3), 315–8.

Flints. In D. Gurney, *Settlement, Religion and Industry on the Fenedge: Three Romano-British Sites in Norfolk*, 22, 72. Gressenhall: East Anglian Archaeology Report 31.

Singer, R. & Wymer, J. On Binford on Klasies River Mouth: response of the excavators. *Current Anthropology* 27(1), 56–57.

1987

The Palaeolithic period in Surrey. In J. & D.G. Bird (eds), *The Archaeology of Surrey to 1540*, 17–30. Guildford: Surrey Archaeological Society.

A pair of bronze palstave moulds from Harling. *Norfolk Archaeology* 40(1), 122–6.

1988

Palaeolithic archaeology and the British Quaternary sequence. *Quaternary Science Reviews* 7, 79–97.

A reassessment of the geographical range of Lower Palaeolithic activity in Britain. In R.J. MacRae & N. Moloney (eds), *Non-flint Stone Tools and the Palaeolithic Occupation of Britain*, 11–23. Oxford: British Archaeological Reports British Series 189.

Flint artifacts. In J. Moss-Eccardt, Archaeological excavations in the Letchworth area 1958–1974. *Proceedings of the Cambridge Antiquarian Society* 77, 96–99.

The shaping of Suffolk; Solid geology; Surface geology; The Palaeolithic period; Late Glacial and Mesolithic hunters. In D. Dymond & E. A. Martin (eds), *An Historical Atlas of Suffolk*, 8–13, 24–27. Ipswich: Suffolk County Council Planning Department in conjunction with the Suffolk Institute of Archaeology and History.

1989

Professor F.W. Shotton. *Lithics* 10, 8.

Shotton, F.W. with Wymer, J.J. Hand-axes of andesitic tuff from beneath the standard Wolstonian succession in Warwickshire. *Lithics* 10, 1–7.

1990

A later Bronze Age cremation cemetery and Beaker pits at East Carleton. *Norfolk Archaeology* 40(1), 122–6.

A cremation burial at Alpington. *Norfolk Archaeology* 41(1), 71–4.

Oxford field meeting, Saturday 13th July 1991. *Lithics* 11, 78–80.

1991

Mesolithic occupation around Hockham Mere. *Norfolk Archaeology* 41(2), 212–3.

Mesolithic Britain. Princes Risborough: Shire Publications.

The Southern Rivers Project. *Lithics* 12, 21–23.

Untitled note on a *bout coupé* handaxe. In T. Gregory, *Excavations in Thetford 1980–82, Fison Way*, 146–7. Gressenhall: East Anglian Archaeology Report 53.

Prehistoric flints. In J.A. Davies, T. Gregory, A.J. Lawson, R. Rickett & A. Rogerson, *The Iron Age Forts of Norfolk*, 13, 24–5. Gressenhall: East Anglian Archaeology Report 54.

The use of hand-axes for dating purposes. In S.G. Lewis, C.A. Whiteman & D. Bridgland (eds), *Central East Anglia and the Fen Basin*, 45–47. London: Quaternary Research Association Field Guide.

Wymer, J.J., Lewis, S.G. & Bridgland, D.R. Warren Hill, Mildenhall, Suffolk. In S.G. Lewis, C.A. Whiteman & D. Bridgland (eds), *Central East Anglia and the Fen Basin*, 127–30. London: Quaternary Research Association Field Guide.

Preece, R.C., Lewis, S.G., Wymer J.J., Bridgland, D.R. & Parfitt, S.A. Beeches Pit, West Stow, Suffolk. In S.G.Lewis, C.A. Whiteman & D.R.Bridgland (eds), *Central East Anglia and the Fen Basin*, 94–104. London: Quaternary Research Association Field Guide.

Hunt, C.O., Lewis, S.G. & Wymer, J.J. Lackford, Suffolk. In S.G.Lewis, C.A. Whiteman & D. Bridgland (eds), *Central East Anglia and the Fen Basin*. London: Quaternary Research Association Field Guide.

1992

Palaeoliths in alluvium. In S. Needham & M. Macklin (eds), *Alluvial Archaeology in Britain*, 229–34. Oxford: Oxbow Monograph 27.

The Southern Rivers Palaeolithic Project. Report No. 1. 1991– 1992. The Upper Thames Valley, the Kennet Valley and the Solent Drainage System. Salisbury: Wessex Archaeology.

Comment on W. Roebroeks, N.J. Conrad & T. van Kolfschoten, Dense forests, cold steppes, and the Palaeolithic settlement of northern Europe. *Current Anthropology* 33(5), 578–9.

1993

The Southern Rivers Palaeolithic Project. Report No. 2. 1992– 1993. The South-West and South of the Thames. Salisbury: Wessex Archaeology.

The Palaeolithic period; Late Glacial and Mesolithic hunters; The Neolithic period. In J. Everett (ed.), *An Historical Atlas of Norfolk*, 22–29. Norwich: Norfolk Museums Service in association with the Federation of Norfolk Historical and Archaeological Organisations.

Singer, R., Gladfelter, B. & Wymer, J.J. *The Lower Palaeolithic Site at Hoxne, England.* Chicago & London: University of Chicago Press.

Lawson, A. & Wymer, J. The Bronze Age. In J. Everett (ed.), *An Historical Atlas of Norfolk*, 30–31. Norwich: Norfolk Museums Service in association with the Federation of Norfolk Historical and Archaeological Organisations.

1994

The Southern Rivers Palaeolithic Project. Report No. 3. 1993– 1994. The Sussex Raised Beaches and the Bristol Avon. Salisbury: Wessex Archaeology.

The Lower Palaeolithic period in the London region. *Transactions of the London and Middlesex Archaeological Society* 42, 1–15.

Introduction: raw materials and petrology – an overview. In N. Ashton & A. David (eds), *Stories in Stone*, 43–4. London: Lithic Studies Society Occasional Paper 4.

Comment on S. Mithen, Technology and society during the Middle Pleistocene: hominid group size, social base and industrial variability. *Cambridge Archaeological Journal* 4(1), 19–20.

Gamble, C. & Wymer, J.J. The protection of Lower Palaeolithic sites in southern Britain. In D. O'Halloran *et al.* (eds), *Geological and Landscape Conservation. Proceedings of the Malvern International Conference 1993*, 443–5. London: Geological Society Publishing House.

Rose, J. & Wymer, J.J. Record of a struck flake and the lithological composition of 'pre-glacial' river deposits at Hengrave, Suffolk,

U.K. *Proceedings of the Suffolk Institute of Archaeology and History* 38(2), 119–25.

Wymer, J.J. & Robins, P.A. A long blade flint industry beneath Boreal peat at Titchwell, Norfolk. *Norfolk Archaeology* 42(1), 13–37.

1995

The contexts of palaeoliths. In A. J. Schofield (ed.), *Lithics in Context. Suggestions for the Future Direction of Lithic Studies*, 45–51. London: Lithic Studies Society Occasional Paper 5.

Palaeolithic archaeology of the Lower Thames region: the Southern and English Rivers Palaeolithic Survey. In D.R. Bridgland, P. Allen & B.A. Haggart (eds), *The Quaternary of the Lower Reaches of the Thames*. Durham: Quaternary Research Association Field Guide.

Wymer, J.J. & Brown, N.R. *Excavations at North Shoebury: Settlement and Economy in South-east Essex 1500 BC-AD 1500.* Chelmsford: East Anglian Archaeology Report 75.

Wymer, J.J. & Robins, P.A. A Mesolithic site at Great Melton. *Norfolk Archaeology* 42(2), 125–47.

Bridgland, D.R., Lewis, S.G. & Wymer, J.J. Middle Pleistocene stratigraphy and archaeology around Mildenhall and Icklingham, Suffolk: a report on a Geologists' Association field meeting, 27th June, 1992. *Proceedings of the Geologists' Association* 106, 57–69.

1996

The English Rivers Palaeolithic Project. Report No. 1. 1994–1995. The Thames Valley and the Warwickshire Avon. Salisbury: Wessex Archaeology.

The English Rivers Palaeolithic Project. Report No. 2. 1995–1996. The Great Ouse Drainage and the Yorkshire and Lincolnshire Wolds. Salisbury: Wessex Archaeology.

The Welsh Lower Palaeolithic Survey. 1996. Salisbury: Wessex Archaeology.

The English Rivers Palaeolithic Survey. In C. Gamble & A.J. Lawson (eds), *The English Palaeolithic Reviewed. Papers from a Day Conference Held at the Society of Antiquaries of London 28 October 1994*, 7–22. Salisbury: Wessex Archaeology.

Barrow Excavations in Norfolk 1984–88. Gressenhall: East Anglian Archaeology Report 77.

The Palaeolithic period in Essex. In O. Bedwin (ed.), *The Archaeology of Essex. Proceedings of the 1993 Writtle Conference*, 1– 9. Chelmsford: Essex County Council Planning Department.

Norfolk and the history of Palaeolithic archaeology in Britain. In S. Margeson, B. Ayers & S. Heywood (eds), *A Festival of Norfolk Archaeology*, 3–10. Norwich: Norfolk and Norwich Archaeological Society.

Shepherd-Thorn, E.R & Wymer, J.J. An Acheulian hand-axe from St Paul's Walden. *Hertfordshire Archaeology* 12 [for 1994– 96], 3–4.

1997

The English Rivers Palaeolithic Project. Report No. 3. 1996–1997. East Anglian Rivers and the Trent Drainage. Salisbury: Wessex Archaeology.